O9-CFS-640

4/11/00

THE EPIC HERO

THE EPIC HERO

Dean A. Miller

THE JOHNS HOPKINS UNIVERSITY PRESS
BALTIMORE AND LONDON

© 2000 The Johns Hopkins University Press
All rights reserved. Published 2000
Printed in the United States of America on acid-free paper
9 8 7 6 5 4 3 2 1

The Johns Hopkins University Press
2715 North Charles Street
Baltimore, Maryland 21218-4363
www.press.jhu.edu

Library of Congress Cataloging-in-Publication Data

Miller, Dean A.
    The epic hero / Dean A. Miller.
        p.   cm.
    Includes bibliographical references and index.
    ISBN 0-8018-6239-6 (alk. paper)
        1. Epic literature—History and criticism—Theory, etc.   2. Heroes
in literature.   I. Title.
    PN56.E65M55   2000
    809'.93352—dc21   99-39582
                                                             CIP

A catalog record for this book is available from the British Library.

CONTENTS

INTRODUCTION:
THE BOOK OF THE HERO

The fame of warriors is built on the destruction of humankind.
—Edward Gibbon, *The Decline and Fall of the Roman Empire*

The first question from any prospective reader will surely be, Why write another book on the hero? Suspicions may immediately be raised as to the essential mental maturity of someone who chooses so grand or grandiloquent a subject at any time, and *a fortiori* in our bland and gentle age of reputed equality, fraternity, and pacificocentrism. The path to this book, insofar as I can trace its rational development, led onward from my postgraduate training in Byzantine (late Roman or East Roman) imperial history and civilization, a training that forced me to investigate and ponder on that most brilliantly articulated and symbolically rich premodern political phenomenon, the office of the Byzantine emperor, the *basileos kai autokratôr Rhomaiôn.* This supercentralizing, powerfully autocratic persona and position had a predictably confrontational relationship with another locus of power and influence in that traditional society, a Byzantine aristocracy intimately joined yet opposed to the emperor and his massive and intricate theology/ideology.[1] One aristocratic phenomenon leads to another; I moved my focus from the Gestalt and thoughtworld of one nobility to the strange but potent sociocultural patterns of other aristocracies, especially to warrior aristocracies as these might be described generally or generically. In addition, we are all captivated by a mystery, and the first mystery of the *aristoi,* wherever located, is their invariant assumption of an inborn and natural superiority, a superiority one might call moral or ethical except that these specific terms are never (or very rarely) articulated. Of course, behind the potently projected dream of an aristocratic dominance lurks the brutal, material fact of the superior force of the weapon wielder and war maker, the warrior; while before him—the aristocrat—is projected the image of the hero, the warrior ideal, encased in the special epic description of his adventures and his fate, known, feared, and admired in so many guises and so many cultures. There is surely some very large part of the mental—that is, the cognitive-imaginal and perceptual—history of humankind to be dealt with here.

It seemed to me that the book of the hero needed to be written, and that I would have something original, or at least pertinent, to say on the heroic subject, who would be "the" absolute hero, in his clearest and starkest outline. Yet because numerous studies already exist, some readers may assume that I felt they were either deficient or incomplete in some way, or did not address the problem in a coherent manner, or were simply wrongheaded in theoretical approach or in extended narrative detail. In fact, almost everything available that might bear on the traditional hero, every attempt at a listing and analysis of his featured adventures and salient characteristics, has had some value, and I have indeed used, and gratefully used, a considerable amount of the available *stoff*, whether I agreed with its author's conclusions or not. Some of my adaptations of the older approaches to the hero are laid out here.

QUESTIONS AND APPROACHES

The broadest treatments of the hero and the hero's acts, rooted in Thomas Carlyle and the early nineteenth century but more familiar to us today under the names of Otto Rank, Lord Raglan, Joseph Campbell, Erich Neumann (and in another vector, the Soviet folklorist-linguist Vladimir Ysaevitch Propp), are always fascinating but, I confess, have been less important to me as directive and invariant guide marks (despite the fact that my own approach is certainly broad-gauge). These earlier, large-scale declarations tend to be too grandly deductive for my taste (this is particularly true of Raglan and Campbell), and *their* hero is too strictly cast in and limited by the image of the hero of myth: the hero mythically expressed and mythically circumscribed, a transcultural or omnicultural, ahistoric, synchronous, and, at his deepest core, symbolic phenomenon. The monolith and the monomyth do not attract me. In the main I limit my focus on the hero to the traditional Indo-European model, as he appears in sources derived from Indo-Europe, Indo-Asia, and this core area's cultural extensions.[2] I chose this areal focus because our heroic data are so frequently based in it and emerge from it: because they are set and maintained, willy-nilly, as part of our unavoidably Eurocentric tradition, which is our *archê;* because a good deal of valuable scholarly attention has been paid over time to individual heroic-epic episodes and their details; and because a theoretical guide into some of these data's recesses, convolutions, and complexities was already close to hand.

My appreciation of the theoretical acuity and the weight and caliber of the labors of the late Georges Dumézil and of some of his students emerges frequently in the following pages, and especially my gratitude for his concept of an Indo-European *idéologie,* expressed in, but not only in, his theory of trifunctionality and its archaic reverberations throughout the old Indo-European-speaking cultures. From time to time in the past twenty years I have published my own explorations into territory mapped by Dumézil, with special attention to his *fonction guerrière,* his Indo-European Second or Warrior Function as it is emergent within the Dumézilian reconstruction of a key tripartitive idea resident and continually renascent, or "reprinted," within the artifacts of the Indo-European thoughtworld.[3] Much of my previous work has been integrated into or is caught and held in the immediate background of the present study, and so I suppose that a Dumézilian flavor is readily apparent here. Dumézil's theoretical structure is precise and elegantly calculated yet generous and not restrictive, and he asks what I think are acutely pertinent questions and always permits others to ask them as well. I also respect and admire his warning about that adjective, and that idea, "Indo-European": "Le mot 'indo-européen' n'est qu'une convention savante pour parler d'un objet d'étude, d'une réalité préhistorique dont la recherche—archéologique, linguistique, mythologique— s'efforce de restituer le plus grand nombre d'éléments."[4] Dumézil, having devised the trifunctional model for this Indo-European *système,* recognized that too rigorous an insistence on its invariability as an Indo-European marker could consitute a theoretical prison, and such scholars as the Rees brothers, N. J. Allen, and Emily Lyle have taken a Dumézilian viewpoint and marked off pathways of their own; Jaan Puhvel has also reread and reformed or modified Dumézil along new lines. This great French scholar had no school, and didn't want one.

The matter and method of deciding what questions are put to the material selected and collected in pursuit of the typological hero seem to me most vital. Obviously I think that the right questions have not been asked with enough rigor, severity, or frequency, especially in respect to a significant definitional problem: the relationship of a central, even archetypic model of *the* hero to the constellation of *heroes,* in their sometimes subtly differentiated modal operations, and guises. There is even space and time available to pay some attention to that anachronism, the "national" hero, by which I mean that we ought to try to decode the specified heroic forms, operations, and styles that one society or another will isolate, celebrate, and iconize out of all the shapes and generic varieties of heroism at hand. It follows that I think that there are variations, configured in what has to be plotted as three-dimensional grid models built to correspond to the main subjects and objects of the heroic *bios,* however tricky a project this may prove to be (see the conclusion to chapter 7). Yet such a complex model must build from, or center on, a true heroic Type—or, to take another image, an irreducible figural being—which is the final shape and essential core of what we expect when we imagine a traditional hero. Or must it?

The questions to which I just referred not only deal with the heroic biography (and even more significantly, his thanatography), important as such a narration must be. They should also be directed to such puzzles as are raised by the companionship attached to this hero, who is most often described as "accompanied but alone," and to the uses and morphisms and special tasks of these companions; to the perverse reluctance of the hero to follow the Oedipal myth (or scenario), one result being that for heroic fathers to kill heroic sons is much more common than the reverse (and I think that this must be a *primary* Indo-European heroic scene and scenario); and to the collection of evocative symbols that define heroism, and to which bards and singers and all the old audiences of admirers and imitators responded. To fill out this very brief list, I believe that our investigations and our tentative theory building should aim toward explaining the peculiar mixture of heroic solidity and stolidity (the typological concreteness or stability) along with that ever shifting mobility that always makes the hero such a frustrating and difficult target to pin down.

These questions inevitably lead to others, and the list that follows is, again, by no means exhaustive. What is the nature of heroic individuality, and why and how is the hero so often defined by means of a code generated by a collectivity or group of his "peers"? How is he simultaneously placed *above* humankind, and therefore somewhere near the gods, and *below* the human, mixed with and mixed into the animal and even the monstrous, the teratic world? Why should a hero—and this is not a trifling matter, for he is so often identified with and by his weapons and especially by his sword—carry not one sword, but two? And, finally, what stands behind or emerges from his perpetual and obsessive *affaire du coeur* with death itself?

ORGANIZATION

The book begins with a history of the hero, an overview of the type revealed for the most part in epic or related genres, from his special and authentic Greek beginnings, when Homer sings his magnificent song, through those exaggerated reports of his death in early modern history and literature, to his agonic renascence in romantic (and national, and *völkisch*) literature and other art forms, even as he and his *esse* is excavated—revealed—and used or misused to support a philosophical construction, whether by a Schopenauer or a Nietzsche. The chapter then moves on to the central source material (mainly, the epic data) that isolates, celebrates, and carries the hero onward, and to epical variations in source, subject, and theory. Finally I examine the contributions of those scholars who have seized on and examined "the hero in our time."

Chapter 2, "The Heroic Biography," takes our old, combative friend from his mysterious generation to his violent end and a famous but often an ambiguous grave, with digressions into his family, his chosen companions in adventure and battle, and the clouded mystery of his sexual nature or patterning. Chapter 3, "The Framework of Adventure," tries to organize him in a spatial dimension, including supernatural space, and in a political mode, in which I have to set him against the king. The two vectors, the spatial and the political, come together in a way in the different types of the Heroic Quest, an activity often (though I believe wrongly) set forth as *the* definitive, the sole and decisive heroic adventure, sometimes declared to be his sole raison d'être.

Chapters 4 through 6 rearrange and reexamine various aspects of the surround of the hero. Chapter 4, "The Hero 'Speaks,'" takes up the vocabulary, syntax, and, to some extent, the semiotic realia projected in the heroic act and presence, from his stylized immobility to the various forces and formulas shaping, even occasionally controlling, the agonic forcefulness and the fatal violence for which he is best known (the forms of communication he uses; the power of the Word in his world, from its declamatory and identificatory dimension to its magical aspect; "rites of combat" and all the ways in which the terrible ceremonies of violence are shaped). Chapter 5, "Foils, Fools, and Antiheroes," looks to those figures, frequently very powerful in their own right, who move near and through the space and time of the heroic life and agonistic art: the trickster, the smith, and certain refactions or exofactions of the hero that show a marvelously mixed origin and character, sometimes extending toward the comic realm, and raising the possibility of the appearance of an antihero or "reversed" hero in the epic context. This chapter also probes the area of color symbolism, which is situated near to yet far from the conceits of heraldry, for the deeper meanings of black knight, red knight, green knight, and so on. Chapter 6, "*Tertium Quid:* Aspects of Liminality," returns to the enigma of the hero placed and acting between nonhuman zones, both animal and divine, in his own tertial territory (as in his maturation he is so often caught and held on the dangerous edge of a fully socialized and fully adult status) and in his unique relationship to what humankind in general tries its best to delay or avoid—death. This often amounts to an obsessive and energetic search.

Chapter 7, "The Final Hero: Beyond Immortality" takes up three problems. First, I am concerned with a key "marker," the *Sohnes Todt* motif, one that seems to proclaim a special nature of the hero within the Indo-European context. Second, I try to isolate "a" traditional hero within the constellation of different heroic refractions, factoring in such images and forces as the supernatural, aging and failure, skills and errors and gifts, even nature and culture. Third, I try to locate and isolate the perennial appeal, the permanent meaning, at the heart of the heroic—the hero's utility and importance in the perceptual field of a society in which he fits so uncomfortably and yet to which he appears to be so necessary. Here I need to pay some tribute to those psychological (and psychoanalytic) suggestions that may pertain to the theoretical concepts built up around charisma and any reverberations therefrom that might be detected in the hero and the heroic, and to the sociopolitical images and ambitions of the hero-imitating social and political elites. Finally I return to the patent power of the epic mode itself and, in a cinematic and unsystematic fashion, review the various epic forms that allow the hero to astound us again.

What I hope to describe, in the chapters that follow, is a structure of archaic heroism—the heroism of the epic, chiefly deployed in this kind of narrative—into which other kinds of information, other discoveries and other instances of a hero's life, poses, acts, and fate, can comfortably and honestly be slotted. In casting my net over so wide an area, I cannot help erring in some detail or another of my treatment of specific problems, topoi, even genres; but I hope that occasional errors in detail will not be used to obliterate the final value of this project.

ACKNOWLEDGMENTS

The epical and saga-borne evidence used in this study obviously has a number of different linguistic origins; most, though by no means all, of the sources have been translated into English or into some other readily accessible European language. (For example, that exotic but important source, the Ossetian Nart tales closely investigated by Georges Dumézil, but which originate in a fairly inaccessible Caucasian tongue, have been translated into French [by Dumézil] and also into Russian.)[5] A special kind of scholarship has also given me important assistance by translating older forms into the modern language, as Old French into the French of today, Middle High German into modern German, and the medieval Russian of the *Slovo o polku Igoreve* into contemporary Russian usage. I have gratefully (if, I hope, carefully) used the translations when and where they were available, and have risked my own readings only where I have the linguistic ability to do so. I, alas, will never claim the linguistic élan of a Dumézil, who once, according to the legend, learned the Quechua Amerindian language of the Andean highlands—on a bet. Therefore I have gratefully accepted expert help when I thought it was called for (as in Old Irish and Anglo-Saxon), when the accuracy and thrust of my argument seemed to depend on correctly decrypting a very particular, exceptionally nuanced source or usage.

This project, in its broadest outlines, has been in train for about twenty years, and a great many individuals, most of them located somewhere in the academy, have, in one way or another, helped me along the way. Their aid and assistance in no way makes them responsible for what I have written or concluded, and some of them may have forgotten that they helped me at all, or in what possible way. The following list is by no means complete: the late Alexandre Bennigsen, Alice Benston, Gerald Bond, Douglas Renfrew Brooks, Edward Calnek, Eugene D. Genovese and Elizabeth Fox-Genovese, William Scott Green, Joël Grisward, Sarah Higley, Donald R. Kelley, the late Christopher Lasch, C. Scott Littleton, Emily Lyle, J. P. Mallory, Elias Mandala, Tetsuo Najita, John Peradotto, Edgar C. Polomé, Fitz John Porter Poole, Jaan Puhvel, Thomas Spence Smith, Traian Stoianovitch, Udo Strutynski, Lawrence Sullivan, and Forrest Vance. In addition I need to express a special appreciation to certain members of the Department of History at the University of Rochester, which I joined more than thirty years ago, when I was lucky enough to find an extraordinary group of fertile, acerbic, critical, and highly individual minds who probably—to reverse the ritual disclaimer I just made—*should* bear some responsibility for whatever appears here, because they started the whole fearsome process moving: Loren Baritz, Marvin Becker, Milton Berman, N. O. Brown, the late Michael Cherniavsky, the late John Christopher, the late Willson Coates, Harry Harootunian, R. James Kaufmann, Sidney Monas, and Hayden V. White.

Then I must express my particular gratitude to William Sayers, whose long and close attention to my book's progress has been invaluable and whose exceptional linguistic skills have always been on call for me; and to David Konstan, without whose enthusiastic aid this whole project might have gone dead in the water. I owe, as well, particular thanks to P. M. Mitchell, formerly curator of the Fiske Icelandic Collection at Cornell University, who materially assisted my research into the Norse sagas, and to Robert Bartlett, now of the University of St. Andrews, whose Medieval Studies Workshop in the Department of History of the University of Chicago gave me, at a key period in the life of this book, an invaluable *locus standi* to assist my ongoing research in the Chicago area. The Department of History of the University of Chicago has also been kind enough to extend to me the status of Visiting Scholar in its department, so that this research would not be significantly interrupted, and this invaluable aid has now been extended by the Center for Middle Eastern Studies based at this university.

To the editors at the Johns Hopkins University Press, and especially to those who felt that this book was worth publishing, above all Douglas Armato and Linda Tripp, I extend my warmest appreciation, as well as to Carol Zimmerman. And to Paul Lipari, who undertook the huge task of editing a massive manuscript, I can only repeat the words of Brendan Gill: "The work of a good editor, like the work of a good teacher, does not reveal itself directly; it is reflected in the accomplishments of others."[6] I owe Mr. Lipari a great debt of gratitude.

To express my appreciation to my own university, and to its officers, the Central and the Collegial administrations in particular, I can only repeat the words of Skalla-Grímr to King Haraldr in *Egils saga:* ég mun eigi gæfu til bera að veita þér þá þjonustu, sem ég myndi vilja og vert væri.[7]

Finally, I must record here my remembrance and my deepest appreciation of the priceless friendship, the unstintingly cooperative spirit, and the brilliant and ever helpful insights of the late Ioan Petru Couliano, of the Divinity School of the University of Chicago, whose powerful and original mind and caring and genial spirit were so brutally torn from us, his saddened friends and colleagues, on 21 May 1991. *Ca Dumnezeu sa aseze sufletul lui unde dreptii se odihnesc.*

THE EPIC HERO

1 THE HERO FROM ON HIGH

"Let us drink to the *pallikars* of all nations."
—Lawrence Durrell, *Bitter Lemons*

AN OVERVIEW OF THE HERO
The Word

The word "hero" projects to us a kind of spurious solidity, so that we use it, and hear it used, as if it actually referred to a single cognitive image. Sometimes, especially in popular usage, the "meaning" of the word is, in superficial terms, made plain enough. An individual is named the "hero" of a particular incident, which means that he or she had intervened in some critical situation in an extraordinary fashion, acting outside, above, or in disregard to normal patterns of behavior, especially in putting his or her life at risk. This person, at least in the Anglo-American journalistic tradition, does not claim to have acted out of some special sense of his or her innately "heroic" character; quite the contrary, the accepted pattern is one of self-deprecation. "Anyone would have done it" is the typically reported claim, however unlikely this modest statement may be in fact. Heroism is also still regarded as a military virtue: after the fact or the act, a hierarchy of clear evidence exposes a "lower" or a "higher" heroism connected to the appropriate award, culminating in the Medal of Honor, *Croix de Guerre,* Victoria Cross, or other decoration signifying the highest degree of heroic resolve, often fatal (to the posthumous awardee) and almost always at the serious risk of life.

On the other hand, mortal risk is usually absent from another common modern use of the word, as in "X was Y's hero." Here hero simply means a model, a kind of ideal to be striven for or imitated to the best of one's abilities. And here I think that the person—the object of what may be called hero worship in the modern sense, or, in a regrettable but necessary buzzword, the "role model"—is replaced by a persona: the object-hero is actually composed of a cluster of admirable and perhaps imitable characteristics (admirable, that is, to someone and in some fashion, for Adolf Hitler, Jesse James, and psychotic serial murderers had and still have their hero worshipers).

Certain rules still govern the definition. We can see this in a literally academic, and relatively early, attempt to nail down the various possibilities in the concept of the hero. The French *Dictionnaire de l'Académie* of 1769 (its fourth edition) already revealed a "progressive degradation" of the term: first, *hero* is given as a "demigod," then "a man who distinguishes himself in war by extraordinary acts," and finally as "a man who, on some occasion, betrays the marks of great pride [*grande fierté*] or of a remarkable nobility."[1] After more than two generations, the American hero of our century probably remains Charles Lindbergh, the incomparable Lone Eagle, yet in this regard it perhaps is worth recalling James Thurber's wonderfully cynical short story, "The Greatest Man in the World," in which a "heroically" enduring solo airman is revealed not as heroically shy, manly, and gracious in the Lindberghian mode, but as a money-hungry, foul-mouthed, drunken bum and braggart.[2] Even in our aeon, some conception of "style" is attached to what "hero" seems to, or ought to, signify.

The point is that our images of heroism and of the hero are inescapably ours, as we form our intelligible thoughtworld, in that part of the historical continuum following on what Michel Foucault has most recently identified as *l'age classique,* that is, our Age of Reason.[3] Living in this moment commits us to the certainty of a rationally ordered universe, one in which magical powers and events, for instance, are not permitted, or must be subjected to alternative explanations demanded by rationality as unimpeachable. In this new view we must disallow much of the very substance of an older, outmoded heroism: setting aside the superhuman and especially the supernatural tints and taints; the crude interventions of gods and the friendship or, even more grotesque, the imagined kinship of the hero with humanlike animals; the encounters with monsters, the magical flights and Otherworld adventures—the heroic defiance, in a word, of physical laws, in the impossible combinations of the human with the animal and the divine. Of course, those most affected by the new rules of the Age of Reason were those we have to call the most reasonable: the classes expanded by urban development, the increasingly literate and educated, the European congregation of "moderns" whom science would invigorate and enthrall: they who were proud to be called the enlightened.

The present study, with its special emphases, might claim to bypass the enlightened, and even the Enlightenment, but of course this is impossible. Though I may declare that the object of my attention is the *archaic, traditional*, or *premodern hero* (each phrase set against the succeeding Age of Reason), I cannot consciously or unconsciously (*n.b.*!) set aside the accumulated cognitive history that stretches from that *age classique* to today. For one thing, there is the intellectual fashion that followed in its turn on the rational triumphs of the Enlightenment, the fashion described as romanticism—and romanticism gave us back our heroes, or at least tried to recover the mind set that had originally created these "powerful" figures, so as to honor them again in an idealized and redrawn past. Whatever the various urges involved in the romantic phenomenon (national feeling, antirational reaction, new forms of art or old fits of nostalgia), the result, in the nineteenth century of our era, was a newly complicated view of the hero.

Perhaps we can take the romantic hint and retrogress, to dive deep and so recover a history of the hero. The word itself is Greek—*hêrôs*—and our initial view of the type is conditioned by ancient Greek definitions. If we turn to another definitional source, Liddell and Scott's *A Greek-English Lexicon*, the magisterial guide to ancient Greek usually used by Anglophones, we find a series of definitions, invested with an admirable clarity while giving a simultaneous hint of difficulties to come, or to overcome. The dictionary's list of definitions lets us believe that a kind of linear development occurred in Greek: from Homer's archaic usage, where "hero" is used for "any free man" or, possibly, any significant man or "gentleman" prominent in the epic or not; to Hesiod, who sets the hero in an age of his own, a past age, marked by impressive, "legendary" place-names used as dramatic foci, such as Troy or Kadmeian Thebes, and anterior to the duller and smaller present; and finally to Pindar, who defines the hero as a semidivine being, above men, below the gods.

Yet surely this list gives us an artificial lexical clarity. Joseph Fontenrose, on the subject of the hero, delivers himself of the following: the hero is "a type of supernatural being, frequent in Italy and Greece, that may be called hero, demigod, godling, daimon, or spirit—*the ancients appear to have been as uncertain as we* [emphasis added] . . . these figures [began] as heroes, i.e., as powerful ghosts."[4] "Powerful ghosts" brings out two key constituents of the image: the heroic connection with death, and the fact that the hero's intermediary power may in fact be something not to seek out or welcome but to fear. Our evidence may consist of strange bits of evidential detritus, and intercept strange incalculable currents in which such detritus floats: the leader of a slave rebellion in Chios, one Drimacus, was respected as a kindly hero after his death;[5] whereas Pausanias tells us that following the advice of the Delphian pythoness the Orchomenians sacrificed to Akteon "at night, as to a hero."[6] His phantom had troubled them after his death. The hint here is of a contrast we will often encounter in the following pages, of heroic flash and brilliance sent out into darkness, *chthôn*. Beneath these literary constructions persists a widely accepted common notion of the "hero" as a mediator, a conduit between the living world and whatever nonhuman powers and zones exist, or the allied conception of the "hero" as simply one of the dead—another and final stage for all humankind, possessed of whatever special powers might inhere in death, that postvital (but perhaps still potent) state. The various uses of the term *hero* carry a number of significances, from a mediative position, even nameless and possibly malignant, to a slightly marked social status (Homer does not confine the term to an Akhilleus or a Hektor), to a figure of a remote and magnified time, and on to that status between the human and the divine.

Homer's epic, the first in our Eurocentric (or Indo-European) tradition, has received more scholarly attention than any other at least partly because his heroes and their kind of heroism set up a series of complicated analytic problems, beginning with the fact just noted that, although the poet may use *hêrôs* in the vague lexical sense, he clearly means to convince his audience of the extraordinary heroic-epic status of Akhilleus and others, like Patroklos and Diomedes, who may also sometimes carry the appellation "best of the Achaeans," together with matched or overmatched players on the Trojan side, like Sarpedon and Hektor.[7] Another problem derives from the fact that although the events described purport to be situated in what we now conventionally call the Mykenean age—the twelfth century B.C. or thereabouts—the ambience of the poem is firmly set in the eighth century B.C., in what has been ingeniously identified as the Greek Middle Ages.[8] In fact, we now know that this eighth century saw the appearance of much of what would define later Greek civilization, including an alphabetic script, the Panhellenic Olympian games, the proto-*polis*, and, most significantly for these purposes, the newly developed hero cult.[9]

Our investigations into this hero cult seem to show what will become a familiar bifurcation in a central idea. One line expresses the heroic ideal as we find it in Homer, the powerful image of the physically perfect young hero dying for fame and escaping maturation (and thus the "bad death" of an impotent and ugly old age) by achieving a "good death" that ends his physical history in combat.[10] Everything in this line is concentrated on the *agôn* of the essentially asocial individual. The second line integrates the cult of the dead hero into the new sociopolitical entity of the Greek city-state, or *polis:* he becomes guarantor and defender of that vital social unit.[11] The first image, with Akhilleus as its most potent representative, stresses the extrasocietal, utterly separated player in the game of death, who seeks by death to earn *kleos aphthiton,* that "eternal fame" or "unfailing praise" that also paradoxically preserves him *athanatos* and *ageraos,* deathless and ageless. Later this is, with some difficulty, attached to a glorious death that is not merely individual but is perceived to defend the *polis:* those dead in battle for the mother-city can be associated with the old heroes, and the two kinds of death, old and new, can be declared equally significant. Another kind of older "political" hero, whose conspicuous *hêrôon* is one of the solid, authenticating signs of civic focus, has prophylactic or, more properly, phylactic powers since, according to Hesiod, the "men of the race of gold" act from under the earth as "royal guardians"—*phulakes*—to mortal men (*Works and Days,* 123). But this is a new and different image.

It is my belief that heroism, to the Greeks, was a multifold concept, but one held together by the power-laden *muthos* of death. In the Akhillean mode the hero both deals violent death and seeks it out, and he remains a solipsist, always apart; in the mediating mode he, even anonymously, acts from within his postmortem place (the *hêrôon*) to fertilize and protect human society, and especially that important new formation, the city-state, so that the extraordinary dead are found to support the ordinary artifacts of the living. Pindar, in his turn, elevates and abstracts both the warlike and the mediating mode, connecting the *agônes* or regularized game combats of the various Panhellenic games to the supreme effort of the warrior in battle, and insists that the athlete's *kleos,* his fame when he is victorious, gives him both personal immortality *and* glorifies the city-state in whose name he strives. Additionally, to Pindar, the "immortality" granted these exceptional human beings does lift them up out of mere humanity and toward a semidivine status.

The idea, however, that the hero must be a major mover in the human drama is more than a little diminished by the popular or folk conception making *all* of the significant dead into heroes. Moreover, the notion that a hero must be someone who has attained fame—immortal and always remembered fame—is undercut by the number of instances of heroes unknown or nameless, whose monument set on the face of the earth (it need not be an actual burial place), the *hêrôon,* seems in a general way to commemorate some particular individual, but reveals itself to be most important as a contact point, where the *energeia* of the anonymous but powerful one seems to inhere. The mound, stone, or other significant reminder exists not just to memorialize but to notify others of that place where the mediating status and force of the hero is known to operate. Those *hêrôa* dedicated "to the unknown hero" make such a point, as does the existence (as recorded by Pausanias in his invaluable guide) of not one but a number of *hêrôa*, widely separated but identified with a potent name, such as that of the Athenian king-hero Theseus. Fame and specific remembrance now give way to a more central aspect of the hero considered as type: his mediation between one zone and another, between this world and an Otherworld. What I call Otherworld may have a nominal connection with divine persons and spiritual potencies (gods or goddesses), or it may be merely indicated as the place of death; either, or both, is possible. We find an exemplar of this combinatory style in the figure of Herakles, god-born but still a mortal finally made immortal, who shows other significant characteristics: his hard death, his earlier raid on Hades' realm, and his other Otherworld adventures betray the connection of this "hero" to different terrains within the extreme testing ground of mortality, the effortful intrusion of this archetypical myth-hero into the imaginal world dominated by death.

Tragic Hero, Epic Hero

Herakles' heroic biography, with its extraordinary range of feats, tests, abasements, confrontations, and disasters, leads us on toward some fascinating, if troubling, areas of further concern. Herakles will be called the *theios hêrôs*, the divine or divinized or godlike hero, and this identification says that he, and he alone, was finally lifted out of his physical humanity up toward the gods—and so Herakles is dead yet not dead.[12] As such he ought to have a cultic mediatory significance even more marked and widespread than other mediatory heroes, and in fact this cultic importance seems to shift and grow over time, to become greater especially in the postclassical (post–fourth century B.C.) Hellenistic world, where the soterificient powers of this extraordinary human-hero-made-god were to be, for many reasons, so especially appealing and so widely appealed to by the inhabitants and subjects of this new world.

But Herakles defined as specifically a human hero also belongs to that group of individuals in the archaic, epicomythic Greek context whose *tragic* potential is readily apparent to a later time and the literary creators of a new Greek genre. So he becomes, or is reinvented as, a hero of tragedy, and our focus must change with the hero. For the (literally) dramatic shift from older, epic hero to hero of Greek tragedy to occur, certain essential features must emerge and be fully recognized. One view of these features, reduced to a formula, was noted by Aristotle, writing after the tragic genre was no longer vital—for the Greek tragic drama, as J.-P. Vernant remarks, was born and died during a time span of little more than a century.[13] Aristotle's formula is perhaps too well known: that in a proper tragedy a "noble" hero, possessed of the hubristic tragic flaw, is destroyed by a divine intervention, and that the audience, exposed to the dramatic crisis, experiences *katharsis:* it is moved to feel "pity and awe."[14]

The philosopher's analysis is not so much wrong as irrelevant to our project. Other more recent lines of investigation point up that the nobility of the tragic hero was less important to the Athenian audience than the fact that he was of the past: the "ancient heroic legend" (separated from the audience's quotidian temporality by such technical apparatuses as the stage itself, the artificial formulas of staging, and the actors' masks, but also by a conceptual separation that invariably recognized "heroic time" as "time past") was worked into the political and social debates of the living *polis* and its citizens.[15] Yet not the last of the ambiguities introduced by the tragic poets into a heroic *muthos* resulted from the "humanizing" and, in the root sense of the word, the politicizing of the hero, when he became part of "a debate with a past that was still alive."[16] In his essential features the tragic hero and the hero described in epic are never the same man; the magnificent fifth-century genre of Greek tragedy simply extracts the epic hero from those archaic—and more rigid?—framings and adapts him for quite other purposes.

The chief of these purposes seems to be to reinforce the ambiguity just mentioned; for tragedy's largest theme is not Aristotelian cathartic closure, but a much harder matter, "the questioning to which there can be no answers."[17] The tragic protagonist agonizes over acts and choices, is torn between alternatives, recognizes (too late) the potent workings of a pollution-creating act, of the fact and pain of tearing guilt, and of the grimmer purposes of the ultimately unknowable gods. All this is utterly foreign to the epic hero, so that Daniel Madelénat, considering the hero of the epic as he is transmuted into a tragic hero, can conclude that the epic hero is antitragic, and the tragic hero antiepic.[18] Ambiguity of the tragic kind does not ever becloud the epic scenery or seize on its actors; the exteriority and *plein aire* marking the epic hero and his drama—even the epic characteristic Madelénat calls a "morale progressiste"—separate the two forms in nearly absolute terms. Tragedy ends by dissolving the individual will and can be called pessimistic *au fond;* the dignified or "worthy" end of the epic hero, no matter how violent, is antitragic, and epic-heroic character, ethos, cannot be tragic. The very mask that marks off the tragic hero from an envisioned reality would be impossible for the epic hero, who, though his face may be radically distorted by battle fury, or obscured and so made nearly anonymous by his war helmet, is never truly masked.[19]

Given that comparatively few plays within the tragic genre have survived to us, as compared with what Aristotle knew, any broad generalization must be tentative, but it seems clear that the Big Three of Greek tragedy, as we have what we have of their body of work, play complex games with essentially new and powerful themes, in dramas more various in plotting and more experimental in their raising of ethical and even, in some important sense, psychological dilemmas, than any older epic tale describing the rough, glory-seeking deeds of the hero-warrior. Even the Dionysian ambience of the theater, it seems fair to say, is essentially foreign to the modes and traditions of the old heroes. We see that a fundamentally theatrical and novel outlook is apparent from the first tragedies of Aeschylus, with their increasingly polyvalent explorations of individual responsibility and guilt, of the possibilities, constrictions, and contradictions inhering in divine and human law, and with their probing into the very core and crux: how mere human powers, heroic or not, can ever perdure when divine powers implacably intervene. And we know that the experimental range possible in the new genre can extend very far, ending, perhaps, with Euripides' strange and powerful *Bacchae*, when the dramatist brings the god Dionysos himself on stage to direct, on a divine whim, the terrible and fatal action against the doomed hero-king Pentheus.[20]

The two kinds of heroism, tragic and epic, are drastically different, the more so when we understand that Greek tragedy, as Vernant correctly insists, shows the hero as *problem* rather than as *model*.[21] When we pass on to the wider and sometimes confused use of the term "tragic hero," as applied to other heroes in other, non-Greek contexts, the difficulties must be multiplied again. Certainly the flawed and ambiguous workings of human will are masterfully explored in Shakespeare's tragedies, in a sea-changed genre that is nevertheless a self-consciously declared continuation of the older tragic tradition; and tragedy as an extreme, hyperemotionalized dramatic form is a staple of the English Jacobean and of Continental stages of the baroque period. Yet the true *tragôidia,* as it is tied to and yet essentially distanced from epic, appeared, was staged, and had its effect only in its Athenian home.

In some other epic-heroic contexts we can detect the possibility of far-off familial resemblances. A circumstantially parallel dramatic situation arises in the Old Irish heroic literature, where a hero like Cú Chulainn or kings like Conaire Mor or Cormac mac Airt can be fatally caught between the unbreakable demands of contradictory *gessa* (prohibitions, taboos), or have their glory condemned and brought down in the end through the machinations of a malignant deity; but there is no sign that the structure of flawed interior heroic will and exterior fatality is or can be fully articulated here as it is in Greek tragedy. These Celtic heroes retain the limited emotionality, freedom from guilt, and clear choices of the archaic hero tale, following on a fatal circumstance with their desperate and enduring, violent and poetic sangfroid.

The Tradition Handed Down

The archaic Greek, and specifically the Homeric, pattern of heroism was the unimpeachable model set for an Augustan production such as the *Aeneid.* Virgil's epic makes no bones about its derivation from "the" original epic, though naturally the Virgilian creation had to have its Roman coloration.[22] In the Mediterranean world the sense of an achieved cultural continuity remained so pervasive, the so-called Hellenistic invention and sustention of a cultural *oikoumenê* so broadly diffused if not deeply rooted, that the heroic model was retained essentially unchanged, even after the Christianization of the Roman Empire. So, at least, it remained for the numerous members of a literate elite; mere history or historical change could not disturb the transmission of this potent epic-heroic inheritance. One of the strangest manifestations of this sense of continuity was the erection of an equestrian statue by Justinian I in Constantinople in the sixth century A.D., showing the emperor himself costumed as the ancient hero Akhilleus.[23] Such a conceit surely follows on the fact that "Byzantine" East Rome, as the great oecumenical continuator of the high culture (especially after the excision of most of its Latin-speaking territories in the fourth to sixth centuries), reconcentrated its intellectual attention all the more strongly on its magnificent Greek thesaural inheritance.[24] A Byzantine mandarin of the tenth or even the fourteenth century would know his heroes well, from Homer through all the epigonal descriptions of and elaborations on Greek heroism, together with the portrayed lives and fates of the "tragic" heroes of more Greek dramas than we have access to today.[25]

Even beyond the Byzantine world the tradition was irregularly emergent. That impressive Mediterranean consciousness of an inheritance that connected literary present firmly to rooted past is finally seen in the *trecento* sensibility of a Dante who, in canto IV of his *Inferno,* locates in the first

Circle a special, bright place for those "honored folk" (*orrevol gente,* 72) whose "honorable fame" (*onrata nominanza,* 76) found favor even with the powers ruling a Christian Heaven. Homer, *poeta sovrano,* is the first named here; Hektor and Aeneas are also present, but the Achaeans are not. The guide Virgil's Roman prejudices must, it seems, still be respected, and Rome was, after all, Troy's guilty child.[26]

Perfect continuity of tradition was not, however, invariably accepted or acceptable. Elsewhere, as the late antique world moved, shook, and melded into an early medieval Europe, the view, elite or popular, of the traditional hero as warrior had to be subjected to serious revision. Christianity, after all, was introduced into an imperial world defended by a strong army, some of whose soldiers—*hoi stratiôtai tou hêgemonos*—had jocularly and brutally assisted with the Crucifixion (Matt. 27.27). Until the reign of Constantine the Great the imperial military was, actually or potentially, the arm of a persecuting imperial state; the oppressors were not warriors of the ancient marque but paid soldiers serving the state, not heroes but *milites, stratiôtai.* The original warrior ethic and a new refraction of the old heroism would only be rediscovered in barbarian Europe beyond the *limes,* in the pullulating, impatient Germanic tribes and on the far, and equally impatient, Celtic edges of an imploding imperial world.

The hero from the extra-Mediterranean, boreal, and truly European liminal zone emerges, we often think, as from a mist; his arrogantly posed and brilliant solidity, which remains forever the veritable mark of his type, contrasts sharply with the spatial and temporal flux and darkness around and behind him. It is a powerful image, and we will often find that an epic-making mind, unknowingly following the Hesiodic model, will simply shove his epical cast of characters back into a timeless, but certainly older, Age of Heroes. Later scholarship will make of this archaizing convention what it can, especially by adducing a probable periodization and locating dates and events in "real time."

Two solidly historical interventions, though of vastly different kinds, will add a particular flavor to this early medieval evidence: the appearance in the European political and religious consciousness of an ideological counterforce to Christianity, in the form of a militant and expansive Islam, and the slightly earlier development and transmission of those consequential technical innovations that allowed the appearance of the first true heavy cavalry in Europe—and so, in time, led to the horsed and armored (and noble) knight as *chevalier, caballero, Ritter.* The first phenomenon provided the tension and groundwork for the creation of a whole genus of "border" epics in which Christian hero confronted his Moslem counterpart: these include a variety of Old French *chansons de geste* from the *Chanson de Roland* on—the Byzantine *Digenid*, the Spanish *Cid*, and numerous Balkan border-epic songs, some sung within the last generation before our own and reflecting (like the earlier Turkish *Danismend* epos) the other side of the border, and a specifically Moslem point of view. The religious (and border) flavor, with an anti-Moslem or anti-Arab bias, has predictably been back-dated into the verses of the archaic Armenian epic, and such a tendency can be detected elsewhere as well, for such was the potential and the real threat of this new enemy—and his value to the epic.[27]

The second development eventually produced the hero as knight, the hero on horseback. This knightly heroic tradition emerges resoundingly in such contexts as the Germanic *Nibelungenlied* (with its connections to the more shadowy Old Germanic epic-mythic themes surrounding the Völsungs), but it will resound most deeply in the Continental hero tales clustered around the figure of the "Briton" Arthur. The Welsh origin of these tales is not in doubt, but the vaster number of Arthurian tales, now and formerly described as the *matière de Bretagne* (with allied decorations and excursions taken from Welsh epics such as the Tristan tale), came from Continental European interpreters increasingly intent on filling out the persona of the truly chivalric hero, the perfect knight's knight. These interpreters, of whom the best known is the twelfth century Frenchman Chrétien de Troyes, not only added important characters to the old inheritance—Lancelot and Galaad being the most egregious—but also shifted the basic Arthurian motif, of hero and king and their conflicts and cooperations, in the direction of an increasingly Christianized theme: the pursuit or quest, by the pick of Arthur's knights, of a sacred object, the Holy Grail. The sequence of tales whose hero began as Peredur, later Perlesvaus-Percival-Parzifal, a "foolish hero" in the Welsh telling, shows this pattern most dramatically: the final edition of the Grail narrative has obscured the cheerful violence of the ordinary chivalric hero behind the Christ-iconic figure of the spiritually triumphant Galaad, who is the perfect (and Christian) knight, and an utterly changed kind of hero.[28]

This may be the best place to note that in another Celtic context, the Irish, contingent to the Welsh but showing a mighty florescence of its own, the "Christianization" of its heroes was dealt with differently but ingeniously: the most important heroes of what had to be accepted as a pagan past, and specifically the great Cú Chulainn himself, were said to have been revived from the dead by Ireland's patron saint, Patrick, and then politely ushered, as national icons, into Paradise.[29] Such a treatment is slightly but significantly different from Dante's address to the heroes of Homer, who are typologically very similar to the Irish.

Chivalry

The production of knightly hero-tales (if not, in the strict sense, of what we can precisely call heroic epic) continues throughout the medieval period and follows the general pattern of creating variations on traditionally received and identified narratives and texts, especially in the Arthurian tradition. The best-known, though not the last of them, is Malory's *Morte d'Arthur*, but Italian "suites chevaleresques" eventually appear as well, like the anonymous *I Narbonesi* or Andrea da Barbarino's *I reale di Francia*, leading off from an earlier French sequence of epics, the *Cycle des Narbonnais*.[30] These later, newly devised or revised knight tales display no smoothly monolithic figure, but instead emphasize one or a number of modular if not ideal characteristics: foolish impetuosity, amorousness, naiveté, even stupidity, and the awkward or perverse figure of the antihero is now possible, for reasons that need more exploration.[31] Even with the appearance of such variations on the old theme, however, there is a typical knightly figure or character still kept in main focus. The hard imaginal core of the chivalric knight, apart from those marginal or epiphenomenal characters and their characteristics just mentioned, was supposed to be composed of physical bravery and *cortoisie*, which is a behavioral or attitudinal code at least to some degree involved in the literary theme of courtly love.[32] This would be an all too easy image to satirize. We will soon recognize a New Age, and although it is not quite fair to say that this New Age, expressing itself in the great intellectual images of Renaissance and Reformation, saw the chivalric ideal only as it was satirically exposed in the person of Cervantes' Don Quixote, the times will be dominated by different and more complex notions of what heroism was or might be.

Something more on the subject of chivalry seems to be called for. This idea of chivalry is complexly bound up with our heroic subject, and yet to some degree escapes the limits of the heroic entirely, to gain an attitudinal life of its own, one showing often contradictory effluxes of its different components. It was initially taken as an attempt (of indifferent success in real terms) to allow the church and to some extent the royal power to subdue or redirect the bellicose energies of a medieval fighting knighthood; but it reaches through the end of the European Middle Ages, energizes certain aspects of the English Civil War,[33] and resurfaces in the self-conscious elite status or "side" of British and Continental cavalry regiments as late as the ninth century.[34] It infected a number of Southern partisans in the American Civil War, and its last forlorn or pathetic gasp seems to have occurred in the legendary charges of Polish lancers against German armor in 1939. In this later, modern reading or use of the concept of chivalry, an aspect of military caste is conjoined with aristocratic assumptions both of superiority and responsibility—at least in a cavalry officer's corps. In terms of military technology, the shift from chivalry to cavalry is naturally a significant one.

The imaginal life of the concept of chivalry, which is surely the more important component, and one that infiltrates the military aspect, re-presents, in one sense, the typical confrontation between individual heroic predilections and the desire of some political center or authority to press forward and hold in place social-hierarchic order and control; the emotional and moral aspects, such as the special relationship to women and a received behavioral code, are mixed in gratis. This means that at any time chivalry might signify either an intensely personal, interiorized behavior, or a kind of public style, attitude, and display. The former emerged in emotional and complicated psychological stances, and especially in the most powerful sense of personal honor, in which the perduring integrity of a combined "name" and "being" mark the individual, an individual ever sensitive to even the slightest hint of derogation or diminution. The latter emphasized a loyalty and service, respect for hierarchy, and shared community. What we have, in fact, is a partial transmutation of the old heroic tension between individual and society, with a new set of symbolic representations.

We can find a specific focus for the combination of chivalric themes and the more or less successful attempts to manipulate them in the Renaissance courts of England and Europe—royal courts with extensive resources in which powerful kings sought to use the imagery of chivalry, with all its variable and available symbols, to support the primacy of the throne. With a fine irony, it was the Burgundian court (a rare creature of feudalism, and not destined to survive the consolidations and ramifications of power politics in sixteenth-century Europe) that served as mentor and model for court-centered chivalric occasions and displays: processions, pageants, and especially tournaments, those simulacra of knightly mounted combat. All of these celebrations were extremely expensive.[35] In this game of imagination Tudor England had the advantage of its Arthurian inheritance; the heir apparent to Henry VII, Prince Arthur, who died in 1502, would presumably have reigned as Arthur II, reviver of the ancient and numinous royal name, and of the legend's images of true-knightly loyalty and obedient, self-denying service.

Yet chivalry is a halter and bit to the knight's private and undisciplined force only up to a point; in the test of war it might prove unavailing, or impertinent, or counterproductive, especially when its second, personal component, boasting the special character and demanded style of the individual fighter, thrusts this individual forward—perhaps to an honorable defeat, even to the death, and with no rational gain achieved. Following the hero's path is no safe going.

Renaissance Complications

The Renaissance, with its increased and even obsessional attention to the recovery of classical learning, would lead to a revivification of classical images of the hero. One can even speak of an open confrontation between two older traditions of the hero, the classical and the Christian-chivalric, a confrontation persisting through the eighteenth and even into the nineteenth century. (The way this confrontation works itself out in the pictorial and sculptural arts, for example, is an enormous theme in itself.) Too much can be made of this rebirth (the recollection and imitation of certain ancient heroic themes had continued, in one form or another, right through the European Middle Ages), but arts and letters reveal in the most obvious way a revived concern for all aspects of antiquity, including the study of the texts that describe the manifold stances, acts, and excellences of the ancient heroes. The recuperated classical heroic model was most popular among the self-identified cognoscenti, the elite and the educated, especially when this influential group compared the recovered classical hero's purer narratives to the Gothick extravagances of an increasingly unappreciated and derogated medieval imagination.

The great literary sea change that suppressed—by nearly drowning out?—our evidence of archaic heroism is already apparent in the Western Middle Ages, with the transformation of the hero tale as an originally oral, and orally transmitted, adventure epic into a literary genre. This led first to the transposition of the oral to a scripted form, and then to the creation of a genre commanded by individual writer-creators exercising their own considerable inventive powers—and thus all the more likely to explore different views of what a hero might be and do (as in Walther von der Vogelweide, Chrétien de Troyes, Sir Thomas Malory, and others). Indeed, we now know that the old bards themselves changed the tales they sang as they sang them, and therefore some modification of the traditional heroic epic's narrative bumps and twists has to be assumed from the very beginning—from the time of Homer himself. We also have before us, still in the classical period, a purpose-built epic like Virgil's *Aeneid;* and the occasional "national" epic (to use an anachronism) may have some individual poet-creator's name attached to it, as in that collection of mythic-folkloric, traditional, historical, and pseudohistorical themes credited to the Persian Ferdausi, and called *Shâh-nâma* (Book of Kings).[36]

Further alterations occur with the Protestant Reformation, which undoubtedly broke the unity, authority, and hierarchical organization of Western European papalist Christendom, and so in a great sense brings to an end a large part of that traditional medieval thoughtworld. At the same time certain other medieval religious tendencies, especially toward achieving spiritual purity and individual responsibility to and before the divine, lay beneath a fair part of the reform, and one powerful effect of it was to reintroduce harsh, individualized, and even absolute differentiae into matters spiritual. Religion-based heroism, self-sacrifice and martyrdom, and the recovery of certain scriptural images of God-justified "heroic" violence, are part of this historical shift. The reform and its consequent sharpening of spiritual or confessional identification and definition, and of a newly identified "heretical" opposition, might be said to have brought to an end that more tolerant aspect of the matured medieval thoughtworld that had produced the "ambiguous epic," with its reversals and doublings of traditional epic personae gathered up into a crop of failed kings and successful villains, and its casual dilution of older heroic themes and values.[37] Hard and sharp and intolerant edges are seen anew, and clearly or even luridly outlined protagonists and antagonists grimly face one another, under battle flags again marked with the cross, and newly sacralized.

Then there is that other legacy of the Renaissance, its intellectually inventive and rational-scientific inclinations and innovations, which will lead to the Age of Reason, which in turn had such an intriguing effect on the persistence of the idea of the hero. The Renaissance leaves behind an ambivalent inheritance, recovering and enriching various antique types and expressions of heroic character, yet putting in train the intellectual attitudes that would stand against, deny, and denigrate much of the archaic hero's glory, as contained in his unthinking, primitive pose and his sincerely irrational, unconstrained joy in the use of force: his argument of blood. And of course it was what we have to call a Renaissance mentality that not only produced the greatest satire on heroic chivalry, in the form of Cervantes' pathetic Don, but also, in Shakespeare, a towering verbal gift that imprinted itself on the very definitional matrix describing dramatic heroism. In the following chapters we see a good number of invented complexities in the collective image of the traditional or epic hero, but very little immediately resembling that psychological subtlety the Elizabethan master poet deployed. I think it is fair to say that heroic drama after Shakespeare may be marked by wider possibilities in terms of theme, but more and more sclerotic narrative and characterization, so that even newly described emotional conflicts are turned toward predictably formulaic conclusions.

Heroic (and Historic) Conquest

The forced transmission or migration of European culture and control across the Western seas (or, in another vector worth investigating, from European Russia out into the Eurasian landmass to the East) shows a cluster of characteristics in which traditional, epic heroism, however perceived and modeled, can often be identified as a salient influence. Such adventurous thematic possibilities as the pursuit of a heroic quest, as well as that very real sort of crusade, the expedition undertaken at least partly for the triumphant engrossment of the faith, are clearly available to the minds of the explorer-conquerors of new lands, as is a powerful greed of gain.

The latter is most particularly visible, or openly admitted, in the Spanish *conquista*, where a close affinity exists between rejoicing in rich booty and the well-earned, tangible rewards of prowess. (See, for example, El Cid Campeador in Spain, and the lust for gold of a Cortés or a Pizarro half a millennium later.)[38] In the case of Cortés and his extraordinary conquest of the Aztec-Mexican Empire, we can even find an implicit recollection and reimaging of that old epic confrontation of the tested and triumphant few as against the ravening, savage, and pagan many, and an explicit, self-conscious parallelism declared between the events of the Conquest and ancient heroic deeds. (The "notable deeds" of the Romans are openly used as a model, for example; and according to the Spanish chronicler and participant Bernal Diaz del Castillo, "ten thousand Trojan Hectors and as many more Roldans" could not have fought any better against monstrous odds than he and his comrades had done in a savagely hostile and pagan Mexico.)[39] We even see a conscious iteration of the heroic-iconic image of El Mio Cid himself in the person of one Juan Velasquez de Léon, whose personal honor seems to reside in the beard by which he swears, in the antique manner of the Campeador.[40] In fact we ought to expect that this heroic mimesis, with real behavior modeled on a fictive image, would not be uncommon in the Age of Conquest, and Martín Menéndez y Pelayo, a seventeenth-century Spaniard serving in the Portuguese Indies, tells us that he knew a Portuguese comrade in India "who believed in the literal truth of the books of chivalry and sought to emulate the deeds of their heroes."[41] Alas, we don't know the fate of this solemn imitator of chivalry, or what Menéndez y Pelayo thought of the imitation.

The great European penetration of the New World, South and Southeast Asia, and eventually most of Africa thus provided a theater for "heroic" individuals, who also tended to be technically superior to the indigens in arms and military organization. The Europeans of the Conquest could thus assume and imitate a heroic role, although they might or might not extend the comparable heroic honor to their opponents—opponents whose thoughtworld was often more truly congruent with that ancient warrior ethos the Europeans merely thought to imitate. The conquerors variously recognized or typed the indigens they met—childlike, feral-animal, wonder-working, and supernaturally adept—but the long-term consequence of the great expansion did make Europe conscious of other, rediscovered perspectives and reflections of heroism, of a great number of primitive tribal societies in which the warrior-heroic ethos was intact and operational, even in barbarous or savage social states. A great part of an archaic or traditionally ordered world, with one of its components a recognizable warrior's world view, was there to be newly revealed, if not admired.

These three great redirective processes in early modern Europe—Renaissance, Reformation, and colonial exploration and empire building—were often complexly interrelated. "Renaissance" epics sometimes attached and shaped antique themes to the central fact of great discoveries, and the Virgilian model especially presented itself as a paradigm of migration and armed conquest. The *Aeneid* obviously influenced Camoes's *Lusiad* and the *Araucaniad* of Alonso de Ercilla y Zuñiga, but it also informed or inflated less obvious and more factitious works, such as Boiardo's *Orlando Innamorato* and Tasso's *Gerusalemme Liberata*.[42] (The *Lusiad* went so far as to echo the god Jupiter's promise of imperial dominion to Aeneas and to Rome, transmuted into an imperial Portugal *de naçoes deferentes triunfando*, and thus was that nation destined for great things, as Rome had once been.)[43] Another provocative borrowing from the received Greco-Roman imaginative treasury converted the newly conquered and colonized lands into that old, mythically prepotent East, an Orient represented by such archaic signs as a threatening and unmanning femininity, the undisciplined surrounding mass of hostile inhabitants (and the perils of "submersion" in foreignness in general), and even luxury and suspiciously easy wealth: Lucan's *Pharsalia* had set the antique pattern for this crochet.[44] Against all these old-yet-new threats, the imperial-epic hero opposed the sturdy masculine claims of the heroic (and European) West. *Verso,* and in reaction, the Protestant Milton saw all this "discovery" as the work of the Devil, since the effort belonged entirely and merely to the "temporal" realm, and in *Paradise Lost,* according to one scholar, he explicitly assigned to Lucifer's damned minions "the aristocratic martial heroism traditional in the epic."[45] We would expect such an attitude in a Puritan and Parliamentarian—yet I have already noted that the heroic-chivalric tradition inflamed some surprising shorn-poll partisans in the English Civil War.[46]

Romantic Recovery

A time of drastic shifts in Europe's thoughtworld through the eighteenth century drowned out or marginalized certain old attitudes toward the hero, manifestly changed others, and yet seemed to leave a reservoir of archaic ideas and images waiting to be revived, retapped, revealed—in history. That recovery or revelation was to be especially important for the century previous to our own, which we are particularly indebted to—or at the mercy of. The nineteenth century firmly set modern Western man in the midst of a new scientific and industrial environment, and equipped or beset him with a rational-positivist intellectual framework and structure inimical, it seemed, to the archaic true-heroic spirit; but it also provided a number of interconnected developments affecting anew our perception of the hero, his works, and his deep essence.

The first and most ambiguous of these was the romantic recovery of national or "folk" heroes, whose deeds were encased in a popular and often illiterate (that is, orally transmitted) context of ballad or primitive song and poetry. Romanticism invoked not only the recovery of a past—the fecund, exciting, and emotionally charged forms of the Middle Ages—but also an archaic, and therefore obviously "pure," communal ethos-in-epos, an identifying national spirit grown and nourished in the heroic past of a true folk. The romantic phenomenon also signified the conversion of many urbanized, bourgeois Europeans to a new and different sense of group loyalty and identity, and this new audience encouraged the emergence of the "operatic" hero, in the dramatic-musical art form that sang of the hero (and the heroine) in new, disguised as old, ways. The culmination of this sung but breathless kind of operatic-heroic and national drama was to be revealed in Verdi and Wagner.[47] The new, large, middle-class or bourgeois audience, in Georg Lukács's view, also was collective midwife and then audience to a new novelistic form, the historical novel, with its factitious recovery and representation of past heroic ages, and of those ages' heroic individuals, all suitably recut and shaped into acceptable models adventuring in acceptable ways, for a new time's sensibilities.[48]

Another development extended from the newly available "ethnography," the human reality revealed in the lands and peoples opened to the European eye, but also derived from the recovered and revalorized *völkische* identities of "old" Europe. This ethnography was the extension of an approach to knowledge by way of a new science's fieldwork—anthropology— entailing the collection and study of the hero tales and myths of a congeries of peoples, whatever their obscure origin or exotic location: one might even say, the more obscure and exotic, the better. The effect of this accumulation was to reify the comparative mode in our view of the hero, that is, to allow the construction of patterns of thought and action defining the hero as a cross-cultural, cross-societal, eternally human phenomenon.

A third development, certainly rooted in the nineteenth century, however dramatic and critical its efflorescence in the twentieth, was the psychoanalytic enterprise, following on the theories of Sigmund Freud but, for our purposes, developing to an even greater degree from those of C. G. Jung. Freud's theory postulated that the ancient thesaurus of myth and the newest creations of an individual's dreamworld were conjoined and coemergent, and the discovery and utilization of certain constructions and projections of the unconscious mind had a literally deepening effect on our sense of the heroic individual's essence, task, and nature. To Jungian adepts the very heart of human individuation, in the maturing of identity, is attached to the hero's eternal scenario, to his testing and his triumph.

What might be called the seriousness of the romantic enterprise is now apparent, because beyond the romanticized aspects of the recovery of a neglected past, of national or ethnic yearnings, of operatic emotionalism, and of a kind of new but reactive irrationalism, are distinctive and powerful intellectual and even philosophic developments, with the idea of "the hero" very often exhibited, though perhaps sometimes in a malformed guise, at their core. Although the Enlightenment saw the triumphant emergence of the properly observing and cogitating individual, nicely suited to a patently reasonable universe, the era after the French Revolution (and especially after Napoleon's destructive but in some sense exhilarating wars) wasn't nearly so sure of reason's puissance. This in turn led to the suspicion that the reason-built, stable works of "reasonable" men were not as important as the sweeping, revolutionary acts of The Great—that is, of "heroes" risen above the ruck; and Carlyle duly notes that "Universal History, the history of what man has accomplished in this world, is at bottom the History of the Great Men who have worked here."[49] From cynosure and model/icon of a warrior society, to representation of the ancient seminal genius and essential character of this or that people, the hero has now become an historiographic and even a philosophic actor and player—and, of course and as usual, a problem. If the European Enlightenment felt itself supported by "the goodness and reasonableness of ordinary men," the new attitude questioned everything, including the value of moral value (that is, of "goodness"), the efficacy of reason, and even the very significance, in human history, of the work or thought of any collectivity of ordinary "good-natured" men.

My study cannot do much more than note in passing the problem of "the hero in history," or all the ramifications of the theory of the "great man" as theme and motor, especially as his individualized powers might be compared to various deterministic forces operating in history.[50] In part there is a definitional difficulty: the hero, imagined as great man, is conceived as one who lifts or forces himself into a dominant place in his society and epoch, and then compels that society and time into new, even unique historical patterns; in the process he will in all likelihood push aside older, outworn representatives of the principle of power and authority—such as tired and shopworn dynastic monarchs. To some degree he thus resembles that archaic theme (given in detail below) of young hero in his resistance and opposition to old king. The young Napoleon to whom Beethoven, in the popular legend, once thought to dedicate his *Eroica* Symphony is an embodiment of the type. However, the hero as we will usually perceive or calculate his potency does not lead his society, though he may die for it: his iconic power rests in the hot core of the human imagination, coupled with his own very special style. As he acts in externalizing his own sense of interior identity, and so follows his own nature ("good" nature is not at all to the point), he also moves clear of fated or determined macropatterns. In this sense the Napoleon victorious at Jena, whom Hegel saw as "the world-soul on horseback," is merely a human sign of the largest historical movements, and he seems both too large and too limited to fit into my own explication of the "hero."

The romantic recovery of the powerful individual thus sets us both a serious and a specifically modern problem, of directed force and passionate individuality versus the grand patterns of history; and it remains in our age as a permanently enticing psychological and even ethical temptation, where recapitulated but often misunderstood archaic patterns can lead, and have led, to the most destructive atavism. That dominant "death theme" so often recalled in the heroic biography, and seized on and enlarged operatically by

Wagner, can and does emerge in a cacophony, in nihilistic, demented political and social maneuvers, as witness a latter-day dark prophet and great man, one who surrounded himself with the pseudomythic apparatus and the fragmented bits and pieces of a "heroic" Germanic past, and then led his nation to a shuddering debacle at least as reminiscent of a gory and gangsterish last act of a *Nibelungenlied* as of any high-mythic *Gotterdämmerung*.[51]

Obviously the new emphasis on irrationality, and its new respectability, could beget strange and dangerously toxic growths, and equally strange and misshapen "reactions," in the new sense of the word reaction. In fact the complexities of the nineteenth-century revulsion against the pervasively optimistic thoughtworld of the Enlightenment are too manifold to give in any great detail here, though I should note that in a fairly strong side current, a whilom influential French Catholic and ultrareactionary like Joseph de Maistre could extol the unamended Holy Civilization of the European Middle Ages, and declare that no "progress" (and in fact nothing of value) had marked human history since those great days of papal authority, accepted hierarchy, and benignly corporative social sensibility—and yet also scorn (in exquisite French) those soft-brained contemporaries of his, inclined to the excesses of romanticism, who viewed that earlier age through the distorting lens of "sentimental enthusiasm."[52] Obviously thinkers in this traditionalist Christian-Catholic vein could not readily accept the revivification of the "pagan" hero, nor could they possibly welcome the new, schismatic national sentiment, however decorated with excavated folkish archaisms, that might crystallize around the tales of these heroes of the reborn ethnos.

The "sentiment" called out in the romantic movement had any number of literary foci. In addition to the recovery and revalorization of ancient heroism and the epic or popular tales describing it, we find the creation of romantic heroes in genres tuned to new modes. This literary phenomenon has to be at least mentioned because it reaches our own day, and affects to some degree our own perception of the hero himself. *In nuce,* the quintessential romantic hero is young, melancholic (alternating between pale and stoic taciturnity and unchecked, passionate outburst), and sensitive (the French *sensible*). The romantic hero of this sort is altogether too easy to mock; like Rousseau's Emile or Goethe's Werther, he seems as much victim as actor, and especially the victim of his self-generated, immoderate, and too often destructive emotions. If Lord Byron is often seen as the prime mover in perpetuating the type, it is not least because he reintroduced, in exotic poems like *The Giaour* and *The Corsair,* the essential separateness and antisocial violence of what he saw in the archaic hero, combined with the split-selved morbid sensibility of the new type, all mounted in distant and picturesque scenery, especially seascapes and mountaintops, inflated with a sense of natural, but exotic and "eastern," grandeur. Certainly the appeal of distance (that is, physical distance specifically shaped and defined) is a new element in the new perception of the hero.[53]

And with Byron in mind we might take a brief side glance into a case where imagination and history flowed together, and were held together by a particular, if wrongheaded, view of the archaic-heroic spirit: the case of the battle for Greek independence, which was achieved, with the reformation of a small but independent Greek state, in 1830. Politicians in power supported legitimacy and the restoration of the old system and order, and they abhorred any revolution anywhere, but a fair proportion of the Western European educated classes identified themselves as Philhellenes and rallied toward the fight for Greek independence precisely because it announced the rebirth of Hellas—and with Hellas the radiant glories of an ancient Greece reborn. Of the leading poetic voices of romanticism, Shelley and Byron in particular propagandized for the Philhellene cause (witness Byron in his *Don Juan*); Byron even died for it, if not particularly heroically. The Philhellene idea was, in profane reality, strongly underwritten and propagandized for by the Greek middle-class mercantile elite in diaspora, and by intellectual inspirators of the revolution like Adamantios Korais, men who were never directly involved in the fighting. In marked contrast, the Greek population on the ground, and *a fortiori* the commanders of the irregular (klephtic or guerrilla) bands who *did* do the fighting, acted from religious motives more than from any sense of national identity; their great dream was *to Romaiko,* the rebirth of the old "Roman" domination, meaning the expulsion of the Moslem Turk and the recovery of an imperial political glory, with its renewed golden capital not in old pagan Athens but in Holy Constantinople.[54]

This millenarian Romaic-Orthodox vision was modified considerably as the war went on, not least because the shrewder Greek commanders and revolutionaries saw how well the Philhellene idea, and the propaganda friendly to a new Hellas, served them and sold abroad.[55] Yet running in parallel to the new idea of a heroically revived Hellas was another, an older popular-heroic tradition, raised around the *klepht, armatolos,* or *pallikar,* the folk-hero-*cum*-bandit, a Greek version of the type seen in every part of the Balkan mountains and elsewhere in the "undeveloped" world of the time. His tradition was carried in the songs (*Klephtika*) in which the young untrammeled *pallikar* customarily (and heroically) denied and flouted the authority of his elders, his community, *and* the Turkish occupiers, all of them, all the "old ones."[56]

The klepht was in fact a bandit (the word in modern Greek has only this meaning), and his image intersects that of the special kind of popular hero, the semicriminal type generated from particular social crises, injustices, and confrontations. In the various wars of national liberation that erupted in the nineteenth century and continued into the twentieth, the more antique figure of the excluded, antisocial bandit has very often been reinterpreted in the popular imagination, and so newly heroized. As the armed, bellicose, but often undisciplined core and origination of many revolutionary upheavals, these rebels usually move desperately through a predictable historical and imaginal parabola. Beginning as the primitive sword's edge against the oppressive enemy of the people, the outlaw-rebels are then either successfully or unsuccessfully co-opted into the wider, more rational and specifically political structure of a national revolution. If successfully co-opted they become acceptably national heroes, but when, as often occurs, they fail to understand the political and social solidification of the triumphant postrevolutionary regime (and its new controlling and compromising "political" principles), they are very likely to return to their outlawry and their old brigandish state and style. Even with this reversion to type they may still exemplify popular visions, ideals, and desiderata shoved aside in the revolution's reorganization of society; so, while still called criminals by those now in power, they retain a considerable popular heroic standing.

Greek klephts, along with Serbian, Macedonian, and Bulgarian *hajduks,* underwent these tests and transformations; the Central and South American rebellions against colonial Spain saw something of the same. In Mexico the long, fierce revolutionary struggle culminating in the years 1910–17 saw a complex, sometimes cooperative, often hostile interplay between more organized revolutionary forces and the ancient Mexican *serrano* (mountaineer) traditions of local rebelliousness and the closely related, antisocial, sporadic bandit activity.[57] In all of these cases a celebratory stratum of popular-heroic literature, evidence in oral form, was laid down, from the Greek *klephtika* to the popular *corridos* of a despairing rural and working-class Mexico, and even to a type of folk song found in Anglophone North America.[58]

The great socioeconomic and political manifestations of the nineteenth and twentieth centuries (industrial capitalism, urbanization, the formation of a world market), as well as world war and world revolution, seem to have created that impersonal but oppressive atmosphere in which another "popular" or folk hero with an ancient pedigree could be made to reappear: the "little man" (little but noble in adversity) who refuses to be defined as powerless by those who hold grand power and wealth, and who finally rebels against inhuman oppression and adversity, thereby becoming an outlaw. Usually the abstract, that is, class-motivated nature of the oppression has little place in the legends of outlaw-heroes, since oppression in this tradition is almost always taken as personal and is answered and avenged personally; this, too, is a far-related relic of archaic heroism. The North American frontier, especially the trans-Mississippi frontier figured and decorated as a quasi-mythical West, provided a gaudily tricked-out stage for the play or display of excluded outlaw-heroes, as well as "border warriors" and some other important refractions of what we can recognize as an old heroic macrotype; again, the difference, in the public eye, between what Eric Hobsbawm called the social bandit and the ordinary criminal is often blurred.[59] Some reverberation of this theme continued into the economically and socially stricken times of the Great Depression of the 1930s, when bank robbers in particular were popularly invested with the persona and aura of this "social bandit," the hero of those who had been betrayed by every kind of old authority.[60]

There is a special aspect of the hero in relation to the idea and fact of revolution, running from the several French Revolutions to the Marxist intellectual legacy, because, in theory, we should not be looking for heroes here. Marxism is generally held to be a sternly determinist philosophy of history, and therefore it should have little room for individual heroes and their heroic antics; yet Karl Marx recognized that "men change circumstances,"[61] and V. I. Lenin, the main architect of the Bolshevik triumph, explicitly displayed that extraordinary manipulative power wielded by the determined, even obsessed individual—acting as a "world spirit incarnate" at least as significant in his time as Hegel's Napoleon. The Soviet revolutionary regime, as it first consolidated power, had to redepict heroism as a strictly proletarian virtue, and it did so with a stubborn and sometimes ludicrous emphasis on the exemplary and didactic social function of this sort of hero. (The Chinese revolutionaries took this pure proletarian emphasis even further.) The acceptable proletarian hero image was also retrojected into the past, resulting, for instance, in the Soviet glorification of the eighteenth-century peasant rebel Pugachev and the Cossack brigand and folk song hero Stepan—Stenka—Razin. Socialist theories and policies will, by definition, have to undergo some marvelous torsions to constrain the individual-heroic potency, while recognizing a "people's hero."

The Heroic Image

There exists any number of candidates for the title of typical romantic hero tale, but my own choice as a paradigm of the genre and of the heroic types contained within it would be the Russian Mikhail Lermontov's *Geroe Nashego Vremeni* (A hero of our time), of 1840, and not just for the title.[62] Lermontov's *Hero* resulted from one of the Western European intellectual and literary currents that, not for the first or last time, eddied into Russia, where they could fertilize growth often both wilder and more true to archaic type than the Western parent; and this loosely articulated collection of five episodic stories displays an unsophisticated but often striking style. The different refractions of what Lermontov himself identified as heroism are displayed in his cast of characters, and include Grushinskii, the man of exterior show, a bit of a pathetic clown, eventually shot by Pechorin, the protagonist, in a bizarre duel; and Maxim Maximitch, the hero's old *bon compagnon*.[63] There is the Serbian Lieutenant Vulich, the gambler, brave, taciturn, with little time for wine and none for women, who plays what must be the first game of Russian roulette in literature, and survives, only to be soon killed more or less by accident;[64] and, of course, Pechorin himself, duelist and solipsist, whose eyes are marked by "deepest melancholy" and whose journal reveals him to be utterly bored, living on only "out of curiosity."[65] Pechorin is no towering literary creation, but Lermontov has taken pains that, once encountered, we will remember him. Lermontov's work is also marked by two thematic characteristics, one new and one much older. The first is his open and expressive appreciation of nature's wild drama, with the mountainous Caucasus as an especially theatrical and "romantic" backdrop; the second makes its appearance in the endemic warfare that is also part of the backdrop, especially as it sets the Russian regular military against a Chechen tribal enemy, with the Chechen *dzigit* (the young hero-warrior) acting the primitive part of the archaic hero and displaying his violent style and values, all rediscovered, rearmed, and restored to life.[66]

From Byron and Lermontov to Zapata and eventually Fidel Castro, the image of the hero comes forward to our own time, carried along in a number of parallel tracks or currents, sometimes contrasting, sometimes openly competing. The collection of heroes continues with the new accessibility of the hero-tale thesauri of diverse peoples—African, Amerindian, Asian, Oceanic—as well as the gathering up of folktale heroes kept alive in oral traditions on the fugitive or isolated edges of European "high" or urban culture: traditions maintained, for example, in the Russian *byliny* or the

Finnish Kalevalic rune verses. The Balkan South Slav lands, especially revealed through the collecting and interpretative work of Milman Parry and Albert Lord and their students, have yielded one of these living oral heroic traditions, important not only for its content but for what it told us about the complex tropes, devices, and techniques of oral performance, and about the processes involved in transmitting the oral tradition.[67] Thus our access to other kinds of tale-telling, other renditions of the hero's life and works, has been vastly enriched. The number of heroes, and of heroic traditions, that we now "know" or know about has stretched, in terms of time *and* space, to make available a collection of source material only barely knowable a century ago, and quite unimaginable a century before that, when the—antiheroic?—intellectual writ of the Enlightenment ran relatively unopposed, and the enlightened Voltaire made belittling remarks about the barbarity of the drama of Shakespeare.

To take one area in which the hero is securely embedded, the *Märchen* or folktale, this genre had a long and lively existence before it was identified within a scholarly frame (as genres always are) and collected, beginning with the nineteenth-century labors of the brothers Grimm. Other European scholars followed in their turn, usually (at first) collecting and collating in their own regions or nations; a typical and important example is Paul Sébillot's five-volume *Le folk-lore de France,* published from 1904 to 1907.[68] The next logical step was to be the invention and superposition of some method for identifying, categorizing, and organizing these folk sources, and reducing their multiplicity to some order. Beginning with Antti Aarne's *Verzeichnis des Märchentypen* (1910), the identification of types (and then more narrowly and precisely, the proliferated motifs) of the folktale culminated, but would by no means conclude, with Stith Thompson's massive *Motif-Index of Folk Literature* (1955–57).[69] Thompson's compendium remains a particularly important tool for research in and on the hero, and not necessarily only for the folk hero of the *Märchen*.

Scholarship (and, indeed, a general interest in the hero) was not to be limited to or by the collection and the thematic organization of the sources directly telling of the hero's feats and fate. In the third section of this chapter, titled "The Hero in Our Time," I expand on the explorations into the heroic that have been more recently launched from various directions, impelled by various disciplinary and other agenda.

THE HERO AND HEROIC LITERATURE
The Heroic Song

We in our time have our being mainly if not absolutely in a literate culture. The written word informs and, by consequence, constrains us. Yet with some notable exceptions our imaginal evidence for the postures, figures, and deeds of heroes is identified and conceived as originally oral, cast in the form of chant, ballad, or song, and sung-and-so-created by specialists in this distinctive genre. Albert Lord's eternal and omnipresent "singer of tales" is our unforgettable active icon: the verbal web weaver catching his audience by his deft peformative magic, his ability to balance the set narrative framework of traditional tale with his own skillful arts and his expansive special knowledge of trope, turn, *tessitura*, pattern, and evocative word. In resinging he continually reinvents and re-presents to his audience the known but new heroic tale.

The special difficulty springing from this description is the obvious one: very little of the (originally) oral, sung epic remains oral, to be expressed or re-created by the bard. Songs have become texts, in more or less the following stages: (a) a performance, which may be casually recorded (that is, recalled in whole or in part) by the auditors;[70] (b) the creation and reception of a firm or standard text, an "edited" version of an originally oral version of the song/epic; (c) the identification and collection of surviving texts, the reconstruction of manuscripts, and other technical operations involved in the reception of text.[71] (In a separate category, epics may also be *created* in a written form, with no initial oral or performative stage, like Virgil's *Aeneid* or Shota Rustaveli's Georgian *Vep'khistqaosani*.) Problems of translation then arise between newer and older forms. Eighth-century B.C. Homeric Greek, for example, was only accessible later if "learned," which is to say studied in its archaic Ionian particularity, even in fifth-century Athens; *Beowulf*'s Anglo-Saxon verses were nearly as impenetrable to Middle English speakers as they are to us, because the verses were not just old but remained in what is essentially another language.

In certain isolated populations, however, and because of unique historical circumstances, the ancient "epic" language might be more widely retained. An Irish Gaelic literacy maintained a knowledge of Old Irish, kept alive apart from the Anglo-Norman and the subsequent Angloglot ascendancy in that land; Iceland's literate population is proud to this day of its strict maintenance of the stern and rockbound language of the Old Norse sagas; and at a slight diagonal, a Hispanophone, or someone familiar with Greek *dēmotikē*, will have comparatively little difficulty with, respectively,

El Cid's epic or the Byzantine period *Digenes Akrites*—medieval border epics created at about the same time but at the two ends of the Mediterranean.

On the whole, however, the reduction of the ephemeral "song" to written form brings its own problems, strictures, and stringencies—as does the removal of the original text into a different language. Will English, French, or German, for example, have a precise or even a comparable term for a word or phrase used in the original? More important, can the idea system encoded in the translator's language encompass conceptions expressed in the original language of the epic? The so-called simplicity or terseness of epical language (but not every epic will show it), along with the formulaic elements prominent in that genre, may seem to ease the process of transmission—but then again, it may not. Dense or semantically thick and heavily allusive epical formations may in fact be the most difficult to transfer to another language frame: the skaldic or poetic interpolations put into the Old Norse sagas, with their often technical, multiple, deep, and occluded meanings and purposely complicated "kenning" phraseology, are an important case in point. Translators will bring widely varying levels of idiosyncracy to the project; and questions of precision versus an immediate understanding of the text, the rendering of style, or even the choice between verse and prose renditions, all must be worked out. Success (or even an acceptable final version) is by no means predetermined.[72]

Because our knowledge of the traditional archaic hero cannot easily be separated from our knowledge of the *descriptio* of his acts, which is usually if not invariably carried in his specific epic source or sources, any modification or distortion of the descriptive epical evidence is liable, in theory, to affect our reading, and therefore our subjective experience, of the hero in his objective and personal immediacy—though allowances have to be made. Few in our time can immediately, by reference to their own experiences, seize on the sensations of Akhilleus angrily defying an Agamemnon, a doomed Hektor fleeing that ravening Akhilleus, or a Beowulf leaping up in the night to seize the grim monster Grendal in Heorot Hall. We are necessarily left with the words of the poet, the singer—and he wasn't there, either. Very often, indeed, "he" was actually "they": with a few exceptions our epical evidence is the product of an anonymous series of singer-redactors.[73] Moreover, it is also likely—and recent evidence from the vivant folk epic traditions (as in the South Slav area) reinforces the point—that the "basic tale" is not just passed diachronically, from singer A to singer B to singer C and so on down the years, but that the primary tale may also be sung by another bard (A') and passed on in this rendition to singers B' and

C'. Here, for our increased confusion, is a synchronous axis, formed of parallel song creations.[74]

The adventures of the heroic life are sung to a special audience, and usually in a specially differentiated and marked poetic form, that is, in an "epic mode." Heroism's characteristically active substance and the singer's style and craft are woven together, and the psychology of the heroic is necessarily remade to fit the critical receptors of the auditors. When a folk epic emerges from the older (?) warrior-heroic ambience and moves off on its own track, we, as separate audience or readership, must accept the Otherness that affects us as receptors.[75] We look in or listen from outside the description. And this is inevitable, for in these particular respects we are "not like" the hero, in whatever epical context he dwells, in terms of space, time, language, culture, and psyche. We are not he.

We also must remember that when an oral epic tale has been converted to the arguably more solid and separated written form, the problematic of transmission is by no means exhausted. The original graphic rendition seldom survives; copies of that original—whatever might exist—may be marred by scribal misunderstanding or error, may be partial, or may include other matters deemed of interest to someone along the axis of transmission, so much so as to change or even to occlude the epic *esse*. A very early example of this appears with the tenth-century Germanic *Walterius,* an "epicoid" experiment familially related to the Nibelung Cycle, but so marked by the monkish mind (especially the intrusive and critical "acid humour") of its author, Ekkehard of St. Gall, that it is deemed to have left the strictly epic mode altogther.[76] And there is no reason why only one version of the "prime" tale was reduced to writing; other versions, at other times, may have been written down—and this was well understood even before it became clear that oral transmission can show the same "synchronous" or parallel production. The scholarly apparatus attached to any modern version of an epic tale will usually include a description of the manuscript tradition, with a *stemma* drawn up that reconstructs what may be known of how that particular epic source descended to us. Of course, scholars are powerfully inclined to find an *Ur-* or "first" version or at least a most authentic, approximately original rendition of the epic they are interested in; such a search depends on our time's essential academic *Geist,* a kind of lust for proven continuity. Sometimes it is successful, but often it is not.

What we have at last is a written text, a version of the epic or other heroic narrative source, variously recrafted and stylized, by which I mean that the ultimate redactor-translator has inserted some sense or reading of a style appropriate to the content, as well as giving us the content, the dramatic assemblage of heroic acts, itself. Are we looking then at historical data, conceived as usable in the distinct historiographical enterprise? Are these heroes real, to the extent that they existed, acted, and were recorded, in real human historical time? That is a question to be differently answered, with strong reverberations and connotations attached to each answer. One response would be that the question has no real meaning because of the strict, more than generic separation between historical narrative and heroic song, but I will set that overnice response aside. To look "through" the epical evidence to some recoverable historical plane ought always to be possible in theory, with variable results.

In pursuit of history's authentic vagaries we can conclude to our satisfaction that Spain's national hero, El Cid, is firmly identified with the actual Rodrigo Diaz, Conde de Vivar, flourishing his "two swords" in the 1050s of our era; eastward in Byzantine Anatolia, with his adventures set in about the same time, another border lord, the hero Basil "Digenes Akrites," has not emerged from the fascinating murk of legend into the certifiably historical light despite the best efforts of interested scholar-researchers.[77] These two epics always seem to provide us with a nice symmetry, as well as some proof that there is no such thing as "the" epic. Such variance is not uncommon as we move through the sources for the heroic "lives," but I want to hold off any detailed discussion of this problem until I have opened the question of that heroic source, the epic; for now the historicist puzzle has to be approached from another angle.

Why is there such concern among historians and others for the detection of verifiable, probative facts, those "real" historical data that might be encased in an epical creation or other source for the heroic? Mainly, I think, we detect the typical historian's deep and schooled distrust of that old enemy, the imagination, of unanchored and unchecked fancy, of time and time's products confused, set adrift willy-nilly in the midst of the anomic patterns and the *entertaining* face of poetry and song. If this positivist bent is less marked and pervasive in the profession than it once was, there remains an abiding professional suspicion that in the realm of the human image-making or fantasizing faculty the rules are too different, too casual, or beyond proof one way or the other—which is perhaps worst of all. Yet what we have learned, after hard effort, is that these entertainments are composites of history in their own way, supplying evidence of ideals, mindsets, even providing a valuable record of fantasy's explorations and limitations at the time: a record of human mind itself, solidified in its own moment.

Let us now move even farther away from the unequivocal fact and toward myth—myth that delights in equivocality.

Myth and Epic

If there is to be an absolute line drawn between the "hero in myth" and the "epic hero" (a line that may very well be forced), it will usually separate that area where the gods and their overarching "cosmic history" operate, and that zone in which man ostensibly stands alone in his unique story, or history, responsible for it and for himself. Definitions of myth, as they stress the grand themes emplaced there, tie the mythic hero in special ways to these divine forces, plans, and confrontations. Strictly speaking this hero is a representative, even a pawn, of the vast inhuman potencies, and his destiny is constrained (and may be formed) by the whim of divine cosmogones and supernatural arbiters. Such a differentiation invites a fairly simple (but eminently usable) structural plan, as we see in Daniel Madelénat's "fundamental" model of the epic, in which he cites the mythological epic (with the example of the great Indic *Mahâbhârata*) where "les héros se lient étroitement aux dieux et la fable s'apparente aux schèmes archétypiques."[78] This scholar's second model is, predictably, the mixed class of the mythico-historical epic, with the Homeric poems recognizable as the perennial *chef d'oeuvre* or *chef de genre*; his third model is the true human historical epic, as worked out or specified in the medieval French *chansons de geste*.

The mythological epic and its archetypical thematic elevates the hero, who is made the shadow partner or the earthly avatar of divinity, to an awesome height, and yet this immanence of the gods "risque" (Madelénat again) "de dévaloriser l'exploit héroique."[79] We can see how this might be true. We also know that some archetypical themes, however distorted, may make their way into other epical contexts, but our usual Western (Eurocentric) declaration, that "man is the measure," seems to demand that the heroic drama will be made more tense and more effective when the player-heroes are clearly human, however imbued with extraordinary and often superhuman (as contrasted with supernatural) powers and attributes. Certainly most of the epical evidence used in this study will be taken from those songs that celebrate plainly human heroic beings, whatever the sometimes strange *parenté*, and the prodigious powers, of these heroes.[80] The use of the mythic hero as a representative of psychological archetypes or deep patterns is another matter, which needs to be given special consideration at other points in this study.

Typing the Epic as Epic

Scholars who have attacked this analytic problem display no sort of una-
nimity in their conclusions, but they have at least constructed a series of
variously usable sets.

In the ideally heroic vehicle, the protagonist is indubitably human, though
almost always invested with oversized and probably superhuman characteristics and powers.[81] A parallel perception places the heroic action described in the song within some identifiably historical context: a frame of
actual (read: possible, understandable) events depicted as occurring in a segment of human history. The historical frame may not be consistent or even
coherent—it may include mixed refractions of a past reality—but the underlying assumption is that it represents a human, not an extrahuman,
essentiality.[82]

The problem is that what one might call potential tensions pull both at
the definition itself and at whatever ideal specimen is isolated. The *Iliad*,
for example, has the stern weight and traditional gravity to qualify it as *the*
grandest heroic epic, the first in our tradition, yet its human actors are begotten, mix with, conflict with, and are aided and manipulated by Homer's
egregious gods, the *athanatoi*, and thus a strong presence of the nonhuman
is introduced into the tale, which is exactly why Madelénat calls it a "mixed"
epic. But yet again, these deathless gods are very particularly and idiosyncratically drawn—not as the immanent-transcendent and omnipotent
deities of "pure" myth, but as a quarreling, dangerously powerful pack of
deities armed with every sort of special agenda and private interest, and
themselves subject to overarching fate. Such may be the unique view and
creative instinct of one epic poet, but we cannot avoid it, and we also know
that the Homeric view of gods and men has detectable parallels or near kin
elsewhere in the epic literature.

SHAMANIST EPIC

We also know that around the core of the heroic tale is a kind of epic already
mentioned, in which mythic representations and confrontations are unquestionably dominant over the human actors. Madelénat, in his division
of categories, uses the immense and multifold Indic *Mahâbhârata* as his
prime example.[83] For Paul Zumthor the identification "mythic" is prefer-
able to an earlier notion espoused by Sir Maurice Bowra, who suggested
the label "shamanist" for that epic type that he specifically contrasts to the
historic-heroic category of epic.[84] The shamanist epic—wherein the central hero or heroes show not only superhuman or wonderful but *magical*

powers, especially displayed in their shape changing, undying vitality, and supernatural velocity—is also given as a folk-epic category by Felix Oinas, whose dependence on Bowra is clear.[85] Oinas's primary text for the type is the finno-Karelian "constructed" epic, the *Kalevala*.[86] In this regard it is only fair to note that Leminkäinen and Väinämöinen, the "shamanist" heroes of the *Kalevala*, are, like other shamans, still identified as human (though they may in fact have been euhemerized from older gods), and thus, in some ways, the narrative telling of the trials and triumphs of the shaman-ist hero rests at a point somewhere between the strictly mythical epic and the historical epic tale. The *Iliad*, with its intermixed gods and human actors, is set into another interstitial place in this theoretical continuum.[87]

MYTHIC-HISTORICAL EPIC

The intermediate mythic-historical epic, with Homer's songs as the prime example, brings to us both rich data and many problems. The heroes, espe-cially of the *Iliad*, are formulaically related to the gods (as they are called *diogenês*, that is, "of the blood of Zeus"); they often boast a direct familial relationship as well, yet they always betray their human autonomy, and their destiny, in an inevitable mortality, as they are then compared at last, and fatally, with the Deathless Ones. The contrapuntal humanization of the Olympian gang in the *Iliad*, its occasionally shocking display of every human emotion writ large, its personal and familial feuds and occasionally undignified, petty, and even comic-burlesque behavior have often been remarked.[88] Whether or not the *moira* of the hero is set by a divine mover (often in a haphazard and changeable fashion, or as a result of an unseemly conflict between two divinities), the working out of this destiny is set in a human space and dimension. But the Homeric epic is the relentless target of so much scholarship that, in one sense, its importance as a source can almost be overstated. I can plead that the *Iliad* is an atypical epic in several respects, as in its insistence on long and discursive speeches by its actors; it is also completely typical as an epic taken in structural detail. It is impor-tant to note that, read as an exercise in divine-human relations, it is not alone in its type. Again we ought to look toward such structurally related heroic contexts as the Irish Celtic, where the heroic Ulster Cycle, while in no way constructed as a unified dramatic narrative with the same degree of divine action and intervention as in Homer's epos, does introduce divine players, especially as progenitors of the hero, as in the case of the brilliant arch-warrior Cú Chulainn; one god is a protector and another a fatal opponent to the hero, who gets both life and death from them. Yet, though with a different coloration, the Old Irish hero tales—at least those of the

Ulster Cycle—are still worked out on a human plane, always dominated by the effulgent glory of the warrior and of the great fame-seeking, war-making kings, queens, and chieftains.[89]

We can detect a next stage if we continue to follow the corpus of Old Irish epic, which features the Fenian Cycle of *fían*-warriors under their paradigmatic chief, Finn mac Cumaill. This stage pushes the gods and goddesses and supernatural powers in general into a separate topos, where they exist in a parallel world, usually though not always enemy to the adventurous, fully human hero in his own zone.[90] The most archaic Welsh Celtic material, as collected in what are called the Four Branches of the *mabinogi* ("tales of heroic youth") and an allied body of hero tales (including the archetypical Welsh Arthurian quest tale, *Culhwch ac Olwen*), contains some Celtic divinities thoroughly euhemerized, or at least much masked, and only recoverable by comparison with the Irish pantheon (the Túatha Dé Danann) who inhabit the Old Irish Mythological Cycle, or with what is known of Gaulish and other Celtic divinities on the Continent.[91] This ancient Welsh world looks, or feels, something like that of the Indic *Mahâbhârata,* with its divine-human, mixed, and often confusing cast of characters.

HISTORICAL EPIC

The historical label seems to refer *in some way* to a narrative structure describing, or at least using as a model, real and human actors and their actions. For Madelénat the identification most closely fits the Old French *chansons de geste;* so the *Chanson de Roland* has at its proven narrative "center" the annihilation of a Frankish force retreating from Spain, ambushed in the Vale of Roncesvalles in A.D. 778, and the name of one of Charlemagne's lords, Roland, "prefect of the Breton march," is in fact briefly noted and linked with this disaster in the contemporary chronicle that survives to us.[92] For Oinas, with his special knowledge of the Finnic, Baltic, and Slavic folk-epic genre (and particularly the Russian *byliny*), the historical tag most closely fits the group of Russian tales telling of those exceptional tsars, such as Ivan *Groznij* or Peter the Great, or, in Yugoslavia, the songs of real bandit-rebels (the *hajduks* or *ushoks*) who warred interminably against the Turks and left their warrior's postmortem fame behind.[93] In this view the problem of the historic is progressively solved as we move forward, toward a contemporary frame, from older hero tales, and our foci can increasingly boast the hard edges of fact agreed upon, however much nonfactual, epical-fictive decorations may still be clustered around these facts.

At the same time, however, the word "historical" need not necessarily imply a strict transcription or organized transmission of "real" events: it may simply be set in sharp contrast to the figures and forces of myth. The role of the supernatural is reduced here, though never completely eliminated, and the protagonist-hero can actually be placed in a more or less identifiable time frame.[94] Within this frame, and as his tale is told, his full humanity is never doubted, and his actions, if enlarged and wonderful to behold, are essentially those of an extraordinary human being.[95]

The Old French *chanson de geste* is taken as a fully developed morphism of the epic, and yet it is never the monolith caricatured (if that is not too strong a word) by Mikhail Bakhtin. Three thematic groupings of this song type have been organized and identified: the "royal" narratives centered on Charlemagne, the "traitor" type (beginning with *Doon de Mayence*), and finally the big and broad cycle of the knight-lord Guillaume d'Orange.[96] The first or "royal" cycle, however, insofar as it reveals an epic hero, can hardly be said to exist, since its most complete and centered narrative (the *Pèlerinage de Charlemagne*) is essentially a comic sendup of the *chanson de geste*-type itself (Jessie Crosland is exactly right to call it "a curious poem"),[97] while the *Chanson de Roland,* the best known of this genre, is extratypic and even aberrant in several important respects. The second group of songs is identified as narrating an "epic of revolt," where the *chanson de geste*'s hero turns decisively against the king (Charlemagne's son Louis or, in one instance, old Charlemagne himself) and sovereignty's pretensions themselves are questioned, derogated, even condemned.[98] Yet this category again has some variation: the derogated sovereign may be depicted as weak but still a skillful manipulator (King Louis in *Raoul de Cambrai*), or as violent, loud-mouthed, and malignant (Charlemagne in *Renaut de Montauban*). *Gormond et Isambard,* though it has a Christian king, Louis, against whom the hero Isembard rebels, also features and favors the pagan king Gormond, who is as much a gallant and chivalric hero as he is, by definition, an *antecrist.*[99] Royalty, as hero's foil or bane, is cast in the *chansons de geste* in a number of different roles, or can wear very different masks, and this feature supports Calin's expansive opinion on "the immense variety to be found in the Old French epic."[100]

These sources also differ from other epic narratives in the important respect of the value they place on kinship and family. The hero's "house" (that is his *geste,* which has a double meaning) contributes its fund of support to the hero's singular tale and plays a significant role. It even generates a host of subthemes, and in this regard it seems to look northward toward the saga. Loyalty to the "house," protection of the inheritance, problems of fosterage and of brotherly solidarity, all run through the narratives (especially *Raoul* and *Renaud*) and are set both against the personal temper and isolated stance of the hero and the political structures dominated by the king. In this respect the *chanson de geste* separates itself from the epic type first set in place by Homer, and from the stream of "songs" continued in the Celtic and Germanic epics, but it also differs from the Old French epic romance that luxuriantly developed in the Arthurian *matière de Bretagne* and other subject cycles. In both the epic genre cast in the traditional mode and in the *roman cortoise* of Chrétien de Troyes and later, the extreme individuality of the hero is a given, and the hero's kin group is either unimportant to the point of near invisibility or inhabits a few, usually important, situations displaying tension and requiring resolution: father against son, brother against brother. Penny Gold, in *The Lady and the Virgin*, adds a perspective acutely drawn from the place of women in the two genres: in the *chanson de geste* the particular role of the hero's mother, especially as his nurturer and adviser, is strongly underscored; in the *roman* the woman (as wife or lover, not as mother) is not a nurturing figure but a competitor or object of competition, though in the main her dramatic role is "contracted" and diminished.[101]

The Old French *chansons de geste*, to return to the theme of historicity, fall somewhere within the loosely drawn bounds of historical reality; the Old French epic romance or *roman* emphatically does not. The historical reality of Roncevaux and that lost contingent of ambushed Franks has already been mentioned; other songs flirt with verifiable fact to a greater or lesser degree, and have a historic locus extending into the tenth century.[102] The Germanic epics certainly have an earlier historical root: their principal setting is the last stages of the *Völkerwanderung*, about the fifth to sixth centuries. They can be pegged to real time at least by the attested historicity of some of their dramatis personae: Attila named as Atli or Etzel, Theodoric-Dietrich (the king of the Ostrogoths), Odovacer, and even, from the list of the Beowulf tale's actors, the genuine Geatish king Hygelac.[103]

The old problem of historicity in the epic can be handled with more or less subtlety. From the very beginning (whenever that may have been), an audience's acceptance of the power of the epic poem has been partially dependent on its acceptance of the reality of the scenes narrated and the actors described. *We* now accept that the scenes and figures were real to this audience: time and place are conjoined in those allowed to "live" the epic. This is another and probably a clumsier way of expressing Zumthor's most perceptive insight, that history in the historical epic is "important less for the data that it provides than the emotion it is able to elicit."[104] True, and yet paradoxically we, who in our time do not immediately experience the epic and its scenery but study it—that is, read it—seem to find an emotional *frisson* in the identification of an epic character as a real (historically existent) person. Perhaps, like Plato, who also lived and thought in a self-constructed atmosphere far from the immediacy of the epic experience, we still do not trust poets.

The Hero in History

But a new question now arises. Even if we accept the essential humanity of these Western medieval heroes, the epic is still considered fiction (a story, that other meaning of *historia* or *histoire*), so of what use is the "historical" in this last type of epic? Jan de Vries, in his *Heroic Song and Heroic Legend*, is of the opinion that the *Nibelungenlied* reflects or contains "three worlds" in its assembly of verse stanzas: the original migration period (fifth-sixth centuries), the twelfth-century courtly ambience out of which our specific poetic rendition of the epic comes, and an atemporal mythic-archaic imaginal world that generated the characters like Sigfrid the Dragon-Killer and the Amazonian Brunhild.[105] These three worlds are not perfectly congruent; disjunctions appear that create perceptual, even psychological strain, as the anachronisms and discomfiting lapses become apparent. (Or they would, if the eye or ear that takes in the tale were constrained to analyze rather than to experience.) In our own age the ordinary reader, casting about in his or her mind for a memorable medieval hero tale, would quite probably fasten on the Arthurian knightly *matière*—but the historical core of this mammoth corpus (the possible real existence of a Romano-Briton war leader at the time of the Saxon migration-incursions in the sixth century A.D.) is nearly invisible. The florescent Arthur tales that survive to us consist of an old core of Welsh inventions (apparent especially in *Culhwch ac Olwen*, the so-called Welsh *Triads*, and a few poetic fragments) and a many-branched concretion of Continental descendants—which may ricochet back to "Britain" to affect later Welsh inventions.[106] This collection of material displays various aspects of the epic hero, but strictly speaking these Continental inventions are not epics.

On the other hand, the Norse-Icelandic *Jómsvíkingasaga* is a clearly epicized version of the real confrontation between Jarl Hákon Sigurdson, briefly ruler of Norway, and King Sveinn Haraldson of Denmark in the late tenth century.[107] Sveinn, portrayed in this saga as a rotten and shiftless *roi fainéant*, persuades the chieftain of the Jomsviking order, which was a kind of Viking warrior brotherhood, to assault Hákon by sea with a force of his Jomsvikings. These include warriors described in almost Homeric terms, like the ferocious Bui Vesetison and his nephew Vagn Akesson, a Viking whose bloodlust and arrogance is almost Akhillean; yet the dénouement of the expedition, the battle of Hjórungavagr, though bloody enough, is curiously truncated and anticlimactic. The Jomsviking battle host's attack is frustrated by a supernatural intervention engineered by Jarl Hákonn; the survivors retreat, and of their redoubtable war chiefs only Bui dies—by suicide; Vagn is captured but survives his scheduled execution.[108] This epiclike saga can best be analyzed as a Norse-Icelandic exercise in antimonarchism—a familiar epic theme.[109] Within the genre of saga, and in terms of the accepted divisions into which the Old Norse–Icelandic sagas are divided, the *Jómsvíkinga* falls somewhere between the legendary type of tale (the *lygisögur* or "lying sagas," sprightly and unfettered inventions) and the historical or family sagas describing the acts, ordinary or extraordinary, of fully identified human actors and their kinfolk.

A larger puzzle extending from the sharply problematic area of the "hero in history" has to do with the deep origins, in human time, of the hero himself. The question is this: what are the historical circumstances that enable the emergence of the epic hero, that is, the hero central to epic, with all his heroic acts? (The qualifier *epic* would again seem to put us outside or beyond the *myth* and its indwellers, of gods and men coexisting, coinvolved in momentous events of cosmic, especially cosmogonic, significance. We must locate our heroic root in human history conscious of itself as such, as irrevocably human—and this is a correlative of that core epic already discussed.) The usual procedure would attach various epic traditions more or less loosely to identifiable historical movements and confrontations and the players involved in them: from the intrusive, charioteering Indic Arya, to the piratical Achaeans of what the archaeologists call the Late Helladic period, to the hairy heroes of the *Völkerwanderung* and the slightly better-dressed knights of the *chansons de geste*.[110] Behind these disparate, casually assigned eruptions of "heroic" activity, and the epics that report them, there may be a macropattern derived from the archaic migrational surges of the oldest Indo-European speakers, and even from the restless genius (however suspect such an image may be) behind the expansion of these peoples, or at least the expansion of this family of languages.[111]

In an early work, H. M. Chadwick laid out "The Causes and Antecedent Conditions of the Heroic Age" as an endpiece to his most ambitious work, *The Heroic Age*. He found his two ideally heroic societies, the Achaean Greek and the Teutonic, to have been brought into being, arguably, by "great movements" or mass migrations (though he recognized that migrations need not always bring about this heroic effect) and by "the influence of a civilized but decaying empire" as attractive adjunct, a kind of magnet to or prey of the new heroic society.[112] Chadwick also cited, as a prime characteristic of his heroic age, a novel "emancipation" from tribal (or kin-based) law, revealing a society "free . . . of restraint"—even divine restraint, as the gods, reduced in their socially ordering potency, could be considered safely set aside, or made less significant in a new and disorderly social cosmos.[113] Chadwick also notes the confluence of "Mars and the Muses": the warlike fixations of such an active age showed that heroic poetry "had a considerable influence upon the spirit of the times."[114]

Half a century later, Maurice Bowra also tackled the etiology of heroism in "The Meaning of a Heroic Age."[115] For Bowra the keynote is the peculiar aggressiveness of his heroes: they "realize their full nature, and display their surpassing gifts, in fighting."[116] A "heroic age" is thus specifically and vividly outlined as an "age of war,"[117] and the tension between societal desiderata, especially the need for the society to police and defend itself, and the irritable and irrepressible forcefulness of the weapon wielder, is all too apparent.

Yet violence occurring in the past is not the only foundation upon which the perception of heroism and its age is built; that perception also looks to the particular spiritual universe of the combatants, who are seen as the disrupters of constricting and limiting forces, responsible as individuals for "a snapping of many ties and obstructions" that had previously curbed the energy of the individual.[118] The old règles du jeu no longer pertain, though in some closely organized early societies (Bowra calls these "theocratic") the element of social control retains its restrictive authority, and some power derived from the gods refuses to allow any newer, fuller exercise of a released or unleashed human nature. The heart of the new spirit is what Bowra calls the "sharp realism of the military outlook," which seems to signify an amendment, even a denial, of any transcendent motives derived from a divine-cosmic plan.[119]

Another paradox now appears, for although the new heroic age may escape the usual patriarchal or royal authority (what Bowra calls the "perils of priestcraft"), it cannot allow a truly uncontrolled heroic potency. This new age demands that its newly emergent "heroic" war leader gather around him others very like himself, so as to be "surrounded by remarkable men" all of the heroic stamp, comprising a "single military caste."[120] Agamemnon, Charlemagne, Arthur are only a few of the epic king-heroes who boast such a following of fighters—champions whose prowess is nearly identical to that of the leader and who will call upon whatever sword power supports his—and their—claim to domination. And there, of course, will be the everlasting rub.

But still we ask: out of what exactly placed concatenation of historical circumstances does the "heroic age" burst into being? Bowra's insights are not without persuasive force and analytic acuity, though I have rearranged and reinterpreted his reconstruction. First, the new phenomenon, vital and unsystematic, may spring up from the dying body of an aging, sclerotic world view, as in the Europe of the late antique period, when the old imperial order fell to pieces and tribes and whole peoples pulled free from the grasp of those decaying controls that had hitherto kept them in place. (A second stage may follow, as when the disintegration of Charlemagne's exiguous imperial pretensions brought forth a new, perhaps tragic, sense of heroism and its possibilities, flowering by reaction out of the ruin of yet another dream of power.)

Second, the migration of protoheroic peoples is seen not just as a "violent break with the past" but actually keeps intact an image of their old homeland perceived both as abandoned territory and as a lost, but psychologically still supportive, spatial ambience. (In Bowra's perhaps oversubtle view, the movement from the old homeland leaves the heroic tale or legend as the only tie with what was left behind. Psychological vulnerability is desperately converted into a reactive "heroic" attitude, and a grave sense of loss underlies one of the emotional constructs of the heroic.)

Third, conquest forces other peoples, caught in the path of the migrant conquerors, out of their old and secure enclaves and elicits a "heroic" reaction, often cast as a last stand against the surge of intrusive newcomers. (Bowra sees such a pattern in the Britanno-Welsh originals of the Arthurian legend, and some of the Serbian tales of the prince-hero Marko Kraljević seem to have a similar root.[121] On the other hand, the Irish Celtic epic cycles, which may retain a few fossilized references both to the migration-invasion of the island by the Goedelic Celts and [anachronistically] to the much later incursions of the Vikings [the rowdy northerners called Lochlannoch, or "men of the lakes"], still carry a self-generated character all of their own, like yet unlike the neighboring Welsh Celtic sources.)

Fourth, the invention of a past "heroic age" may depend from and react to the spirit of a subsequent religious conversion, which, though clearly blessing and saving the converted, left behind a separate, undoubtedly heathen past now conceived specifically as an age of great heroes. (In this instance Bowra points to the Irish Celts and Christianity. He may be right, but parallel situations are not easy to find. Traces of such a notion may be detected in the Persian *Shâh-nâma,* and perhaps in the Norse-Icelandic family sagas, but neither of these two epic or epiclike contexts sets much of a serious stress on the unbelieving past as specially marked, or as identifiably heroic.)[122]

Bowra's thesis has the great advantage (and vulnerability) of stressing psychological patterns and pressures in producing the real sense of a "heroic age." Following this line, we know that the release of the deep and dangerous human propensity toward spasms of uncontrolled violence is certainly prominent in all heroic biographies, though how this bloodthirsty dæmon, once released, is to be reined in again is not quite clear in Bowra's arguments. The consequent or attached problem is that the hero's unbridled essence, always expressive of his individual character, is usually circumscribed only by a code *interior to himself,* and very rarely accessible to sweet reason. What Bowra calls the "sharp realism of the military outlook," though it may have helped to liberate the ancient warrior from the supernatural strictures wielded by some priest-king (if indeed such overarching "theocratic" power ever existed), is not exactly visible in the often unrealistic, gloriously illogical acts that so mark a heroic age. "Military outlook," "military caste," and even "war," when war is defined in abstract terms of strategy and plan, demand order, organization, hierarchy of command, and implicit obedience to that hierarchy—and none of this fits easily into the heroic thoughtworld and its normative forms. We can see the difference semantically (or lexically) in the two words "warrior" and "soldier," even without looking beyond them to the separate, more loaded concept of the "hero." On the other hand, war simply considered as that state of human affairs in which hostile confrontation is enabled and even legitimated—war seen as a fine opportunity for the display of dominating force, for testing oneself, and for joyously beating down and defeating the opponent—will always be attractive to those violence-seeking and perpetually belligerent characters who, willy-nilly, seem to be our heroes.

Bowra is quite right to point to the constellations of "remarkable men" who are drawn to and surround legendary war leaders like Agamemnon, Charlemagne, and Arthur. He is probably also correct to connect this warrior grouping to the Germanic *comitatus* (the Old Irish *fian* would be another example of this sort of fighting-tail). The *comitatus* was held together by the adhesive of mutual honor and aid, formally articulated through a series of oaths sworn between leader and his man, and also by the reinforcement of that view of true honor which obligated the follower not to survive his leader, fallen in battle.[123] Yet it is clear that the great hostings, followings (or gatherings?) described in Homer, and also in the Old French *chansons de geste* and in the Arthurian cycle, are continually beset by cen-

trifugal forces born in and animated by individual heroic pride, and by that
diamantine heroic sense of ultimate selfhood. The epic dramas of enraged
Akhilleus, of prideful Roland or, later, Raoul of Cambrai or Guillaume
d'Orange, or the story of the destructive tensions boiling up between Arthur
and Cei (in the Welsh quest tale *Culhwch ac Olwen*) or Arthur and Lancelot
(in the Continental legends), plainly show the fragility of *any* authority
when it comes into conflict with the ever present, ever ready heroic construction of a personal identity tied to an indissoluble sense of honor. In the
Norse-Icelandic sagas this tension between centrifugal and centripetal tendencies appears to lead to the creation of two warrior hero subtypes: the
Þórr-warrior willing to follow, serve, and represent; and the Óðínn-warrior
absolutely resistant to any form of subordination to a directive principle—
or, more to the dramatic point, unwilling to bow to the personal authority
of any monarch or his agents.[124]

Bowra's final insight is ingenious, though to our age perhaps inevitable:
that the recollected image of what constitutes a "heroic age" also has an economic dimension. It often includes a memory of past plenty, of riches widely
distributed among the warriors and proudly displayed, like the arm rings
worn in the Germanic North.[125] He sees this recollection as most powerful when a culture is pushed from an earlier hegemonic position, as in the
Britanno-Welsh situation in the sixth century, or is constrained to present
an image of a "heroic" past because of the collapse of a more complex political system, like Charlemagne's brief dream of empire renewed, with the
consequent deeply felt loss of what he calls "the sense of limitless possibilities."[126] The point is well taken, but the image of a prosperous "heroic" past
is also probably allied to the nearly universal fantasy-projection of a passed-
away golden age, an age whose gilded economic image is crafted to make
the strongest contrast with present stringency or shapeless poverty. We
should also recall the particular forms that "heroic" wealth usually takes: re-
distribution, especially by the hand of the generous war leader, is important
as the meed and mark of honor, but the greatest economic factor recognized by the warrior-hero is booty—goods or wealth taken from someone
else at the point of the sword. The recollected scene of a fatter economic
age or age of past plenty, in other words, is shot through with the same violent tones as the other images defining a "heroic" era.

Epic and Romance: Derivations

The first instinctive reaction or temptation in looking out at the tangle of
scholarship spread over these two related genres is to locate a nice, simple

dichotomy, or a striking bipolar arrangement, and hang as much of the assembled evidence as possible somewhere on this divided framework. An extension of Schiller's appellative formula might do: the "naive" and the "sentimental" made to refer, respectively, to the epic (formulaic, stripped-down, simplified) and to the romance (complex, ramified and, of course, sentimental).[127] Or, borrowing from the somewhat faded inventions of the late Marshall MacLuhan, and giving his terms an admittedly distorting twist and yank, could we convincingly speak of epic as "cold" (sharp-edged, distanced, sculptural, and stylized despite its bursts of violence) and romance as "hot" (immediate, convoluted, emotionally active)?[128] The oppositive "closed/open" suggests itself; Mikhail Bakhtin's excursus on "Epic and Novel" can be read as an extended polemical declaration specifying the "openness" of the novel and the "closedness" of the epic, a genre "congealed and half-moribund," guarding an "absolute past" that is "sacred . . . walled off absolutely from all subsequent times," possessing a "hopelessly finished quality and . . . immutability," and so on.[129] Bakhtin's absolutist, even totalitarian dictum invites a response, which I will defer for now.

One could even suggest a division of categories based on the Homeric poems, such as Madelénat's description of the *Iliad* ("harsh, somber, where war, anger and violence are deployed") and the *Odyssey* ("sweeter tonalities, more varied adventures"); both are related to the fantasy tale and to the "nonchalance anomique"—a brilliant phrase—of the later romance novel.[130] This analytic statement on epic and, or versus, romance recapitulates an Aristotelian distinction, as drawn in his *Poetics*, and should remind us that it was the rediscovery of the *Poetics* that reignited the controversy in sixteenth-century Italy between ancients and moderns, with the former leagued to protect the unity, purity, and high purposes of the epic, among other old and sanctified "high" genres, while the latter briskly advanced the new and vital "mixed" epic romances like Ariosto's *Orlando Furioso*—a passionately individual and resonantly "romantic" work that audaciously took off and ran with the previously sacrosanct epical figure of the Paladin Roland.[131] Aristotle's revival puts him at the center of an argument with both historical and typological dimensions; and the attitude opposing the maintenance of "high styles" or high genres encourages that very experimentation, openness, and thrust toward diversity that eventually leads through the romance to the modern novel.[132] At the same time, however, Northrup Frye was of the opinion that "the conventions of prose romance," once this form appeared, changed little; the genre remained diachronically resistant and intact despite the energetic florescence of theme and character in the romance type over the centuries.[133]

Clearly the epic is an anterior creation to any romance, even if the *Odyssey* is accepted, as some have suggested, as a romance or protoromance. The romance's relative age is separate, too, from any subjective placement in an "absolute past." This said, complications immediately set in. The *Aeneid* fits into the epic category as a concretization of a heroic past and of a "national" origination and divinely shaped fate; yet its tendentious character, written form, and known authorship, as well as its complex time line mixing epic past, present, and future, put it at very least into a special subcategory of the epic family. When new literary forms appear in that Hellenistic or imperial world eventually dominated politically by Rome, they will include such phenomena as the epic-escapist *Argonautica* of Apollonius Rhodius, created as an epitome and perfect manifestation of the sometimes wildly experimental Hellenistic mind-set. Prior invention or source, epic or mythic, simply provided the narrative matter upon which later authors battened, introducing those novel elements—fantasy, sentimentality, playful sexuality, free and even formless adventure—that take this genre far away from the heroic epic in its strict sense.[134]

A second branch or lineage runs from this late antique root consisting of satire, and then of the looser and more various sons of satire: the parodic and comic literary creations. In terms of the configuration of generic and diegetic connections, the moralistic intent of the satirist puts him in a special place, and his grumpy inventions will eventually connect him to Rabelais and to other satiric, but also comic, writers of the Renaissance and after. By contrast and by definition the comic and the parodic triumphantly display their "low style," and so must oppose the "high" style and purpose of the epic. Bakhtin says that "laughter destroys the epic," and he is quite right, in a way:[135] the two modes may be directly opposed, because of the theft or comic misuse by the parodists of epic or even of mythic themes. (One thinks of Plautus's *Miles Gloriosus* and, later, of those antiheroes who appear in the insinuative mock-chivalric productions of the late medieval period.)[136]

In the next stage of the epic-romantic relationship we are led from the chivalric romances of Chrétien de Troyes through the creations of the later medieval specialists in courtly and knightly themes, like the German *Minnesänger*, with a terminus ad quem somewhere in the Italian Renaissance. Certainly one way to organize this confused (and written, not oral) mass of individualized creativity, and to relate it to the parallel universe of the epic, is to bring back the cyclical image: as the Hellenistic Greek, Byzantine, and certain ingenious Roman litterateurs had selectively extracted and remade a portion of the classical mythic-epical *matière*, so the European talent later would work the lode that included the Arthurian and related source tales, the Old French epics (especially the egregious *Roland*)—and, when they could effectively be fitted in, bits and pieces taken from the older classical thesaurus of epic, translated and reread as knightly tales and romance sources. Any raw material would do; all was grist for this mill.

Behind much of this investigation into types and genres, the connections and disconnections of epic and romance, there flourishes the grim pursuit of that literary snark, the novel—or the first novel, the *Ur*-creation, prime of its numerous and uncontrollably proliferating kind. If the novel must be separated at the root from any epic type to find such an artifact, how can the novel be related—and, if necessary, detached from—the genre of *roman/romance*? The linguistic history that makes *roman*, in French, equivalent to the typic novel brings difficulties, and German usage is more or less parallel, being taken from the French. Russian follows along in this borrowing, but Spanish introduces a special confusion, for its native *romanza* is not equivalent to "romance" as that term is used elsewhere—yet with the great Spanish rebel and rogue Cervantes we have something clearly sea-changed: "the death of one kind of fiction and the birth of another."[137] Such a statement establishes Northrop Frye's position in the old but still hot debate over the novel's first place. (Fortunately this is not a puzzle I am required to solve here.) Epic, *pace* Bakhtin, ought to be visualized as a constellation of distinct images, not as any sort of lump or unbroken monolith, but whatever epic is, it certainly is not a novel[138]—although it does touch the novelistic by way of the mediation of epic romance.

Epic and Romance: Deviations

The most simplistic attempt to identify the romantic epic in the preromantic era will naturally stress the most obvious element: the enhanced component of "love and adventure," for the romance is "almost by definition a love story."[139] Some vision or version of sex, one might say, is superadded to the endemic violence. By "love" we seem to understand that the motivations of the hero will begin to include his desire to *win* a woman (usually but not always a human woman), not merely to possess her, and she then becomes the goal of a variation on the heroic quest theme. A variety of female characters may be extravagantly mixed into the narrative, even including the Amazon (who is an epic figure) or powerful women adept at manipulating supernature (sorceresses and enchantresses), but the realistic, familial-feminine personalities who appear in the *chansons de geste* will very often be excised or forgotten. Closely connected to these redoubtable females, oddly enough, is one who on the surface appears to be an essentially powerless figure: the virgin. She, especially in Frye's view, undertakes to move the narrative action, on one level, *because* she is a woman, for romance rests on, and operates out of, a reversal of the usual secular roles.[140] Woman-as-virgin works through craft, guile, and secrecy, in operations clearly parallel to the magical, and specifically contrasted to the overt and violent force wielded by the hero, so that she achieves her own "happy ending" through the capture of the relatively becalmed, immobilized, even sedated heroic target of her secret affections. This magical or quasi-magical quality, the vivid potentiality of the virgin (male or female but usually female), is seen in her solid placement, over long ages, in both myth and in ritual—a point not missed in his time by Georges Dumézil.[141]

The boundary between human and Otherworld realms becomes permeable in the romance, and indeed the ambiguous suasions and subversive actions of supernatural powers vigorously revivify the romantic (as compared with the epic) scenario. The twinned base motifs of the feminine and the magical-fantastic will thus be much to the fore, but the theme of romantic love—subsumed or contained in the quest, the frustration of quest, and then the triumphant rejoining—can vary in its formulation from area to area and example to example. In the North the category of saga we call fabulous (the *lygasögur,* generally grouped with the *fornaldasögur* or "tales of far-off times") can include wildly comic sexual escapades, as well as highly distinctive heroes who, much like Odysseus, display and glory in the unbounded manipulative, reversing, and masking powers of the true epical trickster.[142] The attainment of the heroic adventurer's final prize, in other words, may be brought about through distinctly unheroic means, not least because the solidities and sharp, firm edges of the epic as epic, our normative-heroic narrative, are bypassed or ignored.

Sometimes a doubled or tripled story line will combine quest adventures pursued by a hero of the true muscular marque with a parallel adventure undertaken by a tricksterish, even a magic-wielding, partner.[143] Or the central hero may be painted in thick, stolid, and lumpish colors, all the while being energetically worked upon by a brilliant constellation of surrounding characters. Sexuality, which is rarely prominent or even particularly relevant in the normative epic, is a complexly powerful but fragmented force here: *in potentia* with the virgin; frustrated in the hero and others; separated off into comic-erotic incidents; combined with a sacrificial theme; partly or completely sublimated in the more formally imitative romances that even boast the ideals of a borrowed southern *cortoisie.*[144] The range of story options obviously is greatly widened.

The feminine element immanent in the romance epic, wherever located, is both subtly disequilibrating and directed toward forming another equilibrium, so as to break and re-form the narrative frame. The epic-romantic palette is richer, and the emotional ambience, as we would expect, is less controlled and certainly less predictable than in that other, strictly and sternly epic form. And with the feminine, in what looks like a natural consequence or congruence, comes the fantastic, again made powerful in its interference, in its open boast of limits transgressed and of order disordered.

The second component, "adventure," which both the romance and the epic share, is specified to be the adventure "out there." In this mode the hero leaves some familiar land or strand and ventures out into a strange zone, indeterminately far from his heroic base, or marked as so sufficiently strange and remote that the unnatural/supernatural is naturally resident there.[145] Again we find the evidence of the collectivity of Norse sagas, these creations from the margin, instructive, because even in a "family saga" like the *Eigla* the saga hero Egill finds his supernatural adventures, in the main, far away from his Icelandic home.[146] Broadly speaking, the zone of adventure is not only spatially distant or constructed imaginally as a transzone, an indeterminate never-never Land, but is structurally different as well. When the hero sails off in pursuit of adventure (as he does in the *barca aventurosa* taken up and detailed by David Quint), he is led into a series of confrontations and incidents that have no necessary or organic closing, because the adventure of romance, as compared with the true quest narrative which it sometimes resembles, really has no shaping principle: the carrying narrative, like the *barca aventurosa* itself, "has no destination but the adventure at hand."[147]

It is a serial and not linear process by which these adventures are invented: each is undertaken for its own sake, in the grand enlargement of the field of narrative possibilities, or even in the multiplication of "marvels" as fantastic accoutrements to the tale. All this separates the romantic epic from the epic proper, which operates in its own enclosed and brutally predictable world in which we know that "nothing is left to chance."[148] The romance intends to be literally diverting, and its diversions don't fit at all well with the linear plotting of epic and the epic's relentlessly etiological imperative.[149] Yet the two genres are continually mixed, if not confused. The mixture need not be merely thematic, as when Chrétien de Troyes draws on some lost epic identified with the original Welsh Arthur; it can be total, as in the exceptional "fusion" of *chanson de geste* and romance, genres absolutely separated at birth, in Ariosto's *Orlando Furioso*.[150]

Epic and Romance: A Social Dimension

The problem of isolating a social dimension in the production of heroic narratives shows two key parts: the first refers to that social configuration from which the particular genre seems to spring; the second refers to shifts within a genre, and how they may reflect social variations.[151] An innovation in genre has its causes, and though it may be assigned to one creative mind (Cervantes is often identified as such a singular inventor) it is better, at least for my purposes, to factor in the broader social dimension. To lay out this social dimension (or operation) again runs the risk of oversimplification, especially if the social element were adduced as the absolute, primary factor in producing these different genres, or if a term like "folk" were simply left to stand as a social marker without sufficient explanation. Instead I see the social situation as intricately connected to, not as explaining, the imaginal artifact: the two coexist.

Some heroic narratives will not easily fit into the columnar categories drawn in table 1. The Virgilian *Aeneid* as a specifically crafted and openly tendentious or propagandistic epic is one; the Persian *Shâh-nâma* combines elements of archaic myth, heroic epic, and folktale: it also builds a historical-chronographic framework to hold it all. The most "archaic" extant Welsh narratives, the so-called *mabinogi,* are mainly mythological, or myth-adventurous, in nature, whereas one of the tales usually put in with them (*Culhwch ac Olwen*) is mythepical, another luxuriantly combinatory specimen. Among the Scandinavian-Icelandic narrative sources, Saxo Grammaticus's narrative "history" stands as a variegated growth, with mythological roots, epic-heroic branches, and even (some claim, however unlikely it may seem) a touch of genuine historicity as well.

Table 1, as it makes social identifications and introduces the element of social causation into a discussion of epic-romantic relationships, also operates along a developmental time line, from archaic past to modern times— or, roughly, the present. The five columns (A–E) are placed more or less arbitrarily, though column B (the saga genre) is purposely set between the epic-aristocratic and folk narrative sources, since it seems to be typologically related to both. What I am aiming for in table 1 is a visualized scheme in which social organization is attached to, and in the broadest sense modifies, literary type or genre, however approximately. The table ought also to serve as a time line template to organize roughly these varieties of heroic discourse—again, very approximately, because some genres are more available for or susceptible to time line organization than others.

EPIC

The epical sources develop *for, out of, because of* a warrior-aristocratic fighting elite, though this elite may be led by a chieftain or war king. The warrior group monopolizes the violent and glorious act of war, and is intensely anomic except for an unwritten code supposedly controlling the individual's behavior, and the associate sense of personal honor to be won or jeal-

Table 1. Heroic Narratives

A (Epic)	B (Saga)	C (Folktale)	D (Romance)
(1) Homeric-Achaean		(1) Archaic folkthemes	
(2) Armenian			
(3) *Aeneid*	(Eddic sources)		(1) Greco-Roman romance
Shâh-nâma			
(4) Germanic	(1) *Völsung saga*		
(5) Old French			
(6) Byzantine Greek	Saxo (?)	(2) oldest *byliny*	
(7) Spanish, Welsh	(2) Family sagas		(2) Continental Arthurian romance
(8) Irish	(3) *lygisögur*		
(9) Serb		(3) Ossete Nart tales	(3) Franco-Italian romances (Ariosto, e.g.)
(10) Caucasian			
			Cervantes
(11) New focus, recovered epics	(4) Recovered, rediscovered saga literature		(4) Novel/ romance
		(4) Serbo-Croat heroic songs	(5) Historical novel

ously guarded. Points 1, 2, and so on in column A show the various surges of epic production, from the archaic Homeric to the late medieval Serbian and Caucasian, but does not try to show how these generated epics might be related, if at all, to one another. The uncorrupted (or unmodified) production of the strict epic type stops, except on the edges of Europe, in around the twelfth century; the rediscovery of the epic belongs mainly to the nineteenth century, and is not manipulated by an aristocratic elite, but rather by a bourgeois (and "national") sensibility. The possibility of a reversion to the epic mode emerges in our own times, in a special and, in one sense, reactionary view stressing the inutility of "individualistic" nineteenth-century literary modes, and reaffirming some sort of archaic-heroic and, oddly enough, simultaneously communitarian or *gemeinschaftlich* model.[152]

SAGA

The saga sources for heroic action, considered as a distinct phenomenon, must be closely connected, at their birth, with the early Germanic epic mode, as with point 1 in column B, the Völsung nexus. In the canonical arrangement, this first manifestation of the northern saga as a prose creation, and separate from the cosmomythical Eddic tradition, is set aside in time (in the *fornaldarsögur*) and has a fairly heavy mythic seasoning. Then the main group of Scandinavian-Icelandic heroic sagas emerges in the social framework, born from an independent smallholder society and mentality, one connected to the identifiable epical-heroic mind-set by a kind of warrior's egalitarianism, a persistently agonic urge and confrontational persuasion, and withal a sense of the individual warrior's unimpeachable honor, and his sense of fatality. The type is kept alive, as a living and vital fossil, through Iceland's long cultural isolation and through the obsessive Icelandic sense of the value of a unique cultural inheritance.[153] Within the general saga mode are subtypes such as the adventures or legendary tales, *lygisögur*, clearly related to the column c in table 1, the folktale.[154]

FOLKTALE

The folktale aggregation containing identifiable heroic evidence probably has its archaic origins deep in the stratum of myth; additionally, the dominant conceptualization of the folk hero carries a stronger hint of the fantastic and of such wish fulfillment themes as the reversal of low social status and the triumph of the downtrodden, and we presuppose the generation and nurturing of the type in a traditional peasant or village-centered "small" society far from the centers of power, creating an imaginal world peopled both with heroes borrowed and transmuted from the "high" epic, and with heroes of its own devising. (The Russian *byliny* of the Novgorodian Cycle even include merchant-heroes, showing a positive image of a part of society ignored or denigrated in the purely epic-heroic tradition.)[155] In the Ossetian Nart tales an invented heroic-mythic past sustained an isolated peasant-herder culture of the Caucasus just barely conscious of its former Scythian greatness (point 3), and in the best-known and most recent example of a nonaristocratic source for heroic narratives, the Moslem Serbo-Croat heroic songs demonstrate, in a remarkable fashion, the persistence of a number of epic-heroic attitudes and themes transformed and repeated for a special audience (point 4). Almost by definition folk sources reveal their resistance to history, as shown in their deep-seated and almost perverse inclination to manipulate and re-form its component data. Part of this tendency toward mixing and confusing temporal markers comes from the originally oral form of the tale. But note that these sources can seldom be merely kept in category as fantastic and fantasizing entertainments.

ROMANCE

Column D, of epic-influenced and other modes of romantic narrative, is most readily organized using a time line, and also seems to require such a chronicled discipline. The congruity comes about, arguably, because the romance genre feeds on and yet reacts from the "high" epical genre: a social group, conceiving of itself as separate, that is, as unwilling or unable to accept the heroic scenarios and other themes of a previously dominant social elite, seems to demand the various releasing mechanisms and experimental modes that romance newly provides. Thus the Greco-Roman (Hellenistic) romance narrative (point 1) appeals to a literate, urbanized—even in one sense, bourgeois—class, but also to a bureaucratic or civil-official class dwelling in the several megalopoleis and other urban centers of a newly imperialized world. The *roman cortoise* and the related forms of medieval epic romance (point 2) have been arbitrarily assigned to the new sensibility of a twelfth-century "new-fashioned," socially reoriented European feudal aristocracy, but the genre grows even more robustly and complexly in the late medieval and Renaissance period, in its newly urbanized social conformations, where another kind of heartily bourgeois literate taste is served—and the taste of an upstart, nonclerical educated elite even more so.[156] From this point complicated, interrelated lines run, with some interruption, to and through the border between novel and romance, and the eventual efflorescence of the new and dominant novelistic genre in the European nineteenth century. At this point the literate European middle class not only begins to generate new literary forms like the historical novel, but seizes on and engrosses what it can of both folk and epic genres, through a new and concentrated process of rediscovery and refocusing.[157]

Where myth and the mythic fit into this creative scheme is worth a moment's reflection. Probably myth feeds all, providing the sustenance for the first efforts of epic, saga, and folktale heroism (and, of course, for some large part of Greek tragedy), and remaining as a potential nutrient, a sort of universal possibility, at any point and in any genre.[158]

THE HERO IN OUR TIME

Our own century, following on the great romantic shift of the preceding century, presents a complicated and multilayered general scheme respecting the hero: a mélange or perhaps a bricolage of different perceptions and aspects. In addition the burden of our own history affects or confounds him, his type, and ourselves. On the one hand catastrophic events, in particular the horrors of the two world wars, struck down much of our nineteenth-century inheritance as it consisted of a positivist, rational-liberal, progressive view or plan for mankind—an effect that simultaneously reduced our sense of the active scope of the free individual viewed as a social construct (or constructor), and strengthened the perceived role of the isolated, fate-chafed, intensely subrational, and furiously active heroic figure. New views both of society and of its often uncontrollable and destructive elements became drastically, dramatically available. The peculiar and sinister "Aryan" pathology of Nazi Germany, and the reactionary and often purposely primitivist hero worship underlying other "national" forms of a fascistic or ultraist ideology between the wars, gave ample evidence of the dark foundations of the warrior-hero's persona, and suggested how a destructive atavism based on these foundations might be recalled and revived. Heroism has no specific susceptibility to moral judgment, but it is easy nevertheless to identify a "bad" heroism in all of this—or heroism in a bad cause.[159] A countervalent heroism was finally produced as well, in the antifascist nations, sufficient at least for the purposes of wartime propaganda, though often marked by that puzzled ambivalence accorded to the marked or exceptional individual in a supposedly egalitarian, democratic society, to say nothing of the strange and simple virtues that "heroism" might have to demonstrate in order to appear congruent with the ideology of a socialist or communistic system.

Behind or beyond the exigencies of *Realpolitik* or other kinds of socially influenced narrative describing the hero in history in our own time, the idea of the hero has been constantly reworked from patterns set in the preceding century, then redivided along a variety of lines: inquiries into social structure (anthropology, sociology); personality and essential character (psychology, especially psychoanalysis and depth psychology); or cognitive expression in spiritual structures (mythographic analysis, *mythologiques*, the study of the history of religions). Naturally these categories will not remain rigid or petrified; the last is especially permeable and often takes in data and analytic suggestions culled from the other two. What might be uncharitably called intellectual faddism also has had the effect of advancing one disciplinary or subdisciplinary approach over another for greater or smaller periods. Nor are these disciplines absolutely unitary and irrefragible: emergent schools within each can operate from quite different theoretical suppositions, and thus demonstrate different approaches to the "problem" of the hero. To some, in fact, he is not even recognizable as a separable or discrete essential or ontological phenomenon.

Anthropology

In our century, anthropology and sociology have not only created a space for themselves in the world of learning but have generated enough information and energy to allow the formation of various theoretical perspectives, separated into the schools just mentioned. Some of these schools have formed around the influential conceptual shifts devised or dominated by particular individuals (Bronislaw Malinowski and Claude Lévi-Strauss in anthropology, Max Weber and Emile Durkheim in sociology); others are built on general, consensual theories of how societies operate and are best observed, recorded, and dissected, like the so-called functional anthropological approach made especially important in British anthropological circles. The primary focus of all, however, is human society or culture, which immediately raises the question of how the image of the hero, with his ambiguous personal situation within the group and his oftentimes disruptive, antisocial individualism, is properly capable of being fitted into any scheme of social operation and cooperative utility. That question remains implicit, in the background, of the paragraphs that follow.

In anthropology, the very large accumulation of observations on existing premodern, non-Western cultures has provided a valuable set of framing materials for what might be called a comparative backdrop to a study of the hero-warrior. Fieldwork has discovered tribalized societies in which the warrior (essentially the armed, usually young male) still maintains a position as society's prime defender-aggressor, and shown us the old matrix within which the image of the hero is formed. Arnold van Gennep assembled quite early the materials for his *Les rites de passage,* including the long segment on initiation rites that is still the starting point for any study of male age-group maturation and process-in-ceremonial, especially the inculcation and recognition of male adult, potentially warrior, status.[160] Other data recovered from the field and connected more directly with violence (more or less organized violence) and the role of the fighting man include studies of the blood feud and the "reciprocal" use of force, the genesis and morphology of headhunting and other rituals of tribal war, weapons taboos, sexual behavior and aberrance as some part of a warrior's code, and the very rich symbolic, ideological imagery connecting man to animal—primarily, in the case of the warrior, to raptor and carnivore images.[161] Another large topic, partially connected to the sociological concern with socially aberrant behavior and crime, deals with the "outlaw," with expulsion from society, or with a precarious existence on society's boundaries, its *limina.* All of these investigations resonate within the imaginal field of the individual hero.[162]

At the same time, Michael Meeker's analysis appears incontrovertible: "anthropologists have not studied how an increasing resort to force and coercion in popular political experience may have affected . . . cultures and societies."[163] Violence and lethal coercion, the cruel opposites of socially adaptive mechanisms, tend to be intrusive and almost unwelcome in the broad flow of the relatively calm and considered anthropological collection and publication.[164] Of course, this pattern of discreet avoidance is not always possible; research done in areas where war making is an ongoing social option—or entertainment—and where the warrior is a prominent player in a particular society's formulations and operations, has had to come to terms both with the active player and with his violent "game." For instance, the fortuitous discovery in the 1930s of the large, populous, but technically neolithic Papua–New Guinea Highlands revealed a number of tribal groups deeply and enthusiastically devoted to war and to the agonistic arts of the warrior. Six decades ago C. H. Wedgewood examined the phenomenon of organized violence in an aboriginal area of Papua–New Guinea, revealing, among other features, a practice in Melanesian warfare that immediately recalled "heroic" behavior as displayed from the *Iliad* onward: the ritualized duel between high-status fighters representing each side.[165] Of course, such a feature of so-called primitive warfare had been noted by observers of "primitive" peoples for a very long time: at the very least, since Caesar toured Gaul.

So it appears that what might be called the anthropology of war, with an attached concern for the stance and behavior of the hero visualized as an "extreme" case of the developed warrior type and personality, is at least an identified subenterprise within the anthropological discipline. Its range includes studies of North Arabian Bedouin tribes caught up in that good old habit of the "heroic" society, the raid on a neighbor's livestock, with an added Homeric reflex in the poems created on the spot to celebrate specific events of heroic prowess.[166] (E. E. Evans-Pritchard's published work on the Nilotic Nuer, though it consists of highly respected texts proceeding from the *doyen* of the British functionalist school of anthropology, and describes a people seriously addicted to cattle raiding and to something like a cult of the spear, contains very little on the actual conduct of hostilities by these Nuer tribesmen.)[167] Other areas in which the anthropologist might emphasize the area of violent competition would include fieldwork carried out among peoples dwelling in marginal, isolated areas, especially barely accessible piedmont or inaccessible mountainous zones, in which tribalized societies might be caught by the investigator in the process of losing their "heroic" traditions—or, in a defiant reversal, in which the very processes of modernization have broken down older cooperative ties that had once damped down aggression, and so encouraged agonistic, violent individual or group confrontation.[168] The anthropology of conflict still retains the character of a stepchild within its discipline, and this cannot be merely because the collection of information in the field can bring the scholarly fieldworker into volatile and perhaps personally dangerous situations.

Far from the nomads and the blood feudists, a special sort of anthropological research has appeared, using classical (Greco-Roman) sources and materials converted into "ethnographic" data. This idea surely descends from Frazer, but the present field of "classical anthropology" (ethnographic inquiry launched into the classical period and its sources) is anchored in the work of Louis Gernet, a remarkable French scholar whose "big book" is his *Droit et société dans la Grèce ancienne* but whose acute investigations, scattered over more than three decades, were collected in *Anthropologie de la Grèce antique*.[169] Gernet used the considerable corpus of sources surviving to us from ancient Greece as materials for describing that society "comme un ethnologue,"[170] and he was followed by a second generation he strongly influenced: Jean-Pierre Vernant, Pierre Vidal-Naquet, Marcel Detienne, Nicole Loraux. (English translations of much of their work followed fairly briskly on their publication in French.) In *The Black Hunter*, a typical study emanating from this group (who has been described as "not exactly an *école* . . . or even an *équipe*"), Vidal-Naquet tries to decrypt the essentiality of the Greek ephebe, the young warrior-in-training.[171] As he brings together the historical-institutional record and the symbolic apparatus devoted to this important figure, the author shows the ephebe encouraged to act the role of an antiwarrior: an ambiguous creature prone to trickery and stealth, moving and thriving in the darkness of night and in the liminoid frontier zone, and dangerous *because* he is unarmored and essentially weaponless—or armed with unorthodox and unwarriorlike weapons.[172] A representative essay by J.-P. Vernant would be one of his studies relating "myth and tragedy," tracing the reworking of Greek myth by the tragic poets, and the social and intellectual currents that ran from one imaginal form to the other.[173] Marcel Detienne has shown a penchant for what, in his *L'invention de la mythologie,* he himself calls "ambiguous borderlines," the zone in which myth makes or marks its place; he has also taken up the most ambiguous and terrifying of the Greek gods, Dionysos, and explores how the most stringent Greek social and religious taboos may be given mediating shape and operative sacrality.[174] All the scholars of this group appear to be deeply concerned with *invention,* that is, creation: how a society contrives to invent or "think" itself, as specifically propounded in Detienne's *The Creation of Mythology* or Nicole Loraux's *L'invention d'Athènes.*[175]

The collected work of this group of scholars does not go unchallenged; Hellenists of a more orthodox, purely classicist, cast have claimed that Vernant *et cie* may mistakenly combine evidential areas that do not in truth conform comfortably together, and the very description of the authentic approach of the *ethnologue* and the rules of his game brings up hard problems of usable source and fair interpretation.[176] Yet these French scholars, as they pursue the anthropological study of the ancient Greek world, provide a useful service that will receive due credit in the chapters that follow, for they add both a material density and a theoretical brilliance to any research into or among the Greek society that invented the word "hero" and that still influences our perceptions of this extraordinary human image and type.

That very large and complex body of work, the *Mythologiques* of Claude Lévi-Strauss, poses another interpretational problem emerging from a new anthropological-ideological megatheorum, one even more provocative and *français* than the multidimensional labors of Vernant, Vidal-Naquet, and the others just described. To the extent that close descriptions of social or cultural patterns are the usual result of the ethnographer-anthropologist's labors, and as these general features of a society and culture are intrinsically contrasted to the special particularity of the hero, the even more abstracted *suraperçu* of Lévi-Strauss would seem to move farther away from the zone where this figure typically operates. Lévi-Strauss emphasizes myth, especially the "pure" myth or mythic thinking automatically generated in preliterate societies as an attempt to understand or mediate the world, but his approach seems to avoid evidence for the hero, except when *mythic* themes are repeated or reflected in the epic. Lévi-Strauss himself has an untrammeled and vastly inclusive view of myth: "we claim under our own usage every manifestation of the mental or social activity of the population studied";[177] and one of his interpreters adds that "a myth is defined as that which is intelligibly communicable."[178] Heroic epic, in this hypersynoptic view, could not be excluded from the already vast Lévi-Straussian estate.

Reaction to this French theorist can all too easily become reactionary, but James Boon's analytic approach to Lévi-Strauss may have useful consequences for our theme. Boon, a semiotic anthropologist, has shaped his frame of study of the French *maître* and his critics according to cognate literary-interpretative models. Lévi-Strauss in this view emerges as affinitive to the French symbolist poets; British functionalist social anthropologists are related to the nineteenth- and twentieth-century realists and naturalists; and such scholars as Clifford Geertz (and presumably Victor Turner as well) become "pragmatist-dramatist" in modality.[179] Boon eventually returns Lévi-Strauss's structuralism to its reciprocal romanticism, the mode and genre that, among other recollective acts, returned to us our archaic hero; and the French anthropologist may be closer to the brilliant and fatal isolation of the hero than one might think.[180]

Whether one agrees or disagrees with this analysis, or indeed with Lévi-Strauss, the latter's significance cannot be denied. No examination, for example, of the crucial narratives dealing with the hero-king Oedipus would be complete without reference to his provocative decoding of the key myth-narrative of Oedipus in his *Structural Anthropology*.[181] In a wider view, the undeniable attraction of Lévi-Strauss comes from his extraordinarily subtle and multiplex way of viewing the techniques and declensions of human intellect, his theory of how the coding and decoding processes of the mind work. However occasionally overcomplicated and even perverse in his pursuit of *les jeux mythogènes*, Lévi-Strauss must be considered a powerful influence on the study and the figures of myth. How this influence works itself out, taken case by case, is another matter.

The hero, obdurately individual, is too often contrary to or apart from the normative social concerns of the anthropologist, who is therefore made uncomfortable. One could even argue that a preponderant number of field-working anthropologists, though rejecting ideology, have constructed an antiheroic ideology when they take up this figure at all,[182] although some of those working in the discipline have at least recognized the problem. Michael Meeker, dealing with an Afghani group possessed of a powerful self-interest in maintaining heroic traditions or pretensions, noted that the creators of the science of society "sought to confirm a moral vision of human experience" and that such a mind-set nearly always tends to overemphasize rationality and to ignore or underplay "counterproductive" aggression, conflict, and "irrational" force and violence.[183] Clearly an optimistic ideological perspective that seeks out and predicts a rational pattern in human social intercourse will probably find such a pattern displayed somewhere, and so irrational heroism, as an act or concept, will cause every sort of problem. Meeker himself has to use the odd, even oxymoronic phrase "heroic tribes" to describe groups who revive and use as social myth their memory of old conquests and successful warlike aggressions. Yet we ought not to be ungrateful, for what the science of man, even as most narrowly conceived, does contribute to any study of the hero is a great weight of real data on war-making, warrior-centered societies, and the social *realia* that underlie and parallel the imagined, projected portraits of heroic personality and deed.

Sociology

It is not always clear how a science of society—sociology—differs essentially from the science of man just briefly examined; certainly the disciplinary roots are practically the same, and the implied division between the culture studied by one and the social structure studied by the other can often appear artificial. For Emile Durkheim, a founding figure of the sociological enterprise, "primitive" culture and "primitive" society were pretty much the same thing.[184] And Durkheim was identified and declared by Lévi-Strauss to be his own didact-predecessor and model, creator (with Marcel Mauss) of what Lévi-Strauss defined as a "social anthropology" at the time he took the first chair in that discipline (as finally established, in 1960, by the Collège de France).[185]

If we say that a sociological enterprise tends to content itself with (or limit itself to) mature social systems, we have probably left the ground where archaic heroism flourishes, as the warrior is finally replaced by the soldier— or by the bureaucrat. Between Durkheim-Mauss and Talcott Parsons (the latter representing an eclectic-functionalist sociology roughly comparable to the functionalist school of social anthropology) we find the massive figure of Max Weber, but Weber had for his province a "coordinated, panhistorical level of macrocomparisons"; and although there is no dominating reason why the asocial or poorly socialized hero might not have attracted Weber's attention, he did not: there is no special heroic figure, no *Helden-*

typus, among Weber's description of *Idealtypen.*[186] However, as he was much concerned with power, worked out or betrayed in concepts such as *interests* and *authority* (two "facing" ideas, contained in a series of confrontations between individuals and groups for possession of this power), his structures describing *domination* must always be part of the analytic background in any pursuit of this concept. Weber's key notion of *Stand* or "status group," to be strictly contrasted to "class" (with its economic valence and "rationally motivated adjustment of interests"), is important for the understanding of any nobility/aristocracy invested with a stubborn psychic-emotional sense of the central importance of its "standing";[187] and in his view feudalism was a "major variant" of traditional domination.[188] Weber also understood the considerable value, in fact the vital place, of those elements that defined a context by opposing it—that is, a society defined by its outsiders, so that communal solidarity is highlighted in opposition to heroic agonism and mobility.[189] Pressing this grand theorist a little further, we might see him come close to something like the heroic persona in his examination of the Old Testament prophets, noting their "patrician origins . . . isolation from family, passionate loneliness," and their opposition both to kingship (secular authority) and to the "credulous masses."[190] There is more than a shadow of similarity to be seen between this figure and the hero, but the prophet naturally remains most significant in a religious context, not in the fatally patterned *sæculum* of the hero.[191]

Where Max Weber does edge into the definitional ambience of the hero in the strictest definition is in his well-known interest in charisma and the charismatic. Briefly, Weber conceived of charisma as "a certain quality of an individual personality by virtue of which he is set apart from ordinary men and treated as endowed with supernatural, superhuman, or at least exceptional powers or qualities."[192] He is aware of what we might call primitive heroic charismatic warrior figures such as Akhilleus or Cú Chulainn; he even sees a reflex of this archaic charisma (my own term) in the Norse *berserkir,* with their "spells of maniac passion," and in the shaman, whose internal projective energy may be fed by a form of epilepsy.[193] But Weber's real object is to connect his charismatic figure genetically to some kind of authority, to show "how the individual is actually regarded by those subject to charismatic authority, by his 'followers' or 'disciples.'"[194] There is more than a little difficulty here, for though Akhilleus was a war king in the old Achaean mode, Cú Chulainn was not even a chieftain but purely a perfect, and perfectly lethal, warrior and champion; and the *berserkir,* as we shall see, sometimes were themselves animalized "followers," if only under special circumstances. Only if we parse "follower" as "imitator" or "admirer" do we approach the peculiar power granted to the hero by those who invented and used his image.

"Charismatic leadership"—one of the three types of legitimate authority Weber postulates—seems to contravene the central idea of herohood: its ambivalent and frequently antagonistic relationship to the very concept of authority. "Hero worship" maintains itself as a special attitude, which in some cases may even be translated into a perennial *cultus*. Yet what Weber also tells us—and we ought to mark this as we track down our archaic subject—is that the charismatic figure "remains outside the realm of every-day routine and the profane sphere" and also that "pure charisma is specifically foreign to economic considerations."[195] We will have reason to recognize both of these characteristics later. Thus charisma, though it may in Weber's phrase be controlled and "routinized," especially in the modalities of kingship, has at its root a powerful irrational presence and immediacy that demands recognition. I return to the problem of charisma in the concluding pages of this study.

A sociological trace also runs in quite another direction, that is, by way of Durkheim and Mauss to a scholar whose conceptual inventions, and especially whose notion of the warrior and his vocation, will appear as most valuable and significant in the chapters that follow. Georges Dumézil built his theory of an Indo-European *idéologie* on the Durkheimian foundation stating that myth, religion, and other ideational constructs grow out of social and cultural structures. In the Indo-European context (and displayed most clearly in the most archaic evidence, so far as this can be precisely located) the conceptual base describes a society divided or dividing itself, or more exactly "thinking" itself, into three functions: the First Function of Sovereignty (leadership, both sacral and secular); a Second Function, the Guardian or Warrior Function; and the Third Function of Sustenance, the forces of life and health.[196] Though each of these *fonctions* (the word is better kept in its French form to avoid confusion with other meanings in English) may have its own heroes, as each projects itself into gods and myths fitted to each tripartite element, the Warrior Function will hold a special place in my analysis of the hero, his life, acts, and *Geistesgestalt*. The importance of Dumézil's theories has special weight in that the data used here are usually, though not invariably, drawn from Indo-Europe, from the group of traditional, premodern, epic-creating societies that belong to this linguistic family or genus; but criticism[197] has tended to concentrate either on (a) the question as to whether the Durkheimian *représentations collectifs* can properly be derived from a linguistic identification or grouping (that is, of all Indo-European speakers) rather than a socially composite entity; (b) whether the tripartitive impulse is not merely a mental "tic" associated with the importance widely attached in any number of societies to the number three; (c) how tripartition can be specifically assigned to Indo-European-speaking cultures when the threefold division seems to appear in other linguistic-cultural contexts as well; or (d) conversely, how to explain the relative absence (or rarity) of that prime marker, trifunctionalism, in certain important, archaic Indo-European-speaking contexts, such as the ancient Greek.

In addition to his many ruminations on the figure, powers, and fate of the warrior, on the hero myths of various Indo-European cultures, and on cross-cultural resemblant patterns of warriorhood as they can reflect an archaic Indo-European impress, Dumézil also provides another theoretical insight useful in the analysis of the hero-warrior. This insight grows from his perception of the significant bifurcation of the Indo-European First or Sovereign Function into two modes: a Mitraic valence of predictive, coercive, overt authority (resident mainly in law and in the sword power) and a Varunaic valence, involving or deploying hidden, mysterious, and covert powers.[198] In his later work, Dumézil tentatively extended the notion of a bifurcated *fonction* to the warrior's vocation, for certain northern sources suggested two contrastive modes of warriorhood, each connected to one of the Norse high gods. In this new view the "warrior of Þórr" (Þórr's place and powers being approximately parallel to the Indic god Mitra's) is the defender of social order and represents legitimated sword-and-law power, whereas the "warrior of Óðinn" (with Óðinn described as a Varunaic god) displays random, hyperindividualistic, antisocial, and especially antihierarchic propensities to irrational violence.[199] Dumézil's suggestion of bifurcate powers has a discernible tie to some essential work done on "dual symbolic classification" as these studies attach particular symbolic value to right hand and left hand, an idea built upon the unfortunately few published studies by another French scholar, also a pupil of Durkheim, Robert Hertz.[200]

Another important figure, one of a scholarly generation just past, is the Belgian Marie Delcourt, whose research on classical Greek mythemes evidenced the transmutation of social-familial themes and crises (matricide, the origins of magic and craft, the submerged workings of pollution and taboo) into a collectivity of mythic representations, confrontations, and solutions. Delcourt was an ingenious and indefatigable researcher whose work often parallels the *ethnologie* of that French group following on Gernet. A typically brisk and combative statement is, "For the Greeks, a hero is quite simply a dead man honored by those not belonging to his family."[201] Her later explorations are more imaginatively fine-tuned, but at all times she retains a clear, cogent, and unpretentious thrust and style.[202] Her influence remains important, though only one of her monographs, on the symbolically potent figure of the hermaphrodite, has so far been translated into English.[203]

The Psychoanalytic Endeavor

The Freudian revolution, now institutionalized and sometimes even banalized, will perforce have an influence on any reconstruction of the hero, if for no other reason than that we, at the end of the twentieth century, cannot escape the net of this influence. Our perceptual or cognitive field is identifiably Freudian in coloration, not necessarily because we subscribe to his doctrine of psychic self-knowledge or revelation by way of the sacred analysis, but because our mental maps or mapping apparatus must show his work. "I am here to talk about Freud," a colleague of mine once announced at the beginning of a lecture, "not the Freud who invented the Oedipus complex, but the Freud who revealed the Unconscious."[204] To have revealed and begun the tracking of this powerful, dangerously ambushed area of the human mind and its deeply perilous forces was no small achievement, for which we must always remain in Freud's debt. And since the hero is a projection of mind, we ought to pay attention to how and why the good Viennese doctor says our mind produces this image—even though, as we will see, the hero himself often seems to have no Unconscious at all—or, at times, even much of a mind.

Something of Freud's invention will have to stand behind any construction of the hero acting as isolated and beleaguered ego, of course; individual against society, a drama all too frequent in the epos, is rather easily cast into Freudian terms as the conflict between "I" and "they," of ego against superego. The destructive (and self-destructive) impulse that so often surfaces in a heroic narrative is not difficult to decode using the constructions of Freudian psychopathology; in fact, when we observe a violent and deadly heroic scenario, it may be difficult to evade the psychoanalytic view and terminology, in which a battle raging in the mind's dark, volatile, and resistant interior is released, displaced, projected outward against an antagonist who is, in psychic fact, oneself—as hero must slay hero.

Freud may very well give us, whether we accept it or not, some of the sharpened instruments with which we probe our subject and his guises. On the actual figure of the hero, however, the father of psychoanalysis is naive and curiously limited and dated. The primary human drama producing a heroic protagonist occurred, for Freud, when the "sons," the members of his curious invention the "primal horde," overthrew the primordial "father," early autocrat and potent monopolist of the women of the tribe. The guilt for this primordial crime was then assumed by one of these "sons," and this crime is replicated and forever identified in the career of the unfortunate King Oedipus.[205] Freud may or may not have taken his aboriginal "primal horde" very seriously, but his poor Oedipus, as myth and as complex, goes marching on.[206] The pivotal point in Freud's reading of the Oedipus narrative, tale, or myth is the theme of mother-son incest, which we will indeed find below as a fairly frequent transgression—not that the hero commits it, or not at all often, but as he is born from an incestuous union of some kind or combination. To follow Freud and take Oedipus as the primary hero figure raises problems both immediately and theoretically, not least because his story or myth describes him as both hero and king, two antiposed types. But Oedipus does recapitulate the hero's dark biographical trace or process, at least up to a point.[207]

Freud is also involved in the biographical drama of the hero in his complicated relationship to Otto Rank and to Rank's still influential reconstruction of the heroic birth myth.[208] And yet Freud preferred, it seems, to change or reinvent myth, and the Oedipus myth in particular, rather than to depend too heavily on, or even thoroughly know and understand, the Greek original, for what does he mean by "the lying fancies of prehistoric times" if not myth?[209] What he does with the myth he re-creates is also important; in his heroic quest the hero goes back, regresses, to find the safety of the womb. Jung's construction and analysis of the heroic quest is quite different in its scope and goal.

The civil (or not so civil) war between the Freudian and the Jungian schools of psychoanalysis could be explicated (I hesitate to use the word analyzed) in depth and *in extenso*, but I am little inclined to do anything more than summarize it. In addition to breaking with the master and the master's sacred *dicta*, Jung also stands accused by orthodox Freudians of "irrationality" and "mysticism" and with a manifest desertion of reason and the proven value of therapeutic sequence and goal. Freudianism, to the Jungian, is narrow and scholastic, caught and stalled in the "personalistic," the limited, occluded, or fragmentary psychic biography of the individual analysand, as well as in its obsessive insistence on the infantile stage of human maturation as the only psychic *archê*. Whatever the value of these counters and characterizations, it is true that Jung and the Jungians have substantially widened the field of inquiry into mythographic patterns, moving from the individual psyche and the dimension of the dream and the unconscious to which the dream gives access into the deep-mythic dimension; then they turn upward toward that individual psyche, laden now with the cargo of myth, to use these myths to explain the active processes of psychic maturation and individuation. The hero makes his entrance here, for the mythic hero's grand biography, in a Jungian interpretation such as Erich Neumann's, is the strict and potent pattern against which each human individual's progress toward full selfhood and conscious identity must be matched.[210]

Some Freudians have taken up the hero, specifically the Greek hero, as subject, but usually only to add some further ramifications to the *mythe à clef,* that of Oedipus. Orestes and even Odysseus have been drawn into this reductionist scheme, ringing the changes on the triad of father-mother-son, and stubbornly focused on incest and parricide.[211] In comparison, Jung's widest net is spread with his theory of the archetypes, his conceptual images that are generated and reflected in each individual's dream, fantasy, imagination, but always connected to humankind's collective unconscious, as this is made evident, especially expressed, in the priceless treasures of myth. The warrior-hero, as we shall see, is not one of Jung's archetypes (though the child hero is), but the archetypal idea itself acts as a vast but problematic nutrient in which "our" hero may or may not flourish.

From Frazer to Campbell

Finally, this century has produced a number of polymaths whose nets have been cast so wide that these broadcasters seem to escape any single category or discipline, though they may show a familial resemblance or attachment to one or another. In a specializing age they have run the risk of being derogated as relict Victorians, amateurs, or dilettantes—Frazer certainly drew this criticism—or, referring to their widecast methodological bent, accused of illicitly or imperfectly combining different disciplinary approaches. They are, in fact, best described as quirky if not downright eccentric scholars, and their usefulness in a study of the hero and his type varies a good deal, as does their continuing influence on scholarship in general. At base they seem to serve both as references and as reference-points, as a permanently interesting backdrop to the problems set and examined below. No study of the hero would be complete without a discussion of J. G. Frazer, F. R. Somerset (Lord Raglan), R. B. Onians, and Joseph Campbell.

Sir James George Frazer, as father (or stepfather) of some part of social anthropology, might have been placed in that discipline's section, but I think he belongs elsewhere, and not least because his aims and techniques have been specifically rejected, or at least marginalized, by latter-day leading lights of the functionalist school of social anthropologists; in their considered view a true science of man—a science they owned—no longer needed to pay much respect to a panscopic theorist with a single outmoded or extraneous theory, and especially one who casually took his data at second hand, "picking up odd details of custom and story."[212] Yet Frazer is still the author, in *The Golden Bough: A Study of Magic and Religion*, of a Great Book manqué. This massive work (the two volumes of 1890 grew to thirteen in the final edition of 1911–15) deploys its evidence to one end, an end all too easily caricatured, as is the resounding and orotund Frazerian style, but at its core lies what James Boon instructively calls "an allegory of a sensational tragic theme that underlies basic religious and political institutions. The officeholder is slain to perpetuate the office."[213]

To some degree any work that seizes on a wide spectrum of cross-cultural *materia* to make its point (including the present study) owes something to Frazer's broad reach and bright vision; certainly this was true of Lord Raglan's essay on *The Hero*. Boon suggests that a valuable bridge between Frazer and the social anthropologists working after Malinowski exists in the work of A. M. Hocart, whose combination of collected field data, together with a theoretically original reading of ritual practice and myth, gave birth to books such as *Kingship* (1927) and *Kings and Councillors* (1936).[214] Nor has Frazer lacked for a latter-day defense of his method and point of view; I. C. Jarvie's *The Revolution in Anthropology* (1967) offers a well-heated appreciation of Frazerian method and an even more calorific assault on the politicized "revolutionaries" whose work and thought, he says, ought to be cast out and undone, as representing the most arrant philistinism.[215] Fifty years and more after his death, Frazer remains either a foil or an inspiration of one sort or another, if not quite the misunderstood tsar-father who, as Jarvie sees it, some red Leninist radicals (not much of an exaggeration here) lust and plot to overthrow.[216] A recent biography by Robert Ackermann, which avoids Jarvie's *parti pris*, does Frazer the honor of considering him for what he was, a massive late Victorian talent in the hardworking Scots mode, who lived on to become an "embarrassment" to succeeding generations—when they even bother to read him.[217] Frazer at least deserves this temperate and civilized judgment.

Frazer was still alive when Lord Raglan published *The Hero: A Study in Tradition, Myth, and Drama*, in 1936.[218] Raglan made no particular obeisance to Frazer, and in fact does not cite him overmuch, but *The Hero* sits comfortably in the Frazerian camp, though Raglan could never be the effortless stylist Frazer was.[219] His book on the hero consists of three sections: "Traditions," "Myth" (which contains his specific thinking on the hero), and "Drama." The first and third of these sections are, on the whole, without much enduring merit. "Traditions" attacks the claimed or putative historicity of a selected batch of so-called folk traditions, first on the grounds that such tales—of King Arthur, or Robin Hood, or the fertile local rumor that "Queen Elizabeth slept here"—are full of interior discrepancies, false or fantasized data, and simple historical impossibilities, and second because the core of these, especially the most enduring, is never "historical" but mythic, and usually a variation on the same base myth. (Frazer's influence is manifest in this second opinion.)[220] In "Drama" Raglan takes that mythic process and roots it firmly in "ritual drama," specifically "royal ritual."[221] This section is even more murky and ill-organized than the rest of the book, and the author admits that his research for it is not exhaustive or even complete. (That would be left to Theodore Gaster, the most obsessive and rigid adherent to the notion that "myth must follow ritual.")[222]

In his second section, Raglan targets "the Hero" after a long discursis, in which we find such strange obiter dicta as that "the savage is interested in nothing which does not impinge upon his senses, and never has a new idea even about the most familiar things."[223] But after a glance at the "Tale of Troy" defined as composed of "myths—that is, ritual narratives," Raglan arrives at what he chooses to call the hero.[224] The heart of his observational scheme is composed of a pattern, of twenty-two "well-marked features and incidents" that describe a heroic biography or, more precisely, the life and acts of a hero-king.[225] The pattern is then fitted, to Raglan's satisfaction, against a series of exemplary lives, from Oedipus through King Arthur, including the gods Zeus, Apollo, and Dionysos. He goes on to interrogate the evidence for the "historical" hero, detouring through Shakespeare's "heroic" Henry V, in order to separate "history" and "tradition"—and cheerfully, in my opinion, ends by beating a dead horse. Yet Raglan's "pattern" has some undoubted and enduring value—this segment of his book has been recently reprinted together with Otto Rank's *The Myth of the Birth of the Hero*—and no synoptic view of the hero, his biography, and his adventures, can afford to be dismissively cavalier about Raglan's comparativism, ill-based, ill-framed, and "super-diffusionist" (in Fontenrose's word) as it surely is.[226]

Raglan, an epigone of Frazer, is even easier to send up than the inventor of the massive structure of the *Golden Bough*, but it is a simple matter to be unfair. He is a prickly eccentric shot through with the narrowest self-satisfied pragmatism along with the widest and wildest syncretic risk taking. The British attitude toward certain sports was once said to inevitably favor the gifted amateur—the gentleman player—over the professional, while at a more rarified Anglian level the advantages of a classical education were rumored to carry all before them.[227] Lord Raglan's case demonstrates the dangers in both assumptions. At the same time, Raglan is certainly an original, despite his vaguely Frazerian coloration, and only rarely is he dull. Finally, according to Fontenrose, "Raglan has put us on our guard about reading history into legends—that is his one sound contribution."

But sometimes the classical education just alluded to really *does* carry all before it, or just about. R. B. Onians's *The Origins of European Thought*, the only book by this classical scholar to reach a wider audience, is a memorable work, and not merely because of the nearly eighteenth-century amplitude of its full title.[228] It was first published in 1951 and reprinted two years later, but even though it did not stay in print long, it maintained a remarkable subterranean reputation as an imaginative and strangely important book. To this day it remains a mine of ingenious perceptions, suggestive connections, and inclusive constructions—making up a true net of thought, which, once experienced, will never be forgotten.

The author's premises are, in an important sense, materialist or, better, "physicalist": beginning with the Homeric evidence, he plunges into the archaic thoughtworld in which *materia*, physically discernible "things," identify and collocate the vital processes of living, feeling, thinking: human *being*, in the widest sense. His book had its beginning, in the 1920s, as an investigation of the classical data, and moved outward from there. Later, Onians drew in other areas, such as the Chinese and the Indic, which he knew rather more glancingly, but nevertheless handled with an impressively wide scholarly scope and skill. As many educated individuals still know their Homer (or at least think they ought to), it is right and proper in Onian's view to begin at this point, with the question "how do Homeric notions of the main processes of consciousness differ from our own?" [229] His first evidence, setting a pattern he will follow throughout the book, results from his locating, palping, and figuratively dissecting "organs" of consciousness, perception, cognition; and it was Onians who first discovered that although certain key concepts identifying life and identity are lodged in somatic locations (*thumos* [breath soul] and consciousness in the lungs, *psuchê* [life soul] in the head, but with important connections elsewhere), a whole range of other perceptual and cognitive functions have very ambiguous bases: the coincident actions of "thinking" and "speaking," or the powerfully physical "moving" aspects and affects of strong emotion. Thus the Homeric word *aiôn*, or "stuff of life," is liquid, or caught in liquid form; Onians describes it as a "thing . . . like *psuchê* persisting *through time*

... a vital substance necessary to living."[230] Eventually it would come to mean "lifetime" and then "eternity"; and from this liquid image Onians follows the very liquidity desired in warm and vital human life, as opposed to the dryness and coldness that sign aging and then death.[231]

Not all of Onians's peregrinations through the connective tissue of archaic thought have been completely accepted. Nevertheless, any study looking to the powerful individual, as he stands and acts in a traditional or archaic society, will be wise to look to Onians to provide a sense of the amplitude and complexity of very different kinds and modes of consciousness, cognition, perception: a world or worlds not always understood or even apprehended without calling on such a guide.

A large part of the present enterprise may be taken as a critique, explicit or not, of Joseph Campbell, the last and most recent of the theoretical broadcasters I have chosen, whose works somehow bear on the image of the hero. Again, like Fraser and to some degree Raglan, Campbell's appeal to a wide (and perhaps unselective) audience, along with the enthusiasm shown him by certain propagandists for a "popular" narcissistic psychology, rasps the nerve ends of any number of scholarly specialists, from historians of religion through students more adept in the various specific mythologies Campbell plundered in his career. He also had the good (or ill) fortune to achieve what Frazer, Raglan, and Rank never could, an adulatory series of television interviews—which, if nothing else, demonstrated the mythopoeic power of this modern apparatus over a receptive middle-brow television audience.

Campbell's first large book, *The Hero with a Thousand Faces* (1949), is patently in the tradition of scholars like Otto Rank,[232] and his emphasis is definitely on the mythic rather than the epic hero. To his portmanteau approach, and in an effort to provide a stouter theoretical underpinning, Campbell added large parts of Jung's theory of archetypes, enabling him to fill out the "monomyth" in which the eternal heroic pattern is made congruent with a cosmic *Überbild*. In the four decades between the publication of *The Hero with a Thousand Faces* and his death, Campbell expanded to the heroic-cosmic schemes of eternity. Moreover, he relentlessly inflated, desecularized, and apotheosized the heroic role: "The hero has died as a modern man; but as eternal man—perfected, universal man—he has been reborn. His second solemn task and deed therefore . . . is to return then to us, transfigured, and teach the lesson he has learned of life renewed."[233] Such didactic, even hieratic language is typically Campbellian. His later work is, again typically, bifurcated; part scholarship of a more or less orthodox Jungian marque, and partly mystagogic proclamations all too redolent of (or too easily parasitized by) New Age "cosmic consciousness," with its posse of fakirs, their attendants, and other latter-day celebrators of a joyous irrationality.[234]

What Campbell does to aid a study of the hero is to set up stages and categories of the heroic biography and experience that can be tested against the data (data of the sort presented in the following chapters). This sounds as if I need him as a stalking horse, and to some extent this is true, because I think that there is a significant error built into his Jungian attribution. As for that error, in the pages that follow, *res ipse dixit.*

2 THE HEROIC BIOGRAPHY

A terrible beauty is born.
—W. B. Yeats, *Easter 1916*

PARENTAGE, CONCEPTION, BIRTH

Because the hero we have in view is attached to humankind, he will not be generated from the tsar's imperial sneeze, as was that Lieutenant Kije of Russian legend. Nor can he come from totally inhuman fertilizations, separated and distinct from the immense cosmogenic potencies contained in the culture hero. A mother and father of some kind are necessary—but the mixture, incongruity, or incompatibility of these two parents will be central to the heroic biography.

Divine Parentage

The oldest source, by convention, for the heroic mode in our Western tradition—the *Iliad*—sets forth some sort of divine parentage for all of its significant players: this is what *diogenês* means—"of the blood of Zeus." This label, like others in the epic ("best of the Achaeans," for example) is a generic, not an individual identification.[1] In fact, at the time of the Trojan War, when "the history of the heroes in 'time' . . . opens," the casual or fatal sexual intervention of Zeus, as a hero's genitor, was calculated to have been some generations past: Patroklos was reckoned a grandson of Zeus, and Telemonian Aias a great-grandson, as was Aias's archer-brother, Teukros.[2] Others of the Immortals who can be genealogically plotted in the ancestries of the heroes of the war include Poseidon, grandsire to Nestor and to Theseus's son Menestheus, and Hermes, who most appropriately figures as

Odysseus *polumêtis*'s great-grandfather on his mother's side. The goddesses among the Deathless Ones are more immediately prominent, "condemned . . . to bear sons to mortal men":[3] Aphrodite herself on the Trojan side (mother of Aeneas), and the divine nymph Thetis on the Achaean side (mother of the hero-cynosure Akhilleus). I will look to what I think to be the special significance of the goddess mother in due course.

To some degree the scenario of the Trojan War points to a detour or diversion in our theme. The *hêrôs* of Homer—a "noble gentleman"—is rather an attenuated refraction of the properly mythic hero type, as I have already remarked. This is not to say that certain key figures in Homer do not show a valid, typic stamp. Akhilleus remains as a model for the sculptural icon of the fighting warrior-noble; Odysseus the Crafty One displays all the unmistakable stigmata of the trickster-hero. In Diomedes the volcanic fury of his father Tydeus may not be much diluted, and we see the dimensions of berserker energy and an unhinged aggressiveness (though he can also be much more of a gentleman than Akhilleus, as in *Il.* VI.215ff.); in Thersites a fragment remains of the satiric gifts that tie him to Celtic personages such as Bricriu Venom-Tongue, or Icelandic warrior-poets like Egill Skalla-grímsson.[4] Nevertheless, despite the divine actors in the *Iliad* and the *Odyssey*, we have to accept that the Athenian king Menestheus, for instance, though present in Homer's tale, has not much of the mythic power and impact of his father Theseus, who was "twice-fathered" and, like Herakles, remains a clear representation of the god-begotten hero who also has a human "father."

The ancient commentators were not so nice in making their distinctions. So far as the mythographer and travel agent Pausanias was concerned, all heroes "as they are called" had two fathers, one human and one divine; in the case of Parnassos Poseidon is the god, Cleopompos is the man, and so on.[5] This is a late convention: for us the hero biographies of Theseus and Herakles show divine parentage in its richest meaning, as an injection of Otherness into the mortal world.[6] For these two (and for Perseus, another son of Zeus) the divine father's seed is contaminative with power, and leads to the first, the birth act of a drama in which the second act is the separation of the hero, his isolation and exile in or into a nonhuman or extrahuman world. Such a separation is shown in those versions of the biography of Herakles, where he is either sent away among shepherds to be raised or exposed after birth and saved by Athena or Hermes. (And why, we might ask, by these particular trickster-divinities?)[7] The expulsion of Perseus is more forthright, as he and his mother are cast into the sea in a *larnax*, a chest, while Theseus, son of Poseidon and of a mortal father Aegeus, king of Athens, remained exiled away in Troizen until his appointed day and its appointed heroic tasks were to begin.[8]

For other high-level miscegenations and engenderings we can turn to other heroic-epic traditions: the Indic hero Karna, in the *Mahâbhârata*, born of a virgin impregnated by the sun-god Sukra, evincing anomalous and potent portents at birth and sent off, like Moses (another one who was "neither god nor man") on a river journey in a little rush-boat;[9] or Pryderi, in the Welsh Celtic tale, who is seized into the Otherworld, probably by his divine father.[10] In parallel with the other heroes in this mythic stratum, Pryderi has both human and divine genitors. We can see a most extreme example of the complexities possible for a "divine" conception in the case of the Tibetan hero Gezar of Ling, where the Tibetan Buddhist context demands for the incarnation of the hero the following sequence: (a) a divine "director" decides that the birth of a hero is necessary, because of the earthly threat of certain demonic powers already incarnated as evil kings; (b) this "director'" persuades the god Thubpa Gawa to be incarnated; (c) but the god sets certain conditions, such as that his "human" father must also be a god, and his human mother one of the *nagas* (semidivine water-spirits). Finally (d) the heroic conception follows the drinking of a magic potion offered the mother by the father, and the hero Gezar is born in the form of an egg, from his mother's head.[11]

Generative anomaly is extraordinarily dominant in this Tibetan narrative, and in a Buddhist context it has to be so. The idea of the unavoidable contamination involved in the normative plan of heroic generation, through the power of a divinity, is secondary here to the accepted Buddhist belief that the processes of profane life are all profoundly contaminating in themselves, and incarnation in this case a tremendous and unlooked-for sacrifice for any divinity. Thus Gezar is an *exemplum* who does not easily fit into the world of the Western, human hero. The editors of his Life properly label it a supernatural life, and the anomalies that cluster around his engendering push it toward the separate category of the culture hero; in the Greek myths such tales occur in the overmyths describing the conception and birth of the gods. In less outrageous circumstances surrounding the extrahuman drama of heroic generation, the statement of divine parentage makes at least two themes clear. The first is obvious: the extraordinary epiphany of a transhuman hero demands an extraordinary, possibly divine, intervention, and the *contactus* of divine potency generates or explains the superior powers of the hero. The second has to do with what we might call the sociology of myth. The isolation of the hero, his separation from normal patterns of familial life, begins with a generation that cannot eventuate in any truly familial formation: a god may be Father but he will never be Papa, or indeed any sort of paterfamilias. The latter role may be taken up by a mortal, or not; the incredible apparition of the hero is naturally most dramatic when no human father is apparent, so that the secular world may see the hero as illegitimate. Another variation on the theme of the divine parent occurs when the mother is a divinity, for she must surely return to her home in some Otherworld; anomaly is even sharper when the mother deserts her child. But other modes of anomaly are even more severe.

Animal Origins, Animal Companions

SNAKE

Humankind and the human realm can be divided, or placed between, the zones of divinity and of the animal, but the figure of the hero very often displays images and potencies, combined or confused, from both of these zones. Such a combination or confusion is drastically apparent when the hero's divine genitor takes on an animal form: Pausanias (who is always good value for his casual recollection of mythic or archaic traditions) tells us that the birth of the Messenian hero Aristomenes came after his mother, Nikoteleia, united with "a spirit or a god" in the form of a snake, "as they say"—his usual formula.[12] The god is not named. In the legendary life of the conqueror-hero Alexander, his strange mother Olympias claimed that a snake, a form of Zeus-Ammon, was involved in his conception.[13] The generation of Alexander, according to Plutarch, also featured other animal signs, especially of the lion, and according to the legendary collection called the *Alexander Romance,* the royal hero-child was born with a lion's pelt and teeth like lion's fangs.[14]

The lion sign is often attached to the noble warrior-hero, and I will return to this and other raptor images; at the moment the snake is still in focus, and the image needs some explanation. Among the multiform images in which serpent and hero are seen together, we probably would be well-advised to set aside, temporarily, the monster-snake, the great adversary or *drakôn* of the great myths. The serpent-mate or hero's serpent-wife (the old French *mélusine*, for example) is another figure to be reserved for later. What *is* particularly pertinent at this point is the twinning of hero and reptile, as revealed, for example, in a French tale in which the snake twin is concealed in a caul on the hero's back.[15] The image of a concealed serpent twin, combined with an imputation of powerful anomaly through multiplication, is also revealed in a Christian Serbian epic: Marko Kraljević's enemy, the uncanny Musa, is revealed at his death as having three hearts, one with a snake wrapped around it.[16] An attenuated version of the snake twin appears in Pausanias's collection, where he records that a certain powerful man of Amphikleia, fearing for his son's life, put him in a jar (*aggeion*) and hid him: the child was protected there by a snake that drove off a wolf. Then the chieftain, seeing the snake, panicked, threw his javelin and killed both the snake-guardian and the child. Both were burned on the same pyre.[17]

Like so much of Pausanias's enormous fund of evidence, the legend from Amphikleia has a rich and troubling texture. The story purports to be a foundation tale, explaining why Ophiteia (Snake Town) came to be so named, but it is also a destiny anecdote of the type of the "Appointment in Samarra"; it shows a father consigning his son to an ophidian, subterranean existence; it shows the serpent's friendly guardianship pitted against the feral powers of the wolf;[18] it may also show a dark reminiscence of that founding sacrifice (of a child) that could actually and literally underlie the establishment of an ancient Greek city-state. At the core is the strange equality of the human and the serpent, united, as in the hero's *hêrôon*, in the precinct of death.

The snake can join the biography of the hero at a number of significant nodal points: at generation and birth, in an occasional symbolic placement, and at death. This ambivalent reptile may also occasionally come into the heroic tale as a healer treating the hero's wounds; in this activity the serpent is paired to the hero's hound (see below), as if both a domestic/non-threatening and a feral/threatening animal's force were necessary to complete the heroic healing process.[19]

HORSE

Another animal, the horse, is much more widely, typically, and closely connected to the human heroic figure, especially in the most dramatically outlined scenarios of life and death. The hero as horse-man is a well-known theme in societies in which this animal is domesticated and used as part of the equipment of war. In the horse-rider ambience of a Central Asian epic (in this case a Segai Turk tale) the hero, Khan Margan, is called the "son of a mare."[20] In the Balkans epic tradition, the attribute "born of a mare" is also possible for the hero,[21] especially in a horse-loving epic context in which a host of heroes is approvingly described as "all horsemen, not a single man on foot."[22] At a slight but perceptible angle we would place a mythic hero like Perithoös, whose divine father is given to be Zeus in stallion form, and who would be a companion, in fact nearly a "twin," to the hero Theseus.[23] In both the archaic reflections of the Celtic hero (the Welsh and the Irish), the twinning of the infant hero and a foal is an important motif. It occurs both in the *mabinogi Pwyll Pendeuic Dyfed* and in the *Compert Con Culainn* (Conception of Cú Chulainn), greatest of Old Irish heroes.[24] I am convinced that these two conception narratives, and a related Caucasian (Ossete) Nart hero tale, display a specific Indo-European motif, most importantly in a series of triplex incidents, including the tripled conception of the hero.[25] The horse in these parallel examples is part of a triad of child, horse, and hound, a triad not uncommon in, for instance, the medieval chivalric literature centering on the—formulaic?—trio of knight, horse, and hound. Here again one animal image is transferred to an adjoining complex, and we will soon need to examine the hero's involvement with the image of the domestic dog and the feral wolf.

A most anomalous variation on the "three beasts" theme is also available in that continuation of the Peredur/Percival narrative called the *Livre de Caradoc;* in this "strange history" (as R. S. Loomis quite properly calls it) the enchanter Eliavres, by his arts, causes King Caradoc to lie on successive nights with a mare, a bitch, and a sow, each of which has been given the form of Caradoc's queen, Isaive. While this enormity is proceeding, Eliavres himself lies with the queen and begets a hero-son, the younger Caradoc. When the king learns of Eliavres' act of lèse majesté, he forces the enchanter to lie with the same three beasts, and three half-human get are the result. The Celtic influence is very strong in this tale, as witnessed by the introduction of the sow, sacred to the old Celts, and the fact that the sow's "son" carries a name similar to that of Twrch Trwyth, the ferocious boar-prince who is hunted down in the Welsh tale *Culhwch ac Olwen*.[26]

The near identification of horse and hero is further demonstrated when the horse shows or imitates human characteristics beyond the animal's natural configuration. Serbian Prince Marko's horse Sarać is "not as other horses," can speak, and it also (heroically) drinks wine.[27] Sarać, who was born with a caul, even imitates the heroic type we will examine later, the "slow" or unpromising hero, for as a colt it was an unattractive "leprous" piebald whose extraordinary qualities were only recognized by Prince Marko.[28] The oracular horse with human speech is already familiar to us from the *Iliad* in the form of Xanthos, one of the chariot horses of Akhilleus.[29] The extranatural qualities of the hero's mount may also be reflected in morphisms that are essentially monstrous: the horse of the Tibetan hero Gezar can not only speak but fly; it is a shape changer.[30] The monster-horse ought to, and usually does, come from an anomalous origination: Perseus's winged Pegasos (and his womb-mate and "twin," the hero Chrysaor, both fathered by Poseidon) sprang from the neck of the decapitated Gorgon.[31] This Poseidon reflex is shown as well in the winged horse Jabučilo, the mount of

Marko's valorous uncle Momčilo, for it was sired by a "stallion from the lake,"[32] while the great hero-horse Kourky or Kourkis Jelaly, in the Armenian epic *Sassowntsi David,* was water-born as well.[33] So, according to one Irish Celtic legend, were the superb chariot horses of the great Cú Chulainn.[34] In the particular instance of the Armenian epic, the "twinning" of horse and hero is at least suggested by the fact that the first heroes of the great House of Sassoon, Sanasar and Baghdasar, were born after their mother, the princess Dzovinar Khanoum, was magically impregnated by the waters of Lake Van.[35]

The monstrosity of the horse may even emerge in its feral, carnivorous behavior, again parallel to a sinister aspect of the hero himself, for the extraordinary mount may entirely escape human control, like the flesh-eating horses of Glaukos who finally killed their master,[36] or the horses of King Diomedes in the Heraklean legend, "the horses of death."[37] Marcel Detienne regards this fearsome aspect as demonic, chthonic, or Gorgonian, demonstrating the essence of fierceness and bellicosity (and the "military force" of the animal); it should be contrasted with the horse tamed by culture-protecting Athena through the technical-cultural aid of the bit and bridle.[38]

Clearly the horse is the animal most closely identified with the hero in many of his biographical episodes. The two come together in the accident of divine or monstrous origin, the possession of extraordinary powers, the attributes of great speed and strength—and a fatal, mutual impulse toward death and destruction. "Le cheval est isomorphe des ténèbres et de l'enfer" is one acute observation, for this animal rightly shows itself both at the beginning and often at the fated end of the heroic biography.[39]

DOG

How important the domestic dog has been in the imagination of humankind can be quickly seen by checking the index of Stith Thompson's *Motif-Index,* where the entries for "dog," "dog's," and "dogs" are considerably more numerous even than those for "hero" or "heroes."[40] The very great range of interaction between human beings and their domestic dogs is clear in this large (though mainly European) folkloric deposit, as in the anthropological literature generally, where the weight of the evidence seems to point to the dog's being often perceived as a liminoid or interstitial beast, not human but not quite animal. In premodern societies in which the dog is more than a casual house pet (used for the economic necessity of hunting), the animal seems to have the highest status: dogs "are treated as human beings" in the Nyanga area of West Africa (Kongo), are buried with ceremony after death, and are even assigned a postmortem significance, leaving behind their dog-ghosts.[41] The Wik-Mungkan people of aboriginal Australia regard dogs as their owner's relatives,[42] while the Ngaju Dyak of Borneo also see the dog, together with some other significant domestic animals, as in some fashion "siblings" to man.[43] Highland Thai tribesmen are recorded as believing that the dog, like the monkey, is a "degraded human being" descended, but also separated from, man,[44] whereas in Brazilian Amazonia the Parare tribespeople put their domestic dogs in the category of the animal world, but because of their barking they are imaged as near speakers and therefore outside, or a little higher than, the category of mere (voiceless) animal.[45]

If the hero evinces the distillation or dramatization of specific human traits, we would expect his relationship to the dog, this primary domestic animal, whose associations are both personal and social, to be significant if not crucial. The *Iliad*, so often our first referent in terms of the epic imagination, sets an antagonistic tone: the fatal result of the wrath of Akhilleus is that the bodies of heroes will be "a spoil for dogs," *helôria . . . kunessin*.[46] The dog in this text is a scavenger that escapes from the zone of culture to feed on dead men, a reversion that nearly falls into the same fearful category as the human werewolf. In the *Iliad* the dog is always a defiled animal according to Paul Friedrich, who interprets accordingly the passage in which Helen characterizes herself in her shame as "a dog, worker of evil, abhorrent" and as "me, the (shameless) dog"—that is, bitch.[47] The Homeric poem displays a strong bias toward the treacherous and also the sexually uncontrolled or even criminal aspect of the animal, in parallel to S. J. Tambiah's observation that in Southeast Asia the dog may be "thought" to fit into the image of a human committer of incest.[48]

Yet the hero and the hound are often brought together in adventures in the world of epic, particularly in the Celtic lands and the Scandinavian North—and in the Balkans, where it is sung of the hero Banovich Strahinja, who had a gray horse and a gray hound, that "you love [Karaman, the hound] more than you love your battle horse."[49] I have already referred to those heroic conception narratives in which heroic child, horse, and hound are knit together; of these the most singular must be that of the Irish Cú Chulainn, the "Hound of Culainn," who was thrice-conceived, with one of his engenderings involving the god Lugh.[50] His human birth name had been Sétantae, but renamed Culann's Hound he set himself to act for a time as guard dog for his smith-fosterer; this special guardian's role is one of the themes of the truly heroic animal. Culann's great hound was not the only one to be killed by a hero in the Irish sources, and the suggestion has been put forward that by killing this near wolf the hero "appropriates its martial spirit."[51] The Irish context continues to provide us with signs of this combination of man and hound in the histories of the *fíanna*, the quasi-mercenary Irish warrior bands, whose adventures are placed some time after the great matters of the Ulster Cycle in which Cú Chulainn spent himself. In the *fían* tales the dog sign is variously parsed; Finn's own hunting dogs were his magically transformed nephew and niece.[52] A symbolic caninism, in the good sense, is attached to the hero-warrior who is supportive of kin, protective to society, and obedient, while the *wolf* is allied to the outlaw, the dangerous stranger, the expelled one. A human individual may also pass from the image of dog to that of wolf—from domesticated culture to feral nature—or the reverse.[53] Those tales in which dogs, snakes, or wolves are identified as the healers of the hero's wounds simply illustrate this transferal and shift on another level of interaction between animal and human hero.[54]

The greatest and most dramatic combinations of hero and hound move into and radiate from the intrusions of these heroes into the wilderness world as the primary dramatic scene of the hunt, where the monster-prey, and every other attractive danger, is so often to be found. Gwyn Jones has given us the heart of the great hunts, for example in the Welsh *Culhwch ac Olwen*, in which Arthur and his men and dogs pursue the monstrous boar, and ex-human, Twrch Trwych. The most fearsome of the hunting hounds in this pursuit are named: Drudwyn, without whom "Twrch Trwych would not be hunted"; Cafall, who is Arthur's own dog; Aved and Aethle, who with grim tenacity followed the great and deadly boar to the last, "straight forward into the sea"; and others.[55] The courage and ferocity of the prey-beast must be matched by the courage and persistence of both hound and hunter. The interaction of man and animal is such that an exchange of personae is more than hinted at, especially since the great hounds of quest and hunt are, to all intents, feral monsters themselves, "wolves" hard to curb or control. Now we pass to the wolfish side of the hero once more, and to the hero's initial movement out of culture and into ferality, into wild-animal morphisms.

WOLF AND BEAR

These are the two threatening wild carnivores of Eurasia, though the archaic (Greek, Persian, Georgian) imagination could still recall the possibility of encountering the Asian lion. The sinister simile of the prowling lion, used in the *Iliad* of Akhilleus and of other warriors, is marvelously to the life, and there may be something more than a mere reminiscence of the Heraklian legend behind the epithet "lionlike" that decorates the last Armenian hero Pokr Mher, or the lion slaying in the Byzantine Greek *Digenid.* We also have numerous lion images in the Persian *Shâh-nâma.*[56] Our data for wolf and bear tend to push us north and west again—the wolf is called the *animal féroce* of the European West—and not least because it is in the Celtic and Germanic-Scandinavian contexts that the most thorough exploration and exfoliation of the relationship between animal and human realms occurs, along with the most dramatic rendering of the passage between these (and other) zones or categories.[57] This is not to say that the Celts and northerners monopolize this drama: we can cite Greek myth and the Indic and Iranian evidence, as well as the Slavic, Caucasian, and Central Asian epics that may sometimes be an extension of the Eurasian. Nor are the Celtic and Germanic-Scandinavian thoughtworlds identical in their imagining of the interpenetrating zones of man and animal, despite the similarity of some themes and a similar refraction of certain archaic Indo-European patterns. The Celtic imagination, for one, leaves the impression of permeable boundaries and reversible valences, the Germanic-Scandinavian a solider sense of identity and of a stricter boundary (though this subjective impression may originate in linguistic patterns, and semantic and semiotic usages). But epical traditions are rich in allusions to the feral associations of the heroes, and most dramatically to the hero's origins in or from the beast of the wilderness, as an exotic, alien enemy to humankind.

The motif of wolf suckling, well-known to us at least from the legend of Romulus and Remus, shows up in Ireland not only in an heroic connection but also in the *vitae* of two saints, one male and one female.[58] So Saint Ailbe and Saint Ciwa demonstrate that the animal world is open to and supportive of the separated, unique personality of the saint, but we know this to be true in the larger context of sainthood, as we recall Saint Francis of Assisi, the wilderness-dwelling saints and holy men of Syria—and the shaggy, wilderness-dwelling Hebrew prophets before them.[59] The two Irish saints are, perhaps, closer to the secular heroic mold, in being actually kin "by the milk" to wolves. The Irish wolf-suckled *hero* is Cormac mac Airt, the archetypal hero-king whose royal reign was marked, for a long while, by Edenic peace and plenty—and also, presumably, by a taming of feral animal potencies.[60]

The stories seem to say that the wolfish connections and projections of the individual hero need not be destructive; for that matter, the individual wolf (as compared with the animal roaming in the wolf pack) may be seen as "good," like the nurturing, maternal wolf bitch—or, as we find in Pausanias, a wolf (in this place acting like a watchdog) that killed a thief who stole gold from the sacred Delphian precinct.[61] The wolf *pack*, on the other hand, seems in the main to be perceived as naturally malignant. As we have seen, this is one image of the Irish *fénidi*, called a "wolf pack" when they escape social control; Germanic images of the *Wilde Jagd* or wild hunt combine supernatural or diabolic, out-of-control human *and* animal potencies; and Baltic folklore gives us the tale of a frenzied lycanthropic mob or pack that attacks isolated homesteads, kills the dwellers—and drinks up all the beer.[62] In one of those fertile and imaginative asides that keep Mircea Eliade's contributions to the study of myth always worth examining, this scholar sees both a social and an individual dimension in lycanthropism, the adoption of a wolfish power and posture.[63] My own examination of the initiatory or group aspect of the heroic assumption of animal (particularly carnivore) guises, and an analysis of the furious or *berserkr* aspect of the hero-warrior character, belongs to a later part of this study.

The bear or ursine image remains (derived, in the North, from at least one etymology of *berserkr*) and here we have at all times an individual transformation. Gwyn Jones's brilliant exposition of the motif of "The Bear's Son" is our good and fluent guide, parsing for us the saga tale of Boðvarr Bjarki, "Warlike Little Bear," out of *Hrólfs saga Kraka*, where the hero is the son of Bjorn and Bera, that is, Bear and She-Bear.[64] Bjorn is forced by sorcery into his theriomorphic disguise; he is man by day but bear by night, and is killed in his bear shape, but Bera gives birth after his death to three sons. Malign sorcery intrudes again and continues the theriomorphic pattern, to the end that of the three the eldest was half man, half elk, the second had a dog's feet, and only Bjarki, the youngest, had no visible animal trace, though he did, as it turns out, have a bear as his hidden animal double. Bjarki the Warlike was also left a human hero's weapon, a sword, but in the course of this tale he is reattached to the feral powers of the animal world when his elk brother gives him blood from his elk leg to drink. The blood draft again revives and reveals the proximity and the potency of that animal world to the human hero; another blood draft is seen later in the story, when Bjarki forces the cowardly Hottr to drink the blood of a Grendal-like monster and eat some of its heart. This grim meal brings Hottr instant courage, as in the parallel instance of the coward knight in the Old French tale *Perlesvaus*, where a coward shows what has to be called self-preservative rationality—a rationality overcome by a brutal immersion in the feral animal world.[65] The reformed coward is but one step short of the animalized warrior, engorged with *wut* or *furor*, for one of the marks of this state is the abandonment of a normal human desire to defend oneself.

This warrior-*berserkr* is all fury-filled attack: shieldless, unarmored, and naked, like a wild animal.

I will return frequently to the associative nexus of hero and animal, but as a last remark here I think that for the hero, *horse* and *snake* morphisms seem to be intrinsic to his narrative and essential being, whereas *wolf* and *bear* are adaptive morphisms for him and his tale. We might also note that, in a psychological significance, the animal-monstrous "double" may be created so as to contain and display characteristics felt to be unfitted or repellent to the true-heroic image.[66]

Incest and Animal Signatures

Finally, the animal connection leads us back to that form of heroic generation caught up between animality and taboo or sacrilege: incest. It is most significant, I think, that incest carries two different signs of extrahumanity: the animal and the sacral. Animality continues to have a place in our analysis as certain animals, especially the dog, may be despised because they obviously ignore those limits that separate male and female in the same family group.[67] This prohibited sexual relationship is often exposed in the myth of the king, and in both simulated and real royal rituals.[68] In the context of royal incest the aim is an ingathering of sacral power through the violation of a normative sociosexual taboo and, as Luc de Heusch notes, "ne semble donc par avoir but de régler un problème de descendence."[69] That is, any suggestion of a royal urge to "keep it in the family," though it might display a kind of vulgar logic, does not make a finally persuasive argument. The difference between royal incest—real or imaginary—and the fundamental *mésalliance* that produces a hero is that the latter union normally occurs only once, and generates the ever singular hero.[70] Dumézil is thus correct in concluding, in a note dealing with a collection of Celtic and Scandinavian heroic conceptions, that "the [generative] incest is either accidental or seen as an exceptional event."[71]

Again, differing heroic narrative contexts will put the incestuous act in wildly divergent dramatic perspectives. The father-daughter incest that reportedly resulted in the birth of the dark "hero" Aegisthus, a player in the drama of and around King Agamemnon after the Trojan adventure, is an enormity meant to create a means of condign revenge by brother against brother, and is fitted to the contorted, terrible history of the House of Pelops;[72] the father-daughter incest that serves as one part of the triple engendering of the Irish Cú Chulainn is almost casual, and is only a portion of a cumulative anomaly.[73] In another Old Irish situation the great clan of the Conaillne was said to be descended from a connection between Conall Costamail and his daughter, the amazonian Credne, and there is no editorial censure placed on it whatsoever.[74] Other Irish tales, in the considered view of the Rees brothers, appear to show incest subsumed under the category of individual reincarnation;[75] and in *Hrólfs saga Kraka*, Helgi unknowingly marries his daughter Yrsa, and Hrólfr, the eponymous hero, is born of the forbidden union. (The old dog-motif appears as well, because Helgi in his youth was disguised as a dog for his own safety, and Yrsa was contemptuously named after her mother's dog.)[76] The dramatic import of the incestuous union in this saga falls somewhere between the incest that generated the misfortune of Aegisthus and that surrounding Cú Chulainn's conception tale.[77] The Persian *Shâh-nâma* gives us the father-daughter incest of King Ardashir with the princess Homây, even authenticating it as "the custom that you call Pahlavi"; and the Prince Dôrâb born of this union bears a number of similarities to Cú Chulainn.[78]

We recognize, or think (after Freud) that we ought to recognize, mother-son incest as *the* malforming event in the troubled history of the human psyche, but it seems fairly rare in our heroic-epic contexts. The Oedipal drama demands the generation of the Theban hero-king's two doomed sons by their mother-grandmother, but Eteokles and Polyneikes, though they display one aspect of the negative fraternal in their deadly rivalry, are still completely enmeshed in Oedipus's complex tale. In the Jungian theory as further developed by Erich Neumann, mother-son incest is a powerful symbolic description of a particular, potentially destructive stage in human psychic development. Mother-son incest tends to appear not on an epic but on a cosmic or cosmogonic level: the great culture-creating tricksters are also great committers of incest,[79] and what Dumézil terms "legitimate" incest is situated in the province or zone of his Indo-European Third Function—the locus of every aspect of sexuality, legitimate or not. In the Germanic-Scandinavian North, for example, the Vanic gods rule as the guardians of sexuality and increase, and the "Vanic" element can be reflected on the human-heroic plane in such instances as the saga of Hadingus, as reported in Saxo, specifically in the hero's quasi-incestuous sexual relationship with his giantess foster mother Harthgrepa.[80]

Sister-brother incest is also important for the generation of heroes, and perhaps the most marked incestuous incident in the North and West of Indo-Europe is a key event in the *Völsungasaga*, the liaison between Sigmund (Sigemond in *Beowulf*) and his sister Signy. "For three nights altogether he lay her next to him" (*Leggr hann hana hjá sér þrjár nætr samt*), resulting in the birth of Sinfjotli. (He is called Fitela in the Anglo-Saxon epic version, where he is described only as Sigemond's sister's son—which, in strict truth, he was.)[81] Just before her self-immolation Signy declares that, with the help of sorcery, she had in fact arranged the nocturnal meeting with her own brother so that their son, bred a super-Völsung, could avenge (*til hefnda*) the death of King Völsung, her and Sigmund's murdered father.[82] The characters, if not the incest, appear in the "southern branch" of this saga, the *Nibelungenlied,* and it is possible that this famous brother-sister incest served as a model for others that occur in the Norse sagas, especially in the marvelously variegated romance adventures or *fornaldarsögur.* On the edges of this focal area we find such evidence as the assertion, in that legendary collection, the *Alexander Romance,* that Alexander's human father, King Phillip, threw out Alexander's mother Olympias and married his own sister; was he seen as trying to generate another heroic son by this interdicted congress?[83]

For incest on the Celtic side, the popular favorite would probably be that fated encounter between Arthur and his half sister Morgaine, resulting in the birth of Modred or Mordred (though we have this scandal only in a late and Continental invention). This resembles the engendering of Aegisthus and, to a lesser degree, Sinfjotli, in terms of the old theme that involves committing a sin, an enormity, so as to carry out a more effective personal revenge in the future. A moral lesson is also preached in the case of Arthur, at least in the late form in which the encounter between him and his fay half sister reaches us. No such moral judgment is ever made in the Old Irish *Coir Anmann,* where the hero Lugaid Sriab nDerg, Lugaid of the Red Stripes, is born as the result of a triple incest by his mother Clothra's three successive unions with her own three brothers.[84]

The Rees brothers make a case for the inclusion of these incest tales in a general narrative configuration describing *social chaos,* a state preceding the establishment of some sort of social cosmos or order.[85] Certainly these stories of hypersexual mating (or, in Lévi-Strauss's sly or ironic term, the "overvaluation of kinship") can be categorized thus, and so can asexual-anomalous unions, such as the Celtic examples cited by the Reeses. In *Tochaid Étain* the heroine Étain, in the form of a fly, is swallowed by the wife of an Ulster champion and then born (or reborn) from her womb.[86] Étain was of the Túatha, and thus of a race described as intermediate between gods and men, and supernatural begettings must surely be more likely with such a tribe. Another unnatural (and, by imputation, incestuous) semination came about when Daolgas, dying, is kissed by his daughter and a spark, flying into her mouth from his, impregnates her.[87]

Such asexual, acutely anomalous inseminations make a handy thematic bridge to another family of heroic tales, those of the Caucasian Ossetes whose heroic band of Narts were an object of much fascination to Dumézil. The birth tales of the most prominent among the heroic Narts are a series of extraordinary, even outrageous anomalies. Their "heroic mother" Satána is born of a dead old woman made living, young, and pregnant by a lecherous god, and other impregnations described in the Nart tales are quite as bizarre. The hero Soslan is born from a rock upon which a lovelorn shepherd had ejaculated; the hero Batradz, with his coating of steel, is taken at term from an abscess in the middle of his father's back.[88]

As we move away from these narratives in which social disorder or archaic chaos may be apparent, we might return to the simple theme of the extraordinary heroic begetting by means of a forbidden sexual union: Roland, the nonpareil paladin of Charlemagne, is in one old source called the illegitimate result of a brother-sister incest, and Charlemagne is made both the hero's uncle—and his father.[89]

THE YOUTH OF THE HERO

For the ordinary human being in a traditional society, more specifically the ordinary male, physical growth and integration into the social group tend to follow a rhythmical or punctual rather than a gradual pattern and time sequence. Separation from childhood and from the female-nurturing world may be made final and catastrophic in specific initiation rituals, and these rituals follow the scenario of *separation/information/reintegration*, or "death"/ "separate existence"/"rebirth." (An identical or similar scenario may be followed when a man is married or at other passage points, such as subordinate initiations: into a secret society, a priestly order, or the shamanic vocation, for example.) Physical death, with a "good death" in the fullness of years, marks the secular terminus of the scenario—but these rhythmic-punctual occasions are distorted almost beyond recognition in the typical heroic biography. Here temporal sequence is displaced or collapsed, beginning with the immediate entrance of the heroic child, or even infant, into a pattern of precocious behavior. The metaphors for this precocity can be drawn from at least three sources, and across an imaginal spectrum: the extraordinary child is following a *supernatural* model, or shows *adult human* characteristics, or is cast in an *animal* process and pattern (that is, his maturation recapitulates the rapid physical maturation of most animal young). Whatever the model or combination of models, the effect is the same. The passage from childhood to adult maturity is "heroically" overleaped; growth and physical prowess are not achieved gradually but immediately, or at least at a greatly accelerated pace.

Moreover, after the hero reaches physical maturity, no further development is necessary, and both sexual and social maturation are reduced to minor significance. (We shall see how heroic sexual relationships are liable to be abnormal, abortive, and immature, while the social utility of the hero is always shadowed by his other side: the asocial, individualized, untamed, combative, and destructive.) Finally, death itself and the final termination (though not annihilation) of the hero's life is pushed forward in human time, and typically that death is self-sought or self-directed by the hero.

Predictable Precosity

The hero's extraordinary engendering is occasionally signaled by an extraordinary pregnancy (close to the mythic or the folktale refraction), as when, in the *Völsungasaga,* the future king and progenitor of a fated line, Völsung himself, was born after a six-year term, and emerged "very well grown, as might be expected."[90] Then the nursing of the hero follows. A late—or modern traditional?—Balkan source tells us that the Serb Moslem hero Smailagić Meho was given three wet nurses, so that he would grow the faster.[91] Heroic growth feeds on appetite, appetite on growth, though the hero may overleap this infantile stage entirely as, in a comic heroization, Rabelais' Gargantua did, born shrieking "A boire! A boire! A boire!"[92] In his brief but hungry nursing stage the hero may also be reconnected to the animal world: to the image of a sheltering and nurturing nature, and with an animal "family" replacing the human and the cultural connection.

Abnormal growth and superhuman strength persist as a nearly inevitable mark of the child-hero. A Welsh warrior-hero is "in stature and girth a warrior but in age a lad,"[93] and the Reeses tell us that "the hero soon abandons childish things, and his triumphant intrusion upon adult society is one of the universal themes of mythology."[94] They add that this stage is not usually explored in detail, though the Celtic world sets aside a special place for the marvel-filled workings of at least two of its greatest heroes: the *macgnimartha,* or "boyhood deeds," of Cú Chulainn and of Finn mac Cumaill. There wonders abound: at the age of four Cú Chulainn (then still named Sétantae) overawes and beats up the whole Boy Troop of King Conchobar, a hundred-and-a-half strong, and soon kills the monster hound of the smith; at seven he is more terrible than any warrior, and has the power not only to kill but to capture and tame wild animals. (On the other hand, Cú

Chulainn's physical size is not agreed upon: one source has him say that "I was their little champion, whom they used to love.")[95] Finn mac Cumaill's exceptional youth is only slightly less furious and fabulous.[96] The animal world persists both as support and as prey for the young hero, as we see again in the Byzantine Greek *Digenid*. This particular epic, which appears to have some on-grafted elements of an ancient Heraklean biographical mythos, sends its hero out rather late, at "twice six," to kill bear, catch and kill deer, and, finally, kill the necessary and iconic lion.[97] ("Stop writing," says the singer of this tale disdainfully, "of Homer and the stories of Achilles.")[98] In the Caucasian (Georgian) epic *Vep'khistqaosani* (*The Lord of the Panther-Skin*) the lion has multiple significances, but one is as the usual prey and proof of truly heroic abilities: when the eponymous hero Tariel was only five "it appeared no labor to slay a lion—it was like a sparrow."[99]

Because war and the hunt are so closely entangled in the usual imaging of heroism we would expect that heroic feats of arms will follow closely on other displays of precocious physical prowess. Venturing as far afield as the Ainu *Kitune Shirka* for a very clear example, we find its young hero arming himself "though he had never seen deeds of war": his warrior's ability is in-born, natural, untaught.[100] An intriguing variation on the theme of heroic size and precocity is available in the Armenian epos; the hero Sanasar, of the House of Sassoon, found a magical warrior's panoply belonging to his heroic family, put it on and grew, while sleeping, to neatly fit the armor—but this epic tradition also contains the usual image of a hero who grew "in a day as much as other children grew in a year."[101] The Icelandic sagas, devoted to real ancestors or other once living exemplars of saga heroism, show these exceptional powers in a slightly attenuated but still recognizable form—although the hero of *Egils saga*, as we shall see, truly belongs in another and a special category, not least because he is called *ljotur*, ugly—and because he is also markedly intelligent."[102]

In fact, one element of Egill Skalla-grímsson's early fund of talents leads us away from the unremittingly physical nature of the signs marking the child-hero, because Egill will be known as a great skald, a creator of poetry, one of an outstanding Icelandic fraternity. Of course, he demonstrates this gift very early, and so connects to a motif seen especially in the Celtic heroic context, the revelation of marvelous poetic talents in figures like Taleisin[103]—although such gifts, in the Celtic lands, are usually allied with precocious wisdom and form a part of the armamentarium of sovereign, kingly figures and their adjuncts, rather than of the warrior-hero and his bloody kind.[104]

Heroic precocity occasionally emerges in a striking naiveté: the twelve-year-old Digenes says scornfully, "What if I wait to grow up, what good is that?—everybody does it."[105] At the same time one scholar has noted that the precocious use of adult arms in childhood by the great Cú Chulainn is matched in "equivalent heroic anomaly" by the "retention of boyhood arms into young adulthood," a most interesting and provocative twist in the heroic fabric.[106]

Unpredictable Unprecocity

The extraordinary precocity of our hero is occasionally balanced by its precise opposite, the main character's refusal to display heroic attributes at all.

The reversal of expected themes is very common in our folkloristic legacy, where we can find a good-sized fund of "laggard" or "unpromising" heroes, such as the type of the "male Cinderella," along with the frequent appearance of the youngest, the smallest, the least significant son, the runt of the litter.[107] In addition to the very natural aim of wish-fulfillment in folk fantasy, these reversals may have a place in comic constructions; the motif of the coward knight or a similar type can be inserted to provide relief from the endlessly proliferating and even dull perfections of the typical warrior-hero or knightly paladin.[108] Moreover, the coward knight or other characters who belong in the fascinating category of the heroic trickster may express, if not arcane wisdom, a commonsensical intelligence, as in the pacific statement "no good comes of war"[109]—although very often they are not characterized as particularly intelligent but, in more than one sense, as retarded. The avoidance of combat, rather than the usual bloodthirsty search for it, marks these "slow heroes" in at least one stage of their biographies.

The type includes some unexpected names, for among the unpromising or "slow" young heroes are the great Beowulf himself and, in Saxo, the legendary Uffi or Offa.[110] Another hero in Saxo, Haldan, regarded as stupid in his youth, seems a kind of natural primitive, essentially undeveloped—not too far from the Welsh Celtic example of the quintessentially naive Peredur;[111] and the Norse sagas display the type frequently. Ormr Stórolfsson, a lazy and unpromising youth, is eventually levered up out of his sloth, demonstrates his great strength, and goes on to a well-filled saga tale of his own.[112] The contrary and perverse saga hero Grettir the Strong contains within himself both meanings of Old Norse *kolbítr* 'coal biter': he is both a torpid layabout (his own father called him lazy and cowardly) and an uncontrolled, nearly demonic *berserkr*.[113] His biography places him at some distance from the slow "dunderhead"—the Serb hero Marko Kraljević is given this label early in his own hero tale—who eventually begins to deploy the agonic excellences of the pure heroic type.[114]

Another Icelandic *Þáttr* provides us with Hreiðar the Foolish, who is tall, fleet of foot, ugly, but clever enough to outwit a king.[115] His character and career provide a bridge between the Grettir-type and the ordinary "unpromising" hero and display a certain resemblance to Egill—or to Saxo's Amleth. We will hear more about them when we encounter the epic trickster.

THE DRAMA OF THE GENERATIONS

In his translated collection, *Contes et legendes des Oubykhs,* Dumézil gives several versions of an Oubykh story in which the old men of this Caucasian tribe are summarily slain by their sons when they reach a certain stage of decrepitude. The liquidation is ended only when the oldsters convince the younger generation that they, the sons, would in time be similarly dealt with by *their* sons and that, in general, "we have need of old men."[116] This tale, with folkish and sly humor, deals with a matter of considerable importance in our heroic frame, and one that is worked out more complexly in our sources than may have been immediately realized.

Fathers and Sons

We expect tension and antagonism, possibly fatal antagonism, between father or genitor and heroic son. Why? We need not be persuaded merely by Freud's reading of the Oedipal conflict; for one thing, heroic sons are very rarely fatal to their fathers. In fact, a quite different pattern is seen: a hero is himself allowed to have a son; this son reveals his own heroic aptitudes far from the paternal home or zone of action; the son eventually returns or otherwise encounters the father, and although the son carries some token to identify him, the sign is revealed too late, and the *son* is slain. This theme is well known as the "Sohrâb and Rostam" or *Vater-Sohns-Kampf* type.[117]

I examine a number of refractions and permutations of this theme, which if not "pan-cosmic" is definitely pan-Indo-European, in the last chapter of this study. Here, and briefly, four full or canonical replications of the confrontation are well known and often cited: Persian (Rostam kills Sohrâb), Irish Celtic (Cú Chulainn slays Connla), Germanic (Hildebrand kills Hadubrand), and Russian Slavic (Il'ya of Murom kills Sokolnichek).[118] Added to these four father-son confrontations *en clair* we have a number of partial or more vague replications of this key theme, extracted from a variety of sources including the Old French *chanson de geste,* Armenian epic, and Icelandic saga. There is enough evidence assembled to lead Jan de Vries to the conclusion that we are in the presence of an Indo-European myth or mytheme,[119] but whether or not this is true (and I am convinced that it is), these encounters, with their "tragic" outcome, are surely part of that thematic subset, ringed by the most stringent taboo, in which kin slay kin— the structural reversal, as Lévi-Strauss would have it, of incest.[120]

The tension generated by the motif of the "talisman of identification" is made manifest for us in the legend of Theseus, who was left two "signs," sandals and a sword, by his human father, Aegeus, and who barely escaped death upon his arrival in Athens, when his father recognized the identifying sword only at the last minute.[121] Theseus evades a threat mounted by the mortal one of his two fathers (the father aided by the sinister exile Queen Medea, whom the Jungians would certainly see as an icon of the Terrible Mother) and will be able to continue his heroic career. Then, in time, he will have to take responsibility for the death of his son Hippolytos; and Herakles, the hero to whom Theseus is most closely tied in imaginal terms, will kill at least some of his Theban children in his madness, though the line of the Herakleidae will be allowed to go on.[122] Sometimes the special isolation of the extraordinary human being is stated, oddly but unmistakably, and another motif is superadded: "I have had no child," says the Armenian hero Pokr Mher, last of the House of the Sassowntsi, "I can have no death."[123]

It may be that the "hero's son" is in fact perceived as an unnatural continuation, an overstatement, of his too specific potency. It is worth noting that the "Sohrâb and Rostam" theme is most likely to be attached to a heroic life near its end, to emphasize not only the surnatural separateness and isolation of the true-heroic biography, and the necessary denial of kin ties, but to definitively frame and close off the hero within his own unique history.[124]

The hero may be detached from his father because the father is unknown, though illegitimacy (a sociolegal term) can of course be read as a sign of divine, or at least nonhuman, generation; but father and son may also be separated by the label of nation or ethnicity. In the Byzantine *Digenid* the hero Basil the Borderer is fathered by a Moslem emir, *amêradôn megiste kai prôte tês Syrias,* "greatest of emirs and first in Syria."[125] Though the narrative demands that the emir promise to convert to Christianity, the paternal presence remains in the Saracen lands, and the hero is set apart both because his paternal generation comes from the foreigner, the enemy, and also because he is the perfect Akritic, the true borderer who straddles the *akra*, the march or battle-borderland. The removal or exile of the heroic child alienates him from his parent by forcing him to be foreign. The rescued Oedipus is raised in Corinth, not Thebes, and believes himself to be a son of the royal house there. Sohrâb is raised among the Turan, and Pokr Mher off among the "Arabians."

When the hero is marked by a double engendering, his mortal father (or a kinsman/stand-in) not infrequently comes to be his enemy. (As the Reeses cogently remark, "the advent of the hero is invariably an embarrassment to someone or other, and an attempt is made to get rid of him"[126]— though if an oracle or some other explanatory or interfering voice or sign has declared that the child will be the human father's bane, "embarrassment" is too light a word.) Theseus barely escaped the deadly plot of his mortal father Aegeus; and Akrisios, the father of Danae, who had already shown his enmity to his own kin by warring against his twin brother, later persecutes his grandson Perseus.[127]

An interesting twist occurs in the Welsh Celtic tales, where the newborn hero-child Pryderi is snatched away and hidden by (presumably) his divine, Otherworld father, though it is unclear who this is or just why the occultation of the hero-child came about.[128] The Otherworld has a great presence in the Celtic tales and, quite fittingly, does not operate according to any ordinary or profane human rule of reason, cause, and process but according to the rules of a true parallel world. Describing this realm requires an extraordinary and difficult effort, but the tale-tellers, especially the Welsh, usually manage to carry it off brilliantly. The many-faceted Persian *Shâh-nâma*, with its often offbeat royal-heroic compounds and confusions, adds a further variation to the abandoned or "child-in-casket" theme in the biography of Dârâb, the child of incest, who was set adrift on the Euphrates by his queen-mother, Homây, not his father.[129]

Again we see that the appearance of the hero-child results from some anomalous generative event or series of events. There is no slow preparatory time of nurturing, instruction, and dependence, but a swift and *heroic* headlong assault on those limits and limitations that describe the adult world of constraints—a world for which the father unmistakably stands. Adult maturity as a desirable end is often the object of heroic derision; so in the Irish tales of Finn mac Cumaill the hero Finn, here acting as *rígfénnid* or "chief of the warrior band," quarrels with his son Oisín. Finn contemptuously dismisses the chances in war of the immature *óclach* or young warrior, while Oisín retorts that the palsy of age has cut down the powers of Finn's spear: "the óclach is at the peak of his form, while the old man has already peaked."[130] Finn is also contemned by his son for becoming a chieftain, and thus someone who has been drawn too far into the old (and unheroic) Establishment.

Mythic theory and observable fact tell us that the rivalry between father and heroic son is inevitable. The Icelandic saga tales, where the tone of the narratives often sets the characters midway between a personal and historical human context and a magical or supernatural world of darker or at least greater powers, example the youth of Egill and his confrontation with his father, Bald Grímr Kveld-Úlfsson. Already displaying both physical prowess and skaldic skills, twelve-year-old Egill finds himself and a companion facing Skalla-Grímr in the ballgame called *knatt-leikr*.[131] Egill and his friend outplay the older man until the sun begins to set, whereupon the uncanny, trollish powers that marked Skalla (that is, "Bald") Grímr and his father before him commence to grow with the growing darkness; he seizes Egill's companion and kills him. Egill himself only escapes death when a slave woman of Skalla-Grímr's household, a known sorceress who had fostered Egill, intervenes; Grímr, now deep in his sinister, crepuscular mood and powers, pursues and kills the woman in place of his son.[132] Egill then retaliates for the deaths of his friend and the bondwoman. The trial of wills between son and father ends only when young Egill is separated from his uncanny parent, and allowed to sail off to find adventure in Norway.

In Grettir the Strong's saga, the challenge by Grettir to his father Ásmundr's status and expectations takes the form of unheroic and perversely antisocial behavior; the result is the same as in Egill's tale, as the son successfully escapes his father's control and sails off on the first stage of his own adventures.[133] *Völsungasaga*, with its rich magical ambience, has a confrontation between Sigmund and his "sister's son" Sinfjotli, whom the father considered "still too young to wreck vengeance with him."[134] Father and son first engage in outlawry—they "killed men for their money"—and then go abroad as wolf-men, dressing in skins that changed them into wolves. In this guise they roam the woods, and encounter two situations in which the help of the other is needed (in his peril Wolf-Sigmund howls for help, but Wolf-Sinfjotli does not). Later the son meets and defeats even longer odds, and kills all of his opponents, but when he brags of this his humiliated and enraged wolf-father bites him in the throat. The wounded Sinfjotli is healed only when his father discovers and uses a magical cure.[135]

Such a near fatal confrontation seems to put an indelible mark against Sinfjotli's destiny, for after the two have avenged the old death of King Völsung, Sigmund marries and fathers more sons. But Sinfjotli kills the brother of Sigmund's wife Queen Borghild; she avenges him by poisoning the young man, with Sigmund, the father, as an accomplice. Óðinn, in this case taking up the ancient role of Ferryman of the Dead, carries the body of Sinfjotli away. Sigurd, Sigmund's other extraordinary son, is born after Sigmund dies in battle, so like other posthumous heroes he is completely relieved of the ancient father-son antagonism, at least in its simplest form.[136]

As a final note to what Grégoire called this "cosmic theme" we see that in two of these father-son confrontations the older hero-father takes advantage of a significant, unsporting "edge" over the younger. In the combat of Sohrâb and Rostam, the father asks God to return his "vigor" to him, which seems to be a sort of superhuman weight or *gravitas;* in the fight between Cú Chulainn and his son, the father at last uses his unique and irresistible weapon, the *gae bolga.*[137]

Hero and Mother's Brother

When the tension or enforced separation between heroic son and father seems to allow no positive or creative tie between the two generations, the epic context often deflects the fathering relationship toward the mother's brother. In the Balkans we find that the Serb hero Marko Kraljević, though his name translates as Marko the King's Son, is said to have taken his heroic character not from his father Vukasin but from his uncle, Momčilo.[138] The Moslem Serb border-warrior Smailagić Meho, hero of the remarkable oral narrative created by the *guslar* Avdo Mededović and recorded by Milman Parry, is called the heir both of his father and of his uncle Hasan; he is the "only child" of both,[139] which is to say he is the inheritor from older males in both the maternal and paternal lines. A great deal further afield, the Tibetan hero Gezar of Ling, who as we saw is surely separated from any earthly paternal tie because of the complexities of his incarnation, says even before his appearance on earth that he ought to have there as an ally "an uncle who is energetic and a clever strategist."[140]

The uncle-nephew bond is also very prominent in Western medieval hero tales. The theme is stated simply in the medieval Spanish epic of *El Cid Campeador,* for the Cid has no sons, and the kinsmen who always aid him are his nephews: Félix Muñoz, Minaya Alvar Fáñez, and Pedro Bermúdez, his standard-bearer.[141] The same is true of the French hero Guillaume d'Orange's cycle of *chansons de geste.*[142] W. O. Farnsworth supplies a fairly complete list in his study of the avuncular relationship in these songs; the most famous is the hero of the well-known (but, in many ways atypical) hero tale, the *Chanson de Roland,* for Roland is the sister's son of Charlemagne the king.[143] In the epical romances or chivalric tales and their root

narratives we find important uncle-nephew ties, as between Peredur/Per-
lesvaus and the Fisher-King,[144] while in Slavic Eurasia a Russian *bylina*
called "The Tsar Resolves to Slay His Son" has it that Ivan the Terrible's
son, the Tsarevitch, was not (as indeed actually occurred) killed by his grim
father's order but was saved from execution by his uncle, his mother's
brother.[145]

An important dimension of the uncle-nephew relationship in the hero
tale is the tabooed incestuous union of brother and sister which, as in the
Völsungasaga, produces a hero who is simultaneously son and sister's son,
while the father is also the mother's brother. The tale of the Völsungs does
not assign a good fate to Sinfjotli, the result of this incest, and the brother-
sister (really half sister) incest that makes Arthur both father and uncle to
Mordred also has a bad end. The Irish hero Cú Chulainn also displays, in
his engendering, a hint of brother-sister incest, but this is not made of great
moment: his tripled conception is the significant, the overwhelming generative anomaly.[146]

Of all the peoples generating and sustaining themselves on hero tales,
the Celts seems to have made the most of the mother's brother–sister's son
tie, though the ancient Germans, as Tacitus bears witness, were already
notable for the respect they gave this connection: "the sons of sisters [*nepotes*]
are as highly honored by their uncles as by their own fathers. Some tribes
even consider the former tie the closer and more sacred of the two."[147] Tacitus's ancient evidence is in parallel to the relationship described in Marko's
Serbian legend. The old Irish narratives crystallize the mother's brother–
sister's son tie in the term *gormac,* which carries the meaning of one, the
son (*mac*), who acts properly toward family: "who has been adopted for the
purpose of maintaining the adopter."[148] Specifically, the sister's son must
act properly toward his *maternal* kin. Cú Chulainn's loyalty to and support
of King Conchobar (his mother's brother) and the Ulstermen is unquestioned, but fortunately for the beleaguered warriors of Ulster his human
father, Sualdam, was an outsider, so neither he nor his extraordinary son-
champion was affected by the *ces,* the curse-brought "debility" that lay so
hard on the Ulstermen.[149] But Cú Chulainn has little else from, or to do
with, his human father or his father's kin. Before we leave this hero I should
note that he has another uncle, Fergus mac Roich the exile, who as the *Táin*
narrative shows cannot act openly against his kin tie (*condalb*) or against Cú
Chulainn, who is also his sister's son.[150]

Other Irish sister's sons may, however, differ. The Reeses, describing the
class of heroic adventures called *aithoda* or Elopements, point out that two
well-known Irish elopement tales, the *Longes mac n-Uislenn* (Exile of the

sons of Uisliu) and the *Tóruigheacht Dhiarmada agus Ghráinne* (Pursuit of Diarmaid and Gráinne) in the Fenian Cycle, both involve sister's sons who betray their uncles.[151] In the "Exile" the young Noisiu runs off with Derdriu, the ill-fated maiden whom King Conchobar has kept apart for his own bed. The king responds to this betrayal of the kin tie by a betrayal of his own once he has Noisiu in his hands: the nephew is slain by his order, whereupon Derdriu kills herself. In the *Pursuit* Gráinne is to marry the old *rígfénnid* Finn mac Cumaill, but she has other plans, and she escapes with young Diarmaid. After many adventures the two are retaken; Finn and Diarmaid seem to be reconciled but when the younger man is wounded (actually poisoned) and only Finn's magical ministrations can save him, Finn withholds his aid.[152] Another tale with clear parallels to the two Irish Celtic elopements is that of Tristan (Drystan in the oldest Welsh sources) and Iseult, Welsh Esyllt.[153] Tristan is King Mark's sister's son, and the only deviation from the two Irish narratives shown in the Tristan legend is that Mark is not responsible for Tristan's death, at least not in the tale as we usually know and recall it—though in at least one other, later reflex the old king is made Tristan's final bane.[154]

These three young Celtic lovers and their (sexually transmitted?) fates strike an intriguing but complicating note. To have seductive and winning ways with women is not a typical or desirable heroic trait, and the men in these narratives seem to have the empathetic, flexible, seductive qualities that make them especially attractive to women—particularly women promised to old men, old kings, or old warriors. These heroes are "feminine . . . not effeminate" as the Rees brothers perceptively remark;[155] or, in Jungian terms, they have introjected the *anima,* the feminine part of the psyche. They also have very marked tricksterish characteristics, Tristan in particular. The most important point about them is that they can be persuaded, or can persuade themselves, to set aside the codes both of kin loyalty and of the true warrior's primitive or basic fealty to his chief.

The generally supportive role played by the epical hero's mother's brother does not quite fit with at least one theory of the avunculate: Neumann's Jungian excursus, based in the "fearful" matriarchate, states that the mother's brother, acting as "bearer of the authority complex in the matriarchate" and representing "duty, prohibition and coercion," is necessarily hostile to the hero (as Ego). (This relationship is eventually replaced by the father-son antagonism.)[156] But Neumann's scenario is rarely respected or followed by our heroes, and the anthropological kinship data, with its varieties of "structural" schemes, allows our epical avunculate (the mother's brother computed as the good uncle) to be placed comfortably into one of its categories.[157]

Fosterage

In the fostering relationship a young hero is taken away from his immediate family; yet again, the hero's primary paternal relationship is not with his father but with a father substitute, a simulated or classificatory paternal figure. Fostering is an important Indo-European institution, especially for royalty and nobility, to the point that Émile Benveniste, in his important *Indo-European Language and Society*, derives the Germanic *edel* 'noble' from an archaic root signifying "fostered."[158] The fostering tie for the hero may have a very different cast, however: it often begins when the hero-child is kept in the care of a wet nurse, who might very well be an uncanny woman. *Egils saga* hints that some of this ugly hero's alterity came from the milk of his nurse, the sorceress (and his father's victim) Þórgerdr; another sorceress, Busla, is foster mother to the brothers Bósi and Smidr in the romance *Þáttr* "Bósa ok Herrauðr."[159] In the saga of Hadingus, as extracted from Saxo's pages, the hero's nurse is the giantess Harthgrepa, who as a "Vanic" figure offers Hadingus the incestuous union that Saxo finds so unseemly and Dumézil was at such pains to explain.[160] The Irish hero Finn mac Cumaill, born after his father's death, is taken in by a mysterious and powerful woman, Bodhmall, sometimes joined by an even stranger female, the Luath Lúachra or Grey One of Luchair.[161] All of these foster women may have a nurturing and definitely have a protective function—replacing guardianship within the family—but they can also provide the hero with a special and select kind of training or education. In "Bósa ok Herrauðr," Smidr is said to have learned all of his considerable powers in magic from Busla, while his brother Bósi learned some tricks but, for his own reasons, rejected the full course of sorcery offered. Finn's fosterer was much more than a female nurturer and protective presence: she was both a *benfénnid* ("female member of the *fían*" or woman warrior) and a *bendrui* ("female druid"). Bodhmall passed on to Finn the skills of warlike prowess, *fénnidecht*, as well as the more abstract mental (or spiritual) skills of those important "knowers," the Irish druids and poets.[162] We might recall as well the training that the Irish hero Cú Chulainn received from the uncanny Scathach, another woman warrior and witch figure.[163]

Sources in the Germanic-Scandinavian context show mother's-side fosterage from Beowulf on (Beowulf was fostered by his uncle Hrethel).[164] In

Egils saga we read that King Haraldr lúfa had been fostered by his mother's brother Guttorm,[165] and in *Viga-Glúms saga* Killer-Glúmr flees Iceland and sails to the hall of Vígfuss, his mother's father, in Norway.[166] Fosterage in the sagas, however, has a wide range of rationales and usages. A child, and not always a son, may be fostered by someone wishing to attach himself to the child's more politically or socially powerful father and family;[167] or a feud may be avoided when one party agrees to foster the offspring of another—though, depending on the dynamics of the situation, this fosterage might signify leaving the child as a hostage. In the late Norse collection and source, the *Sturlunga saga,* a farmer is given the option of fostering the plaintiff's son or being taken to law, but in this case fosterage is a barely concealed, quasi-legal punishment, a sort of dragooning levied on the reluctant fosterer.[168]

In ancient Greece the most extraordinary fosterer was surely the Centaur Kheiron, half man and half horse, begotten by old Kronos in divine stallion shape: he fostered Iason, though not alone.[169] Deep powers of the forest and mountain wilderness, and of the chthonic and mysterious cave, the *spêlaion,* are all combined in this old story, but Kheiron is called wisest of the Centaurs; one supposes that he tried to pass this wisdom to other foster children, who included Peleus, Akhilleus's father, and then Akhilleus himself.[170] Most of the fosterers in the ancient Greek hero tales are closer to the human family than the monstrous Centaur, and they are almost invariably situated on the maternal side, either as mother's brother or mother's father.[171] To introduce the mother's father as a player in these dramas may seem arbitrary, but both the terminology and the affective connection relating mother's brother (uncle) and mother's father (grandfather) to ego (the mother's child) seems to describe just one perceived relationship: some sort of male "partner" (or, in Louis Gernet's terminology, a survival of kinship) on the maternal side.[172] Energetic research into the kin terms used has unearthed what may be a Proto-Indo-European (P-I-E) terminological level, built on such hints as the fact that the Latin *avus,* grandfather, gives rise to *avunculus,* "little grandfather" or uncle, most particularly the maternal uncle,[173] or that Old Irish *gormac* at one time meant either mother's father or mother's brother. (Indeed there are two traditions bearing on the conception and birth of the hero Cú Chulainn, one identifying King Conchobar as the boy-hero's uncle, the other as his grandfather.)[174]

All or most of the fostering incidents just cited fall into the category of overt fosterage, agreed on for one of a variety of social or micropolitical reasons. Fosterage may also, more dramatically, be covert, undertaken to protect the fosterling from any number of dangers threatening his extraordinary childhood. From the oldest stratum of materials making up the Arthurian legend we have the fact that Arthur was secretly fostered in the house of Cei (*Caer Gai*), where we can easily infer that he absorbed and abstracted a great deal of his own latterly power and stature from that warrior-hero who showed himself so prominently in the early Welsh sources.[175] The fostering of Finn mac Cumaill shows a clear case of this protective-covert care: not only is the fosterling guarded and nurtured by an anomalous fosterer, the powerful kenning woman Bodhmall, but he is taken for his protective fosterage into the extrasocietal and liminal zone of the wilderness. There he is both guarded and trained in what is essentially an animal/natural placement or topos; and indeed, because the *fían*-warriors are always in process, always crossing the *limen* between the society they are supposed to protect and the wild zone where their feral skills are honed, it is right that they be known as great fosterers themselves, taking adolescent males from the *túatha,* the more or less stable tribal kingdoms, and initiating and educating them in warlike and other adult skills.[176] Here we have an exact parallel to the fosterage of Kheiron the Centaur, half human and half animal.

We are no longer much inclined to see the survival of a suppositious "matriarchy" in the close relationship of maternal, cognate kin to the hero, but it is true that, as the central character of the hero quickly solidifies, his open assault on the identity and powers of the paternal side is increasingly obvious and insistent, though rarely is that assault deadly to the father.[177] If the hero means to replace his father, as he must try to do, and proclaim his own place and identity, he should expect little cooperation from that father, and may look forward to open antagonism and confrontation. A male from the maternal side thus stands for the Jungian Good Father, or, as the Reeses identify him for the Celtic context, "a kind of female father."[178]

One other variation in the avunculate ought to be outlined: the situation of the "other" uncle, that is ego's father's brother. We have an unambiguous hint on this taken from the assembled anthropological data, telling us that the Nilotic Nuer regard the father's brother as the "bad uncle," the mother's brother as the "good uncle."[179] Is antagonism to the father thus displaced toward his brother? The Nuer refer to the maternal uncle as "both a father and a mother," but he is more frequently assimilated to the mother, as a "protective" kinsman. Evidently because he combines maternal with paternal (or at least masculine) powers, his curse is especially potent so far as the nephew is concerned.[180] Marie Delcourt is of the opinion that in a patriarchal system the father's brother is really a duplicate of the father, as demonstrated in the levirate, which reinforces the idea that the son-ego will have a negative view of his paternal uncle, who carries in himself the pro-scriptive aspect of paternity without any buffer of affection derived from a true, generant fatherhood.[181]

In fact we would expect to find, in the widely recorded folkloric motif of the wicked uncle, the element of a conflict between two brothers, with the conflict extended to the son(s) of one of them.[182] This is exactly what we encounter in the Hamlet mytheme, as disclosed early on by Saxo Gram-maticus in his story of the brothers Orvendil and Fergi, and of Orvendil's son Amleth.[183] Saxo also gives us the tale of Olaf Ingelsson's two sons Frothi and Harald: Frothi had his brother killed and then savagely pursued his brother's two sons, Harald and Haldan.[184] The two escaped (saved by animal disguises similar to those used to protect the young Finn from his pursuers) and eventually came back to kill their evil uncle.[185] We also see without surprise that most of the entries in Stith Thompson's *Motif-Index* under the heading "cruel uncle" (S.71) are father's brothers.

SINGULAR HERO AND HERO'S SIB

The hero is the product of such special circumstances, of the interaction of such potent—and very often tabooed—generating forces, that his singu-larity is usually taken for granted: there is little room for other birth mates. Nevertheless they do occur, to roil the narrative and perturb the plot.

Variant Births

The gods who beget offspring on mortal women may return to Earth occa-sionally to propagate more of those "of the blood of Zeus," but they dispose of their favors to one partner at a time. Indeed the god's favor may prove deadly, as when Zeus burned up poor Semele in his divine and incandes-cent embrace. Nor do the straying goddesses remain long in the human realm to form any sort of household with their mortal lovers. The divine power will be concentrated to create a single human-divine result, the hero-child, and the same is true when the (human) father dies before the son's birth, as with Siegfried, Finn, or Raoul of Cambrai in his own story among the *chansons de geste*.[186] In Tristan's case, not only is the father dead but the mother dies as he is born, and the infant is "hid away from all eyes" by his guardian.

When the hero-child is born and the mother dies in childbed we may be seeing a kind of imagined sacrifice: a death pays toll for the extraordi-nary birth, even though this death of the mother must have been common in traditional societies. Then there is the birth by Caesarian section, perceived as unnatural: Shakespeare's Macduff is "not born of woman" because "from his mother's womb untimely rip't," and thus he was fit (and fated) to be the invulnerable Macbeth's bane.[187] The Persian hero Rostam is born by a kind of magical Caesarian, and although his mother Rudaba is made whole again, it is implied that she will bear no other child.[188] A particularly anomalous birth occurs when the mother is already dead; such a motif is set out in the Ossetian Nart tales, in which the "mother of the Narts," Satána, issues from a union between the sky-god Uastyrdji and a woman already old when she died. Parallels to this bizarre generation will be found elsewhere,[189] but if we are looking for absolute anomaly and singularity the generation of a heroic life from a dead mother must be well to the fore.

When a hero is born from an incestuous union his uniqueness is, again, made explicit. A variation in the revenge theme is suggested by Arthur's unknowing incest, but in this instance the act is not only planned by the woman but is meant to rebound on the violating male: the emphasis is not on the sacral potency of the act but on its unnatural, contaminated, or sinful gravity. The father-daughter incest seen in Saxo's redaction of the events leading up to the birth of the hero-king Hrólfr Kraka combines both of these themes, of extrapotency and sin: Hrólfr's father Helgi unknowingly commits incest with his own daughter, and when he realizes what he had done, he goes off at once to seek his death in battle. All this has been engineered for her own revenge by Thora, a woman Helgi had once casually deflowered and impregnated. Yet the hero Hrólfr is born of such an incestuous union, and, as Saxo proclaims, "So his father's blunder was favorable as it was infamous, and subsequently atoned for by his marvelous son in a blaze of glory."[190]

Companion Birth Mates

By rights and by definition, the hero should be one of a kind, or even kinless. The *spartoi* or "sown men," sons of the dragon's teeth in the ancient Greek myth of Kadmos, would be the perfect martial heroes: parentless, signed or stamped as they are by the clear mark of the war spear. Heroes, however, may not only have siblings, but certain scenarios in the heroic life seem to demand them; the hero then stands against, or in contrast to, a sibling who appears as companion birth mate. A Spanish "romance of chivalry," the egregious *Amadís de Gaula*, adds a fillip to the spectrum of heroic-fraternal relationships by having two separated brothers, Amadís and Galaor, each unknown to the other, who encounter and oppose each other in battle and elsewhere.[191] So the uniqueness of the central hero is established not because he stands alone but because he is put next to a coeval who is different from him in some significant way.

A complete difference between hero and birth mate appears when the god-begotten child is born with a human-begotten "twin." The instance most likely to spring to mind is that of Herakles, whose powerful but human brother Iphikles was born of Alkmene by her human husband Amphitryon, yet Iphikles had very little to do in the great legend of his brother. The Dioskouroi, the "ideal" twins Kastor and Polydeukes, though known as the sons of Zeus and Leda, turn out to be of the same mixed generation; Polydeukes begotten of Zeus and Kastor by the human seed of Tyndareos. The two separate fathers, however, are not brought into the myth until very late, almost as an afterthought, when, in fighting another set of twins (the Messenians Idas and Lynkaeus), Kastor, the human twin, is speared and mortally wounded.[192]

Kastor dies because his twinned enemies complement each other with their gifts: Lynkaeus "the Lynx-Eyed" sees and comprehends what he sees; Idas is the strong-arm thug who carries out the plan. This balanced complementarity of the planner and the actor will play out in many another heroic script. In contrast, a kind of beneficent complementarity shows itself in the archaic or mythic-primeval twinship of Amphion and Zethos, the one endowed with musical and contemplative gifts, the second known as a great warrior and hunter; both are "founding" heroes of note.[193] Finally, we have twins as an entity, as inseparable and therefore seen to have a doubled heroic strength, as in the pair Kteatos and Eurytos, the heroic get of Poseidon the Earthshaker, whom Herakles himself could not overcome without an act of treachery most shaming to this hero.[194] On the other side, the ancient Greek context also gives us our archetypal case of twins-as-antagonists in Akrisios and Proitos, who fought "even in their mother's womb."[195] In fact the motif of the first fratricide itself is assigned, in Greek myth, to primeval twins, Ismenos and Kaanthes, with an incest-theme added, since Kaanthes killed his brother over their sister, Melia.[196]

What is often marked in the tales of heroic twins is the animal image, which may be, oddly enough, conjoined to divine parentage: the double birth is taken as a human anomaly, but also one that connects the newborn to the multiple births of animals. Of course, Zeus in bird shape begets the Dioskouroi (or one of them) on Leda, but it is dark Poseidon who is, literally, the chief of the stud, fathering in his stallion shape Aidos and Boiotos on Mellanippe (the "Black Mare"), Meleus and Pelias on Tyro, and then Kteatos and Eurytos who would be Herakles' victims.[197] The nonhuman element is especially strong in the tale of Meleus and Pelias, who are literally cast off by their mother and, when they come to land, are suckled by animals, one by a dog bitch and one by a mare. The occultation of the hero and his nurturing by an animal wet nurse are here simply doubled, within a most familiar heroic sequence. In terms of heroic themes the animal mothers themselves, the bitch and the mare, are already known to us as well.

The notion that a hero may be born with an animal brother, or at least an animal "companion," has appeared earlier in these pages. (The Irish Celtic Cú Chulainn and the Welsh Celtic Pryderi, both with foal companions at birth, illustrate the motif most clearly.) When we turn to the legendary Boðvarr Bjarki in the Icelandic-Scandinavian context, we see a situation in which a magical intervention produces a human child with a theriomorphic potential and two more completely animalized brothers; the three make up a trifunctional set fitted to the Dumézilian model, although most of our attention is of course focused on the "ideal warrior" Bjarki.

Youngest Son or the Last-Born

When the hero is born alone, of some exceptional and noteworthy coupling, his essential solipsism is overt and complete, but the circumstances of his begetting must place him into some kind of family or other cluster of kin—which may prove either supportive or antagonistic. The hero who appears as a younger son seems likely to display a deeper, even three-dimensional pattern of heroic action, especially as compared with an older, less complex brother (or chosen companion); and as Boðvarr Bjarki was the third of the extraordinary brothers to be born in that story included in King Hrólfr's saga, he provides a fitting bridge to the complex of the youngest son as it appears in the heroic narratives.

The successful, triumphant last-born appears very frequently in the folktale's vast narrative corpus, and reasons are easy to point to. Scripture tells us that "the last shall be first," and popular feeling has always cheered on the underdog or the runt of the litter—two very conspicuously animal images.[198] The perception of the younger son as a superior rather than inferior creation also reaches far into the ideology of kingship, especially in the Near East, where we have the biblical story of Esau and Jacob, the tradition that Davidic (archetypal) Israelitic kingship was constructed on the image of the last-born of the sons of Jesse, and, on the cosmological level, the idea that the first creation was a faulted one, with the initial appearance of a monstrous or animalized, and so unfit or inferior, cosmic order.[199] Roman tradition (as caught in the *Aeneid*) had Silvius, who would be the last-born son of Aeneas, identified as "king and father of kings" (*regem regumque parentum*, VI.763ff.).

I have claimed elsewhere that ultimogeniture (a specifically Indo-European arrangement?) may embody the politicization of this myth of the younger son, and had strong roots in the notion that a more symbolically "feminized" son—the one farthest away from the father—would display the proper mixture of symbolic genders.[200] In real political terms this idea doesn't seem very deeply imbedded in the so-called patriarchal systems of the Indo-European thoughtworld, but the aspect of the younger son in the heroic context still produces important, rich and variable resonances. In one retelling of the Heraklean legend this hero inherits his specifically heroic, as compared with kingly, role when the goddess Hera's jealous plot delayed his birth, so that another boy-child (his human brother Iphikles) would assume the kingship, not Herakles.[201] (The perceived paternalism of the king figure will always continue to agitate parts of the heroic biography.) What we might call complex or alteriform heroes often evince ways in which fraternity can be dissected and reformulated: in *Egils saga* the second-born Egill, very like his trollish father (who also was a second son), makes a specific contrast, both in appearance and in talents and powers, to his older brother, who is named Þórólfr in both generations. Each Þórólfr in this saga is a king's man, drawn to the significant but dangerously exposed role of king's champion, yet neither has much luck—that important Norse concept, maintained as part of the personality—in his service.

COMPANIONS IN ADVENTURE

The solitary, isolated hero or lone knight errant of the imaginal cliché is often nothing of the kind. In contrast to the king of myth, who must by the definition of monarchy stand alone, the hero frequently has partners, companions, or a supporting cast of characters fitted to his feats, though some will be only modest ancillaries in the heroic adventurous enterprise. I will try to develop the whole constellation of heroic subtypes in another chapter, but at the risk of repetition it seems to me necessary that some of the shapes and permutations of heroic companionship be fitted in here. Keep in mind, however, in Daniel Melia's ambiguous but accurate description, that the warrior-in-battle (in this case Irish) undergoes his supreme test "accompanied but alone." The companion is important, or may be important, but the final test must be passed or failed by the solitary hero.[202]

Pairs and Triads

When we think of the motif of hero and companion we are quickly drawn to sources in which the heroic dyads are identified, flower as part of the dynamic of the drama, and then—usually—die. The *Iliad* and the *Chanson de Roland* are perfect examples. The friendship of the hero Akhilleus with Patroklos is said to express the most perfect *philotês*—"warrior's friendship"—which is called upon, in vain, to bring Akhilleus back to the war from which his terrible and selfish wrath had driven him. This *philotês* then inspires or ignites Akhilleus, after Patroklos's death, to the battle fury that will bear down Hektor, first champion of the besieged Trojans.[203] In this reading Akhilleus is truly Patroklos' bane; and in this epic among epics the hero's partner, though older and presumably more experienced, represents and projects an insufficiently heroic force and excellence, so that to try to take the place of his more powerful companion surely must mean his own destruction.

In Roland's *chanson de geste* the heroic pair, Roland and Olivier, are paladins of the most perfect mold, but each is ingenuously given a mark and character of his own: "Roland's a hero / and Olivier is wise."[204] Part of Olivier's wisdom is to recognize that his friend is too quick-tempered to go to the Saracens as an envoy and much too reckless as well. Roland's refusal to recall the main divisions of Charlemagne's Frankish host by sounding the oliphant dooms the beleaguered rear guard, and when Roland realizes his fault Olivier is not quick to forgive. Olivier knows a brave dolt when he sees one, and perhaps his resentful percipience is behind the solid sword blow he gives Roland—accidentally—as he is dying.[205] The epic is Roland's, however, and in the later or alternative chivalric epic the voice of wisdom or even of common sense seldom carries the day over true-knightly bravery. (Witness the case of the coward knight, who appears, has his comic and his heroic moment, and so dies, in the story of *Perlesvaus*.)[206]

The Old French *matières* are full of heroic partnerships, which set this epic tradition apart from a superficially similar epic creation like the *Shâhnâma*. This Persian epic, full of outsized heroes described in the most unbuttoned and gaudiest detail, has only one brief entry in the category of heroic companionship: the "happy-starred warrior" Bizhan is said to go adventuring "accompanied by Gorgin son of Milâd, his companion in battle and his adjunct when succor was required." Gorgin, however, turns uncooperative ten lines after his first mention and loses no time after that in betraying Bizhan to the enemy Turk.[207] We can therefore set the Iranian epic aside, but the ancestral forms of the narratives from which some of the *chansons de geste* and more of the chivalric tales descend are much richer in pairings.

Before the Welsh Celtic Cei was transmogrified into the ridiculous Sir Kay of the Old French Arthurian romances (for a primary example, in Chrétien de Troyes's twelfth-century romances), he was a figure who towered at least as high as Arthur himself, and his warriorhood and other powers were unquestioned.[208] Cei displays himself in a variety of roles, and he will be frequently brought up as an exemplar in any study of the hero, but at this point I have in view his place in a heroic dyad, paired with another warrior, and centrally cast in the greatest of the old Welsh quest tales, *Culhwch ac Olwen*. His warrior partner is Bedwyr, occasionally and aptly named "the Square," a sword hero of mighty and mindless brawn. In *Culhwch ac Olwen*, Cei and Bedwyr are knitted together into a narrative fabric in which one "impossible" task is tied to another, and the two show themselves most fully complementary in the undoing of Dillus Farfawg, Dillus "the Bearded."[209] Even more to the point, however, is that Cei is a sort of pair unto himself, although to understand this point we must turn to another example of a "paired" warrior, the saga hero Egill Skalla-grímsson.

In the Scandinavian-Icelandic body of epic, Egill, central to the *Eigla,* is indeed a figure of some fascination. Ugly, contrary, quarrelsome, and violent, he is also a superbly talented skald, master of the poetic gift so highly valued in the saga world. In fact he represents one face of warriorhood, presented against or in contrast to another type. Egill, like his father Bald Grímr, is an Óðinn warrior: he has the mysterious, sometimes perverse or reversed, highly individualized and often antisocial potencies represented in the god. Egill's brother (and Grímr's brother, Egill's uncle) are Þórr warriors: they are clearly integrated into society, men of loyalty especially to the king, and both will pay for their loyalty with their lives.[210]

What is so remarkable about Cei is that it is possible to see him as an actor who can take up both the "Óðinnic" warriorhood of Egill and the "Þórr" warriorhood of the two Þórólfrs. Cei is not split but contains a dyad within himself: he was granted, according to the text of *Culhwch ac Olwen*, two gifts, the first to be cold and unyielding (a champion's role, and "there shall never be server or officer like him"), the second to be "hot," a shape changer, a figure much closer to the choleric and individualistic Egill and his father Skalla-Grímr.[211] In the Celtic world this archaic, doubled persona is retained, and we can find it not only in Cei but in a slightly more exiguous Old Irish form in someone like Finn mac Cumaill.[212] These Cel-

tic heroes, as is often the case in this context, add certain specialties or sin-
gularities to their duplex character.

The Charioteer

A special epical figure, the charioteer serves as the hero-warrior's aide and
adjunct in three immediately identifiable Indo-European heroic traditions:
the Indic, the Irish Celtic, and the Homeric Greek. Clear similarities and
intriguing differences are equally apparent among their tasks and situations.

The Indic war charioteer is cast in a noncombatant role, so that when,
in the *Mahâbhârata,* individuals of the *suta* or charioteer caste actively involve themselves in war making, their actions are deprecated and seen as
unfitting.[213] In fact the charioteer caste itself was, according to the *Laws of
Manu,* an anomalous one in origin, owing its existence to a faulted and in-
acceptable hypergamy.[214] The *suta* caste also includes bards, that third
estate that presumably escapes direct involvement in war in order to report,
to whatever audience, the feats and triumphs of the true chariot warriors;
but a baron (of *kšatriya* caste) may sometimes act as a charioteer: in one
episode of the *Mahâbhârata* a king's heir, Prince Uttara, is converted from
his originally timorous posture to become, willy-nilly, the charioteer of the
ever-perfect warrior, the Pandava, tigerlike Arjuna.[215] This particular case
has an element of the comic about it (parallel to the profession and the
conversion of the coward knight in *Perlesvaus*), but other cases of warrior-
charioteers are known. We ought to note in passing that the Indic source's
charioteer is not quite made the warrior's standard-bearer; the identifying
or protoheraldic standard of the hero is fixed on the chariot itself.

In the Irish Celtic heroic narratives, as in the great *Táin Bó Cúalgne,*
where chariot warfare somewhat resembles the Indic example (though without the use of the war bow, which is the great heroic weapon of the Indic
epic), the charioteer again is the ancillary helper to the hero, and, again, a
noncombatant. (Cú Chulain himself stated that "charioteers or messengers
or men unarmed" would be exempt from attack.)[216] The ordinary charioteer is given no remembered name, and may be addressed with the more or
less dismissive diminutive *gilla,* or "boy." Cú Chulainn's own charioteer,
Láeg mac Riangabra, is of course named, and Láeg has a particular inter-
mediatory role that fits him into a pattern somewhat similar to the Indic:
he is an observer and describer who in certain narrative episodes reports
the outward appearance of a stranger, whom Cú Chulainn then identifies

by name.[217] In another of the Irish tales, the *Togail Bruidne Da Derga* (part of the Old Irish Mythological Cycle), there are chariots but no identified charioteers, and the "observer" or reporter named is both a chieftain and a spy: Ingcél Cáech reports what he sees to the other raider-chieftains before their assault on the *bruidne*, Da Derga's fatal hostel and trap.[218]

Homeric chariot warfare is very different. The terms *hêniokhos* 'charioteer' and *therapôn* 'squire', are used together (as in *Il.* V.580 and VIII.119) with the simple imputation of personal service to the hero and horse-handling combined. Yet the *Iliad* doesn't necessarily distinguish between driver and warrior, as in the scene of furious battle in book V, where the death of a Trojan "squire and charioteer," Mydon, is closely followed by Hektor's slaying of two Achaeans, "well skilled in combat," who were riding in one chariot.[219] Nor, as this evidence thoroughly demonstrates, were charioteers spared when the missiles were flying, for the horse handler can be and is speared or cut down as he drives. Then, too, great warriors were perfectly capable of taking the reins themselves, like Aeneas in this same affray (V.230–31) or old King Nestor in another (VIII.12).[220]

Both historically and epically, the charioteer and his chariot will have a limited run, ending when the "knight," the rider, the warrior-horseman, appears. While they are available, however, the driver and his chariot present a mixed character and set of narrational possibilities. The war car itself may either be a platform from which the warrior-passenger displays his strenuous skills, or a conveyance to battle (which is waged on foot), or both. The archaic Celtic context, which is usually regarded as typologically close to the Indic, separates the charioteer from his warrior-partner as the Indic epic does, but also makes the chariot into an acrobat's stage: "feats" of balance and risk taking dear to the Irish charioteer-warrior's heart (balancing and even dancing on the pole at speed) are described here in detail.[221] The harder, or less decorated, language of the Homeric poet has little room for athletic tricks and displays, but plunges the combatants straight "into the mouth of bloody war," where no one is safe, even the Immortals, should they chance to interfere or interpose themselves. Yet a remnant of a separate category ascribed to the chariot handler is still detectable in both the Celtic and the Greek heroic narratives, though fainter in the latter: the charioteer takes a kind of "squire"'s place beside the warrior.

Heroic Triads

Another permutation of the motif of hero and helpers presents the following shape or pattern: a pair of heroic figures, each with a specific valence or talent, is joined by a third figure whose powers are drawn from a manifestly different, usually supernatural, source. The Icelandic *Þáttr* "Bósa ok Her-rauðr," for example, is best described as a breezy adventure tale of warriors and warlocks, one in which Herrauðr has the role of the normative or "straight" actor while Bósi is a freer spirit, a bit of a trickster, and an unin-hibited sexual adventurer. The *tertium quid* is Bósi's brother Smidr, who possesses all the tricks of a magician with all the associated gifts of shape changing and sorcery.[222] In the course of their wanderings the two heroes (Bósi approximately parallel to Welsh Cei and Herrauðr to Bedwyr in the Welsh sources) may find themselves in need of supernatural assistance, which is provided either by Smidr or by the old fosteress-sorceress Busla. Eventually all of the magic workers, black or white, are eliminated, and at the tale's conclusion Bósi and Herrauðr are left as sole survivors.

The magic-making *female* member included in the heroic triad, merely sketched or suggested in a few of our saga sources, appears in clearest out-line in the Balkan heroic songs, where the typical adventurous threesome consists of a hero, his standard-bearer, and a female helper who may be either a supernatural sprite or *vila* or a very human "tavern maid." The Serbian *vila*, like the Albanian *zonia*, is a spirit of the wild—of mountain, tree, or lake—who dwells in a supernatural substratum well-known to both Christian and Moslem bards. The Moslem hero Mujo, with his friend Omer, is aided on several occasions by a *vila* who is called his *posestrune*, or "sister-in-god."[223] Prince Marko Kraljević has several hero-companions,[224] but he also requires help from his own guardian *vila* in his fight with the eerie opponent Musa the Highwayman.[225] And no list of Balkan herodom would be complete without mentioning the egregious Tale of Orasacs, the great trickster-figure of the Moslem hero-songs. Though a paragon of often comic reversal he maintains the tradition of the heroic triad, with his rascally standard-bearer Radovan (or at other times "Woe-Bringer" Belaj), while his female assistant seems to be his mad sister Aziza. The character of the "tavern maid" who aids the Moslem hero and his partner carries, like the supernatural *vila*, a cargo of anomaly: she is female, her occupation is tabooed because she works in the inn or "place of strangers," and she is often a Christian, or at least bears a Christian name, like Mara or Ruza.[226] (Tale the Trickster is said to have been aided by one of these tavern maids, one named Mara, at a point in his collective adventures or epos.) In another part of the Slavic world, a Russian *bylina* on the subject of the picaresque scoundrel Van'ka Kain gives Van'ka a companion-dupe, the thief called "Kamchatka," and an unnamed servant girl who renders magical aid.[227] A water-nixie (a kind of *vila*) even appears in the Germanic *Nibelungenlied*, where she and her sisters are bullied by Hagen into helping this savage Burgundian knight.[228]

The female player in these heroic triads seems to be there to provide esoteric advice and assistance, based in the supernatural realm or in a liminal femininity tabooed or at least thought to be inaccessible to ordinary social intercourse. There is no connotation of sexual play or availability so far as the "tavern maid" helper is concerned, though the *vila*, as a water-spirit, is typologically identical to the *mélusine*, or magic-working snake-lady of Western European chivalric tale and folklore (I treat her when I eventually deal with the motif of the "supernatural wife"). The heroic triad may also carry an echo of Dumézil's Indo-European trifunctional division: the central hero identified as a First Function "leader" standing for the sovereign, the standardbearer as a warrior-functional aid and support (as he so often is in the Icelandic-Scandinavian context), and the *vila* or female helper as an advising, healing, and magical figure emergent from the Third-Functional zone. On the other hand, C. Scott Littleton has advanced the theory that a female character, especially a sister, is attached to a dioscuric hero pair (as Helen was to her brothers, the original *dios kouroi*, Kastor and Polydeukes), and that such a triple grouping itself marks a Third Function statement or operation in the *Iliad*; Littleton relies for reinforcement on Donald Ward's research into the theme of hero twins and a woman, which he has located in a number of Indic, Germanic, Baltic, and other Indo-European contexts.[229] I should note that in a latter-day epic-poetic source like Avdo Mejedović's *Wedding of Smailagić Meho*, the supernatural heroic helper is not present, though Smail, father of Meho-Mehmed, has a standard-bearer named Osman, who had served Smail on the border for twenty-seven years but is still referred to as a "youth." Is this a faraway reflex of the Irish Celtic *gilla*? More than likely it is.[230]

SEX AND MARRIAGE

The sexual-biological aspect (or imperative) of the human condition ought to have its impact in the heroic biography, and so it does—sometimes, and with enormous variation. Even as a marginal theme in the epic tradition, it is occasionally rejected by the searching scholar: Charles Muscatine, in examining the phenomenon of forthright or vulgar, sexually explicit language in "courtly" romances, noted that "The epic tradition has little to do with the subject matter that concerns us here."[231] Nevertheless, as in other parts of this heroic biography, we can perceive and organize patterns that give a sharper edge to the collectivity of heroic individuals and their stories.

Three in particular seem significant: asexuality, sexuality as agon, and predatory sexuality.

Asexuality and Singularity

We have already broken down the image of the "typical" hero and introduced a rich, or perhaps confusing, range of heroic permutations, and yet our focus keeps returning to a central figure who is self-described, self-contained, isolate, solipsistic. This is *the* hero. Certainly the foreground of the heroic stage is dominated by characters like the ancient Starkaðr, scarred, grizzled, and obdurately solitary, whose marvelous exposition of the rules of true heroic behavior has no room for tenderness, to say nothing of sexual passion, though he does have a proper guardian's soft spot for the legitimate married bliss accorded to true kings.[232] A Celtic hero like Cei has, we are told, a son Garanwyn and a daughter Celemon, a "leading lady of this Island,"[233] but no wife is named. (In the later French Arthurian *matière* he displays a sour misogyny, but there he is sour about almost everything.) Beowulf, though he became a king, never married—this at least is the consensus of the experts on his epic.[234] The Akhillean warrior is likely to stand well clear of regularized marriage, though Akhilleus himself had a son—and what a son—by an early, unhoused union; and furious Akhilleus can display a pathologically active sexual bent, as in the accusation that after he had slain the Amazon Penthesilea he "loved her after her death." In this as in other problematic or debatable areas, this hero demonstrates an exceedingly complicated character and force.[235] Indeed Ahhilleus, who never formally married, displays more sexual energy than we ever see in a married epic hero like the later, Byzantine Greek Digenes.[236] Digenes, though wed to a girl called, appropriately, Korê or the virgin, shows little trace of the romantic, to say nothing of the sensual, so far as his mate is concerned, and after his one well-known fall from grace (with the woman-warrior Maximo), he is so stricken by remorse that he kills his partner-opponent—a formulaic reversal, it seems, of Akhilleus's rumored necrophilia.[237] The deep-psychic confusion involved in combat and copulation, of what is acceptable and nonacceptable in sex or violence, appears in the epical contexts often enough to attract remark: the Serb hero Marko is helped to escape captivity by the "daughter of the Moorish King," but when she also offers him her sexual favors he is revolted (supposedly by her color) and kills her.[238] In the Ainu epic *Kitune Shirka*, an exhausted hero is approached by a beautiful girl who threatens his life, but the hero's own Amazon companion bespells the attacker. The hero then makes a sexual gesture to the second Amazon—and kills her. At this point his own Amazonian companion says reproachfully that "women should fight women."[239] This Ainu tale, which may have a connection to Central Asian Amazon narratives, demonstrates some of the complexity possible in male-female, lover-fighter pairings and connections.

"My strength is as the strength of ten / Because my heart is pure." The Tennysonian Sir Galahad really is a revolting little prig, but the celibate hero is, if not absolutely typical, certainly very common in the heroic mythotype. One part of this sexual mythology says that when a warrior flees battle, and deserts his true fighter's function, he acts either from cowardice or from an unwonted concupiscence and sensual desire—what we might call the Mark Anthony complex. There is also the old notion that abstention from sex provides the ingathering of powers necessary to the successful fighter, which is widely current in the belief systems or traditions of many warrior societies; a whole host of taboos can be collected from cultures in which male warriorhood and war making are given pride of place. I will return to this subject in due time.

Sexuality as Agon

"We marry those we fight" is a saying enshrined in the anthropological lore, and it refers, among other things, to the pleasurable perils of contracting an exogamous marriage. But by now we ought to expect the hero to identify and deal with every social rule very much in his own way: usually by ignoring, exceeding, or in some other way violating this rule. The women of the enemy (not merely the extrakin group) are an irresistible target, as in both Moslem and Christian heroic songs of the Balkans, where the rape and abduction of the enemy's women is a common theme.[240] The Byzantine hero Digenes Akrites is born of just such an abduction and union, and rapes of this sort will clearly be part of an inevitable (or at least very frequent) scenario on the embattled "border" between traditional enemies. A heroic quest, with its frequent theme of penetrating a hostile territory in order to overcome an enemy and seize a valuable prize, is easily transmuted into the stealing of a prized woman, the archetypal princess *lointaine*. Such a theme is dramatically and psychologically strengthened when the enemy is envisaged as a female opponent: with the woman warrior we enter the realm of Amazonia, and not for the last time.

The woman warrior, in my view, usually fits into the first of three distinct Amazonian categories, the second being the Amazon queen, a ruler who may have magical powers, and the third the revenging partner, who takes up a man's arms and persona in order to recover or avenge her mate; the three categories sometimes can be seen to overlap.[241] The Amazonian warrior is commonly described as outsized to match the typical hero: the Amazons in the *Alexander Romance* exceed "in size and beauty all other women."[242] The sword maiden Brunhilde we know to be of serious heft, as witness her hard treatment of King Gunther in the *Nibelungenlied;* so, in a Russian *bylina,* is the Amazonian Nastas'ya, Dunaj's conquest, whose story complicates and reverses the love-death theme of the *Digenid:* in the Russian tale the hero kills the heroine and then himself.[243]

Heroic size, explicitly described or implicit, is often accompanied by other signs of warlike excellence: the tribe of Amazons that appears in the *Alexander Romance* consists of great horse riders, and the daughters of Danaos, in Greek myth, were skilled in driving the war chariot. The horse eponym was also frequent among them, like Hippolyte whose girdle Herakles sought (Hippolyte's sister is named Melanippe, or "Black Mare"), and signs of the mare undoubtedly have a perceptible psychological significance in the heroic complex.[244] Another Hippolyte, who was Theseus's foe in his own war with the Amazons, eventually became the mother of Theseus's son, the ill-fated Hippolytos.[245] We can follow the equine connection into the *Aeneid,* where the woman warrior (*bellatrix*) Camilla was raised by her father in the Italian mountain fastnesses and was nursed by a wild mare (*equae mammis et lacte ferino nutribat*),[246] and even into Balkan Moslem heroic songs, where the Christian Amazon and Queen, the redoubtable Mara of Confez, has a magical winged horse.[247]

The fighting Amazon may also, like the hero, act as part of a dyad. The Armenian woman warrior Khantout is the sister of a sinister maiden enchantress, and the hero Baghdasar "the Small," brother of Sanasar "the Large" of Sassoon, must overcome both Amazonian strength and a paired power deploying certain feminine magical stratagems, in order to defeat the two of them.[248]

Another Amazonian characteristic, which must echo the ideal celibacy of the male warrior-hero, is her special and vital virginity. In the *Nibelungenlied* Brunhilde's considerable physical strength fails only after her virginity is taken.[249] In Central Asia, in an Oghuz Turk epic, the woman warrior Banu Chicheck fights the hero Bey Bamsi Beyrek, but after she is defeated—and that not easily—the Bey's father warns him that such a girl should never be a wife but only a companion to the victor.[250] In like wise, the virgin huntress and man-killer Atalante is, in one version of her myth story, turned into a lioness (an animal chaste by definition,) and Robert Eisler, pursuing a psychoanalytic course into the myth, reads her service to Artemis Lykaie, the Wolf-Goddess, as demonstrating that the Amazon huntress must be asexual, a hunting companion only, to the hero.[251] Certainly her asexual character can be dangerous to man: as Artemis's votary she "imitates the goddess," "swings over to total animality," and "becom[es] the fierce huntress who pursues and massacres the male she ought to marry."[252] Harthgrepa, the Norse hero Starkaðr's giant foster-mother, solves the problem of concupiscence by dividing her fierce and destructive side from her sensual side: when she "desires the embraces of men" she shrinks down to a desirable size from a giantess' normal, fearful grossness.[253]

But it is the usual though not invariable fate of the warlike Amazon to be defeated and mated, in some fashion, to the hero—although the latter's victory may have to be accomplished by manipulative trickery, and it may not bode well for the future. The ex-Amazon may be transmuted, as wife and mother, into a paragon, like the "proud maiden" Oryo in *Beowulf* and certain examples described by Saxo, but the normative patterns are less happy.[254] In Theseus's liaison with Hippolyte (or Antiope) the broken Artemisian chastity of the mother seems to be tied to the eventual doom of the son, Hippolytos, and Theseus's sexual conquest of the Amazon is arguably one of his "three sins"—those sins so often committed, as Dumézil saw it, against each of the three Indo-European functions by the adventuring Indo-European hero-warrior.[255] On the other hand, an Amazonian mother might merely be part of that very special genetic inheritance of the hero: such a parentage is casually inserted into the Norse tale of the brothers Bósi and Smidr.[256] In the Norse *fornaldarsaga* called the *Saga Heiðreks Konungs ins Vitra* (The saga of King Heidrek the Wise), a sequence of potent descent and anomalous inheritance begins with the berserk Angantyr, then moves to Angantyr's Valkyrie daughter Hervor, a fearless killer who takes her father's sword from his grave howe. Hervor eventually marries and settles down "to fine work with her hands," but her favorite son is Heiðrekr, a trickster and mischief-maker whose daughter (another Hervor) also is an Amazon, and probably the reincarnation of the first woman warrior of that name.[257] The Amazon or Valkyrie figures who appear in several other sagas possess this reincarnate persona and boast the inheritance of special powers.[258]

The Amazon as heroic opponent condenses within one outline the sharpest images of the heroic sexual conflict. When the hero is on a quest, and his prize is a woman, the woman warrior is a prize capable of defending itself (herself). But her position is fragilely based, and sometimes she goes too far. In the Serbian epic of Marko Kraljević three suitors are confronted by Rosanda, the "sister of Leka Kapitan," who roundly insults all of them: Marko is called a Turkish minion, Dark Miloš is "horse-born," and Relija is stigmatized as illegitimate and "suckled by a gypsy."[259] Marko punishes these verbal outrages by attacking and mutilating this virago, putting out her eyes and cutting off her right arm, a barbarity that silences her satires (we can compare her, in a way, to poor Thersites) and which has a flavor of violent countermagic about it. The Amazonian "aberrance" is, or can be, dangerous both to the hero and to a rival woman warrior, not least because of the confusion of sexual roles and because the sexuality of the hero himself is often so confused or inchoate.

Predatory Sexuality

In this mode the emphasis is on the practice of the sexual game itself: not on the seizure, rape, or forceful conquest of the woman (or sometimes the boy) but on the theme of seduction and seductiveness.[260] We might be surprised by some of the heroic figures who turn up in this compromising sexual situation.

One of the most archaic layers of the Welsh Celtic evidence bearing on the Arthurian legend, the *Trioedd Ynys Prydein* (Triads of the Island of Britain), describes the future King Arthur as a notorious womanizer who, at one point, is caught out by a warrior-rival "in woman's clothing and dancing with the women" as part of his obsessive pursuit of the sex.[261] This is the same Arthur who will later, in a different narrative context, act the old cuckold's part, when Guinevere the Queen is conquered by Arthur's younger alter ego, Lancelot. (We have already glanced at this ancient theme of the older or prospective husband whose woman is seduced away by a younger man, usually with deadly consequences.) Tristan, King Mark of Cornwall's sister's son, is always well to the fore as the icon of the young seducer, though in the fully developed tale, as in Gottfried of Strassburg's German version, he plays more the part of a trickster whose tricks go awry; Isolde/Yseult takes charge of the action and actually dominates most of the latter part of the narrative.[262] Another great seducer, Ilium's Paris, who had a true hero's upbringing (including exposure in the wilderness and nurturing by wild beasts), also had a hero's name, Alexandros or "repeller of men," because he fought off robbers while he had been a shepherd in his youth;[263] yet ever since the Trojan War he has been roundly contemned: for his arrant—if sensible—cowardice in the face of an enraged Menelaus, for his part in the death of great Akhilleus (striking at the hero from a distance and from behind with his coward's arrow), and, worst of all, for his seduction and abduction of Helen, thereby causing the war and the ultimate destruction of his own family and city.[264]

In the Dumézilian perspective the warrior-hero who practices the seductive arts always originates in, or slides into, the Indo-European Third Function, where sexuality is a structural component and a propellant motif. (In addition, Paris/Alexandros can probably be twinned to Hektor, so displaying that reflex of the divine twins that seems to mark this particular *fonction*.)[265] This characteristic is most plainly visible in some of the later cycles of the Old French *chansons de geste,* instanced in the *Cycle des Narbonnais* thoroughly and ingeniously studied (through a Dumézilian lens) by Joël Grisward.[266] In the epic songs composing this cycle of tales, Hernaut and Garin, those "sons of Aymeri" set into the Third Function, carry the marks of physical beauty, impetuosity—and long, red hair.[267] In the long, feminine hair of Hernaut in particular we can see, perhaps, an exact oppositive reversal of the male-imitating Amazonian image, the woman warrior aspiring to the Indo-European Second or Warrior Function. Male beauty is routinely ascribed to the hero, but when it stands alone, that is, is not included in a cluster of formulaic expressions (along with impressive physical size and the other usual distinguishing marks), it appears to signal the subject's position in the Third Function, not the Second Function, and, at least in the Western medieval context, it is often accompanied by unwarriorlike stigmata, such as cowardly behavior.[268] An Icelandic *þáttr* like "Bósa ok Herrauðr" may include a playful and unbridled sexuality with a comic turn to it, and Bósi—revealing another dimension of the warrior in the Third Function—is not put down by the tale-teller for his rowdy sexual adventurousness, but other and more serious heroic traditions bend strongly, if not invariably, toward the view that women are, in a number of ways, very dangerous to the warrior, and that congress with them may be more parlous than any hard-fought battle.

Homoeroticism/The Married Hero

The epic traditions we work with, and any reading of the sexual mores expressed in them, places these two sexual modes at opposite poles: the one involving a close emotional and, explicitly or implicitly, sexual relationship between males; the other describing the hero within the circumscriptions and expectations of a regularized family life. The evidence seems to suggest that any homosexual relationship, when it is made at all apparent in our sources, is ordinarily seen and defined as temporary and extrasocietal:

not as an intrinsic and expectable episode in a broader process of social maturation for the young warrior, but as an attachment with some situated value within the nonfamilial, male warrior cohort or group. In fact it is uncommon even in the Greek epic-heroic sources. Marriage, on the other hand, is imagined and stated to be a more or less permanent, socialized, and socializing heterosexual relationship, with the production and nurturing of the next generation as one main goal. But the married hero is not common, either.

We have already seen how the power of the sexual drive is channeled and re-formed in the heroic imagination, or, more precisely, in the imaginal structure regarding and bearing on heroes (that structure emplaced in and projected by the epic singer's imaginative creation). If the heroic world is essentially homocentric (using both the Greek and the Latin meanings of the prefix), the alterity, perhaps the frightening or inflaming alterity, of the female could push the warrior toward his own kind. The fixing of the hero in a "powerful adolescent" mode, within a totally masculinized affective frame, would evidently reinforce the possibility of homosexual attachment. Yet the only "significant" evidence concerns not homosexuality as such but the specifically pederastic pairing sometimes connected to the process of initiation in real or reconstructed warrior "societies," to the individual "instruction" in arms and the warrior ethos by an older and directed to a younger male, with a sexual connotation perhaps implied. Thus in the *Aeneid* Nisus was the comrade (*comes*) of Euryalus, and "one love [*unus amor*] was theirs" (IX.179, 182). This relationship seems to be unambiguous enough, but what do we make, much later, of Gawain, in Chrétien's romance *Yvain*, pleading for *compagnie*—that is, for male companionship—and for a true *compainz*?[269] The scholarship is in considerable disagreement on the subject.

In an attempt to describe a homosexual, and specifically a pederastic, relationship as it may have had its roots in an archaic Indo-European warrior-initiation practice, Jan Bremmer can single out only the Greek evidence for this practice, and that only among the Dorians, especially in Sparta and in "archaic" Crete.[270] There is evidence—or the accusation—of similar behavior among some Germanic tribes and possibly among the Celts, though no indication of such practices persists in the old Irish and Welsh narratives—narratives that of course have been passed through a Christian cognitive and moral lens.[271] Earlier Greek myth remains uneasy and ambiguous on the subject; the imprimatur of Zeus the Father-God himself was put on the ravishing of the beautiful boy Ganymede, yet it is part of the darker legend of the fate of the House of Kadmos that Laius,

Oedipus's father, brought pederasty to human society when he pursued and carried off Chrysippos, Pelops's son.[272] This act brought him no good result: his sexual inversion was seen to be one of the sins paid for by his own death at his son's hand, and sexual crime of another sort was continued in the next, more deeply damned generation of the Kadmian House.[273]

Bremmer says that the pederastic act or element in initiation, if it ever existed among Indo-European-speakers, was disapprobated and so disappeared, first because of the humiliation involved for one partner in occupying a passive homosexual role, and more importantly because of the elimination or transformation of the warrior-initiation process that might have temporarily fostered and encouraged such practices.[274] The appearance, and then the occlusion or disappearance, of a regularized, hypermasculinized initiatory mechanism surely must influence how a given society sees male homosexual relationships. This could explain why, in the highly individualized and agonic (yet familial and, in its own fashion, legalistic) context of the Norse-Icelandic sagas, any hint or inference that an individual had accepted the passive homosexual role was a hot and grievous insult, a killing matter for accuser or accused.[275] Here the accusation or implication of derogated sexual passivity in the male, of an unnatural inversion of the normal sexual or gender relationship, might even be generalized and directed toward a married man whose wife appears to be dominant in the partnership: in *Egils saga* Egill raises a *niðstong* or "pole of insult" against the Norwegian king Eiríkr Blood-Ax because of his perceived unmanliness and compliance in respect to his supposedly dominant partner, Queen Gunnhildr.[276] Any remnant either of the old Germanic *Geheimbund* (warrior society) or of homosexual initiatory rituals had long since disappeared in the Sandinavian north and the Icelandic west-over-sea. Alongside the irrefragable individuality of the saga heroes, which is one of the unmistakable marks of these sources, sits the ordinary life of the family, which makes up a primary, complementary, but also complicating motif. Both would be antagonistic to any hint of man-love, the latter defined in both cases as a "perversion."[277]

There is no incontrovertible proof that the *philotês* between Akhilleus and Patroklos contained a sexual element, and the myths of such paradigmatic heroes as Theseus and Herakles (or Roland and Olivier) have no hint of a homosexual element. In general such an "element" can be found only by reading it into texts for which there is no clear warrant. This would be especially true of the *chansons de geste* and chivalric tales emanating from a warrior culture overlaid, however lightly at times, by a Christian ethos antagonistic to homosexuality. Pressing farther afield in the pursuit of evidence available or readable for our topic, the old Georgian epic *The Lord of the Panther-Skin* is unique (even in a heavily Persified culture) in its strongly emotional and affective narrative tone. Its heroes are not at all the stoic and marmoreal characters seen in other heroic tales, but this startlingly decorated, sometimes almost risible quality simply marks a singularity of the old Georgian context, or possibly of the author, the poet and aristo Shota Rustaveli. If one wants to speak of repression and transference, one may, but the bulk of the heroic narratives descending to us are in the main missing the motif of homosexual affection.

Nevertheless there remains that disjunction, for whatever reason, between the anthropological data we have on the allowance and even encouragement of some male homosexual experience in certain societies, and the heroic images generated, in myth and in epic, in those same or parallel societies. The disciplinary or punitive element inherent in an initiatory-group experience doesn't explain this disjunction. In Papua–New Guinea and Melanesia generally, socially accepted forms of male homosexuality can be seen far beyond the temporal limits of the initiatory experience, and male-bonding misogyny as a social given can extend into and even interrupt the married state; sexual customs there (and, almost certainly, kinship definitions and processes) have moved at a marked eccentric away from forms recognizable even in similarly warrior-dominated, male-centered groups found elsewhere, and most specifically in the European Old World.[278]

There remains the question of whether the unleashed potency of the warrior, with his possible violation of every limit, might lead him to an expression of victorious dominance through homosexual rape (though I am aware that this should be considered an expression of aggressive mastery and superpotency, not sexuality.) The epics known to me give no evidence at all for this; the *Iliad,* for example, which contains some of the strongest and most violent images in literature, hints at terrible acts of rage and revenge (including cannibalism) and speaks openly of corpse mutilation and human sacrifice, but says nothing of any specifically sexual humiliation inflicted on a defeated enemy. Both internal and external censorship certainly may be at work, but in the end the solid evidence is simply not there.

Now what of the married hero, fully integrated, in theory, into his society? Heroes do occasionally marry: the Achaean trickster Odysseus had a wife, and successful quests for the maiden as "treasure" or for the bride of brides may eventuate in legitimate wedlock for the hero. Ulster's Cú Chulainn, too, was married once, and mated twice more, though in his case it is said, significantly, that the other Ulstermen wanted him married "that he might have an heir, knowing that his rebirth would be of himself." Cú

Chulainn did sire this heroic heir of his body, but no good came of it.[279] In the Irish tales of the *fianna* we find that Finn mac Cumaill engendered his son Oisín on the Otherwordly woman Blaí Derg, who had the form of a deer: here the ordinary mating is put far off, and unabashed strangeness takes its place.[280] On the other hand, in the Georgian epic all three heroes, who are also kings, marry and take possession of their rightful kingdoms; and in the Welsh tradition, we are finally told that "that night [Culhwch] slept with Olwen; as long as he lived she was his only wife," and the *Culhwch ac Olwen*, one of the greatest, if oddest, of the heroic quest tales, ends in extraordinary completion.[281]

By and large the heroic drama lies directly and essentially in *action*, in the quest or the wooing of the woman; and Cú Chulainn's wooing of Emer, for example, is laid out (in the Old Irish *Tochmarc Emire*) with such elaborate verbal exchanges, such word play, illusive allusions, japes, and uncontrolled metaphoric displays, that it is obvious that the game, to the poet-narrator, is in the verbal pyrotechnics, the play rather than the ending.[282] On the other hand, though thematic-generic similarities are often pointed out between the Celtic and the Icelandic–Scandinavian–North Germanic thoughtworlds, a signal saga wooing such as that between Oláfr the Peacock and Þórgerdr Egill's-daughter in *Laxdæla saga* consists of her challenge, his riposte, and for the rest "no one could hear what they were saying."[283] In the North, to the taciturn belong the fair, at least in this instance.

That conclusion is perhaps simplistic. In the Icelandic family sagas, with their acute and often powerfully complex treatment of the dynamics of family and social group and—or against—the individual, marriage can certainly add a disquieting dimension of dissension, rivalry, and conflict to the story. Among other potent themes, *Laxdæla* displays the destructive *eros* wielded by the beautiful, man-eating Guðrún;[284] in *Gísla saga Súrssonar* a tragic outcome emerges from the close and strong bond constructed between Gísli and his wife's brother, and the subsequent alienation of Gísli's own blood kin from him.[285] In the magnificent *Njála* a strong secondary theme develops around the fateful but attractive figure of the "thief-eyed" woman Hallgerðr, married in turn to three husbands and the bane of each. In the end she refuses to aid her husband Gunnarr, Njáll's friend, in his last extremity and seems fully to merit, at least in the saga's own terms, the description of "evil woman" put on her by the *sagamaðr* (by way, we note, of another woman's comment).[286] Yet we ought to remember that many of the women of the sagas, even when they are not Amazons outright, are often very strong characters, for good or ill, so that the saga heroes can easily find their lives fatefully (or even fatally) complicated by marriage or some other relationship contracted with one of these females.

The married hero, in the epic traditions set outside the more "realistic" sagas, seems to be the special victim of two thematic possibilities, in both of which he stands outside the *regula* of the usual heroic biography; either (1) he assumes roles of patriarchal domination, of sovereignty *in parvo*, over his family, or (2) he is caught by marriage and remains held in place, with his heroic freedom of movement lost. In the first deviation from the heroic norm the hero advances to a directive familial role suited to the older, matured adult man. But by escaping his youth alive, and taking up the husband's and father's role, he is already in clear violation of the typical heroic creed; by surviving, he has gone over, the heroic ethos might say, to the enemy. An old hero is another sort of anomaly, unless he is already an extraordinary figure like Starkaðr; he might as well be a king, and often he is. His advanced years, where respect should be expected, are curiously converted to become the object of epic derision, especially as he is forced to appear in marital dramas pointing up that most unpromising role of an older man tied to a younger woman. Arthur in his rampaging youth is called (according to the Welsh *Triads*) the Red Ravager, and here he is a potent, tireless, and sly womanizer; Arthur as king will at last be a pathetic if majestic cuckold. Ulster's King Conchobar is betrayed by his sister's son, the lover of Deirdre; the magnificent Finn mac Cumaill, in his position of authority as *rígfénnid*, is manipulated and befooled by an attractive younger woman. When the hero manages or is fated to move into the generation of husbands and fathers, he can become the target of that which he once was: representing order, stability, social integration, and direction, he is now the derisive object of the anarchic and terrifying energy, and also the green and springing sexuality, of the younger hero.

The second deviation places the hero, now married and responsible, into the trap constructed by culture. The best and most affect-laden image of such a trapped or "emplaced" fate is surely the Trojan hero Hektor,[287] "guardian of the perishable joys" in Rachel Bespaloff's memorable phrase.[288] Caught in the city under siege, tied to wife, child, royal parents, and realm, he is the object of Akhilleus's savage and unlimited warlike skills, and he will die before his city, too, perishes. Akhilleus, "whom force has made half god, and violence half beast," makes certain that Ilium will have no saving champion, certainly not Hektor, who makes the mistake of wanting some further good (or a different sort of good) beyond the fame and frame of the warrior-hero. In the heroic tradition as we usually encounter and parse it, the city is a trap for heroism. So is marriage, which usually means submission to the ideal systems of contractual kinship, continuation, and social rules. Thus in the Armenian *David of Sassoon*, the eponymous hero is betrothed to a woman who represents the cultural-familial focus; he is "beguiled" into sleeping with her, but soon leaves to pursue, more heroically, the Amazonian maiden Khantout. Eventually the casual product of his first liaison, a daughter, will ambush and kill him.[289] In the usual epic scenario, the hero is prepared to go to any lengths to avoid the fate of Hektor—not death, but death on the defensive, trapped in the constricting bonds and artifacts of culture, rather than death on the offensive, assaulting that culture. His fate, of course, is to be caught in exactly that sort of cultural trap, a subject to which we will now turn.[290]

DEATH AND THE HERO

According to Marie Delcourt, "Pour des Grecs, un héros est donc simplement un mort honoré par des personnes étrangères à sa famille."[291] Several intriguing questions are immediately thrown up by such a definition, but for now let me concentrate our attention on one of them, which might be stated as: is the only good hero a dead hero?

The Good Death

The hero deals in death, and for the most part he accepts that death will be his inescapable portion. "Be dead, then"—*tethnathi*—says the pitiless Akhilleus to Hektor (*Il.* XXII.365), but he must know that his own death awaits soon enough; when it comes he will surely remember his statement that the war-god Ares is always just: "he kills those who kill." Death being the currency in which heroism deals, some deaths are more acceptable than others. The best of all is the great battle death.

> Our ancestors have left us no other good
> The death of none of us should be on the blanket
> But with swords to die singing[292]

So goes an Albanian war song, and there are many very like it in the great fund of epic. Evidently the alternative is dreadful to contemplate: according to Q. Curtius Rufus, Alexander the Great, a conscious imitator of the heroic life, feared when he was taken sick in Babylon that he might die not by an enemy hand but had lost his life "taking a bath."[293] Old Starkaðr—Saxo's Starcatherus—is reported to have been of much the same opinion, for "dying through illness was once thought as discreditable . . . by individuals who were dedicated to warfare."[294] The Icelander Kormák in his own saga bitterly regrets his impending "straw death" in bed, though in truth he is mortally wounded, and will die of his wound quite soon enough.[295] And the whole matter is almost too blithely put to verse in John Dryden's libretto to Purcell's *King Arthur*:

> Brave souls to be renown'd in Story
> Honour prizing
> Death despising
> Fame acquiring
> By expiring.
> Die, and reap the fruit of Glory
> Brave souls to be renown'd in Story.

Well sung! and the "good death"—the proper or fitting death—for the hero is violent, for he *is* the incarnation of deadly force. The heroic opinion, in this area as in so many others, contradicts the normative opinion of society, which tends to define a good death for humankind as one coming in the slow accumulated fullness of years, and as "natural," not violent.[296] The heroic "good death" is *supposed* to be violent, a sword death—and it is voluntary (though Homer, read carefully, supplies a more emotionally complicated mixture of reactions to the young hero's death than most of our epic poets). Mary Douglas believes, and I think quite correctly, that part of the mysterious and lasting potency of the heroic individual comes from his voluntary submission to death: the hero wills himself to accept and even to welcome the danger of death, and at the very end to don the *lainon khitôna*, the "coat of stone" in one of Homer's many striking images of the end of heroic life.[297] This power of velleity may be turned around: an old one-eyed man (the god Óðinn in his usual disguise) tells the hero Hadingus, in Saxo's version of the story, that he would never die "except of his own will," and finally Hadingus, weighed down by age and weakness and his adventures, does kill himself, by hanging.[298] In the North the "warrior of Óðinn" tends to live longer than his opposite or counterpart, the "warrior of Þórr," as we see in the legend of Starkaðr, who is given three lifetimes by his god; in the end, utterly weary of his prolonged life, he tricks a young companion into killing him.[299] Even a quasi-historical figure in the Icelandic sagas, like Egill, an exemplary Óðinn-warrior to be sure, will eventually tire of his survival into a nearly helpless and unattractive old age; he curses the god who had taken his favorite son, and he finally dies, blind but still stubbornly, skillfully making his stark poetry, through the great gift given him by that same old, unknowable, and ever treacherous chief god.[300] Another variant on the motif of heroic aging is provided by Joël Grisward: the father figure Aimeri (in the Old French *Cycle des Narbonnais*) is one "whose drama . . . is that of a man who doesn't want to grow old."[301] The theme of the self-willed death has also been found and analyzed by Dumézil in the *Mahâbhârata* where the hero Bhiṣma gave up both rule (his right to the throne) and the promise of progeny to take up his heroic warrior's role. We hear again an older echo of the Armenian hero Pokr Mher's declaration, "I have had no child, I can have no death." Bhisma gained immortality, until at last he made a personal choice to die.[302]

Heroic longevity not only obtrudes into the typical biographic drama of the hero, but can bring its own woes; it is a double-edged gift, and not necessarily a welcome one. Thus it fits the bivalent and shadowy potency of a northern god like Óðinn. We may even see a situation where the very essence of a markedly stoic heroism will not rest on and resonate in the bright blaze of early feats and a glorious sword death, but on a resigned acceptance of the burden of old age. But other themes often enter into this ideational complex, including the tricksterish quality frequently seen in the Óðinn warrior (Egill in the *Eigla* absolutely shows this quality)—and we recall that the heroic trickster is the likeliest of all to be a survivor. The Welsh Cei, of the Two Gifts, once a rewarded champion among champions, may have survived much longer in the later Arthurian *matière* than he might have wished.

Killing the Hero

How to kill a hero? Even if he accepts death, his extraordinary prowess, his exceptional physical qualities and manifest perfections, must make this no easy task. When part of his genetic inheritance is divine or Otherworldly, mere men indeed may wonder. Nevertheless he must and will be killed: it is necessary to his essence, and the epics do not stint in bringing their fated heroes to the "iron sleep," the "die-cast of Mars," the "end of war and life" (all citations from the *Aeneid* alone, another rich repository of well-crafted poetic tropes).[303] Perhaps the plainest and starkest prediction is given to the Serb hero-prince Marko Kraljević: "you will die by the hand of God, the old killer."[304] What follows is a compilation, extensive but not all-inclusive, of ways and means by which the hero is done down at last.

OVERPOWERING ODDS

One of the grimmer pleasures of the epic poet is to give the hero a bloody death surrounded by his last sword harvest, the high-piled bodies of his enemies. Roland, Olivier, and all the paladins of Charlemagne's rear guard were slain, but only after a monstrous slaughter: "four thousand pagans / by these few Franks were slain" or "When Charlemagne comes to this bat-tlefield / He'll see the hosts of slaughtered Saracens / For each of us some fifteen pagans dead."[305] In the *Nibelungenlied* the Burgundians, great killers all, who were trapped and besieged at Etzel's court, throw out four thou-sand Hunnish bodies (*aventure* 34) before the last of Dietrich's warriors are slain, and of these Burgundians all save Gunther and Hagen lie dead (*aventure* 38). When the Irish hero-king Conaire Mor was trapped in Da Derga's hostel, he killed "six hundred before reaching for his weapons and another six hundred afterward"—but he will fall himself on that fatal night.[306] The theme of the hero finally overpowered by tremendous odds can easily be condensed, made more realistic, and inserted into such a framework as the Icelandic family saga: according to Þorkell Elfara-Poet, Gunnarr, in the *Njála*, "wounded sixteen men / and killed two others," be-fore he, fighting alone, was cut down "with many terrible wounds" (chap. 77). And when the saturnine and unlucky saga hero Grettir is at last brought down, eighteen men band together to kill him and his brother on Drang Isle. Even then, black sorcery must be used against him before he falls.[307]

The Last Stands of the heroes pit many ordinary warriors against the doomed single adversary, so that numbers (and fate, another force and com-plication) overbalance and quell him and his deadly powers. Though they represent necessity, and even inevitability, the hero's multiple enemies usu-ally are said to gain little honor for themselves when they pull down the singular hero-warrior, though in truth few other options are open to them, and obviously the sanguinary end of the hero's tale is not often meant to reflect much credit on his slayers, however useful their terminal enmity may be to the age-long rumor and high fame of his story.

THE BETTER MAN

When a series of confrontations between heroes is made part of an epic narrative, as in the archepical *Iliad*, one hero will fall to another superior in skill, or sometimes in luck. Patrokles, even tricked out in Akhilleus's armor, is not Akhilleus; he falls to Hektor (or to Hektor and the god Apollo). Hek-tor is also deemed "better"—*polu phҽrteros*—than Menelaus (VII.104–5) and bests and wounds Agamemnon as well, but in killing Patrokles he reactivates, with fatal consequences for himself, the raging champion who is indisputably, whenever he claims the title, "best of the Achaeans," *aristos Akhaiôn.*[308] This resounding phrase, as Gregory Nagy has demonstrated, is awarded to more than one of the Greeks, but Akhilleus is truly the non-pareil warrior, and Hektor will be no match for him and his divine-animal anger.[309] The *Iliad,* as we know, also pits god against god and, under certain odd circumstances, god against human, as when Diomedes, at the peak of his furious and battle-blind form, wounds both Ares and Aphrodite. Athena is also allowed to intervene in the duel between Akhilleus and Hektor, but at the end it is raging Akhilleus whose own unquestionably superior warlike might triumphs.

Sometimes the *agôn* of hero against hero is slightly skewed. Marko Kraljević met the mighty Musa the Highwayman, he of the Three Hearts:

> and hero held hero by the bones
> and chased and tumbled over the green grass
> and hero has fallen on hero.[310]

He only kills Musa, however, with the aid of his guardian *vila.* Musa's full hero's strength had not been tested and overcome by Marko alone, so Marko laments: "I have killed one better than myself!"[311] The redoubtable Cú Chulainn is the greatest warrior of Ulster, and he will kill innumerable heroes of Connaght in the sanguinary course of the *Táin.* The boylike, beardless hero, the Warped One, is a warrior so tremendous that there can be none better, though it is fair to note that he must use strange and unfit means to fell certain of his opponents, as when he killed Ferdiad, who was practically his twin, with the secret weapon called the *gae bolga* (see below, p. 213). He himself will die only because he is fatefully caught by the net of the prohibitions, the *gessa* levied even on him.

The paradox of the heroic singularity conjoined with the interchangeability of hero to hero emerges markedly in this image of death by the better man. All of the language of the epics decorates and inflates the persona of each warrior-hero, and each of them carries his cargo of burnished excellences into fierce confrontation and battle. Why one of them should take the meed of glory and be called the best, therefore, may not always be clear or cogently argued, but as in the cases of Akhilleus and Cú Chulainn, the extraordinary combination of *divinity* and *animality* is very much emphasized: the terrifying warp-spasms or distortions of Cú Chulainn, the leaping fury of Akhilleus, the deerlike fleetness of Finn mac Cumaill. Mere physical strength and hardihood is not enough to compass a full description of these cynosures, and certainly not enough even for an upstanding, ordinarily heroic warrior-opponent who thinks to overcome them.

THE WEAKER COMPANION

In some dramatic cases the death of the hero seems to come not because the epic sees the central hero as himself failing or losing his consummate power, but because the hero is united in a symbiotic relationship to a weaker partner, whose death affects or drains away some of the supreme prowess of the stronger figure. Such is at least suggested in the last battle of Roland, after Olivier has died; part of Roland's strength is invested in his responsibility for his less powerful companion: "Since you are dead, it is hard that I still live" (*Quant tu es mor, dulur est que jo vif*).[312] Roland is responsible not only for Olivier's death but, as Olivier bitterly reminded him, for those of all the others in the Frankish rear guard: "We Franks are dead from your recklessness" (*Franceis sunt morz par vostre legerie*).[313] Roland finally dies from a combination of his own pride, the overwhelming numbers of his foes, and because his closest, his "twinned" comrade had fallen. A clearer image of this inanition of the hero appears in the Byzantine Greek *Digenid*, where the hero's sole companion is the Korê, the girl with whom, as a partner, Digenes lives what appears to be a remarkably chaste life. The hero, after bathing, which may be a reflex of Alexander's purported end, falls ill of a disease "called *opisthotonos*" whose symptoms resemble poisoning (here as in some other episodes the *Digenid* likes to imitate the Heraklean legend). He seems to be slowly dying,[314] whereupon the Korê, unable to bear "boundless grief," dies suddenly in the hero's sight; Digenes immediately follows her.[315] In both cases, and in the latter more openly, the perfection of the hero is closely attached to a less-perfect partner. The partner's death breaks the unbreakable frame of the hero's life and penetrates the impenetrable, so that black death can finally triumph.

TRICKERY, TREACHERY, AND MAGIC

We have seen that to accomplish certain tasks the hero must sometimes be paired with a colleague able to think as well as act, one who might possibly add the trickster's multiform and ingratiating skills to the purely heroic forceful endeavor. Yet the more complex, extraheroic world of manipulation, masking, trickery, and indirection can also be used against the hero, to become his bane.

All of the mechanisms listed here spring from a reversal of, or deviation from, the true heroic system. Trickery is covert, irregular, off-key, unbalancing; treachery violates the code of heroic solidarity or attacks some asso-

ciated bond (like family or marriage); magic emerges from a totally different category or universe from the human. All three may be variously combined, or added to other elements, to pull down the fate-held hero. In the
Nibelungenlied Hagen, who is already meditating treachery, tricks Brunhilde into revealing the secret of Siegfried's only point of vulnerability; soon
he attacks (by penetrating a magical but still vulnerable barrier with knowledge gained through trickery) and fatally wounds the hero.[316] The supernatural world also takes its place in the fatal wounding of Akhilleus: Paris's
arrow is guided from afar by Apollo's malevolent, or perhaps merely fatally
fulfilling, divine eye and will, and it pierces a magical covering or barrier
of invulnerability.[317] The triumph of magic is especially clear in the destruction of the typecast hero Herakles, but here we also see how heroic
force rebounds against its wielder, for the blood of Nessos, once mortally
wounded by Herakles, is Herakles' bane: the blood of a monster or supernatural being kills rather than, as in other cases, protecting and proofing
the hero.[318] A deadly trick (of false information and misdirection) played
by Nessos on Deianeira is also involved in the end of this mythic hero.

The innumerable armed confrontations of the northern sagas allow for
every kind of violent death. In *Njáls saga* we have already seen how Gunnarr Hámundarsson was felled by many wounds inflicted by numerous
opponents, but his enemies were surely helped by the treachery of his bitch-
wife, Hallgerðr.[319] Sorcery and magic are not uncommonly injected into the
sagas, though they tend to operate around the periphery of the lives of the
central heroes. Someone like Grettir, however, encounters a run of ill luck
or fatality almost certainly stemming from his frequent bouts with the
transnatural world, his willingness literally to face up to and battle its powers. Then his terrible wrestling match with the horrifying *draugr*, the malevolent walking revenant of the thrall Glámr, proved to crystallize all of the
forces ranged against him: this *contactus* with an evil thing, though one he
still managed to overcome by main force, seems to have injected a slow psychic venom that continued to poison him up to his saga's end.

The inevitable death of the hero is played out in more sonorous tones
when the solid structures of the heroic persona are undermined by perverse
circumstance, reversals and indirect attacks, forces from the hero's own
shadow (his hidden counterself), or forces from the Otherworld he may
oppose but cannot control. (The working of a shadow or "double" is apparent in the death of Finn's father Cumall, betrayed and slain by his own follower, and with his own sword.)[320] There is also the theme of the insidious
unheroic enemy, the trifling opponent whose small-souled enmity to the
hero can creep up and work drastic harm, especially when it is ignored by

the hero or invisible to him (as is often the case). Even a slave can prove fatal to a hero.

SELF-LIMITATION

This road to death is mainly, though not exclusively, seen in the Irish Celtic epos.[321] In this context the *geis* (pl., *gessa*)—the "prohibited matter" or taboo—is built directly into the heroic biography: "it might almost be inferred that a hero is safe from harm, while his *gessa* remain inviolate."[322] These *gessa* may be both subtle and direct; according to the Irish *Acallamh na Seanórach*, the champion Finn had a *geis* that forbade him to "see a corpse, unless it had been killed by weapons."[323] The ordinary dead are taboo for Finn. The most phenomenal of the Irish heroes, Cú Chulainn, must carry with him a set of prohibitions that can circumscribe his tremendous powers. This appears to be no great matter until his hero narrative moves toward its finale, when the clear heroic path, won and dominated with such irresistible might, suddenly throws up terrible choices—and every choice comes to have a deadly outcome. One of Cú Chulainn's *gessa* forbids him to eat dog—an obvious taboo, given his adopted name—but another commands him never to refuse a meal, and, of course, he eats the forbidden meat. He is prohibited from giving away his weapons, yet a threat of shaming satire (the quasi-magical criticism against which no one is proof) makes him do precisely that, so his enemies can fatally wound him with his own great death-dealing spear. One reflex of his legend says that at the very end he kills another dog (as he had begun his heroic career by killing the hound of Culann the Smith); he must surely and finally die after that.[324]

The Irish sources furnish us with another emblematic drama of *gessa*, as they describe the death of Conaire Mor in the *Togail Bruidne Da Derga* (Destruction of Da Derga's hostel).[325] There are at least eight prohibitions set on him after he becomes high king, and all are sequentially violated when he goes on his fated way to his death in the hostel. In both his and Cú Chulainn's case, fate and malignant sorcery combine: the hero is caught between invariable and unbreakable heroic rules and some equally important stricture or demand.

It is quite possible to read a kind of *geis* into other heroic deaths outside the Irish tradition. It is *geis* for Roland, as a paladin, to summon aid by blowing the oliphant; it is *geis* for Bui Digre, in the *Jómsvíkingasaga*, to deny his own chieftainship and accept the plain fact that his oath to fight for King Svein had been rendered void, after his own lord had prudently retired from the fight.[326] In *Egils saga* we may see *geis* in the fact that Þórólfr the Elder could not act as anything less than he was, a king's man and champion who could easily be mistaken for a king; but he is constricted by his sense both of self and of plain duty, and finally the jealous king himself gives him his deathblow.[327] Perhaps this is fate and personality joined. It is true that the Irish death tales, as compared with other epics, put such a cloud of final death-bound misadventure over the hero, and evince such complex combinations of fatality, magic, accident, and individual quirk, that they are difficult to imitate.

LOVE AND DEATH

A "curious" feature of the Celtic death tales, according to the Reeses, emerges when a sexual aspect is introduced into the terminal episode of the hero's life: some element of an active feminine sexuality fatally intrudes to assist and hasten his end.[328] To understand this better we might first examine the Germanic-Norse Valkyrie, who Ellis Davidson rightly stresses has a "wide and complex nature."[329] She may play a supernaturally protective but also personal and human part in a hero's life, (as in the *Helgakviða Hjorvardssonar* of the *Poetic Edda* [Helga Poems]), or act very like the guardian sprite or *vila* of the Serbo-Croat heroic tales. She may also be a battle-loving and bloodthirsty female, almost a demon, but the Valkyrie's power is connected to the fact that half of the battle dead are said to be given over to Freya—identified as the Third Function, Vanic goddess of sexuality and increase.[330] In Gísli's story, a Valkyrie seems to be the "bride" who in a dream shows Gísli a soft bed and promises "here you shall certainly come when you die," at which time Gísli will have "riches and the women also," as the goddess Freya permits.[331] The Valkyrie may thus intervene both before and after the hero's death, and her character as shield-maiden can emphasize either or both: the shield (and the good battle death), or the maiden (and sexuality).

The Irish Celtic interposition of a sexual element into the hero's death day can have a similar cast but an even deeper and darker symbolism. Fergus mac Roich is killed by a foe's spear cast while swimming in a lake with Queen Medb (a femme fatale in several senses) "entwined" around him;[332] and a version of Cumall's death (Finn's father) has this hero ambushed and killed while swimming to a beautiful woman on a lake isle.[333] There is a clear resemblance between these two deaths and that of the Armenian hero David of Sassoon, killed by the treacherous bow shot of an Amazonian foe—his own daughter—while he, too, is swimming.[334] The feminine symbolism is clear for enfolding water, and the copulatory significance of the act of the male swimming therein is not hard to find. But sexual congress can also be shown to break that code of celibacy that so often protects and extends the hero's fell but fragile invulnerability. A "mysterious woman," or women, partakes of the last adventure of the hero in Cú Chulainn's case, and when Conchobar succumbs to the sexual invitation of the women of Connaught just before he is killed, and again when Conaire violates one of his *gessa* and admits to Da Derga's hostel the dreadful dæmonic female whose name (Cailb) and nature are, as the Rees brothers acutely observe, very like to the terrible Indic death-goddess Kali.[335]

Sex is somehow fastened to that old sequence of ruptures, anomalies, and fateful signs that leads at last to the violent separation of all these heroes from the world. In other epic contexts the sexual element may be connected to the destined death of the hero by a long chain of events, with a sexual lapse at the beginning of the chain. The "heroic" Arthur who appears in the more archaic Welsh sources is a sexual predator (among other characteristics later deleted from the portrait of the "kingly" Arthur), but at least one sexual lapse also is allowed to persist as a fatal part of his later legend: his liaison with the witch-woman Morgaine, who proves to be his own half sister. The champion Tristan, too, is led to violate his king's champion role (and the close ascriptive tie of sister's son to his king, Mark), which will inevitably, albeit after a long delay, lead to his death. The Armenian hero David's fate has just been mentioned. Such "long chain" sequences spring from or are marked by a causative logic that does not quite fit the Irish situation, in which ambiguity and contrariety combine the sexual aspect, with its disintegrative power emphasized, into other forces and fated elements. "How to kill a hero" at the end of the heroic biography is, typically, answered or solved by an interlocking cluster of causes: the heroic stance and character, superhuman in his boasted strength and prowess, is brought low by a varied assault. No single opposing element can pull down a Roland or a Grettir; only a combination of forces, springing both from external enmity and interior faults, can do so. The Irish tales extend this complex ambiguity in many directions and into many modalities as the heroic personal cosmos is disintegrated, and the ambiguous and temporary order brought to the world by the hero's unique powers collapses.

BEYOND DEATH

Deathlessness and Sleep

In the usual heroic life pattern, the Akhillean hero trades his early death for immortal fame. Fame will bring the only immortality that the hero can enjoy, since his physical death is emphatically assigned as the inevitable heroic portion. Still, under certain circumstances the powers of the hero do not in fact die, and he receives a meed of years, a suspended death sentence—or an existence beyond death. In some cases the deathlessness of the hero is confused or conflated with the archaic sign of the "sleeping king"; lacking (or distrusting) a strong monarchic image, a folk may invest the sempiternal potency of the king figure in a strongly focused, perdurable heroic image. The Serbian Christian "sleeping hero" Prince Marko and the Armenian Pokr Mher, also a sleeper in the mountain, are almost certainly examples of such a perceptual shift.[336]

When we speak of a hero whose powers are thought to survive his death, it should be noted, we are not referring to that special situation, the Greek cult of the hero, with its hero's position in a postmortem intermediary place, moderately sacralized and usually marked on earth by his *hêrôon* or, in an even more important idea formation, where his powers "founded" and are based in, honored, and continued by the Greek *polis,* the city-state itself. The heroes I have in view at this point are said to wait, and may return in bodily form. Given the essentially doubled valence of the hero type when alive, it is not surprising that the hero can return as a "bad" revenant or as a "good" one.

Bad Death and Revenance

Examples of the bad, or destructive, returned hero must spring from the inevitably potential antisocial force of the warrior-hero when he was alive, and possibly from a "bad death," that is, a death figured as anomalous or, in heroic terms, unnatural. I have written elsewhere in some detail on this phenomenon of "bad death," and particularly as it may unfold a pattern characteristic of Indo-European-speaking groups. If my hypothesis has merit, the Dumézilian Second Function (*fonction guerrière*) projects or reforms these heroic victims as revenants who still pursue the strenuous careers cut short by their supposed death.[337] A sizable number of these unpleasant undead are seen in the Icelandic-Scandinavian North, in the form of a *draugr,* the malignant walking corpse, not a spirit at all but an unpleasantly solid entity who shows up in a dozen sagas and *Þáttir.* Beyond the northern evidence we can find parallel instances in Greek herodom: the Hero of Temesa mentioned in Pausanias, and Akteon—even Orestes. All of these "dark" warriors betray the characteristics of a "bad death" suffered, and they return in a palpable, physical form, with a nasty taste for postmortem violence: Temesa's "hero" is finally put down in a hand-to-hand combat; Akteon reappears as a kind of poltergeist; Agamemnon's son

Orestes, very far from his high tragic persona, assaults and beats up night travelers.[338]

The other side of the type of the undead hero may be more familiar: the warrior-hero passes from the view of men, but with the implicit charge laid on him that he must await some cataclysmic disaster among his folk and will return at that time to take up his defense. The last of the House of Sassoon, Pokr Mher, is confined (or rests) in a cave until his time comes again;[339] the Serbian Prince Marko, after his death, either is "carried overseas" to a holy burial ground in Mt. Athos (making that death journey by water seen extensively in other death tales) or is "asleep in Sarplanina" or "in the mountain" and will awake when Serbia is born again.[340] The hero Theseus may have remained, living, in the Hades he raided, as a punishment, but in another account he fell into the sea and disappeared off the island of Skyros. Having fallen and gone forth into myth, he reappeared in history: he was seen with the Athenian hoplites at the wave edge at Marathon, facing the Persians, and his supposed bones, those of "a man of gigantic size" and so fitted to a well-rehearsed heroic physical image, were brought from Skyros to Athens in 473 B.C.[341] Another hero, Aristomenes of Messenia, also once fell from a great height but miraculously survived the fall, and this evidence of a surnatural power evidently led Pausanias to relate that Aristomenes, too, appeared after his supposedly real or final death to aid the Messenians against their ancient enemy, Sparta, at the battle of Leuktra.[342] In all of these instances the warrior-hero is expected to return, or does return from his resting place, armed again and called back to battle; his actively intermediary place is resumed, and his powers are perceived as sufficient to survive any death and dissolution.

To Die for Glory?

We simply assume that the hero usually but very dramatically dies in the earnest hope of a kind of survival or even a persistence close to immortality, as a name to live on in fame and glory, so we parse and analyze the sentences in which the honorific descriptions are embedded. El Cid's faithful men have won "such honor" (*tan ondradas*); the knights of the *Nibelungenlied* will fight for "praiseful honor" (*lobelichen êren*); the reckless paladin Roland will fight to protect "my good name" (*mun los*), but also urges his men to fight so that no "malicious song" (*male chançun*—that is, a satire?) might ever be sung about them.[343] In the Byzantine Greek epic a very young Digenes says, "I want fame now, to light my line"; in fact, he will have no "line" to light, only the poem, which illuminates him forever.[344] The Irish hero Cú Chulainn is "renowned in song" (*cardda raind*)—as his uncle Fergus mac Roich is "famed in song" (*deroichet raind*)—and when he is given the name Hound of Culann (*Cú Chulainn*), Cathbad the Druid (who names him) swears that "the men of Ireland and Scotland shall hear of that name," and it shall be "ever on [their] lips."[345] The Old Irish vocabulary is very rich in synonyms for "fame, renown, glory," nearly as rich—though not nearly as precise—as the names for desired and hard-won fame in the *Iliad*, where the interactions and permutations of "name" and "fame" and "death" are most thoroughly and insistently worked out.

In fact, fame may or may not end or celebrate the heroic parabolic life, in its furious pace and action, its stylized confrontations, and its ideal brevity, but the hero, in another of the paradoxes linked to him or contained within him, does not really care. To him the past means little, the future not much more—or even less. The present, the instant, is all.

3 THE FRAMEWORK OF ADVENTURE

"I've quite lost my way," said Lancelot.
"Lost in a dark wood," Sir Roger agreed.
"With every possibility of misadventure."

—Donald Barthelme, *The King*

THE HERO IN SPACE

The first constraining element in the framework of heroic adventure is the space in which the adventures occur. This spatial dimension can be visualized as a horizontal plane (extension), a natural or untamed space (wilderness), an intrinsically "other" space or extension (such as the sea), an enclosed or cultural space (city or center), as liminal space (defined or identified in edges, boundaries, and borders), or even as an interior-psychic or mental space, especially as a theater for heroic madness. The last, however, is a very special space constituting the supernatural or Otherworld topos; I shall consider it separately, and in more detail, in chapter 7.

The Extensive Plane

One of the persistent and controlling images of *kingship* is the king's possession of and dominion over the royal city, that topical point in which the various powers of the sovereign are concentrated. The ideal zone for the *hero* extends outward and horizontally from that "civilized" royal control point. Otherwise there is no guarantee that the hero, in his exploratory zest or motile fury, will stay on the horizontal plane: he is perfectly capable, in his *Himmelstürmer* mood or mode, of assaulting the realm of the upper air and its prepotencies, or of descending to thunder at the gates of Hell, especially when Hell/Hel/Hades is designated as the Realm of the Dead—with which he has much to do. But the horizontal plane is where he exercises most of his powers, and it provides the ground, and the scenery, for the bulk of his venturing.

The typical pattern often begins with his birth drama, when as infant-hero he is sent away from "here" and taken "out there," where other imaginal topoi of exile and alterity may be superadded (the mountain fastness, the wilderness, the abandoned desert, or the alien and dangerous fluidity of river, lake, or especially sea). After a time it is from "out there" that he comes back to whatever center, and its controlling authority, sent him forth, or to other centers of enclosed, rigid, restricting, old, and impacted power. He appears over the horizon, riding or striding, alone or companioned, and he reacquaints the settled people with his name, or with *a* name. So young Culhwch rides forth in the Welsh tale to see his royal Cousin Arthur: "Such was the ease of the steed's motion under him, making toward Arthur's court."[1] Or the Persian hero Zâl in the *Shâh-nâma*, brought from the mountains by the great bird, the Simogh, and set down to disagreeably surprise his unaffectionate father.[2] In the biography of Finn mac Cumaill, for instructive contrast, the wild place "out there" where the Irish child-hero is hidden away will be the permanent stage for Finn as warrior-hero, whose wilderness adventures and antics will attract a good deal of our attention.

The extensive plane can also have another, more strictly physical or socio-geographic significance: this is the zone in which horse nomads raid and fight one another or from whence, uniting their savage hosts of horsemen or camel riders, they swoop down on the city or on its ambient zone of culture. In this nomadic-heroic zone, unbounded planar space is marked off and validated by the cattle or other prized and guarded herd animals that graze on it, and by the personal presence of the mounted hero, his allies, and the "enemy"—who also possesses these precious mobile goods. The ethnographic data collected in the last hundred years have illuminated the mind world of raiding pastoralists, including African, Central Asian, and North Arabian types, and although some difficulty remains in applying these data against the archaic reality of Indo-European pastoral nomadism and its presence in heroic myth, the information we do have is at very least suggestive of parallels.[3] The Bedouin of North Arabia, for example, were free of any significant external governance as late as the First World War; they cheerfully continued the pattern established when herd animals (and, later, riding beasts) were domesticated in this barren area millennia before. In one of their tales we read: "shortly afterward he undertook a new raid against the Rwala . . . and took all their camels together with the 'Alya herd." Soon came the inevitable response: "the Rwala came like a whirlwind, attacking the camp, and possessed themselves of all the herds there."[4] Obviously we are looking at nomadic raiding considered as a game, however violent, with set and well-known rules—one of which is that the settled area is *not* included in the game. In the nomadic-pastoralist view, such an area is marked as *prey*, not so much antagonistic as anomistic, a zone dominated by utterly different mores:

> Woe to their chief in his reign! Long has it endured in his kin
> And he might peacefully rest in the irrigated depressions
> Thou hast begun a war with a tribe that can strike from afar
> As even the hardest iron yields when thou takest pains to bore it.[5]

The woeful chief of the civilized foe is settled both in time and in place, but the fruitful, protected solidity of his "irrigated depressions" is attacked and broken by those raiders who will "strike [him] from afar." The spatial dimension in this pastoral-raider view consists of utter horizontality without feature, 360 degrees in sweep, an extension equated both with opportunity (the settled area, the target) and threat (other hostile nomads). The essential spirit of the featureless, extended plain always is conquered by movement, the slow drift of grazing animals, the sudden galloping onset of the raider.

Wilderness

The nomads' favorite zone of steppe or plain must have had its effect on early Indo-European pastoralists, perhaps generating the "cattle-raiding myth" that continued to surface in areas so far removed from the steppe as Celtic Ireland.[6] Wilderness has a more active, darker, and deeper image than the extensive plain/plane: to the tamed area of cultural construction and political control, it counterposes another kind of presence and power. The wilderness is not bare or featureless: it has its own verdant growth and ancient, natural constructions, its trees, groves, and plant "life" so very foreign to the life of man. It is also inhabited by beasts, whether beasts of the hunt or beasts of prey, enemies to one another and to man as well, however close he may draw to them in his articulated imaginal world. Wilderness is the place of a kind of rich but suspicious chaos, and it has its own specific and salient color: green. It is also, of course, the special place of the hero: here he is at home, if he is at home anywhere.

This is substantially a European notion and image, though it also has parallels in the African image of the wild "bush," among South American rainforest aboriginals, and in the jungles of Southeast Asia; and any hero with feral, animal tendencies will naturally be comfortable in the wild. Bjorn the Bear, the father of the legendary hero Boðvarr Bjarki, had to retreat to a wilderness cave in his bear's shape; and one of Bjarki's theriomorph brothers, the half-elk-shaped Elk-frothi Bjornsson, always remained in the animal world beyond men's halls and fields.[7] The hero in his frequent headlong pursuit of game or prey animal will also perforce be found in wild places, where he is liable in his haste to violate and cross the feared border into the Otherworld; this occurs especially in certain quest tales. Other adventures will also depend from this invasion and transgression.

In an image that considerably extends our vista, the Byzantine Greek hero Digenes Akrites seems to spend his time far from civilization, but his epic says he dwells in a "strange grove"—*alsos xenon*—which greatly resembles a royal park or Paradise. Indeed it is called exactly that (*thaumastou . . . paradeisou*), though the Borderer has a secret place for emergencies as well, as he once conceals his virginal wife in "the hideout on the hill."[8] Digenes' wilderness life is active enough, but the signs and symbols of ferality are muted. They become somewhat decorous in his story—which may betray the influence of the Greek idyll or pastoral poem.

The Italic tribes who settled in their oddly shaped peninsula had their own versions of the war-god the Romans called Mars, part of whose complicated potency dwelt deep in the forests—the area beyond the city's sacred boundary, and traversed when war-as-raid was in season. Mars (taking on a dual role we will soon identify in the Irish warrior *fían*) also protected society against the supernatural perils of the *silva*,[9] and he is at times closely connected with Sylvanus, the woodland-god. (We remember that the last-born son of the migrant hero Aeneas was Silvius, "king and father of kings," who was raised—*educet silvius*—in a forest by Aeneas's wife Lavinia.)[10] The Romans, and the Italic peoples with them, differentiated among those forests that sharply contrasted to man's own zone, the cultivated, controlled, and settled place. Some of this wilderness was not quite so wild, but beyond the helpful and accessible woodland was the true "*terra incognita* . . . (and) foreign parts, with their great and uncontrollable dangers."[11]

Leaving Italy to establish an empire, the Romans found a particularly ferocious enemy, the Germanic tribes, in command of large segments of these foreign and threatening landscapes. Their affinity for the wilderness was very clear to the observer and early anthropologist Tacitus: the grim land "generally either bristles with forests or reeks with swamps"; the tribesmen "consecrate woods and groves to their gods"; and they *lived* in forests like the vast and alien Hyrcanian, dwelling distrustfully apart from one another in crude homesteads and resembling (in Roman eyes at least) something like the much later image-ideal of the Noble (if bloodthirsty) Savage.[12] The Germanic-Scandinavian hero will long maintain his wilderness connections: the threatened Sigmund in the old saga of the Völsungs escapes into the woods to live in a subterranean earth house. (Tacitus had already remarked on the hidden underground chambers dug by the Teutons.)[13] There he and his son Sinfjotli will be doubly concealed, by the forest and by the covering earth they pile over themselves: the two heroes in their assumed wolf shape will occupy a wolf's den—a space even farther from and more foreign to the human social cosmos.

Other barbarians who had already come to Caesar's attention were the forest-dwelling Gauls (*aedificio circumdato silva, ut sunt fere domicilia Gallorum*), whose land, like that of the Germans, boasted nearly impenetrable forests of an incredible and intimidating aspect and extent.[14] In these forests, like the *silva Arduenna* in which Caesar found (or didn't find) the sly Gauls scattered "in hidden valley or wooded place or trackless swamp," the woods appeared to be the perfectly Celtic place of safe refuge from which they might plan to threaten their Roman conquerors anew.[15] This sheltering wilderness can also be the special place of the non-Continental, Goidel Celtic hero.

This Irish Celtic "hero in the wilderness" appears preeminently as the *fénnid*, the young Irish warrior who, with the sworn companions of his *fian*, is placed in the wild area, which he maintains not only as a protective belt against all his tribal enemies but against threatening incursions from the nonhuman Otherworld as well.[16] The *fénnidi* were once, according to the Irish myth, granted by divine fiat that portion of Ireland "of woods, wilderness and game"; their drama will still be set there, especially that of Finn mac Cumaill, the greatest *fénnid* of them all.[17] All of the excellences and faults of the *fénnid* and of *fénnidecht*, the special craft of the wild warrior, are signed and reinforced in Finn, with his anomalous birth and his strange isolated fosterage by weird women, his animal powers and associations, and his skill at all the ancillary crafts. Among other things, Finn is a druid, a smith, and above all a *fili*, a poet whose craft knowledge—called *imbas*—originated, according to the best tradition, in a tree or a grove.[18] The central process in Finn's life is a fruitful, or sometimes a harmful, confusion of opposites, as when he combines warrior with poet or, even more dramatically, warrior with druid; the *fian*-men who imitate him are both sturdy outlaws and ordinary younger members of the tribe or *túath*, who simultaneously guard their own society and are thought to threaten it. Ragged but rugged masters of the zone outside and the zone between, they are "forever denied adult status"; nevertheless, as they are often fosterers and admitted experts in initiation, the "professional" *fénnidi* have the power to assist other young men of the *túath* to mature and so to enter adult society.[19]

The Fenian tales elaborately describe the characteristics of these wild warriors, and it is not difficult to see here a strong connection to the general and accepted theme of the male initiation cohort subtracted from society, forcibly set apart in the wild, trained, initiated, and then reintegrated into that society.[20] The Celtic image of wilderness and of its special, resident warrior personnel displays very familiar elements: a triumph of formlessness and of combined and confused categories, with Finn as a hero both in and outside society, as a "servant" *and* as a "chief," at home in nature (he was once called "Lad of the Skins") but also skilled in manipulating various of his culture's valued crafts.[21] He gains his knowledge "from extreme mobility and extreme immobility," and finally he is positioned "between youth and senility." His "boyhood deeds never end"; he can reverse time and revert to childhood; and the tale says he may even be able to resist and avoid the final pang of death itself.[22] I shall investigate this theme of extended boyhood a little later; for now let me note only that *somewhere* here in the imaginal persistence of adolescence is one of the truest keys to the sempiternal image of herodom.

Water and Otherness

The fluid world, like the forested wilderness, is ruled by inhuman potencies and the strangest forces, and the hero must be prepared, like Beowulf, to dive in and attack the monstrous enemy hidden deep down there. The male hero may intrude into this watery element, which is often conceived of as feminine, to win a reward—which is surprisingly often a horse.[23] In a schematic reverse, we have the dying hero who takes his treasure into the watery depths to safeguard it forever, as the obdurate Bui digre, Bui the Stout, does in the *Jómsvíkingasaga*.[24] The deeps thus possess either threat or opportunity, monster or treasure—Broad Bui is said to have become a sea snake guarding that treasure he took down below with him—and a clear parallel is shown to the Otherworld marked as Underworld, when the hero penetrates down and into another kind or degree of absolute alterity.

The extensive surface of the watery element displays another variety of threat-and-opportunity as well, but one still very similar to our view of the telluric wilderness. In a Viking society, for example, heroic nomadism became sea-borne following the technical conquest of the northern waters in prehistoric times by means of the arcane crafts of shipbuilding and navigation. The *Beowulf* poet's Anglo-Saxon vocabulary was already well furnished with the kennings or special word usages that tie the sea and seafaring to other kinds of journey (whale road, sail road), and Beowulf's voyage to Heorot Hall indeed begins as "heroes thrust out the well-braced vessel on their welcome adventure."[25] The greatest and perhaps oddest of the Norse warrior skalds, Egill Skalla-grímsson, made his first poem on the delights he looked forward to as a youthful Viking marauder: "standing high in the stern / I'll scour for plunder. . . . Then home to harbour / After hewing down a man or two."[26] Egill's ship is the "wave horse," *unnar hesti*, which is his to guide where he will, except when malign sorcery takes a hand against him.[27] The perils and joys of this risky seafaring will be often seen elsewhere in the hero's cosmos, most memorably when sly Odysseus is made to suffer because of Poseidon's *kholos* ("bitter wrath"), so that this trickster-hero must "go wandering over the deep."[28] The long-haired Achaeans had, of course, come in their hollow ships to Troy; as in the far North, the sea was their road to plunder and revenge, as it was the high road to quest and adventure for the Argonauts in their own mythepic. Yet the sea, like the wilderness, can be the most dire foe, or serve as the elemental source from which daunting enemies come. In Celtic Ireland the archetypal enemy in the Mythological Cycle of tales is the strange Fomoire who battle the Children of the Goddess (the half-divine, half-heroic Túatha Dé Danaan) and are "associated with the sea and the islands." Their opposed and hostile power, frequently dark and magical, also has a strongly feminized flavor.[29]

The sea, conceived of as deep or flowing water, is finally tied both to the beginning and to the end of a number of heroes' histories, as the heroic birth narratives and death tales given have already shown. The ambivalence of the watery element is well to the fore: a newborn hero-child like Perseus is tossed into the sea in his *larnax* so that he will be borne away and destroyed, but the wave bears him up and rescues him, taking him safely to another, perhaps a safer land; in a strong contrast the mythical Moses theme (repeated in the Persian *Shâh-nâma* and elsewhere) uses the river's flow and current as a concealing, protective, and also estranging feature for the hero-child castaway. Equally, at the end of the hero's life a last sea journey may transport a dead or dying hero to another place. Óðinn as a boatman takes the dead Sinfjotli to another, unknown destination in the *Völsungasaga*; the body of Marko Kraljević is taken by sea to the Holy Mountain of Athos.[30] The last voyage of Arthur the hero-king is even better known, as is the dramatic-heroic Viking funeral, with the dead warrior's ship sent burning out to sea—although as Ellis Davidson has shown, there is comparatively little specific evidence in the North for such a practice. Archaeology has revealed ship burials, and naviform howe burials, but the sagas themselves do not dramatically expand on the subject, and this distinguished scholar of the northern world thinks that the old *sagamenn* recalled the custom but had "no recollection of the beliefs that prompted it."[31] The Norse *Prose Edda* does provide a brief but rich description of the congregation of the gods who attended the last rites of the dead young god, Baldur, sending him to sea burning on his ship-pyre, and other hints and fragments reveal the old pagan death voyage and the god Óðinn's part in it.[32] The combinatory vision of death and water is even seen in the Norse warrior's duel, for the very word for duel, *hólmgangr*, presumes that the fighters will go off to an "island" to fight. And in the Ossetian Nart tales, where Dumézil found in the high Caucasus a number of fascinating affinities to European tales of the North and far West, one of the Nart heroes, upon growing old and decrepit, asks to be cast into the sea in a "coffin," presumably to float away to his death; in fact, he does not die.[33]

Center, Gate, and Wall

If the deep wilderness and the deeper sea are aspects and reflections of space in the hero's world, the *enclosed* place is opposed and antithetical to the hero's position, for it displays a three-dimensional solidity replacing or obtruding into his zone of simple spatial freedom and extension. In the hero tale the city as solid center is a dramatic image strongly shaped by those narratives that isolate an important but ambiguous connective and reactive link between king and hero. Here in the walled city the sovereign usually commands: he organizes his dealings with men and gods, stores the treasures appropriate to the dignity of his office, demands appropriate submission, and punishes defiance. At least one part of the heroic ethos contradicts each of these presumptions. (Even submission to his king's authority can only be on the hero's own terms; and defiance is his very nature.) More essentially still, the sovereign, at least in the myth-borne and perfect pattern, aims to guide and balance his realm with an eye to the gains of fruitful peace, while the warrior-hero's obsessive concern is nearly always with confrontation, force, war, and the trial and judgment of blood. Assuredly the sovereign figure, occupying the space and wielding the powers of the first of Dumézil's three *fonctions*, often rises out of the warrior mold itself, and as assuredly his powers and the society he dominates must be defended by warriors obeying his command. (I will soon examine the king's champion as an important if ambivalent hero type.) Nevertheless the king remains a figure fundamentally extraneous to the wild heart of the heroic enterprise and to the demands of the heroic style, and the unstable tie connecting the two is powerfully symbolized by the hero's ambiguous or dubious attitude toward the king's special place: to city, palace, or even to his hall.

This attitude is naively but precisely stated in the Byzantine *Digenid;* having stolen away his chosen girl from her father's house in the city, Digenes as hero-raptor warns her that "brave men are killed by lanes and byways," and immediately urges her out into the safer open country (*eis de tous kampous*).[34] The borderer Digenes himself will never again be seen in the wicked city: when "Basil the Blessed," the king of the Romans, wishes to hold converse with the young but renowned Borderer (who is also named Basil), the king comes to the border to meet the hero; there is no obedience expected to any imperious summons to the imperial capital.[35] In the older Greek heroic tradition the strong contrast between the isolated, ever violent hero (whom Jackson calls the "hero-intruder") and the defensive, immobile, even "victimal" mass of fighters in the threatened city is first made in the *Iliad;* walled and towered Ilium is the real prey of the furious besiegers, the Achaeans, though Troy's defenders usually fight outside the walls or right at its towered gates.[36] Hektor's tremendous courage is trapped as much by the burden of the city he must guard as by the other perishable joys (wife and child and family) that have already been described.[37]

The well-walled center, held to be the king's space, need not be an entire city; in the North the royal person has his hall or hall complex, which the hero finds just as deadly—and despicable. Hrothgar's Heorot Hall in *Beowulf* is no protection for the Dane king's men; in strict fact it presents and serves them up as a dreadful smorgasbord for the ogrish Grendel, who will finally be done down not by a Dane or a king's man but by the Geatish foreigner, Beowulf (himself, by his name, a feral bear-warrior).[38] The lay of the Nibelungs comes to its end with the Burgundian guests trapped in Etzel's court: "These traitors [Etzel's men] brought a vast army to that building from which the young foreigners offered a spirited defense," and slaughter is piled on slaughter. Eventually the hall, with slain warriors' blood "flowing away everywhere through the waterspouts into the gutters," is fired by Queen Kriemhild's order ("do not let them out of the hall, thirsting for bloody revenge!"), and so we go on to the stark end of the tale.[39] Weak kings, obdurate heroes, personal hatred, and terrible revenge—all are concentrated in a burning hall in which bloodthirsty valiance is trapped, overwhelmed at last, and slain.

The *Þattr* "Bósa ok Herrauðr" tells of two foster brothers, one of whom,

Herrauðr, is clearly a hero of the strong-arm (and faintly obtuse) type, while the other, Bósi, is as much a canny trickster as anything else. Kings are not friendly to these two, nor are they friendly to kings, even though Herrauðr is a king's son; and their varied adventures with royalty lead them into three inimical, confining structures in which special gifts other than physical strength and heroic courage must be brought to bear to overcome the spatial-constrictive perils: a king's dungeon, a strange "temple" belonging to a witch-king, and the hall of another king-foe, Godmundr. The two foster brothers are released from their deep dungeon because of the intervention and threats against the king by an old sorceress, Bósi's foster mother Busla; they invade the strange "temple" and overcome its perils through a combination of strength and trickery; and in Godmundr's hall—hundred-doored, with two vigilant watchmen at every door—Bósi the Trickster magicks and befools the assembled king's company with the music of his harp.[40] Thereafter Herrauðr plays *his* proper part by punching King God-mundr on the nose and creating a diversion, which lets the conspirators haul their princess prize and themselves up (in a magical escape) through the hall's smoke hole.[41]

Even when the intruding hero is not directly threatened in the royal hall, his heroic ethos may be challenged or negated there. A good example of a hero's reaction to "culture," cast almost as caricature, appears in Saxo Gram-maticus's legendary, grimly scarred old warrior Starkaðr or Starcatherus, who attacks the lascivious sensuality of the decadent young king's court, along with the overrefined (that is, German!) cuisine—especially those "abominable sausages"! Even the too delicate tones of the queen's flautist, at whom the old hero hurls a contemptuous gnawed bone, comes in for ridicule.[42] This unseemly *luxe* is set quite apart from the fact that Starkaðr/Starcatherus's primitive heroic display and strenuous objurgations are aimed equally at the king's political compromise with the murderer of his own father (he had married the murderer's daughter). All these faults are of a piece; this is the sort of thing that bad kings do.

Other Baits, Other Traps

The theme of the trapped hero is associated not only with kings and their doomful halls or prideful palaces but extends far into the wide imaginal stream of heroic combative confrontation. A great cluster of images is concentrated here, from the animal (as when the hero is "driven to earth") to the supernatural; the prime element of destructive, devouring fire is often seen, and feminine images, especially attached to or reinforcing the idea of the perilous snare, will seldom be far off. Of course, in practical terms the superlative powers of the hero may only be confronted and matched by his enemies under special circumstances, as when these powers are spatially limited, restricted, or hemmed in. Indeed this theme appears early in the mythic heroic (as contrasted to the epic heroic) sources.

In the Welsh tale *Branwen Uerch Lyr,* an ogrish pair of giants is lured into an iron house, whereupon "all there were of blacksmiths in Ireland" worked their bellows on the burning coals surrounding the house, until it was heated white-hot.[43] The unearthly couple manages to break out and escape nevertheless. This Irish connection (unique in the Welsh *mabinogi*) is of particular interest to us because the "firetrap" motif in hero tales, in which the hero or hero-king is surrounded by his enemies after he has been lured into a *bruidhne* or hostel and treated to a complicated death, is very prominent in Irish scenarios.[44] The best-known is the *Togail Bruidne Da Derga* (Destruction of Da Derga's hostel) in which the victim is the once perfect or ideal Irish king, Conaire Mor. The elaborate *gessa* that were laid on Conaire, and the fell consequences of his serial violation of these taboos, have already been discussed; here the disintegration of Conaire's powers is finally completed in the surrounded hostel, which is thrice fired by Conaire's assailants.[45] The "elemental" end of Conaire the king is repeated with additional, thematically important details in the deaths of the kings Diarmaid mac Fergus and Muirchetach mac Erca, where the evidence suggests that these sovereign (that is, First Function) figures find their kingly center turned against them, even converted into the trap usually reserved for the hero. The two latter kings also die multiple, ambiguous deaths, while Conaire Mor is given a warrior's sword death by beheading (though other powers are also invoked and must hold sway here: the royal head does not immediately die).[46] The death of Noísiu, who stole the beautiful Derdriu from the old king Conchobar, is closer to the clear, unadulterated model; the young warrior is trapped at last by the old king's treachery in Emain Macha, Conchobar's fort, and he is killed there with his brothers.

Tight straits (literally) can also test the hero in another way, threatening certainly but not necessarily fatal. The old Fenian tales that involve Finn and his warrior-*fénnidi* are rich in *bruidhne* encounters. This Irish topos is a dwelling place into which an outsider or stranger can be admitted, but the usual tensions and threats arising from such a locus may, with luck, be relieved by an elaborate code of host-guest behavior. Food and drink must be provided; proper social intercourse must be maintained and honor duly and mutually observed; the physical safety of both host and guest must be assured, and particularly that of the guest, as he is the more vulnerable in this setting. The crux of confrontation in the Fenian *bruidhne* stories emerges especially when the hostel's host or hosts turn out to be supernatural beings, probably malignant and certainly not constrained by any normal, human ethos, and the rules of the guest-host situation are perilously threatened, perverted, overturned. Food may be unacceptable—and in several cases the guests themselves face the possibility of becoming the meal of a cannibal host; hospitality is replaced by supernatural hostility. The men of the *fían* do not fare well in these adventures, and they are fortunate to escape with their lives. (Although they usually do, and escape itself is a motif often introduced in these stories when the horses of the *fénnidi,* their particular means of mobility, are stolen to complete the effectiveness of the trap.)

In these *fían*-tales the thematic significance of this "threat without fatality" is of an uncertain utility. It may replicate but partially conceal an archaic heroic testing or initiatory passage; it may also be the imaginal remnant of a shamanic spirit journey.[47] Of course, the theme of a supposed shelter that turns out to be the den of a malignant or at least inhuman potency is widely known in the folkloric record; the Ossetian Nart hero tales, with their tint of folkloric ambience but also with their frequent and well-remarked affinities to the Celtic narratives, include a story very much like the Irish. In this story a mysterious white deer leads a hunting-party of hero Narts to a tower occupied by seven giants, who with sinister cheer welcome the Narts as two-footed "beasts of the mountain" who have invited themselves in to be eaten.[48]

In the Scandinavian North, which is so often imaginally tied and closely related to the ancient Celtic world, the motif of the heroic penetration of a supernatural and threatening spatial enclosure usually takes the shape of the visit by a hero (or heroine) to a grave mound, there to challenge and fight a dead-undead inhabitant, the *haugr,* who resists the invasion, usually for a prize of treasure or extraordinary weapons. Hewing more closely to the old theme of the "firetrap," however, the Icelandic-Scandinavian context provides a remarkably widespread set and sequence of events, where protagonist (or antagonist) is caught in his own homestead by his enemies and either burned or otherwise slain in the assault. Historical reality here reinforces the epic theme. Such incidents are listed matter-of-factly in the chapters of *Landnámabók,* as they are said to have occurred both earlier, in Norway, and after the Icelandic land-taking. In a revenge-killing, the *goði* or priest-chieftain Grímr is burned in his home in Norway. (Another Norwegian *brenna* is recorded, of Þororm, one of King Haraldr's men, after which the perpetrator very wisely fled to Iceland; and a Gotaland burning is recalled as well.)[49] One of Ketill Trout's nephews, Snjallsteinn, is forced out of his homestead by fire and killed outside, and "Þjódólfr (Karlasson) burnt Kari at a place now called Brenna."[50] And more: Þorvaldr, a son of Tongue-Oddr, "was responsible for the burning of Blund-Ketill," a fatal incident more fully described in *Hænsa-Þoris saga*.[51] In *Vatnsdæla saga* Þórólfr sleggja is burned out, or smoked out, by the sons of Ingimundr and then killed;[52] *Hallfreðar saga* begins with the burning of Ottar Þorvaldsson's father and foster-father by the Viking Sokki, an enormity that Ottar soon avenges.[53] *Eyrbyggja saga* features the very unpleasant Þórólfr Twist-Foot (*Bægifótr*), who got six of his slaves drunk and persuaded them to set fire to his rival Ulfar's house with Ulfar inside (a rather different and more cowardly arsonous assault, according to the saga ethos, than fire setting combined with an attack under arms), but the plan miscarried.[54] (This Þórólfr became a malignant *draugr* after his timely death, and no wonder.) After Iceland was thoroughly Christianized, burnings still were known to occur: in the later *Sturlunga saga* collection *Gðomundar saga dyri* tells us that Onundr Þorkelsson was burned to death in his house by Guðmundr dyri and his men, and that Onundr's sons, two of whom were Christian priests, took two years (the saga notes this delay indignantly) to decide to exact their blood vengeance.[55] In *Hrafns saga Sveinbjarnarssonar,* included in the same collection of later (thirteenth-century) sagas, Hrafn is caught in his burning house by his feud enemy Þorvaldr, bargains with his own life for the lives of those caught with him, saves them, and is finally beheaded by Þorvaldr's command.[56] And, of course, no discussion of arson in the sagas can be considered complete without some mention of *Njáls saga* (the tale fully named as *Brennu-Njáls saga,* the saga of Burnt Njáll), arguably the greatest, and certainly the most thoroughly investigated, of all of the family sagas,[57] in which peace-loving Njáll is done in by the intransigence of his sons, the interference of troublemakers like Hrapp and the vicious Morðr, and the violent concatenation of what one scholar calls "feud-chains."[58]

Burning is not absolutely vital to the scenario of the trapped saga-hero: in *Laxdæla* the feuding Helgi Harðbeinsson is surrounded by his enemies in an outbuilding, and they have to tear the structure apart to get at him.[59] Nevertheless the firetrap theme in the Icelandic-Scandinavian sources is met frequently enough that it might cause one to reconsider our portrayal of the typologic warrior-hero as mobile and unencumbered. In fact, the Norse sagas deploy at least two spatial strategies. The first celebrates what we would recognize as the normative, peripatetic hero: outlaws like Grettir and Gísli (and Gunnarr Hámundarsson of *Njáls saga*), wanderers and

Viking skalds like Egill, and the far-traveled heroes of the *lygisögur* and the romances, all of whom are avid avoiders of hearth and home. The second differs by means of its forthright quasi-historical treatment of the land taking in Iceland, the laying out of homesteads (their sites often chosen by a ritual appeal to the god Þórr as a "social" god), the continued requirements of property holding and family, and the intricate network of familial, social, and political relationships within a violence-prone, heavily armed society whose members always had the option of the recourse to armed force. A "heroic" theme, then, can be at least partially domesticated in the sagas; a protagonist or his enemy may be trapped and destroyed within his own structure, his own domestic space.

Durance Vile

The imprisonment of a hero for any period is an extraordinary epic event; we usually expect him to be either free or dead. Indeed, to ring the hero round with prison walls, to keep him away from his venturing, requires an overwhelming power of some sort. The authority of a king or another sovereign figure may be enough for a time, as it is when Bósi and Herrauðr, in their *Þáttr*, are endungeoned, but we recall that it is sorcery and not legal or judicial leniency that brings them out again. Sorcery, and the potencies of the Otherworld, seem invariably to be involved when the hero is caught and "put away."

The Welsh Celtic narratives underscore the extreme and usually the supernatural aspect of the imprisonment or even the simple temporary detention of the hero. In *Culhwch ac Olwen* the sequential process of the great quest demands the freeing of Mabon mab Modron, who had been kept in Caer Logw ever since he had been taken "from between his mother and the wall" when he was only three days (or nights) old;[60] but this imprisonment has been very odd and ultrasecretive, because even the most ancient animals of the land are quizzed for their knowledge of where he might have been murred up, and only the very oldest of them, the eagle, has any idea.[61] (After the deliverance of Mabon—and after Cei has taken himself out of the quest, enraged at the king—Arthur sets free another figure, Greid son of Eri, whose imprisonment had been mentioned by Mabon.)[62] Often the Welsh hero is kept both "out of time" and "out of space" in his detention: Pryderi (in the myth tale *Pwyll Pendeuic Dyvet*) was a newborn child rapt away by a power, and to a place, unknown, and he remained there "out of time," that is, permanently an infant.[63] The Otherworld interposed itself again when Pryderi, in the *mabinogi* called *Manawydan mab Llyr*, was caught up in the toils of magic and, with his mother Rhiannon, was made to disappear—together with all the man-made or cultural features of the whole cantref or principality.[64] They would only be returned when the magician responsible for this, or rather his wife, was physically restrained and the husband forced by his love for her to undo the "holding" spells he had cast. Celtic captivity, when the supernatural realm is brought into the tale (which happens often), displays the characteristics of indeterminacy and also imminence: the hero is taken into an atopic, timeless zone through some temporary opening in the perforable wall of profane reality. Reasons are not always given, at least in our present form of the narrative.[65]

Some other characteristics of heroic captivity are also outlined in a forthright and simple fashion in the Serbo-Croat heroic songs: here some hero is seized by a powerful enemy, and he is cast into a prison where he stays for an incredible length of secular years under impossible (that is, supernatural) conditions—entirely without food or drink, and surrounded by snakes, scorpions, and other loathsome companions. He can only be released from this magical captivity through the skill of another magician. (A fatal modification of the snake-filled dungeon theme occurs in the biography of the legendary saga-hero Ragnar Lodbrök, whose death is finally accomplished when he is taken by an enemy and thrown into a pit filled with sea snakes.)[66]

Another possible interpretation of the captivity-and-death theme would make it part of the threefold death motif related to Indo-European trifunctionalism. The Old Irish context gives us "wounding and hanging and imprisonment" (or "wounding and pits and gallows") as a description of three juridically correct deaths; each of these fates is connected to a function, in the Dumézilian reading, and also to a zone (aerial, terrestrial, aquatic or subterranean). It would appear that when a hero, whose freedom in space is primary and necessary to him, is held in or gobbled up by the subterranean, he has been made the victim of a Third Function operation or death. This is unfitted to his Second Function, and such a fate exacerbates the anomaly and terror of his detention.[67]

Scenes of the Border

The border is very often a transitional or liminal topos between the human, profane world and a supernatural zone or Otherworld; and one obsession of the hero, to find and penetrate into threatening or unknown places and terrains, with the near certainty of encountering alterity in the form either of hostile human, animal, or supernatural forces, is absolutely a key feature in his biography. The place of the hero on the border is thus almost a cliché: liminality is all but a given.

The bordering hero makes the most vivid impression on us when he is simply defined as such. The Byzantine Greek Digenes, for example, is specifically named Akrites, the Borderer, and his position is imperially confirmed:

> *kai ezousian nemô soi tou diokein tas akras*
> *tauta de eis khrusoboullon sôa epikorôsô*
>
> I give you the authority to rule the borders;
> These things I will ratify in a Golden Bull.[68]

This kingly confirmation of Digenes' place is only a franking of the hero's own choice, for he has already said "on the borders (I) chose to live alone."[69] Digenes' border in theory separates the Christian world from that of the unbeliever, but this separation is casual and even trifling, as various features of the tale demonstrate.[70] The roll of those attending the hero's funeral, for example, include "elect Bagdadis . . . Nobles from Babylon, many from Amida," as well as *arkhontes* from all the Byzantine Asiatic military provinces. In fact, only by inference can we conclude that Digenes is a defender of the Roman emperor's borders; most of his combats in this epic are with the *apelatai*, the rievers or rustlers who infest what is obviously a lawless zone or march, and with whom Digenes really and readily identifies himself.[71]

At the other end of the Mediterranean another *limes* was drawn between Islamic and Christian lands, and another border lord was celebrated there in his own Spanish epic (although he was not quite contemporary with Digenes).[72] El Cid Campeador, in contrast to the youthful Akritic, is a mature man, "he of the great beard," and he is conventionally married, with two daughters.[73] He is not a solitary knight, but fights with a full complement of vassals, admirers, fellow spirits, and relatives (especially nephews). The *Poema del Mio Cid* is firmly set in the real geography of an identifiable border region, and the Cid's various expeditions are easily traceable by the (usually) fully identified towns and fortresses of the Marches, whether Christian or Moorish; the physical setting of the *Digenid*, on the other hand, remains geographically vague and spatially ambiguous despite the long labor of such scholars as the late Henri Grégoire.[74] The overall tone of the two epics is equally dissimilar, for the *Digenid* is a romance fantasy embedded with bits and pieces of more archaic Greek and Near Eastern themes, while the Spanish epic *Poema* is in many ways realistic, human, earthy, and naive in a different way from that of the the Byzantine epic.

Nevertheless there are strong lines of affinity between the two border-songs. Despite the Cid's Christian faith, the confraternal air of the border zone is very marked: the hero has Moorish vassals and close Moorish friends, and even in his hot pursuit of the Moorish king Bucar the Cid cries "Let us kiss and be friends!"—an offer the Moor, unfortunately for him, refuses.[75] The Christian king, Alfonso, is also drawn in unflattering strokes: he exiles El Cid because the hero had been falsely traduced by an influential enemy at court; he returns El Cid to favor only because the hero sends him large gifts of captured booty; and he recommends the marriage of the Cid's two daughters to the awful princes (the Infantes) of Carrión.[76] We have to conclude that although Rodrigo, El Cid Campeador, is a loyal subject, his king is not much of a prize; this is a prime characteristic of the developed medieval *chanson de geste* and epic, and *a fortiori* of the heroic border song. We also take from the *Poema del Mio Cid* a sense of uncluttered heroic individuality: all strong and valiant men are equally acceptable on the border; El Cid is equal to the king himself; and the cowardly princes of Carrión are not allowed to boast or plead their aristocratic high rank at court in their confrontation with My Cid.[77]

Those other paradigmatic border songs, the Moslem Serbo-Croat heroic songs, are widely known because of Parry and Lord's influential (if arguable) theories relating to oral composition, and also because they were sung and collected within modern memory.[78] Even though they are often atypical of the genre, they, too, proclaim that the border is the natural arena and theater of heroic excellence, that central authority (the Ottoman sultanate based in far-off Istanbul) is respected but regarded as abstract or otiose, and that the sultan's adviser-representatives, such as the wicked Vizier of Buda in the *Smailagić Meho* song, carry the true contamination of the center, and are likely to be corrupt and even treasonous.[79] The enemy, to the songs' heroes, is not only the "Magyar and German" Christian who stands on the infidel side of the border, but a wrongfully and corruptly exercised central authority. The border heroes are horsemen ("all horsemen, not a single man on foot" is the formulaic phrase), and their mobility is unhindered; but the topographic or geographic reality in these songs varies according to the knowledge or interest of the individual bard and the traditional lore to which he has access.[80]

We might also consider the Old Russian *Slovo o polku Igoreve* (Song of Igor's host), where the focus of epic action is the "boundless plain" (*velikaya polya*) reaching to the river Don, a bleak wilderness in which black carrion birds foretell the coming disaster.[81] The enemy is the "strong, iron host of the Polovtsi" led by the great barbarian war chieftains Gza and Konchak, and the leaders of the Russian hosting are both heroes and architects of the disaster: their internecine feuding has opened the Russian border so that the "triumphant" pagans can invade from all sides.[82] Like the *Chanson de Roland*, the *Slovo* presents a picture of defeat; and a political theme, the obduracy and selfishness of the feuding Russian princes, is combined with contrasting, emotive images of the natural and supernatural world. The "wolf in the ravine" welcomes the bloody slaughter, while the evil Div or demon bird "swoops on the land."[83]

Given the geographical facts of Scandinavia and Iceland, the spatial locality or zone of the border was usually imaged by the sea, with its own special valences of threat and opportunity and its collection of Otherworldly marks (the road of the dead, the place of anomaly and transmutation, the place of marine and submarine powers and monsters). Some memory of a land-border adventure persists, however, in the withdrawal of certain Icelandic outlaws to the area beyond society or human use, to the barren upland fells or, in the case of Grettir the Strong, the isolated and fatal Drang Isle. The saga of Egill Skalla-grímsson allows its hero to have a true border adventure on his last sortie out of Iceland to Norway, when Egill undertakes to travel to Vermaland, a wild border district between the Norwegian and Swedish kingdoms. He is acting here in an unfamiliar role, on grudging behalf of the "good" King Hákon, but more directly to help a kinsman; in fact it is king's men who conspire to send him into mortal danger.[84] The treacherous Vermalanders are frustrated by Egill; one tries to get him drunk—a vain hope—and after skirmishes in the vast Eida Wood, where Egill girds on stone armor (!) to defeat the Vermalanders' weapons, he emerges from their ambushes with great credit, performing a little rune magic along the way. The trollish and treacherous borderland, in this particular saga, is a terrain in which a trickster-warrior's skills (which Egill preeminently possesses) are needed to combat both human and inhuman perils.

Interior Space: Lost Moorings

The mind of the hero is usually solid, if not actually lithic; its most fervent bent is simply on confrontation, hard-won fame, and personal honor, and it possesses few "neurotic" interstices in which complications and frustrations could lodge to produce the disoriented images of mental illness. The warrior-hero can, however, display the enraged, blood-red signs of *wut* or *furor,* when feral animal energies and even an animal persona may utterly overbear the heroic mind and even his exiguous humanity; and even under certain less dramatic conditions the hero's mental moorings may indeed be lost. As before, the loss of human reason often signals the onset of an animal persona revealed in aimlessness, wandering, and causeless violence.

The most famous madman among the heroes of the ancient Greeks was Herakles, to whom ever vengeful Hera sent Lyssa or Mania (insanity) so that he thought himself in one place when he was actually in another.[85] Part of the Oedipus legend says that it was the madness of the old malediction on the House of Kadmos that made blind Oedipus curse his sons, after which he wandered the land with his sister-daughter Antigone as his guide.[86] In these cases, heroic madness shows itself as an intensification or hypertrophy of the hero's normal bent toward movement from place to place and adventure to adventure. Madness and wandering turn up frequently in the medieval romances, where the afflicted knight is sent mad not by the gods but because of his ladylove: Chrétien de Troyes's Yvain strips off his clothes and "flees across the meadows and fields," and thereafter "lies in wait for the beasts in the woods, killing them, and then eating the venison raw" like an animal or a savage.[87] The same sort of insanity strikes Tariel, the wilderness lord of the Georgian *Lord of the Panther-Skin;* here madness and animality combine to produce an aimless quest, which in reality is a search both for a lost ladylove and for the Georgian knight's own mental balance. We may also glance at the great Don Quixote here, but *his* wanderings are called mad not because of space or place but because of time: careless history's newly invented course and "modern" style had made his quest not only redundant but crazy.

Heroic Space, Heroic Blood: In Conclusion

The space in which the hero acts can be topologically varied according to the context within which he is drawn, but certain primary themes are likely to be common to all sources and contexts. The necessary horizontal plane of adventure begins where settlement and the solidities of culture, political order, and secular authority end. The green presence of wilderness signifies both opportunity and threat: the animal world here holds enemy and prey together, and may provide a model or even an instructor. The *limites* between the zone the hero is supposed to defend and the zone of alterity, however described, may be variously placed. We are told that the relatively small territories making up the Irish *túatha,* the "tribal" kingdoms, are seemingly designed and planned so as to be threatened on all sides, or to provide the opportunity for raiding on all sides, so the warrior-*fénnidi* can always find permanent occupation on these multiplied and vulnerable peripheries. A single differentiating border presumes a linear differentiation, but one that sets up more of a *zone* than a line, and although the opposing sides who confront each other along this border may be marked by what might be mistaken for an absolute or ideological difference (Christian-Moslem, Christian-pagan, or Iranian-Turanian), the real and substantive separation is always between those who fight on the border and those who dwell elsewhere. The center, defined as a complex of solid structures, is essentially opposed to the border. The center, also threatens the heroic world by its abstractness and impersonality, and by its dangerous potential for turning into a final and fatal trap for the hero. The hero's space is where his excellences—youth, daring or arrogance, animal energy, and personal prowess—can best be deployed; or as the Old Russian *Slovo* declares, the barrier to the hovering threat of the Polovtsi horde is not river or trackless waste but the "blood-red shields" of the warriors of Rus'.[88]

THE HERO AND THE OTHERWORLD

We can regard the air of threat and opportunity that so thoroughly permeates the hero as a natural extension of his interposition between ordinary men and supernatural, possibly divine, powers. We know that he may be generated by the union of a mortal and a divine parent, and that even when he is not, every kind of prodigy points him toward a special career, where it is confidently expected that he will sometimes hazard himself in or against the Otherworld in one of its many aspects. These confrontations may vary from the complete immersion of the hero in an atmosphere of supernatural potency invested with its own laws, logic, time, and space to a series of tests or set pieces, exceptional to be sure but imbued with little or no element of the supernatural. He may be surrounded by the rich changeability and alterite powers of the Celtic narratives, or in the strictly human-bound, secular dramas of the *Poema* of the Cid or the French *chansons de geste*, where the matter of wonder is contained in the prodigious and superhuman, not the supernatural; or in a rich selection of other adventures placed more or less marvelously in between.

Gods and Men: Gods as Men

For the clearest image of a mortal ethos cast in a divine *morphos*, Homer again is our epic poet of choice. Brigades of scholars have moiled and toiled over the question of how idiosyncratic the religious views of this first singer of tales are; for my part, I think them more or less congruent with patterns seen in numerous other heroic epical-narrative contexts. In Homer the passions of men—partisanship, jealousy, vengefulness, anger, lust—are extended to or from the embroiled and disputatious family of the divine *athanatoi*. The heroes earn or collect, as part of their destinies, the friendship or enmity of individual gods: Akhilleus has Athena on his side but cannot finally escape Apollo; Odysseus makes an enemy of Poseidon but is ever aided by the great virgin goddess who manipulates wiliness, *mêtis*.[89] The mother of the gods is implacable against the defenders of Troy, the father of the gods rather more measured, and others of the Olympians take one side or the other. They or their messengers freely interpose themselves in the action, and the Deathless Ones may therefore even be put at physical risk, as when the battle-maddened Achaean hero Diomedes wounds an interfering Aphrodite and then spears divine Ares himself. These gods, their special tricks and masking powers withal, are palpably *there* in the Homeric narrative; they are part of the physicality, the ready, depthless, hard texture of the great battle tale that Erich Auerbach described so cogently.[90]

Gods and goddesses acting as mortals and on the earth are not limited to the ancient Greek heroic milieu, but the open and undisguised Homeric interposition of divinities in human affairs is not as common in other epics. One of the Nart tales of the Caucasian Ossetes has the sun-god, Uastyrdji, come down to earth to insist on an anomalous mating with a dead mortal woman who for some reason had caught his divine eye when alive, but these Ossete tales more commonly demonstrate a peculiarly mixed array or catalog of human-superhuman characters and categories. In this Ossete imagining, human and superhuman heroes easily pass into other realms (such as the sea-god's kingdom), while the sun and other divine powers are personified but absent. There is a smith-god who like other smiths fosters a hero, while an otiose "high god" is also spoken of; "*djinn* and spirits" attack the Narts and are attacked in return, and so on.[91]

In Norse-Icelandic saga, at least one of the gods, Óðinn, will be active on the earth. The "Varunaic" sovereign god of the Aesir usually makes his appearance first as an often perverse designer or weaver of men's fates, and second, as a northern Kheiron, who may ferry the dead hero to his last home. In the legends of grim Starkaðr, Óðinn debates with the god Þórr about the destiny of this warrior-hero, an exceptional event not least because Þórr makes no other appearance in any of the surviving sagas.[92] Óðinn, as "a man in a little boat," carries off Sinfjotli in *Völsungasaga*, and in Saxo he conducts the hero Hadingus on a supernatural death journey over the sea; for the rest, there is a puzzling reference in one of the sagas to the appearance of what seems to be a god or spirit of vulcanism, and in *Laxdæla saga* Oláfr pái apparently sees an angry goddess Freya in a fateful dream.[93] This Norse-Icelandic vagueness about, and the incomplete outline of, the old divinities may have something to do with poor recollection (or a Christian suspicion) of an old pagan past. (Cultic activity, such as Þórólfr Mostur-Beard's priestcraft within the formal cult worship of Þórr in *Eyrbyggja saga,* or the adherence of Hrafnkel Frey's-Priest to Freyr-worship, is another matter.)[94]

The other supernatural, if not specifically divine, beings of the Norse sagas are the Valkyries, involved (as servitors of both Óðinn *and* Freya) in both war and, occasionally, love. Some Valkyries "choose the slain and . . . rule the battle";[95] others are married to heroes or have the swan shape that likens them more or less to the water-spirit, the winged *vila* or *zonia,* of the Balkan tales. Their association with an individual's destiny, death, or both, also reveals a familial resemblance to the Norse notion of the *fylgja* 'fetch', the animal or female figure who appears in order to mark off the crucial moments in a man's (or a family's) fate or existence. H. R. Ellis Davidson is probably correct in thinking that more than one tradition bearing on these creatures had been merged, and some old beliefs submerged or forgotten, by the time of Snorri Sturlusson and the later, Christian *sagamenn.*[96]

The Celtic tradition regarding the interaction of hero and Otherworld figure displays what I cannot avoid calling a typically Celtic subtlety, confusion, and ambiguity.[97] The Welsh *mabinogi,* specifically the canonical Four Branches of that ancient collection, have descended to us in a format in which divinities freely mix with humankind, but often in such disguises that the divinity can only be guessed at. The story of *Pwyll Pendeuic Dyuet* includes an exchange of places and personalities between Pwyll and Arawn, the prince—or god—of the Otherworld, and a central character is Rhiannon, whose name is an allonym of Epona, the Celtic horse-goddess; but Rhiannon is not depicted as a divinity in any way, though she is certainly a strong personality and a wise woman. Other figures described in the Four Branches are onomastically associated with their divine cousins in Celtic Ireland: Manawydan and Llyr to the pagan Irish sea-gods Manannan and Lir, Lleu to the great Irish hero-god Lugh, the goddess Don to the Irish goddess whose own people are the Túatha Dé Danaan, and so on.[98] The Welsh *mabinogi* seem to fall somewhere between the Old Irish Supernatural Cycle and the succeeding heroic cycles of Ireland, the Ulster Cycle and the Fenian tales. Gods and goddesses, sometimes disguised and sometimes in full view, dodge in and out of these Welsh narratives, while another supernatural component, the activities of great and potent magicians or sorcerers, is introduced, especially in the Fourth Branch of the collection, *Math mab Mathonwy.*

The gods are usually peripheral to the narrative in Irish sequences such as the heroic Ulster Cycle. Lugh is involved in the triple conception of Cú Chulainn, hero of heroes, and he has a walk-on part during Cú Chulainn's defense of Ulster against Queen Medb's army of southern cattle rustlers. In addition, this superlative hero's death is partly caused by the machinations and enmity of the death-and-battle-goddess, the Badb or Morrigan, whom he had once defeated and mortally insulted.[99] In the later, Fennian tales the lords and ladies of the supernatural clans have retreated, or been forced, into the rath, hill, or *síd*, a place best understood as a fortress of the Otherworld folk, from which its dwellers may make forays into the world of men. It is up to the warrior *fénnidi*, bivouacked in their interposed "wild" zone, to ward off these attacks, above all the liminoid hero Finn, who is trained and can act in the three contiguous worlds: of ordinary men, of *fénnidi*, and of the Otherworld powers.[100] Penetrating into the Otherworld is always both a dangerous and a potentially empowering venture; Finn in one tale is said to gain his great poetic powers when he is "caught in the door" of a *síd* while pursuing an Otherworld raider; in another adventure he wins a weapon, the spear called Birga, from a *síd*.[101] A price, as we expect, will be paid for the power gained: dealing with Otherworld potencies leaves its mark or demands some token. At one point Finn lost his virile vigor; when it was restored, he was gray-haired, and thus marked by a sign of the premature onset of old age.[102] In other encounters with the Otherworld, heroic hair—even skin—is lost or left behind; the *fennid* Conán Mael is forced to leave part of his hide in the (Otherworld) Hostel of Rowan, and so becomes "bald of skin"—*máel*.[103] To be *máel* or, in another translation, "shorn-haired" was the mark of the churl, the complete outsider—and yet it might also be the sign of the Celtic druid, the master of secret lore. (We are reminded of the *Iliad*'s Thersites, the ugly crop-head who is such a contrast to the long-haired Achaeans, and who also seems to bear and boast the contemned talents of the satirist, the "blame poet.")[104] We know, too, that the talented maker or craft hero, like the smith who is so often allied to the venturing hero, may be characterized by physical deformities, grime, or other marks—prices—of his special skill or secret knowledge. I return to the tertial or intermediate placement of the hero type, between this world and the Otherworld, in chapter 6 of this study.

The Opening to the Otherworld

Before proceeding with the hero tale in the strict sense, we ought to re-member that the folk imagination and the popular mind (if these are in fact separate) also conceive of lower-or underworlds in which a separate reality perdures, and into which a hero or heroine may intrude or be projected for whatever reason: Louis Carroll undoubtedly tapped this imaginative vein when he dropped his Alice into the rabbit hole. Any reasonably compre-hensive collection of *Märchen* is likely to have at least one subterranean adventure, and in a typical tale appearing in the *Contes Lazes* translated by Dumézil, a heroic youngest son (a familiar folk hero figure) follows a wounded *div* or demon down a well, and eventually lives happily ever after with the maiden he finds a forlorn prisoner there, and whom he releases.[105]

In the heroic context, however, the Otherworld is almost always a dan-gerous place to explore, with fitting gains or predictable consequences. In the ancient Greek hero tales the place of alterity, and also the goal of some uniquely heroic venturing, is Hades, the world of the dead, although at times the Greek view of this topos is very subtle. Perseus had to wend his way into a deep cave to find the Gorgons, only one of whom could be slain; he returned with Medusa's head and with the magical-monstrous Pegasus, the winged horse who had sprung from her severed neck.[106] The lightless landscape at the end of the world, where the cave was to be found, was as close to Hades as this particular myth-hero had to come. Iason, who jour-neyed into the unknown at the other end, geographically speaking, of the Greek world, discovered another Otherworld, and there tasted death in the dragon's mouth; when *he* returned to the world of the living, he brought Medea, the princess-sorceress, and the stolen fleece—along with an evil destiny.

Often we find that the heroic temperament is profoundly suited to a jour-ney where living men should never walk, and numerous Greek heroes (Odysseus, Herakles, Theseus, Orpheus) pass the dread barriers guarding the Otherworld of the dead. Odysseus, following the directions of Kirke, sailed to the Groves of Persephone, and there found the house of Hades (*Od.* X.509), where the rivers of Hades flowed. He did not have to go down to the Dead: the Dead came to him, *ótrunen gar agauê Persephoneia:* "august Persephone sent them forth" (XI.224). Odysseus seems to be in an Other-world, not an Underworld, a "joyless place" as it is called by the seer Teiresias (XI.94), where the light of the sun is gone. Teiresias also gives Odysseus his fit reward for disturbing the dead in a prophecy of further wandering, a sour and violent homecoming, and a death far from his island kingdom of Ithaka

(XI.111ff.). Nevertheless, Odysseus *polumêtis* is not your typical strongarm hero, and his visit to the realm of the dead is accomplished quite neatly, with a handy and friendly sorceress pointing the way.

Odysseus sailed to the end of Okeanos to find the Otherworld, to a place where the rivers of Erebos flow together roaring. These marine and riverine signs mark the proximity of Hades but do not exactly guard it. Herakles had to travel by land to the uttermost end of Greece, Tainaron, where there was a cavern entrance to the Underworld and, barring the land of the dead, another infernal river and its gloomy and ancient ferryman, Kharon.[107] Kerényi's synoptic account gives a vivid impression of how the brash hero of heroes is said to have behaved there, blundering about, sword and bow in hand, frightening the poor ghosts and overturning the timeless set order of Hades with its dark rulers. Herakles will triumph, leading Kerberos back to the king who had set him this labor, but of course he, too, had to pay in the form of a sinister knowledge that would eventually encompass his mortal death. And he is "grimly altered" by his dark journey; the dead may have marked him with madness. His apotheosis would come, to be sure, but an ambiguity remains: did he really escape death? For in Hades Odysseus met the *eidôlon* of Herakles, still weeping over the twelve labors, and especially the terrible one that sent him down into the darkness to find the guardian hound (*Od.* XI.602ff., 617–26).

The king-hero Theseus's rumored descent to Hades with his friend Perithoös was even rasher and more hubristic than that of Herakles. The two took the same route as the other hero, through Tainaron, but *their* mad aim was to seize and carry off Persephone herself, the queen of Hades. They were trapped, for one of the rules of the Otherworld is: if you are human, hero or not, always keep moving; the two paused and sat down outside the dark king's palace, and there they stuck fast.[108] Herakles managed to rescue at least one of them, though Theseus—exactly like Conán Mael in the Fenian tale—may have left a fleshly souvenir behind. (Theseus's legend is often related to that of Herakles,[109] as in Euripides' *Madness of Herakles*, where Theseus acts the part of a just king relieving the guilt of the other hero—though no mention is made of any previous rescue from Hades.) It is not to be wondered at that after his death Theseus, in one tradition at least, was returned to his punishment seat in Hades. I have described Theseus elsewhere as the true *hypermachic* hero, a great traveler and raider and ravisher of women, and it may well fit the very end of his legend that he is sometimes seen forever fastened, like an unwilling limpet, to that stony seat in the gloomy kingdom of the dead.[110]

Orpheus's descent to Hades must be called a special case: he is less a

heroic figure than a supreme poet-singer and magician armed with powerful song magic, a favorite of Apollo and nearly his mortal double, who pursues the dead Eurydike not with arms and belligerence, but with potent
voice and the sweet sound of his lyre. His skills, which are clearly magical
as they rest at the heart of the poetic craft, give him true power over the
darkness, so when he followed the road of the dead to land's end at Tainaron,
he seems to have had a chance to recover his lifeless wife from Hades. He
failed, nevertheless, and in addition appears to have attracted the dangerous enmity of Dionysos (who had his own cryptic place among the divine
powers resident in the Underworld).[111]

Aeneas, survivor of the sack of Troy and hero of Virgil's great epical
Latin propaganda piece, also penetrated the barriers of Hades, and his
journey greatly resembles that of Odysseus. He found the same infernal
rivers, although he entered by the Cumaean cave in Italy; he is guided by
the Cumaean Sibyl, whereas Odysseus had directions from Kirke; and he
carries as a protective trophy a golden bough, to be left as a hostess gift for
Proserpine. Kerényi believes that some remnants of older strata (as of the
Heraklean descent into Hades) may be detectable in Virgil's account, but
the furious and destructive energy of the Greek hero's assault on the kingdom of the dead is totally absent from the *Aeneid:* this Trojan hero's Aver-
nan expedition seems aimed largely toward that great vision of the imperial political future of Rome as solemnly revealed to Aeneas by Anchises.[112]
There is no sinister note, unless it is the appearance of the justifiably angry
shade of the suicide, the jilted Carthaginian queen Dido; and despite the
Sibyl's warning about the difficulty of escaping shadowy Avernus, Aeneas
quickly leaves that realm by the Ivory Gate.

If we except the poetically brilliant but tendentious scenario of the Aenean
descent, the antique heroes are all severely tested in their visits to the Otherworld. The underlying assumption is that only heroes of the most extraordinary marque can attempt this fearful journey, and that they will have
to retribute a suitably heavy price. The topos of this Otherworld is marked
by threat and grim darkness, with ambiguous barriers (the Styx is in fact
marshy, neither flowing water nor firm earth), guardian monsters, and deep
secrets that may bring no true good to those who learn them or try to carry
them back to the living world. The Greek hero tales establish the rule: the
hero is always involved in death, it is his sign, but only rarely can even he
visit its kingdom and return. And if not the hero, who?

The Hill and the Howe

Two other heroic traditions, the Celtic and the Icelandic-Scandinavian, provide us a considerable selection of instances in which the hero is able to cross the gulf between this world and the Otherworld. They differ in that the Celtic hero will enter, or be lured into, a place (usually a hill or rath) that is in fact a *síd*, whose fairy folk (called by the same name) are perilous supernatural beings, only slightly related to humankind, though living in a matched or parallel world;[113] whereas the hero in the Norse-Icelandic sagas almost always tempts the supernatural by entering a grave mound or howe. There he confronts the dead, or at least one dead but still vital and belligerent opponent.[114] (In an interesting variation, the Celtic supernatural beings may sometimes leave the *síd* and come among men, as when a *síd* being, Crónánach, emerged from the fairy fort of Munster and visited Finn mac Cumaill on Finn's hunting mound, and there sang him his destiny. These beings of the Otherworld can also shape-shift when they leave their own realm; Crónánach was a "black, mis-shapen churl" when he arrived at night, but the light of day changed him into one with "a delightful beauty upon him," his appearance both youthful and kingly.)[115]

Time and again the Old Irish *fian* warriors have to deal with the *síd* dwellers—sometimes invading the *síd*, sometimes defending the folk of one rath against the supernatural powers of another. Rather more often the *fénnidi* must defend, as part of their primary function, the tribe's settled world against Otherworldly antagonists based in their *síd*-fort. Sometimes the supernatural beings strike back at what must be seen as a provocation: once King Ailill absentmindedly let his horses graze on the side of a *síd* on the dangerous and sacred Semain-eve; the horses, of course, disappeared, and the *fénnid* Fergus had to go to the aid of the king to recover them.[116] Sometimes the people of the *síd* raid far from their base, and it requires such special skills as the superhuman footwork of a Finn to catch and overmatch them, as in the case of the unearthly Cúldub, who snatches food from the camp of the *fian* and runs away.[117] Finn follows after him and kills the supernatural thief with a spear cast at the very gate of the fairy fort; he also uses a special "named" spear against the hostile *síd* warriors in another incident in which the two worlds, human and supernatural, are embroiled.[118]

The Irish *síd* deploy a variable charge of supernatural voltage. They have their warriors and their women, their chieftains and their nobles, and they are at least as prone to violence and venery as their human counterparts. They also, of course, can lay claim to magical knowledge and oracular gifts—which they may pass on to a particularly deserving hero such as Finn.

Their art and power of *lommrad*, 'laying bare', making everything man-made or cultural disappear in a selected place, is also notable in the Welsh sources, and ought to be seen as a supermagical *apocosmesis*, that is, demonstrating that sacral power capable of returning man-created being to nothingness. Night or day can also have a variable, usually a reversing, effect on the folk of the Otherworld. On another point: the Irish Fenian narratives aver that the special place and talents of a great *fénnid* chieftain like Finn mac Cumaill allow him to penetrate into and perhaps neutralize the supernature contained in the *síd* (as at one point he evidently wins treasure from a *síd*), but objects taken from the Otherworld can be as chancy and contaminated here as in other heroic tales, or in the folkloric record.[119] The supernatural drinking cup or horn brought to Finn by Crónánach of Síd ar Femuin, together with the tale of his destiny, eventually caused a fatal quarrel among his warriors, which seems to have marked the end of the hero Finn's earthly existence.[120]

The Otherworld (inhuman or unhuman) depicted in the Norse-Icelandic materials, the sagas in particular, is nearly always the topos of the dead, located in the grave barrow or burial howe: "on" rather than "in" the earth, though a natural hill or mountain may hold the dead, especially the revenant dead, as well.[121] In a typical scenario the intrepid saga hero enters a grave howe because he wants something, often a sword, that was buried with the dead. Because some of the enhowed dead maintain a postmortem consciousness, even if they do not walk abroad as *draugar*, the howe-dweller may resist the despoiler, and a duel with the dead ensues. Grettir the Strong invaded the howe of Kar the Old and got treasure, for which he had to fight the revenant and cut off its head (officially this was a *haugr*, although evidently the dead Kar had been "walking" abroad with evil intent as well); one item in Kar's hoarded treasure was a magnificent seax or short sword, brought out from the grave mound and used later by the hero.[122] In the *Landnámabók*, a great Viking and occasional merchant named Midfjord-Skeggi broke into the ancient barrow of King Hrólfr Kraki in Denmark, removing the king's sword Skofnung, but he could not bring out Boðvarr Bjarki's sword; the implication is that the dead hero had fought Skeggi for the weapon, and won.[123] In the *þáttr* "Egill ok Ásmunðr," the latter of these two heroes meets and becomes a blood-sworn brother of one Aran, a king's son, and the two make certain agreements as to what the one must do if the other dies. When Aran does die, Ásmunðr raises his grave mound and, according to the agreement they had sworn, goes into the mound to stay for three nights. Dead Aran wakes, devours the living animals also deposited with his corpse, and on the third night attacks Ásmunðr. Ásmunðr loses his ears but manages to behead the revenant; afterward he burns the body (chaps. 6, 7). In Saxo's version of the same story, Ásmunðr's "friend" is called Asvith, son of King Bjorn; Ásmunðr impales rather than burns the beheaded, demonic body (V.150–51). Ásmunðr's injuries are congruent with other tales of Otherworldly encounters and combats and the marks, both physical and psychic, that may scar the survivor.

A peculiar but informative variation on the Norse barrow raid concerns Oláfr, the legendary king of Geirstað, who seems to have been singularly unimpressive as a sovereign and warrior; nevertheless his people sacrificed to him after his death "for plenty, and they called him *Geirstaðaalfr*"— Geirstad-Elf.[124] Many complications hover over this tale, including how *alfar* or elves were viewed in the North and what special powers they had.[125] The focus of Oláfr Geirstað-Elf's story is on his connection with the Christian king (and eventually saint) Oláfr, for it seems that in some way the old pagan king "quickened" the later king's pregnant mother, after certain objects had been brought out of Geirstað's mound.[126] Whether the first Christian king of Norway was a reincarnation of a pagan *haugr* king was a point about which not even the second king, the Oláfr later called the Saint, cared to hear any idle speculation.[127]

Only occasionally do the sagas conceal the dead in a natural feature. *Eyrbyggja saga* does contain the story of Þórólfr Mostur-Beard, a Þórr's priest in Norway who brought his vocation as *goði*, and some of the sacred furniture of the god's precinct, to Iceland. Near where he settled, Þórólfr duly identified a particular mountain as *Helgafell* or Holy Mountain, "and believed that he and his kinsmen would go into it when they died."[128] After Þórólfr died, his son Þorsteinn Cod-Biter also died by drowning; thereafter one of his men reportedly saw the mountain open and Þorsteinn welcomed into a scene of feasting and drinking, to sit opposite his dead father.[129] A similar story is told in *Njáls saga* about Svanr of Svanhill, identified as a dangerous sorcerer, who was drowned and thereafter seen by some fishermen being welcomed into Kaldbakhorn Mountain.[130] These mountains may have opened for Þorstein and Svanr because no bodies were recovered to be enhowed (though this must have happened quite frequently in Iceland's waters), but we can also see a traditionalistic retrieval of older themes: in Þorsteinn's case even a vision of the heroes' *Valhöll* itself.

Before leaving the scene of the mound and the dead we ought to recall the classical heroic *hêrôon* which, as our evidence now insists, *may* be, but usually isn't, the burial place of the hero; instead it memorializes his place and task of mediation between the worlds of the living and the dead. In fact, certain *hêrôa* were not mounds but trees or springs, and the central idea contained in these markers or topoi is not that the hero is memorialized here but, as one scholar (Fontenrose) believes, has been transformed.[131]

In those scenarios in which the hero travels to or penetrates an Other-world, whether the topos of supernatural beings or the place of the dead, he is marked, again, by his tertiary quiddity, his own essential otherness. Born out of or in close association with extrahuman potentiality, he is driven to confront and reconfront this power: his fate is often to have an agonistic relationship with supernature as well as death. In many of the heroic traditions the beings he faces are near images of himself, and he deals with them according to his own code, place, and time: the warrior Diomedes wounds the war-god Ares, Finn mac Cumaill spears Cúldub at the very gate of his *síd*, Grettir fights and rekills Kar the Old in his grave mound. He also accepts the fact that a price must, and will, be paid; and prizes won from the place of alterity are often fatally contaminated by that irrefragable and dangerous alterity. Finn's cup, a gift from the *síd*, marks his inevitable mortality; Grettir's tenuous luck, his *gæfa*, increasingly fails after his second encounter (he fought the undead-dead not once but twice). The very weapons of herodom, when sought and brought from places where their potency was radiated by inhuman associations, can turn, betray, or take the hero deeper into danger than even he should go. This is the great peril of those weapons' once-hidden power.

ASPECTS OF THE QUEST

The quest is so firmly connected with the hero, his emblematic acts, and his essential character that some scholars can identify a hero only if he is so engaged. This is an extreme position, in my view, but excusable, for undoubtedly the quest *is* the hero's special business.

Definition and Structure

A barebones scenario for the hero and his part in the quest would be: Someone extraordinary / Goes or is sent / To search for and retrieve / Something important. This may seem very general, but I believe it is well-nigh universal.

Walter Burkert defines the quest plot as "the deepest deep structure of a tale," always directing the hero to "go out, ask, find out, fight for, take and run";[132] this is a lively reconstruction, but somewhat misleading in detail. Who or what, for example, prompts or impels this sequence of acts? (From such a skeletal formula we can make a long arm to Vladimir Propp's thirty-one segmental functions—"stable, constant elements in folktales, independent of who performs them"—that make up in their collectivity what Propp calls a kind of quest.)[133]

Joseph Campbell's "monomyth," his "nuclear unit" in heroic tales, thus describes *his* version of the quest: "A hero ventures forth from the world of common day into a region of supernatural wonder: fabulous forces are there encountered and a decisive victory is won: the hero comes back from this mysterious adventure with the power to bestow boons on his fellow man."[134] I think that we will find that this "Otherworld" quest comprises only one part of the whole. In an understandable attempt to find a middle way between Campbell's "overgeneralized" mythic nucleus and the "rigid formulations" of von Hahn, Rank, and Raglan, the Irish scholar Tomás Ó Cathasaigh is drawn to de Vries's biographical sequence, in which we can identify segments of a quest in the dragon fight (VI), winning of maiden (VII), and Underworld expedition (VIII).[135] Perhaps it is best simply to lay out what appear to be consistent constituent factors in the quest, from key actors through the temporal and spatial dimensions; after this we can try to test our structure against a selection of specific quest narratives.

A Charactery of the Quest Hero

Of the massive collection of typological characteristics assigned to or displayed by the hero, the following aspects seem to be particularly well fitted both to his questing role and to the quest taken as process or "test:"

1. The hero is unique and isolate. His mark is his strong and deadly arm, but a particular quest may demand a hero capable of *cooperative* venturing, an actor deploying plan and persuasion rather than unthinking and violent action. At the same time:
2. The hero is devoted to combat and confrontation: he must be prepared to seek out, or at least never avoid, those aspects of the quest involving "blocking" strategies, threats, and finally violence. He is both physically and morally prepared for such violence: a risk taker, superlatively courageous, honorable, single-minded in purpose—and probably, or even necessarily, without much imagination.
3. The hero is detached from cultural and social place, is mobile and uncommonly swift. As a figure of extraordinary *celeritas* he is thus easily capable of taking up the challenge posed by time and distance either in this world or another.

4. Precisely because the hero is easily detached from the societal matrix, he is often as dangerous to the social fabric as he is useful in defending it. Indeed, in the end, he is more useful outside of society and displaying his excellences elsewhere—that is, on a quest.

There may be other significant morphisms of the questing hero, such as the childlike, naive pursuivant, like Peredur-Percival-Parzifal, who evidently represents the innocent last who shall be first, but in the typical quest these primary characteristics, with others that may be demanded in special circumstances, project the hero into the adventure's space and time.

The Spatial Dimension: The Geography of the Quest

The canonical form of the quest moves the hero toward the deepest exploration of his *extensive* space; he will go "far away," to and into strange, threatening, dangerous lands. Yet despite the fact that he often leaves behind the constricted or punctual space dominated by other powers (especially those of the king), the quest frequently demands that he confront and willingly enter another kind of enclosed space: grim castle or uncanny city, close-guarded shrine or deadly place where his goal, or the prize, is securely kept.

But other spatial features are also woven into the quest. The hero has the opportunity to overleap every sort of boundary, but especially that *limen* separating cultural from natural (or supernatural) zone. The quest may be pursued into wilderness or wasteland, like the *gaste terre* of the Graal narratives. (Not infrequently the strangeness of the wild zone is more manifestly supernatural in flavor, but in any case ordinary humanity is definitely proscribed here, repelled by difference, shadow and darkness, tracklessness, and the pervasive air of threat and hidden doom.) When the questing hero takes ship he also passes an absolute boundary separating land-bound mankind from a completely foreign element ruled by its own prepotent guardians, and his movements on the measureless deep are more than usually random and perhaps out of his control. (The Otherworld may be set here, and even when the perils of the sea are defined as merely natural, the hero must brave fog, storm, or the winds that can bring his ship to wreck.) Finally, we have mountains bristling forth their towering, salient dangers: threatening height, bitter cold, a malignant and merciless terrain even without the nonhuman beings who are said to dominate cliff, cave, narrow path, and treacherous pass, those physical phenomena in which the mere shape of terrain and geologic accident is translated into utter foreignness.

When the sea is described as Other Place, other images are recalled as well, especially of a supernatural topos (emplaced on islands in the sea, or in a submarine domain). Here again we are likely to find those two kinds of Otherworld, though not infrequently confused: the land of death, and the place of alterity. The land of death, as we have seen, is often but not always an underworld, which the hero penetrates in order to win back someone or something absolutely lost. Its signs are distance, another element, other and inhuman powers, and death or the threat of death.

The Celts give us the fullest development of the notion of an Otherworld formed as a place of alterity. They also vary their notions of the locatability, the "where" of this Otherworld most ingeniously, whereas the Greek and Roman imaginations demand a physical, identifiable route and a well-marked passageway. For the Celts the Otherworld Islands are placed in the sea, and usually to the West, in the direction of the setting (dying) sun; but if the realm of the Other is located in the *síd*, it may be scattered among men and approached by a strait gate. The Celts also, however, sometimes picture their Otherworld as a real but physically nonlocatable parallel universe, connected to this world by a sort of permeable membrane; the venturing heroes or Otherworld beings pass back and forth through this membrane according to the private logic of the narrative. The Welsh tales especially seem to delight in an Otherworld, an Otherwhere, that is Nowhere, and into which human beings can disappear without a trace. Often when a questing hero is taken up into this unmarked Otherworld, we have an interruption in his adventure; he remains completely inactive both in space and in time, which also is unmarked, a temporal vacuum or narrative blank.

Temporality and the Quest

I have suggested that a questing hero's spatial referent may also be connected to a time marker. To some extent this separation is arbitrary, especially in respect to the non-human Otherworld, which unveils appropriately enigmatic features to which I will return. Initially I want to lay out another series of interactions between questing hero and the notations and permutations of time in the quest: quest as a *random* event; as the most important event in a sequence of *maturation;* as the *completion* of a sequence; and as an *extratemporal* event.

QUEST AS RANDOM MOMENT

When the context in which the quest occurs is less mythic or legendary than epical—when the quest is appreciably reduced and made incidental in its intrinsic dramatic significance—a questing adventure may be randomly or casually inserted into the hero's framework of adventures, as a thematic afterthought or possibly even a survival of a more archaic narrative formulation. Such a disconnected quest sequence seems to be inserted into the Norse-Icelandic *Egils saga* in a late stage of the saga's action: this hero ventures into a border wilderness, encounters treacherous foes, deals with them using quasi-magical means (wearing stone armor and wielding a tree-trunk club) and (more or less) recovers a king's treasure.[136] This "quest" is really peripheral to the main sequences of Egill's tale—although sea voyages are so common in the sagas that any deeper resonance is unlikely in this epical context. At the same time, the "death voyage" by sea is certainly known, if not common, in the North.

QUEST IN A MATURATIONAL SEQUENCE

Here the hero is required to "go and find" something as an essential part of his growth into and self-identification within the "matured" state of herohood. Some association with the process of the *rite de passage* seems clear enough: the hero follows that sequence of *separation, testing,* and *reintegration* common to those initiatory rites that mark the passage between ascriptive childhood or adolescence and full male adulthood. A subtype of this maturational adventure is provided in those sagas in which the "contrary" protagonist (Egill again, or Grettir the Strong) defies a paternal injunction, so as to embark on adult adventures such as voyaging and raiding at an improbable (heroically young) age. More typically, we see the young Theseus following (and carrying) his "signs" from Troizen through the perils of the Isthmus, to be recognized, after other perils, by his mortal father Aigeus as king's heir in Athens.[137] When the hero quests for the maiden or princess, another theme may be broached: this quest usually has less to do with sexual maturation than with other symbolic significances, such as the prize of the true king.

QUEST ENABLING A COMPLETION OF SEQUENCE

In this case the conclusion of the quest brings its hero back from the perils of the search to take up a prize won by his success. Often the prize is "rightful kingship" or at least the recognition of the hero's special character; again, a woman or maiden may have to be won. How psychologically and mythically complicated such a quest may be can be seen in the Oedipus tale, when the hero unknowingly returns to take up his kingship and the woman attached to or authenticating this kingly role. The terrible fatality accompanying the end of the quest of this Theban king underscores the point that the process of quest, however strenuous, may be less dangerous than its often ambiguous reward. The place of the woman in enabling the hero's completion of his quest may also be fraught with ambiguity and betray a dark *telos:* Kerényi reminds us that women from the transhuman world may be necessary to accomplish the goal of the hero's quest, as Medea, for example, was to Iason—"but not to his lasting happiness."[138]

THE TEMPORALITY OF THE QUEST

In time as in space, the movement of the quest's process outside or beyond the quotidian world frequently induces a perturbation or even a rupture in the normal time signature and sequence of a heroic adventure. On the simplest level, certain times of the day are given over to or dominated by Otherworldly powers: night is a tenebrous time when the Other is strong, and to extend a quest past the onset of night virtually guarantees some sort of supernatural intervention or occurrence. (A passage through the curtain that separates this world from the next is very likely to occur at night.)[139] Certain nights may also be more parlous than others; adventuring in the Celtic world on the seasonal markers of Beltain and Semain (May Eve, November Eve) when the gates of the Otherworld are open will almost certainly lead to a volatile mixture of human and nonhuman beings, with special opportunities and equally marked dangers made available for the questing hero. The distortion in ordinary time likely to accompany any penetration into the Otherworld may discover a limbo in time as in space (the adventurer disappears into No-time as into Nowhere), but the more dramatic variation from human time happens when a single night (or some longer but still relatively short period spent in the Otherworld) is revealed, on the adventurer's return to the human world, as a year or even a century or more in sequential, quotidian human time. In any extreme form, such a (literal) contretemps would of course break the frame of the quest.[140]

Players in the Quest

The full or efficient complement for a typical quest ought to be reducible to four players: hero, heroic helper, the sovereign, and the woman. The last three figures, who have already been parsed to greater or lesser degrees, will be integrated into the quest as follows.

THE HEROIC HELPER

Very few quests are undertaken solely by the hero, and we have already encountered a range of helper types; the specific kind attached to the narrative should fit in with the special exigencies of the quest. The hero may be backed by a strong-arm warrior or one with other martial skills, but more often the quest companion is equipped with tricksterish talents, and is a satellite capable of guile and subterfuge—or at least of some degree of low but effective cunning. Often enough the plot's calculus demands that a quest companion (especially the almost-sufficient, hypermuscular heroic helper) fall or fail, leaving the central hero to take a final test alone; such a turn of plot probably shows a development from a more archaic root form in which the unaccompanied hero must first fail, then succeed in his aim (fails and dies, is revived, and returns to a final triumph).

Heroic helpers may also come from the animal world, like the magical horse or other beast endowed with prescience or some other quality or special knowledge separate from simple animality. This aiding animal will be the necessary reverse of that animal monster who impedes the quest, but animal "guardianship" can be either benign or malign, in the same way as human figures may be either helpful or opposed to the questing hero. Finally, a subtype of quest adventure assembles a mutually cooperative group, a heroic *équipe*, to achieve the goal: Iason's quest undertaken with the Argonauts and the Welsh *Culhwch ac Olwen*, both analyzed a little farther on in this chapter, are two examples. The type is uncommon, and when it does appear, the "cooperative" quest stretches the concept and limits of heroic character and talent, often in a fantastic atmosphere.

THE SOVEREIGN

The king is very familiar to the quest adventure, and he too can be either benign or malign. As the "bad king" (the more common avatar), he is the hero's enemy, possessor and guardian of the treasure sought; he is imagined as the holdfast dragon full of venomous powers, who must be fought or fooled (or both) for the hero to gain his goal. As the "good king" he can be the orchestrator or *maître en scène* of the quest's process, and the arbiter of a fit reward when the adventure is over. (The "sovereign" again displays a double valence so far as the *warrior*-hero is concerned: as directive and rooted wisdom, or as a glowering and malignant oppressive force.) When the quest is directed toward the reward represented by sovereignty itself, and the hero seeks to authenticate his own kingly destiny, the old king must stand in the gateway or sit in the palace to baulk him, or at least to test him.

THE WOMAN

The woman, we know well, makes up a complex knot of roles and modes in the quest, but in the simplest arrangement these will be to act as *goal* of the quest, as *assistant* in the quest, or as *enemy* (temptress, sorceress, evil queen). In the first role she is often linked with the treasure; she may even be the human prize sought and fought for by the hero. The intense ambivalence of her intrinsic powers shows up in the opposed roles of helper and enemy; different versions of the same quest narrative may identify her as either. Sometimes, in a warrior-Amazonian persona, her aid to the hero is direct and similar to that of a hero's strong-arm companion, but usually she possesses special secrets or hidden knowledge: Ariadne is the lady of the labyrinth, Medea knows the way to the prize of the fleece, the *vila* of the Balkan tales or the *mélusine* of the medieval French tales puts her extraordinary powers at the hero's service. It is a very short leap from this special knowledge to the darker arts of the obstructive sorceress, and the very humanness and "denseness" of the hero (Iason again comes to mind) may lead him to trigger a shift in her helpfulness, when he misunderstands or fatally ignores her doubled and therefore dangerous powers. In the language of signs, she can be door or trap-door—and be either lady or tiger.

Master Motifs: A Selection

I have arbitrarily chosen the following quest scenarios to demonstrate as many variations in process and kind as possible for the adventure. All of these quest narratives are well known—the Graal-quest especially has generated a huge descriptive and analytic literature—except perhaps for the last, the eccentric and energetic Georgian *Vep'khistqaosani* or *Lord of the Panther-Skin*.

THE DEADLY QUEST

The tale of Iason, the Argonauts, and the golden fleece is surely a treasure quest, but one into which other important thematic elements are deeply impressed. (The quest for the fleece is also a test for the rightful king, as the young king-hero who succeeds in his venture is to replace the old; and the treasure's guardian, the dragon, has a number of conflated roles.) The quest itself, with the Argo and its hero-crew, resembles a point-to-point hunt, in which the specific skills and gifts of Iason's companions are deployed in turn to advance the expedition past one peril after another. It is probably significant that two other great heroes, Theseus and Herakles, are sometimes associated with the quest early on but cannot be included in the complete drama: the sole responsibility for this quest, for good or ill, must finally be Iason's. And two kings are part of the primary tale: Pelias as instigator and enemy, King Aietes as a dark power, a treasure hoarder resembling, in Kerényi's considered view, other Underworld lords of death.[141] (Kerényi believes that the additional three tasks set by King Aietes in Kolchis were "idle inventions," inserted to associate Iason with other risk-taking heroes such as Kadmos.)[142]

Of course Iason's success in far Kolchis is not the end of the story. The golden treasure has a fell power of its own, and in fact, as Kerényi observed, there can be no good end to this quest. Iason's own heroic powers are not sufficient to gain the fleece: he has to be helped by Aietes' daughter Medea, a very dangerous companion. Once she allies herself to her hero, no compunction restrains her: Medea betrays her father and sacrifices her own brother to delay Aietes' pursuit. When she arrives in Iolchos with Iason and the fleece, she contrives such an abominable death for King Pelias (his own daughters are tricked into killing him in hopes of magically "cooking" him back to a renewed youth) that it is impossible for Iason to keep the kingship he had more or less fairly won.[143] Now it seems as if the purposive venturing and heroic mobility that enable Iason's quest has gone septic; the hero and the princess move on to Corinth and there, when Iason plans to marry the king's daughter, Medea brings about the terrible death of king, king's daughter—and her own sons by Iason.

The constituent mythemes of the fleece quest describe a heroic adventure eventually drowned in fatality. As Oedipus's quest for his own rightful identity will come to a bitter end, so Iason's pursuit of the Fleece entangles him in the powerful will of an Otherworld woman. Through her he will lose everything he had sought, and be finally reduced to impotence and a blackened name: the questing hero becomes the feeble and shameful pawn. And yet, of course, as a true hero he *had* to undertake this quest: given his nature as hero, he had no other option.

THE SACRED QUEST

In the large cluster of Western medieval narratives describing a knight-warrior's search for a sacred vessel, a Holy Graal or Grail, we find a dense and complicated mixture of themes. Such a weight of opinion and scholarship has descended on these narratives (especially owing to their connection to the Arthurian *muthos*) that any attempt at paring or recondensation must risk the deletion of important insights.[144] Here I have followed a kind of literary-inventive history in dividing this quest into three narrative segments: a Welsh base text or set of master motifs; non-Welsh (mainly Continental) narrative extensions, inventions, and redactions; and a final, distilled, deheroized, and "spiritualized" version, in which the quest's personnel and events are all bent to one sacred end, to the revelation of the *San Graal* in all its salvific Christian potency.

The pedigree of the Welsh *Historia Peredur mab Efrawc* is gnarled indeed; and even it is not the identified original or *Ur*-Graal narrative but a Welsh "romantic" redaction of a French source. (The Continental Perceval narratives evidently drew on the same source.)[145] The Cymric quality of *Peredur* is apparent enough in the close resemblance of its key motifs to those seen in older, or more clearly Welsh, sources: the canonical *mabinogi* or the quest tale *Culhwch ac Olwen*—a quest story usually grouped with the *mabinogi* type. The Celtic coloration is deepened when we pick up parallels between Peredur's progress and the Irish evidence, particularly the adventures of Finn mac Cumaill.[146] The attention of the Welsh *Peredur*-tale is focused on this hero's peregrination from primitive and indeed unpromising beginnings (following the "slow" hero type already familiar to us) to a final and full self-knowledge, either equated with or symbolized by the signs of royal sovereignty. The hero's onward course is both enabled and tested by Otherworld powers, and this ambivalent combining of threat and aid is also seen in the simulacra of femininity, which have key places in the tale, especially the black maiden and the empress-queen (Gwenhwyfer).[147] The cup or vessel in *Peredur* is a talisman of sovereignty well known from other Indo-European sources, and here it signifies an organic completion and maturation; other elements and signs, like the sword and even the bleeding lance, might suggest the conflation or intersection in this tale of other Celtic themes such as the vengeance quest.[148]

The Continental continuators of this quest type, of whom the first in place is the twelfth-century master-poet Chrétien de Troyes, add characters absent from the Welsh (such as Lancelot, who has already been borrowed for the *Perlesvaus*). Chrétien and his successors very clearly identify the Christian and Arthurian foci of the quest, and tie them together by means of the dominant sign of the Graal, now indubitably taken as the true Vessel of the Precious Blood identified with the original *Passio* of Christ.[149] In Chrétien de Troyes and those who continue him, magical events stand almost invariably as tests (as compared to their marking stages in the necessary training and maturation of the hero, which we find in *Peredur*).[150] New figures will appear, and older characters may take on new and more complex tasks and masks (Sir Gawain is a case in point), but with all the florescence of incident and byplay, the main thrust of this redaction is always the discovery and recovery of the sacred Graal.

The third formulation of the sacred quest is now most often labeled as a

"Cistercian" monastic version, one transformed by the dominating ideas of a particular period in the religious-intellectual exfoliation of the Western medieval world. Spiritualized, as one scholar believes, and even theologized, the organic themes worked out in *Peredur* and then *Perlesvaus* are now stood on their heads.[151] The very figure of the hero of the quest is completely changed: Perceval the Innocent, by reason of his comparatively paltry sins, is still considered too flawed to complete the quest, so he is replaced by Galaad, a perfect and in fact sinless Christlike knight. Given the extraordinarily rich fabric of narrative inherited by the creators of the Cistercian version, not every theme can be purified or completely spiritualized. Nevertheless, we can recognize two major shifts: the Otherworld is demonized, and the ancient figure of the woman finds her ambivalent powers degraded or reversed; woman's beauty no longer can stand for sovereignty's achievement and prize, but only as occasioning sin and temptation.

In the sacred quest whose transformations I have pursued to this point, with its Celtic origin and its posterior medieval *dénouement,* we can see the venturing quest hero made progressively less active and significant. In Dumézilian terms, the Second Function warrior-hero has been brought under the stern control, at least in imagination, of a sacred first function figure, not kingly but sacerdotal (King Arthur's significance at the last is vaguely directive but not central). Galaad is a constructed vision of Knight-as-Christ,[152] and the object of the sacred quest has become more important than the subject, who once was the active, questing hero. Of course, all this began with the great fund of Celtic myth, itself already equipped with the prototypical objects central to the Christianized quest, especially the cup (usually connected to sovereignty, but often closely related to the ancient Celtic cauldron of life or regeneration), but also the lance, which deals a debilitating or emasculating blow in Celtic myth, paralleling or foreshadowing the fate of the wounded Fisher King, Percival's uncle.[153] The Celtic original also sets the tone, emphasizing the importance not only of testing but of processual increments; in addition it underscores those vital Otherworld potencies that will eventually be derogated, demonized, or replaced.

A SEQUENTIAL QUEST

The hero in the Welsh *Culhwch ac Olwen* is a king's son who first appears in a mildly folklorized setting and whose "quest" after the maiden Olwen, the giant's daughter, originates in an evil stepmother's curse. Culhwch sets off for the court of his cousin Arthur to obtain Arthur's aid, to which Arthur, as kinsman, naturally must agree. Eventually a scouting party, including Culhwch, finds the *caer* or fort of Ysbadadden Chief Giant; there Culhwch meets the beauteous Olwen and her monstrous father, who sets the correctly impossible terms of the quest proper.[154]

The Chief Giant's demands number thirty-nine (or forty),[155] the first twenty of which refer to what must be done to prepare for the wedding between Culhwch and Olwen, which the canny giant is sure will never take place—fields miraculously cleared and crops grown thereon, special honey procured, a magical bottomless hamper found to provide for the wedding feast, and so on. But the bride's father must also be properly turned out, and the essential items for his toilet are "the comb and shears that are between the ears of Twrch Trwyth," the mighty boar-king.[156] The hunt for this great pig will involve all of the remaining actors and other desiderata necessary to the quest—dog after dog, huntsmen of a particular tenacity and skill, finally the sword of another giant, Wrnach. When the list is finished, and Culhwch has blithely responded to each item with the phrase "easy to do" (*hawd yw genhyf*), the questers depart. At this point Culhwch, the optimistic respondent, abruptly leaves the quest. His "noble kinsman Arthur," he says, will accomplish all, and that is exactly what happens.[157]

No particular order is kept in the achieving of the Chief Giant's demands: the last item in the list—the sword of Wrnach—is taken first. Then other elements, mainly having to do with preparations for the hunting of the boar, are pursued, such as the liberation of Mabon son of Modron, the obtaining of the two pups of the bitch Rymhi, and hairs from the beard of Dillus Farfawg to make a leash for them. It is after the completion of this last, as always an "impossible" task, that Arthur inexplicably insults Cei, who retires from the quest in a justifiable huff.[158] After Arthur and his men have completed eight of the quest's sequential elements, the mythic great hunt of Twrch Trwyth begins. This hunt is more of a war, fought on the dead run in both Wales and Ireland, with losses on either side (the boar's savage offspring fight on his side). Finally the knights prevail, Ysbadadden is brutally "shaved" and beheaded, and Culhwch wins Olwen—and yet he remains the *beneficiary* of all these actions performed by others. Even Ysbadadden is dispatched not by Culhwch but by the revenge-seeking son of Custennin, one of the giant's victims.[159] Because of this, *Culhwch ac Olwen* might also be called an enigmatic quest, whose first puzzle springs from the character of the suppositious star and hero.

As a quest tale *Culhwch ac Olwen* is a rich pastry, and we know neither the cook nor much about the original recipe, that is, what was intended in its composition. As Gwyn Jones says, the tale, when reduced to its barest core, is a version of "a widely dispersed and long-flourishing wondertale," in the category called Six go through the World.[160] (It is a great deal more than that, of course, though Jones, whose Welsh-accented prose provides a fine, expressive, and genial guide to it, is frank about the narrative's failings.)[161] The embarrassment of riches in Culhwch's pell-mell enumeration of *all* of Arthur's knights, the multiplication of description in certain adventures and the paucity of detail in others, the continual, nearly obsessional pairing of persons and themes (which, as we shall see, may have another significance), and other textual incongruities and narrative stumblings may express either the tooth of time or the carelessness of creator-narrators. One scholar has recently set out to show that the tale's thrust is at base ironic and parodic, combined with the occasional antic burst of "custard-pie humour," but the results of this effort are dubious.[162] Another attempt at decoding the narrative, directed out of the Jungian school of depth psychology by John Layard, has the twin virtues of explaining both the early displacement of Culhwch out of his own tale (Arthur emerges as "Self, on which Culhwch is to rely for the attainment of his goal") and the sense or pattern underlying the persistent doubling of elements in the story.[163] This approach may even take *Culhwch ac Olwen too* seriously, yet as the enigmatic quest par excellence, the Welsh tale may be permitted to be both parodic and deep. Its narrative segments are sometimes disconnected and even disconcerting, but its efflorescent humor still gives delight not least because, as the king of Siam would say, it is "a puzzlement."

AN ECCENTRIC QUEST

Its most recent translator into English has called the Georgian *Vep'khist-qaosani* (*The Lord of the Panther-Skin*) "a Georgian Romance of Chivalry," and in the grossest sense, this is correct.[164] In fact, the Georgian narrative, created by a thirteenth-century noble and bard of Caucasian Iberia named Shota Rustaveli, is both a quest tale powered and advanced by conventional themes, and an exotic inventory of inventions—passing strange at first to readers more familiar with the less decorated epic traditions of the West, but worth, I think, the trip.[165]

The *Lord,* in structural-narrative terms, is a doubled quest. The king of the Arabs briefly catches sight of a strange, abstracted, but attractive knight, so he sends the hero, Avtandil, to search this knight out. Deep in the wilderness Avtandil finds Tariel, the wild and distrait lord of the epic's title, who has been sent mad, in the form of an extreme melancholia, because he is bereft of his love, the Indian king's daughter Nestan-Darejan. This "sun-fair lady" has herself disappeared, so Avtandil is involved in a second quest—with Tariel—to find her.[166] Avtandil, "one thinking ever of two," is now torn between his own love (for the maiden Tinatin) and his knightly loyalty to his new comrade.[167] After reporting back to his king, Avtandil disobediently returns to the wilderness, where Tiriel has been wounded, and then sets out on the track of the Indian maid, passing through the kingdom of another hero, Pridon, or Nuradin-Pridon, the lord of Mudghazanzar.[168] Disguised now as a merchant, Avtandil reaches the City of Roses, where he tarries with the Lady Fatima, a comic-realistic female both bibulous and adulterous, and cast rather along the brassy lines of the Wife of Bath; he also finds that Nestan-Darejan, after many vicissitudes, had been finally rapt away by the sinister, demonesque Kajes, "adept at sorcery," to their evil queen's city.[169] Returning to Tariel, the heroes (who now include Pridon) form a small expedition equipped with magical weapons (providentially left by the Divs whose wilderness cave Tariel had appropriated); they reach the Kajeti, fight, and free Nestan-Darejan without further ado. A series of marriages and reconciliations follows (among others, the heroically disobedient Avtandil is reconciled with his king), and the three heroes, now become three kings, reign "in glory and splendor."[170]

The *Lord* is a tale neatly articulated in its thematic mechanisms, but covered with such a rich frosting of unconventional phraseology that the reader may overlook the skillful construction of its poet-aristo, Rustaveli. R. H. Stevenson, as editor-translator, is at pains to show how other, Western medieval courtly epics can parallel the *Lord* in emotive and open "demonstrative gesture," but an all too typical line in the Georgian poem— "They were all bereft of their senses; they deemed it an honor to swoon for his sake"—surely marks a strikingly different sensibility from that of the sterner normative epic.[171] At the same time, Rustaveli can slyly drop the Lady Fatima into his tale, a marvelously "common" and comic character whose good heart and sense will assist in the successful recovery of the kidnapped maiden. The supernatural realm has a fairly limited place here (the sorcerer's skills of the Kaje hold no real threat or bite, and are easily countered by the bits of magical equipment left in Tariel's cave), yet other epic themes and personae are more dramatically marked. Tariel's animalization, his absolute rejection of human society, is made abundantly clear, and this condition is catching, for at one point both Tariel and Avtandil become "as wild in heart themselves as any brutes."[172] Avtandil also seems to command an Orphic power with his song over both beasts and men; and finally, this tale fits into the usual political relationship specific to heroes: both Tariel and Avtandil are obliged to defy their sovereigns in order to pursue what they see as other, more authentic knightly-chivalric obligations, be it love of woman or loyalty to comrade.[173] The double pursuit contained in the *Lord* provides a structurally uncomplicated if grandly emotional finale to the theme of heroic quest; and its base notes, love and loyalty, develop naturally from other romances of the area (especially the influential Persian romance tales) and period.[174]

Conclusion

Even this small sampling of quest types illustrates the rich variability possible in this sort of heroic adventure, which is so often the central heroic adventure. The hero remains at the heart of the action, and seems to lose nothing of his adamantine essence, but he is not, and cannot be, solitary; and the simpler formulas of heroic birth narrative or death scenario, the very simplicity (a boring simplicity?) of the heroic isolation, character, and act are strongly modified, and may be remodeled to allow complex failures and fateful impasses experienced in the heroic *periêgêsis*. Much of the credit for this fruitful complication of the heroic quest belongs to the separate possibilities of the ancillary figures, a complex constellation of secondary players through whom the boisterous heroic *energeia* is channeled, enabled, diverted, or blocked. The end product is a branching florescence of individualized quests.

The four quests included here—Celtic, Greek, Celto-Medieval, Caucasian-Georgian-Iberian—demonstrate the considerable possibilities of differential development, but even within a single cultural context the "core" adventure may permutate into decidedly disparate end forms. The ancient Greek context, for example, provides us not only with the Iason/Argonaut narrative but also the Perseus tale, a "maturation quest" richly susceptible to Jungian analysis, especially in its pairs of malignant/benignant deities and monsters.[175] Then we can turn to the arch-hero Theseus, whose career is projected as a discrete series of quests, often generated by his particular restless *brio* (a quest for his rightful kingship in Athens, the treading of the Labyrinth guided by Ariadne, and adventures with his hero-twin Perithoös, including that reckless raid on Hades from which one tradition says he was unable to return.)[176] And of course there is always Odysseus, the trickster-hero who runs a gantlet of threatening situations in a highly unified narrative yet whose descent into the Otherworld, which should be his darkest trial, is merely an easy detour made for the purpose of obtaining certain information from the shades of the Dead,[177] and who encounters a plethora of feminine types along the way. Yet his quest, too, is ultimately unsuccessful: not even Odysseus can go home again, or not for long.

THE POLITICS OF HEROISM
Problems of the Evidence

To lay out a segment of inquiry dealing with the politics of heroism brings us back to solid earth with a thump and a jar—and a problem. To begin with, the very sources we rely on to provide a picture of the heroic enterprise and the interior calculus of the heroic personality are extraordinarily suspect as indicators of political valence and act, because the evidential narratives (generally, the epics) by definition express only the warrior-heroic point of view. They are not only biased in terms of their focus on a central character type but also thoroughly imbued with a value system blindly—and purposefully—ignorant of what we would call Realpolitik, read as political reality. As documents, they display every characteristic contrary, even inimical, to the colder data of the political force field: they are affective and conventionally emotional, they are constructs of the imagination and often of the highly charged fantastic imagination, they are self-consciously divorced from the dissective-analytic aspect of intelligence, and they are obdurately and proudly impractical. Nevertheless they remain analyzable political documents in that they contain evidence reflecting some particular view of power, authority, or both, however indirectly; and thus they can also be read as document narratives bodying forth some vision or reflection of a responsibility for social construction, direction, or control.

When they are assessed as political documents, the heroic sources we ordinarily use betray an especially restricted view of the political field or arena of action: the main players are by and large the only players shown and known. Society at large, the faceless mass beyond or under the epical scope or field of view, is meaningless and indeed almost invisible in this heroic context. "I don't know the numbers of peasants and rabble" (*Ní [f]edar cia líon do aithechaib 7 do drabarslúag*) who died in this great battle, says Lóch Lethglas in the Old Irish *Cath Maige Tuired* (Second battle of Meg Tuired).[178] Such unconcern, the normative epic attitude, is seldom breached. (In the Old French source *Raoul de Cambrai*, peasants "armed and carrying bright shields" reinforce the feud party of the Sons of Herbert, but this democratic sight does not recur in *any* other *chansons de geste*.)[179] The German medieval context can offer some rare examples of a knight-imitating peasant "epic" narrative, as in *Meier von Helmbrecht* and *Der arme Heinrich*, but these tales are extrageneric, and so far as we know they had no descendants apart, possibly, from the folkloric.[180] The very numbers of the nonnoble people, the ignored mass, may seem to define their unimportance to the epic, for singular figures, in the several senses of that term, are the actors ever in view on the epic stage.[181] The drama of confrontation, the *machê*, excludes all but the heroic perspective, and this is seen from Homer, where the fighting mass commanded by the heroic cast of characters is nameless, faceless, and speechless, to the Serbian heroic songs, in which the attempt of the people to enlist themselves in warlike adventure is firmly denied. And the Ossetian Nart hero tales add a mixture of images in their term *san lag*, which translates as "black men" and signifies those inferiors and "common men" who may occasionally be opponents of the heroic Narts, but who are usually of no significance in the narrative.[182]

Political action, tension, and rivalry in the epic context is handed over solely to the hero and the king. In terms of the Dumézilian formulations, the First Function of Sovereignty and the Second or Warrior Function continually confront each other for the prize of power or ultimate dominance. (The Third Function, however described or designed, is consigned to a political role either minor, barely supportive, suspiciously out of order, or nonexistent.) King and hero continually intrude on each other's narrative turf, as the collection of quest tales just examined demonstrates; and although it may be possible to think of a kingless heroic scenario, it would not be easy. The figure of this "other" powerful persona is in every sense present: contrasting, abutting, reacting, and interacting with the hero. It is our duty now, however, to isolate king and hero in some sort of political dimension, and identify their relationships within a more or less strictly defined program of clearly political command and response. The question may be boiled down to, Who is in charge? Or will there even be any agreement as to what "in charge" means? Once again we must go back to the epic sources themselves.

Monarchs, Antimonarchs, and Anarchs

The relationship between king and hero can be drawn from a number of perspectives or lines of assumption, from the essential/ontological to the accidental/dramatic. The two figures clearly emerge from the same *genus*, of that "powerful" individual detached from the norms of social practice, standing "apart" from and "above" the field of normative, cooperative social interaction. Sometimes they may be compressed into one: a king may pass through a heroic stage, especially as a young man to be educated or tested for his final role and invested at last with legitimated power.[183] Or he may assume a posture that intrudes into the heroic zone, and so maintains a doubled character or identity permeated with ambiguity: the king (*wanax*) of the *Iliad* usually appears in the role of war leader (and war hero), and the key rivalries in the great Homeric tale are about heroic prestige and honor, not the valences and balances of royal power.

Nevertheless, we do find political "reality" expressed in a number of epical contexts. The American translator of the Georgian *Lord* notes that the figure of the king is treated with respect there; and although loyalty to a liege lord provides a thematic tension against which the loyalty of knight to knight or knight to his ladylove is tested, the king-sovereign remains just that. Indeed all of this Georgian epic's knight-heroes are promoted to royal status, and in general the creator of this tale showed himself "the son of a people which . . . had risen to greatness under the leadership of a strong monarchy" and so respected the idea and the fact of a monarch's powers and responsibilities.[184] The Persian thoughtworld that so influenced the Georgian often intermixes images of hero and king, as the emblematic *Shâh-nâma* demonstrates, though the two figures may also be drawn as opponents.[185] The *Nibelungenlied* presents another thematic variation when Siegfried's initial "heroic" boast about his intention to take away King Gunther's lands and castles is softened and his antagonistic posture relaxed, and he is transmuted into Gunther's champion against the invading Saxons, converted to "a powerful man acting responsibly in defense of legitimate authority."[186] (At the same time, however, the *Nibelungenlied* also gives us Etzel, the uncertain and vacillating Hunnish monarch overinfluenced by a savagely vengeful woman; and Gunther himself [the not terribly bright] is easily swayed by the barely controlled ferocity of his counselor Hagen of Troneck.)

In the chivalric *chansons de geste*, W. T. H. Jackson discerns two types or cycles. The first includes the "noble king"—Charlemagne specifically—who endures as the icon of the conquering Christian overking, and yet who is ultimately held responsible for the deaths of Roland and Olivier and their knights.[187] (Erich Auerbach, for his part, is rather harsher on the old king, seeing in him "an admixture of passive, martyrlike, and sonambulistically paralyzed traits" all emphasized when Roland is assigned to command the Frankish afterguard.)[188] Jackson even sees Olivier made a victim of his "heroic" friendship for Roland but also as one who displays, contrary to Roland, a "kingly" sense of the "good of the general cause."[189] Olivier, perhaps unsurprisingly, dies caught between these two opposed imperatives, the personal and the political.

In Jackson's second cyclic type, respect for the sovereign power, is severely diluted and faded: the king has become "weak, even shifty," and may indeed appear as a classic *roi fainéant*. Thus we find a perceptual shift in the Old French *Cycle des Narbonnais* closely and fruitfully studied by Grisward, a shift that the *chansons de geste* also reflect in their derogatory view of Charlemagne's son Louis, who is "le négatif de son pére, une manière d'anti-roi."[190] This is so despite the fact that kingship as such is respected, even by the champion Guillaume d'Orange (called Fierabrace, or "au Cort Nez"), whose epic adventures occupy four of the tales in the Narbonnais Cycle.[191] It is undoubtedly true that a view of the king specific to the medieval West (and particularly, Jackson avers, to the epics of the twelfth and thirteenth centuries) rings with a certain harsher tone, identified by this scholar as a new fear and suspicion of the king who doesn't act as a proper king should toward his knights and vassals.[192] At the northern edge of the medieval world, monarchy is given even shorter shrift by the Norse-Icelandic *sagamenn*.

The peculiarities attendant on the production of the sagas, especially the historical or "family" sagas, are well known: though written down in Iceland from the beginning of the thirteenth century, they refer to events or, more precisely, to the persons involved in these events, dating back to the ninth century: to the land taking in Iceland when that island, or at least its coastal areas, was gradually occupied by Viking colonists, almost all of them sailing west from Norway. The actual or historically verifiable reasons for the migration to Iceland are not agreed on, but the sagas themselves bear fertile evidence of the powerfully antimonarchic sentiments of a number of important colonists, who set up a "republic" for themselves governed, more or less, by an orally transmitted code of law or legal procedure. (The island would fall under the crown of Norway only in the early twelfth century.) That king regarded as a particular foe of the good *bonðr*-Viking or the emigrant *goði* (specifically meaning a priest but broadly taken as the local chieftain) was King Haraldr Halfdansson, at first nicknamed *lúfa* or Shaggy, and then *hárfagri*, Fair Hair, after he had "neatened," in one hard way or another, his turbulent kingdom. That important text, the *Landnámabók*, makes a point of mentioning this king as the direct cause of an individual or family removal to Iceland some fifteen times, often with the stock phrase "because of the oppression [*ofríki*] of King Haraldr"—though other involuntary emigrants may simply have chosen the wrong side in a brutal civil war, as Haraldr was long engaged in this hard and bloody process of uniting Norway under his crown.[193] One of those specifically called an enemy of King Haraldr was Þórólfr Mostur-Beard, the Þórr's priest, a founding figure in the first pages of *Eyrbyggja saga*, but the family whose saga is most openly devoted to the antimonarchic principle or tendency is that of the Kveld-Ulfrs, in *Egils saga skallagrímssonar*.[194]

The central figure, Egill, the warrior-skald, is a stubborn enemy of Norway's kings, and his saga lays out a comprehensive list of their sins, to wit:

that they are unjust, tyrannical, and treacherous (like King Haraldr, who is all but depicted as a *berserkr*), or weak, ungenerous, and treacherous (like Haraldr's successor Eiríkr Blood-Ax). Egill's saga goes on to shape the Norse-Icelandic distrust of and opposition to kings in terms of these classic models and images,[195] and similarly antagonistic themes emerge in other sagas as well. In the pseudohistorical *Jómsvíkingasaga*, the devious and manipulative royal machinations of Denmark's King Sveinn Haraldsson are confronted and matched by the evil, magical acts and supernatural connections of Norway's cowardly Jarl Hákon, and the warrior order of the Jómsviking brotherhood, itself badly led, is caught between these two unworthy monarchs.[196] In the genus of sagas called *lygisögur*—"legendary" or literally "lying" sagas—the imagined king-figures are heavily skewed toward either the evil sorcerer-king or the weak and ineffective ruler ever dominated by his bad councillors.[197]

The Icelandic *sagamaðr's* grumpy vision of the "bad king" almost certainly springs from an old Indo-European inheritance and connection, as I have tried to demonstrate elsewhere,[198] but the Norse-Icelandic sources do have room for some idea of "good" kingship, as shown in the Life of King Oláfr the Saint in the *Heimskringla*. Saint Oláfr, however, is no Charlemagnean mirror of royal *Christianitas;* he is a good old Norse warrior-king with more than his share of ferocity and bloody-mindedness. The pagan King Haraldr seems rather more the typical imaginal monarch of the northern sources: erratic, savage, and untrustworthy, the Viking fighter writ large: in Dumézilian terms, an essentially Second Function figure or, at best, a rather misshapen representative of the sword-king type, on the Mitraic rather than the Varunaic side of a bifurcated Sovereign Function.[199] While the wind is in the North, incidentally, we should also note the peculiar authorial sensibility of a source like Saxo Grammaticus, whose Danish kings, legendary or historical, are displayed as curiosities who act very curiously indeed, perhaps all the more so in the author's (curious) atmosphere of Latinate moralizing.[200]

In sum, the king is triply damned in heroic eyes. First, he directs or manages a social order from which the hero is self-excluded or which he follows only on his own terms. Second, he may affect to stand above all secular or profane codes, ignoring or reversing the social or legal order he demands from others. Third, he may misuse his power through incompetence or because clearly defined boundaries are absent; and he may even intrude into the heroic persona itself. In schematic terms the heroic mode makes a strong political objection to the monarch because the latter establishes a vertical and metonymical structure, set in terms and forms of a hierarchy and the intensive control of this hierarchy, and yet the monarch may evade or violate that structure, pushing himself into the horizontal and the metaphorical patterns shaping and dominating the heart of the heroic idea. The confusion of the two types brings less gain to the hero than to the king.

Champion and Bad King

The first role of the hero as *champion* is to stand for the king; he is the hero fastened into the structure of kingship, usually placed between the sovereign and external threat, or sometimes taking the place of the king in certain legal and quasi-legal proceedings. The king's champion operates within that Mitraic valence of monarchy (sovereignty) in which kingly power can in fact be delegated.[201] In both real and symbolic terms the champion's heroic potency is converted into an instrumentality not under his own control, and therefore he is made vulnerable in certain specific ways. This vulnerability is taken up as the core theme of certain epic treatments, and the unfortunate results for the hero-champion are exemplified in the fate of Roland and Olivier in the *Chanson de Roland* (though we should always recall that part of Roland's fate undoubtedly stems from his own implacable and belligerent warrior's ego, to say nothing of his refusal to accept anything resembling a commonsense estimation of his parlous tactical situation). Other epic traditions provide a further refining of the thematic type.

Georges Dumézil originally located the two modalities of northern warrior activity, the Þórr-warrior and the Óðinn-warrior, in one of his analyses of the Indo-European *fonction guerrière,* specifically in sources describing the legendary Danish hero Starcatherus-Starkaðr.[202] The first indication of this bifurcation appears when the young Starkaðr is the object of a debate between two of the divine Aesir, Þórr and Óðinn, and his fate, as worked out in his long, grimly heroic life, is shaped by this divine difference of opinion;[203] but in *Egils saga* the two modalities are much more fully and dramatically drawn. The generations of the Kveld-Úlfssons are divided between personifications of Óðinn-warriorhood (Kveld-Úlfr himself, his son Skalla-Grímr, Skalla-Grímr's son Egill) and exemplars of the Þórr-warrior (Grímr's brother Þórólfr and Egill's brother of the same name). One of the arguments of this richly detailed saga is that the two Þórólfrs are drawn to royal service, to "championhood" or Þórr-warriorhood, and both die because of their choice. The elder Þórólfr is the personal victim of Haraldr lúfa's red envy and his perverse inclination toward taking bad counsel; the younger Þórólfr continues the tradition of having "no luck [*ekki gæfu*] from the king": he is killed in battle, fighting in a king's cause. Other aspects to this bifurcation of types include the attractive physical qualities of the Þórólfrs compared with the unattractive, even trollish, Óðinnic Kveld-Úlfssons, but the chief lesson to be learned is the danger—in fact the fatality—likely to accompany the role of king's champion.[204] (A last interpretive and clarifying point might be made in contrasting the rather cold, calculating quality of an Óðinn-warrior like Egill with the antimonarchic *démesuré* who sometimes appears in the Old French sources, the knight figure called "unmeasured" in his mindless reactive violence against the king.)[205]

Another main context and arena for the activity of the king's champion appears in the Celtic sources and their medieval continuations. Here the older Irish Celtic narrative cycles give us the outrageously heroic figure of Cú Chulainn, but this warrior, although called *ferg* or *níad*, a champion of the Ulad, never appears controlled by Ulster's King Conchobar, though Tomás Ó Cathasaigh reminds us that the role of king's champion "is the proper role of the sister's son" of the king, which is what Cú Chulainn is to Cochobar, and there are other passages in the *Táin* that reinforce the champion's place for Cú Chulainn, as compared with the dæmonic, warped "madman's" apparition we can see blazing up in one morphism of this nonpareil hero.[206] It is usually this ancient Irish warrior's uncontrollable explosiveness, not any sort of subordination to a king's command, that impels the narrative of the *Táin,* and any limitations on Cú Chulainn's actions will emerge inevitably from his own character, and from the *gessa* or taboos that must inevitably and fatally circumscribe his hyperheroic powers.[207] Other Irish tales may depict a mortal tension between a king and his "man," as when a champion's loyalty to his chief is broken because of a woman, but in these cases the dividing gravamen arises from an eruption of heroic ego and personal emotion, not from any reason of state imprinted in the king. In the cycle of tales devoted to Finn mac Cumaill and the warriors of the *fianna* there is no question but that Finn is a king's champion, as he is head of the guard corps, the *fénnidi,* placed to protect his society from its various threatening or impinging enemies.[208]

The Welsh Celtic materials devoted to Arthur, and their medieval continuations, articulate the most complex interactions of king and hero-champion, and the most dramatic example emerges in those old adventures dealing with the figures of Arthur and Cei. The latter is already identified in the most archaic (meaning archaic in sense and tone, not certifiably first-recorded) surviving Welsh sources, like the *Trioedd Ynys Prydein* or *Triads,* in which he is called a true battle champion; Arthur's image in these Triads is singularly different from any later portrait, for here he is made out to be a violent, jealous, sexually rapacious fighting chieftain.[209] In fact, these figures seem to appear as two refractions of the same heroic reality; in the archaically toned sources, they are nearly "twinned."[210] At the same time, Cei's place as king's champion is clear, as in the old, fragmentary Welsh poem *Pa Gur*, in which Cei is also paired with Bedwyr, a champion of a different but undoubtedly familiar strong-arm kind.[211]

Bedwyr the Square provides the unthinking and obedient musculature of the king's champion; he must have some characteristics that connect him to the type of the Þórr-warrior in the North. Cei himself, however, is bifurcated, according to the evidence of *Culhwch ac Olwen*, in which his connective apposition to Arthur undergoes the most startling transformation. In this tale we find Cei "of the Two Gifts," one described as the perfect king's instrument, cold and controlled ("there shall be no server or officer like him"), the other an extraordinary planner, trickster-magician, and "hot" shape changer—a figure, in sum, possessed of an impressive personal voltage.[212] Before the tale is fully told, in fact before the great hunt even begins, both of Cei's sets of gifts will be rejected by Arthur, who (most interestingly) reverts to the ambiguous and unpleasant satirical bent he was said to have boasted according to the evidence of the old *Triads*.[213] Arthur insults his champion in both of Cei's potential modes, and Cei, as we have seen, angrily withdraws from the quest.

In the later (or further) developments of the Arthurian corpus, Cei or Sir Kay moves farther and farther away from the prominent place he once held as a warrior-hero. Already in the Welsh *Peredur* he has taken up the evil temper and bad manners that invariably mark him in the exfoliated Continental redactions of the *matière de Bretagne*;[214] and eventually Cei the Battle-Diademed, foremost in fighting, will be transformed into Sir Kay the Porter (or Doorward), which at least retains some trace of the old champion's posture, in a position of risk or threat between the king and the exterior world. In the end, however, the old warrior and champion declines into Sir Kay the Seneschal, the butler of the knightly paladins, holding a derogated, menial position, and projecting an angry, incompetent, spiteful, silly—and cowardly—nature.[215]

It is unclear why this pathetic declension takes place, although it may be analogous to that process Gregory Nagy has proposed for the *Iliad*, in which the older figure of a satirist and blame poet with considerable critical and perhaps magical powers (powers certainly retained, as we shall soon see, in the Irish Celtic view of the satirist) is reduced to the scorned, ugly, comic-pathetic—and severely truncated—figure of a Thersites. In any event, Cei's fate illustrates one possibility for the champion: to have his heroic potency leached out, with the (formidable) warrior-champion's voluntary service and loyal adhesion to the king (with whom he was once all but twinned) finally made all too predictable and trivial.

Cei's championhood, with its latterly amendments and declines, forms an intricate scenario, but interestingly enough, Arthur himself is trivialized to some extent in his simultaneous ascent to mythic and romantic status. The energetic, erratic, and sometimes immoral and even "bad" king of the Welsh *Triads* becomes the king figure who ponderously plays out a high drama of sin and redemption, but so far as Arthur's primary champion in the Continental tales is concerned (the paladin Sir Lancelot, who does not exist in the Welsh sources), the tension between sovereign and warrior is reduced to the familiar and banal triangle with its sexual and generational focus: old king, younger queen, young warrior. Inevitably the king emerges diminished. Such a scenario is well known to us in another narrative based in the Welsh; in fact Tristan (as Drystan) is identified in the same *Triad* of heroes as Cei, one of three "battle-diademed men" or foremost fighters of the host.[216] (Also like Cei, in one of his personae, Tristan/Drystan has distinctly tricksterish abilities, although these seem to be pared away as he becomes more firmly ensnared in his illicit liaison with Isolde.)[217] It is certainly worth noting that Lancelot, of the Continental amendment of the *matière*, appears to fill out the features of each of those named in that old Welsh *Triad*, for he is king's champion, like Cei; he is the younger man with the older man's wife, like Tristan; and he is a rival to Arthur, as Huail Mac Caw had once been.[218]

Of course, Lancelot and Tristan are best remembered as part of a love triangle, and these young heroes, by allowing the emotional and sexual attraction between themselves and forbidden women to move forward, reinstate or reconstitute the personal, individual, and competitive heroic essence. They also confront or contradict a system, the collectivity of rules governing social artifact and hierarchy.

The hero revives the heroic propensity for risk and danger. He violates not only the rules governing the articulation of loyalty and trust between First and Second Functional figures, but also those rules creating and governing familial solidarity. Again he acts against the metonymic ordering principle of monarchy, and impudently substitutes for it a dangerous metaphoric image: the hero-champion stands—or falls—on behalf of the king.[219] And finally he may, though perhaps unknowingly, resuscitate the archaic theme in which the queen represents the sovereignty of the land, and a younger man presses strongly forward as a rival to the older for that sovereignty.[220]

The Political Hero?

Obviously, despite the limitations I mentioned at the beginning of this section, the sources we use (mainly the heroic epos) do contain at least one implied political statement: the heroic individual is depicted, however crudely, as the most significant actor regardless of his "political" standing or lack of it. We also know that these epical treatments and sources are likely to emanate from a particular sociopolitical grouping, aristocratic or nobiliary, and the attentive creativity of its artistic parasites or mouthpieces—more politely, its singers. The epic is a projection into imagination of a very real sense of dominative place, that is, of essential political power, but such a sense of dominance is stated in special terms loaded with an unanalyzably solipsistic charge: the hero or dominant figure "is what he is," and dominates because of what he always claims to be. This solipsism avoids or actively stands against that systematic social logic by which a particular group is constituted and operates thereafter. (Joseph Nagy adds an important element to this conflict in arguing that the Irish Finn mac Cumaill and the band of the *fianna* can only accumulate those powers which allow them to protect the settled place by their training and experience in the most dramatically unsettled place, the restless wild in which animal and supernatural potencies jostle one another, persist, and dominate.)[221]

W. T. H. Jackson sees the central epic conflict as one "between settled king and intruder-hero . . . essentially a study of transfer of power or . . . of the problem of kingship,"[222] yet the gravamen of most epics does not rest in kingship's operations but in the intransigent egoism of its epic hero. The weakness of the epical king detected by Jackson is not accentuated in the narrative to show how a transition to a stronger, more effective king comes about—though this shift may occasionally occur—but to suggest the most serious doubt about the rightful nature of kingship itself, a doubt very strongly held both by the epic's creators and by its audience. The *totalitarianisme* found by Dumézil at the very heart of his theorized Warrior Function, the essentially bellicose *fonction guerrière*, needs, and if necessary creates, the biased portrait of its "bad king," as in another context the myth-history created for the Roman Republic dominated by the nobiliary order of the *patres* demanded its story of a tyrannical and lecherous last king, Tarquin the Proud, to condemn and righteously overthrow. I think it significant that the Second, Warrior Function, through the means of its epic-heroic propaganda, insists on attacking a political problem not by political counter-argument nor by the theoretical or practical construction of a different system, but through the strongly affective arts of the narrative imagination, through *stories* that support the symbolic presentation and position of the hero.

Political order, in the heroic epic, is forever evanescent and vain to pursue. The destructive potentiality of the hero—his negative valence, the uncontrolled operation of his enweaponed, fulminating, and lethal ego—produces typical scenarios in which every attempt at social stability, any demanded obedience to rule and order, is dissolved. In the end it must always, so far as the hero is concerned, falter and fail.

4 THE HERO "SPEAKS"

Opponents should be spurned with words first, weapons afterward.
—Saxo Grammaticus, *Gesta Danorum*

What do paladins talk of at dinner? They boast as usual.
—Italo Calvino, *The Nonexistent Knight*

Speech may be the distinguishing trait of the human species, but ordinary speech seems to be self-consciously circumscribed and "coded" by the heroic ethos. Here again the exponents of unbridled individuality are seen to limit, even to repress themselves in their use of a basic technique of communication, so that whole areas of linguistic exchange are either avoided or transferred away to some sort of specialist in oration. The remaining kinds of heroic speech, involving self-identification, self-advertisement, challenge and response, threat or counterthreat, and a limited selection of statements of choice or opinion, are combined with somatic and behavioral signs to communicate with those thought to be worth communicating with—and only with them. More precisely than any semiotician, the warrior-hero encodes and decodes the signs that identify his communicative cosmos.

To reach the point where the hero actually opens his mouth and speaks, I detour through some gestic and behavioral byways, in which we again see a prime paradox of heroism: the perpetual claim of unmistakable identity and absolute heroic difference, combined with that interior, essential resemblance of one hero to another that requires an exterior mark or unambiguous sign, so as to distinguish, in the simplest terms, one hero from another.

HEROIC STANCE

The first descriptive convention of the heroic tale is to show the hero as he stands, confidently displaying the glory of his exterior appearance.

Indeed his separation from other men is signed overtly and without am-

biguity through his extraordinary equipage, the costly and glittering surface he always turns toward the profane world. In one way our understanding of the heroic stance or pose is deepened by modern research into
the instinctive, coded poses of various animals, the more so as one aspect
of the supposedly human warrior-hero surely is contained in *to thêriades,*
"the beast in man." The human hero adds an artifactual element to his
stance, however: all the way from the *Iliad,* three thousand years old, to the
Serbian heroic songs sung (and so reinvented) a mere generation ago, the
description of heroic self-display or pose seems to vary only according to
minor conventions and local habits.

In the *Iliad* "godly" Paris-Alexandros fits on his "goodly" armor (*teukhea
kala dios Alexandros*): the beautiful greaves with silver fittings, the silver-
studded bronze sword, the great helmet with its crest that "nodded terribly"—*deinon de lophos . . . eneuen*—and of course his death-dealing spear,
the heroic weapon of choice in Homer's Iliadic action (*Il.* III.329–36). The
Serbian bard Avdo Medjedović, singing his own epic in the 1950s, may
add horse and rifle to the heroic equipage, but his purpose and studied effect
are essentially the same. We behold the young hero Mehmed, being dressed,
as it happens, by his mother: "Then she girded on him two Tripolitan sashes
and his braided belt of arms. . . . Therein were his two Venetian pistols
forged of pure gold. . . . Between them was a two-edged sword which sev-
ers heroes' hearts. . . . Down the front hung four cords, braided of 'fined
gold . . . mingling with his sword-thong which held his fierce Persian
blade."[1] Compare the young Byzantine hero Digenes in full fig, "flashing
like the sun" (*hôs hêlios astraptôn*), who holds a spear of "Arabian green" with
a gold pennant, and was a beautiful (*hôraios*) sight.[2] Or as Culhwch of the
Welsh *Culhwch ac Olwen* rides off to seek his kinsman Arthur: "He had two
sharp silver-mounted spears in his hand. A sword in his hand twice the
length of a man's forearm; it would bring blood from the wind. . . . On
his hip a gold-hilted sword, edged in gold, with a gold-chased cross on it,
colored with the brilliance of the heavens and inlaid with ivory. Before him,
a pair of spotted white-breasted hunting hounds."[3] And so on. The epical
extravagance of the Indic *Mahâbhârata* is represented *pars pro toto* by a
description such as "On Sûryadata's armor a hundred lotuses and *saugh-
andikas* were embossed, and it was gold-plated and bright as the sun."[4]

Some epic contexts, it is true, are more inhibited in their decorative
images. The *Poema del Mio Cid* maintains a certain Iberian reticence about
the appearance of its eponymous hero until late in the poem, though we do
know him to be spectacularly bearded, since he is so often named "he of
the great beard," *el de la barba grant.* (The hero is more fully described when

he turns out for a final appearance before King Alfonso and his Court.)[5] In the Scandinavian North extravagant description is uncommon; the saga heroes are usually described only as large and powerful men, though in *Laxdæla saga* Oláfr Hóskuldsson, called Oláfr pái or Peacock, was "the most handsome man people had ever set eyes on . . . [who] always wore the finest clothing and weapons"; the latter are briefly described.[6] The Norse-Icelandic sagas do employ a varied and often realistic vocabulary of physical depiction (recall the vivid ugliness of certain heroes from *Egils saga*), but this is often keyed to reflect important emotional or psychological characteristics. In general, however, an uninhibited, efflorescent, even baroque appreciation of the hero's physical appearance, accoutrements, and appropriate weaponry is a widely seen feature of epic description, and this detailing of the exterior appearance of the hero has more than one use. For the "original" epic poet-creator, lavish verbal illustration is at least partially formulaic, enabling the bard to thicken his song-sequences and catch his mental breath before advancing the action of his narrative.[7] But ego, display, and the advertisement of bardic skills may also play a part, along with a fondness for sheer, untrammeled fantasy. If and when a particular narrative is transferred to a written form, elaborate descriptions, however modified, will remain as an expected feature of the genre.

The Sculptural Hero

I have suggested elsewhere that certain views of the hero appear to find him statuesque or sculpted, posed and immobile, a veritable manikin-image clothed in the high fashion suited to heroism, "image du guerrier qui n'est que style";[8] and I have theorized that particularly in our 'primitive' examples of epic (Irish Celtic tales like the *Táin*, or Serbo-Croat bardic songs) we can see, under the naively multiplied layers of decorative phrase, an assumption that in their covered, even submerged selves "the heroes" are all equal, and perhaps interchangeable. Accidents of political allegiance will make no difference. Both Trojans and Achaeans display the same personal array *de luxe;* the champions of the Paynim are as superbly turned out as the Paladins of Charlemagne in the Old French *chansons de geste* (perhaps even more so, which raises another diverting question).[9] The epic subtype set on the border places puts its narrative attention on the essential isomorphism of the "border warrior" of either side or even of either faith; and so on once again. The paradox of the "unique" hero is that he usually looks, and acts, like any other hero. Nevertheless, certain variations in heroic costume and decoration are worth at least a brief look.

The element of individual and personal taste, which is largely absent from our usual range of Eurasiatic, Indo-European hero tales, is strongly inter-jected into the "medieval" Japanese version of the true hero-warrior. The *Heike Monogatari* is typical: "That day Tsunemasu wore a purple battle robe and armor laced with green silk cords, shaded from light to dark green. A gold-studded sword hung at his side, and a quiver of twenty-four arrows with black and white feathers was strapped to his back. Under his arm he carried a bow bound in black and red lacquered rattan."[10] At first glance we might be reminded of Serbian Mehmed or the Welsh Culhwch, but there is a curious difference. The old tale of the doomed Heike clan, as thoroughly blood-soaked and violent as any *chanson de geste* or saga, includes a con-vention that the warrior chooses and is responsible for his own appearance (note the phrase "that day [he] wore"), down to the color of his armor lac-ing and the tasteful fletching of his deadly arrows. A forceful elegance, and a nice sense of color and textural contrast, mark the warrior-killer in this particular Japanese context, but nothing resembling such subtlety of per-sonal choice and taste is perceptible, so far as I am aware, in the epic-heroic contexts of the West.[11] Richness of apparel, the cost and distinctiveness of arms and armor, perhaps their value as heirlooms—these are stressed in our usual sources, while in our gaudier examples (such as the Serbo-Croat description of the youthful Mehmed) the hero is dressed *by someone else,* evidently with the aim of creating and presenting his exceptional status: the more outrageously, even naively colored, costly, and glittering the con-structed result, the higher the apparent heroic standing. One narrative as-sumption is that these young men (Mehmed, Culhwch, Digenes, whoever) must be identified as heroes when they move out into the world; they carry, as a sort of signboard, and often for the first time, that scintillant and costly weight of their true heroic surface.[12]

Heroic Color Codes

Although none of our familiar epic contexts approaches the forthright style of the Japanese, occasional details of dress or accoutrement do convey cer-tain meanings. (So does the use of a precious substance like gold, as an index of rarity or richness.) A little later in this study I take up the color symbol-ism of the knight-warrior-hero; for now I want to explore the pursuit and identification of those "dress-coded" details of heroic narrative in which color has a clear place.

The Norse-Icelandic sagas are conventional when they present a warrior-hero in red equipment or ceremonial clothing (red is the strongly marked

designating color of the Second or Warrior Function according to Dumézil).[13] Steinþórr of Eyrr, a "fine-looking warrior" in *Eyrbyggja saga*, is
described as bravely turned out in a scarlet tunic, and carrying a gold-
mounted sword, though his too-decorative weapon proves sadly deficient
when wielded in a real fight.[14] The king's son Aran in the *Þáttr* "Egill ok
Ásmunðr" wears a scarlet cloak—though this may be meant as a predictive
sign of his eerie, postmortem ferocity: he will eventually become an evil
haugr or grave-mound revenant.[15] A suggestion of extrahuman powers
associated with this color is even clearer in the tale "Örvar-Oddr," for Oddr's
magical protective silk tunic is red.[16] And Oláfr pái, the Peacock, whose
handsome presence does not, in the end, bring him much luck in *Laxdæla
saga*, is at one point painted and posed in the recognizably heroic style with
gold-mounted armor and a red shield.[17] The warrior's color, the color of
blood and of bravery, evokes in the sagas a number of affective suggestions:
self-conscious self-display, possibly a lack of self-control—and maybe a
consequent doom of misfortune or ill luck. In *Njáls saga* the knightly saga
hero Gunnarr and his company ride to the Alþing "so well dressed that no
one there could compare with them," but at this same Alþing Gunnarr
meets Hallgerðr, the "fatal" woman who as his wife will help to bring him
his death—and it is Hallgerðr, the future wife, who wears a red tunic and
scarlet cloak. Is this also a bloody prevision?[18]

The Norse saga sources suggest a few other conventional or conventionally symbolic valences attached to color: white (*hvitr*) may simply describe a pale blond or tow-headed individual, without derogation, but elsewhere and otherwise *hvitr* signifies pale cowardice, that is, an emotional
exsanguination, a loss of the red and wrathful warrior's color. White, in the
canonical Indo-European color scheme, is the color of the sovereign First
Function, and this may possibly combine with the normative Icelandic anti-
monarchical slant or operating mode.[19] The tale *Hrólfs saga Kraka* applies
the color white to the king without any editorial comment, while the champion's identifying color is red-brown, the color of dried blood.[20] Another
color with an emotive value in the sagas is *bla*, which translates into the
whole range of the dark spectrum from blue through black. It is a death
color, the color of Hel, and is introduced especially when deadly violence
is contemplated. In *Gísla saga*, the protagonist goes to commit retributive
murder wearing a blue cape;[21] in *Hrafnkels saga*, when Hrafnkell sets out to
kill the shepherd Einarr and is later seen on the track of revenge, he is identified as "a tall man in blue";[22] and, in a nicely symbolic remnant, in the
Landnámabók the raven, the carrion bird that feeds on the dead, is identified as blue-feathered.[23]

In the Old Irish narratives as well, red is specifically attached to Cú Chulainn as the superb warrior-hero. His "red" persona is foretold first to Connacht's Medb and Ailill by the prophetess Fedelm, and his dress uniform is described as a red "warrior's apron" and red shield.[24] Despite the polychromatic palette used in heroic description by the poet, Cú Chulainn monopolizes the color of blood; his own color, when the warlike excitement takes him, is crimson.[25] In fact, only one other Ulster hero is to be described as wearing red clothing.[26]

We might note in passing, incidentally, that stylistically the Old Irish cycles are in a class of their own, and this is reflected in their construction and imaging of the hero. Rich and dense wordplay is the delight of these poet-creators, whether Christian or not; serial, conjoined, and expansive phrase descriptions set forth the hero's brilliant and superlative individuality, with a special emphasis given to action, movement, and astonishing skills. Such a grand hero as Cú Chulainn stands at the opposite end of the heroic continuum from the Apollonian or "posed" hero (even his physical integrity is not solid but capable of fearsome distortions when the battle fury fills him, and he will accurately be called the Warped One);[27] and at times, indeed, especially in a source like the *Táin*, the subjective image of the hero can be overtaken, even devoured, by the poet's art.

Prodigious Physicality

Again we should remember the ambiguity of heroism: the hero's exterior persona either reflects an interior, ontogenetic reality, or is the essential collection of characteristics that constitute their subject totally: whereupon there is no interior to reflect. The very peak of drama seen in the presentation of the hero, with emphasis on surface, pose, costume, and act (terms taken, advisedly, from the world of the stage), causes us to ask, though perhaps too soon, if there will be ever found any "deep" purpose to this invention of human society. Is the hero only an actor? Is he only a man painted, or sculpted, drawn as merely larger than life? And to what end?

At this point we should examine an element of the heroic appearance not yet touched on in detail: the physical size of the hero. The *Iliad* assures us that its heroes are *megas*, "great" or "tall"; sometimes they are even *pelôrios*: huge, prodigious—or monstrous—like Hektor, Akhilleus, and Telemonian Aias.[28] Aias is described in detail, "towering over the Argives with head and broad shoulders," though Homer does not always give mere size the advantage: Menelaus kills Ereuthalion, "tallest and strongest" (*megistôn kai kartistôn*) of all the Trojans.[29] We would expect the *Aeneid*, as it frequently follows the *Iliad*'s epic model, to use the same sort of physical epithets; so Turnus is "taller than everyone by a head," *toto vertice supra est;* Aeneas himself is *ingentem*, "mighty"; and Mezentius, more or less a parallel type to Aias, is *vastis*, "huge."[30] The poets of the *Iliad* and *Aeneid* are fairly restrained, for elsewhere the poetic reconstruction of the hero more than occasionally breaks out into prodigies, as when the unequaled Persian *pahlevan* Rostam "grew to the height of eight men."[31] Such being the case, the height and bulk of Sohrâb, Rostam's son, whom he killed, was naturally prodigious as well—in fact it identified him to his hero-father, though not soon enough, in their fatal duel.[32] In the North the heroes of "far off times" maintain the pattern of exceptional size: Sigurd in the *Völsungasaga* is about twice an ordinary man's size and bulk, according to a very roundabout description;[33] and in Saxo's account, Starkaðr the Old is physically immense even in extreme old age.[34] Superhuman size in the hero may also have another meaning: the two Celtic champions, Cú Chulainn and Cei, are both presented as shape changers, and each may increase his physical size in a prodigious way—although Cei seems to have control of his shape-shifting ("he could be as tall as the tallest tree in the forest when it pleased him"), whereas Cú Chulainn does not.[35] For the Irish hero a violent physical distortion and expansion is part of his "warp spasm," triggered by battle rage or an anticipation of combat.

In the heroic epic, if we can in fact detect a pattern, sheer physical bulk is not always a heroic mark: great size, for example, may mark the hero's sinister opponent, the black monster figure who may be threatening, but also a bit stupid, even a gull. (See the Cyclops or the giants in the Welsh *Culhwch ac Olwen*, or the Irish *Fled Bricrend*, or other giants descended or ascended from folklore into the Norse *lygisögur*, or acting the part of the pagan monster-enemy in the Old French *chansons de geste*.) In Chrétien's *Erec et Enide* the character Mabonagrain is disallowed knightly status because he is simply too big.[36] Another possibility, revealed in *Raoul de Cambrai*, shows a neat reversal-construction: after his death the heart of the hero Raoul is compared with the heart of the giant he kills; the giant's heart is small, whereas the hero's heart "was very large—like that of an ox."[37] In the epic's descriptive formulas size is not as significant, I believe, as significant anomaly. We have already seen the young hero so quickly matured that he gains a warrior's full powers at a green age, or the boylike figure possessed of death-dealing gifts past any human measurement, powers often defined in terms of whirling speed. Cú Chulainn, who becomes the very embodiment of *celeritas* in what he himself calls "my savage sport,"[38] would be the best example here; and in this Old Irish case the game has gone far past the confrontational *agôn* in which the hero-warrior is conventionally involved, and has reached what Roger Caillois calls *ilinx:* vertiginous speed or the "whirling."[39]

When we move from pose to play we pick up that heroic characteristic of violent movement, the special kind of *celeritas* just noted for Cú Chulainn, but never restricted only to him. "I never saw his equal for swiftness, for vigor, for fury, for hardness, for boldness, for heroism in slaying hosts and multitudes," declares his old feud enemy Fer-tai of the younger Finn mac Cumaill.[40] The Caucasian Ossete vocabulary, in describing their archetypically heroic Narts, uses the word *pakat'ar,* meaning a "true violent hero," and the Narts, especially the irrepressible Batradz, do display a violent rapidity of movement and abrupt action when fully aroused.[41] The Byzantine epic, on the other hand, presents this heroic celerity with plain, folktale-like naiveté and expectable metaphors: young Digenes "flew like an eagle," "shot off like a leopard," and declared that "no horse ever beat me running."[42] He duels, in his tale, but has no proper battles; and his velocity has something of the innocent verve and flavor of the Welsh Peredur-Percival, whose "strength and fleetness of foot" were such that he would capture and herd the deer of the forest, thinking them to be hornless strayed goats.[43] But naturally the *Iliad* both begins and complicates this image of heroic fleetness. Aeneas is called "swift of foot" (XIII.482) in attack, but the merciless Akhilleus scorns him for this very swiftness; yet "swift of foot" is in fact formulaic for Akhilleus, who bounds "like a lion" and runs like the fastest horse. Most memorable of all is his great, fury-filled, but inexorable pursuit of Hektor, when the two circle Troy's walls three times, one hero fleeing, one implacably following close after (XXI.137ff.). To focus on Akhilleus brings out the ambiguity of celerity: it can mark both the onrushing attacker and the one who flees in great fear of his life. Headlong flight from a terrifying foe is the obverse of the rage-filled speed of the attacking warrior-hero, and may sometimes be remarked as part of the experience of the same man.[44] Heroic swiftness, essential for the full meaning of the hero's violent "game," is not an unmixed gift: though emblematic of heroic rapidity conquering space, it also may bring the hero that much sooner to his own final stillness.[45] In addition, it is concocted together with such signs as that of the horse, the imaged animal of death.

The Hero's Hair

This physical attribute is rather more pertinent to our inquiry than might at first be supposed. In Bernard of Clairvaux's *De laude novae militiae* the saint refers in disparaging terms to those knights of his time (twelfth century) who ornament themselves like women, and, "nurturing a mass of hair which hides your sight," are figures of pride, vanity, and excess who cannot compare with the new and more admirable sort of *miles*, the ascetic soldier-monk, recruited to the service of the Temple—who ideally would be tonsured.[46] In one reading (Dumézilian), this is a critique of those members of the *fonction guerrière* who have somehow slipped toward the *luxe* of the third function rather than placing their warriors' abilities at the sacred service of the First—and yet Saxo Grammaticus, a near contemporary of Bernard's, puts very similar strictures in the mouth of the sour old hero Starcatherus or Starkaðr, who, in a general rage at the latter-day laxness of King Ingel's court, points to a courtier-wastrel who "unknots his spreading hair and allows his unbraided tresses to float." The implication is that a real man and warrior may indeed have long hair, but he keeps it disciplined into a braid or knot or both.[47]

The matter of heroic hair begins for us, again, with the *Iliad* and the formula everyone knows, those "long-haired"—*komoôntes*—Achaeans. The epithet establishes one term or pole in what Joël Grisward calls the "mythologie de la chevelure," that is, when the "mane" of long hair worn by the male can be a sign either of *force* or of *beauté* in the male; the biblical referents for each mode would be Samson and Absalom.[48] Presumably the long-haired Achaeans would be seen to represent the pole of force. Two millennia later, Gregory of Tours mentions the *reges criniti*, the "long-haired kings" whom the old Franks had "put over themselves" (*super se creavisse*); it seems fairly clear that these were *heerkönige*, warchiefs who commanded and deployed military force.[49] Yet Gregory also tells us that these chosen *reges* were "of the first and most noble family" among the Franks, which may argue their descent in the line of some form of sacral authority. In yet another twist, the Old Irish sources tell us that long but wild and shaggy hair was *not* particularly heroic: there it was the mark of the *crosán* or "entertainer," an ambiguous, marginal, and perhaps feared figure.[50]

The long-haired hero may reactivate another image, that of the animal: either the "natural" and feral pelt wearer or the horse (especially with the word "mane" in mind), who becomes his twin once again. The familiar, animal image of the mane is already present in Diodorus Siculus's view of the Celts, whose fighters bleach their hair and wear it pulled or teased back to resemble that of Satyrs and Pans, but it also is very similar to "the horses' mane" (*khaites hippôn*).[51] The Old Irish narratives give us a rich assortment of hirsute usages, colors, and styles; Cú Chulainn is again typical, even mythotypical in that his hair is described in the *Táin* as of three colors: dark, blood red, and golden blond.[52] Cú Chulainn's long hair (and lack of beard) is paralleled by the adolescent warriors in the tales of the Irish *fianna*, who also may have styled their hair "to give a lupine or ursine effect" and so reinforce the raptor reflex.[53] The added "natural" image in the Irish Celtic sources, however, is what Sayers calls "a thorough-going but underlying correspondence between human hair and vegetation, especially branches and grasses."[54] Heroic hair, whether wild or tamed, is attached to a whole battery of deeper images, reaching on from this signing of a florescent natural and vegetal vigor, or of an animal virility.

Finally, the matter of hair length can have a social, even a class dimension and reverberation. The *Iliad*'s highly ridiculed Thersites is crude, oafish, lower class—and bald. In the Old Irish sources the adjective *mael* (crop-headed, shorn, or bald) is "primarily a sign of servility and low social status."[55] And when, in the medieval German tale, the peasant-born and *faux* knightly Meier Helmbrecht is finally humiliated and forcibly returned to his true, lowly social status, his tormenters yank out the long, aristocratic tresses he had boasted and leave him fittingly "bald and bare."[56]

At the last our hairy hero seems to be left, as he is so often, to balance between polarities and to give solid form to a florescent ambiguity. A warrior-hero's long hair represents force, animality, social status—and of course virility. (The beard is even more important in this last regard.) At the same time, however, hair worn long may surreptitiously announce the androgyny and sexual ambivalence that can be part of the warrior-hero's sexual stance. In addition, although long hair may present itself as part of the heroic persona or costume, it should not become a cosmetic concern. The long-haired hero can display his *chevelure*, but he should not display a *coiffure*, hair too elaborately fashioned. The latter would move him much too far toward the cultural and the artificial, and even toward the moralists' label of effeminacy.

GESTURE AS PERSONAL RITUAL
Identifications

First the hero must declare himself, so that all may know him. But in fact the epical evidence often gives us the hero's name or identification indirectly, or follows a formulaic style in which the subject (that is, the surface of the subject) is described in minute detail, and a name is only attached at the very last. Such a kind of identification is the rule in the Old Irish *Táin*, but in fact indirect identification is much more common than direct identification in many of our sources. (Among other reasons, oblique nomination allows more space for efflorescent poetic invention, especially when some intermediary or insulating figure describes the incomer, and the proper name then "solves" this puzzle of, Who is this who comes?) In the Byzantine Greek *Digenid* the intermediation is carried to considerable lengths. The hero's love object, the virgin girl or Korê, sees and recognizes Digenes but passes the acknowledgment of his presence and return of greeting on to him by way of her intermediating nurse, and obliquely: "If you are Basil, Twyborn Borderer," and so on.[57] The collocation of attributes, the formulas pointing out all the excellences of bearing, are made to seem more important than the individual name—and indeed the true hero would appear to be identifiable *as a hero* without any name at all.

Recognition of the heroic attributes therefore takes pride of place over the more particularized and perhaps abstract bit of data that happens to be the heroic appellation: "fame" replaces "name," or nearly so. And marks of nobility, which rank among the ineluctable attributes of heroism, are detectable at any distance: the Byzantine hero Digenes is naturally recognized by his enemies because of his "daring and much gallantry," and the king-emperor knows that he faces a hero, "for beauty so compounded shows bravery."[58] In fact an important trope is revealed here that recurs frequently throughout the epic literature. Thus in the *Nibelungenlied*, Hagen avers that the magnificent knight who had just ridden up to Gunther's court must be Siegfried, "though I have never seen him."[59] Exactly the same instant recognition occurs in the *Chanson de Roland*, when the pagan Grandoine, soon to fall to the hero, surely knows him, "though I have never seen him."[60] Peredur, upon his approach to Arthur's court, is identified by a dwarf and a she-dwarf there, much to the disgust of Cei, who is acting as mayor domo;[61] and so on.

Occasionally these telltale exterior signs of identification can be misleading, as when Patroklos is armed and disguised as Akhilleus in the sixteenth book of the *Iliad*—though this impersonation does not last very long. Ordinarily, however, impersonation or false identification belongs more to the adventure mode of the heroic trickster, following on the ancient tradition of wily Odysseus, who named himself *Outis*, No-Man, to Polyphemos—and yet we can see this same trick played in the Norse-Icelandic tale "Bósa ok Herrauðr," in which Bósi disguises himself by physically, not magically, taking on the exterior appearance of a poor peeled devil named Sigurdr "even to the skin on his face" and then goes on to play his nasty tricks in the hall of unlucky King Gudmundr.[62]

Kings are ever vulnerable: as Jackson has suggested, the "settled" king in his central place and position receives the "intruder-warrior," who brings with him all the ambiguous potencies of the exterior topical zone, the perilous "outside." Heroes approaching kings are expected to pass through the intervening or insulating spaces manned against them, most typically by royal doorwards. Thus Beowulf, as he approaches Hrothgar's hall, first passes a coast guard to whom he identifies himself only as a Geat and as Egtheow's son; after this he gives his full name to the king's herald, Wulfgar.[63] Celtic sources are particularly rich in these "entrance" encounters; the Welsh narratives (beginning with the fragmentary old poem called *Pa gur* [What Man]) feature the great doorward, Glewlwyd Mighty-Grasp, who guards "the house" of the king and demands the names of those of Arthur's men who enter.[64] In *Culhwch ac Olwen*, Glewlwyd has become Arthur's own porter and quizzes Culhwch when that sprightly and froward young man rides to Arthur's court; knight-errant and doorward then perform an elaborate word exchange, and Culhwch, irritated, finally threatens a magical resort, to satirize and "shout down" court and cantrap and all.[65] Glewlwyd thereafter carries to Arthur his favorable description of the young visitor, who is admitted at last—but only after more verbal interplay with the king does he supply his name and lineage.[66] (Cei the Champion inserts himself into this exchange in a puzzling way, advising Arthur not to "break the custom of your court" for this young man; in later Continental offshoots of the Arthurian legend Cei will himself, as Sir Kay, become an obnoxious and obstructive porter to the king.)[67] The gate exchange between intruder and gate-guard also appears in the Old Irish *Cath Maige Tuired*, a part of the mythic cycle involving the heroic-supernatural Túatha Dé Danann and their varied adventures, although here the applicant at the royal gate (Lugh) is admitted only because of the ten "arts" (*dán*) he can simultaneously proffer.[68] When Cú Chulainn (whose divine father is this same Lugh) first approaches King Conchobar's hold at Emain, the child-hero is introduced by an extraordinary act: he sows distruction among the king's Boy Troop and displays his warp spasm. There is no wordplay to serve as as passport, and the hero-child eventually gives the king his old birth name of Sétantae.[69] In a Caucasian parallel that points to the connections between this area and the Celtic world seen in other (specifically Ossete) evidence, the Armenian *Sassowntsi David* tells us how David of Sassoon impressed the old porter Korkig when he, David, rode in heroic wise and guise up to the castle of the Lady Khantout Khanoum.[70]

Gesture, stance and stature, physical beauty, behavior—all demonstrate the true and ever recognizable hero-noble. Be careful with that young warrior, the men of the Emir (Digenes' father) say, watch out for him, for he shows "skill as well as courage," and thus he is almost certainly someone of note.[71] Character always identifies, and such an attitude connects the *Digenid* to the chivalric *chansons de geste*, in which nobility is reputedly "recognizable at sight" whether it be Christian or Saracen. "The noble quality cannot be hidden," in Norman Daniel's words.[72] This scholar offers a wealth of supporting material from the *chansons de geste*, remarking that the conventional attributes regarded as praiseworthy (*franc, cortois, gentis hom et de grant fierte, de grant nobilite*) are quickly and easily attached to those Saracen knights otherwise and elsewhere derogated as *felon* and even, grossly, *fil a putain*.[73] We might also note that in the *chansons de geste*, lineage or *molt haut parente* is very often declared in the naming of the hero-knight, at least to the extent of the father's name and rank, but such is not always the case elsewhere.

Identifying declaration may be connected to plot line if an important kin tie is claimed, as when Culhwch can claim Arthur's help because he is Arthur's own cousin and thus entitled by customary usage to such aid.[74] Another convolution of plot may demand a false declaration or concealed relationship, as when heroic fathers (often fatally) unknowingly confront their own sons: this very important heroic theme is examined in detail in chapter 6. In the genera of epics we mainly have in view, it is probably the warrior-farmers of the Icelandic sagas who most carefully plot genealogical detail, giving their audiences that long list of begats that connects the players both to family (on both sides) and to place.[75] Such connections often serve to reach back to the "founding," the peopling of the Quarters of the island itemized in such detail in the *Landnámabók*, but one or another saga may provide certain details on Norwegian roots, and very occasionally an exceptional genealogy reaches back to the Norse Dreamtime, to heroic progenitors housed in legend rather than history. But "good family" (or at least "old family" carefully enumerated) and descent clearly drawn is the common rule here. Bastardy is rare in these sources: of those we could name as principal players in the surviving family sagas, only Oláfr the Peacock, in *Laxdæla saga*, is admitted to be illegitimate—but then his slave mother's father was, as we are plainly told, an Irish king.[76]

In the end, however, lineage (like so much else in the epical ethos) can be a mixed blessing. Family identification may actually interfere with the full sense of heroic individual worth and interior essence, just as it simultaneously supports or franks the blood-carried "nobility" of the true hero. (Two kinds of interiority are detectable in this.) In any event, most epics have a narrow or shallow sense of family line: "There are no long genealogies," as Daniel remarks of the stalwarts in the *chansons de geste*. "Nobility might almost be spontaneously generated."[77]

Challenge and Threat

Once the hero is named, described, and physically present, ready to advance the action of the narrative, a king or other sovereign figure typically appears. (Remember Jackson's thesis of the interactional field of intruder-warrior facing settled king.) In *Culhwch ac Olwen* the young Culhwch has already threatened Arthur, literally, with his big mouth ("I will raise three shouts at the entrance of this gate," *A mi a dodaf teir diaspart ar drws y porth*) with awful effect if he is not immediately admitted.[78] The Byzantine hero Digenes' meeting with the king (always called king here, *basileus*, never emperor of the Romans or *basileus kai autokratôr*—his real, high-ritual great title)[79] takes place on neutral ground, at Digenes' request. This is somewhat unusual, but Digenes' thinly veiled threat against the king's establishment is highly representative. If some of the king's "inexperienced" soldiers happened to say the wrong thing to him, he announces, "I would surely make you miss these unfortunates."[80]

Such a threat or derogation toward the king is also visible in *Beowulf*, but again directed obliquely, not at Hrothgar but at the boastful *Pyle* Unferth: Beowulf turns Unferth's challenge back on him and questions the ability of the Danes (and clearly, by extension, their king) to withstand Grendel's dark and trollish might.[81] A challenge to the king, again indirect, appears in the Georgian *Lord of the Panther-Skin,* at the first appearance of Tariel, the strange Wandering Lord. Seeing Tariel, who is (as usual) weeping bitterly, King Rostevan sends an attendant to fetch him, but to no avail; armed men then follow, but the mournful knight does not wish to be interrogated even by a king while he is so dramatically caught up in the tearful spasms of his grief—so he kills the retainers, one and all.[82] To this rebuff one can add the already noted visit of Grímr's Gang to King Haraldr lúfa in *Egils saga;* Skalla-Grímr responds to the king's invitation to become one of his men with "I know I haven't the luck to serve you as you deserve."[83] Haraldr quite correctly interprets this statement as a threat to his royal self, though it is worth noting that in this most antimonarchic of sagas no king is ever physically attacked by the violent party among the Kveld-Úlfssons.[84]

The most notorious example of outright threat posed by the aggressive hero was isolated as a type by Jackson, as when Siegfried appeared openly to threaten the Burgundian King Gunther. The Nibelung hero quickly gets down to cases: "I will take by force everything you have / Your land and castles will be subject to me."[85] Another kind of more subtle challenge appears when the hero pushes himself forward as a critic of royal behavior or as a didact prepared and self-offered to instruct the monarch in proper kingly behavior. In the Byzantine *Digenid*, at the meeting on the Euphrates between the hero and the king, Digenes the Borderer delivers himself of a homily asking the king to be just and merciful (to "forgive unintended faults"), with an emphasis on the rewards, to rulers, of acting justly.[86] Armed with such good attitudes, the king will always wield *hopla dikaiosunês*—the "weapons of righteousness"—for only God and not worldly power supports "rule and kingship."[87] According to this epic the king is suitably impressed. (The young hero, Cú Chulainn–like, also performs a number of picturesque feats for the king.) Digenes' statement is an unexceptionable, mainstream summation of the necessary (in fact, Indo-European) preeminence of true "justice" in the ideological underpinning of sovereignty.

Starkaðr the Old delivers his critique to King Frothi's son Ingel in the form of a long poem; the young king is sternly castigated by the old warrior for cowardice (failing to avenge his father) and for unregally falling into every sin of the contemptible flesh. "Seeking a brave man, I found a king / devoted solely to vice and voracity."[88] Ingel's lavish and unnatural feasting is Starkaðr's chief target; the generosity of the laden royal table is painted in the most scathing terms, and the result of the diatribe is that Ingel "exchanged shameful conviviality for extreme savagery" and immediately butchered his father's killers as they sat at the royal table.[89] The sour old hero is mightily pleased at this bloody, and inhospitable, result of his objurgations.

A more complicated case occurs in the *Couronnement de Louis*, part of the epic cycle featuring the knight-champion Guillaume d'Orange (called Fierabrace, or au Cort Nez). This includes several more or less similar recipes for correct kingly behavior, encased in a complicated narrative sequence. The Frankish crown is being passed from Charlemagne to his son, and it is the old king who sets out to instruct his heir on how a king should act: to avoid "sin or wrong," allow no man to be wrongfully attainted, never "seize the fief of a young orphaned baron."[90] The list is expanded in laisse IX, repeated with variations in laisse X, and provided again in laisse XIII; its enumeration is comprehensive, encompassing patience, wisdom, fair and just rule, respect for the church, and correction of the arrogant. (By and large these formulas are conformable to the sovereign's omnifunctional powers as described in the usual Dumézilian formulation.) But Louis ("young Louis," "little Louis" as he is called) is too immature, and poor Guillaume is made responsible for upholding his youthful rule.[91] In fact, he is Louis's own champion, and must see to it that the new king continues to hold his royal inheritance despite being "such a fool," and ungrateful to boot.[92] Alas, Louis's careless ingratitude to his champion is made all too clear in *Aliscans,*[93] another song in the Guillaume Cycle, and in this *chanson de geste* Guillaume delivers a diatribe that connects him immediately to the moralizing Starkaðr—yet the diatribe is directed not at Louis but at Louis's queen Blancheflor, who is Guillaume's sister. Here Guillaume indicts the queen, and by extension Louis, for gluttony and sensual vice in combination.[94]

The *monstratio* or challenge takes at least two forms, then: the hero seen as "beardless boy" performing, dancing like David before his king; and the Old Hero, case-hardened in battle, like Starkaðr and Guillaume, who stands for the pure warrior ethos and sternly reprehends any slippage by the king into the softer, more seductive tones of the Third Function. In Caillois's terms, the young hero represents unfettered *celeritas* or *ilinx;* the old hero the stern rigors of *agôn* and necessary confrontation.[95]

Gestures of Domination and Submission

The parade of warriors, a procession out of which the hero naturally will distinguish himself, differs from the heroic stance only because the subject is moving; the formality of the presentation retains the same importance.[96] A particularly apt form of this parade is the Germanic *bohort,* a circular ride that can break up into individual knightly challenges and serious lance breaking; this is a feature of the *Nibelungenlied* and is also inserted by Gottfried von Strassburg into his *Tristan.*[97] A hero in this demonstration displays his visible excellences and his skill at *faux* combat, but there is also a perceptible anti-kingly effect: the ride is circular, without precedence or order, composed solely of movement and the clear probability of confrontation.

In real combat the presentational gesture involves the act of showing or demanding primacy, the exceptional warrior running ahead of the battle: he who "first rushed forth," like Agamemnon or various other impatient warrior-heroes of the *Iliad.*[98] In the Celtic lands the champion or "battle-diademed man" evidently was marked off to emphasize his chosen first place before the line of the battle host; according to the Welsh *Trioedd* those three supreme champions in "the island of Britain" were our familiar Cei, Drystan (Tristan), and Arthur's old enemy Huail mac Caw.[99] Such Celtic displays of championhood reach both to history and to epic, the former recorded in various places in Caesar, Polybius, and Diodorus Siculus.[100]

The theme of the single champion of the host is noted as far afield as the Old Testament, in the case of the giant Goliath and the boy David; we see the rich opportunities it provides for rare drama in battle.[101] A most intricate reworking of the theme in real life occurred at the battle of Hastings, when the minstrel (or juggler) Taillefer is said to have ridden out from the Norman ranks, demanding from the Norman Duke William (a.k.a. the Conqueror, or the Bastard) that he be allowed to give *le cop premier* of the forthcoming battle.[102] As William Sayers describes the various sources in which Taillefer's "epical" exploit is celebrated, the knight seems variously a juggler playing with his weapons as Cú Chulainn did (or, for that matter, Turnus in the *Aeneid*) or a minstrel calling up the sacred heroic image of embattled Roland: *tunc cantilena Rolandi inchoata*, according to the evidence of William of Malmsbury.[103] Taillefer may have been a Breton, and according to one account he took the head of a slain Saxon enemy, thus following *that* good old Celtic—and pagan—war custom.[104] A densely crowded matrix of traditional motifs clusters around Taillefer, not the least of which is the immolation of the man sacrificed for luck in battle, the warrior who stands forth and dies for the king. Here we move into another antique scenario; the single combat between warrior-kings intended to decide the outcome of a confrontation has a long history, extending back at least from Hastings (where Harold Godwinson is said to have refused it) to Troy, where Hektor suggests it in book VII of the *Iliad* (VII.66).

In epic battle, as long as the combatant stands, or can stand again, he is evidently thought capable of fighting on and will continue to do so. The hero on horseback, in any serious combat, will eventually dismount; so the chariot-riding Celts and the Achaean or Trojan warriors of the *Iliad* (although the chariot-mounted barons of the Indic *Mahâbhârata* make their elaborate bow play while the chariot is in motion). To remain standing—and fighting—maintains the heroic pose and intention, possibly as a gesture of final defiance, as in the semihistorical circumstances described in the Anglo-Saxon "Battle of Maldon":

> Mind must be firmer, heart the more fierce
> Courage the greater, as our numbers grow smaller[105]

or in the laisse that describes Roland's "last stand":

> Count Roland feels that he is going blind.
> Now he stands upright using what strength remains.[106]

Sometimes the hero, though standing, is rendered incapable of movement by the press of his enemies; such an immobilization by pressure of numbers is not infrequently found in the sagas, when an enraged hero can be captured only by being hemmed in by his more numerous foes. Thus the ferocious young fighter Vagn Akesson is finally captured on shipboard in the last act of the battle of Hjórungavagr described in the *Jómsvíkinga saga*;[107] Grettir the Strong's murderers capture Grettir's brother Illugi in the same way.[108] Similarly but individually, the bloodthirsty Hagen, in the *Nibelungenlied*, is overcome by Dietrich, lord of the Amelungs, who "locked Hagen of Troneck in his arms," and Dietrich evidently overcame King Gunther in this way.[109]

Intermediate postures, neither standing nor lying, are ambiguous, possibly (or especially) because they are detached, whether voluntarily or not, from an erect fighting stance. Grettir's killers are scorned because they slew a dying man (who could not stand upright because of his useless leg, poisoned by witchcraft); survivors in the Jomsviking saga, sitting disarmed and helpless, are beheaded one at a time by an axman until Vagn trips up and manages to kill the executioner with his own ax.[110] Even under less violent circumstances, who sits where among the powerful, and why, can be a very important question. (Sitting—an aspect of enthronement—is assigned to the royal mode; and Edward Irving, taking up the motif of the "old king," remarks that this seated posture, in the epic, conventionally symbolizes inactivity, passivity, even impotence on the king's part.)[111] Tensions can arise—again—between hero and king when the two figures are joined in the important theme of "feasting in the hall." Here the king can either avoid or commit error, and in the latter case be derogated in the epic evidence, because he designates where the warrior-hero will sit. When Starkaðr issues his verbal blast against the effete King Ingel, he naturally refers in sarcastic vein to the inferior and dishonorable place in which he, King Frothi's old champion, had been seated, but the ancient hero also tries to reassert an ethical line by attacking the royal eating habits and, by extension, the king's lengthy sedentary posture at table. Starkaðr's claim seems to be that truly heroic viands are prepared rapidly and consumed without waste of time: "burn, gobble, and bolt" would seem to be his motto.[112]

The other intermediate posture is *kneeling*, and again heroic-ethical and royal-hierarchic definitions and statements come into contrast, if not into open conflict. Within the strictly metaphoric and agonic *Weltbild* of the hero, kneeling is likely to be part of the misfortunate ritual of asking for mercy from a victorious opponent. The gesture, so persistent in its affective associations, may involve bowing the head in submission, but it is more importantly directed toward the knees of the victor—the place, if Onians and others are correct, of "life and the life-soul."[113] And the "appeal to life" may certainly be refused, as the merciless Akhilleus refuses the suppliant who had clasped his knees: *labe gounōn, ellisseto gounōn* (*Il.* XXI.65, 71).

If mercy is refused or never sought, then the opponent, whether hero or simply victim, is laid low. *Keisai,* "there you lie," says Akhilleus to the slain warrior Otrynteos, though he uses the same phrase, with more pathos, of his dead friend Patroklos (XX.389; XXIII.210–11). Those killed by the young, beardless, but unstoppable Cú Chulainn are "faces cast down / in the bristling battle."[114] The opponent of a vigorous saga hero like Egill is likely to end his career like Ljotr, the professional duelist and berserk: "Ljotr dropped and died on the spot" (*Féll Ljótur þa og var þegar þrendur*).[115] Or as the *Nibelungenlied* (a source noted more for the violent energy of its descriptions than for any poetic pathos) puts so strikingly the death of the betrayed and stricken Siegfried: "The lady Kriemhild's lord sank among the flowers."[116]

HERO AND WEAPON

The images connected with the armed hero and his weapons form a vital nodal point in this study, not least because of the wealth of information to hand. An individual epic may vary quite widely from the norm in terms of its emphasis on personal, social, even psychological elements in the heroic makeup, but the hero's weapons, the tools and markers of his grim trade, are almost always there, and they are almost invariably described in full, intricate, nearly obsessive detail. Indeed in the weaponry of the typologic hero we can detect a dreadful and wonderful congruence between human imagination and human skill; between symbol and solid fact, fancied notion and finished craft. Given the range encompassed by human talent and ingenuity, with *homo faber* unleashed in terms of his devising and his use of killing tools, the hero of whatever culture ought to be found with an almost unlimited choice of weapons suited to his special character, from the hardwood club of Polynesia to the medieval war hammer and mace, the thrusting spear and javelin, the horseman's lance, sling, bow and war arrow, and every kind of sword for cutting or thrusting—counting only those weapons invented before the introduction of the vulgar and noisy gunpowder. Nevertheless, this overwhelming variety can in most cases be reduced to two categories: the weapon of force on (or in) one hand, and the weapon of skill on (or in) the other.

The hero is always, and must be, a prodigy at weapon play, but his combats and confrontations tend signally to emphasize the trial of strength (especially with the sword in Europe, Eurasia, and the Near East) or the trial of skill or accuracy (meaning, in the same area, the thrown spear or possibly the drawn bow). The hero-knight of the medieval canon, horsed and armored, can combine the two in his skillful manipulation of the lance from the saddle. The bow—not ordinarily, in the West, regarded as a gentleman's arm—can occasionally be seen in the same focus, as when the (admittedly ambiguous) trickster-hero Odysseus has the physical strength to string and draw his mighty bow, and the skill to direct its arrows accurately and to deadly effect. In the *Iliad* the bow is assigned to Alexandros-Paris or to Teukros, "knowing well the bow," *toxón eu eidôs,* though Teukros is also called a good man for hand-to-hand combat, *en spadiê hisminê.*[117] Only in the Celtic tradition (the adventures of the champion Cú Chulainn and the earlier tales of the Túatha Dé Danaan) is the slingshot regarded as a heroic missile weapon.[118] It is the sword, however, that predominates in the evidence of the epical milieu of Europe and Eurasia.

The Named Sword

It has been suggested, with considerable grounding, that only after the development of the so-called damascened or faggot-forged sword blade, probably in the sixth or seventh century, did this weapon achieve its exceptional yet conventional place as a nearly ubiquitous partner to the warrior-hero—and, like the hero, its name.[119] (The smith, whose close association with the warrior as his "blackened" alter ego reaches deep into antiquity, now seems to have produced a weapon whose "personality" or character is strongly suggested by a given name.)[120] Some support for a Frankish origin of this exceptional sword blade is provided by the efflorescence of "named" blades in the north and west of Europe, but particularly in the Old French epics, the Arthurian *matière,* some Germanic epics, and in the Old Norse sagas, though in one of the latter the prized swords are, for whatever reason, called *valskra sverða,* "Welsh swords."[121] Named (and often magical) swords do make their appearance elsewhere; in the Celtic narratives at least one shows up in the Old Irish Ulster Cycle (Cú Chulainn's sword Crúadan in the *Mesca Ulaid*),[122] and in another Old Irish source King Fergus mac Leide wields Caladcolg or Caladbolg, the "best blade that was then in Ireland."[123] In the Welsh *Culhwch ac Olwen* Arthur "names" his sword, spear, shield, and knife (these may be back-formations derived from the Continental Arthurian narratives), and another magical and named knife also is part of this tale.[124] In the Serbo-Croat song *The Wedding of Smailagić Meho* the hero is given a "Persian sword" that has been to Mecca and is named "Hadji Persian Sword";[125] In Spain El Cid Campeador boasts the two swords Colada and Tizón.[126]

The preponderant image of the named sword is revealed in French, German and Scandinavian epic sources. The *Chanson de Roland* gives us Roland's Durendal, Olivier's Halteclere, Turpin's Almace, and, on the other side, Ganelon's Murglaine and Balagant's Precieuse. We know that Charlemagne's own sword, Joyeuse, was eventually passed to his (and his son's) champion Guillaume d'Orange. In the Sigurd/Siegfried Cycle (Germanic and Scandinavian) there is the great sword Gram, broken by Óðinn, reforged by Sigurd's foster-father, the smith Regin, and used by Sigurd to kill the dragon Fafnir.[127] It was evidently destroyed in the death pyre that consumed Sigurd and Brynhild.[128] In the *Nibelungenlied*, in the southern branch of this saga cycle, Siegfried's sword is Balmung, taken by his slayer Hagen, and fated to be Hagen's bane.[129] The hero Beowulf is given the sword Hrunting when he goes to fight Grendel's Dam (line 1457), while his "heirloom sword," Nægling, shatters and fails him in line 2681 of this epic; in Saxo the hero Haldan, after killing twelve opponents with a homemade club, demands and receives his grandfather Ingel's swords, Lyusing and Hviting, which he uses in a fatal duel with his half brother Hildiger.[130]

The Norse sagas also contain a whole armory of "named" weapons. Even a glancing overview gives us Grettir the Strong's Aetartangi, Egill Skallagrímsson's Adder and Dragvendil, Þórkell Eyjolfsson's Skofnung (in *Laxdæla saga*, but originally a blade owned by the legendary King Hrólfr Kraki), Bersi's Hvitingr in *Kormáks saga*, and a great many others.[131] Rather than continue and prolong this list of weapons, however, I would rather probe more deeply into the essential relationship between hero and sword, following in my own way a percipient suggestion made by H. R. Ellis Davidson, along with other hints.

Sword and Swords

When one reaches for the icon and symbol of the Indo-European Second Function warrior-hero, the sword is central, dominant—and even alive. The brilliant translator of the *Nibelungenlied*, A. T. Hatto, included the sword Balmung in his glossary of the characters' names—because, he says plainly, "in heroic poetry swords are persons."[132] Such must surely be the case as well in the epic of the Serb hero Marko Kraljević, whose saber is called Sentient: it "knows its own master" and would not let itself be drawn from the scabbard until it came into Prince Marko's own hand.[133] The same quality of sentience must also appear in the sword of Meho or Mehmed (Ismail's son in the Moslem Serb song), which had been sent on pilgrimage as if it were human and carries, in its name, the honorific Moslem title of *hadji*. A magical sentience is equally found in one of the Irish Celtic sources: the swords of the Ulstermen will, it is said, turn against their own masters if these warriors should lie.[134] Roland's Durendal is not merely a tool for dealing death: it is so much a part of Roland's persona that, dying, he must try to destroy it; it must "die" with him, as his comrade Olivier had already died.[135] He fails, but the Serb hero Prince Marko succeeds; on the point of expiring, he breaks his "razor sword" in four pieces so that no Turk can ever have it.[136] The idea is translated into historical, artifactual terms if we recall that weapons actually deposited in Bronze Age or Iron Age warrior graves may be first "killed" by being bent or broken. Yet although it is true that the hero *is* his weapon, it is also apparent that we again have evidence of the emergence of an essential ambiguity in the hero's character; and we encounter the two-sworded hero so often that some important idea or ideas must surely be realized in the theme.

Egill Skalla-grímsson carries two swords, Adder (*Naður*) and Drag-vendil. The first is appropriate to the death dealer, an extension of his specific, Óðinn-patterned nature and of his battle-hardened fatality: he won it from another foe. But Dragvendil is a family or heirloom sword, passed on by way of the Þórólfrs (Egill's uncle and brother) and his father Skalla-Grímr. It was originally the sword of Ketill Trout, a great Viking and Icelandic settler and an important near kinsman of the Kveld-Úlfssons.[137] The hero Boðvarr Bjarki, as his career is discovered in Saxo, also has two swords, Lovi (Laufr) and Svirtir.[138] The former is the family blade (it shows up in King Hrólfr's burial mound, according to *Landnámabók,* chap. 174), but the latter was Bjarki's own, and from it, he says, "I received my name of Warrior."[139] In *Gunnlaugs saga ormstungu* the hero uses two swords, but as a form of countermagical trickery: his opponent is the kind of dangerous northern warrior-warlock whose mere look can blunt sword edges, so Gunnlaugr shows one of his weapons to his dangerous enemy but uses the other against him.[140] But a more powerful ambiguity hovers about Grettir the Strong. Grettir is given the sword Aettartangi by his mother Asdis (Aettartangi translates as "tang" or "hilt of the generations," though the sword's other name in the saga context is *Jokulsnautr,* the Gift of Jokull, a sword familiar to us from *Vatnsdæla saga*),[141] but he took his second sword from a grave mound in Norway after a fearful combat with the dead occupant-owner, Kar the Old, the *haugr* or howe revenant.[142] The combat is Grettir's first with an undead foe (his ill-omened second fight is with the *draugr*

Glámr), and from this point the saga hero's fearless energy, his willingness to confront either the supernaturally potent dead or the inimical living, must turn against him, and assist his eventual expulsion from society (and family), and at last his own death.

As a footnote to the formulaic usage of the "two swords," Saxo may have been responding to an even more archaic reflex of the motif in his description of Halvdan's two weapons. Both of them are grandfather Ingel's, yet one, probably the "shining" weapon (Lysingi) is used to kill Halvdan's half brother.[143] By implication, the sword used to kill a kinsman ought to be marked as the "individual" sword, the extension of the hero's most isolate, afamilial, and personal character; the second sword remains as a true family heirloom, representing social structure and familial adhesion.

Ellis Davidson's provocative study on "The Sword at the Wedding" is mainly concerned with the sword as emblematic of social and familial integrity, and she finds it especially meaningful that the sword as a "mother's gift" appears as often as it does in the Norse material, citing Grettir, Killer-Glúmr in *Víga-Glúms saga,* and Oláfr, later King Oláfr the Holy, who received a sword from his mother, Asta, that had belonged to another King Oláfr; Ellis Davidson misses the instance in Saxo I just cited, for Halvdan got his grandfather's swords by way of his mother as well.[144] These cases make concrete and personal the abstraction of familial solidarity seemingly expressed in one of the hero's two swords, but other important signs can be detected in or behind the data she has gathered. Thus in the legendary tale *Hjalmþers saga ok Olvis,* the hero Hjalmþer meets "a creature called a *finngalkn*"—a monstrous female figure with a horse's head, mane, and tail.[145] This creature has a fine sword, which she offers to the hero if he will kiss her. She sets a further complication by throwing the sword in the air, so that Hjalmþer has to embrace her before the sword falls. He manages to accomplish this feat, and gains the sword and after it both "luck and victory." In this fairly obscure *lygisaga* we have not only a sword emergent from the supernatural zone but an exact parallel (on the warrior function level) with that salient theme of the First or Sovereign Function, marriage with sovereignty, which appears so prominently in the Old Irish sources. There the putative king must kiss or even lie with the ugly hag, and rightful sovereignty is thereby won and becomes his through passing the test.[146] In Hjalmþer's saga special features reinforce the specific functional Gestalt of the incident: the horse shape of the weird *finngalkn* represents the second functional aspects of the warrior's mount, and the embrace itself is put under the deadly risk of the falling sword. Bravery and celerity, risk taking and act, are rewarded, and a pact is made, as Ellis Davidson suggests: the hero is finally joined to his (Second Functional) supernatural protectress.[147]

If one of the swords wielded by the hero symbolizes social usefulness and familial solidity, the other is usually marked by more mysterious and perhaps powerful qualities. Skofnung, for example, a named blade that shows up in *Laxdæla saga* and elsewhere, was a moundsword, taken from the grave howe of the legendary King Hrólfr Kraki, and it has obviously magical characteristics: "such is the nature of the sword . . . that the sun must never shine on its hilt, and it must never be drawn in the presence of a woman."[148] These strictures can be read in several ways: must the sword always be in hand and ready for use, so that the hilt is hidden from the sun, or is it a weapon only to be used at night? The former seems more likely; a night weapon would be a weapon of *morðr*, of hidden and thus illicit death dealing, like those in the section to follow. More important is the qualification that Skofnung never be drawn in a woman's presence, which not only reflects the archaic belief that a woman's potentiality can contaminate a weapon (by weakening its essence?), but separates Skofnung from the feminine-familial sword gift and type. Another magical adjunct of Skofnung is the healing stone that accompanies it, a stone capable of curing the wounds the sword might deal. More important, *Laxdæla* tells us that the sword is taken up (by Þórkell Eyjolfsson) to avenge a kin slaying, but although the hero duels with and wounds the man involved in the slaying, he also heals his opponent's wound with the healing stone, and the two come to form a personal friendship. The personal warrior's tie, in this case, sets aside the dictates of familial solidarity (and the concomitant requirement for blood vengeance); and Skofnung presents itself as an *expressive* heroic weapon, like Egill's *Niður* or Grettir's short sword won from old Kar's mound.

I believe that a clear connective link exists between the two swords and the Second Functional, geminated images of Óðinn-warrior and Þórr-warrior: the "individual" blade fitted to the destructive and disconnected aspect of its patron Óðinn, and the "familial" blade to the integrative and social orientation of Þórr. A weapon (the sword of Þórr) descending from or as the gift of *feminine* powers will be touched by a cohesive social dimensionality, though not—which is another option—a magical capacity. The Óðinnic blade is likely to be aligned with alterity: thus the short-sword or *seax* is foreign in origin, and the weapon taken from a mound has rested deep in death's shadowy realm. (Grettir's unnamed blade is both.) But we should always remember that in either orientation we are looking at artifacts of violence and death (whatever the arguable societal and integrative aspect of the

Þórr-blade), and that absolutely consistent categories are rarely maintained intact in our sources. To give one example, the sword Dragvendil, in *Egils saga,* passes through the generations as if to knot together the two strains so unambiguously marked in this saga, until it comes into Egill's own possession. Then, when Egill confronts Atli the Short over an inheritance, Egill's own ambiguous potency becomes clear: he appeals first to law and then to force, offering *onnur log,* "another law"—that is, a duel.[149] When the family sword can't bite on Atli, Egill discards it, throws his opponent down, and kills him by tearing out his throat with his teeth. This extraordinary victory is richly ambiguous: in his self-congratulatory stanza Egill exculpates himself by implying that Atli was after all a sorcerer, whose magical eye could blunt edged weapons. We could also see the wordsmith, the skald, using his mouth as a deadly weapon as he had earlier used it to shield himself, by way of his skaldic skills, from King Eiríkr's wrath. But it is also possible that Dragvendil, as a weapon "of the right hand" (that is, a Þórrsword), was ineffective in a situation in which Egill's Óðinnic nature was so dominant, thus forcing our hero to fall back on a purely animal ferocity.[150]

Fated and Anomalous Weapons

If Skofnung is a weapon representing heroic independence and untrammeled act, and Dragvendil is a blade suited to familial inheritance and cohesion, there are still other weapons whose essential character is not only actively antifamilial, and thus destructive to family bonds, but also fatal, in several senses of the word, even to the heroic wielder.

"Leg-Biter" (*Fótbit*), from *Laxdæla,* is described as "never rusting,"[151] and Geirmundr the Noisy (his cognomen *gnyr* seems to refer to "noise of war," the clash of weapons) always carried it in his hand, like the sword Skofnung just mentioned. He married Oláfr pái's daughter Þuríðr, but the match, though it produced a daughter, was not happy one. Geirmundr prepared to sail to Norway but would leave no money behind to support his wife and child; Þuríðr, as he left, managed to exchange the child for the sword, and Geirmundr thereupon cursed the weapon, predicting that it would bring about "the death of the man in your family who would be the greatest loss."[152] So it comes to pass. Indeed, the curse is later compounded or doubled when Oláfr pái manages to offend the goddess Freya and the sword becomes the fatal instrument.[153] (Another unlucky weapon is Tyrfing, taken from her father's grave by an Amazonian daughter in *Herverar saga.* Is this, like *Fótbít,* another sword contaminated by a woman's touch?)[154]

Then there is the ill-fated, kin-slaying *Grásiða* or Grayflank, which plays such a deadly role in *Gísla saga súrssonar*. Grayflank begins in anomaly, with a feminine name and as the property of a slave. (Old Norse sword names are invariably masculine, and thralls do not as a rule carry swords, particularly named swords.) Further anomaly abounds: Gísli, the uncle of the eponymous saga hero, borrows the sword to fight a berserk but won't return it; and when the bondman resents this and attacks the older Gísli, both men are killed, and Grayflank is broken.[155] The pieces are reforged by a sinister figure named Þórgrimr Neb, and turned into a weapon apt for dark doings: a short-hafted, easily concealable spear, used (presumably by or on the order of Gísli's brother-in-law, Þorgrímr Þorsteinsson) to kill Vesteinn, another brother-in-law, and then used by Gísli himself to kill Þorgrímr. Both deaths are night murders, secret killings, *morðir*.[156] Gísli is eventually outlawed for his vengeance slaying, and the saga draws on to his death. The violence in this saga, as in the *Njála* and other sagas, is sparked by rivalries among women, but the gravamen rests in cognatic-agnatic relationships, and the anomalous *Grásiða* enables the most heinous acts of kin murder.

Fatal or unlucky Norse weapons are ordinary human artifacts, however infused or infected with unnatural powers, yet parallel to them and their effect is a strange heroic weapon taken from the Old Irish Ulster Cycle, the extraordinary *gae bolga* possessed by Cú Chulainn. Just what this weapon was is only suggested in the sources available to us; even the meaning of the name is still contended. It certainly was a kind of spear (*gae*), probably forked or barbed or both.[157] When Cú Chulainn uses it he is always standing in water (a river's ford, or the sea) and therefore it is possible that somewhere in its deadly ancestry lurked something as banal as a fish spear or harpoon. More to the point is how the great Irish hero uses it, which is only in situations where he confronts a warrior equal to himself in all respects but one: the knowledge of how to wield this peculiarly fatal device, taught to Cú Chulainn alone by the witch-warrior Scathach. The hero uses it three times in the *Táin* and its related narratives: against his foster brothers Loch and Ferdiad, and then against his own son, Connla.[158]

The special marks of this anomalous weapon, as summarized by Sayers, are worth noting: it was "part of an alien culture, was learned from a woman, and was, perhaps, as a hunting and not martial weapon, considered less than honorable to use in the ritualized battle of equally matched warriors, *particularly if it should result in the slaying of kin or near-kin*."[159] The morphological resemblance of Cú Chulainn's *gae bolga* to the other two fated weapons can be laid out precisely: the alien culture is clear in *Grásiða*'s case (it belonged to a thrall) and at least implied in that of *Fótbit* (brought by Geirmundr from Norway). Women are implicated only in terms of the marital complexities of the two Norse examples—though *Fótbit*, once possessed by a woman, is cursed by its owner, her husband, and *Grásiða* carries a feminine name. The latter weapon is certainly converted into something "considered less than honorable," but the vital point is the involvement of all three weapons in the death "of kin or near-kin." Like the *gae bolga*, the Norse fated weapons are not invested with what we can call supernatural powers; all are weapons caught up in human action and reaction. But they are used most particularly in those cases where the bonds of kinship (already at risk in many heroic epical contexts) are evaded and destroyed by deadly will and tabooed violence.

Armor and "Scant Protection"

As we have seen, the most heroic champion may boast (literally) *no* protective covering, except possibly a shield: this is the extreme display of his risk-taking championhood, and his naked contempt for the opponents' weapons is matched (on the other, the animalized side of the warrior complex) by the *berserkr*, who may reveal himself in his frenzied state by abandoning his shield to "hew with both hands." The élan of the hero is directed aggressively and with more than human force, and only rarely does body-armor of any kind decide a combat by warding off this fury, once the hero has fully become what one author aptly calls *vaillants brise-crâne*, "head-breaking braves."[160] In fact, the more complete and comprehensive the protective covering of an opponent, the more dramatically the battle-engorged hero will carve, crush, or pierce it: "nor did the corselet of bronze that he wore avail him, but the spear was fixed full in his belly" (*Il.* XIII.371–72), a phrase repeated with variations many times in the *Iliad;* bronze armor "that had before kept death from his body" is sundered by the spear and "rang harshly," *auon ausen,* as he falls.[161] A true hero makes nothing of his opponent's armored defense: the enraged Lord of the Panther-Skin in the Georgian epic "tore armor in pieces; chain mail gave in his hands."[162] In the final bloodbath enthusiastically described in the *Nibelungenlied* "mighty Hagen" breaks helmets as does "bold Volker"; Iring the Dane takes a deadly wound from Hagen "through shield and corselet"; Rudiger and Gernot hew at each other, each "shielding his vital parts, for their swords were so keen nothing could withstand them."[163] (*Si tâten in dem sturme diu vil herlichen werch,* "What glorious deeds they did in that fight!" the poet enthuses.)[164] Roland deals the pagan Grandoine a true paladin's mighty sword cut: "The sword-blade cleaves his whole helmet down to the nose-piece / through nose and mouth and teeth down through his body" and on through saddle, unlucky mount and all.[165] In another laisse the bellicose churchman, Turpin, "strikes the Berber such a tremendous blow / His shield split open the chain-mail flies apart."[166] Guillaume Fierbrace takes a blow from Guy of Alemagne that shatters his helmet, and he strikes back, so that "even [Guy's] chest is cut through and pierced."[167] The nonpareil Persian *pahlivan* Rostam strikes Kâfur ("The Infidel") on the head "which crushed it and his helmet and shoulders together, so that his brain gushed out of his nostrils."[168] Armor, like the Irish warrior Ferdiad's "horn skin" or other protective coverings and presumed invulnerabilities, does not avail, regardless of the supposedly magical powers it or they may sometimes be invested with in this or that particular epic.[169]

The significance of the warrior's shield, on the other hand, can be usefully marked and multivalent. It is often paired with the sword: "with sword and shield" defines the warrior-hero prepared for the fray even after the horsed warrior or knight becomes the heroic norm; and as the Welsh Taliesin's *Cad Goddeu,* in similes, aligns the two in a heroic identification: "I was a sword in hand, I was a shield in battle."[170] Thus the shield bodies forth some of the personal identifying marks of the hero and will often become his alone. The trademarked shield is already hinted at in the *Iliad,* where Agamemnon lifts his great shield, many-ringed and bossed with twenty bosses, and bearing the Gorgon's head "and about her Terror and Rout," which clearly demonstrates the Achaean king's own protoheraldic device— and we won't even speak of Akhilleus's divinely crafted, mythologically oriented shield.[171] The greatest display of shield devices in ancient Greek literature probably appears in the expanded Theban *muthos;* there is no certainty but a strong likelihood that the symbol-laden shields displayed in Aeschylus's *Seven against Thebes* betray an origin in the epical sources of this conflict, however reworked by the dramatist. Evidence from ancient Greek vase paintings supports this contention.[172]

In the Old Irish narratives shields are often described: Lugh mac Ethenn (the god who was Cú Chulainn's divine father) has "a knob of gold on his black shield" while other warriors have "curved scallop-edged shields" or shields "graven with gold animals." All these are formulaic descriptions.[173] Cú Chulainn and his great opponent Ferdiad are given multiple shields in the *Táin,* as they also carry dramatically multiplied weapons; these greatest of heroes escape the normal with their "two feat-playing shields" and "eight shields with sharp rims," as the bard enlarges his theme of epic battle past all ordinary restrictive bounds.[174] Some of these shields are themselves "death dealing," not defensive but anomalously offensive, and thus they are given a place both in battle and in the hero's "feats," as when the athletic Cú Chulainn leaps onto the shield rim of Ferdiad and is effortlessly shaken off by his opponent.[175] Yet shields have no special place in another Celtic context, in the mythological-magical field spread out in the Welsh *mabinogi*, though they are at least mentioned there.[176] They are of more importance in the sagas, at least to the extent that the skalds address "shield songs" to them, and so use the fighter's shield as an excuse for verbal-poetic displays.[177] Elsewhere in the epical frame the Iranian heroes, who are bow masters as well as hand fighters, make little of the shield, though Rostam and his son Sohrâb are both protected by "leopard-skin shields," which are not elaborated on. Possibly the wild-animal skin was imagined to have a magical-prophylactic power here in old Persia.[178]

When at last we pursue the shield as heroic adjunct into the range of chivalric epic, it is notable that our first assay, of the *Chanson de Roland*, may betray a revivified Indo-European trifunctional schema. This work, like the *Iliad*, retains a hint of Dumézil's hypothesized interfunctional confrontation: the Franks are always roaring for grim war, whereas the wealthy Saracens are softer, less warlike, more committed to life and luxury (although individual pagan warriors may certainly be worthy opponents). This much is signified in the shields of the Saracens, as when their crystal or gold bosses are shattered by the war-fury of the Frankish paladins, or even more plainly when "Moriane's emir receives Duke Samson's charge" and "flowers and gold will not defend his shield."[179] The emir's device (if, as I feel certain, a shield device is indeed being described here) casts him circumstantially into a derogated, "rich" Third Function, and this derogation is seen elsewhere in the French epical cycles, as when in *Raoul de Cambrai* the ferocious old warrior Guerri the Red hewed at Ernaut and "scattered the flowers and precious stones" decorating his armor.[180] Beyond the early medieval epic the shield is increasingly involved in both personal and perhaps symbolic identification, and shifts over to the true bourn of heraldry.

The hero's defensive armament ought to project and reflect his glittering persona and to increase his visual effect (and, of course, display the developed word skills of the bard or epic poet). The high and terrible crests of the Homeric warriors, their gleaming bronze corselets, and even their leg armor (thus the "well-greaved Achaeans") are part of a warrior's costume made spectacular and aweful, and only the egregious "warrior of reversal" is other than physically impressive in body and equipage. Very often, however, the magnificence of the warrior's carapace is so fully described because it will soon tumble clashing into the bloody dust, like that of the greatest of the *Iliad*'s fated combatants, Hektor *koruthaiolos*, "of the flashing helm" (XI.315).

The defensive shield or other protection always gives way to the sword in the violent heat and percussive beat of the heroic narrative.

THE RITES OF COMBAT

The clash of arms is what the warrior-hero is made and imagined for; it is what he stands for in several senses of that verb. The hero's gestic vocabulary is not completely exhausted by these spasms of duel and onset and battle, but he is obviously and often an actor here, in confrontational circumstances I have roughly divided into five scenes or tropes.

The Presentation of the Opponents

The first and most important desideratum in combat is *worthiness*, for just as in sacrifice (to which this ritual of blood is closely and clearly related), the opponent/victim must be worth fighting: he must be judged to be some sort of equal to the hero in essential warriorhood. Even monstrous, animalized, or ogrish half men, relict of myth or folktale, are still regarded as worthy battle opponents, and indeed a hero may gain even more credit by opposing and defeating them. Those who are not considered worthy to take part in the deadly game are only rarely named, probably because they are literally nonentities, and so are quite outside the frame of the heroic narrative. The Georgian *Lord* remarks in passing that peasants do not concern themselves in war; nor, according to the same source, do traders or merchants.[181] An offer by the loyal lower classes to take part with the Serbian Moslem *bulyukbašas* in a great border expedition is more or less politely declined in one of the Serbo-Croat heroic songs.[182] The great majority of hero tales have no place for the mass of the people (the Norse-Icelandic sagas present a special problem here, coming as they do from a small and relatively unstratified population, and a "republican" tradition that, perhaps ingenuously, stressed social equality). True, when heroes meet, they sometimes levy the most fearful charges against one another, even of low birth, illegitimacy, and unheroic behavior of every sort including cowardice. But it seems to be accepted that if a man enters this "flyting" contest (of which I will have more to say in the next section), he has the right to do so; he is already deemed worthy to take part either in word combat *or* in weapon play.

The mutual recognition of the opponents, and their worthiness to act the warrior (or to die), may be decorated in various ways, but afterward the fate of the players, and especially of the central player or hero, rests in the narrative itself, and in an unfolding often already known to the hearers of the heroic tale. Patroklos will meet Hektor, and Hektor Akhilleus; Gísli and Grettir the Strong will be pulled down by implacable feud enemies in their sagas, while Gunnarr Hámundarsson, surrounded and betrayed, will finally be slain in the first part of the *Njála:* all these ends are well known. Roland and his men will perish at Roncevalles; the knightly followers of Gunther will die in a welter of blood and broken helmets at Etzel's court. If the heroic tale falls into the category of a fatal death-drama, all confrontations must build to the downfall of the central figure or figures. At the same time, however, the epic poet, for his own creative sense purposes, may begin his tale *in medias res:* my Cid rides through the gates of Bivar on his way to an undeserved exile; Chalemagne has long been at war in Spain; the Achaeans have fought for years before the walls of Troy; but all the chief personalities must still be made recognizable and must be recognized by the auditors. The players must be posed, not merely poised, before the fury of the action begins and swiftly overtakes everything.

The Power of Blood

This pose or presentation is all the more necessary because of what can happen in the heroic narrative once combat has been joined, especially once the battle fury seizes the fighters. *Furor, ferg, wut, margon* or *aristeia, berserksgangr* all signify that the warrior-hero is out of control, has escaped the set limits of combat conducted as a ritual, and may have passed into a killing trance, quite possibly to the point where he cannot distinguish between friend and foe, or kinsman and nonkinsman.

In its most extreme morphism the *furor* even changes the physical form of the warrior; Dumézil acutely described it as "une sorte de démonophane" on the battlefield.[183] Seized up in this demonic state, the champion Cú Chulainn undergoes what Kinsella translates as his "warp-spasm," a complete and grotesque distortion of his bodily integrity. "The first warp-spasm seized Cú Chulainn, and made him into a monstrous thing, hideous and shapeless, unheard of"—a depiction ending as "a straight spout of black blood darkly and magically smoking" shoots upward from the top of his skull, for the very surge of blood in his heroic veins cannot be contained by his body.[184] Later, in the great duel with Ferdiad, Cú Chulainn's warp-spasm is triggered both by criticism from his own charioteer, Laeg, and by Ferdiad's obviously equal prowess, and so he "blew up and swelled . . . bent himself in a fearful hideous arch, mottled and terrifying, and the huge high hero loomed straight up over Ferdia"; his rage-fed distortion is such that his youthful stature (earlier his opponent Ferdiad had tossed him off his shield "like a little boy") is gigantified, made monstrous.[185] How can Ferdiad stand against this transformed hero, even with his own "horn skin and red rage"?[186] Lesser distortions in other epical contexts are still remarkable, as when the Moslem Serb hero Meho is seized with irrepressible anger: "my heart danced," he says, "and my breastplate shattered."[187] Hektor in a battle rage ("gone berserk," *mainetai*) foams at the mouth and his eyes blaze fire (*Il.* XV.608ff.). Even the tighter and more laconic narrative atmosphere of the sagas betrays some evidence of these perturbations: besides the frequent appearance of *berserkir* in a number of sagas, we find Egill Skallagrímsson's less controlled kinsmen described as "frenzied" (*homoðisk*) when they undertake a murderous revenge, and Egill himself distorts his appearance (probably in imitation of one-eyed Óðinn), just as he "swells" with grief at the death of his son Boðvarr.[188] And in the *Njála*, when Þorhall Ásgrimsson, Njál's foster son, heard of the Burning, his body swelled and blood burst from his ears.[189]

Beyond these fantastic or hyperdramatized images is the plain edge of that bloodlust that can impel the hero past any set limit—any ritual or customary control of warrior violence—with the result that his own people, or indeed his family, can be at risk. Even undisturbed or unwarped, Cú Chulainn's nature is so aggressive that anyone in his path may be severely damaged: "A man in a chariot advancing upon us," reports the watcher in Emain Macha. "He'll spill the blood of the whole court unless you see to him and send naked women to meet him."[190] The women of Ulster's King Conchobar's court are called to bare their breasts at the hero (which shames and "detoxifies" him); he is then doused in three vats of cold water until his extraordinary calor is cooled and he can safely be received among his own Ulster folk. The Achaean hero Diomedes, who occasionally bears the accolade "best of the Achaeans" and who is a son of the ferocious Tydeus, will assault the gods themselves if they happen to be in his war path, as in book V of the *Iliad*, when he wounds divine Aphrodite (335ff.). Fleeing, the goddess complains to Ares that Diomedes "would now fight even with Father Zeus," and indeed when the furious hero meets Zeus's son Ares a little later (855ff.), he spears *him*, though admittedly the goddess Athena has a sly part in this affray.

Such uncontrolled aggressiveness makes all the more amazing Diomedes' polite and restrained encounter with the Trojan Glaukos in the next book of the epic (VI.119ff.): each is a guest-friend whom the other is forbidden to slay. Michael Nagler has examined this incident, along with a number of others from the collected epical evidence, extracting, among other violent themes, one "on almost killing your friends."[191] He locates a case (in von Eschenbach's *Parzifal*) in which the hero, after his achievement of knightly status, more or less innocently makes a career of assaulting his relatives; [192] and in the massive Indic epic *Mahâbhârata* the supreme warrior-hero Arjuna recognizes that battle can only be joined and finally won at the "price of . . . all kinds of kin."[193] Can heroic bloodshed be limited, especially when it might involve the enormity of kin slaying? It seems not, given the nearly invariant inner nature of the warrior—and therefore, as Nagler sees it, several traditions try to convert warfare, or inhibit violence, by interpolating a stronger ritual function, especially the blood-ritual of sacrifice.[194]

Yet any control over the warrior, societal or self-induced, is tentative and fragile; and once he is fully launched into the ruck and risks of combat, his sacred rage may make nothing of other sacralities, even including the kin or blood tie. Thus when the warrior is faced with an opponent whom we, by way of the epic narrator, know to be some sort of real or classificatory kinsman, three possibilities are available: (1) the kin tie or *philia* is recognized, as with Glaukos and Diomedes, and combat is avoided; (2) the tie goes unrecognized, and the death of either fighter brings an ultimate pollution discovered later; (3) the tie is known but the fight goes on anyway. Cú Chulainn recognizes his son Connla, but he must kill him nevertheless "for the honor of Ulster."[195] Polyneikes and Eteokles spear each other and bring to a bloody end the terrible persistent anger that indelibly marks the line of Oedipus. In the hero tale the unthinkable is doable, and ever is done.[196]

Death and Dying

The mutual slaying of brother by brother at the end of the expedition of the Seven against Thebes is called a suicide, *autoktonos*, by the poet Aeschylus.[197] Beyond that mythically prepotent instance the warrior's epic tale often displays well-marked evidence that its hero is playing out a suicidal scenario, that he has devised or accepted a confrontation from which he cannot possibly escape alive. In terms of a ritual of sacrifice he presents himself as victim, but he will not go quietly, and most often he will not go alone; the hero is dangerous to be around at this moment, and not just to his enemies. In the *Chanson de Roland* the song's hero dooms himself and his men: Olivier says,

> The pagan might is great
> It seems to me our Franks are very few!
> Roland, my friend it's time to sound your horn.[198]

To which the hero replies,

> You must think I've gone mad!
> In all sweet France I'd forfeit my good name!
> No! I will strike great blows with Durendal."

All is summed up in a laisse not much farther on: "Roland's a hero and Olivier is wise" (*Rodlanz est proz ed Oliviers est sages*) though the epic's poet is most probably revealing in this line a resonance of the old theme of the two "heroic partners," like Cei and Bedwyr or Diomedes and Odysseus. We see that Olivier's reputed wisdom has no effect on his friend, although again (in laisse CXXVIII, line 1693) Roland, looking out over bloody disaster, asks Olivier what his counsel might be, and is told in succeeding laisses that his "blind pride" will kill all of them and that second thoughts are impossible: "we are all the victims of your great prowess now!"[199] Any final remorse on Roland's part, though the poem may suggest it, does not set aside or mitigate the effectively suicidal pose he has assumed, with the death of all who stand with him as he takes *his* last stand.

Given the rules (in fact, the unwritten law) governing Icelandic feuds, decisions made by certain saga heroes must also be counted as suicidal in intent. Gísli, Grettir, and Gunnarr have been mentioned earlier; each, having been outlawed (in the most severe degree of outlawry), could only save himself by flight from Iceland, yet each of them rejects such a flight. They are then brought to bay by enemies acting ostensibly in the name of ordered society and its rules, and the sagas can ring unexpectedly subtle changes on this theme. A man like Gísli may emerge as what Theodore Andersson calls "the well-known protagonist of heroic poetry who knows his fate and acquires his stature by standing against it."[200] And Gísli (who is, after all, certainly guilty of a reprehensible secret murder, whatever his excuse for this ugly deed) is not only a subject of the powerfully individualizing impulse of the heroic tale, but is himself equipped with the poetic skills to create his own poetic commentary on his opponents and on his doom:

> I fought a lone fateful
> Fight, this was my nightmare
> Single, not soon was I
> slain by their main power.[201]

Armed with his skaldic gifts, Gísli establishes his superiority over the many enemies who finally bring him down; and through his errant self-will (which effectively caused his death) and his personal prowess he escapes the ordinary constrictions of the social framework. His death, and to some extent Grettir's, is an elevated suicide, and a commentary as well on the way the word-gifted hero stands against society considered as a mass—and against the law or rule of that mass.

Hagen, in the *Nibelungenlied*, is another warrior whose very nature inclines or pushes a narrative toward destruction: once he has injected his bloodthirsty will into the tale, the term "fatality" takes on a new and doubled significance. The Norse *sagamenn*, too, display various kinds and subtypes of the heroic protagonist-as-suicide: Þorgeirr Hávarsson of *Fostbrœðra saga* is a warrior whose sheer aggressiveness against a whole series of individuals—against "the community at large," in Andersson's view—must finally result in his death.[202] Ferocious Þorgeirr is only marginally different from that saga type the *ójafnaðarmaðr*, the sociopathic "man of violent injustice," compulsively devoted to anti-social acts and obsessive troublemaking. This ornery, destructive type is more perverse and more complex than the *berserkr*, but makes a bridge to that animalized, asocial persona, one seemingly bereft of thought itself, and therefore suicidal in a special and mindless sense.

Victory and Mercy

If the hero triumphs over someone nearly equal to himself, he may perhaps assume a chivalric stance, pitying the ill fortune of the fallen or regretting the confrontation that took the opponent's life—though we need not expect much of this gallant behavior in the merciless *Iliad*, where *peithos* or pity is overwhelmed and any fallen foe is exulted over without apology. "But for you," Hektor says to the dying Patroklos, "vultures will eat you here" (XVI.836); Idomeneos mocks a dying enemy, Othryoneos (XIII.374ff.); and of course Akhilleus, in his turn, "exulted" over Hektor, twice promising his antagonist that "dogs and birds shall rend you apart" (XXII.330, 335–36, 353). The more intransigent of the Norse saga heroes is only a little less exultant over the bodies of fallen foes, though they often prefer a well-crafted poetic sendoff, as when Egill trenchantly refers to "The leg of Ljótur / Lanced off by the bard";[203] or, as Grettir the Strong describes the end of his enemy Þorbjorn Oxen-Might:

> The "Oxen-Might" showed
> His last insolence . . .

Þorbjorn got his reward
When he embraced the fair earth.[204]

But other heroic contexts express more pity, or at least some small regret, for the fallen enemy. King Gunther in the *Nibelungenlied* can regret the fate of his brother, just cut down by Rudiger, and yet even he can note of that opponent, when he is finally slain in his turn, "I shall always mourn for noble Rudiger." (We would not encounter such chivalric softness from red-raging Hagen of Troneck.)[205] The Old Irish *Táin* describes at length Cú Chulainn grieving over the body of Ferdiad, whom he had (unfairly) killed with his sinister and ultimate trick of the *Gae Bolga:* "Alas Ferdia! Woe for you." and "You have fallen to the Hound / I cry for it, little calf / The shield didn't save you / That you brought to the fray."[206] Ferdiad was Cú Chulainn's foster-brother, a classificatory kinsman, as Kjartan was the *fostbroðr* of Bolli in *Laxdæla saga;* after he had given Kjartan his death wound, Bolli "at once regretted bitterly what he had done."[207] In the *Shâh-nâma* the death of the Turanian champion Forud is mourned by the Iranians, but then Forud was one-quarter Persian.[208] There are the occasional "good Saracens" in the *chansons de geste,* like Ferragu, who is *Saracins frere* to Roland in the *Entrée d'Espagne*—but Roland still tricks and kills him. (In the chivalric confrontation between Renouart and the Saracen Loquifer, each defends his own faith and respects the prowess of the other—but Rainouart is a comic character.)[209]

Why will different epic-heroic traditions allow different attitudes toward a fallen or slain enemy? The open, ferocious Homeric exultation over a foe might seem to support the idea of the survival of "primitive" elements in the poem, a notion evoked by other barbarities in the *Iliad,* such as the mutilation of a slain enemy's body, head taking, and even the suggestion of cannibalism. Another possibility, one I find tempting and even persuasive, is that the violent antipathy shown to the dead in the *Iliad* tends to support the idea that a mythogenetic Indo-European interfunctional war is presented here in this epic in some significant remnant. The two warring groups are not, despite their similarities, merely players in the *agôn* of war; each is regarded as essentially "other," in Functional terms, with the Achaeans representing pitiless war and the bloodthirst of the Second Function, and the warriors of Ilium acting from and defending the softer place, the comity and *richesse* of the Third Function.[210] The situation in the sagas is rather more complicated. Egill and Grettir are not what we would call gentlemen, and it isn't expected that they, in their narratives, will act like gentlemen;

they both are warrior-skalds and they, especially Egill, have a strongly marked tricksterish tint or taint about them; the *sagamaðr* allows them un-fettered, even perverse personalities, and a free rein to express their fierce and open delight in the death of their foes. Another kind of Óðinnic in-fluence may emerge in these two: that perception of the dark and enigmatic god who apportions destruction however he wills, or who withdraws his favor whenever he sees fit. Thus they use Óðinn's gift to celebrate their own, perhaps temporary, survival, and another's fall. In contrast, *Laxdæla*'s nar-rative is permeated with a more romantic-chivalric viewpoint, and Oláfr pái and his son and foster son are drawn as more knightly figures;[211] and in our other examples, the chivalric view of the equality of combatants is more or less implicit: the opponents face one another in a deadly game with equal players—an attitude that can occasionally penetrate even to the duels of Saracen and Christian.

There may be a ritualized release or "break" in the epic violence, when one combatant, obviously defeated, asks for and receives mercy from the victor. Or not. Such an event almost happens even in the bloody *Iliad:* "but Adrastos did Menelaus take alive," because the Trojan, trapped and fallen, "clasped him by the knees" (VI.37, 45). Menelaus, however, is only briefly beguiled by a faint access of mercy; brother Agamemnon interferes, Mene-laus pushes Adrastos away, and Agamemnon spears the suppliant (62–63). The appeal "to the knees," even better known in the Roman context in which the knees also serve as a sign of life and generation, is unsuccessfully put forward by Hektor (*Il.* XXII.338), when he implores the bitter killer Akhilleus "by your life and knees and begetters" (*huper psukhês kai gounôn sôn te tokêôn*). When Diomedes and Odysseus bring Dolon to bay and the terrified spy begs for mercy, he promises them a rich ransom; but after the two Achaeans, and especially wily Odysseus, strip him of whatever infor-mation he has on the battle dispositions of the Trojans, another plea is cut short by Diomedes' sword.[212] The *Aeneid*, tending as it does to echo Iliadic attitudes, is no more merciful: Liger pleads but Aeneas refuses: ("die, don't desert your dead brother," *morere et fratrem ne desere frater*).[213] Nor does the Roman hero show any mercy to defeated Magus, who also "embraced his knees" (*genua amplectens*).[214]

Ordinarily, the grounding of weapons by one opponent is meant to acti-vate the merciful generosity of the recognized victor: the "game" is acknowl-edged to be lost. Occasionally this outcome is actually recorded in the epic, as in the *mabinogi Lludd ac Lleuelys*, when a monstrous visitor, defeated by Lludd, "sought protection from him."[215] Peredur, in the Welsh genesis tale of the Graal narrative sequence, overthrows knight after knight, and after them he faces an armed and armored witch-hag who, defeated, delivers the proper formula: "Thy mercy . . . and the mercy of God!"[216] The Irish Celtic evidence, on the other hand, strongly deprecates any request for quarter: it is "womanly" and cowardly and has no place in a proper warrior's behavior.[217] In the *Nibelungenlied* Siegfried wounds and grants mercy to the Danish King Luidegast, though the inhabitants of this epic are not noted otherwise for their chivalric behavior.[218]

A knightly man may also take the unhorsing of an opponent as a plea for mercy, though unspoken. In Chrétien de Troyes's *Erec et Enide,* Erec confronts a foe who, knowing he cannot fight the hero, throws away shield and lance and hurriedly dismounts, and Eric "no longer cared to pursue him."[219] Similarly in the *Shâh-nâma,* when Rostam had overthrown the demon-warrior Pulâdvand, "the links of his spirit" were clearly seen to be broken, and the greatest Iranian epic hero can thereafter ignore him.[220] Yet Rostam had just slain a captured and helpless enemy, a Koshani.[221] Knightly mercy, it seems, can never be taken for granted, and at any given time or place the epic poets may always exalt heroic mercilessness.

Prize and Trophy

The complex of gestures that proves an epic victory very often includes the despoiling of the victim. In fact we can descry at least four stages in claiming or advertising the defeat of a foe: (1) defeated, yet still alive, the opponent surrenders his warrior's weapons and gear to the winner; (2) dead, the loser's equipment falls to the victor by right; (3) the possession of the stripped body of a foe is taken as an additional sign of triumph over the fallen; (4) the removal of the head of the corpse as a trophy provides a final proof of victory, a widely seen barbarity almost certainly quasi-magical in origin. (Most of these possibilities already occur in the *Iliad.*) I suggest that the deep structure of this sequence can be traced as follows: removal of the signs of warrior status, especially weapons (thus signing the foe's "social death"?); physical death and the concomitant removal of those signs, over which the dead now have no control; removal or abstraction of the body (forgoing the normative postmortem, honorable disposal, and social treatment of the dead); mutilation or animalization, when most of the body is treated as carrion but the head continues to be identifiable, individual, and probably perceived as a powerful relic.

As we have seen, the exterior, usually decorative carapace, the hero's uniform and mark, along with the primary weapons of the warrior, is regarded as differentiating and individualizing. The *Iliad,* with its plethora of combats, slayings, and victories is full of minor variations on stage (2) and (3), the seizing of armor and the dead body, beginning when Menelaus throws the helmet of Paris-Alexandros, clearly a victor's spoil, to his men (III.369ff.). The phrase "despoil him of armor," *teukhe esula,* is frequently set into the poem, and especially into the long segment describing the death of Patroklos and the series of confrontations between Achaeans and Trojans over his corpse in books XVI–XVIII.[222] This sequence begins with Hektor and Patroklos contesting the dead body of Hektor's charioteer Kebriones, Hektor at the head and Patroklos grasping the foot, in a ghastly tug-of-war (XVI.762–63). After Patroklos is speared, first by Euphorbos and then by Hektor (XVI.806–29), Menelaus guards Patroklos's body for a time (and kills Euphorbos, who evidently tried to claim it, XVII.3ff), initiating a veritable beggar-my-neighbor series of attempts to take the armor of the slain. Hektor finally gains the armor but is cheated of the head; and the Trojan Glaukos (the erstwhile chivalric opponent of Diomedes) chides Hektor for so softly giving way and abandoning the chance of trading Patroklos's body for the armor and corpse of his own close companion, the late Sarpedon (125–26, 162–63). So it continues, the poet's narrative almost transfixed on the *enara brotoenta . . . haimatoeis,* the "bloody spoils" of this or that dead warrior. The sequence extends to the very end of book XVII—when it is time for Akhilleus's terrible revenge and the spoiling of Hektor's corpse. The Virgilian *Aeneid,* again, echoes the Iliadic custom of spoiling or stripping the warrior, as when the arms of great Mezentius are set up by Aeneas as a *tropeaeum,* or Pallas's spear and helmet are carried in his funeral cortege, but his killer, Turnus, had taken "the rest."[223]

In the North, *Beowulf* instances the stripping off of a fallen foe's accoutrements (2985ff.), while the later chivalric medieval epic narratives are full of the lifting of the armor of the defeated. A useful if anomalous example occurs in the Welsh romance "The Lady of the Fountain," in which Owein and Gwalchmei (the Continental Gawain) joust furiously but no clear victory can be claimed; at last each courteously insists that the other is the victor, and so should have "my sword and armour."[224] The recovery of the body of a leader's corpse is also mooted in the *Nibelungenlied:* the vassals of Etzel ask for the body of Rudiger "dead as he is," but the savage Burgundian knight Volker the Fiddler will not allow this. "Come and get him" (*Nemt in*) is the coarse reply, and more sanguinary swordplay and noisy helmet-smashing naturally ensue.[225]

To preserve the corpses of one's own warriors, for whatever appropriate funeral ceremonies, is a matter of great moment in the *Iliad;* the obverse is that an enemy's body should rightly (or "naturally") be kept from that sacred ritual, that one ought to "work shame upon his body" (XVI.559) and "feed dogs and birds" with it. This may not be as barbaric as it seems, at least to our eyes; in any case heroic head taking, with its range of causes and valences, is a recurring theme in the epic literature. We have already noted the beheading of Dolon, the "trickster," whose unfortunate story (and the head-hunting theme) is elaborated in Euripedes' *Rhesus*, where Dolon, setting off to spy out the Achaeans' ships, brags that he will return "with slain Odysseus's head"—or that of Diomedes.[226] At another point in the *Iliad* the warrior Pindaros says "may some alien take my head from me" if he does not fulfil a vow (V.215). The *Aeneid* implies that such trophy taking is more likely done by the ferocious Turnus, who in fact takes heads on two occasions.[227] In the bloody *Nibelungenlied* Kriemhilde wants Hagen's head, and offers to reward whoever brings it to her: *unde mîr sin houbet her für mich trüege*.[228] In the Russo-Slavic *byliny* the hero Il'ya of Murom is said to take heads,[229] and head taking appears even in the relatively chivalric air of the Persian *Shâh-nâma*, where the Iranian Bizhan kills and decapitates the Turanian warrior Palâshân and takes the head back to Giv, the victor's father, who had expressed some doubt about his son's warlike abilities.[230] Indeed the threat, at least, of beheading is seen even in the Old French *Raoul de Cambrai*, where an enraged Gautier wants to behead Bernier, and in Chrétien de Troyes's *Erec et Enide* (Erec is insulted by a knight, defeats him, and "would have cut off his head"—but at last forbears).[231]

The slayers of Grettir the Strong, in his saga, take his head; he was an outlaw and there was a price on it, but no honor is said to have come to the man who did this deed.[232] Beheading is also seen in the sagas as a mode of execution (as in *Jómsvíkingasaga*), and, more significantly, as a kind of super–slaying ritual when the opponent is one of the undead-dead, like a *haugr* guarding his howe and its contents. Grettir the Strong himself dealt with Kar the Old in this way; Ásmunðr must rekill his erstwhile comrade Aran in the adventure tale "Egill ok Ásmunðr"; and we can cite as well the strange case of King Oláfr Geirstadsaalfr of Vestfold, another lively howe dweller.[233] In *Gislis saga* the young Gisli takes the head of a feud enemy after killing him, and there is the faint trace of a "ritual" beheading here. Gisli had previously hewed off the man's leg in a duel; the defeated opponent, Skeggi of Saxa, had then gathered men and burnt out Gisli and his family, killing some dependents; so "this time" Gisli took his enemy's head, presumably to make an end of the feud.[234]

The Celtic warrior-heroes, however, are by far the greatest head takers, and beheadings great and small are crowded into the Old Irish cycles. Here the head is clearly the mark and trophy of victory, the place where the iden-

tity of the dead warrior was seated, and presumably where some power—
for good or ill—still was felt to supersist. One old tale included in the
Ulster Cycle tells us that the men of Ulster used to "cut off the tip of the
tongue of a foe whom [they] had killed" and keep it in a pouch, to be enumerated and bragged over later.[235] (Such a practice, though it may be only
a poet's conceit, was certainly handier than collecting the whole head, and
must be connected, as fact or legendary factoid, to the old Celtic belief that
true "life," fully human vitality, was surely expressed in "speech": the dead
warriors resuscitated in those magical Welsh cauldrons of Regeneration
could fight but not speak.)[236] Heads, nevertheless, taken in the usual blithe
Celtic fashion, were the great battle prize. Cú Chulainn is the champion in
this as in other warriorly deeds: the celebration of his *macgnimartha* or
"boyhood deeds" tells us that he, as a mere child, had already cut off the
heads of grown warriors for his trophies.[237] In the *Mesca Ulad* (The Intox-
ication of the Ulstermen), Cú Chulainn slew Crimthanu Nia Nair "and
carried away his head and his gear," while in the great combats and broils
of *Fled Bricrend* (Bricriu's feast) this peerless warrior killed "three nines"
and made a cairn of their relics, of "heads and goods."[238] The *Táin* is full
of these decapitations: Cú Chulainn decorates a tree fork with four heads,
or slays and takes heads at the ford so baneful for Eirenn.[239] Then he will
kill the fabulous warrior Cú Roi mac Dairi himself and behead him; and,
outside the bounds of the *Táin*, he will himself be finally slain by Cú Roi's
son Lugaid, and his own head removed in its turn.[240]

Other Irish tales of confrontation or revenge contain the same theme:
we see Conaire the king beheaded at Da Derga's hostel and the champion
Mac Cecht avenging him by killing and beheading those responsible, or
The Pursuit of Diarmuid and Gráinme in the Fenian Cycle, where the full
revenge of old Finn demands young Diarmuid's head.[241] Perhaps the grimmest tale, *Scéla Mucce Meic Dathó*, which translates as a misleadingly anec-
dotal *The Story of Mac Datho's Pig*, concerns a feast and the great dispute
waged there over the champion's portion, the tidbit of meat to be claimed
by the best warrior in hall. The bullying Connachtman Cet mac Matach
puts down the claimant Munremur mac Gerreind by reminding him that
he (Cet) had taken three heads of Munremur's warriors "together with the
head of thy firstborn son," but Cet is humbled himself by the entrance of
Conall the Victorious.[242] "I have never," says Conall, "slept without the head
of a Connachtman under my knee." Cet then gives way, but in bad grace,
petulantly referring to his big brother: "but if Anluan mac Matach were in
the house" Conall would meet his match. "He is," is Conall's reply, and

throws Anluan's severed head at his brother.[243] With this condign bully's reward and this enormity we can leave the Celts and their heroic head-taking obsession—except to note that the Celtic view of the head trophy does *not* animalize the foe: he (or it) retains some human spark, which makes for its greater value. If Strabo and other contemporary observers and recorders were correct, the continental Celts carefully preserved the heads of great foes to grace the homes of the prominent warrior or chieftain.[244] According to one of their beliefs, the heads of extremely powerful individuals might retain their potency—and even, in legend, the power of speech—after decapitation. (See the story of King Conmaire Mor in *Da Derga's Hostel*, or the Welsh tale *Manawydan mab Llyr*, in which the talking head of Bran the Blessed [Bendigeidfan] is buried somewhere under London "with its face toward France" to protect the Briton realm.)[245]

A final note about decapitation concerns the practice as it is modified in other contexts, especially but not only in the chivalric romances, becoming part of a "game," and one with a strongly magical element. In the "head game" found in both the *Fled Bricrend* (in which Cú Chulainn again is involved) and *Sir Gawain and the Green Knight*, a monstrous or supernatural figure dominates the game, which is a supreme test of the truly heroic posture, a malignant twist on the old scenario of "blow for blow," which might be called "You take my head—then I'll take yours!" A later formulation intriguingly substitutes the beard for the head, either accentuating one aspect of the monstrous part of the contest or removing the contest entirely. In the *Tristan* of Thomas of Britain, an African giant named Orgillos boasts a "cloak of beards" provided by the notables he had slain; this may well be connected, however distantly, to the figure of Ogmundr Eythjolf's-Killer in the Norse romance saga and fantasy "Örvar-Oddr," for Ogmundr too has a cloak made up precisely in the same way, though his beards are taken "from all the kings east of the Baltic" as tribute.[246] We are also immediately reminded of *Culhwch ac Olwen*, where Dillus Farfawg's beard is shaved off while he is still alive by Cei and Bedwyr. (Dillus, it is implied, is another giant, for "the biggest hole in the world" is dug by the two to trap and hold him, unconscious, while his beard is removed.)[247] In fact, the major secondary goal of *Culhwch ac Olwen* is to obtain the instruments to "shave" Ysbadadden Chief-Giant, the maid Olwen's monster-father. Thus forcible shaving of an enemy's beard may precede decapitation, or be a shaming substitute for it.

In any case, the head taker is now a giant, or the act involves giants, as these are monsters, Otherworldly creatures, all in postures of threat. The bloody image of decapitation is both obscured and softened *and* mythicized; and the warrior's act is replaced by a dishonoring one that seems peculiarly inhuman.

THE HERO SPEAKS AT LAST

When the hero does speak, his speech has a peculiar—a violent—tone. "Verbal aggression" is now a more or less polite and even academic term for the substitution of verbal for physical violence, in a relatively ordered society fearful of and at the same time vulnerable to that violence. In the heroic milieu, however, speech (especially on the part of the hero) is an extension or a preparation for violence, not a substitute; and like the gestic plays and posturings just analyzed, it is often meant simply to identify its author. In our epic sources, speech as a mark of a true human intelligence, encompassing dialogue, rational argument, and the subtleties of communication, is usually left to a "tricksterish" adjunct of the hero—about whom we shall learn more in chapter 5.

Shout and Sound

The first vocal theme is the war cry, as the warrior announces his proud and hostile presence.[248] A garden-variety war cry is one thing (*boên agathos*, "good at the war cry," is usually or formulaically attached both to Menelaus [*Il.* II.585, IV.220, XVII.246] and to Diomedes [V.320, 347, 432]), but something more potent is also a part of the heroic vocabulary. Menelaus "utters a piercing shout" (*diaprusion:* XVII.246), and Odysseus does the same (XI.462);[249] Aeneas cries "a terrible cry" (*smerdalea iakhôn:* V.302); Akhilleus "shouts mightily" (*megal' iakhe:* XVIII.228); and Hektor's cry in battle has a hot, fiery quality, "like to the flame of Hephaistos that no man can quench" (XVII.88).[250] All these are terrible, daunting cries, whether they come from man or divinity, as witnessed by the fell goddess Eris's cry (XI.10).

What the cry says or "means" rarely needs to be glossed: the warrior's fearsome sound becomes a weapon in itself, as when the hero, in the Georgian epic, Tariel, gives mighty voice and "warriors dropped to the ground."[251] The Armenian tradition gives vent to an even deadlier vocality: as the hero David of Sassoon lies mortally wounded, his terrible dying cry kills his assailant—his own daughter.[252] The Irish *fían* produced an *esnad* or "hum," a threatening, wordless noise that seems to be the male warrior's virile counterpart to the wailing of women;[253] and the mighty Dietrich in the *Nibelungenlied* shouts "so that his voice resounded like a wisent-horn."[254] (More on this horn in a moment.) In the Old Russian *Slovo,* the *Song of Igor's Campaign,*[255] the men-at-arms of the ferocious Rurik "roar like wild bulls" (*rykauit', aky turi*) in fratricidal combat; and the images of the Persian *Shâhnâma* become even more baroque. Koshan "roared in a voice like a drumbeat" as he presented his boast and challenge; the Iranian hero Rahham "roared out and began to boil like the sea"; and the "elephant-bodied" Rostam advances, "roaring" (appropriately) "like an elephant enraged."[256]

As to the Celtic evidence, we first can cite historical fact according to Polybius, who reported that the Gaulish warriors worked up their martial spirit with horns and trumpets, with all the fighters "shouting together" or "giving the paean together" (*sumpaianizontos*) to create a screaming noise (*kraugên*) so extraordinary that it sounded as if "coming from the place [the earth?] itself."[257] From the extraordinary we move to the superhuman, for one of Cú Chulainn's special heroic feats is the "hero's scream": "he gave the hero's scream from his throat, so that devils and goblins of the glen and fiends of the air replied, so hideous was the call he uttered on high."[258] Such a cry has gone beyond any human zone, to draw on and affect the supernatural realm. Another such magical shout is threatened by Culhwch at Arthur's gate, when he says that he will "raise three shouts" audible from Cornwall to Ireland, so that "all the women in the court that are pregnant will abort" and those women not pregnant will become sterile.[259] (But another Celtic hero, Noisiu, perversely boasts a war cry "which gave pleasure to all who heard it" and made the cows of the realm give two-thirds more milk!)[260]

Shouts may be either percussive or piercing. (The latter dominate in the *Iliad,* whose war cries are akin to the flung spear that finds and transfixes the well-cuirassed bodies and loosens the knees of stricken heroes.) Cries resembling those of animals or the potencies of nature are also common: thunder, the crashing of the sea, or the trumpeting of the elephant above. The Celtic warrior's cry may even reach beyond the natural world itself, to agitate the Otherworld and supernaturally affect those who hear it. Then there is the horn.

In the Welsh *Culhwch ac Olwen* three hunters are described whose blown horns are combined with the shouts of their family and followers "until no one could care if the sky fell in on the earth";[261] and in the *Nibelungenlied,* as we have already seen, Dietrich makes a sound so loud that it might be mistaken for a horn. Thus the natural (or unnatural) human voice is transferred to another adjunct of the hero: his horn. The most famous of these, Roland's oliphant, has a central place in his last battle because Roland refuses to sound it until too late—at which point his mighty effort in blowing it is described in two successive laisses.[262] It is broken in Roland's final moments of life. In the Norse-Icelandic *Hamoðismál* the horn's power to cut through the casual feasters' noise "in hall" is explicit ("Til the warrior hardy sounded his horn," *aðr hair hugfullr i horn um paut*);[263] and the "horn of challenge" is commonly or formulaically encountered in later chivalric narratives: hung at a convenient spot, it is sounded to announce that some knight errant has stopped by, ready to fight the horn's owner.

What is signified in the hero's shout? If the human voice (as the Celts appear to believe) carries the proof of intelligence and therefore of a living vitality specific to humanity, the warrior's shout announces a retrograde act, moving back or down into animality or even into the inanimate (a drum-beat, the sound of the sea). At the same time it may be an instrument, essentially a weapon, piercing the air and the ear, and as such it is an individual projection of the hero's own mixture of hostility, threat, presumption, and declared proof of his overwhelming persona. Consider the particularity of the short Welsh tale "Lludd ac Lleulys," in which three mischiefs or oppressions afflict the Isle of Britain. Dumézil has shown that these three *fléaux* (*gormes* in the Welsh) carry a trifunctional valence.[264] The second oppression, corresponding to collective images of the second function, consists of a terrible battle between two dragons, one "of the Isle" and one foreign, the former crying such a terrible cry that "men lost their color and their strength, woman miscarried, sons and daughters lost their senses, and all animals, forests, earth and waters were left barren."[265] The cure for this disaster was to bait a trap for the multiform monsters, to capture them (in the shape of "two young pigs") and secure them in a stone chest "in the strongest place you can find in [the] kingdom," after which "no oppression shall visit the isle of Britain from another place."[266]

This Welsh narrative, dense in allusion and in fragmentary, archaic signs (the dragons appear on the Celtic holy day of *Beltain* or May Even, and the two young pigs surely connect to an ancient Celtic cult), presents a highly original critique of the hero-warrior and a solution to his perennial threat, here projected in and by the "terrible cry."[267] Uncontrolled, the destructive potentiality of his Function wreaks havoc in his own society, and terror and barrenness follow. Controlled, enclosed, and muted, his martial force acts as a prophylactic against foreign threat. The war shout (or "dragon's cry") is potentially as dangerous or aidful as the warrior's sword—or its wielder.

Boast and Challenge

The overall pattern of this indubitably heroic activity presents a central or typical exchange, thematic variations of which will be shaped by variations in the calculus of heroic identification (of both self and opponent) and of the special potencies encased in different heroic-epic traditions. For example, the Old French *chansons de geste,* drawn out of the conflict between the Moslem and Christian worlds, rarely present a clear contest of boasts and challenges, because our sources cannot accept the essential equality of the combatants. The Saracen enemy is so often converted into an ogrish or near ogrish figure that the tension between fighters equal in their essence is usually lost. Bragging or boasting on one side, the Saracen is aligned only with "that hideous strength," or with an impressive if barely martial display or superiority in numbers, in contrast to the spare (and laconic) Christian knight. "It would seem," says Olivier in the *Chanson de Roland* as he faces overwhelming numbers, "That we will have some Saracens to fight."[268] This epic is not generally known for its sense of ironical understatement.

In a very different category is the boasting among fellow warriors, a kind of preparatory ritual or game played with no serious thought of opposition or true confrontation. In a Serbo-Croat heroic song "the men of the border began their boasting, who had won the most combats . . . who had done the most to broaden the border . . . which family was better than another, which hero stronger than another" or "who was a better hero than another, who had killed more enemies or won more duels."[269] From these phrases two themes emerge: that the border warriors are equal ("you could not tell who was the best lord among them") and that this game of self-display strongly agitated the young hero Meho, who in fact had nothing as yet to brag of.[270] Because the heroic epic so frequently has a young man, the precocious hero-in-the-making, as its controlling figure, the boasting of others may isolate him and set up a contrast of youth and potentiality against the long and hard experience of older, more seasoned warriors. Another kind of verbal confrontation with an ascending level of violent possibility arises in the Old Irish *Scéla Mucce Meic Dathó.* Here the warriors again debate over the champion's portion: "Each of them brought up his exploits in the face of the other," and the Connachtman Cet mac Matach for a time carries all before him with his scornful boast that he has humiliated this or that fighter of Ulster.[271] (Cet, as we have seen, will finally be worsted by the tremendous Conall Cernach, who will triumphantly win and take the portion, which is merely a bit of meat, but meat richly flavored with honor.) In this case the verbal exchange only marginally or temporarily preempts the outbreak of sword play, for in fact the tale ends with a bloody battle royal between the hosts of "all the provinces of Ireland." Scandinavian feasting also can lead to "scenes of struggles of precedence, of boasting, which can quickly turn into quarrels," as in that mythical battle among the gods, the *Lokasenna*.[272]

The classic confrontation between heroic warrior and his counterpart, with the hyperbolic declaration of his own powers and prowess and the denigration of his opponent, may or may not give way to violence and the proving of one boast and boaster over the other. Beowulf is the target of Unferth's belittling insults in Hrothgar's hall (lines 506ff.), and the hero retaliates with a *gilp* or brag demonstrating his own prowess. He begins by mildly chiding Unferth for being drunk and ends by accusing him of kin murder (587–88), yet there is no movement by either of the two warriors toward further, physical aggression.[273] This soft (or at least nonphysical) ending occurs in hall; on the battlefield the passage from word to weapon play is much more likely. "Lionhearted chieftain," Esfandiyâr begins, most politely, to Rostam in the *Shâh-nâma*, "I have heard . . . that Dastân [Rostam's father] was of evil stock, born of a Div" and he proceeds to insult his opponent's antecedents in some detail.[274] Bloodshed follows. More simply, in the same epic, Palâshan declaims: "I am the lion-breaker, he that holds demons in thrall. Tell me plainly what your name is, for your star is about to shed tears over you." To this his opponent replies: "I am Bizhan. In battle I am an elephant with a body of bronze. . . . Even now I can perceive victory before me. . . . You will be eating smoke, ashes and blood."[275] The vaunting soon gives way to violent combat, which ends when the victorious Bizhan takes his fallen opponent's head. Another example from the Persian provides a somewhat less noble version of the warrior's brag: Juya (which means "Seeker," as in "Seeker after fame") is characterized as "a man of much talk" who cannot back up his brags; he is defeated by the peerless Rustam without much difficulty.[276]

The *Iliad*, of course, is rich in these ritualized challenges. In the climactic combats Akhilleus assaults Aeneas with his challenge, accusing him of standing forth so bravely because he hopes to inherit Priam's kingship, and reminding him of an earlier encounter, when Aeneas "ran headlong down from Ida's slopes"—and "you never looked back as you fled" (XX.188–89). To Hektor he is even more tersely sinister: "Come closer, so that you may the sooner be destroyed" (XX.929). The responses of both Aeneas and Hektor begin identically: "Don't think to frighten me with words as if I were a child; I too know how to make taunts and insulting speech . . ."[277] Aeneas goes on at some length, the gist of *his* speech being that each already knows well the other's history and parentage, and that bandying words like children or women does not suit a true warrior, whereas hand-to-hand fighting does. Hektor is briefer, and more resigned: their fates are "on the knees of the gods" (XX.435). Although the *Aeneid,* despite its Iliadic modeling, lacks this efflorescence of insult, we do have Turnus's contemptuous verbal attack on Aeneas as a "Phrygian eunuch" (*semi viri:* XII.371), which seems to echo the flyting speech of the Rutulian Numanus Remulus in book IX, who calls Aeneas's men the "twice-conquered Phrygians" or the "Phrygian women."[278]

The greatest flyting (mutual insult, or praise of oneself and contemptuous dispraise of the other) found in the Old Irish narratives introduces the combat between Cú Chulainn and his foster-brother and near double, Ferdiad, in the *Táin.*[279] Chanting alternately, the two praise themselves and dispraise the other. *Ferdiad:* "You'll regret you came / You're a fire without fuel." *Cú Chulainn:* "Like a great boar . . . I'll overwhelm you." *Ferdiad:* "It is I who will kill / I who will destroy / I who will drive Ulster's hero to flight." Despite all this, Cú Chulainn pleads with Ferdiad to forgo the combat, and is rejected: "Forget that we were foster brothers / Squinter, you are past help!"[280] Their duel, however, is a chivalric one, and evenly matched— until Cú Chulainn illicitly uses his deadly and secret weapon, the *gae bolga.*

In the *Táin Bó Cúalgne,* Cú Chulainn and Ferdiad are given a fitting poetic talent along with their superlative warriorhood, so that the preamble to their fight is artistically textured. In the Norse-Icelandic sagas boasting and ridicule are also often assigned to those with a skaldic gift, and verbal assault and invective take on the marks of a complexly articulated and sometimes perverse word skill. Given the antimonarchic bias of the Icelanders, it is not surprising that the skald-warrior frequently obtrudes his talent into the relationship between men and king with verses aimed at the monarch's pretensions to power. Such *vísur* are, of course, open challenges to the king and his men, all the sharper because the skald should be expected to serve (according to the Dumézilian schematic) as a First Function adjunct or support—which, in fact, he sometimes does.[281] And yet Gunnlaugr Serpent's-Tongue (in his saga) lives up to his cognomen in an exchange with the Norwegian ruler, Jarl Eiríkr, unleashing what Theodore Andersson calls "one of the most deadly and intemperate insults to be found in the sagas, rich as they are in edged words."[282] Egill Skalla-grímsson is another "uncontrollable" skald, as he shows in his insulting verses directed at King Eiríkr Blood-Ax and his witch-queen, and at the ineptitude of the king's men.[283] In truth, however, these skaldic assaults do not quite fit our formulaic pattern of hero against hero: they are governed by a different protocol.

The *sagamenn* have a special affection for the true warrior-skald who can wield both sharp weapon and sharp versifying tongue, but these fighting poets are not likely to be measured and moderate personalities. Egill is an anomaly both because he manages to survive to a great age and because he has something of the manipulative and ever-surviving trickster in him. Grettir, however, and Gunnlaugr Serpent's-Tongue seem destined always to go too far, making enemies where no enemy was before. They delight in saying those things better left unsaid, and Óðinn's divine gift, which is the word-weaving skill of these skalds, tempts them to the point where, inevitably, another kind of retributive violence is stirred and fatally released. The kind of challenge and response that goes even beyond the rough and elastic boundaries of saga propriety shows up in *Bjarnar saga Hítdælakappa*, in which the two antagonists, Bjorn Champion-of-the-Hitadalers and his opponent Þórdr embark on a series of ridiculing verses whose gross themes include accusations of sodomy, claims that one (Bjorn) is the father of the other's son, and insulting invective against each other's wives; the versification is increasingly interspersed with physical violence. Bjorn the Champion is portrayed in this saga as a good and moderate man by and large, but clearly, as Andersson remarks, his *visur* are "at least as scurrilous as Þórdr's," and "the *treníð* [slander] goes beyond what is permissible in polite feuding."[284] The saga ends abruptly with the "good" Bjorn's death at the hands of his poet-rival; the gamelike quality of the exchanges is underscored by a late attempt at reconciliation that fails because Þórdr demands that all the verses be repeated and counted, and Bjorn is found to be literally and fatally one up.[285] The tradition of trading strong insults in the Germanic North goes back at least to the *Völsungasaga*, where we find Sinfjotli, who "knew how to talk with kings," accusing King Granmar of the grossest offenses against the natural order, including shape changing and sex changing, with the underlying imputation of passive homosexuality; all in all, this exchange, in which Granmar turns Sinfjotli's accusation of monstrous shape changing back against him, has the air of a magical assault or duel, an attempt at depotentializing the foe, closer to the Old Irish satirical assault.[286] Neither participant in this strange episode tries to praise or defend himself; each is pure attack.

Satire

It is worth repeating that insult is generally *intended* to heat and overheat the fighting blood, especially on the field of battle, when the warrior is already het up and mutual insult makes him hotter;[287] and that the insult barrage and exchange is only undertaken *by equals*. Despite the sometimes abominable charges flung hither and yon, it is taken for granted that the two warriors implicitly recognize each other as suitable targets: men of a similar terrible kind. Mutuality must be assured, especially when sharp weapons are unsheathed and used—unless one of those (verbal) weapons is satire.

In the heroic context, as we might expect, satire and the satirist are most prominent and have the most singular powers in Ireland and Wales. Ferdiad is persuaded to do battle by Queen Medb in the *Táin*, who sends "poets and bards and satirists to bring the blushes to his cheek with mockery and insult and ridicule, so that there would be nowhere in the world for him to lay his head in peace."[288] This assault, *to which Ferdiad cannot reply*, is what brings him to the royal tent of Medb and Ailill, there to agree finally to fight for "the four provinces of Ireland" ruled by the two, although afterward he is also baited with rich gifts and the promise by Medb of her own sexual favors.[289] The essential quality of satire in this heroic epical context is that it is undertaken in such a way that no immediate response in kind is possible for the satirized warrior, because the core of its power is outrageous and irrational exaggeration, an extreme torsion of the heroic enterprise and persona—in other words, "criticism in comic form."[290] Satire is separate from the hyperbolic self-praise and dispraise of the opponent involved in heroic flyting; and because of its radical distortions and unreasonable, even utterly unbelievable statements, it is assumed to have a magical potency, the more so as it is likely to be cast in a poetic (artificial, crafted, devised) form. Satire, however, is usually the province of specialists, who are often feared; when it remains part of heroic verbal assault (in other heroic contexts, like the sagas and the *chansons de geste*), it can merge into the flyting brag.

This satire in its most distilled guise would seem to provide a means of controlling or persuading heroic-warrior violence, pushing the warrior-hero off the pivot of his own autonomy, interrupting his self-generated patterns of grim purpose and action. Rather than remaining certain of the frame and meaning of his being, the warrior hero becomes ashamed, meaning that he is aware of the ethical scrutiny of someone (not necessarily his peer), or at least is made conscious of the social frame in which he exists. The wielders of satire (again, in its distilled form) are specialists in this agitation of the heroic ethical sense: they are the "poets and bards and satirists" who threaten and afflict and at last influence Cú Chulainn's great antagonist, and they are directed, in this case, from a sovereign (First Function) power. The Celtic examples descend, one may say, from the mythic—and magical—confrontation in the *Cath Maige Tuired*, in which Lugh's poet offers to "make a *glám dícenn* against them [the Formorian enemy], and I will satirize them and shame them so that . . . they will offer no resistance to warriors"—to create, in fact, a sort of magical, depotentializing propaganda.[291]

Differences emerge, however, when our evidence comes from a culture in which the warrior (the Second Function actor) has finally become the dominant sociopolitical (and imaginal) player: satirical power then devolves to some degree on the warrior, or on certain especially skilled poet-warriors—though not in the *Iliad*, where, as Gregory Nagy has persuasively argued, a relict of the satirist as "blame-poet" surfaces only in the unlovely person of the pitiable, clownish Thersites.[292] That strange hero Culhwch in the Welsh quest tale *Culhwch ac Olwen* may act as a *symbolon* of the juncture of two valences when he threatens the king's gateward, saying that he will "satirize your lord and give you a bad name" and threatening to "raise three shouts" with all their magical-destructive power.[293] The warrior-skalds described by the Norse *sagamenn* combine these gifts of magical satire and warrior boasting: Egill, Grettir the Strong, Gunnlaugr Serpent's-Tongue, and Bjorn and Þórdr in *Bjarnar saga Híitdælakappa* display the poetic-satiric power reduced, or at least shifted, so that it is at the service of the word-duelist, and becomes flyting. In other heroic literary contexts the warrior may fear shaming verbal attacks either from his fellows *or* from the poets who are supposed to celebrate their deeds: the *Chanson de Roland* and the *Battle of Maldon* have been cited in this regard, and I gladly accept the suggestion.[294]

The salient point is that the heroic-warrior function is to some degree kept in check by the power of the word, usually but not invariably manipulated by a specialist in "shame" and "blame" as well as praise. Poetic satire may be magical in its form and effect but it is *always,* so far as its target is concerned, unanswerable. To some degree an essential part of heroism in the strictest sense is ever vulnerable to this sort of powerful comment and control, especially if the hero is defined as laconic, self-limited in his use and manipulation of words except for certain ritualized outcries. It is to heroic laconism that I now turn.

Laconism and the Hero

The term "laconic," taking its name from the stern military-aristocratic ethic of Laconian Sparta, may have been partly invented by Athenian observers or ideologues of the aristophilic right, wishing to create an antitype to present against the noisy, over verbal, and incessantly discursive *dêmos* of Athens. Such a laconic individual, in this invention, speaks little or not at all, even (or especially) in situations where the ordinary mortal would speak. Here we find the legendary image of the young Spartiate-in-training refusing to utter a word even with the captured fox gnawing at his vitals, or the marvelous heroic-imaginal terseness of the Spartan inscription to their dead (or from their dead) at Thermopylae. The medieval knightly-chivalric ethic maintained the tradition, as when the old knight Gorrement de Gohort in *La conte du Graal* teaches the young Perceval that "loquacity is a sin."[295] At least as late as the classicist revival reaching into the eighteenth century of our era, this laconic image resurrects or recollects the "strong, silent" hero.

Heroes, beginning with the Homeric reflex, may babble like brooks, as we have seen, though in Homer himself we also find at least one candidate for the title *aristos Akhaiôn*, "best of the Achaeans," in Diomedes, who tends to sum up the situation confronting the Achaeans in a reasonable and succinct manner[296] (though in fact Telemonian Aias is even better known for his terseness).[297] Moreover, Diomedes is often set as partner to the irrepressible Odysseus of Many Wiles, making up half of the pairing so frequently seen in the epics, of a "strong arm" figure whose forte is force, motion, and action, and a "planner," or even someone encased in a tricksterish persona; the Welsh Cei and Bedwyr always come to mind as a comparable pairing.[298] In Homer there is also a formulaic treatment that hints at heroic laconism: *herkos odontôn*, the "barrier of teeth" behind which speech should be kept. At first glance this may merely seem a poetic expansion of another formula, usually rendered as "what a word you have spoken!" (*Il*. IV.25, VIII.152), but surely it offers a further endorsement for withholding speech, especially angry or immoderate speech, behind the barrier where it can do no harm.[299] We also have the evidence of IV.431–36, where the disciplined silence of the advancing Greeks is favorably contrasted with the "sheeplike" noise of the panicked Trojans.[300]

Despite the impression of spare and even terse phrasing that the Norse-Icelandic sagas impart, there is no particular bias there toward the word-sparing hero. Perhaps the status and dramatic significance of the warrior skilled in skaldcraft, or the importance to social peace of the knowledgable speaker or law adviser, influenced the *sagamenn*. In *Eyrbyggja saga* a character named Þórarinn the Black is introduced, a man who is "taciturn, normally very quiet."[301] Þórarinn is immediately juxtaposed to the repulsive Oddr Katlason, "loud-mouthed . . . given to gossip and slander," and a sorceress's son to boot.[302] Yet Þórarinn's peaceable nature is sorely tried; he is involved in a quarrel that leads to violence, kills his foe, and is even inspired to make a poem celebrating his triumph. Eventually he and his allies kill

Oddr (and Oddr's sorceress mother), but unfortunately Þórarinn, in the process of finding his new talents, runs afoul of Snorri the *goði*, the central and manipulative "political" figure in this saga, and is forced into exile.[303] The gift for skaldship (and violence) uncovered in the previously concise and pacific Þórarinn svarti seems to do him little good in the end, though he is certainly a more memorable saga character because of it.

A hero may be silent because of special circumstances built into a particular epic: the knight Tariel in the Georgian *Lord of the Panther's Skin* will not speak, when he is first sighted, because of an emotional trauma (to use an anachronism) that has left him at least partly crazy. But the epic also suggests that he is silent because he has taken on an animal's persona; the knight has become "wild as any beast" and thus cannot speak like a human being.[304] In this guise, Tariel, assimilated for a time to the non speaking animal world, bears some resemblance to the wordless Norse *berserkr*, to the dead-undead *haugr* or howe dweller, and to the revivified Celtic cauldron warrior: a resident or emergent animal aspect in the hero can render him dumb, unable to communicate with or in the human world.[305]

Laconism, in Dumézil's theory at least, is built into the Function in which the warrior-hero acts, whereas the innate communicative power of words is assigned to the First or Sovereign Function—or to the magical and quasi-magical gifts of that partner of the true hero, the Odyssean trickster.[306] This leads to the further complication that if "words," considered generically, are assigned to a function outside the heroic, the abstracted potency of the *written* word must be even farther from the hero's use or control. The attitude of the hero often can be bluntly stated: writing lies, falsifies, or conceals the truth. In the *chanson de geste* entitled *The Conquest of Orange*, the warrior Guillaume insists that his narrative is a "true song," and "I think that no clerk will belie me / nor any writing that is found in a book."[307] Writing can assume another kind or dimension of fatal power, as when, in the Armenian *Sassowntsi David*, we meet a supernatural figure named Krogh—"Scribe"—who writes out . . . the death warrants of human beings.[308] On another tack, in the Balkans, where the orally transmitted epic and a tradition of oral-epic creativity in a mostly illiterate population came down to very recent times, the written communication is accorded a special, in fact a magical, value (its effect lies outside of any rational communicative valence). Thus the "well-written letter" is emphasized in the Moslem epos, and the same kind of power-laden missive appears in the Serb epic of Marko Kraljević, especially in the form of letters either written or signed in blood.[309]

In the Irish Celtic context, with its extraordinary emphasis on skilled word weaving, the separation of written from oral "truth" is worked out with all the ambiguity and complexity one might expect. The archaic rule, as summarized by Prionsias MacCana, is that writing, even when used by the *fili* or *file* (the court poet who at one time also had a juridical role), was always subordinate to oral speech, perceived as a "living dynamic medium" as contrasted to "static" and therefore inferior graphism.[310] (This is a precise reversal of the Balkan view.) Dumézil connected this Irish tradition directly to Caesar's remark that the Gaulish Druids refused to commit their "sayings" to writing (*Neque fas esse existimant ea [versuum] litteris mandare)*; he (Dumézil) also believes that Caesar invented the reasons in order to rationalize the practice.[311] The crucial test in the Irish tradition came when the "perfect reign" of Cormac mac Airt was broken; according to the Book of Ballymole, Cormac distributed the juridical powers of the *filid* (the power and responsibility of recollecting and repeating legal precedent), and in an especially dramatic case the unwisdom of this decision was made clear. The ownership of a sword—the weapon of the warrior—came to be disputed; the memory of a *file* was opposed to a different name found written on the sword hilt, and the true owner was defrauded because an artisan had put down the wrong name. "The Dead," according to this tradition, now "witness against the Living."[312]

We have not, as yet, been searching for a "typical" hero, but if we had been, this chapter might well have provided a model. The neatly presented paradoxes of sculptural, marmoreal stance suddenly broken by leaping speed and shattering violence, the solemn presentation and preservation of ego combined with death seeking and the urge toward self-annihilation, perfect style and manner side by side with unthinkable atrociousness, deliberate silence or laconism set against the war scream. Paradox there may be, but little ambiguity. The fell-handed hero moves and works *en clair;* his paradoxes describe him but they never soften his adamantine outline. The range of his emotions, as revealed in his epic story, is limited and without subtlety, and all the emotional peaks—of sorrow, rage, joy—are connected to the one crux of agonic confrontation. When the hero is given speech, that gift considered most human (along, perhaps, with the urge to slaughter one's own kind), he simplifies this complex system of signs.

Our heroic portraits, of course, are drawn by others; it is the free-flowing and designed phrases of the epic poet that give us the laconic hero or, conversely, the controlled and self-limited formularies of the epic that release these great bursts of movement and of violence. Herein is an apt description of the problem surrounding the coding, and codes, of the hero.

5 FOILS, FOOLS, AND ANTIHEROES

Agamemnon is a fool to offer to command Achilles; Achilles is a fool to
be commanded of Agamemnon; Thersites is a fool to serve such a fool;
and Patroclus is a fool positive.

—Thersites, in *Troilus and Cressida*, II.iii.64

The acts and talents of a series of loosely connected characters can support,
or occasionally interfere with, the accepted base patterns of the heroic
career. Each character plays the role in his own way. The trickster is always
a valuable foil and adjunct to the heroic career, but he is a figure with his
own purposive and narrative peculiarities. The poet-skald or satirist defines
or clarifies matters heroic in one way or another. The smith is a mysterious, often magic-working partner to the hero, and one whose creative arts
are probably deeper than any Indo-European structure can comfortably
contain. "Blackened" and comic figures add their own complexity through
a conscious reversal of the heroic style—which is also, of course, the province of the trickster. Finally, the surface of the heroic type is subject to
other, in this case chromatic, shifts and symbolic readjustments, as the shift
and variance in the heroic character is displayed in the color he adopts or
the color assigned to him.

HERO AND HEROIC TRICKSTER

As a signifier in the semiotic sense, "trickster" comes to us less heavily laden
than "hero." Although the *Iliad* contains a suspicious character whose name,
Dolon, translates as "Trickster," and although this same archepic (along
with its companion tale of quest and final homecoming, the *Odyssey*) gives
us, in Odysseus, the very model of the wily one, the focus on the trickster
has not sharpened until our own century.[1] Even then it was anthropologists
and students of comparative religion who first descried and described the

trickster-as-type and his multivariant activities. These investigators identified, in the myths of a series of "primitive" or traditional cultures, a figure,
often in animal form or disguise but possessing (at the other contrastive
extreme) divine or semidivine powers, who "plays" and yet creates—something. He—trickster—is not so much a cosmogonic as a *cosmotactic* figure
(in David Bynum's inventive word), one "who . . . orders or changes the
world" and who occupies an important if thoroughly ambiguous and trans-
liminal place in myth and in all its generic narrational relatives.[2]

The trickster, as he is found and constrained within the heroic-epical
context, cannot be dissected from the wider, and deeper, drama of his great
relative, the divine or mythogenic Dancing God, the boundary-breaking
being who, as Barbara Babcock says, "muddles all models": Epimetheus, for
example, Titan-brother to Prometheus in Greek myth, the "scatter-brained
one" who "first was a mischief to men who eat bread," according to Hesiod.[3] Very often the energy of what we have to call a trickster-hero is
drawn from or radiates from that other, powerfully energized and forma-
tive mythic realm, and his plans and acts display the closest conformance
to patterns originally set by his mythic kinsman, and reflect the identical
strategies, especially of violating boundaries, confusing categories, and perversely reversing norm and rule—whatever that norm or rule might be.
As Karl Kerényi wrote about the Norse god Loki, he manipulates power
"through the strength of (his) weakness and the boldness of (his) cowardice," and is "related to the monsters," yet remains thoroughly human in
his perverse powers of invention.[4]

Differences must still be clearly identified. The trickster-hero should be
fully human, as his partners and, occasionally, his foils are, though he himself tends to be able to move more freely than most into and through the
supernatural zone, and he often acts as an intermediary between that zone
and the zone of heroic human action. Inasmuch as the warrior-hero already
seems to stand in a space between categories, his trickster affiliate often
emerges as an even more complex interzone interloper and intermediary,
one whose scenarios of intermediation may not always be easy to intercept
and clarify. And rarely if ever will the trickster-hero, despite his connection
to the mythic and mythogenic trickster, be equipped with the full range of
tricksterish powers and emanations. It would take a constellation of individual tricksters to do that.

Thus our examples will extend from an archaic, multiform figure like
Tale of Orasacs in the Moslem Serbo-Croat songs, through Celtic trickster-
magicians and Germanic warrior-tricksters, to the attenuated Homeric
context whose tricksters are tightly, even suspiciously controlled, almost

excluded from the dramatic, warrior-heroic ethos of our first surviving epic. We will also encounter degenerate or "part-time" tricksters, whose powers may be reduced or even rendered useless in the course of the narrative.[5]

Hero and Trickster Paired

At the significant risk of fatally dissecting a character type whose salient features tend to merge, and who delights in making a shambles of categories, I will try to divide our "heroic" trickster into the following subtypes or acting modes: partner (and partner in opposition), reversed figure, and solitary figure.

PARTNER

The trickster-partner presses against his hero: you couldn't miss him, even if his stance and his acts were not as outrageous and contrary to custom as they usually are. But the partnership I speak of here is quite different from that other kind of warrior partnership formed by Akhilleus and Patroklos, or Roland and Olivier, or hero and standard-bearer in the Serbo-Croat songs.[6] In those warrior-pairings there is a dominant and a less dominant or supportive figure, but the hero-trickster partnership is of essential equals, sometimes almost ludicrous in their differing characteristics, but parallel in their placement and potency. So the *Iliad*—once again our starting point— matches Diomedes with Odysseus. Diomedes is the hot-spur knight, as chivalrous as any of the braves in this poem is likely to get: the direct, commonsensical (though also sometimes berserk), and uncomplicated warrior we are used to. Odysseus, on the other hand, is the manipulator, the calculating master of *mêtis,* the devious word smith who yet must be considered a warrior-king[7]—and who will always give rise to difficulties. He makes strange errors, especially in his own tale, where he stands alone, or is perhaps "doubled" within his own character, like our good Welsh friend Cei; and whether he is considered a "warrior" or a "trickster," he will predict the sort of mistakes he is liable to make.[8]

Another, typologically identical kind of partnership is that of Cei and Bedwyr in the early Welsh Celtic formulation of the Arthurian narratives. Almost invariably named together, the two undertake adventures in which the "square" Bedwyr contributes might and muscle, whereas Cei operates in the zone of craft, special knowledge, and magical manipulation. (This is Cei's alternative or second role, for he is also, as we have seen, a king's champion; and the two roles are often conflated or compounded, as the quest tale *Culhwch ac Olwen* clearly shows.) Another kind of partnership, from another epic-heroic tradition, appears in the Norse romance saga or *lygisaga* "Bósa ok Herrauðr." This tale, which is very rich, for its size, in the variety of personae provided, has as partners not only the two Vikings of the title, who are called foster brothers for the purposes of the story, but a complicating third.[9] Herrauðr is a knightly, loyal king's son, though he is rather cruder than the usual fairy-tale prince; Bósi is a mischief-making but talented, priapic, and adventurous schemer; and Bósi's brother Smidr ("Smith"), a true warlock and shape changer, adds a particular twist to the tale. Bósi intermediates between his strong-arm partner and his sorcerer-brother, a position he specifically chose when he refused to take the complete curriculum in sorcery offered by his foster mother Busla, for "he didn't want it written in his saga that he'd carried anything through by trickery instead of relying on his own manhood."[10] In fact Bósi will not be in any way averse to trickery, disguises, and other more or less magical tricks and japes in his headlong pursuit of adventure—especially erotic adventure.

The Norse-Icelandic materials also provide us with another sort of partnership that might be called "partners in opposition," and which reflects another side of the "warrior of Óðinn, warrior of Þórr" relationship. Here the Þórr-warrior (most clearly exemplified by the two Þórólfrs in *Egils saga*) takes on the posture of the "straight," socially adaptive and useful warrior, while the brothers of the two Þórólfrs, Skalla-Grímr and Egill, are edgy, prickly, talented individualists with a strong whiff of the supernatural but little sense of social solidarity or group loyalty, except, minimally, to their own family. In the North, as we have already seen, the simultaneous similarity and differentiation between the two warrior-types become part of an anti-monarchic theme, a dominant note in a number of the sagas.[11] The scenario of paired and related warriors divided by their *ideological* support for or opposition to kingship is also seen in the semihistorical *Jómsvíking-asaga*, where the Þórr-type (and victim) is surely represented by Aki Tókasson and the Óðinn-warrior by Palna-Tóki, a regicide and eventually the founder of the Jomsburg warrior order.[12] These two sources (Egill's saga and the Jomsviking narrative) are also united by other similarities, especially the fact that a murderous monarch is persuaded to distrust and eventually to kill a king's man, a loyal supporter of the explicit Þórr-warrior type, and is urged toward this betrayal by "bad councillors" (the malignant and illegitimate Hlidiridarsons in *Egils saga*, Fjolnir Tókasson in the *Jómsvíkingasaga*).[13]

Beyond the sagas, where it appears likely that antimonarchic political concerns push on or assist the development of the Þórr-warrior/Óðinn-warrior bivalence, the "paired opposites" *may* emerge for us in Priam's two sons, Hektor and Alexandros-Paris, the first as the gallant and expert warrior of Troy doomed to die at Akhilleus's hand, the second the unwarrior-like sensualist and sly bowman, Akhilleus's bane, who will survive his greater brother for a little while.[14] Tricksterish partners (see Bósi, above) are frequently invested with excessive sexual energy.[15]

REVERSED FIGURES

Two figures are concerned here, who in very loose terms could be labeled "villain." In essence the first, like the wretched Aegisthus who helped Klytemnestra murder Agamemnon, displays an interfunctional type of reversal, meaning that the potencies characteristic of the Third Function (especially sexuality) energize his assault on the first two Functions (Agamemnon as king and as warrior). The second figure, the "reversal hero," like Tale in the Moslem Serbo-Croat heroic songs, displays his reversals intrafunctionally, within that heroic *fonction guerrière* that dominates or at least frames his adventure narratives on the border.

Aegisthus is odd man out in the Greek heroic scene, and his strange biography, so far as we can reconstruct it, emphasizes the perverse, the ambiguous, and the liminal. He is Agamemnon's cousin and foster brother (the son of Thyestes by the incestuous union of Thyestes with his own daughter), and Atreus's foster son and murderer. I have suggested elsewhere[16] that in one reading Aegisthus is the last in the gloomy and doom-laden but potent line of the Pelopid "magical kings" (a seminal term provided by Luc de Heusch and further developed by Claire Préaux), with that king's deep-seated enmity to legitimated (delegated and Zeus-authenticated) power "on the Right Hand." He is an anti-warrior as well, preferring secret assassination to open confrontation, at least according to those sources that are hardest on him, the Greek tragedies.[17] Indeed, his position is firmly based in the Dumézilian Third Function, but wrong-way-to: "His ground is a perversion or reversal of the forces resident in the Third Function: sexual jealousy, trickery and 'craft' as it applies to human relationships, greediness of gain."[18] Aegisthus is not afraid to commit a triple crime that, at one blow, violates all three of the *regula* of the Functions: helping to kill a king (attacking a First Function, Sovereign power), but by stealth and trickery (contrary to a Second Function norm describing correct warrior behavior), motivated by an illicit passion for the king's wife (a perverse torsion of Third Function sexuality). Such a multipotent act attaches him to what in the North would be called an Óðinnic mode or, in Dumézil's alternative schematic structure, to the mysterious, Varunaic sources of sovereign power. In fact the crime of loathly Aegisthus has its parallel, oddly enough, in the career of the Scandinavian old hero or servant-hero, Starkaðr.

The reversals of Tale (Tale of Orasacs, Tale Ibrahim, Tale Budalin or "the Fool") included in the Serbo-Croat and Albanian Moslem heroic songs cover a broad and comprehensive range. Tale has no specific partner but is called upon by all the warriors of the border to act for them as trickster. Later he is enlisted to aid the Moslem *bulyukbašas* in their campaigns. Tale's very appearance is a gross parody of the usual hero's persona: riding a mouse-gray and mangy horse, sidesaddle like a woman or a peasant, he wears goatskin trousers out at the knee, and either a wolfskin cap with his "Turkish" queue protruding through a hole or a piece of tattered cloth that pretends to be a turban.[19] When he makes his first appearance in the *guslar* Avdo's long, indeed epic-length song, *The Wedding of Smailagić Meho*, he is "filthy, his hands black, his beard has clots of dust in it; his pistols in his belt of rushes dirty his bare belly."[20] (Precisely this reversal of the usual hero's glorious scintillation is copied by another Tale-like figure, Jurisić Janko, who rides off "on a poor nag and with a blunt sword" in the Christian Serb tale called "The Marriage of Dušan.")[21] No reversal is alien to Tale.

In Tale's heroic fighting tail he boasts either Radovan "the deserter," the "rogue without equal" who hasn't a good word for anyone, or the sinister Belaj, "woe-bringer," who carries Tale's standard reversed and, like Radovan, rides backward. Occasionally Tale may be associated either with a mysterious "ragged man"—more decrepit even than Tale—who has magical powers and superhuman strength, or with a priest who seems to support him from the side of a more orthodox Islamic wisdom but who is also a bit of a rogue magician.[22] Finally, a female figure sometimes joins his entourage, his mad sister Aziza, although Tale also calls on the special gifts and powers of the Balkan water-sprite or *vila*, frequent companion to the hero in her own way.

Withal, the special powers that Tale wields, once he has been bribed by someone with "'fined gold" (a substance he is very fond of) are considerable. These powers are absolutely closed off to the true heroes of the border, and are best divided, I think, between the two clusters of meaning for the word *craft*. First, Tale is the strategist of the "army" of border heroes, its director (insofar as it has one) as well as the chief military-intelligence officer and spy.[23] He is also the master gunner, the adept in the use of the cannon, that technically complicated weapon of siegecraft and mass destruction that the border heroes do not and cannot, in all honor, use.[24] Second, he has important gifts as a prescient and as a weather master, and has very useful connections to the supernatural zone.[25] And only he, with a blow of his favorite mace, can loose the chains of captives.[26] We even find that in one of Tale's activities both aspects of the "craft" he knows emerge and merge: when he counts the host of Moslem warriors by passing them through a gate in a field, he is performing an abstract task, one separate from merely naming and identifying all the heroes; at the same time he is probably increasing their powers by a process that enhances their martial prowess, the direct reversal of that depotentializing ritual, well known in Rome, of passing the captured warrior "under the yoke," not just to humiliate but to devitalize him.[27] In this "counting" episode Trickster Tale is, almost literally, pumping up his fighting host with warlike valor.

Tale is not alone in the Balkan heroic-trickster frame: the Christian Serb hero Marko Kraljević shows a variation on the type, combining the usual heroic bravery and puissance with a distinctly unheroic array of talents. His epic songs refer to him as "crafty"; he uses disguises; and at one point he tricks a Moorish princess with a false oath.[28] When he encounters the Perilous Bogdan, Marko is (unheroically if justifiably) afraid of this fearsome warrior, and in another encounter he cannot win his ultimate champion's duel against the uncanny Musa the Highwayman except through trickery—though even a hero's hero such as the Irish Cú Chulainn is known to have an ultimate, fell recourse to tricks, as we already know, and especially to sinister, unfair weapons and crafty maneuvers.[29] Marko also displays a residue of magical powers, especially in connection with animals and that omnipresent Otherworld (half-human) female spirit, the *vila*.[30] He most resembles Tale, however, when he executes an individual in cold blood, which a true border *agha* would never do).[31] Both Tale and Marko, it seems, can bend the hero's honor.

Tale is painted in strokes so comically broad and yet so detailed, and with such a full-blooded narrative *brio*, that he can serve us as an ideal centerpiece for a collectivity of tricksterish modalities and personalities. His "blackened" persona attaches him to others of this same antiheroic coloration. His ugliness pushes him into modal contact with near-tricksterish figures like the northerners Egill Skalla-Grímsson and the legendary Starkaðr, and both these features form a connective filament to the smith—though in this regard, too, Tale plays the game of reversal: when we meet him in the *Smailagić* epic song he is furiously busy at desmithing (deconstructing?) his sword, or threatening to do so.[32] Naturally his appearance and his uninhibited language put him into the larger and different category of a comic invention, and though the Serbo-Croat songs are generally restrained, even puritanical, in their sexual references, Tale at least suggests a comic-erotic subtext when he claims that the marriage of the young hero Meho cannot go forward because the bride had been promised to him, Tale.[33] Finally, Tale's unheroic, commonsensical, and rational streak emerges in statements about the cost and futility of war that we will recall when we come to another egregious antihero, the coward knight.

THE SOLITARY

The stuff that makes up the trickster's fund of motifs is exceedingly variable, and because the type is thoroughly unafraid of reversal and anomaly, odd, unpredictable, and intriguing combinations are very likely to occur. Some tricksters unheroically seek out amorous adventures; others, like Tale, act as if drunk even though they do not take wine, as real heroes do. No trickster type, however, is more complicated or difficult to define than the "solitary"; and indeed this very term can only be approximate: this class of heroic trickster separates itself more by what it *isn't*. Its figures are not twinned with a strong-arm warrior, nor are they precisely like Tale, who comes out of the Moslem-Serb border tales as a perverse and reversing but effective instrument of his society, rather easily integrated into an articulated social order. Our "solitary" is an isolate but not a monolith, and his characteristics are mixed and confused. One example is the Nart hero Soslan, who has no partner except the furious and incandescent Batradz. Soslan is not only violent and cunning: "his enemies styled him forsworn and untrustworthy,"[34] and his appearance reveals several unheroic faults and defects. He is not quite the Loki-like "reverser" of the Nart narratives, for that position must belong to the eccentric Syrdon, but he is certainly ambiguously drawn as a heroic figure.

The solitary is perhaps the most ambiguous trickster-figure of all, one who offers service (to a king, ordinarily, rather than to another warrior or war group) but whose position and powers are never completely reliable, and never end in a clear or convincing resolution. The choice of the old and familiar fighter Starkaðr as an examplar is bound to be attended with difficulties, and yet few others could illustrate complexity and ambiguity so well. His origins, especially his giant's ancestry, are nonhuman; he is both a warrior, unmistakably, *and* a king's champion (roles that uneasily go together, and the latter of which makes him a royal surrogate at very least); and he even commits the three great sins of the warrior: regicide, cowardice, and murder for gain. That is only the beginning: Starkaðr also employs all the "rational" wiles usually associated with the trickster when he produces his *speculum principis* and grumpily thrusts it at the unworthy King Ingel; and he lives the hyperextended, unheroically long life typical of the trickster, which he ends by a kind of suicide. Indeed he can be set into a category that includes Aegisthus and Oedipus: all of them are "sinners" who demonstrate marked tricksterish characteristics.[35] Dumézil himself chose Starkaðr as one of his *echt*-warrior folk, all of them Second Function examplars of the "warrior sinner";[36] and ambiguity (richness? confusion?) even surrounds the *type* of warrior he is. It is Óðinn who seems to sponsor him, as against the enmity of Þórr,[37] yet at one time Dumézil identified Starkaðr as a "hero of Þórr" (see specifically his advice poem to King Ingel in Saxo, *Gesta Danorum*, VI.187–95), mainly because the old man serves as an example for and tutor to young warrior-kings.

Poetry and Magic

The scumbling of definitions and the confusion of categories is the trickster's special game and glory, but when we come to the *poetic* celebration of the hero and his cohorts—when we ask, specifically, how the poetic function may be integrated into or with the trickster's multiform talents—we may start sinking into quicksand. The hero is, after all, "invented" by the epic poets from the available raw material; these bards, occasionally but usually not identifiable as individuals, create most of the imaginal heroic world and its inhabitants, including the warrior-trickster. But one facet of this trickster-type encountered again and again in the literature is the manipulation of words, not only in "ordinary" speech (as if anything having to do with the trickster could be ordinary!) but in songs, spells, and celebratory poems; and because of this we may encounter singular difficulty in separating subject or creator from object or epical act-narration.

In an effort to clarify the interaction of trickster and poet, I want to develop the dimensions of tricksterdom in three different kinds of poetic activity, even though these activities are primarily focused not on the trickster but on the hero. The image of the "maker" of poetry or song within the various heroic traditions is joined to that aspect of the trickster acting as manipulator, as creator of other elements advancing the heroic adventure-biography. (Once more he may be compared with the smith, whose enigmatic skills will be dealt with in due course.) In the first of these poetic interventions the poet and his craft are shown as an entity separate from bloodshed and war-making, though the same character may be both poet and warrior; in the second the poetic insight is intermixed or combined with the fighter's act and ethos; and in the third the heroic narrative is depoeticized: the bard creates his cast of heroic images from the *exterior*, and he does not celebrate poetic activity *within* the poem.[38]

WAR APART FROM VERSE

An excellent example of the separation of these two crafts emerges in the Old Irish Fenian Cycle, and is crystallized into the character of the *rígfénnid*, the leader of the band, Finn mac Cumaill himself. Finn inherits from his grandfather a version of that old man's druidic-poetic powers, and from his father his warlike prowess: these two modes are separately visible in Finn's two half brothers, one of them skilled in warlike *fénnideacht*, the other in poetic *filideacht*.[39] Finn is fully expert and active in both modes by the time he has finished his *macgnimartha* (or *macnímrada*), his extraordinary "boyhood deeds."[40]

Other *filid* were court poets and encomiasts closely associated, I would think, with the sovereign First Function, and it seems clear that the Celtic druid, with his coded wisdom and his mantic powers, was meant to be defined as a First Function figure; so was the Old Irish *ollam* or master poet, called "equal to the king before the law."[41] (Even in Finn's turbulent time, abstract truth—*fír*—continued to be "normally incarnated in a poetico-musical form" in Ireland, and, implicitly, the *fili* had a special means of access to this essential, an ideally ruling or guiding truth.)[42] Finn, however, is not a court poet, yet after he gained the special insight and magical talents explicitly preparatory for making a poem, his first lay—strangely for such a warrior?—was apparently, according to our sources, a description of nature, beginning with "May-Day, season surpassing! Splendid is color then."[43] This effusion might be considered a simple virtuoso piece on nature, if the poem did not so stress the opening of life after the sacred Celtic day-marker of Beltain, and if Finn's doubled connection to the natural world *and* to the Otherworld was not given such weight in his biography.[44] Other products of Finn's magical-poetic talent include, at the end of his life, the prophetic or fatalist lays described in the narrative *Fianaigecht* (Death of Finn).[45]

The sources we possess describing Finn mac Cumaill's adventures weave his skill as a *fili* into those necessary scenes of his great battle prowess, but the two aspects or talents, death dealing and word weaving, are defined separately and come from two separate sources or inheritances. This presupposition, in the Fenian Cycle, is differentiated from that displayed in the Ulster Cycle's delineation of its great hero, Cú Chulainn, whose typical poetic effort would be shown in the combat-boast contest with Ferdiad, or his mourning song or keen for this foster brother whom he had to slay:

Cú Chulainn's verses flow directly from that superlative warrior's tensions, crises, or special situations. On the other hand, the later Irish Ossianic Cycle presumes that *filid* have another identity and set of distinguishing marks, perhaps, as Joseph Nagy suggests, "darker and more powerful" than the combative and glittering warrior will usually boast.[46]

WAR AND VERSE

In the medieval German *Nibelungenlied* one of King Gunther's more bloody-minded Burgundian nobles, apt partner for the fearsome Hagen of Troneck, is Volker *der videlaere,* "the Fiddler." "Brave Volker" entertains his friends with sweet notes, *sô süezlich erklanc,* but soon he seems to be wielding his fiddle bow as if it were a sword: *sine züge die sint rôt,* "his bow is blood red" and cuts *durch den herten stâl,* "through the hardest steel."[47] Whether or not the *Nibelungenlied's* poet actually intended to have this rather grim warrior cut down his foes with a fiddle bow, he creates a memorable icon of the warrior as a sort of deadly minstrel and adumbrates the important Germanic-Scandinavian image of the warrior-skald. Here the creative talent may sometimes be allied to that of the heroic fighter, and make up part of his integral essence.

Northward, and like enough to the Celtic *fili,* the Norse-Icelandic skald may sometimes act as a court poet—a praise poet, encomiast, or remembrancer to the sovereign—though certain sagas clearly depict this relationship as fragile and easily turned to mutual enmity. The two I have in mind—*Jómsvíkingasaga* and *Þórleifs saga Jarlskaldi*—both display a deep antimonarchic bias and a strong imaginative and even fantastic component. The target in both is Norway's tenth-century ruler Jarl Hákon of Hladir, though the Jomsviking account also has little good to say about Denmark's king at the time, Sveinn Haraldsson, Jarl Hákon's enemy. The short saga of Þórleif Jarls-poet tells how Jarl Hákon "unlawfully" seized his skald's goods, and what happens later. The skald Þórleif leaves in anger for the court of Sveinn of Denmark, but returns shortly thereafter (thinly disguised as Scurrilous-Scoffer, son of Screamer) and delivers a devastating satiric poem that strikes precisely at each *fonction* in the Indo-European canon but has its strongest effect in the Third Function, attacking Hákon's sexual powers.[48] In *Jómsvíkinga* the same ruler, who seems to have his strongest imaginal roots and affinities in some dark aspect of the Third Function rather than in any aspect of the First or Sovereign Function, has another skald in his court, Skjaldmayjar-Einarr, widely considered the greatest of his kind; to keep this poet by his side, Hákon bribes him with rich gifts and thus avoids a repetition of that satiric-magical assault his old skald Þórlief had directed at him.[49] Perhaps he had learned his lesson.

Another source, our familiar and rowdy adventure-saga "Bósa ok Herrauðr," has two examples of the magical song or chant, the first (called *Buslabein* or Busla's Prayer) delivered against King Hring (another monarch with firm ties to the Third Function) by the sorceress Busla, the second (a series of songs) sung by a disguised Bósi in King Godmundr's court.[50] Both magical songs or verses resonate powerfully in the Third Function, again threatening King Hring's sexual performance, and then making the guests and for that matter all the objects in Godmundr's hall dance wildly. Here, surely, we have some significant hint of the heart of the truly magical satire, the power to turn everything topsy-turvy, threatening the solidity of the quotidian world, making people and things change their aspect or entirely break down. The "first satire ever made in Ireland," according to the Old Irish *Cath Maige Tuired*, was of this potent sort, and was directed against the ungenerous King Bres, so that "nought but decay was on him from that time."[51] What we can see of satire in the Norse world closely follows this theme: when directed against a king its most serious effects are on the kingdom's vitality and growth. Even the "bad name" (*drygeir*) that Culhwch in the Welsh quest tale threatens to put on Arthur is almost certainly intended to preclude royal ungenerosity, or possibly the nonrecognition of kinship, both of which defects can be neatly assigned to the key assumptions of the Third Function.[52] We see here as elsewhere that although magic may not entirely *originate* in this Third Function, magical activity is very frequently based in or operative near it.[53] Satire is a very powerful weapon, perhaps all the more so because it can be launched even by the lowliest carl, one armed only with some sort of ability to manipulate "bad words." Indeed it is often not clear exactly what social status the professional satirist may possess or have been granted.

The Norse skald as a word weaver may either attack or defend and enhance the power of kings, and in either mode this is where any magical talents he might possess are likely to betray themselves. Egill Skalla-Grímsson in his saga is forced to stave off the black-magical machinations of King Eiríkr's Lappish (or Permian) witch-queen Gunnhildr, but he does so by wonderfully concentrating his mind—his head being truly at risk—and producing a grand if utterly hypocritical praise poem for the unworthy king, in a sonorous, skillfully wrought *drápa* of twenty verses.[54] Egill too has some knowledge of and skill in the practice of magical manipulation, for he comes from a most uncanny line, but his warrior-skaldship usually takes a more secular form. Poetry and magic take slightly different paths in the tale of this particular trickster-skald and his family.[55]

WAR AND THE POET

The preceding examples differ from the majority of epic songs and tales of the Indo-European inheritance, in which the only poetry is that of the poet-narrator himself, not of any character within the original creation. Thus in the *Iliad*, the word "singer"—*aoidos*—does not appear until late in the last book, where it evidently refers to professional mourners, in Troy, who are called in to sing the proper obsequies for dead Hektor.[56] If Gregory Nagy is correct, the Homeric poet also excises from his song all but relics and hints of the original "blame poet," that intrinsically dangerous satirist who would be called *scop* or "scoffer" in the Old English sources, or skald—"scolder"—in the Norse-Icelandic tradition.[57] What we can infer to have been Thersites' dangerous bardic skills are reduced to a malignant sniping—and it is Odysseus, the sly deviser and warrior-trickster, who roundly and physically chastises him. The Homeric creation seems to deny one function of the bard that appears elsewhere, the choice of singing condign praise *or* blame of the hero; and the pattern set by the *Iliad* has been kept intact up to the most recently discovered oral epics and epic singers in the various European traditions. Thus modern if tradition-bound Serbo-Croat *guslari*, whose traditional songs have so invigorated the study of the epic-heroic genre, seem equally uninterested in creating or repeating any song *within* the song as they entertain their audience.

The same is true of the singers of the greatest of the Old French *chansons de geste*, though I have already mentioned Roland's reaction to the possibility that any "shaming" songs might be sung about him. (There is also a reference in the poem to the enigmatic *Gesta Francorum*, which "sings of our emperor / that he was served by heroes.")[58] Beowulf's epic speaks of a scop who "sang clear-voiced in Heort" (lines 496–97), and the most complete version of the Byzantine Greek *Digenid* says that the Emir, the hero Digenes' father, on leaving his bride "began to sing to comfort the girl"; the song itself resembles a fragment of a love ballad.[59] Shota Rustaveli introduces no subsidiary song-making or bardic skills into his Georgian knight's tale, the *Vep'khistqaosani*, but his case, in terms of epical creation, is different: the poem itself is indubitably his, claimed by him to nearly the extent that Virgil claims his epic, with *cano* 'I sing'—though there is no first-person Georgian verb to lead off his song.

In the end, the manipulative-creative skills *of the poet* put him directly into the tricksterish category of *craft*; and even more notably, the poet, like the smith, has the power either to create *or* to destroy the very fabric of the hero, his essence: he can hammer him with words.

The Trickster: Life and Death

The questionable or even perilous areas of the comic and erotic are very often explored by a heroic trickster, and not by the hero himself, but the trickster also plays a special role in the heroic death theme and its permutations.

COMEDY AND EROS

It is a very tricky business to isolate, define, and interpret the "comic" as it manifests itself in another language and culture, but those confusing-reversing tendencies of the trickster almost invariably seem to create, or at least sketch, a comic situation, with what we can recognize as potentially comic energies emergent and deployed. Certainly the archaic and powerful near kin of our particular trickster-type, the mythic-divine or culture-hero tricksters, are often involved in wildly disorderly and comical-chaotic episodes, with a strong emphasis on excretory and erotic acts and functions—and capricious combinations thereof.[60]

In the Moslem Serbo-Croat songs, Tale the Fool's grubby persona is reinforced by his outrageous speech, his unbridled greed and gluttony, his excremental and obscene oaths.[61] And this Tale the Repulsive is one who, according to the important evidence of one of the *guslari,* "made himself ugly": he had once been as conventionally handsome as all the other warriorly *bulyukbašas* of the border.[62] (In this he has a number of near relations scattered through the epic sources.) Some time past I had cause to comment on his typological near fellow in the Irish Celtic *Táin,* the decrepit and even absurd figure of old Iliach mac Cass, who rides to battle in his broken-down chariot without a charioteer (behind two "old, decrepit, mangy" horses), obscene and ridiculous in appearance: "his private parts hung down through the chariot."[63] But we also note that Iliach's ignominious appearance echoes the mythical but equally questionable appearance of Dagda the Good God, in the Irish Mythological Cycle, whose private parts could also be shamefully and comically exposed.[64] The lecherous and appetitive Dagda can be understood as a perfect trickster-god (as his brother Ogma is a matched warrior-god); I have already underlined his resemblance to the mortal Tale Budalin, especially as Tale can wield his favorite mace precisely as Dagda wields his magic staff, either to kill or to cure. To further thicken the mass of resemblances, Iliach the aged anti-warrior fights with stones and bare hands, and his death reminds us (yet again) of our old friend the scarred and misshapen Starkaðr, for Iliach too commanded his own death by letting himself be beheaded.[65]

In the Norse fantasy sagas, the trickster figure is most likely to have some sort of Otherworld connections, and occasionally Otherworld origins, as with Bósi and his blood brother Smidr, who are both fostered and aided in their adventuring by the old sorceress, Busla.[66] Even an allegedly historical "family" saga like Egill's reflects this tendency: the sagamaðr accepts that the Kveld-Úlfssons, at least those in the Óðinnic-warrior mode, have some sort of uncanny nature and ancestry, as Kveld-Úlfr ("evening-wolf") more than hints at in his name; Skalla-Grímr displays powers that increase as night comes on; and Egill himself has his own pet sorceress-mentor, the bondwoman Þórgerdr Brak, who, like Busla, gave her life for her old pupil.[67] There is little of the erotic in Egill's career (in fact, there are no important women in this tale, a rare exception in the "family" category of sagas), but Egill's unseemly greediness is clearly delineated: "land and money's at stake!" he frankly declaims in one of his *visur*, and both Egill and his father Skalla-Grímr are at some miserly, or perhaps magicianly, pains to take their accumulated treasure with them when they die, by hiding this wealth.[68] Egill's personal appetites are displayed in other ways: he is always a great drinker, and his drinking game at Barðr the king's man's board is rife with outrageous and violent black humor, especially at the end, when Egill runs Barðr through and makes his escape, trailing sulfurous insulting verses about King Eiríkr and his malignant witch-spouse behind him.[69] Even Egill's physical appearance, the typical ugliness of the trickster (the satyr-like Bósi was said to be "swarthy and not so handsome"), is referred to with a comic edge, for though respected as the long-lived founder of a renowned Icelandic family line, he left his genetic tokens behind: "the men of Mylar were outstandingly ugly."[70] Egill's trollish physical appearance was natural and inherited, and evidently he passed it on; unlike Tale, he did not need to disfigure himself.

Egill's prowess as a warrior is always first and foremost in his saga (and in most others): skaldship and tricksterish talents and inclinations are seamlessly attached to his fighter's part and role. Certain other epic northern characters, however, are even more markedly tricksterish, and prime among them is Saxo's "hero" Amleth. This Amleth, who supplied a later poet with certain key themes, is by no means an introspective and melancholy Dane, but a very dangerous, crafty, and lecherous young man, whose frequently unsavory activities are reported by Saxo with extraordinary gusto even in the Latin. Amleth's feigned imbecility, accompanied by a disguising coat of grime, is described in detail, and we find ourselves in a more outrageously violent world than that of Shakespeare's play: the spy whom Amleth discovers in his mother Garutha's chamber is not merely killed but butchered, and the bloody parts are thrown into a sewer.[71] Sent to England by Fengi (the wicked uncle in Saxo's account), he gets rid of two of Fengi's parasites (Shakespeare's Rosenkranz and Gildenstern) by tampering with Fengi's betraying message—and adds a forged request that the English king be so kind as to marry his daughter to the young and lusty ambassador. And after returning to Denmark and killing Fengi in a barbarous manner, Amleth is congratulated by Saxo as "worthy [*dignus*] of everlasting fame!"[72]

In Saxo's fourth book of the *Gesta Danorum* Amleth's adventures are continued, though now turned toward what Ellis Davidson, the most recent editor of an English-language *Gesta,* describes as motifs more markedly influenced by folk-tale themes.[73] But to complete our picture of this model of the unbuttoned trickster, we can add that Amleth boasts of two wives (the second a Scottish princess of the old-tale-type whose unsuccessful suitors are beheaded by her father), and that the hero, once besieged, defeats the British king by trickery, mocking up his dead as living warriors manning the fortress's walls.[74] Altogether we *could* say, if our tastes ran in that vein, that the later, Shakespearean Amleth is in some ways less interesting than this more primitive model, whose uncircumscribed character and wild craftiness are very little disguised in Saxo's florid appreciation. In fact we might even think of the earlier Amleth as growing, or declining, into the posture of a half- or part-time trickster in Shakespeare's version, which would ally him to two other hero figures we have already met: Tristan and Cei.

Tristan (or Drystan) is made into a great champion in the archaic Welsh sources, prominently listed as one of the three "battle-diademed men" in the *Trioedd Ynys Prydein* or Welsh *Triads*—and thus rated equal to the magnificent Cei himself. There he is called a "stubborn man," a "peer" or great man of the Island, and of course the lover or *screhawc* of the Lady Essyllt.[75] But he is also given a more ambiguous role as one of three "powerful swineherds," fitting him to the ancient Celtic prominence of this elsewhere lowly position: watching over the sacred swine.[76] The full-figure portrait of Tristan later assembled by Gottfried von Strassburg provides us with even more detail: Tristan had an exotic (northern) origin and was trained there in certain skills and crafts he then introduced to King Mark's court.[77] It is in the two trips he makes to Ireland, in Gottfried's tale, that his unmasked tricksterish aspect emerges. Tristan comes self-identified by a false name, and self-confessed as a skilled liar well equipped "to save his own skin," but there is more: he requires the magical services of the elder Queen Isolde (in parallel to the Serbo-Croat heroes and their supernatural female helpers, and perhaps reminiscent of Odysseus and others); he is specifically called a trickster (*paratiere*) by his enemies, King Mark's courtiers; and at times he displays a nearly comic ineptitude, as in his botched fight with the obligatory dragon. All this shows very clearly what he is really intended to be.[78]

The well-known erotic element enters his tale with the younger Isolde, but at this point Tristan's tricksterish nature and skills begin to be obscured, and in truth it is Isolde who becomes the craftier and more powerful partner of the two fated lovers. It is she who connives to hide the loss of her maidenhead to Tristan, and she who manipulates old King Mark by tricking speech and even by a doctored oath.[79] Tristan himself is now, it seems, simply swept along in the torrent of the narrative, and in dealing with the two Isoldes, mother and daughter, both of whom deploy magical-manipulative powers greater than his own, he becomes increasingly a pawn and even a victim. The Tristan who, like Cei, had been a champion in battle, loses this part of his older, hero-warrior's persona, although (again like Cei) to a different kind of power or influence. The later Tristan, in the German *minnesinger*'s rendering, retains much of the trickster's character, but even then he is made subordinate to a female power wielding a formidable magical skill he himself lacks. Cei, who deteriorates into the bad-tempered Sir Kay the Seneschal, will eventually appear as a buffoon, and the powerfully tricksterish aspect he carried into a tale like *Culhwch ac Olwen* is denatured into meanness and rudeness—though even in the latter emanation something of the old Cei breaks through, for he openly says what he thinks, which of course can itself have a comic effect in the formalaic, even predictable context of an epic.

The comic-erotic strain that enters into the trickster type thus expresses itself, in the epics and other heroic narratives, both in content and in style. For elements of *content* we can descry priapic sexual adventuring without any of the later trappings of chivalry, along with greed and appetitiveness, episodes of skillful trickery and crafty manipulation, and adventures that go drastically wrong. As for form or tricksterish *style*, we see the extremes of word and gesture: outrageous exaggeration, lies advertised as truth (or boldly asserted to be lies), comic effect achieved by simply saying what others will not say (that is, speaking openly and brazenly), and the vulgar sign and even contemptuous gesture, the *bras d'honneur* made toward the entire heroic world and its gullible audiences.

THE TRICKSTER AND DEATH

The archaic, mythic, and cosmogonic or cosmotactic trickster, the trickster of the macrocosm, is deeply involved in the mythic enigma of death, mainly because he is said to release or even to create the power or actuality of death, through his insatiable curiosity and his cackhanded maladvertance.[80] But the heroic trickster, too, has a very special place in respect to death and its key dramas: he is often able to defeat or at least delay death for himself—or, by significant contrast, to *will* it, and thus to stand apart from a directed or destined fate. His distinction from the normative hero, with his fitting, his "good" and early hero's death, should be clear enough. Odysseus in his own story does not seek out danger and the threat of death, but manipulates his skills (especially his skill with words) and plays with fate itself, to defeat death in the form of monstrous and cannibal beings like Polyphemos (who lead to the "nightmare world" of Hades), and to escape a "symbolic death" in the form of sweet forgetfulness or the potent sexual nets or enchantments of Kirke or Kalypso.[81] It is only what we would expect of a son of Sisyphos, who according to one myth had chained up Death himself, and who at another time had even escaped from Hades' queen and from that black and joyless realm.[82] And Sisyphos—perhaps—died of old age. Odysseus died, either the same way, as an aged and retired trickster, or perhaps in a strange shoreline combat with his own son by Kirke, neither son nor father known to the other. It is another complex reversal of the heroic norm that tricksters usually do have a son—and the son may kill the father rather than the other, heroic way around.[83]

In the Balkans, an archetypical trickster like Tale the Fool does not die at all, within the corpus of tales available to us: Tale to some degree made himself, and he perdures, in one of his personae, as nearly invincible and immortal as any icon of the Dirty Old Man would be. According to one of the lists included in the Welsh *Culhwch ac Olwen*, Two-Gifted Cei was killed, and his death was avenged by Arthur, but this must have been in his other, warrior manifestation; in the Continental elaboration of the *matière de Bretagne*, he lives on as a cranky and ill-fortuned old man, who seems in fact to be about the same age as Arthur, his quondam "twin."[84] We might conclude that the old king and the old trickster have different mythic roots but roughly the same age relationship, in contrast to the always young, because ever death-seeking, hero. Again, insofar as Starkaðr the Old has some of the trickster's characteristics (partly resting in the ambiguity of his relationship to Óðinn), we are not surprised to learn that he was given three lifetimes by that mystery-spinning god, and lived to greatly regret the "gift." The northern evidence also gives us the biography of the real, not legendary forefather Egill Skalla-Grímsson, whose unpleasant old age is laid out in his saga in unstinting detail. As this warrior-skald grew older his contrary and mischief-making propensities increased, but in the end, like Sisyphos or (perhaps) Odysseus, he could no longer keep death at bay even by trickery, being too enfeebled.

The trickster-hero definitely commands death; he will not be made a victim of it, at least until the very end of a long tale of years, an old age that is unheroic by definition. But he will also not become ennobled by his years because, I believe, he had given up that option when he turned to the trickster's ways, and thus he cannot take up the respected role of the old king. Starkaðr's death was actually purchased by the old man, who found a young warrior of the right lineage (who could also be persuaded to the deed because Starkaðr had killed his father), and the battered old man dies, at the end of his three long lifetimes, by the sword, but in a sort of clumsy execution and not a proper battlefield death.[85] Exactly the same death is invited by Iliach mac Cass, the aged and shameless grandfather-warrior in his decrepit old chariot, who is beheaded at his command by one of his own Ulstermen at the end of his first and last day of strange combat in the *Táin*. Oedipus, the warrior-king whom I have already associated with the images of Starkaðr, is given a long, tortured life after his sins are discovered, a life consonant with the trickster mode, and one he finally abandons himself through a sort of self-sacrifice or suicide.[86] Within the collectivity of trickster-hero motifs, however, Oedipus hews rather closer to the heroic line: his wisdom (as Kerényi notes) is flawed and faulty, and his great and distinguishing mark—as also that of his line—is *orgê*, "furious pride," the red hero's pride that ever masters and deludes him.

With his healthy taint of the comic and erotic, his odd unbalanced powers and occasional awful failures, the trickster-hero puts spice, contrast, even a dimension of our old humanity into the marmoreal perfection of the hero's presence and story. A good many epic poets are wise, skilled, or traditional enough to use him and his tricks when they can, and our accounts of the warrior-hero would surely be the poorer without the raucous complications and the original solutions that the trickster occasionally brings.

SMITHS AND OTHERS
The Smith and the Hero

The cluster of images subsumed under or gathered around the figure of the metalworking smith extends deep into the myths of the history of creation or "making" itself. Connected, technically, with the discovery and expansion of true metallurgy, the smith is thrust back into the very womb of creation, as Mircea Eliade impressively and convincingly demonstrated: his dark craft is associated with the perilous mysteries of sexuality, of "male" ore found in "female" earth, or of "male" tools and weapons—especially weapons—fabricated in an arcane process often symbolically equated with the even more ancient mysteries of human copulation and parturition.[87] A number of these symbolic relationships are carried forward into the relationship of the smith to the warrior and his epic tale, in that the smith may be praised or blamed as the very creator of culture itself, aligned with the forces both of life and of death—as the warrior-hero, in another way, is an image projective and expressive both of cultural-protective and of hostile-"demonic" valences.

The non-Christian or pre-Christian heroic epics I am mainly using as sources in this study often include a divine or semidivine smith among those powers concerned with man, or with whom man is concerned. After the Christianizing of Europe, however, the smith-god, with his suspicious mastery of fire, is pushed toward a demonic allegiance or alliance or even a diabolic origin.[88] On the other hand, the extraordinary (or ambiguous) creative powers of the human smith can be edited entirely out of our epic-narrative record: the Otherworld origin of particularly important or power-laden weapons may be stated as a simple fact, with the assumption that no merely human power or craft was involved in their making. Such a theme is given a peculiar twist in *Beowulf*, since the champion's sword that the hero brings with him from the upper world will not bite on the monstrous mother of Grendel, and he must fight with a sword he finds below, "giant-made, long ago"; even with this supernatural origin, it loses its blade after the deathblow, "burnt up by the poisonous hot blood" of the monster-mother.[89]

Another thematic reversal of the power of the smith, as seen in myth, occurs when the creative weapon-magic of the artificer is not deemed strong enough, or is blocked or overcome by some earlier, more primitive, or deeper counterforce. In his fight with the ferocious, trollish, and uncivilized Gaimon, who "eats meat raw and drinks blood," the Norse romance-saga hero Hrólfr Gautreksson triumphs with wooden clubs and rocks, like the caveman. The uselessness of a weapon forged of ordinary metal may be variously expressed, but Hrólfr's saga displays a typical folktalelike formulation: ogres, sorcerers, and other supernatural beings may not be vulnerable to man's ordinary or smith-made weapons, crafted by a higher "culture."[90] Such an idea is already visible in Beowulf's poem, for to defeat Grendel the

hero puts aside his war gear and forgoes using his sword against this particular monster.[91] One of the Serbo-Croat *guslari* turns this notion toward
a rather different image by declaring at one point that the heroic *aghas* of
the border can never be overcome by commonplace modern weapons but
only by "wood and stones" hurled at them.[92] In fact, in the same Serbo-
Croat narrative we find a tricephalic monster, "Troglov Aropin," armed only
with the club-mace he throws at Omer, son of the hero Mujo.[93] The use of
a primitive weapon, when the hero wields it, may of course also mark him
as one of the slow, foolish, or backward heroes (clumsy Rainouart in the
French *chanson* cycle of Guillaume d'Orange is a fine example) who pro-
fess to know nothing of more civilized or effective weaponry. And finally
there is the "natural" club of Herakles, the *hêrôs theos* or hero-god (who is
equally *theos anêr,* divine man) whose specific, iconic weapon, his club, has
been identified as expressing his dactylic or phallic power, marking him as
"sprung from the earth and phallic" in the ultimate core of his origins.[94]

Herakles leads us to Hephaistos and some of the mysteries of divine fabrication and of the deep nature of the smith-god. According to Apollodoros, the young hero Herakles received a bow from Apollo, a mantle from
Athena, but from Hephaistos a golden cuirass; it was Hermes the trickster-
god who gave the hero his sword.[95] Evidently Apollodoros, in this case as
often elsewhere, had access to and repeats exceptionally archaic Greek materials. Hephaistos does not make offensive weapons, though as a smith-
god he can fabricate anything else, and as a "binding" god, crippled or not,
he has potent dominion over both life and death.[96] He is represented with
a bundle of attributes diametrically opposite to the war-god's, and his human or semihuman imitators are likely to carry these as well: the smith of
Greek mythology is crippled, dwarfish, ugly, and impotent. Yet he gains
power over many of humankind's activities by his free passage between two
worlds, and by his power-enhancing "fall" from heaven, his mutilation, and
self-sacrifice: he will later be named as the god who has the power to intervene in sexual activity, initiation, the death drama, and in other human mysteries as well.

THE PLACE OF THE SMITH

The particular powers of the human smith, who surely can be called the
ultimate distillation of *homo faber,* are easy enough to detail but often difficult to explain; his anomalies may confuse us even more than they confused
the early societies in which he labored. Genetic myths tell us that his ascribed status in a society may vary wildly, from establishing him in place as
the First Smith whose crafting powers are regarded as sufficient to "make"

or found a kingdom (a number of African examples) to cases in which the smith is assigned to the lowest possible social level, or even made outcaste—as a contemned nonperson, as dangerous as the slave in his grubby, negative potentiality.[97] Neither of these extremes is to be easily found in Indo-Europe and its extensions, though the Persian *Shâh-nâma* says, first, that the "primeval king" of Iran, the cosmotact Hûshang, invented the craft of smithing, and that this favor was later returned by one Kâva the Blacksmith, who helped to "make" the king by supporting the rightful ruler, Faridun, and who also provided the royal palladium, the Kâviâni Banner made of his own blacksmith's apron, which would always be the "royal emblem of majesty" in Persia's kingdom.[98] Whatever the varied data from our separate sources, the smith's powerful ambiguities are very present and are not easily ignored.

From whence does this power spring? Laura Makarius says that the powers, both negative and positive, associated with the "blacksmith complex" are explained by the smith's continual violation of the blood taboo; the fluid of life in a number of its numinous aspects is associated with the smithing enterprise, and especially with the red, hot iron worked by the smith.[99] It is not just the dangerous uses that will be made of the metal weapons he forges, but the ambient field of forbidden conjunctions around them that impresses and disturbs humankind, for the weapons forged must be and often are invested with more than merely technical force and utility: they are all made by and through what are perceived as magical transformations, and so implicitly are inclined to magical ends. Makarius particularizes her theory out of a range of possible affects surrounding, or incorporated into, the figure of the smith, and her theory does manage to put an anthropological and (to some extent) a historical frame around the smith and his powers.[100] Mircea Eliade, in *his* portrait, paints the smith in broader and less exclusive strokes, drawing connecting lines between him and the other secret masters: masters of fire, masters of fabrication and intermediation (like the shaman), and finally to that transmuter extraordinary, the alchemist, a shadowy and much misunderstood figure who has also attracted C. G. Jung's close attention.[101]

In the post-Neolithic barbarian—that is, the heroic—societies of Indo-Europe the smith may lose some of his generalized and "sacred" force, but he retains large parts of his innate power and secretive significance as the warrior-hero's own artificer, and as a master of other mysterious, taboo-laden, but necessary arts. Our ancient Greek sources locate metalworkers in groups or gangs with old, odd, and evocative names: Corybantes, Telchines, Kuretes, Daktyls, Kabeiroi. There is a good deal of evidence pointing to pre-Greek (and therefore pre-Indo-European) origins of these names, identifying an indeterminate number of beings, perhaps human, who manipulate or deal in a variety of activities, but who are all clearly "mythical metallurgists."[102] All these groups have deep telluric powers, shaped or expressed in various ways: the Daktyls and the Kuretes (or Korybantes) were the earthborn guardians of the infant god Zeus, and the Daktylic mark—especially indicative of hypersexuality and equivocal earth-magical powers—is plainly stamped on a number of our less orthodox, elder myth-heroes, including Herakles and Oedipus. The Telchines as a group possess "a more markedly Underworld character" as well as a penchant for darker or even malignant magic, though later Hellenistic commentators divided the Daktyls, too, into two cohorts, "left hand" and "right hand," with one cohort devoted to good (plain, hard-laboring smiths) and the other to evil designs (black-magicians, workers in the forbidden).[103] All are primitive in morphism, and usually swarthy and dwarfish in appearance; other associations include the magical, rhythmic, and percussive dance (Kuretes, Korybantes) and (in the case of the Kuretes) involvement in the initiation rites of young men (*kouroi*). One salient fact about all these groups is their foreign, non-Hellenic, and in general anomalous and suspect origin and social placement; and as these masters were separated in myth as dangerous (that is, sacred) beings invested with dangerous and unknowable powers, so did their human followers take up a similar position in terms of the main lines of Greek social and social-imaginal development: *technê* (the artisan's craft) is ever marked by what Pierre Vidal-Naquet accurately calls "the Greek ambivalence toward their 'specialists.'"[104]

The mysterious castes, made up of these masters of *technê*, slip into the same mythic field of ambivalence and suspicion as Hephaistos, the lame "binding god," or Prometheus, the Titan trickster and old enemy of a jealous Zeus. Of course, the fire masters' lessons in artisanry cannot be completely rejected or forgotten by the Greeks: the *polis*, the city-state, whether they liked it or not, was at least partially built on these technical foundations. Other lessons from the zone of ambiguity may also be summoned at various stages in the social life of the Greek polity: thus the educational legends of the war-dancing, wild Kuretes may be ritualized to aid in the dangerous process of initiating and socially reintegrating adolescent warriors-in-training.

In addition, mysterious smiths may be taken up by folklore and deposited back in the depths of the earth, as dwarf-smiths are in the North, or "fairy" or Otherworld beings are elsewhere.[105] In mining, always seen as a highly specialized form of mysterious and perilous activity under the earth, the nonhuman being who may be either an ally or an enemy of the human miner continues to have a telluric force "down in the mine" to the present day. Surely these beings and these ancient-rooted beliefs spring from the oldest, most truly subterranean levels of one mythicized aspect or root of human technology.[106]

FUNCTIONAL ASPECTS OF THE SMITH?

Starkaðr the Old, that strange, sour servant-hero to several generations of Danish kings, is not as crabbed about smiths as he is about almost everything else in the unsatisfactory world he observed and inhabited for so long, but he can still be scathing, especially about the goldsmith who works the rich and yielding yellow metal, his hands "endowed . . . with extreme art" but his character soft, sensual, and craven. Starkaðr even assaults one of these skilled pariahs with his sword, cutting him a shaming blow across the buttocks but, in contempt, not killing him. In his subsequent self-congratulatory verses, the old puritan characterizes the wounded goldsmith as compact of lechery, lower-class insolent ambition, and the dirt of the smithy; this worker in the luxurious metal is not only given a set of Third Function negative marks but is caught illicitly disporting himself with royalty, the undiscriminating princess Helga.[107] Thus Saxo has Starkaðr propagandize for his own warrior caste and its supportive or "true" ironsmiths ("they are superior who forge swords and shields for the battles of men").[108]

Elsewhere in the North, and especially in colonized Iceland, smithing seems to have been a craft widely known and practiced by the farmer-*bondar* and by the Icelandic settlers out of their own necessity, but the citations we have on smithcraft as such in the sagas often have a peculiar ring to them. Kveld-Úlfr, Skalla-Grímr, and Egill, three generations in *Egils saga*, are all smiths—and all are uncanny men: *þursam* or "trollish" is the term a saga maker once used for them.[109] Then there is the case of the reforging of the sinister weapon *Grásiða* in Gisli's saga by the sorcerer Þorgrímr Neb, and what sounds like a contemptuous reference to smithing in *Njáls saga*.[110] The character Smidr in the *lygisaga* "Bósa ok Herrauðr" is not a smith, despite his name, but a magician; the only other Smidr known to me appears in *Landnámabók*, and he is illegitimate.[111] Yet *Landnámabók* also gives us the odd case of the smith Steinrod the Strong, who in legend is credited with saving "a good many people" from monsters, and who bested a witch-hag and shape shifter named Geirhildr, using an iron pole he presumably forged himself.[112] Clearly some other, and friendlier, aspect of the smith's power is reverberant here.

Nevertheless, the wariness with which the smith is treated in the sagas

emerges suggestively in the fact that rarely if ever is a weapon actually com-
missioned from a smith-artificer: swords of significance (the named swords,
a fortiori) are inherited, found in grave mounds, taken in combat abroad, if
their origins are mentioned at all. The technical, artifactual origin of the
named swords in the *chansons de geste* and the epic romances is even cloudier,
and the later romances continue this pattern. The nature of the evidence
from our Indo-European epical narratives suggests that the smith's craft
and his associated powers have elements linking them to each of the Dumézilian *fonctions*, with the strongest attraction or bent toward the Second
and Third Functions, but the specific gravity of the smith's art tends to move
it beyond any of these, and arguably toward a Fourth Function: an ectopic
function marked by "what is other, beyond or outside," in N. J. Allen's
words.[113] (Smiths and metalworkers were actually found in Ireland in
what was identified there as a fourth social segment.)[114] The Dumézilian
surthéorie posits a division between a magicoreligious (Varunaic) and a
judicial-contractual (Mitraic) mode in the First or Sovereign Function, and
this subfunctional division can almost certainly be extended to the other
two *fonctions* as well; but Allen (and others, especially the Rees brothers)
proposes a Fourth Function that represents "what stands outside the forces
that ensure continuity,"[115] a function "not self-sufficient but relational."[116]
This would be exterior to or separate from the Varunaic-Mitraic division,
based on a significant variation in emphasis.[117]

"Making" the Warrior-Hero

Whatever his ultimate placement and disposition, the smith is very deeply
involved in "making," if not at times completely fabricating, the hero. He
does so in three ways: by *fostering*; by *initiating*; and, in a magical or at least
a symbolic-manipulative modality, by *forging* the hero.

FOSTERAGE

The fosterage of hero by smith is a widely encountered epic theme, seen
at least as far as Tibet, where the superhuman magician-king (and hero)
Gezar of Ling, after that elaborate series of birth-incarnatory experiences
necessary in a Lamaist Buddhist context, finally takes the human form of
an abandoned child—who is adopted by a smith. Gezar, whose supernatural adventures easily escape the familiar boundaries of our usual Eurocentric or Indo-Eurocentric focus, also has an inborn knowledge of the
skills necessary to the smith, and thus needs no tutelage in the craft.[118]
Although the fostering of a divine child by a smith reenters the mythic

frame from which I ordinarily restrict myself, we can look at the guardian-ship of the infant Zeus in this wise, as the dancing Kuretes, with their iron weapons and telluric kinship, protect the newborn, divine son of ravening old Kronos.[119]

A more useful example of smith fosterage occurs in the Ossetic tradition of the Caucasus, where gods and human heroes are almost as thoroughly mixed and confused as they are in the *Iliad*: here the Nart Amzor is fos-tered by the smith-god Kurdælagon.[120] The Old Irish Cycle of the Túatha Dé Danann tells us that Balor of the Evil Eye, who was the god-hero Lugh's grandfather (playing that dark role Erich Neumann calls the part of the "negative father," and recalling the grim role of grandfather Akrisios in the Perseus myth), tried but failed to prevent the birth of the god Lugh, who was then taken away and brought up by Gavida the Smith, who was also the boy-god's maternal uncle.[121] Smith fosterage runs in Lugh's fam-ily, for this very god was the young hero Sétantae's divine father, involved in the hero's triple conception, long before Sétantae killed the smith Cu-lann's guard-dog and afterward was self-named Cú Chulainn, "Hound of Culann"—both guardian of and fosterling within the smith's house. In the *macgnimartha*, the "boyhood deeds" of the hero Finn mac Cumaill, a smith has a rather more attenuated role, merely offering the young hero hospi-tality, his daughter, and well-made weapons; a separate tradition claims that Finn himself was skilled in the smith's art.[122] Another Celtic smith foster-ing is that of Morann, who as an infant escaped a watery grave because he already had the power of speech (he would later become chief judge, or law speaker, of Ireland) and was taken to be fostered by a smith.[123] He was eventually returned to the father who had once ordered him drowned.

The smith is inserted into the fostering tale or episode in a way that rein-forces his multivalent pose. His most salient role is that of guardianship; the smith's special protection is extended over the helpless infant, child-hero, or godling. The Celtic sources play with and rearrange several facets of this old theme: Lugh is made safe in the care of the smith-god; Man-annan mac Lir, the sea god and divine father of Mongain (who would be a king of the Ulad), takes his son away to the Otherworld after his birth; and so with only a slight change of emphasis we have returned to imitate the plots of the mythepical Welsh *mabinogi*, specifically the tale *Pwyll Pendeuic Dyuet*, and the birth and occultation of the hero of that tale, Pryderi.[124]

Smith fosterage also can remove a child from secular time and place, and thus stands thematically with an Otherworld occultation and guardianship, where time and place have their own rules. In addition the smith may take up fosterage because of his ambiguous (deficient might be the more appropriate word) sexuality, expressed in a non-threatening masculine gender. From the impotent god Hephaistos on, the smith is imagined as one who has sacrificed much to learn his strange art and craft, and thus he has denied himself offspring of his own body. Even his Daktylic-phallic supervirility remains symbolic, sterile, seedless. As another example, in the Irish Celtic sources kings often have strange begettings, but the "perfect king" and hero Cormac mac Airt was born of Etain, daughter of the smith OlcAcha; here we see a smith providing the receptacle (his daughter's womb) for the future king. We and the source recognize that a "great honour" comes at this point both to and from the smith, but only indirectly.[125] (The childless smith is rather more common.) This characteristic—of being a generational isolate—resembles what we often see in the hero, but springs from a different rationale: "the smith," as the Reeses say, "is husband to his forge."[126] The most likely scenario to describe the fostering smith establishes him as a true protector; he guards and maintains the identity of the fostered hero, and this guardianship differs from his instructional-initiatory role, where the hero will be helped by a smith to change his name and find his mature heroic persona, character, and calling.

INITIATION

The smith deals with the initiation of the hero not as a guardian but as a prover, or tester, and also as one who may help to form the vital being of the hero in his last, fully emergent phase or *imago*. Initiation, as we have largely agreed since the appearance of Arnold van Gennep's *Les rites de passage* in 1913, typically if not invariably involves a series of processes and processual stages or points: *separation* from the social matrix, *experience* of extraordinary, destabilizing rites and processes (involving what Eliade calls "the temporary return to Chaos"), and *return* or *reintegration* of group or individual into the order and plenitude of the adult social fabric.[127] The smith appears to act as a coadjutor or guide in the initiatory process for the same reason he fits into other parts of the heroic scenario: because he himself is not a firm part of the social cosmesis and order, but peripheral to or even outside it. He also wields special talents for which he has paid some significant price, and he is often the "maker" par excellence in the heroic biography. In the heart of the transmutation of the hero from a preparatory or potential stage to full, multipotent or omnipotent ability, the artifact-making smith appears as a "friendly monster" who represents both the positive, socially useful assistant in the processes that guard and thus continue life, and the darker, anomic, or even acosmic forces pressing in against and continually threatening these positive processes. In this he is analogous to the hero himself.

One of our problems may be precisely to identify and track this heroic initiatory process; first, because the hero typically follows an extraordinary, temporally distorted process of maturation, and second, because of the hero's uncomfortable position in any peer group or cohort. (Both Cú Chulainn and Finn mac Cumaill, for example, are reported to have set on their supposed peers of the royal Boy Troops, defeating and nearly destroying them all—an incident also repeated in one of the Ossetian Nart hero tales that so often mirror the Celtic narrative evidence.)[128] A kind of group initiation for heroes may be hinted at in the sources, as when the mythic-archetypic centaur, cave-dwelling Kheiron, is said to be responsible for the sequestration, and by inference some form of initiation, of certain Greek heroes including Iason, Akhilleus (and his father Peleus before him), and others—even the healer and hero-god Asklepios.[129] Certainly Kheiron counts as a "friendly monster," but his initiatory supervision (if that is what it is) also brings his young charges into important contact both with feral animals and with the tamed horse, the hero's primary mount or animal adjunct. The horse sign, as Eliade has shown, often brings smith and initiand together: the young warrior-in-training finally breaks through into full warriorhood and adulthood when given his full equipage of horse and weapons, so now a new identity can be crafted, and new and determinate adult responsibilities assigned.[130] The hero, in contrast to the ordinary, adolescent male initiate, is not restricted temporally: he does not merely pass *through* a stage marked by the experience of destructive and acosmetic forces (fire, darkness, the wild, monstrous animality), but rather adopts and internalizes, so as to reproject them. Moreover, he never really emerges from the initiatory phase because he is never (and never can be) fully reintegrated into the normal social matrix. Yet at the same time his symbolic situation is important: the hero, according to the Reeses, "seems to personify not only the initiate but the inner meaning of initiation. He is the victory, the embodiment of a spirit which no boundaries can contain."[131]

FORGING AND TRANSFORMING

The smith usually tends to stand a little apart from the hero he arms and equips, and he may even be an opponent, as Prokrustes, called by Kerényi the "death-dealing smith," was Theseus's grimmest enemy in his first set of adventures.[132] The solidity of the artifacts the smith forges for the warrior-hero contrasts with the shifting and unstable affinity between the two as human types, and that insubstantial tie is perhaps best expressed in and by the element of fire itself. Fire manipulated by the smith is renewable, a tamed and controlled element; the internal fire (*furor, wut, ferg, mênos*) of the hero may be partially willed but is not completely controlled even by those who can make manifest its terrible, upsurging power—and its destructive effect can eventually consume its heroic human container altogether. That internal fire of the warrior may blaze gloriously but has a short, hot life, as indeed does the normative hero. The smith, on the other hand, is meant to survive and usually does, hidden again, back in the earth, or possibly withdrawing into the Fourth Function—the zone of the opposite, the "uncanny, mysterious, otherworldly and paradoxical."[133] Nevertheless, there are concrete realities attached to the smith and his art that may emplace him firmly into a social-cosmetic order, whereas the hero always penetrates into and wanders through another zone, an essentially acosmetic world.

The smith needs a place to do his fabrication: he is tied down to this place even if it is located "elsewhere," outside the social cosmos, in a forest, a cave, in some isolated spot where the noise won't disturb the neighbors. In this workshop and forge the solid ore-stuff taken out of the earth is transmuted through the synergy of fire and air, and by the smith's hard, grubby, repetitive, and rhythmical efforts remarkable objects are produced, to be passed to the hero to use. When the hero is set some task, the smith's workplace may be his first stop, as it is situated between the setting of the task and its fulfillment—and in numerous cases the task could not be accomplished without the tools the smith will provide. Afterward those artifacts will be carried to the ends of the earth—and, like the smith who made them, they will probably survive the hero they serve. "No man must have you," says dying Roland to Durendal, but the hero can't manage to break the sword from "Moriana's Vale"—where, one supposes, Otherworld smiths had been at work on its forging.[134] Other weapons, everlasting, pass from hero to hero, are even taken out of burial howes, dealing death again and again when brought back out from the place of death.[135]

Despite all this, however, the invulnerability of the hero is signed most extraordinarily when he is born already armored, with an integument of steel—like those extraordinary weapons of his that appear without human intervention. The strange and tormented hero Karṇa, great foe of the Pâṇḍavas in the *Mahâbhârata*, is born thus, but it is symptomatic of his equivocal situation that the god Indra later ripped off this protective covering.[136] In addition to Karṇa, our look at the "forged" hero ought to begin with one of the extraordinary Ossetian Nart heroes, the superwarrior Batradz, who, like others in this family or Great House of heroes, had a very strange conception and birth.[137] While still in his anomalous womb—an abscess on his father's back—Batradz "burned," and at birth he emerged blazing and already armored in two kinds of steel, so that he had to be immediately doused or tempered in vats of cold water.[138] The similarity between this tempering and a famous incident in the early career of the Ulster Cycle hero Cú Chulainn did not escape Dumézil, who saw here a concrete example of a *motivbild* binding together the old Celtic world and the equally archaic themes held and fossilized in a primitive, isolated Ossetian enclave in the Caucasus, where the ancient Scythian spirit and its mythic consciousness still lived.[139] This incident, which Eliade and the Reeses consider the "initiation" of this heroic figure, has the overheated child-hero first shamed or, more likely, magically depotentialized by the presence of half-naked women, and then dunked in the three vats of cold water hurriedly made ready for him.[140] (Cú Chulainn is not the only warrior-hero of the Old Irish Ulster Cycle to be "tempered" when his heat or fury becomes too dangerous: in the *Fled Bricrend* [Bricriu's Feast], Queen Medb orders cauldrons of cold water prepared for all three of the great heroes who are "heatedly" contending for the Champion's Portion: Loegaire Duadach, Conall Cernach, and Cú Chulainn himself.)[141] But Cú Chulainn's affinity with the imaginal world of the smithy goes well beyond this "tempering" and his close connection to his own fosterer, the smith Culann.

In the tale *Tochmarc Emire* (The Wooing of Emer) we are told that Cú Chulainn, accompanied by the great warriors Loegaire and Conall and perhaps Conchobar the King as well, once traveled to Scotland to be trained in martial arts by Donall the Soldierly. Some of this training was very odd indeed: "they were taught by him to blow a leathern bellows under the flagstone of the small hole" (which sounds very much like the pumping of a smith's furnace bellows), and "on it they would perform until their soles were black or livid," which seems to imply a hot-foot dance of some sort. Moreover, Donall's gruesome daughter Big Fist (whose feet were reversed back to front, and who had a jet-black face and bright red hair) fell in love with Cú Chulainn.[142] This awful creature is very like a spirit of the forge, soot-black and fire-red, and her torsion is precisely that of Cú Chulainn himself when he is described as undergoing his warp-spasm in the *Táin:* "his body made a furious twist inside his skin, so that his feet and shins and knees switched to the rear and his heels and calves switched to the front."[143] Other drastic distortions occur to this hero as well, which to William Sayers have a particular associative connection to "the generation of heat, and reciprocal and serial movement—in short, to the imagery of the smithy."[144] Cú Chulainn, unlike Karṇa and Batradz, was not born with his armor but is himself well and truly forged, and his ungovernable internal heat, calor, *ferg* takes on or reflects the potency of the smith's furnace fire. It cannot be said what he is at this point, hot hero or well-forged weapon; but, like a weapon, he can and will turn even against his own, pursuing a victory over the torn bodies of his closest foster brothers and of his own son, Connla, once he is provided with the mysterious and ever deadly *gae bolga*—by some artificer never named.

This superhuman, nonpareil Irish hero stands in the midst of the smith's myth and mystery, close to the symbolic smithery noted in certain tribal initiation ceremonies, in which a smith figure ritually reenacts the "hammering out" of the transmuted initiates, taking them forcefully from chaotic potentiality to full adult realization in society. The parallel force or potency associated with the smith, his smithy, and his heat and other images is that of human sexuality; thus we see young Cú Chulainn pursued by a sexually inflamed fire-spirit ogress, or Finn offered Lochan the master smith's daughter in the course of his "boyhood deeds." He accepts her body—along with the two spears forged by her father.

COWARD KNIGHT AND OTHERS

Who is ever going to laugh at a hero?

As I try to organize the constellation of types and figures surrounding the hero, and especially as I develop the ligatures binding the heroic trickster, the smith, and other "reversing" figures, I must move back into what is arguably the most difficult affect to frame and analyze in the heroic narrative zone: the contained element of the foolish or the comic. In the broadest sense the very act of reversing heroic patterns, turning them on their heads, would seem to be intrinsically and irrepressibly comic. The chosen heroic field of furious action, with its hyperbolic effects, strenuous efforts, and grand-operatic gestures, surely invites a parodic treatment, yet in a great many epic-heroic narratives that invitation to parodize is not accepted. We might wonder why.

THE BLACKENED HERO

When I introduced, in two other studies,[145] what I called the "blackened hero" (my examples were the Serbian Tale of Orasacs and the old Ulsterman Iliach mac Cass), I connected him directly to the trickster, though he has affective links as well to the smith-artificer on the one hand and to the "slow," foolish, or primitive hero on the other. At the extreme, negative edge of this "blackened" persona is the semifolkloric image of the ogrish enemy to humankind, the black monster who often carries some racial taint (of semihumanity and utter separation personified) in his narrative descriptions, and who is usually meant to be a foil to, and to be defeated by, the knightly-heroic protagonist. We see this above all in the *Chanson de Roland* and certain other *chansons de geste*, and in the romance epics.[146] Aside from this primeval or primitive monster-opponent, the blackened persona carries part of its comic effect in a free description of a literally dirty old man, whose dishevelment or decrepitude is starkly contrasted to the prismatic glory of the young heroes of the epic center and surround. In the North our old friend Egill has connections to this "blackened" persona, as does such a saga character as Hrieðar the Halfwit, who is ugly, dirty, and yet clever enough to make kings his conies.[147] Another way to move from description toward analysis has been suggested by Ellis Davidson, who derives from three different figures in northern myth and legend (Óðinn, Loki, and the egregious Amleth who appears in Saxo) an explanation of some of the variations possible in the trickster trade. Óðinn, she notes, has an overarching and ruthless power; his tricks are likely to be deadly; his secretive wisdom knows, and to a large if not complete extent, controls Fate itself. He only distantly resembles the portrait of the trickster first drawn by Paul Radin and considerably expanded by Jung and Kerényi, for his divine power is too overawing; Loki, "mischievous and lewd as well as cunning," is much better suited for that trickster's role among the Norse gods.[148] Indeed Loki is especially prone to that convoluted trickery that ends by ensnaring the trickster, and his antic shape-changing and taboo-fracturing have a desperate hilarity to them, although Ellis Davidson properly identifies another side, in which a Loki with deeper roots in the giant-world is seen to have "an ancient power" and a hard old wisdom perhaps equal even to Óðinn's.[149] Amleth, in her view, combines something of both models, while adding to them a hint of the "wise fool," a riddler with a savage, leering humor.[150]

Thus the North may again provide, as it so often does, surviving fragments of an ancient core of Indo-European *idéologie;* and the two facets of tricksterdom, Óðinnic and Lokian, can be readjusted and fine-tuned to explain the ambiguous career of a character like Cei in the Welsh Arthurian materials. Cei's trickster activity, most markedly in the quest tale *Culhwch ac Olwen,* is of the ruthless, crafty, and Óðinnic kind, but by the time he appears in *Peredur,* he has shifted into something more resembling the role and style of a depleted Loki: self-deluded, verbose, and foolish, a "knight" whose mean and frantic tricks tend to turn back on him. A similar declension is visible in the late years of Egill Skalla-Grímsson: his former craftiness and perverse potencies are transformed into spiteful and faintly ridiculous plotting and a near senile nastiness, though the *sagamaðr*, our recording and creating saga man, also seems to be making a realistic statement about the price to be paid by any hero's survival into old age, and in rather a different way from that of the creator of the superb *Njála*, which also has an old man at its burning center.

The first point to be drawn from the Óðinn-Loki comparison is that the core character of the trickster, or at least the human refraction of the trickster, is not solid, crystalline, and impenetrable like that of the normative hero, but changeable, even deliquescent. The volatile energies that must go into this role seem almost certain to disequilibrate the performer, and any imitation of the god Óðinn is particularly and predictably difficult to maintain over time. The second is that the craft of the Óðinn-trickster is in no way comic, at least not in any sense we would usually recognize, whereas the antics of the Loki-trickster may be. Cei's posing as a sword cleaner and then beheading Wrnach the Giant with his own sword, or tumbling the insensible Dillus the Bearded, giant champion of champions, into the trap pit so that his beard-hairs can be plucked and he mercilessly slain ("and then they killed him there," *A gwedy hynny y lad yn gwby*), has a very grim and deadly humor about him: Sir Kay the Seneschal inciting a better knight than he is with rash words, and then being lance-struck out of his boastful saddle, is both foolish and cruelly funny.[151]

King's Fool and Foolish Hero

The king's fool or royal jester again presents a constellation of characters and characteristics (Lear's Fool, for example, falls well beyond the scope of this study). One old aspect of the trickster makes him a clown-servant, as Dumézil saw when he aimed his examining lens at the Ossete tales and found the egregious Nart Syrdon, who serves the other, heroic Narts as a domestic—a valet and commissary—though he is also a malignant shape changer *and* a counselor to the heroes at need; he is even accompanied by an *équipe des grands profondeurs*.[152] Evidence from elsewhere differentiates the king's fool in other ways, as in the Old Irish *Mesca Ulad*, where King Conchobar's irresistible fool, plainly named Rómit Royal-Fool, has "a smooth, blue, Ethiopian's face"—that is, he is a Negro, originating in another race and place entirely.[153]

Yet another social-artistic context, perhaps Indo-Europeanized to some degree through a migrating Indic-Hindu influence, might give us some constructive hints: this is the very exotic Javanese. The relationship between king and clown was highly developed in traditional Javanese culture, both court-bred and popular. In the Javanese narrative imagination the *pana-kawan* or clown is made a mentor to the king, and is able to give good counsel because he is closer to the gods than his royal master: he is "blood kin" to the highest god, and even "equal to Kresna," that is, Krishna.[154] In the plot of one puppet play or *wayang*, the clown Petrick turns against a "proud king" and even leads an army of giants to defeat him and "all the great *pan-dawas*"—the king's warrior-paladins.[155] Yet the Javanese *panakawan*'s very high imaginal status is belied by his gross appearance, outrageous behavior, and especially his language, which is drawn straight from the lowest gutter. The symbolic orientation of this clown figure is arranged on a vertical axis, as he stretches up past his purported master to the highest gods, but also reaches down into the subcaste depths where he finds his incontinent and lewd "plain speech." The symbolic orientation of the foolish hero in most other contexts, on the other hand, is expressed in compact, dense, and unambiguous terms, much like those describing related heroic morphisms and actors: if there is directionality for this figure, it is, as is usual with the hero, horizontal or planar.[156]

The king's clown type often employs gutter speech, tabooed expressions, insulting and plainly vulgar signs, but he may also encrypt his wisdom or commentary in opacities difficult to decode. In either case he avoids what we would call the ordinary modes of epic language, with its open and unambiguous signs and its attempt to form clear and well-lit meanings. The foolish hero also uses ordinary language most of the time, though it may be careless and naive, and his "foolishness" consists mainly of his childlike innocence. In clear contrast to the usual untaught self-knowledge of the hero, the more comic heroic figure self-admittedly knows very little, and is quite unashamed of this ignorance. As a result of his innocence he may speak out frankly, without any sort of social filter, pose, or pretense (though he differs nonetheless from that special kind of "slow hero" who, like Grettir the Strong in his saga, refuses to accept responsibility and mature patterns of behavior out of a malignant, or at least a perverse and notional, self-esteem), and the comic effect is exposed when the willfully immature hero reveals his heroic abilities in suitably naive ways. Young Peredur (the Welsh original of the Continental Perlesvaus/Percival/Parzifal), who has deliberately been kept ignorant by his mother, pursues and is able to capture wild deer, thinking that they are exceptionally recalcitrant goats, and has no idea what a "knight" might be.[157] Another youth, Rainouart of the Guillaume d'Orange Cycle, literally is a blackened hero in two senses, being a Saracen, born swarthy, and also serving as a kitchen churl "blackened and soiled with the fire-shovel," who fights at first with a huge club, like a folk ogre, and who has an even more monstrous appetite for food and drink.[158] When he mounts a horse for the first time, he of course faces the wrong way (this must be an extremely ancient jape); when he finally uses a sword he is delighted "that such a small weapon can have such force."[159] In like wise the young Armenian hero Mher, last of the magnificent House of Sassoon, exhibits stubbornness, foolishness, and heroic superstrength all combined when he insists, despite ridicule, on carrying his horse rather than letting the beast carry him.[160] The tone of each narrative context can be made to vary more or less subtly in dealing with the "backward" hero.

The innocent foolishness of these heroes, of course, comically reverses the norms of herodom; the type is also often recognizable by his great (heroic) physical size coupled with a childish lack of control—or by a lack of control, period. According to his *macgnimartha,* even young Finn mac Cumall, still called Demne (in fact called Demne the Bald; for a time he has this unattractive physical mark of a "reversed" hero) killed nine youths by "accidentally" drowning them, a deed resembling the child-hero Cú Chulainn's fatal (for the other lads) first encounter with King Conchobar's Boy Troop.[161] Rainouart's club (which does not appear to be a Heraklean or Daktylic weapon) will appear in the unschooled hands of other "slow" heroes and might well be used, like Rainouart's, against monstrous and supernatural foes, who are proof against ordinary heroism and its customary or canonical weapons. Innocence by its very nature can take on a magical force or counterforce when inserted into certain aspects of or confrontations within the heroic tradition.[162]

The Coward Knight

The naive, open, and uncoded speech of the young "foolish hero" brings us to a final morphism of the comic-reversing hero: that of the coward knight. Here the primary and essential reversal of heroism is easily detected in the name, as the grossest and most manifest fault for any Second Function warrior-hero must be a lack of physical courage.[163] (A *fonction* devoted to death dealing, after all, should never shrink from the frequently dangerous or fatal personal consequences of that devotion.) Nevertheless, the coward will occasionally appear in the epic and its generic relations, though sometimes this characteristic is blended with a minor-league or ineffective villainy, and other times is simon-pure in its open refusal to be heroically brave.

The great Spanish narrative poem describing the deeds of El Cid Campeador is decorated with two loathly characters who play out part of the coward knight's scenario. The Princes or Infantes of Carrión, Per and Ferrant Gonzalvez, display their cowardice both in battle and elsewhere, and are responsible for the *affrente* or Outrage of Corpes (canto III) in which they brutally attack and then desert their wives, El Cid's two daughters, in a wilderness.[164] Although the two are repulsive enough, they reveal themselves in many respects as failed or inept tricksters, in the style of a much enfeebled or attenuated Loki. They plot to kill a Moorish friend of El Cid's but bungle it, and they are equally unsuccessful in their plan to have the wild beasts of the forest do their dirty work in the Robledo de Corpes. The Infantes are finally brought to book, have to give up large dowries, fall stricken (but do not die) in a juridical combat, and in general have their overweening pride made small. They stand out as a pair of comic-villain exemplars, a couple of cads and bounders, interesting to us not least because of the explicit social criticism voiced in this epic at their boastful *hidalguia*. Their claim that because "By birth we are of the purest blood of counts" (*De natura somos de los comdes más linpios*) they cannot possibly be challenged by the likes of the Cid is scornfully ridiculed, and El Cid Campeador, the sometimes outlaw fighting lord sprung from a lower social order, is obviously favored over them by the epic's poet. For that matter, he is also favored over the king.[165]

The coward knight *de sang pur* operates in a different mode from that of the false noble princes of Carrión, who pretend to be something they are not. He appears under his own name—*li Coarz Chevaliers*—in the first part of *Perlesvaus*, proclaiming: "I am the Coward Knight."[166] In fact he is not alone, especially in the later Arthurian *matière*, but no other coward knight has quite so complex and model a career—not even Leriadus *le Coaurd*, called "the greatest poltroon in Logres," or those who must be seated at Arthur's Court at the Table of Chevaliers Moins Prisiés, a place conveniently set aside for those knights utterly lacking in courage.[167]

Our particular and emblematic coward knight shows himself first off as a perfect icon of reversal, riding backward with lance and shield turned arsy-versy and his knightly armor hanging uselessly around his neck, and declares that he has no interest at all in knightly combat. "Nothing good comes of war" (*Il ne vient de guerre se max non*), he says to Gawain, and when the two part company he hands his lance over, "for I have nothing to do with it."[168] But later this coward knight makes another, typical appearance in *Perlesvaus*, as he is found in headlong flight from a knight who "has so fierce a look I thought I was dead"; after this disaster *li Couarz Cheva-*

liers comes under the harsh tutilege of Perceval himself, who forces him to fight a robber knight. This unmannerly villain knocks the coward about until the coward knight, outraged at the sight of his own blood, strikes the miscreant down, beheads him, and presents the trophy to Perceval. Perceval immediately renames him *Le Hardi Chevalier,* and the newly minted brave knight wonderingly says, "I never believed I could become heroic so fast."[169] But the erstwhile coward does not survive long in his new, heroic role; he is soon mortally wounded in a fight against a sorcerer-knight named Aristor, is taken off to a hermitage to be shriven, and soon thereafter dies.

Three aspects of this chivalric cautionary episode are particularly notable: the *didactic* element, the matter of *plain speech,* and the description of and reaction to *physical appearance.*

The coward emerges clearly as an undoubted antitype to the heroic norm who cannot be allowed to spread his heretical pacifism through *Perlesvaus,* so he falls under or into the hand of a knightly tutor. (Perceval himself was a "slow hero," and had to be taught the simplest chivalric skills.) The conversion of the arrant coward to full warriorhood has more than a little of the heroic-initiatory process about it, particularly in the brutal testing of combat, or the magical meal of monstrous or unusual animal flesh and blood, with this anomalous meal's parallels in various folk legend traditions, and specifically in other, mainly legendary, Norse sagas.[170] A key element, the change of name, displays and reinforces the new character or persona of the changed, reintegrated, and now newly heroic initiate; and all of these elements appear in *Hrólfs saga Kraka,* although in this case the elements are rearranged slightly in a wondertale atmosphere. The hero, Boðvarr Bjarki, finds a craven named Hottr cowering under a hail of bones thrown by the bullies in the hall of King Hrólfr; he drags the coward off to help him battle a "winged monster." After killing the monster, Bjarki "made Hottr drink of its blood and eat of its meat," whereupon Hottr turned "strong and brave" and was renamed Hjalti, or Sword-hilt.[171] (Much of the same information, with an unlikely bear substituted for the monster, is included in Saxo's *Gesta Danorum.*)[172]

As for the matter of plain speech, the statements openly disdainful of war and true-knightly behavior delivered by the coward knight closely fit one aspect of our comic-heroic trickster. Thus when Tale of Orasacs is promised the good Moslem's Paradise and its attendant houris if he died in battle, he is not much impressed: "O priest, forget about the houris of paradise . . . ! What good will your houris of paradise do for me, when my children begin to die from hunger?"[173] Simple reason of this sort stands both against the heroic code *and* its coded language, each of which exalts unthinking (not to say mindless) bravery and the headlong pursuit of a good sword-death. Recall the wisdom (as the *chanson de geste* itself refers to it) of Olivier at Roncesvalles when he saw the vast pagan force ranked against the few if puissant paladins of the Frankish rear guard—and its obverse in Roland's fatal, but all too typical, refusal to take any prudent advice from anyone. What might be identified as a humorously common-sensical, if not exactly wise reaction on the part of a knightly figure is also seen in one version of the *Carados* tale, where the young Carados, after agreeing to take part in the probably fatal beheading game, is asked if he is the bravest of Arthur's knights. "Not at all," he replies, "but the most fool-ish" (*Certes, mes au plus fol*).[174]

The third point, the "face" of heroism (in several senses of the word), is also well illustrated by *Perlesvaus*. The conventional-adjectival system of the French epics, and to some degree of chivalric romances as well, makes its heroes all *biaus* (handsome), *sages* (wise), and *hardis* (brave), a descrip-tion or adduction that easily fits the Dumézilian tripartitive theory. The coward knight betrays his anomaly in his combination of a *biaus* appear-ance or "face" with a *couarz* character (he is also called the "Good-looking Coward," *Biaus Couarz*); and another heroic subtype sometimes appears in the *chansons de geste* called *Lez Hardi*, or the Ugly Brave, whose ugliness is caused specifically by wounds and scars. Gawain, the great womanizer of the Arthurian legends (appropriately named as *le Chevaliers as Dames e as Damoiseles*) is, as the coward knight observes, well scarred because of all the many encounters marking his heroic career, but not so severely disfigured as to rate the tag of *Lez Hardi*.[175] We, the latter-day audience, get the im-pression that the hero should be handsome, but not too much so.

The unscarred coward knight, with his outspoken pacifist poltroonery and reversed character, is an effective comic type and invention. Yet none of the characters we have passed in review is univocal, even in the simplest text, and working below the coward's comicality—or with it—are other potentialities. In another cycle of *chansons de geste*, the *Cycle des Narbonnais* closely analyzed by Grisward, one of the Seven Sons of Aymeri, Hernaut, is called "le personnage comique de la bande."[176] He is a seneschal, like the later (and Continental) Sir Kay: the keeper and distributor of nourishment and riches, a Third Function figure. In the medieval view, Grisward assures us, riches and cowardice as a characteral mark were invariably thought to march together.[177] Even our old and pathetic friend Cei or Kay, when he had at last declined into the seneschalate, is derogated both as a coward and as a sensualist, at least in one of the later Gawain-romances.[178] What is being described, from the point of view of a Second Function (epic or epic romantic) source, is a Third Function persona, and the coward knight must belong or be placed, to some degree, in that Function.

But he cannot quite remain there, as the coward knight (now renamed *le Hardi Chevalier*) and his confrontation with the grim Aristor will attest. This unpleasant personage is something more than a mere villain: he abducts and marries (?) a maiden a year and decapitates her at the end of that time, the act not merely of a scoundrel but of a sorcerer. He also focuses his malefic attention on Perceval and his family, and uses "black" powers—which I believe is the key. The coward knight is aimed against him because this knight still retains vestiges of a "white" magician's *potentia*, a power somehow related to the sexual (or, more properly, to the gender) component of the Third Function. Our ambiguous coward-hero, with his almost feminine handsomeness, his questionable relationship with the strange Demoiselle of the Cart, and various other telltale signs, subsists in the anomalous zone between sexes, bodying forth parts of each, and because of this he can confront the sexual predator and sorcerer Aristor in a way in which the knightly and strong-arm Perceval cannot.[179] A relic of a magical relationship is attached to the didactic element in this tale, though well concealed behind what Grisward has perceptively called the "totalitarianisme" of the Second, Warrior Function, with its propensity toward seizing, changing, reforming, and reusing certain traits native to the other two Indo-European *fonctions*, always to its own ends.[180]

The coward knight's complexities are not wholly obscured by his forced recruitment into a bellicose, if fatal, heroism: he has a full and distinctive persona not found elsewhere in our sources.[181] All of the figures discussed in this section—"blackened" hero, imitator of Loki, foolish hero, semi-villain, coward knight—create certain comic effects by their intended or unintended rebuttal or ignoring of heroic norms and *regula*, but they remain attached to the heroic mode, however indifferently or inefficiently. They cannot be confused with the comic hero, still less with the "hero of comedy," and to illustrate the difference one need only point (in our own time) to Jaroslav Hašek's Good Soldier Schweik or Joseph Heller's Yossarian. What may be less obvious is their provenance, for ultimately both are descended from none other than Odysseus the Versatile.

In the *Iliad* the tricksterish characteristics of Odysseus are usually clear enough, but a different protagonist emerges in the *Odyssey*, or at least is given room to develop another part of his persona, as R. M. Torrance demonstrates in *The Comic Hero*.[182] Now Odysseus becomes the survivor, using every trick and ruse in his arsenal to avoid death—and other diversions—

and win home to his wife and kingdom. To achieve his end he deploys "a sober and flexible heroism," according to Torrance, that is clearly at odds with the behavior of any of "the best of the Achaeans."[183] Odysseus the survivor can be thought of as the *Urtypus* of the life-seeking, death-avoiding man—not in any wise the true hero—who trails a reluctant weapon through the ages. And who is more reluctant than Shakespeare's Falstaff, especially when he delivers the quintessential reluctant warrior's opinion on heroism and one of its prime components and motors: honor. The fat old man's pungent exordium is worth repeating at some length. "Can honour set to a leg? No. Or an arm? No. Or take away the grief of a wound? No. . . . What is honour? A word. . . . Who hath it? He that died a' Wednesday. Doth he feel it? No. Doth he hear it? No. . . . Therefore I'll none of it, honour is a mere scutcheon. And so ends my catechism."[184]

COLOR AND CALOR

This study has already isolated several aspects of the hero's exterior image or "face," his faceted brilliance, the variety and richness of his equipage, and so on. Certain other coloristic themes have just emerged with his cohorts, but now I want to deal more strictly with the codes and signals expressed in or on the glinting surface of certain heroic types.

The Uses of Color Symbolism

Physiologically speaking, the mechanism of the human eye comes equipped with complex receptor organs able to distinguish a very wide range of chromatic differences—colors—at least in the daylight, and the human mind has probably been investing its received and reconstructed cosmos with symbolically "colorized" values for some thousands of years—perhaps from the beginning of culture most broadly defined.[185] Certainly the red ochre spread over Neanderthal bones must have had some special, even some spiritual significance for the survivors, while anthropology and cultural history can provide us with the complex color signs—cosmetic in the root sense—used by human societies ranging from the hunter-gatherer and hunter-agriculturist to the gigantically yet subtly colored human and divine universes described in Mayan, ancient Chinese, or Hittite civilization, to name three examples ready to hand.

Even a glancing view at human cosmotincture invites the grand theory. At the primary level of symbol building, *green* (the color of vegetation) will predictably be figured as nature, and the *red* of human blood will stand for humanity and its construct, culture. But what if green equals earth, and blue equals heaven? Ancient imperial China posited a seasonal and directional color code: green-red-yellow-black-white, with yellow placed at the center of the cosmic and human spaces and black derogated as the noncolor of dead winter, and of the suspect North.[186] The ancient Mayan term for earth and for sky, according to the arcane formulas of the *Popul Vuh,* is the same: *raxa,* or blue-green.[187] The Campa Amerindians of the eastern Peruvian rain forest accept red as the true-human sign, and white, its opposite, as the mark of those nonhuman ghosts, the pale Caucasians known to lurk up in the Peruvian highlands, born in lakes, always malignant.[188] Climate and "nature" may provide nothing more than a start-up code for a multiflorient human urge toward signing and encoding in color. Sir Edmund Leach has offered us a concise appreciation of this coding, warning that there appear to be no universal patterns, that reversals are very common, and that the "*set* of contrasts" is often the vital feature in reading color symbolisms.[189] His admonitions or guidelines should certainly be kept in mind—as, for example, when recording the perception, in the Aztec-Mexica thought-world, that precious human blood was "formally" designated not red but blue-green, which to the Aztecs was "the precious color of jade and of vegetable growth."[190]

Here I focus on the color system and code specific to Indo-Europe, and the information pertinent to this project of describing the hero's world. Such a condensation and reduction in the target area reduces but by no means eliminates the base problem. The Indo-European trifunctional system has long been associated with a triplicate color scheme, but although the First and Second Function colors are usually very stable (white and red respectively), the compound complexities of the Third Function are reflected in various assigned color values.[191] An Indic caste-identification scheme assigned yellow to the *vaisya* (herders and agriculturists) and black to the outcaste *sudra,* who are completely extruded from the regular Indic societal order.[192] A Hittite tricolor identification substitutes blue as a marker for the third (functional) classification, but the dominant or orthodox Indo-European "ideological" color scheme is set at *white, red,* and *green*— with green standing for growth, and the springing powers of fecundity.[193] This tricolored Indo-European schematic is already known from the *albati, russati, virides,* the so-called circus parties who sported their "colors" in that ritualized Byzantine chariot-race recorded by John Lydus in the sixth century A.D.; it is further worked out in the folklore collected and explicated by Lucien Gershel, and most recently we have had it used in an elegant dissection of the *Quête du Saint Graal* by Joël Grisward. Variations and refinements still abound: in the northern lands, for example, blue and green, or dark blue and black, may register as more or less the same color; and to our Eurocentric eyes, the yellow assigned to the Indic *vaisya* would probably appear yellow-green. My main concern, however, is with the second or warrior function, within which three adjunctive subtypes are of particular importance: black knight, red knight, and green knight.

BLACK KNIGHT

We have already identified a number of assigned symbolic valences for this color (or absence of color, noncolor). In the Scandinavian-Germanic North it may be the color of death, so that a *draugr,* the walking dead, may be described as "black as Hel," and to be dark or blackened shows a declension from fully human status (like a thrall, or another type of nonperson put under a malign spell).[194] Black (actually blue-black) is also used as the metaphorized color of revenge or anticipated violence: it is made to mark the color of an expected fatality. Generally and transculturally, blackened figures are connected both to the reversed, comic persona, and to the ambiguous character of the smith. It we move off the fully human continuum, black also marks the *teras* or monster, who is simultaneously made black, anomalously shaped, and inhumanly hideous. The topic place of the black figure may be underground or otherwise detached from the civilized zone *en plein aire;* and the adolescent Athenian "Black Hunter" studied by Pierre Vidal-Naquet boasts a concatenation of motifs connected to the unassimilated or nonintegrated male youth: exclusion from society, involvement in hunting and fighting at night with the ambiguous aid of snares and tricks, and placement in the zone beyond where full civilization comfortably flourishes.[195] Melanthos, the Black One, taken from Greek myth, is the paradigmatic hero of this dark complex.[196]

The associational constellation identified with the black knight thus can display every kind and degree of Otherness, from telluric powers or the darkness of the night to a placement beyond order and cosmesis, even the penumbrous, hyperactive, uncontrolled stage in which a young warrior-initiate subsists before he is made a full "daylit" member of adult male society. Magic—but not necessarily "black" magic—may be added to the mixture of darker possibilities. (Nor should we be surprised to find a source like the Persian *Shâh-nâma* advancing the dualistic vision of black as projecting a mythic and cosmic opposition to Light and the Good: "Ahriman . . . is a black serpent, with wide-open mouth," and his grim army is an "army of night.")[197] All of these combinations, and perhaps more, can be found in the Arthurian prose *matière,* which among other riches gives us the following: (a) the knights Agrovadan, Cormaduc, Crois, Esclamor, Helain, Heliz, and Pharan are all called "le Noir," though none has any specific attributes (Brunor and his son Brunor, for example, both labeled "le Noir," are also called "good" and "fearless"). One thinks of these characters as being merely black-haired or brunette; (b) Caliman called le Noir has "an evil character"; Nador le Noir (and Chevalier de l'Isle Noire) is probably identical with Maduc, Arthur's enemy; Mauduit is evil (as we note his name); Priadan le Noir is the champion of a wicked woman and is defeated by Bohor; Yvain le Noir is a semi-villain defeated by Guiron; (c) Baruc le Noir is probably a dark-skinned pagan or perhaps a Jew; Golistan le Noir may have supernatural connections; Nabon le Noir is a giant, killed by Tristan; and finally we have Lucifer himself, who is portentously named "le Noir Hermite."[198] The sequence, from a simple differentiating description, through attributed evil, to foreignness, to supernatural and Otherworldly associations, seems almost predictable, and we could add to it, for further confusion, the "black" (that is, blank) disguise often adopted by a knightly hero who wishes to remain anonymous, becoming "No Man" by assuming this coloration, and so betraying a little of the masking, Odyssean mode.

The cognomen *inn svartr*, "the Black," is not very common in the Icelandic-Scandinavian material, but of course names there, at least in the "historical" family sagas, purport to identify real people. Of the "Blacks" listed in the *Landnámabók*, a goodly number have Þórr-names, for reasons I cannot guess at: Þorbjorn *inn svartr* of Skeljabrekka, Þórarinn of Mavahlidr, Þórir (a feud victim), Þorkell of Hleiðargardr, and Þorsteinn Black, also called "the Wise," who appears in *Laxdæla saga* as well.[199] Then there are Bárðr *inn svartr*, Helgi the Black (a grandson of Ketill Trout), and the well-known Illugi the Black; Þorkell the Black of Hleiðargardr had a son named Ongul the Black.[200] The usual assumption would be that this cognomen referred to black hair or, possibly, swarthy skin, though other cognomina such as Coal-Brow and Coal-Beard appear as well, and *Laxdæla saga* has two brothers, An the Black and An the White. (The former, for what it is worth, was a smith.)[201] Finally, the *Landnámabók*, reaching back to legendary material for one of its sources, tells us of two illegitimate sons of a Permian princess who had been made a bondwoman, Geirmundr and Hammundr. Both were very swarthy, and were called Hel-Skins; they had a bad character, as well.[202] Perm is the uncanny Northern land frequently mentioned in the sprightlier Norse adventure romances like "Bósa ok Herrauðr."

The *black* label retains an unstable, multivalent significance, and part of this significance is to have no significance at all, or none we can immediately decipher. Black may mean power *in potentia,* or it may sign the hero's opponent on a number of levels. It can also mean burned or Tartarean; be affiliated with the fire powers of the magical or quasi-magical smith; or suggest negative or black fire, the obscuring fire of sorcery. It settles down to no absolute and invariable meaning revealed for our analytic pleasure.

RED KNIGHT

Red, as we have seen, is the prime color-code marker for the Indo-European Second Function: its significances are frequently *opposite* rather than unstable. The color may be displayed as simply as in *Landnámabók,* where a versifying fighter uses red as a shorthand marker for war: "The soldiers don't worry me, waving their red shields."[203] (See also "the blood-red shield on the back of the hero Conall Cernach" in Da Derga's fatal hostel.)[204] In examining the costume of the hero, we encountered a number of heroes associated with red: Cú Chulainn, Peredur, Sigurd in *Völsungasaga,* Lancelot in a typical citation ("he of yesterday with the vermillion arms").[205] The color red is attached to these and numerous other warrior-heroes, but predictably it is invested with all the ambivalence of the hero himself: red is always a dangerous color, reflecting the doubled potencies of blood and fire, or of their combination in the "hot blood" of the furious warrior-hero. We can easily expand the list of "red-hot" heroes: Mstislav, a red-haired (and red-faced and intemperate) Kievan warrior-prince in a Slavic source;[206] the irate Guerri *li Sors,* "the Red," in *Raoul de Cambrai,* also called the Red Knight, a hostile and atypical uncle to Raoul;[207] Esclados the Red in Chrétien's *Yvain,* "more blazing with wrath than a burning log";[208] and so on until the eyes grow red.

To be identified as a red knight *in the essence,* however, and not merely wearing the heroic scarlet livery, appears to indicate too obviously or too deeply the destructively heated potentiality of the warrior. To the medieval mind the red-haired man was an object of suspicion (or even, according to Joël Grisward, a "disgrace"), not just because the red-headed man was invariably considered choleric, quarrelsome, or aggressive, but because he was likely to be "méchant" or "félon." Judas was known to have been red-haired, and so, at the very End of Days, would be the Antichrist himself.[209] The ancient Greek and the Roman-Hellenistic imagination ran on very similar lines so far as a suspicion of the red-haired was concerned (a people fitted to servile status might either be southern, and dark-skinned, or northern, possibly with red hair and pale skin, but neither was chromatically median, like the light-brown Mediterranean type).[210] The Irish Celtic sources tell us that Cú Chulainn the Furious, the distorted one swollen red with blood and fury, was still a "black-browed man" in his occasional repose.[211] The canonical fault or *délit* in the Second Function usually is cowardice, a lack of that unthinking bravery that should be the warrior's prime earmark, but it may also be what I have described elsewhere as *hypermachy*, an overloading of the combat circuitry in the martial man, an unbalancing movement toward bellicosity for its own bloody sake.[212] The "red" warrior's persona may break out of any modifying or controlling ethos, not just from disequilibrating anger but out of its own sense of distinct, uncontrolled individuality. When Akhilleus, in his youth, is briefly disguised as a girl he is called Pyrrha, "red head." It is this same "red" essence that underlies his brittle savagery in the *Iliad*.[213]

In the Arthurian sequence of narratives dealing with Peredur-Perlesvaus-Percival-Parzifal, the knight as innocent, there is a Red Knight who undergoes a strange transformation. In *Peredur* and in the Percival emendations of the Welsh tale, the Red Knight is a brutal enemy to Arthur and even more so to Gwenhwyfar the Queen (the "Fair" or "White"). He is also connected to the Otherworld and its powers, specifically to fire, and in *Peredur* he threatens "to burn the kingdom."[214] Percival, in order to fight off this Red Knight and his threat, literally fights fire with fire, trying to "burn" this knight out of his armor; he also throws the Red Knight's mother (a witch) on a fire after killing her. By the time of Eschenbach's *Parzifal*, however, the Red Knight, now named Ither von Gaheviz, is a "flower of chivalry," decked out in red armor—still to be killed by Parzifal, but in a fair joust.[215] The supernatural threat has leached away; a Balor-like figure, wielding the destructive power of red fire, has become a mere unfortunate opponent to the ever victorious hero.[216]

We can certainly identify, then, more than one reflex of the red knight. The simplest to deal with is the hypermachic "red one," the pursuer of violence for its own sake, though the "sense of distinct individuality" just mentioned can take another and stranger course. In this the subject takes up violence in a perverse, even a tricksterish (but not a comic) way; there is an uncanny urge toward destructiveness, a contrariety that breaks free of every constraint, accompanied by impression that every perverse move made by this figure is not merely reactive and fiercely impulsive, but carefully thought out. We are speaking of something that, freely adapted from the terminology of Jung, might be called the working of a "red Shadow," specifically in the following extraordinary figures:

Hagen of Troneck. In the *Nibelungenlied*, he is the marshal (*scharmeister*) of the Burgundian host—a sage adviser to the king who even has a degree of prescience.[217] Like Sir Kay, he also seems to be employed as the seneschal, "supplying everyone's wants"; and he is *kameraere,* or the king's treasurer.[218] Of course he also arranges for the death of Siegfried "secretly and effectively," but in the end, as D. G. Mowatt notes, he manages to destroy, through his "cold" and perverse fury, all the Burgundian knights, the Nibelung treasure, his king, and himself, all in the holocaust at Etzel's court.[219]

Efnisien (from one of the Welsh *mabinogi, Branwen Uerch Lyr*). He is twinned with a peaceable brother, Nisien, who is "positive" in intent and valence. Motivated, so far as we can tell or are told, by the fact that his half sister Branwen had been married to the king of Ireland without his consent, he sadistically mutilated the Irish king's horses.[220] While in Ireland he foils a plot against his brother Bendigeidfran but then, seizing his half-Irish nephew (Branwen's son), he thrusts the boy into a fire and kills him. Fighting immediately breaks out between the Irish and Welsh parties, but the Irish army gains the advantage because their dead are cooked back to life in one of those Celtic cauldrons of immortality. Efnisien feigns death and is put into the cauldron, but it bursts (evidently because he was still alive), "and his heart bursts also."[221]

Skarpheðinn (a son of Njáll in *Njáls saga*). This saturnine redhead (*járpr*) is the prime reactor and murderer after his foster brother Hoskulðr is killed. He also delivers a series of increasingly nasty insults to the Alþing, beginning with accusations of cowardice against various chieftains and of disgusting behavior involving Þórkel Braggart; finally he puts paid to any chance of a peaceful settlement by accusing Flosi Þórdarson of passive homosexuality.[222] Skarpheðinn will die in the attack by his united feud-foes, in the Burning that follows inevitably on the subsequent isolation of Njáll and his family.[223]

Dubtach Doeltenga ("Chafer Tongue"). He appears in a number of the Old Irish Ulster Cycle tales, first in *Togail Bruidne Da Derga* as the typical warrior figure in a fairly neat trifunctional grouping along with Sencha the Judge and Goibniu the Smith.[224] This warrior holds the spear "quenched in poison," the sign and mark of his own sort of behavior, though the *Mesca Ulad* says he is "doubled" (he has a fierce expression in one eye, a gentle look in the other)—but still "he never merited thanks from anyone."[225] His mischief-making is actually articulated in the bloody *Fled Bricrend:* he agitates to get the champion's portion assigned to some hero other than the three who directly vie for it, and he implies that no warrior will step up to play the deadly "beheading game" with the ogrish *bachlach* and survive.[226] His final fate is not known; Chafer Tongue seems to have been in exile from Ulster during the narrated action of the *Táin Bó Cúalgne.*

The individualistic, perverse, and purposive mischief-making of a particular kind of red knight is carried so far in these four characters that it would not be too great a stretch to call them red tricksters, given all of their primary characteristics. Certainly they illustrate what might be termed dramatic variation: Skarpheðinn is shown more as the Grettir type, noble but perverse and impetuous, whereas Dubtach is indubitably a kind of champion. (He is called "a hero and man of war" for the king Fergus mac Ilide in a later tale, and he resembles the Welsh champion Cei in his divided character and declination from a true Champion's role.)[227] The ligature connecting all of them is their untrammeled and self-willed choler, or calor, for they seem to leap toward an identification with fire and burning: Hagen to the burning hall, the trap finally set at Etzel's court; Skarpheðinn to the *brenna* of Njáll and most of his household; Efnisien committing "what will seem an outrage to the family" when he thrusts his sister's son into the fire, and who then bursts open the heated, magical cauldron and dies; Dubtach armed with his terrible weapon-twin, the fiery spear that must be kept quenched in venom. In every instance except that of the quasi-champion Dubtach, the red knights are consumed in the fires they ignite: they seem to willfully maneuver fate, or the epic story, to this very end.[228] These characters are closest to the Jungian configuration of a destructive and reversing part of the human psyche, not dark but fiery, an oppositive and finally self-immolating aspect of the already potent heroic ego.[229]

Perversity can be variously detected and decocted in any number of ways in our heroic tales; it almost escapes the poles of positive or negative and takes on a pure power of its own. Perverse reversals can be comic, as often in the trickster's typical antics, but they can also be very serious. In the Old Irish Fenian Cycle we find Conón, "the buffoon of the Fianna . . . but also the source of continual strife and destruction," whose character is always in opposition to Finn.[230] He seems to be closer to Hagen, or to the uncontrolled and uncontrollable "red" killers who stalk the sagas and other narratives; and in the Old Irish context he is specifically contrasted to Finn's son Oisín, the "defender-hero," as well as to Finn himself, who has attained (or been doomed to) the comparatively rare posture of an old warrior, whose primary color has faded away . . . to gray.

GREEN KNIGHT

It is not difficult to accept the application of green to the Third Function; it is the goddess Venus's color, the green of fertile growth and lustful venery. Stith Thompson's *Motif-Index* also shows the color widely assigned in folktale not just to the natural world but to the Otherworld and to the zone of magic generally.[231] We have already seen the Otherworld, specifically in the Old Irish epical narrations, marked by green, like the green cloak of the god Lugh and the green clothing of Otherworld beings mentioned in the *Táin*, the Otherworld woman named Sín who appears in the *Aided Muirchertaig meic Erca*, or the six men "of the *síde*" in their green cloaks who appear in the *Togail Bruidne Da Derga*.[232] Occasionally supportive data arrives from out-of-the-way sources and in a roundabout fashion. In the Ulster Cycle tale of Da Derga's hostel we find listed "three champions from the *Síd*," but these make up a trio decked out (surprisingly?) in red. They are red-haired besides, but soon we discover that they had "wrought falsehood in the *Síd*" and were being punished; thus their livery had changed from cool Otherworld green to the hot, combative red of the human warrior.[233]

The use of color in the epic will often penetrate to deep—even mythic—symbolizations: the red sign for an epic hero like Cú Chulainn is directly connected to his "red-enraged" and "red-warrior" character and role. Indeed, Ross Arthur writes that "People are known in the world of epic battle by sign and countersign, and the presuppositions of the signifying system are left unquestioned."[234] If a color-sign is used and visible, its signification will be unmediated and direct. The chivalric romance or later epic-romantic tradition, however, introduces a considerable bent toward ambiguity and the *mutability* of the sign.[235] Precisely at that time when the system of identifying signs and colors we call "heraldry" is introduced to the knightly context, the literary imagination appears to be unwilling to adopt it. Ronald Dennys, a student and analyst of the "heraldic imagination," and himself a professional in the art and craft of heraldry, notes that the Arthurian romances of Chrétien de Troyes, considered as protoheraldic sources, "show a remarkably untidy approach to heraldry."[236] This untidiness is made clear in Chrétien's *Cligés*, where the hero sends his servant to London to buy three sets of arms—black, red, and green.[237] (Will Chrétien's hero now choose his shield to fit his mood or the pattern of an adventure he has undertaken?) Mutability has made a very dramatic entrance, and we are already well prepared for what Professor Arthur calls "the multiple imposition of meanings."[238] Yet these multiplied impositions of meaning are more likely to be seen when a single color is brought forward, and its varied possibilities as sign allowed to effloresce.

Compared with other tinctures, green (heraldic *vert*) is not at all common in medieval coats and their blazons. Its associative field is not firmly set; according to Dennys, Sicily Herald's early (fourteenth century) heraldic tract reads *vert* as a sign of "jolliness and youth, but also of beauty and shame."[239] A light or pale green might also be read as "emblematic of death."[240] The color is most likely to be seen when the medieval fictive imagination was well engaged: Arthur the King was assigned a shield with a green field, while his father Uther Pendragon had a shield invented for him with two green—Welsh?—dragons addorsed. A reminiscence of the old Celtic world's supernatural green counterpart may be reflected at this point, but what do we do with the (again, imaginatively concocted) coat called the Shield of the Passion of Christ, which displays a green cross on a red field? Here the color green probably refers to renewed life, placed on the red field signing the salvific blood shed for sinners—and yet the green cross might also harken back to that idea of the "color beyond nature." *Vert,* the green color of the romances and of the most imaginative heraldry, emerges as a most ambiguous tincture, and never so simple as to sign merely the "natural." Sir Bercilak, Gawain's Green Knight, may represent the potency of a "Celtic Underworld," but he also wears the hunting green, and the hunter may be the Evil One, trawling or tricking for a catch or quarry of souls.[241]

In any case the Otherworldly hint attached to the color does continue in that best known of all of the fraternity of green knights, garbed in "enker-green" or "vivid green," and "al grayþed in grene þis gome and his wedes": that foe with whom the hero has to grapple in *Sir Gawain and the Green Knight*.[242] At the heart of this poem lies a "beheading game" we recognize at once from the Old Irish *Fled Bricrend*, but here, instead of a dark, grim, and ogrish *bachlach*, we have a mysterious but decidedly knightly green-clad figure armed with an ax, who pops up in Arthur's court on New Year's Eve.[243] Gawain agrees to play his game, and beheads the Green Knight— who is little disconcerted by the stroke—after also agreeing to search him out a year hence and endure the return blow, at the Knight's Green Chapel. When the time comes, he resignedly fares forth to his fate and eventually finds a castle, sinister enough but inhabited by a friendly host and two ladies, one old and ugly and the other—the host's wife—very beautiful indeed. He also discovers out that the Green Chapel he has long been seeking is not far away.[244] The host and Gawain agree that each will give the other what he finds that day, the host in the hunt and Gawain in the castle. On three successive days the host goes off to hunt, and each day his lovely wife lays siege to Gawain's honor. Gawain resists, accepting only a reasonably chaste kiss—"Bot þat 3e be Gawan, hit gotz in mynde," she says, for the lady cannot believe that this so-proper knight really *is* Gawain, the famous, lusty great lover of Arthur's court.[245] On her third visit she gives Gawain a green scarf, and then the Green Knight appears, who of course turns out to be her husband, and who handles his ax in a threatening fashion but lets Gawain off with only a nick.[246]

The Green Knight of the poem fits easily into the rich complex threaded throughout the Indo-European Third Function. He appears not in martial armor but in a resplendent costume, "Folden in wyth fildore abote þe fayre grene," of green picked out with gold.[247] Clearly he is from Other-where, as that place is architecturally imaged in the Green Chapel for which Gawain must search, though he is *not* a folkloric Green Man or a primitive Wild Man of the Woods, two other popular medieval images representing a verdant "nature."[248] The "play" at the castle of Bercilak de Hautdesert, as he finally calls himself, is full of unsubtle references to the double meaning of "venery": the knightly host pursuing game out-of-doors, and his fair lady pursuing Gawain indoors. "I sende hir to asay þe" says the Green Knight jovially, and Gawain passes this "asay" as well as any imperfect mortal might. (Some of the dramatic tension emergent in these scenes must inhere in our medieval audience's knowledge of Gawain's wide and well-deserved reputation as an assiduous gallant: he is no virginal and incorruptible Galaad.)[249] There is, again, a certain play between red and green: in his human guise as Bercilac de Hautdesert the host-knight had a red (or red-brown) beard in clear contrast to his other color and role. Chivalric fantasy here finds the color green ("dedicated to Venus," as John Lydus had written in the sixth century) reemergent in its primary significance: of sexual games and florescent life, and, beyond these, of nature and "its" sphere—though it also, of course, retains the potency of an extracultural, wild, and possibly Otherworldly power.[250]

The three kinds and colors of knight appear to take valences found freefloating around the warrior-hero and solidify them into fully rounded characters. The heat—calor—marking the Second Function can be transmuted by what it works with or on, as the various color-codes we find will reflect. In fact, this Function's active heat betrays itself in the ease with which our characters move between modes; and although red can be taken as the marker for the active-destructive processes of culture, it can also be cooled, moderated, and tamed. The tale of Sir Gawain and the Green Knight dramatizes the migration of color and calor: traveling in winter (marked both as bitter cold and by the non-colors black and white), and moving away from Arthur's court (where white will be the sign of sovereignty), Gawain encounters his host-knight Bercilac. Red or reddish, *bevier hwed* in his manly beard, the host engages himself in the simulacrum of war, cutting down a boar with his sword, while the passionate Gawain is being tempted and agitated within. Gawain takes his hostess' green scarf or girdle, a dangerous act, but in the final "green" scene, despite the threat of violent death, all is tempered and cooled again.[251] The host-knight will change from red to green and back, glissading each way from culture to nature, but he reminds us of other Third Function figures (like the warrior threesome expelled from the *Síd* in Da Derga's hostel) who may well have been punished by assigning them the scarlet color of action and aggression. A warrior may carry any of these color markings. Cold black displays the most ambiguity, but we can also read in it that "the fire is out"; red shows an easily adopted destructive and heated rage; green in some sense interposes itself between the two. I have said nothing of any white knight: white is a noncolor, so it must be assumed that a white knight is no knight at all. Instead he is a condensation of First Function traits and will display more than a hint of nonreaction, neutrality, or coldness.

Color: Some Final Notes

The white-red-black sequence, undoubtedly imprinted deeply into the Indo-European image-making faculty, can reemerge in our narratives in a way best described as casually formulaic, with only the faintest echo of any imprinted trifunctional meaning. For example, when Flosi was goaded in the *Njála* and powerful emotion overtook him, he went from "red as blood" to "pale as withered grass" to "black as death."[252] It is possible that in this image the *sagamaðr* wanted to signal, first, the ordinary rush of blood to the face in anger, then a quick thought or mental activity (his pallor), and finally the "black" and Hel-like color signing an intended or impending death—for someone. A trifunctional recollection is certainly conceivable here. Another use of white-red-black is to form a physical, not an emotional, description: a hero or heroine may be given black hair or brows, white skin, red lips or cheeks. An example occurs in the Welsh *Peredur,* where the questing hero meets a maiden with skin "whiter . . . than flowers of the whitest crystal," hair and brows "blacker . . . than any jet," and two "small red spots on her cheeks, redder than aught reddest."[253] Similar tricolored descriptions could be cited from as far afield as the Georgian or Persian epics, or as close as the Irish Celtic: the theme is so widespread (and has penetrated so deeply into folklore) that it has been made a Disneyesque cliché. Whether any trace might remain in it of the Indo-European trifunctional marker is moot: at its heart-root it might signify a perfect or complete triad or ensemble, a cosmic or mythic pattern reduced to a literally cosmetic formula. On the other hand, some significant part of our evidence displays a dualistic or binary, not a triplex, tendency contrasting "fair" or "bright" with "dark," and identifying the hero with the first quality. In a Russian context, the "true" warrior (and also the warrior-wizard Vseslav, who has his own epic) is called the "bright falcon"; his enemy is called the black-feathered raven.[254] In the Old Irish tradition the opposition naturally emerges in the adventures of Finn (*fionn* 'fair'), whose enemy is *dubh* 'black'. (Arca Dubh was the killer of Finn's father Cumall.)[255] In fact, Prionsias MacCana sees the veritable descent of Finn the Fenian from a Gaulish-Celtic "bright god," and the light-versus-darkness theme, with mythic reverberations detectable or not, will be found widely emplaced elsewhere in the epic record.[256] Finally, the heraldic black or *sable*, according to at least one medieval heraldic tractate, has the expected value of dolor or sadness, but it is also assigned to "the religious" and therefore escapes the knightly context altogether. Yet another medieval guide to heraldic minutiae places both white and black at the top of his symbolic color hierarchy, as they are primary and all other colors come from them: white in this evidence is termed the "noblest tincture."[257]

BETWEEN COLORS

The peculiar resonance of the color gray has already been observed in descriptions of some of the more mysterious figures circling around the hero: Iliach mac Cass's rough, gray sword in the *Táin*, for example, or the grubby gray appearance of the tricksterish Tale of Orasacs. Not only has gray a negative cosmetic significance (it is not-white, begrimed, dimmed as light may be dimmed), it also has an assigned value as a mark of the uncanny, especially in the North. Although Hagen of Troneck belongs in the "red shadow," it seems to be worth noting that this extraordinary character has hair flecked with gray (*gemischet was sin hâr, mit einer grisen varwe*) "and his gaze [was] terrible" (*und eislich sin gesihene*).[258] In Grettir's saga Glámr, the thrall, has this appearance even before he meets a suspicious and "bad" death and becomes one of the walking-dead *draugar*: "very strange looking, with glaring gray eyes and a head of wolf-gray hair."[259] The hero Grettir's violent but gloomy saga is peculiarly gray in its associated tone; his grandfather was Þorgrímr Grayhead and his father, with whom Grettir fell early into enmity, was called Ásmunðr Gray-Locks because he had turned prematurely gray.[260] A "wolf-gray" coloration ties this intermediate color to a feral, a lupine aspect: we recall that Egill Skalla-grímsson's grandfather, suspected of being a shape changer, was called Kveld-Úlfr, "Evening Wolf," and that Egill's trollish father, Bald-Grímr, had superhuman powers that waxed as night came on. For all of that, Egill describes his poll (in the "head-poem" that saved him from King Eiríkr's wrath) as *úlfgrátt*, "wolf-gray."[261] The crepuscular time of day, when light and color are all weakened and turn to gray, was the prime time for all three of these strange men—and for the gray prowling wolf, which might be called their totem.

A weapon may be recognized as an uncanny arm by its color, like old Iliach's sword, but we see this especially in Grásiða, "Gray-Flank," of *Gísla saga Súrssonar*, which was crafted specifically for secret night-murder. Such an appellation contrasts dramatically with those sword names celebrating brightness, showing the burnished shining steel of the battle day, like "Hviting." Grásiða instead is the dull steel ex-sword, finally dedicated only to ill-fated killing, a secret weapon imbued with avenging powers.

An uncanny or even supernatural animal is almost always gray. Trickster Tale's horse is "mouse-gray"; no one else among the gleaming warriors of the border will be so dingily mounted. In the "Death Tale of Cú Chulainn" the prescient gift and special character of Cú Chulainn's first chariot horse, the Gray of Macha, is underscored. After it was mortally speared in the warrior's last fight, the horse and Cú Chulainn "bade each other farewell," and the Gray "went into the Gray's Linn in Sliab Fuait"—"into the mountain," returning to the subterrain of the Otherworld.[262] After Raoul's fall in the Old French *Raoul de Cambrai*, the three surviving Sons of Herbert, who had been responsible for his death, and who have now become the targets of Gautier's condign vengeance, are said to be mounted on "a dappled steed, a gray . . . and . . . on the black horse" that had been Raoul's: these surely are three unlucky mounts.[263] And in the Gawain romance *Le chevalier à l'epée*, the sinister Knight who leads errant adventurers off to undergo a particular and usually fatal trial rides an uncanny "iron-gray" horse, a *cheval ferrant*.[264]

The Norse-Icelandic sources might be expected to be full of these ambiguously colored beasts, and they do not disappoint. *Landnámabók* gives us a dapple-gray (*gra-eplottr*) that turns out to be a supernatural "water horse" (this mysterious creature will appear repeatedly in other Nordic sources); it also presents us with a sorcerer named Orn who, after his suicide, returned reincarnate as a "gray, black-maned stallion."[265] *Eyrbyggja saga* concludes the tale of the malignant Þórolfr Bægifot when an uncanny, "dapple-gray" bullcalf gores and kills the man who had finally burned Þórolfr's *draugr*-form, his undead body, to ashes;[266] and so on. The northern information reinforces our perception of this intermediate near color as it is associated with uncertain, unlucky, uncanny materials (the dull-gray ash left after the fire has died, or weapon-steel not burnished but allowed to dull), with feral and threatening animals such as the wolf, even with a time of day (the crepuscular twilight). Dappling introduces an irregular, even more anomalous coloration, not solid but shifting and uncertain. The very color of a man's hair, when it is not naturally but prematurely gray, seems to catch the *sagamaðr*'s attention and imagination, implying a character not quite wholly human, and perhaps inflated with strange instinct or uncanny power.[267] The color/noncolor appears to threaten, by obscuring, the bright effulgence of the hero, and in the best interpretation will display, at least in the north, an Otherworldly or inhuman connection.

Each value-laden specific color has its own drama, and washes over and permeates the heroic sphere, marking and painting our hero not just as a mere metaphor would. Even the typical, gleaming-surfaced, corruscating hero, pursuivant of his blood-red goal, can be faced and modified with other colors and their significances blocked or frustrated by black, tempted or diverted by green. Moreover, the troop of his supporters, foes, and other characters who surround our icon have *their* own colors or calors and the supporting signs and significances of these colors. Our spectroscopic or chromoscopic view can detect very significant matters, coded by color, in the great onrush of epic and related narratives.

6 TERTIUM QUID: ASPECTS OF LIMINALITY

> Adolescence is the sparring phase. After that enmities are—or should
> be—channeled outward on to the adversary.
> The "war boys" are the ones who never grow up.
>
> —Bruce Chatwin, *The Songlines*

Both the hero and the shaman are liminal specialists. The shaman usually
operates in that human-heroic world between animal and god. For the hero,
his liminal nature may appear in a high-flown, hubristic assault on heaven
in the one direction, and his risky penetration of the Netherworld in the
other, with all of the rich, ambiguous powers they represent or contain. The
hero may stand (or deliquesce?) between genders and generations, or
between the realms of life and death. In this chapter I explore the concept
of liminality and bring into sharper focus the shamanic and the heroic character identified as liminal.

DEFINITIONS AND OPERATIONS

The concept of *liminality* is drawn both in and from a particular anthropological inquiry, begun by those theorists in this very modern discipline
who were working to define interstructural or systemic relationships in human societies. Here *limen,* the Latin word for "threshold," may be a point
but more probably is a sequential symbolization, time period, or other intermediating place, or sometimes an interpart of some ongoing process.
(Or, as Victor Turner so poetically phrased it, "Liminal entities are neither
here nor there; they are betwixt and between the positions assigned and
arrayed by law, custom, convention and ceremonial.")[1] *Tertium quid,* of
course (as defined, for example, by the lexicographical experts of the *Oxford
English Dictionary*), is "something (indefinite or left undefined) related in
some way to two (definite or known) things, but distinct from both." In

this chapter I want to return to the hero and investigate how he slips or is placed into this role of "third thing"—which ought to be exceedingly familiar to us from the variety of descriptions hinted at or provided outright in the earlier pages of this study.

One difficulty with this descriptive phrase (which this same much respected dictionary presumes to be a Latinizing of the Greek *triton ti*) is its essentially Aristotelian modality. In that logical, lexical, and semiotic-symbolic system, great emphasis will always be placed on specificity, correct category, and the firm and consistent outlines of the latter. In an Aristotelian system, a "thing"—Latin *quid* or Greek *tis*—or anything that exists between categories will be considered questionable in its essence, and therefore will be identified as a lesser or inferior entity. Yet our central figure, as we have so often seen, escapes an entire society of categories or configurations, including those of time (which takes a variety of guises in its own right), sequence, space, and, of course, every kind of "society" itself. In the very heart of the category in which he acts and dwells, the definitional solidity of the hero may well disintegrate or dissolve, so that the hard-edged, brilliant, and unidimensional icon of perfect heroism is increasingly reduced, to be surrounded by a three-dimensional constellation of associated figures, personae, and refracted subimages (a situation and placement summed up in chapter 7). The hard problem of pinning down a correct definition of the hero soon leaves behind the luxury, even the option, of positing an absolute category, and must perforce turn toward a relational schematic, a theoretical move I have already detected in and shamelessly (but with thanks) borrowed from N. J. Allen and his hypothesized Indo-European Fourth Function.[2] The hero can also fit rather easily and securely into the broader classificatory systematic suggested by the anthropologist Edmund Leach, which exposes the potency, or sacrality, generated when "the edge of Category A turns into the edge of Category Not-A."[3] At very least a structuralist-oriented anthropology hints at a way to decode the situation occupied by the extraordinary entity or human being between categories, including not only his placement and action (or pendular movement) between absolute categories but also between categories in which the second is defined only as a negation of the first: "not-A." The power invested in the interstitial or liminal state may be all the greater when the categories are clearly and strictly defined, but it will still be apparent, if perhaps more difficult to isolate, when those categories are vague or difficult to define.

Between Animal and God: The Specialist

SHAMANS AND THE SHAMANIC

The shaman is an individual, usually self-chosen and often trained and initiated by superhuman means, who assumes an intermediary position between the human and divine zones. He is the most important mediating sacral figure in a widely distributed group of archaic, tribal, traditional cultures; and although we have taken his title and the broad features of his sacral-dramatic art from Central Asia and Siberia, he is certainly not limited to that zone. Very prominent and spiritually potent in the steppe cultures that appeared on the eastern edge of the Indo-European thought-world or oecumene, shamanism is almost entirely obscured in the myths and early religious practices we identify for Indo-Europe. Mircea Eliade's synoptic and inclusive work on the shapes and forces of the shamanistic specialty has to tease out certain "essential features" of this sacred enterprise in order to locate anything like the type as it might be seen in Indo-Europe, and he properly identifies these extrapolated features as fairly faint and vestigial compared to the complete, integrated display of shamanist personalities, operations, and ideology traceable in Siberia or aboriginal North and South America.[4]

What he describes as essential features or aspects include the shaman's spirit journey (either ascending to or descending from, but in either case leaving the human plane "on Earth"); the intimate and dramatic involvement of various animal helpers or familiars in the shaman's enterprise; and the shaman's "mastery over fire." (The last ties him suggestively to the smith, who of course has his own complex relationship to the central drama of the hero.)

Eliade believes that the ancient shift or development that would separate any Proto-Indo-European culture (so closely allied in so many ways with the equally nomadic Turco-Tatar horse-and-steppe cultures) from these more evolved later nomadic cultures was precisely the florescence of that Indo-European tripartitive impulse so often and so widely found in this linguistic family's base sources, and so clearly described by Georges Dumézil and his associative group of scholars.[5] In this situation, what Eliade calls "shamanic traditions" tended to be compressed over time, mainly into one aspect: the Varunaic-Óðinnic, the primal expression of the First Function "terrifying sovereign" and immanent binding god. We must keep in mind, however, that some magical (and possibly shamanistic) practices also survive in the always enigmatic and difficult recesses of the Indo-European Third Function, especially in its potent sexual dramas and vectors. In terms of the present study, we seem to see the warrior-hero's Second Function operation bracketed, even isolated, by the marked concentration of magical-manipulative (and, perhaps, relict shamanist?) potencies in some part of the other two *fonctions*.

The ecstasy, a critical state of "standing outside" that specifically marks the shaman, and the spirit journeys that take the shaman heavenward or into the depths of the Underworld in pursuit of his unique cure of human souls, is not a heroic attribute or goal: we usually see the starkest mark of the hero as his physical and psychic perfection, in which spirit and body are not only complete in themselves but welded solidly together until death. The heroic scenario and experience is in no way an "out-of-body" but most emphatically an "in-body" experience. Nevertheless, these two personae may interact to produce a variety of fascinating patterns and modalities, and our picture of the marmoreal, absolutely externalized hero can then be extensively modified.

The withdrawal of the shaman *in potentia* from his own society into the Wild, his absorption into some part of the animal world, and even his temporary assumption of animal appetites resembles or recalls important elements of the hero's *archê*. The "shaman-specialist"'s continued reliance on, or manipulation of, the animal world (with wild beasts used as messengers, mounts, instructors, and so on) obviously parallels a number of heroic animal alliances (think of all those magical or monstrous horses that aid the hero, from Perseus and his Bellerophon to the Armenian epic's lake-born Korkis Jelaly, or Serbian Prince Marko's talkative mount Sarać, or Cú Chulainn's finest chariot horse, the uncanny and prescient Gray of Macha);[6] and dramatically shaped animal energies can and do enter into the aggregated potencies of both of these extraordinary human types. Animal partnerships reinforce the fact that hero *and* shaman can claim to achieve the conquest of space, mapped both horizontally and vertically: superhuman mobility and velocity frequently appear in their adventures. In addition, both can either be partnered with animals or take on animal personae and energies. Hero and shaman frequently discard or disregard the settled topos, and are surely connected in some way to a borderless, mobile, or migratory primordium. Eliade also cites the ingathering of "extreme heat" (the Indic *tapas*) that marks the ascetic magician, the shamanistic "master of fire"— and, of course, the hero in his red-raging and swollen battle fury.[7]

Nevertheless, these figures are decidedly at variance, and the fact that the shaman represents a religious or spiritual operation whereas the hero, in most cases, is unquestionably this-worldly and secular is only the most obvious difference. Presentation will also be markedly separate, and most assemblages of shamanistic characteristics and powers, when filtered through heroic narratives, will be strongly if not inevitably subjected to two additional processes: *displacement* and *refraction*.

Shamanistic magical operations, the manipulation by this figure of covert, "unknowable" forces, are likely to be displaced in our Indo-European epical context toward the First and Third Functions. The Norse-Germanic evidence declares both that the god Óðinn will display himself as a recognizably "shamanic" figure, and that parts of his magic (the suspect spells and secret acts called *seiðr*) were taught him by the goddess Freya, whose secretive, magically feminine powers are unmistakably Third Function.[8] But the Norse adventure romances (*lygisögur*) frequently attach the shamanistic powers of flight and theriomorphism to "black" magician-kings,[9] just as the Indic evidence attributes the shaman's powers of "ascension" (flight in the air, rapid movement, the ability to vanquish physically) to "arhats, kings and magicians": First Function figures again. Eliade also points to the ancient instance, reported in Polyaenus, of a Thracian priest-king whose *vita* shows openly shamanistic overtones; indeed the mythic Orpheus himself—singing his magical songs, exerting a fascinating glamour over animals, undergoing a "soul journey," then torn and dismembered at last—is surely shamanistic in his tonality, and he, too, belongs without question to some part of the Indo-European First Function.[10]

When shamanic powers are placed directly into the warrior-world of the Second Function, they will be governed in many cases, if not invariably, by the processes of refraction: we can see the shifting of the various component elements of shamanism into the ambivalent zone of sorcery, which at best lies outside human control (or can only be controlled with great effort) and at worst is "black" and inimical to any sort of humanity, even heroic superhumanity. The Norse-Icelandic sources, which often betray an uneasy fascination with extrahuman potencies, often turn theriomorphic sorcerers against one another: their powers cancel out, and their essential in- or anti-humanity disappears in the confrontation. Two sorcerers fight each other in animal form in *Sturlaugs saga Starfsama*, for example, and the old *Landnámabók* provides us with the brief tale of a magician named Dufthak, who takes on the shape of a bull and fights another uncanny figure, his neighbor Storolfr, who has assumed a bear's shape.[11] The Norse sources seem to treat sorcerers warily but in an offhand manner, and thus in *Landnámabók* again (whose entries are provocatively succinct) we find that an old settler and known sorcerer named Orn turned into a "gray, black-maned stallion" after his death, and that Oddr Arngeirsson, who killed and ate a polar bear because the bear had killed his father and brother, became "a very evil man" and a "great shape changer" by means of this forbidden meal.[12]

The sorcerers who crop up in the sagas, whether male or female, are often identified with powers sometimes, if arguably, shamanistic, but they are rarely central to the plot. They can, however, cause a smaller or greater amount of mischief. Witness the wizard Kotkell and his ugly brood in *Laxdæla*, horse masters and evil practitioners of black *seiðr*, who are eventually killed by the saga hero Oláfr Hoskuldsson;[13] Þórgrímr Neb, another evil *seiðrmaðr*, who reforged the sword Grásiða specifically as a murder weapon and was finally stoned to death (a typical sorcerer's death) by Gísli in his saga;[14] Katla and her son Oddr in *Eyrbyggja saga*;[15] or the dwarf Mondul in the romance fantasy *Göngu-Hrolfs saga*, who was nastily adept at evil binding-magic.[16] *Göngu-Hrolfs saga* gives us a strange permutation of the theme: four of its berserks, "men" of the sea-king Eirik, are not only berserks but sorcerers: "big, strong, and ugly to deal with, sorcerers . . . brimful of witchcraft."[17] Obviously the inventors of this adventure saga were perfectly prepared to confuse or mix the extreme reflex of an enraged heroism, the berserk state, with malignant magic making.

One of the most important sources, however, for refractions of shamanic practices in the North is the *Eigla*.[18] I have already outlined the position of Kveld-Úlfr, his son Skalla-Grímr, and his grandson Egill as they assume the role of "Óðinn-warrior," strong partisans of the ambiguous, panmorphic Norse chief god, but deeper tonalities are also apparent. Kveld-Úlfr is suspected of being a shape changer; both Grímr and Egill inherit his "trollish" character; and all three are not only skald-singers but also smiths or metalworkers of one kind or another.[19] It may be possible, therefore, to extract fragments of the shaman's disguise and activities from the story of this odd family, perhaps nowhere more clearly than in Egill's nervous rivalry with the sinister and sexy Gunnhildr, wife of the rather feeble King Eiríkr. This "Permian woman" and royal nymphomaniac appears in several sagas, and her maleficent shape-changing abilities are noted, or at least strongly suspected, here.

Gunnhildr's Permian origin makes her especially suspect in the imaginative context of the sagas: it is in the far North (inhabited by the always questionable "Sami" or Lappish reindeer herdsmen) and in Permia farther to the East that sorcery, and some firmer traces of the old, true shamanism, both abide and make their powers known. *Landnámabók* tells us that one Jarl Ingimundr of Gautland, invited by Norway's ambitious King Haraldr lúfa to leave his country for the country's good, "sent two Lapps on a magic ride to Iceland" to reconnoitre the island for him, thus confusing but enriching our image of the archaic Lapp shaman, who at this point appears to be under Jarl Ingimundr's orders.[20] The Norse romance fantasies, which so often feature wide-faring adventures and numerous fantastic adversaries, are also much taken up with the Lappish or sorcerer's (or shaman's) magical interventions. The tale (*Þáttr*) "Halfðan Eysteinsson" introduces two Lappish kings, called Finn and Floki, both of them magicians;[21] and in the romance "Örvar-Oddr" (Arrow-Odd) the hero Oddr encounters both Permians who weave spells that can raise their own dead and weather-wizard Lapps in whose uncanny land "all sorts of magic and sorcery are taught."[22] These lessons are in fact taught by the grisly Ogmundr Eyjolfr's-Killer, a monstrous Permian man-troll who by his magical arts can pass his body through water and earth and who has a strange cape "edged with the beards of kings." This creature kills with his teeth like an animal and must, in some way, be near kin to the shaman, though he is admittedly a terrifying "black" mode of that figure.[23] Permia—or Bjarmaland—is a veritable nest of witchkings, the most sinister of whom, King Harekr, appears in three tales: "Örvar-Oddr" (as the father of that fearsome Ogmundr), "Halfðan Eysteinsson," and "Bósa ok Herrauðr." In the last he is a villainous shape changer with a beautiful daughter whom Bósi eventually weds; Bósi himself acts suspiciously like a shaman in some of his complicated maneuvers and weird powers. So does his brother, Smidr.

Thus the Norse-Icelandic *lygisögur* invest Permia, and Lappland even more so, with the kinds of magical inclinations and dangerous potencies in which a form of shamanism is detectable. This makes considerable sense, because it was on this very edge of the Scandinavian-Icelandic world that shamanism actually flourished.[24] Scandinavian migrants and warrior-traders journeying into the East Slav lands almost certainly encountered the same or similar traditions, and we can find late evidence of it in, for example, the twelfth-century epos of Prince Vseslav of Polotsk. (Vseslav was a figure of mixed characteristics—hero-magician and werewolf—who could "keep [his] body dead" [comatose?] and fly abroad or hunt in a spirit-form.)[25] Farther afield, or deeper and more westward into Indo-Europe, the shamanistic modality or specialization will be much more difficult to detect. Shape changers, as we recall, are not unknown in the Celtic sources, but their allomorphisms seldom seem to fit the shaman's career. For example, in the Welsh *mabinogi* the tale called *Math mab Mathonwy* is full of shape shifting as well as other strange and magical doings, but whether or not this "Celtic magic," with its strong flavor of the mythopoetic, more than superficially resembles the true shaman's powers is not at all clear or final.

Math, the great magician of this tale, punishes the sexual sin committed by his two nephews by turning them into mating pairs of three animal species in turn, and then turning their anomalous offspring into what are called the "Three sons of wicked Gilfaethwy / *Three true champions* / Bleiddwn, Hyddwn, and Hychdwr Hir" (emphasis added).[26] A *heroic* generation (in fact, three of them) is the real focus of this strange narrative, and Math himself, who was strictly speaking a Celtic god, produces good out of a mixed evil through magical powers over both the human and animal worlds. The peculiar morphisms of Lleu Llaw Gyffes, in the same tale, especially his flight as an eagle after his wounding, also seem to have a shamanic coloration— but he too is a Celtic divinity, strictly cognate to Lugh, the Irish god-of-all-trades.[27]

In another and related Celtic context, the training sequences included among the "boyhood deeds," the *macgnimartha,* of Finn mac Cumaill have been likened to the shaman's initiatory excercises,[28] and the immense distortions of the champion Cú Chulainn, which may recall the actions of a smith who twists and re-forms hot metal, have also been likened to the corporeal self-disassembly undertaken by the shaman.[29] And in the Welsh Arthurian materials we once again find the important figure of the "great warlock-warrior" Cei (in Gwyn Jones's fine and apt phrase), whose activity in *Culhwch ac Olwen,* particularly his salmon ride upriver to find the imprisoned Mabon ap Modron, is a scarcely distorted "soul-search." In fact, at least one reading of Cei's character would easily support a Jungian exposition of the tale's deep significance—a reading in which a cluster of genuinely shamanic attributes could easily find a place.[30]

There is probably enough evidence in these separate Indo-European heroic-epical contexts to suggest the occasional interpenetration of shamanic with heroic acts and themes: certain heroic figures, as part of their special repertoire, may evince certain powers that have a clear parallel in shamanist practices. I suggest that the two modes are drawn together by the *individual* character of their enterprises, by the fact that the shaman and hero must be *separated* from society even though they may eventually act or move toward a social good or end (this is more marked for the shaman), and by the *intermediation* they accomplish between disparate realms, especially between the sociocultural and the extrahuman or natural zones. What most differentiates the two modes is their vastly different connection to the supernatural (spiritual, religious) zone, which remains essentially foreign and exterior to the hero and to which he is often opposed, as to so much else in his immediate surround. The shamanic specialist, if we can so identify him, reaches toward the heroic scenario mainly as a purveyor of magical powers, as a "black" or a "white" magic worker, familiar but never quite familial, and never truly kin to the hero. Indeed the control exercised by the shaman over Otherworldly powers must, almost by definition, remove him from the main line of heroic effort, for in the heroic cosmos and *agôn*, the conclusive exigency of human being and fate must rule.

EXTRAHUMAN EXTREMES: A CASE OF COMPARISON

Another formulation of the "third something" includes situations in which the hero is drastically altered in his somatic integument, escaping that old image of his physical balance and perfection, to achieve a strange and contrasted social purpose and utility through the distorted, inhuman masks or morphisms he can sometimes present.

The physical size of the hero has already been discussed: the *Iliad*'s major warriors are already large-bodied (*megalos* or *megas*), if not superlatively so (Hektor, Akhilleus, and Telemonian Aias are described as *pelôrios*),[31] and a more unbuttoned epic imagination gives us the Persian *Shâh-nâma*, whose hero Rostam is described, again formulaically, as "elephant-bodied"; eventually we learn that he "grew to the height of eight men."[32] The image of the hero as physically imposing also can glissade, after he and his age have died and gone, into a nostalgic afterthought or afterimage: when Fergus mac Roich, Cú Chulainn's uncle, one of the stars of the so-called Ulster Cycle, is called back from death's realm by Saint Patrick's holy magic to appear in a later and perceptibly lesser (though believing) age, he is naturally seen as physically immense compared to his Christian Irish *epigoni*.[33]

The limits ordinarily set for the heroic, human body can be overcome, even grotesquely so, in various ways, and to illustrate the possibilities I again want to set nature against culture, in order to highlight certain directing formulas aimed at modifying the physical integrity of the hero. In the Norse *Hrólfs saga Kraka* the hero Boðvarr Bjarki ("Warlike Little Bear") is born into a drama well known in folklore and the wonder tale: he is one of three brothers, but the only one who travels in a completely human form most of the time.[34] The latter part of this fantastic saga shows Boðvarr as a theriomorph, but of a kind that combines a hint of the shaman's animal disguise with the Norse concept of the *fylgja* or "fetch," the animal and physical (but in no way the "spirit") embodiment of a particular family's fortune or luck. (Sometimes the *fylgja* appears as a woman.) Boðvarr the hero acts as king's champion to King Hrólfr, but in the king's last battle his doubled persona is fatefully revealed. A great white bear is slaughtering the king's foes, despite the fact that these foes have their own supernatural assistant, but then the human Boðvarr is accidentally discovered sitting far from the fighting, in the king's hall, and when he is forced to join the battle in his own less impressive human form the great bear-double disappears, sealing Boðvarr Bjarki's doom and the defeat of King Hrólfr's forces.[35]

The second case of heroic shape changing is the dramatic and well-known Distortion (*ríastrad*) of Cú Chulainn, in which the Old Irish Ulster Cycle hero undergoes a monstrous transformation under certain conditions of battle or when pricked, pressed, or threatened in other ways. Even the shorter description of his distortion (from the *Táin Bó Cúalgne*) is terrific: "the warp-spasm overtook him: it seemed each hair was hammered into his head, so sharply they shot upright. You would swear a fire-speck tipped each hair. He squeezed one eye narrower than the eye of a needle; he opened the other wider than the mouth of a goblet. He bared his teeth to the ear; he peeled back his lips to the eye-teeth till his gullet showed. The hero-halo rose up from the crown of his head."[36]

A second and longer itemization adds even more extraordinary details: "His body made a furious twist inside his skin, so that his feet and shins and knees switched to the rear and his heels and calves switched to the front," and at last "tall and thick, steady and strong, high as the mast of a noble ship, rose up from the dead center of his skull a straight spout of black blood darkly and magically smoking."[37] In this prodigious heroic transmutation Cú Chulainn becomes the very icon of battle fury: a young, handsome (and, it seems, relatively short-statured) "beardless boy" is refracted into a hideous object, a battle thing, a monster or monstrous creation in every sense, though this last statement reflects a perceptible difficulty. In the shorter description of his transmutation the hero is shown as initiating and controlling his distortion, but in the longer and more extreme description this is by no means clear, nor do we know just how far the distortion, springing from his *ríastarthae* or battle fury, will go.[38]

I have chosen these two warrior-heroes because they are outrageous, although Boðvarr Bjarki, oddly enough, is less so than Cú Chulainn; shape shifters who take on animal morphisms, either as a reflection of what we could call shamanist influence or for some other reason, are not uncommon in the epics, and are more frequently encountered in the North. These transmorphisms are not, however, so extreme that they completely escape all category: the hero with his theriomorphic "projection" from King Hrólfr's saga is akin to other well-known man-animals, especially the feral, animalized warrior-*berserkr*, while swellings, changes in color, and gross distortions often mark the enraged and *furor*-infected warrior-hero. What these two examples *do* demonstrate circles back to the relational nexus of culture and nature. The Western, Eurocentric attitude holds that Culture, the artifactual and manufactured cosmos of *homo faber*, is a prime human aim and essential human good, and that nature, ordinarily figured as a hostile or at least a recalcitrant zone or extrahuman force, is to be conquered and put under the domination of man and his culture. Our two heroic "third things," each in his own way caught between human and nonhuman, demonstrate how this egregious assumption can be turned back on itself.

Cú Chulainn's distortion is part of an associational complex dominated by the sign of the Smith; his enormous warp-spasm is connected, as William Sayers convincingly argues, "to the imagery of the smithy."[39] The Irish hero's ties to the smith and his torsive and percussive work are so clear, in fact, that he is very like a product of the weapon maker: his insensate red fury may have to be tempered by cold water, and when he has become a thing, fully charged with blind, hot energy, he will strike at both friend or foe, son or foster brother, without discrimination or any sort of guiding, alleviating human intelligence. The smith or symbolized smith powers, and thus culture, has fabricated in him a supremely dangerous and destructive animated weapon.

Boðvarr Bjarki embodies the working of the opposite principle. Separately existing in both the animal and the human realms, this "good *berserkr*" serves as a barrier against powers originating outside the human/cultural zone; by a kind of homeopathic reaction he can fend off potencies inimical to the human realm. The animal-natural morphism in Warlike Little Bear's case is self-controlled, benificent, protective of culture, though it is born in and compassed by the unhuman.

Before leaving this discussion of heroic hypostases or hypermorphisms, I ought to take note of the ambiguity that again may be imprinted on and expressed in the hero's physicality. The audience for the heroic tale occasionally seems to expect and demand that its extraordinary subjects be simultaneously available both as heroically immense in body and as an adolescent stripling, bulking less rather than more as compared with the ordinary warriorhood surrounding them. Cú Chulainn is a prime example of this odd somatic confusion: his wild distortions blow him up to a fearsome size, yet other details, especially of his arming and panoply, show him to have the expected, ordinary heroic heft when undistorted. Yet he is called the "beardless stripling" (*gan olchain*) beloved of the Ulstermen; he is their "little champion."[40] According to one observer, the very weapons this Celtic champion uses can project this confusion with or survival of a juvenile state.[41] The *Iliad*'s Akhilleus, the perfect hero, also hints at this doubled or confused somatic image; he is conventionally *pelôrios*, huge, and yet at the beginning of the Trojan expedition he is termed *nepios*, a "child" (IX.440–

41), and there remains about him what Katherine Callen King calls "a sense of extreme youth" that we might read as signifying a not-yet-grown, adolescent bodily size as well; we remember that his friend Patroklos was older than he.[42] I don't think we can assign any relational value to these two opposed characteristics, or to make one rather than the other a more archaic or deeper-sourced descriptive. At a guess, the emphasized description of a smaller or "miniature" hero is connected to his great speed, to the heroic feat of extraordinary *celeritas*. In any event, this doubled and contradictory somatic characteristic adds to our image of the hero as one capable of confusing, rather than being constricted by, strict definitional boundaries.

DIVINE FAVORITES

Searching out the heroic essence's quiddity will quickly involve us in questions of a nearly theological signification, especially when we judge the intermixture of divine and human realms and actors in any given heroic-epic context. If the narrative cleaves its hero to the human pole of the human/supernatural axis, no exceptional difficulty arises; the hero may be extruded from the ordinary human mold by a variety of extrahuman interventions (at conception, at birth, or at some later point in his biography), but that may be the extent of his connection. If the hero moves toward the supernatural pole of that axis, however, more complex scenarios will probably result. Then the question becomes: how far can the supernatural intervene before the special human quality of the heroic is disturbed, misshapen, or lost?

Divine Interventions

When gods or divinities of whatsoever stripe interfere dramatically in the heroic drama or biography, a new set of queries and perturbations will arise. The least complex (and to a degree the least meaningful) relationship occurs in those epical contexts in which one or another of the dominant monotheistic religions (Christianity, Islam) appears—or, more to the point, when a particular emphasis is placed, in a specific narrative, on the hero's True Faith.[43] Yet little need be made even of this identification. The Old French *chansons de geste* themselves, when their Christian Frankish nobility are heroically arrayed against an invariably caricatured *payennerie*, evince little real sense of Holy War, though we may be told that "the poets [of the *chansons de geste*] established their orthodoxy abundantly, with sincerity and simplicity."[44] That archetypal epic, the *Chanson de Roland*, offers only the simplest statement: "their cause is evil and we are in the right," or (addressing the pagans) "you're in the wrong" (*li torz*).[45] The Christian God's aid is often invoked, but the effective element in the tale's action is still placed in the knightly fighter and his hard, if sometimes extravagant, handstrokes. That overpowering, fanatical, and terrible slogan, *Deus vult!* is not heard here; these heroes are human and not divinely inspired.[46] This aspect is even more pronounced in the heroic "border ballads": the hero of the *Poema del Mio Cid* thanks God "and all of his saints" for the booty won and, perhaps as an afterthought, for a victory.[47] My Cid may vow to establish a bishopric (?) in Valencia to reward "this good Christian," the genial and hard-fighting Bishop Jerome,[48] but the modern reader will probably receive the impression that the Cid's virile and symbolically potent *grant barba* is more important to him than any divine favor granted because he is a true, believing Christian. Political or at least military-tactical alignments are more important than true faith in the narrative of the *Poema,* as they are, by and large, in other border songs, such as our often-cited parallel sources, the Serbo-Croat songs or the Byzantine *Digenid.*

The gods, especially identified as the *athanatoi,* are an obvious and often a dramatic presence in the Homeric poems, and they have their favorites and their enemies among the human players—though they cannot protect even those they love. Indeed a warrior-hero chosen by a god is very likely to be doomed.[49] It was *theôn iotêti*—"through the will of the gods"—that Argive and Trojan fought and suffered many grievous woes at Troy;[50] and although at times the gods act only as powerful aid bringers to a favorite involved in the press of human-heroic plots and combats, at other times the feuds and fancies of the Deathless Ones, their old quarrels and sly alliances, drag the heroes down. There is no need to rehearse at inordinate length all of the permutations of the *Iliad*'s intermixture of gods and men: we know that Love and War, Aphrodite and Ares, descended from Olympus to help Troy, as did Apollo and his sister Artemis, whereas Athena and Poseidon were implacably pro-Achaean. Hera is another potent figure whose divine and mysterious anger is set strongly against Troy and its defenders, presumably because of that Eris-influenced Judgment of Paris, though other and older antagonisms may be working here as well. At any rate the queen of the gods was prepared to let Zeus deal "hatefully" with three of her favorite cities if the Cloud Gatherer would let her devise the worst sort of ills—*kaka*—for all that belonged to the ever-hateful King Priam of Troy.[51] And Zeus can easily be persuaded into a grudging sort of neutrality, in which he does bad things to *both* sides.

But apart from this very rough tactical map of divine allegiances, what is the effect of a personal bond between divinity and hero? The fact that so many warriors of both loyalties were of godly parentage on one side definitely adds a personal element, but not even an immortal parent can indefinitely save those heroes who are all called *diogenês* 'of the blood of Zeus'. Eos the dawn-goddess could not shield her son Memnon; the sea-nymph Thetis could not guard Akhilleus from the death arrow guided by Apollo—although in this case Akhilleus had already chosen death and fame.[52] Aphrodite does manage to rescue Aeneas for another fate elsewhere, and Athena, related to Odysseus by mutual inclination and the power of *métis* if not by actual blood kinship, finally brings her favorite home to Ithaka. Yet even if he doesn't die, Odysseus still proves the rule that when the Immortals take a dislike to someone, his fate is usually sealed, for after the hero angered Poseidon by tricking and blinding the god's ogrish son Polyphemos, he had to pit his (and Athena's) guile and persistence over and over against the raw and thunderous power of the enigmatic sea-god. Nevertheless this trickster-hero did win through in the end, more or less, though with a good deal of divine help. The other Greek Aias, the Lokrian, twinned to gigantic Telemonian Aias in a fashion that recalls the trickster and strong arm-pairing seen in other epics, is (fatally) less successful in defying Poseidon's powerful hatred.[53]

The fact that the Greek gods posture, speak and argue, seem to hate and love like human beings writ large may make us forget the vital difference: humankind and the gods operate in different zones, and in the end they can never be confused. The gods of Homer are not *dei otiosi*, but for all their manifold doings and combinations with mortals, they are not mortal, and neither side can ever forget this: the most brutal barriers stand between them. Men are fated to be ultimately unhappy, and—or because?—they will die; the gods have power over men, but never is the reverse true. "Right order," the *diké* overseen by Zeus, maintains the status of both camps. Yet it is the desire of the greatest heroes to assault this barrier, not only as a battle-maddened Diomedes spears and wounds Ares and Aphrodite, but also to overcome the "system" that sets each in his place. Of course, the Immortals slyly connive at this hubristic enterprise—up to a point. The gods affect and perturb what we have to call the psychology of an Agamemnon or an Akhilleus; as Hugh Lloyd-Jones has cogently discerned, both Akhilleus *and* Zeus are jointly responsible for the "savage" *thumos* of the hero that so disturbs and harms the Achaean cause.[54] Every heroic attempt to achieve any lasting control over human circumstance will ultimately and inevitably be frustrated, and even the greatest of these human heroes will be thrust back to "the humble place where they belong."[55] Their fame will remain, but always dearly won. This, too, is the nature of heroism.

Celtic Specialties

In a considerable contrast to the harder and clearer outlines of the Greek epic, the interaction of gods and heroes in the archaic Celtic sources is loosely governed by the same characteristic I announced earlier: the frequent mixture, confusion, or interpenetration of their respective realms or zones. It is not easy even to sketch a topography of the Celtic Otherworld in its relationship to the world of men, and as for clearly recognizing the gods and goddesses and other nonhuman beings for what they are, our sources delight in tossing them into the surviving narratives without identifying their special place, or only rarely making such an identification. It has long been one task of a concerned scholarship to descry the old gods of the Celts within the names and attributes mentioned in the Celtic heroic tales, sometimes aided by the protohistorical evidence of Roman and Greek-Hellenistic commentators, sometimes by archaeology's more or less successful pursuit of solid remnants and artifacts, and always by inspired guesswork. The Celtic hero tale emerges from a very confused matrix, especially in the most archaic Welsh sources, where the hero *qua* hero is often difficult to detach from a dense surround of supernatural signs and Otherworldly figures.

For example, in *Pwyll Pendeuic Dyuet*, the First Branch of the canonical *mabinogi*, we have a cast of characters including Arawn, lord of the Underworld, and the queenly Rhiannon, an avatar of the Celtic horse-goddess (though she will not be clearly identified as such a divinity here), but the emphasis of the tale is on the conception, birth, occultation, and eventual recovery of the hero, Pryderi. Another branch, *Branwen uerch Llyr,* introduces and intermixes what must be ancient Celtic sea-gods, for Manawydan mab Llyr is the Irish sea-god Manannan mac Lir, and Bran the Blessed has a direct Irish cognate, as the god-hero of a famous *immram* or voyage.[56] But this tale, too has another aim, to tell how stark enmity rose between Ireland and Britain, and thus brings in that notable mischief-maker or red trickster, Efnisien. The identifiable acts and certain biographical notes referent to other Celtic divinities (such as Math the Great Magician, of whom I have already spoken) can be found in or read into all of the archaic Four Branches, but only in very dense, complex, and enigmatic configurations, and with many a gap and caesura.

The Irish Celtic sources, by contrast, follow a "historical" line somewhat more strictly delineated, in which the hero is depicted and accepted precisely because he intervenes between gods and men—a place, of course, of frequent and awful peril. "The hero belongs to this third category," as Tomás Ó Cathasaigh succinctly states before he goes on to examine the emblematic lives of the martial hero Cú Chulainn and the "king-hero" Conaire Mor.[57] Both of his subjects were generated by Otherwordly interventions (Cú Chulainn from his well-known "tripled" conception), and at critical moments in their lives the Otherworld will interpose itself again, for good or ill according to its own unknowable calculus. Cú Chulainn's divine genitor, the green-caped and many-talented god Lugh, appears to the greatest hero in the *Táin* as "your father from the *síd*." He heals his son's grave battle wounds, but he also brings the dangerous and double-edged power always implicit in a god's intervention, for while Cú Chulainn is in his three-day healing coma his young companions, King Conchobar's Boy Troop, rashly attack the army of Medb and Ailill and are slaughtered.[58] In the most famous of the Irish *tána bó*, the heroic cattle raids, Cú Chulainn will also meet the Morrigan or Morigu, the death-goddess so deeply concerned with his exploits, as he is by far the greatest and most fell-handed of the tale's heroic killers. Indeed, in the tale called "The Death of Cú Chulainn," she— and his adamant *gessa*—will finally bring him down. (Some reminiscence of a Homeric attitude or motif may linger in this death, which is accomplished when the Irish hero's essentially human nature, expressed or defined by his *gessa* or constraining taboos, combines with the final jealous malignity of a supernatural being.)[59]

Conaire Mor, king and hero, is also engendered by an Otherworld father, and after a "perfect" and pacific utopian reign (the ideology of peace is, oddly enough, supposed to be central to the Irish High Kingship) he is destroyed in the holocaust at Da Derga's hostel. This is another conjunction of mortal space and Otherworld, because the king's long and "truthful rule" (*fír flatha*) was finally contaminated and ended by his own fatal, taboo-violating decisions.[60]

In the narratives of the later Fenian Cycle, the realms of men and of the supernatural *síd* are further made disjoint and separate, but they continue to abut or adjoin.[61] Finn mac Cumaill is of a predictably ambiguous though not divine begetting, and the spatial frame of men and of Otherworld beings is more strictly defined in his cycle of tales. Finn's heroic-superhuman traits are more than a match for those of the green-clad warriors of the faery *síd*, who have descended in several senses from the divinities of earlier narrative cycles. As *Mesca Ulad* says, "the Túatha Dé Danaan went into the hills and fairy places. . . . They left five of their number before the five provinces of Erin, to incite war and conflict and valor and strife between the sons of Mil"[62]—although it must be noted that the kings and warriors of Erin rarely needed inciting to war and conflict from anyone. These raths and mounds, exemplified by the *bruig* in which Cú Chulainn himself was conceived or the *bruiden* in which Conaire the Great met his fiery end, are portentous features "immediately visible on the landscape,"[63] physical-topographical reminders of the extrusion of the Otherworld into man's space, but for Finn and his fellows they are also a place of confrontation and adventure. Assaults are launched from or against the *síd* as if they were indeed fortresses held by the supernatural foe, in that military sense invented by war-making man.

In closing we might note that the intermediary, extrahuman, and high imaginal status of at least some of the Irish Celtic heroes was by no means excised by the believers but rather extended into the Christian period. King Cochobar, joyfully murderous at all times in a good old chieftainly way, was nevertheless deemed "one of the two men that believed in God in Ireland before the coming of the Faith," and thus his soul would be saved.[64] Fergus mac Roich achieved the same posthumous glory, while the great Cú Chulainn himself, in the legend, was awakened and interrogated by the sainted Patrick, who finally and charitably arranged that "Heaven was decreed for Cú Chulainn."[65]

Germanic Hints

The system of northern Germanic, Norse-Icelandic belief in pre-Christian gods is reasonably well known, but the extrapolation of such a system into the world of the Germanic warriors and the Norse-Icelandic saga heroes is not a simple task. It might help, at this point, to return to the Óðinn-warrior, whose portrait was first developed by Dumézil as an *imitatio dei*, a human hero either setting himself or being set into a special, and always very risky, relationship with one of the most potent and perilous of the old Norse gods.

Óðinn is the god whose cosmotactic acts are described so powerfully in the Eddic prose and poetry; he is a mighty figure in Norse myth, but he is also known to mix in the affairs of later humankind, that is, of epic or saga time. Óðinn can make his mysterious appearance not only in the legendary *fornaldar sögur* or Norse romance tales: even in the family sagas, though they are ostensibly historical and record events that are supposed to have occurred in real time, he can direct, or at least bend, the destinies of the human players. No other figure in the Norse-Germanic pantheon seems to do this: certainly not Þórr, whose religious *cultus* was widespread in pagan times, but who makes no distinct appearance in strictly human affairs, apart from his brief role in Starkaðr's tale as it is laid out in the legend narrative *Gautreks saga*.[66] In Dumézilian terms, Óðinn is an ideal god of the First Function Varunaic type: a god of inspiration and skaldship, a "binding god" to whom sacrifices are made "for power and victory" but whose cult is essentially expressed in ferocious war, and even more in the fitting battle death made as a sacrifice to him.[67] His sovereignty is an enigmatic one compact of mighty but unknowable forces; his religious focus is in what the old Romans would call *religio*, the zone of dangerous and probably uncontrollable nonhuman prepotency. Human beings who would identify with Óðinn, or be identified with him, must always be in harm's way, like any warrior, but they also should display traits that set them apart from others in the heroic-warrior vocation. In my view, three aspects of this special Óðinn-warriorhood suggest themselves: the archaic, the heroic-trickster-ish, and the tragic; and three saga heroes suggestively fit each aspect: Starkaðr, Egill Skalla-grímsson, and Grettir the Strong.

STARKAÐR THE ARCHAIC

The archaic Óðinn-warrior Starkaðr defined the type as Dumézil first perceived it, despite the strongly marked ambiguities in his character. We already know that this giant-born warrior is the subject of a midnight debate and contest between Óðinn and Þórr before a council of the other gods, a debate recorded in *Gautreks saga* (chap. 7); in the course of the divine conclave the hero is given a series of powers and benefits (from Óðinn) and a contrasting, oppositive list of sins and maledictions (from Þórr). There are incongruous features to the list, and Óðinn's agenda is never really clear; we also see Þórr speaking in the name of the common people, as the "social" god, depriving Starkaðr of "land and estates," and decreeing his lack of progeny—all of which ought, one expects, to be the province of Freyr or another of the Vanir, whose Third Function powers and judgments have perhaps been excised from the narrative.[68] Starkaðr's lengthy career or *vita*, fully described in the account of Saxo Grammaticus, then fulfills the fate decreed by the two gods: living on and on, "surly, brutal, errant, solitary," he will commit his three *niðingsverkar* in line with the formula Dumézil has called the "three sins of the Warrior."[69]

As an archaic Óðinn-warrior this hero's character is curiously mixed. Compared with later manifestations of the type he is marginally malleable and even socially cooperative: Starkaðr is willing to do service for kings, though he will betray them too, and such features as his childlessness liken him to the ill-fated, "serviceable" Þórr-warrior. In fact, when his full biography is pieced together, it is difficult to assign him entirely to one mode of warriorhood or the other. Edgar Polomé, in tracing the final shape of these patterns, finds good evidence for both modes, depending on the source used and the perspective assumed, but he concludes (with Dumézil, who went through several shifts of opinion on the subject) that Starkaðr ends, on balance, as an Óðinnic hero, "linked with the dark side of that complex god," even to his own description of his gray and scarred and battered personal appearance.[70] Such an appearance, in fact, makes him iconic kin to the second kind of Óðinn-warrior, below.

EGILL THE TRICKSTERISH

Egill son of Bald Grímr, like Starkaðr, has already been cited numerous times in this study of the hero's permutations. He is definitely Óðinn's man: both skald and fell-handed warrior, grim opponent to kings, tricksterish survivor, ugly and individualistic, perverse, long-lived and appetitive, especially thirsty for Óðinn's own good brew, the feasting ale, but also greedy for gold and land, and loot and rich inheritances. I have described elsewhere the intricacies of the division within the Kveldulfsson clan, between the monarchophobic Óðinn-warriors (Kveld-Úlfr, Skalla-Grímr, Egill) and the two Þórólfrs, Grímr's and then Egill's brothers, both Þórr-warriors who have "no luck" (ekki gæfu) from kings, and who die in and by service to them.[71] In Egill the uncanny powers of his father and grandfather are somewhat diluted, though Egill can manipulate spells and make rune magic (which he does, for example, in protecting himself against a poisoned drink).[72] When Egill mentions the gods at all he invokes Óðinn (along with Freyr and Njordr when he thoroughly curses King Eiríkr).[73] At one point he seems to draw a causative (even germinative) connection between the enemies' blood he had spilled or would spill as if it were seed on "Óðinn's wife, the earth," and the rich booty that, as Óðinn's votary, he could expect to carry off by right.[74] All in all, Egill displays the violent talents to be expected of one touched by this powerful but unsavory Norse high god, and he returns many bloody battle offerings, the corpses of his enemies, fittingly sent to the hungry god who always, eagerly, awaits such sacrifices. He also has the ambiguously marked career, with the dramatic mixture of good and ill, of one all too close to a god whose attention, and gifts, are not at all safe for any man to boast of, be he hero or not.

GRETTIR THE TRAGIC

The same parlous situation is even more marked in the tale of Grettir the Strong. To some extent, as Edward Fox and Hermann Pálsson are constrained to note, his tragedy comes about because "he is born too late, and into a Christian and civilized world, where the heroic virtues are no longer sufficient."[75] His saga does in fact accept Christianity as an ideological given, if not a deep-rooted spiritual one, and presumably Grettir was a Christian of sorts; at one point in his story he fasts for Lent, and there are other casual indications of his faith.[76] The old gods are never mentioned directly, though Grettir's tale is full of supernatural beings: the dead-undead, like the *haugr* Kar the Old and the fell *draugr* Glámr, then a she-troll, and an earth-giant. Grettir defeats and destroys them all, though in time he will pay a full price, especially for his hard-won victory over the terrible, undead Glamr, but there is another strange character in Grettir's saga, a character first called Lopt and then Hallmundr. This being, who wears "a big hat which concealed his face," is described as even stronger than Grettir, a great swordsman and skald who lived at Ball Glacier, where "Hallmundr had a large cave, and a brawny and impressive-looking daughter"—and he is undoubtedly meant to be the god Óðinn himself.[77] In this saga Lopt or Hallmundr is mortally wounded when he attempts a common burglary—the old gods have fallen low!—but it is not this suppositious and temporary alliance with a much-diminished old god that marks Grettir as one of Óðinn's warriors, and a "tragic" one at that. The main theme in the narrative is the combination of Grettir's extraordinary physical gifts (combined, of course, with an asocial, pigheaded, and turbulent personality), and the "bad luck" that shades and obviates his every act of heroic courage and warriorly fortitude. In Egill's saga Kveld-Úlfr says that his kin will get "no luck" from any king, but Grettir's fate is a good deal bleaker: in his saga he is increasingly and specifically marked as an *ógæfumaðr* or "luckless man," a warrior of force suited to the antique Viking past but now beset again and again by supernatural opponents (much as Boðvarr Bjarki's animal morphism is opposed to an enemy's malignancy in beast form). Grettir is brought down, at the very end, by a fatal combination of his own social isolation in outlawry, the persistent malice of his enemies, an act of the lurking, still undefeated supernatural—and perhaps by the fact that the ancient Óðinn, a shadow of his former perilous self, can no longer extend aid even to his own hero, even if he wanted to.

Having reset the hero in his position among humanity, the animal, and the supernatural worlds, I now want to fit him—still considered as a *tertium quid*—back into humankind's categories, to explore his tertiality there.

BETWEEN GENERATIONS AND GENDERS
Fathers and Sons

We have seen this primary kin tie (certainly primary in any patrilineal society) reset, reoriented, and deformed in a number of ways and directions, assuming a variety of morphisms in our Indo-European epic context. The first overview seems to inform us that the hero will be separated from his mortal male parent by means of various strategies, from the human father who is missing or unknown or dead, through an eruption of an early heroic rebellion and the young hero's confrontational withdrawal from patriarchal control, to the creation of substituted affective ties with a foster parent or maternal male—the mother's brother, composed in ties of the avunculate. In addition, beyond the family, the hero as social misfit and obstreperous or errant rebel remains fitted into a doubtful, fragile, tense filiation to the king-father, insofar as we can read an abstracted paternity into the king's sociopolitical role.

Yet two further points have to be made. There are very few echoes of son against father, or of son actually replacing father, in our sources, and heroic parricide is extremely rare. The hero seems to require the definition-by-opposition of himself and his persona that a constraining paternal presence affords, though perhaps by contrast and contradiction (I will expand on this situation in the last part of this study). The same is true of the king. Regicide may be one of the "three sins" of the archetypal warrior-hero, and yet, of the three paradigmatic heroes Dumézil uses to flesh out and exemplify his theory, only one, Starkaðr/Starcatherus, actually commits this ultimate violence, and then his act is triggered, controlled, and surrounded by extraordinary and ambiguous circumstance.[78]

The long persistence of what ought to be seen as something close to a regicidal taboo is most obvious in a saga like Egill's, in which the strong antimonarchic bias of the Norse narrative cannot be doubted. Egill aims fatal violence against king's agents, against someone who closely resembles the king, against the king's son—but not against the king himself, however he might despise that royal person.[79] Elsewhere in our epic materials the same or similar scenarios are frequently played out: Siegfried threatens King Gunther in the most unambiguous terms when he first "intrudes" into the Burgundian court, but he ends as a king's man and is slain through the treachery of another king's man, Hagen. And we have seen that the fatality that accompanies heroic service to kings—in obedience to the Father?—is so pervasive that it has to be identified as a prime theme in, and cause of, the hero's death.

But if son rarely kills father, "father" does kill "son." And here we do have a dramatic dominant in the epic-heroic narratives, the confrontation of Sohrâb and Rostam, a pattern so persistent and commanding that I think it can, with some care, be identified as a genuine Indo-European relict.[80] The tension that exists between the hero and his father may be differently expressed or deflected, recrystallized, ritualized, or mythicized, but the generational *muthos* within which the typical hero operates permits, if indeed it doesn't demand, the hero to be childless, even if he has to kill his own son, who might expect to inherit his heroic exceptionality. The hero can maintain himself *in his aeon,* his strictly limited and demarcated and fated time, by eliminating the next heroic generation.[81] His own accelerated maturity and physical prowess still seem to leave him dependent on a paternal figure, even if he is in firm opposition to that figure, but in most cases he cannot be replaced by another heroic generation, or is allowed to abort or remove violently that filial replacement. Thus he becomes interstitial. Here as elsewhere the heroic *muthos,* the organized collective of significant patterns as they are developed in epic, moves off at a tangent from those mythic "charters" that support the healthy continuity of a society. Indeed the specifically *heroic* mythepical construct may be completely different in essence from the mythic-cosmogonic.[82]

Insofar as our hero is fitted into a generational sequence, his individuality constrains him to be neither a good son nor a good father—yet he is typically better at the former, everything considered, than at the latter! Only very occasionally is either the paternal connection or the filial connection significant in defining the "structure" of the heroic: the perfect solipsism of the hero is kept safe from challenge, succession, process, replacement, or that profane and looming temporality (expressed in the very term "generation") that afflicts lesser humankind, those who have sons and grow old and die. In this way the hero's search for self-immolation in his bloody "good death," in return for that great jewel of general memory we call fame, can be complete.

Man and Woman

If most of the warrior-heroes we have examined live and act within the Indo-European frame or *idéologie,* their Second Functionality and the central characteristics of that Function could predictably be said to block, or at least to inhibit, the expression of those potencies resident in the Third Function—such as, most obviously, the force of normal sexuality. The heroic distrust, disdain for, or plain imperious ignoring of this fruitful *fonction*, however the attitude is manifested, is well and thoroughly documented in our sources. The Third Function seems to be regarded, by the "warrior" Second, as a zone dominated by essentially foreign or exotic mores; and one of its primary marks, that of wealth and riches, is compromised because it was not "heroically" won, as booty or rightful reward. Those even more primary and important functional acts, such as growing crops or herding animals, are derogated or, again, ignored, and the farmer or the herdsman is "obviously" sprung from a lower and contemned creation.[83] Even when we can identify a "hero of the Third Function," as we not uncommonly might, we see him, as in the frame of the *Iliad,* represented by a Hektor, the victim of Akhilleus, respected by all means but also "caught" in the close net of city and family—or by Hektor's brother Paris-Alexandros, the sensualist and hapless coward of this epic.

Paris-Alexandros certainly recalls the other great mark of this *fonction,* sensuality as affect and sexuality as life process. The normative heroic attitude toward sexuality has already been described. If we bracket, for a moment, the Norse sagas, in which the familial structure and its valences are a given and a complication (though even in this context a number of sagas, like that of Grettir the Strong, still lift up and celebrate the old pattern of the warrior-hero-isolate), and if we elide the special case of romance epic and some folk epics, we are left with epical heroes who maintain a singular aloofness from ordinary familial heterosexuality. In the episodic, condensed, "hot" epic adventures, such as those of Beowulf and Roland, no significant women appear; the Byzantine *Digenid* boasts a married hero but one unmarked by anything resembling a normal sexual consciousness, as the Maximo or Amazonian encounter in this tale most emphatically demonstrates (the hero has sex with Maximo and then, guilt-stricken, kills her). If the French chivalric romances, with and after Chrétien de Troyes, inject sexuality or at least sexual tensions into our evidential stream, they also demand a significant degree of displacement and frustration—and in theory, or in some theories, their finest flower and icon will eventually be Sir Galaad, sexless and sinless. In the Celtic epics Cú Chulainn has several wives, or mates, but his hero's "heat" is truly and absolutely released only in battle, and beyond or behind this terrific prowess he remains a "beardless boy"—and thus, in one reading, presexual. Finn mac Cumaill and his *fénnidi,* as we have seen, make up an excluded war band devoted to adventures on the threatened (and therefore, to them, the satisfying) edge of any normal social and familial life. And Siegfried, in the *Nibelungenlied*, eventually pays with his life for his sexual "taming" of the Amazon Brunhilde—a task he undertook as a king's man and, in fact, enacted in King Gunther's physical guise.

In some part the hero-warrior's sexual inactivity can easily be connected to the notion, very widely current in warrior-dominated societies, that sexual abstinence secures and defends the heat and vital energy necessary to the fighter's deadly art; that in fact this energy can properly have no other outlet than battle and war. A concomitant theory holds that women, by their particular and deeply opposite powers, can contaminate a warrior's weapons; therefore the hero who is metaphorically "forged" as a weapon would be absolutely deenergized by a woman's sexual powers. Beyond this lies the easily unearthed male suspicion of woman as unknown and unknowable, as a being who holds sway in a shadowy dominion and whose physical essence and depths contain the awesome magic that makes a new life. "What do women want?" asks the father of the science of the unconscious, and all of this can be articulated into the meaning behind the strange boast of the Armenian hero Pokr Mher, last of the heroic house of the Sassowntsi: "I have had no child, I can have no death." The death Mher has avoided is the death of "succession"—or again, generation; his fear is the fear of time. Thus, in the end, we have a typical hero composed of a fearsome physical force and precocity, man-not-child, yet with a marginal social concern and sexual maturity: child-not-man.

The Valences of Adolescence?

In Erich Neumann's *The Origins and History of Consciousness* this talented follower of C. G. Jung explores, by way of the collective of heroic myth, the psychic growth that ideally produces the truly individuated, fully formed human "consciousness"—the complete, whole and healthy self. According to Neumann, the details that construct the myth of the hero follow the sequence of hard-fought victories over powerful and destructive forces that allow the conscious ego to coalesce and form itself, or to be formed—or in other words, the hero's mythic biography replicates and dramatizes the processes by which full human individuation is reached, demonstrating how self or ego is freed from the close toils of archaic or "deep" prepotencies, and especially from the dark and negative aspects of the archetypic imagos of Mother and Father. Neumann provides a concise but dense reading of the workings of such a process in his description and analysis of the profoundest core of the myth of Perseus: "The killing of the transpersonal mother and father (the Medusa and the sea monster) precedes the rescue of the captive, Andromeda. His father a god and his mother the bride of a god, a personal father who hates him, then the killing of the transpersonal First Parents, and finally the liberation of the captive—these are the stages that mark the progress of the hero."[84] Alas, the difficulty of applying this Jungian pattern against the typical epic-heroic life ought to be obvious by this point, because we know that heroic biography tends either to abort or to avoid important parts of the process of normal individuation, or displays a hypertrophic or skewed development of other parts; and above all, the *telos* of the epic hero is rarely the achievement of a mature personal and social integration but his death. If anything the hero has a strong and grimly insistent bent toward self-annihilation at an early age: surely this is contrary to the achievement of an integrated and mature individuation of the self?

Where does this leave us? With two possibilities, I think: either the marked precocity of the hero includes or attains a significantly premature individuation and the construction of an early, but complete, structure of self, or the solid exterior integument of the epic hero, his marmoreal or monolithic quality, conceals a mixed and confused or incomplete psychic structure, and especially a poorly developed and even scarcely detectable dimension of the unconscious. And of course it is precisely this quality of exteriority and depthlessness that the epic creators cultivated: in the hero what you see *is* what you get, neither more nor less. Instant experience and outer act is all, at least in the ideal. Moreover, myth and epic have different realms and rationales, which ought to lead us to expect different, and differently constituted, heroes. Finally, what Neumann calls the victory of spiritualization in ego or self may be won by the epic hero in his own way: his *kleios* or *timê* or *fama* forever perdures when his physical entity is gone. Indeed, as the peerless heroes Akhilleus and Cú Chulainn bluntly admit, this is the bargain they accept or even insist on when they take up the hero's role. So the goal of continuity, of an extended ego expressed "beyond" if not "within" his consciousness or vital life, *can* somehow eventually be achieved.

All of this evokes a hero who is caught between maturational states, who in fact ought to be properly placed in the adolescent state or maturational *limen*. At least one scholar (Robert Eisner) has made this specific identification of the "essentially adolescent psychology" of the hero.[85] In addition to what we have already summarized, consider the heroic insistence on exteriority and self-display, the marked disvaluation of any sort of graduated, learned, or accumulated experience, the agonistic definition of self versus group, and perhaps we are reaching to another Jungian discovery: the shadow. For the hero, the mythotypic adolescent forever set between categories and zones, can be called the prince—and the victim—of the shadow.

BETWEEN LIFE AND DEATH
The Hero in the Shadow

Jung identified the shadow as one of the archetypes of the collective unconscious projected into and perpetually taking form in the conscious human mind.[86] A partial and rather disorganized list of these archetypes from the volume in which he examines the concept in most detail reveals "the *shadow,* the *wise old man,* the *child* (including the child hero), the *mother* . . . and her counterpart the *maiden,* and lastly the *anima* in man and the *animus* in woman"[87] (all emphases in the original). We have to take at least cursory note of the "child hero" on this list, whose deep-psychic significance, for Jung, lies in his imaging of the supposedly powerless ("smaller than small") being who performs superhuman deeds, deeds that "point to the conquest of the dark." But our particular, paradigmatic hero is only temporarily attached to this child-archetype: he may look to conquer the dark, but he also remains *in* that dark.

Jung sometimes uses the term "shadow" merely to signify some part of the psyche unilluminated by or unknown to full consciousness, as when he points to the young male whose psyche has, inaccessible to consciousness, "wide areas that still lie in the shadow."[88] To some degree such a description fits the hero—certainly the epic hero—with his purposive avoidance of any "deep" self-examination. However, as an archetype the shadow is not merely a sign of denial or absence. One Jungian scholar, Marie-Louise von Franz, takes the shadow to be "the inferior aspects of the conscious personality" ("laziness, greed, envy, jealousy, the desire for prestige, aggressiveness"), and again we recognize a number of pertinent aspects of our hero—in particular the last two, which, in a Jungian analysis, would be considered dæmonic influences.[89] But Jung himself was not quite satisfied with the label ascribing "inferiority" to the shadow and its components, and another of his disciples rediscovers an intermediating aspect. Erich Neumann sees a part of the shadow as "those elements of the personality that the ego condemns as negative values," but more significantly, the shadow is part of—and "midway between"—the personal and the collective unconscious.[90] It, as shadow, may show itself mythically as the antagonist or the hostile one, but more often it is manifested as what Neumann calls the "dark brother": "in myths the shadow often appears as a twin, for he is not just the 'hostile brother,' but the companion and friend, and it is sometimes difficult to tell whether this twin is the shadow or the self, the deathless 'other.'"[91] Here, in the shadow, is the "incorporation of aggressive tendencies" and that "dark side" of the human personality that lies under "its readiness to defend itself or to attack"—and, most significantly, the "capacity to mark itself off from the collective and maintain its 'otherness' in the face of the leveling demands of the community."[92]

The epic hero fits into this psychic shadow because of his constellation of aggressive and socially unassimilated characteristics, his strange and dramatic vacillation between the light and the darkness, and (though here, I must admit, Jung has another and less pessimistic opinion) his search for death, in which his incomplete and unexamined but very powerful ego will at once be negated and dissolved, and transmuted, made eternal. And remember the evil of which Neumann speaks: the grim but seductive power of violence and destruction lies ready to the hero's sword hand, and blood is always his argument, an argument raised exactly against life itself. Since I have frequently spoken of an icon or image of the hero, we might think of Dürer's famous etching, *Ritter, Tod und Teufel;* it seems that the engraven Knight is less the mere prey of Death and the Devil than their confrère and willing accomplice. And the limned shadows that dramatically suffuse this extraordinary icon of the doomed hero-knight are entirely appropriate to him.

The Opposition—and Death

To go further: as we have frequently seen, heroic violence is only rarely directed against what we would call a distinct power of evil in any theological sense. To some extent this must be because evil is, as it were, "in the family": it may be conceived as the shadowy realm of the antagonist, who is himself heroic. There is, of course, the definition of evil as absolutely something else: an utterly alien, malign, or antihuman force or personification, some "thing" purely opposite and Other to the human. But in fact the theme of most epics is heroic opposition not to forces outside the human frame but, ideally, to *other* superhuman images and forces, forces defined as heroic in their interior nature. The hero fights his own—even himself, in a sense. The hero's opponent may wear or declare some *differ-*

entia identified with the Other, or even of evil, but usually he is simply the hero's mirror image.

To some extent (therefore) the agonistic game being played need not summon a clear victory for our hero: the gestural complex of opposition is what truly matters. *Ergon* (act) rather than *telos* (end) dictates: the deed rather than the end is the norm. Possibly this ergocentric attitude issues from the particular pessimistic thoughtworld of the epic, where the "happily ever after" of the fantasy folktale is decidedly the exception and not the rule. The transitory nature of mortal life, especially the life lived heroically, is explicit in our evidence from the *Iliad* on, though not every epic is as pessimistic as that one.

The implacable thrust of the hero toward death is shown, with reality and unreality mixed, in his final moments, when he moves toward and then seizes death. From a threatening stance, boldly vertical and erect, signing his heroic masculinity and terrible isolation, the *Iliad* brings him crashing noisily to earth: *arabêse de teukhe,* "and the armor clanged" says the poet again and again. We are reminded that the hero, once felled, will never rise again, though he may occasionally take a little time to die.[93] To be sure, heroes are wounded in the *Iliad,* as in XIX.47ff., where three of the greatest—Diomedes, Odysseus, and Agamemnon—lean painfully on their spears. But they have not fallen: to fall here, to take one's last place on the horizontal plane, is to perish—or, in a phrase we still use today, to "bite the dust." Some heroic epics, especially upon the appearance of the knight on horseback, modify the drama of the "fall" in various ways: *Roland*'s obstinate hero dies, as it seems, sitting or partly reclining, and like his most important paladins of the rear guard, he has not one "knee-loosing" mortal wound, as in the *Iliad,* but a great many. It is as if he had been slowly bitten to death by a swarm of enemies figured as animals or even insects: here are the signs of an inimical Otherness presented with a vengeance. The great plunging death may still be dealt, as to a horsed enemy cloven down to or beyond the saddle, or pierced and thrust from his horse by a champion lance, but it is fair to say that this later knight-hero dies: he is not killed. He leaves his life a little more slowly, though there is some variety in the death scenes.

Yet the Germanic epic, returning to a focus on fighters who battle on foot in the last gory adventures of the *Nibelungenlied,* tends to cut them down in the old Homeric way, and with an open and unapologetic bloodlust very visible through the narrative net of formulaic tropes. Again, very few are merely wounded here: Krumhild's revenge will kill Gunther and

everyone who rode with him to Etzel's fortress—even, and finally, her ferocious foe Hagen, who dies at her own hand. Only in the sagas, with their
admixture of realistic combat, will a deadly encounter end in the serious
wounding but recovery of a principle character (Bersi Ozurarson in *Hænsa-
Þóris saga*, for example, though there is an imputed shame and derogation
added to his recovery in this case; and Kari Solmundarson, Njáll's son-in-
law, escapes unwounded from the last fatal trap, the Burning, in the *Njála*).[94]
The sagas are famous for their broad spectrum of heroic final acts, from
Kormák's self-regretted "straw death"—a slow death in bed—to the strange
but fitting demise of the "old hero," Egill, to every sort of fatal trauma,
accompanied, on more than one occasion, by black-humorous wisecracks
("I don't know if Gunnarr is here," says a mortally stricken feud-foe, "but
his halberd certainly is").[95] Death is not merely death for these Icelandic
warriors: it is always an opportunity as well.

Act versus Thought

What we have found, or what we can conclude, is that heroic act puts the
hero in the interesting position of denying both conscious, rational thought
and plan on the one hand, and any possible colorations of the unconscious
on the other. The hero fights; reason and strategy are either ignored or left
to ancillary figures like the heroic trickster. The deep psychic area, defined
for my purposes in terms of its *archetypal* forms, and especially accessible
through myth, dream, or vision, is closed off to the hero in a variety of ways.

First, the supernatural element dominant in myth is progressively leached
out of the heroic-epic vision and frame. Second, the epic treats the dream
episode not as another reality connected to the deep mythic zone but as an
event in itself, in which the constituent elements and dramatis personae of
the dream are thoroughly objectified: they are treated as if they emerge not
from deep within the dreamer but outside him. The dream as dreamed in
the *Iliad* (as Erich Auerbach, E. R. Dodds, and R. B. Onians have unequivocally pointed out) is not something the dreamer "has" but something he
"sees," carried to him by a power exterior to himself, and explicitly identified as such. At the other end of the epic sequence and type, the northern
sagas easily and even carelessly confuse dream (the experience of a sleeping state) and vision (a kind of exceptional "sight" experienced while awake).
Thus the dead, when carrying some sort of message to the living, "appear"
to them, but it is always uncertain whether the living, at that moment, are
asleep or awake. Prime examples of this uncertainty crop up in the *Njála*
(with the postmortem apparition of Gunnarr Hamundarson near his grave

howe) and in *Landnámabók*.[96] The separation and objectifying of dream figures is common in traditional and folk belief generally, so in this instance, at least, the epic or saga attitude is not unique.

Despite the unwillingness of the heroic-epic sensibility to commit or even connect itself to a deep-psychic dimension, that dimension and its forces certainly have access to the heroic being. Indeed it might be argued that such access is facilitated because no rational-conscious structure or stricture stands in the way: the hero is open to the currents of what we, in this instance erroneously, call instinct, and particularly to the thanatic force surging up against life. As a result, one of the hero's strongest and most irrepressible urges is to kill, and if possible to die while taking a final victim.

Peculiar Reversals: The Hero as Healer

But one other mark or facet of the icon of herodom is worth inserting at this point, though it happens fairly seldom: that powerful reversal of character and act that can make the killer a healer. Such a dramatic reversal is visible even in the deadly and implacable fighter Akhilleus, for he had a healing gift learned from his monstrous tutor, the centaur Kheiron. (This gift is one of the reasons Callen King calls this hero the "most complex warrior" among the Achaean host.)[97] The poet does not, however, show him using this skill; instead he teaches it to his friend Patroklos, who does use it (II.831–32). In fact Akhilleus is never called *iêtêr* 'healer', and this lapse or indirection is not, I suspect, accidental. The same indirection can be discerned in an incident in the Old Irish *Táin*, where the superb and merciless warrior-killer Cú Chulainn assists the old seer-curer (*fáthlíaig*) Fíntin to temporarily heal the wounds of another warrior of the Ulad. (Cú Chulainn's odd assistance is accomplished after he raids the camp of Eirenn, drives off all the cattle he can find, and makes a medicinal marrow-mash [*smirammair*] of the captured animals by squashing "flesh and bones and hides all together.")[98] Heroic healing is also a part of the legendary career of the warrior Finn mac Cumaill, who was trained as a seer among his wealth of mysterious powers; and in the *Tórnigheacht Dhiarmada agus Ghráinne* the wounded Diarmaid asks Finn to give him a healing drink, for "to whomsoever you should give a drink from your palms would be perfectly sound . . . after that."[99] We should note, however, that Finn the *rígfénnid*, to complete his revenge against his younger nephew and rival, withheld the curing draught until Diarmaid had died.

Finn's failure to use his curative power is very much in line with those (infrequent) heroic narratives in which a hero is granted, or learns, the healing or curative art, for it is clear that heroic healing or life giving is too thoroughly contaminated by the chief and most dominant attribute of the hero to be of much real use: the hero's business is always to deal out death. It is also true that Finn's withholding of the cure he held, literally, in his hands somewhat resembles the incident in the Persian *Shâh-nâma* in which, after Rostam had mortally wounded his son Sohrâb, King Kâvus refused to send the royal healing panacea Rostam asked for.[100] In this instance, at least, it is possible that the leader of the *fénnidi* is cast partially into the role of a king substitute, and his refusal of the cure at his command becomes part of the old antagonistic tension between king and hero.

Sharp Outline and Chosen End

Any age, to some extent, will admire the hero's immediate and ferocious reaction to all opposition or frustration, his ability to sweep aside complexity and ambiguity by forceful reaction—the glamour, in other words, of a swift and irrevocable solution to the intricate frustrations of life in society. Death supplies an ultimate solution. It is also contagious, yet the hero not only "catches" it: he goes well out of his way to do so. Our first order of business now is to track the extraordinary, not to say irrational, attraction of an eternal theme: the self-chosen early death of a young, strong, and healthy male—his thanatography, if you will.

We are human, so we all await, more or less patiently and "rationally," our own inevitable end. The normative, civilized view of a "good death," at least as it surfaced in the classical Mediterranean imaginal context, sets the typical pattern: a death in peaceful circumstances at a "ripe old age," in which the dying one tranquilly undergoes a nearly organic (even vegetative) transmutation after the arc of his life is complete. (It surpasses all irony that this study of the model "good death," Wilhelm Schultze's monograph "Der Tod des Kambyses," appeared in 1912,[101] barely two years before a wave of violent death and mechanical horror on an unprecedented scale engulfed the European system and thoughtworld—a thoughtworld self-consciously rooted in the classical inheritance—and that this wave of death all but eliminated an entire generation of young men.) In this social perspective of what comprises a "good death," any violent or unexpected interference with this natural process will be called unnatural and therefore "bad."[102] A "bad death" interrupts the possibility of regeneration. It may even lead to what might be seen as "bad regeneration," since an unhappy human spirit, released in the wrong way or at the wrong time, can return to vex the living, and special prophylactic measures may be necessary to protect the surviving kin, and the wider society as well, from this harassment. Suicide, as self-murder, is very often stigmatized as the worst sort of "bad death," and not only in terms of the strictures of orthodox Christian tradition and dogma. All in all the subject is thoroughly complicated (and in its way diverting), and considerable scholarly attention has been paid in recent years to the anthropology of death.[103]

The hero, of course, makes mincemeat of the normative pattern, and reshapes the social definition of the "proper" end to fit his own death myth. A "bad death" for him is precisely the reverse of society's stated desideratum: he unmistakably demands his own violent and early end, and almost invariably he gets what he demands. On the other hand, very seldom does a hero commit suicide in the technical sense (taking his own life with his own weapons or in some other obvious or overt manner). An incident of suicide does appear in, or around, the Homeric epos (as reported in the *Odyssey*), in which Telemonian Aias kills himself with his own sword after the funeral games for Akhilleus,[104] but even this death can be construed as heroic. It is the fatal conclusion of a wildly off-trail contretemps in which Odysseus, at these games, takes the honors as "best of the Achaeans" after dead Akhilleus, and is rewarded with the dead hero's armor. Aias, named second in warlike prowess after Akhilleus, and who had borne his dead body out of the bloody ruck at the Skaian gate, is almost apoplectic in his outrage that this ultimate honor should go to *Odysseus*, who was all but an open enemy to Akhilleus, "hateful" in the eyes of the central star, and even more hateful to Aias himself. To him, the judges had trampled on the honor's core of Aias and violated every heroic self-image and precept. There was nothing for it but suicide, for the calculus of heroic honor demanded no less extreme a gesture.

Because in combat death is the heroic goal, the occasional "old hero" in heroic narratives brings out a special problem. In the North the hero type called the Óðinn-warrior may imitate the old god by surviving, to end up as an old man; and of course Starkaðr, the archetypal old hero (who, as I have just suggested above, was also an archaic Óðinn-warrior), lives three men's lives. Finally he suffers the terrible decrepitude that old age brings and convinces (and bribes) a younger warrior to give him his death blow, saying "a man may righteously choose / to anticipate Destiny's law."[105] Hagen of Troneck, in the *Nibelungenlied,* also has many of the grimmer characteristics of the Óðinn-warrior, and he, too, rates a special death: it is his victim Siegfried's sword in the hands of an avenging woman, Queen Kriemhild, that finally takes his head and his life.[106] Under certain circumstances, therefore—an unbearable captivity, or the fallibilities of a despised old age—a hero may escape by forcing his own execution, knowing full well, one would suspect, that in the game of heroic honor the executioner, who kills a disarmed warrior, will ultimately be dishonored by the deed. Thus we seem to see that the hero has, once again, "won" out even in death.

As we have seen, there are many ways to kill a hero, though sometimes the epic doesn't actually show his death. Typological and even, perhaps, topological variants built into heroic-epic narratives can modify the heroic thanatography. On occasion we find that one of the plain, stripped-down, strong-arm kind of killers simply moves out of the saga or song: the ancient Greek sources do not depict any sort of dramatic end for Diomedes, nor the Welsh Celtic for Bedwyr.[107] Perhaps this partner is somehow influenced by his association with the trickster figure (Odysseus and Cei respectively in these examples), who is ever the professional survivor; or perhaps the strong-arm warrior, in his simple and forthrightly violent image, is missing some important complicating feature, some self-perception or descriptive quality necessary to a full playing-out of the final death-drama. In the border epic, too, the hero seems less rather than more likely to die violently: El Cid, the Byzantine Digenes, the heroes of the Serbo-Croat songs, even Prince Igor in the Old Russian *Slovo,* all survive in the end.[108] The topos (or *limen*) of the border may be perceived as an arena for permanent agonic competition and opposition, a zone perpetually agitated, and therefore not fitted to the scheme of an overpoweringly specific and individual heroic death.

We have already seen the various ways in which the supernatural may overcome the superhuman hero, but in the epic context at least, a divine or other supernatural power (whether wielded by god, magician, or sorcerer) usually must work through a human agency. Apollo may guide Paris-Alexandros's arrow toward death-marked Akhilleus, but this is not the Far Darter's own divine arrow; and the Morrigan, the Irish death-goddess, does not herself slay Cú Chulainn. This "king of the heroes of Erin" is pressed and maneuvered so that he must violate *geis;* in the end he loses his own spears in order not to violate another taboo, and one of these mighty spears, wielded by an enemy, brings him down.[109] (Again, though we must stress that both of these heroes bargained for early death to gain undying fame.) A cluster of tales like the Ossetian Nart legends, on the other hand, creates heroes of such intermixed supernatural and superhuman origins and abilities, and in general betrays such a wild combination of genres, that the act of killing off the Nart hero can take exceptional doing. The superlative Nart hero Soslan falls into the category of the "almost invulnerable" warrior, like Siegfried or Akhilleus, but Batradz is the Nart superhero, the *homme d'acier;* it will require a specific and direct supernatural intervention, in fact several levels of intervention, to bring about his final, fatal downfall.

Supernatural interventions aside, it is easily said that a hero agrees—indeed, looks—to die. This is not to say that every epic, even the purest among the type, will display the same heroic attitude to death. Jasper Griffin correctly descries the exceptional attitudinal divide that exists between the *Iliad* and the epics or lays of the Germanic North: the former exhibits complex views of death and even an admitted fear of dying, whereas the latter are marked by a nonreactive fatalism or even an unimaginative fearlessness.[110] Certainly the *Iliad* is the "poem of death," and its players have their own deaths constantly in view, to which they react in richly differing ways.[111] There is heroic pathos, resentment, anger at betrayal—and fear; they may even "rage, rage against the dying of the light," against going into darkness, *neesthai hupo zophon êeroenta,* as in book XXIII.51. Of course, unlike the gifted Welsh poet's father, the warriors in the *Iliad* who are taken by death are in the main young men, and despite the gory and even grotesque ways in which so many of them perish ("the armor availing not" when they are pierced and cut and bloodily fall), they still are truly "granted . . . the single privilege of dying a hero's death, not a random or undignified one."[112]

The *Iliad,* the first and in many ways the most complicated of the epics in our Indo-European tradition (setting aside the massive Indic *Mahâbhârata,* which, as its champions grandly but accurately say, "contains everything"), truly is the exception that proves the rule insofar as the theme of epic-heroic death is concerned. The pitiableness of young death, a death far from home, a death mourned by father or others—this is a Homeric conceit or epical decoration, affecting and sophisticated as it may be, on the great and terrible necessity of the heroic end in battle. As in other areas and emphases—for example, in the strange, irresponsible, powerful and yet powerless Immortals who infest it—the *Iliad* is a towering work of epic art but not, at least in its wide-ranging reaction to death, a typical one. So much the worse for the typical epic, one might say, except that the *Iliad*'s master-poet intrudes his conceits in such a brilliant way as to divert us from the pattern we are after: the clear image of the coming of a heroic death, in which the *timor mortis* is so rarely admitted as a factor.

Thus we return to Griffin's valuable hint: the hero's death should never be "random or undignified" in its essential marking and character. The deadly moment seizes an extraordinary young male, at the very peak of his considerable physical powers, a beautiful and terrible presence, self-isolated, utterly confident and yet conscious of the gravest and most fatal risk—and takes him down into the darkness. There is no blurring of out-line here, but the hardest and most contrastive "present," its features as sharp as steel or the *Iliad*'s well-honed bronze: first furious life and glory, then the swoop of the black wings of death. And more glory, the hero hopes and predicts: glory at the last, glory that inevitably must follow his demise.

SOCIAL LIFE, HEROIC DEATH
Configuring Opposites

Probably the great attraction of the hero as he acts for his society or social frame is also his great paradox: all the good things that human society openly provides or stands for are openly contradicted in him. As society de-mands a degree of routine, stability, and predictability, so the hero repre-sents the dramatic interruption of continuity: a disturbingly antithetical *celeritas* versus the norms of social settlement and *gravitas*. And then as society must also induce or expect a degree of flexibility in its forms, and possess some ability to change and to adapt, so the hero resists and stands fast: he is an uncompromising and unchanging figure of iconic *permanence*.

Even more: the economic, political, and integrative social mechanisms by which a society nourishes and controls itself are also modified and contradicted "heroically." As a given society articulates a framework of economic production, distribution, and exchange, so the hero evades, con-temns, and derogates most parts of the normal economic system and framework. To him, earth's husbandmen and producers are either prey or simply nonexistent, and those who exchange goods and take a profit, the mercantile specialists, are if anything even less significant. Only "honor-able" distribution is admitted in the heroic view, but here the hero demands his award according to his own valuation of himself. He expects condign award, not any "earned" reward received (typically) from the "ring-giving" chieftain or properly generous war king. To accumulate wealth is not usu-ally thought of as a heroic trait or aim, and yet booty won can be a marker of honor, closely related, in the *Iliad,* to the Homeric notion of honor fig-ured as *timê*.[113] (He who has can then pass on to others, thereby accumu-lating even greater personal credit.) And heroic "consumption" can never be planned or rationalized: it appears as both conspicuous and heroically wasteful in the epics and heroic songs.[114]

We know that the hero's insecure and belligerent placement in the nor-mative familial structure, where he and his sense of superior selfhood early on escapes or is expelled from adult or paternal control, is extended to the wider political system. His heroic type is set against that of the king, who holds the articulated framework of the traditional political world together; the hero's spontaneous and agonistic propensities continually abrade and threaten the structure of political organization. Of course he may be called upon to defend his king or his king's "people," but the hero regards this as a game, not a task set for him. He takes up and plays it in his own way, and nearly always by his own deceptively simple rules—which is to say, ever vigilant of his own self-worth, even or especially after the death he earns, and ever conscious and tempted by the fierce joy of bloody confrontation entered into for its own sake. He is rarely constrained by society and its tendency to integration, and in his view the personalized and affective ties or rivalries of man to man to man are predominant. Akhilleus set the mold when his wrath, his *mênis,* fed by his outraged sense of diminished honor, took him in his anger right out of the Achaean host and the long siege. Social control of the hero can never be predictive or formulaic, by which I mean rational or organizational; it must be exercised either by force (usually in vain, because force and its consequences are what he understands best, lives with continually, and does not fear) or, more successfully, through the techniques of verbal magic: through the devices of satire, shame, and "blame."

Self and Group

He who has the power to blame, the satirist, controls and even reconnects the hero to society in a reversed fashion to the work of the epic poet, whose songs implicitly describe and valorize the heroic group code even as they explicitly depict the full-length portrait of the isolated, individual hero. The satirist is more direct, and it is his satiric "blame" that the paladin Roland fears more than any enemy, that the Welsh Culhwch threatens and Arthur actually uses (against Cei in the *Culhwch ac Olwen*), and that someone like crop-headed and contrary Thersites must once have had the right to use against those long-haired Achaean warrior-princes. The satiric power thrusts against that hard epidermic casing of the qualities making up heroic "face," and so the heroic paradox continues: the heart of heroism is not interior but exterior, and the hero *as* hero resembles and even replicates every other hero. Nevertheless he also stands for the most stubborn sense of ego and self, an absolute identity, a perfect and deadly solipsism.

To speak of a warrior-heroic *code* is to perpetuate this heroic paradox. The word code reverberates with the image of law, legitimate social regulation, even Scriptural rule or commandment. What guides the hero is not any sense of what his warrior-heroic group or class demands as part of its communal definition of identity (or at very least he cannot under any circumstances admit this control), but precisely his own reflection of *what is done*. This perception of right act and pose is never, or very rarely, learned: it must be felt, innate, set into his character. How a society over which he temporarily stands guard, or how some warrior collective in which he seems to have a place, estimates or judges him is impertinent, in his own terms. The hero is contemptuous of the mass.

On the other hand, the imputation of fame and honor, the very substances that define heroism, is a matter of supreme concern and moment. Again the *Iliad* calculates and calibrates these descriptive awards more carefully and precisely than any other epic, and it appears that individual *timê*, translated as "honor," is evaluative and relational. It is caught up in the zero-sum equation that marks the heroic *agôn*, for if one hero gains *timê*, another must lose it,[115] and the judgment (of the individual) by other warrior-heroes is, in this particular respect, significant. In this definition, honor stands in contrast to *kudos* and *kleios*, two other attributed qualities in this epic. The former is described as personal and accumulative or inflative, an "enlargement of the person"—that is, of personal reputation—that has no continuation after death, yet which is invariably related to the physical description of the typical (oversized) hero described as *megas* or *megalos*.[116] *Kleios*, however, does continue after death: it is exactly what an Akhilleus or Roland or Cú Chulainn bargains for by accepting, even seeking, the sure and early death.[117] And it is the epic poet who may make the heroic name *kluta*, "famous," though some fame may cluster even around a nameless hero or, more exactly, around his familiar *hêrôon*, his memorial marker or mediatory topos. Here we return to another primary heroic death theme: the dead hero has earned not only fame among men but a mediatory access to the powers of the death-god or -goddess he served so well.

Timê, kudos, kleios are attributive specifications in the *Iliad* that again demonstrate the liminoid, interstitial character of our hero. Even if the archaic, epical hero does not answer to any moral command or stricture, he nevertheless requires the concentrated attention, if not the moral approbation, of someone exterior to himself. The fleeting and fragile concept of honor captures him, as he balances uneasily between perfect and fearless self-confidence and the possibly shaming judgment of a peer or peers. Akhilleus at one point offers to give the game old warrior Phoenix *hêmisu . . . timês*, "half of my honor" (*Il.* IX.616), and with the offer he sets a perfect mark on this characteristic, both ferociously jealous and humorously profligate of this, his own portion of personal repute.

The Hero's Revenge on History

Honor and death: do they ever cease to be joined? The personal death of the archaic, epic hero was generalized and abstracted into something that ended with the end of traditional heroism, the declared "waning" of the Middle Ages and the beginning of our modern aeon—or so it seemed. Cervantes' Don Quixote, the comic and pathetic old knight errant, placed "on the border between what is and what ought to be," may have crystallized the sensibility and excited the laughter of those reasonable men who no longer thought that they required any hero or his boastful heroism; political power moved away from the sword aristocracies of feudal Europe, and even war itself shifted toward the lower realm and the ignoble skills of the artificer—and, eventually, of the drill sergeant. Epic, the vehicle and voice of traditional heroism, was supposedly found to be too limited, too rigid and stilted, and its imaginal frame was replaced by the more flexible and generous art of the novel, the *roman*, itself sprung from forms of "romance" that had challenged the imaginative primacy of the epic-heroic formulas centuries before.

Again, so it seemed. Just how simplistic such a meliatory and evolutionist, rational, even Enlightened viewpoint may be is at least touched on in the first chapter of this study. In fact the heroic act and biography continued to flourish on the unilluminated edges of Europe, in the long and deep if often distorting memories of the folk, and in areas Europe once had no knowledge of at all; then, just after great political eruptions had appeared to sweep away the last vestigial remnants of feudal aristocracy and of *ancien* monarchy altogether, the hero made his own perverse, triumphant return. Trivialized by history and abandoned, at least in the high culture, by the artistic imagination, he was nevertheless revived by a curious concatenation of forces, above all the "romantic" reaction against the rationality of the so-called Enlightenment; and as a result, the past two centuries have seen the hero popularized (that is, his folk roots rediscovered and reemphasized), romanticized (attached to a particular cult of emotional personality), depth-analyzed, and canonized as a philosophic or pseudophilosophic locus. For a figure so rigid and unidimensional, so impacted in its iconic being, and so resistant to history itself, the result of all this fevered interest has been a farrago of partial refractions and confused and even fantastic half images.

Yet somehow the old epical hero, in all his sharp and bloody dignity, his posture of insouciant threat, his core of perpetual challenge and hopeless and furious bravery, has managed to survive. It doesn't even seem to have been that difficult. The most naive epic description still has the power to catch and hold us: all of us, not merely the old sword nobilities that once generated these images and songs. To the ominous flow of history as profane time, the ever young hero—we are all older than the oldest hero—opposes his hard, extreme, and tested fatal excellence. Whether this recrudescence of the icon of the irrational, the violent, and the death-centered was entirely a good thing is not altogether clear.

THE MESSENGER AND THE MESSAGE

The hero continues as the one "placed between," and in this final segment I want to examine some of the other forms and modes of his intervention: the hero is simultaneously *messenger* and *message*. The messenger of long historical tradition, of course, is dispatched by a superior and carries words or items meant to be passed on to someone else. Such a one is the *kêrux*, the herald of the Greeks, and it might be instructive to compare him, as a representative of the species, with the hero.

Hero and Herald

The herald really resembles the hero only in movement, in his similarly free mobility between zones and realms, his penetration and crossing of boundaries; but he does not move of his own will: instead he is impelled by the will of another. The herald is also protected from violence by sacred custom, and he explicitly does not commit it; his job is solely to go from and return to whatever directive power sent him out. The hero also moves and crosses *limina*, but he is his own message; message and messenger are one, and the message itself is made perfectly evident in his actions. Indeed he is all action and no words: deed defines him, not end. Heroic movement itself may sometimes appear to be controlled, as in the varieties of quest we have already examined, yet a closer analysis of the quest pattern reveals no simple "there and back again." Odysseus regains his kingdom at last, but only temporarily, and that most certainly because of what he is: part vengeful and prideful warrior, part sly, masking trickster, always friend to one god but enemy to another. Iason brings back what proves to be the sinister golden fleece, yet because of what has happened *in process*, he cannot win his rightful kingdom. His heroism is deflected and contaminated by

Medea's terrible powers, though without her his quest would have failed. (Something similar happens in the "quest" undertaken by Tristan, who is also caught in a web of magic and sex that he cannot escape in the end.) The peculiar sequential quest in *Culhwch ac Olwen* breaks out of its track of assigned order, loses its nominal "hero" early on, and turns into a mad fighting scramble across much of *ynys Pridein* under Arthur, who acts as head huntsman and war chief. Other examples are there for the picking.

The hero is certainly willing and formed—even "programmed" perhaps—to risk, to move, to venture, but his movement is uncircumscribed and even random: he continually stumbles into episodic diversions, unforeseen crises, and sudden imminent dangers, and foils any "rules" set for him. Indeed, in a very real sense, movement or the possibility of movement, especially minatory attack, is another part of the hero's message; and unless he is somehow controlled, overruled, imprisoned, or rendered impotent by magic, his message is usually threatening. This threat stems in part from his original topos, which we know to be the Other: wilderness, exile, foreign parts, parts unknown. His precipitate appearance, crossing the *limen* or *limina* separating the known from the unknown, brings the dangerous potentiality of his Otherness into, and against, settlement, society, and order. All this was well understood by W. T. H. Jackson, and underlies his study of *The Hero and the King*. What evidently is less understood and perhaps less understandable is that the hero as hero has no deep interest in seizing control of that settled or royal place; he is rather more likely to show up there in order to try to destroy it.

Yet another part of his inherent or implicit message is contained in the instrument for destruction he carries sheathed or ready to hand, and the red fury he so blithely releases over the settled land, its rulers, and its inhabitants. On foot, or in his archaic war chariot, or perhaps especially on horse (the ancient symbol of death and the sure movement toward death), his heroic rapidity throws down the limitations of space; and the cosmetic and enclosed spatial order of house, hall, castle, or walled city ever may be his target and his prey. Moving in this dangerous way, the hero carries with him, and all too readily displays, every iconic representation of disaster and destruction. Examples proliferate, from the angry shield-devices of the heroic-dæmonic seven chieftains who assaulted Thebes (the sinister inscription on one shield is *prêso polin*, "I will burn the city"),[118] to Akhilleus, who is said to have sacked twelve cities by sea and eleven in the Troad (*Il.* IX.328–29) even before he set sail for Troy, to Egill Skalla-Grímsson, suddenly appearing in the feasting hall of some pathetic king's man, ready to deal out death or, in a verse produced for his fellow raiders, advising them "let's off to Lund!"—where the saga tells us that the taking, looting, and burning of that Danish town will follow inevitably on his words.[119]

Words, in the narrative form of the epic, have to follow the hero as he delivers his deadly message. They form the only net that can finally catch and hold him until he reaches his self-chosen goal, which is typically the end of his short, turbulent, "hot," and parabolic life. The epic itself, as a medium, continues our tertial or interliminal image, as it carries its heroes from their specific time-bound existences, their violent secular dramas, on to a wider and longer glory. The epic solves the problem of time for the hero, while bringing forward other problems of its own; it at last establishes a sure point, a resting place or *locus standi* for one who could not abide or rest in the static or punctual terms of his own "lived" life. In other words, the always moving hero has found the narrative frame that forever repeats and recapitulates his thrusting movement, and then forever describes or inscribes, for him and for us, the final and fated cessation of that movement, in his death.

Sacrifice and Sacralization

The image of the sacrifice adjoins or abuts on the image of the heroic death in a number of ways; the coincidence survives even in the banal, or at least secularized, assertion that some latter-day hero "sacrificed" himself or herself for some altruistic purpose. What I have in mind is a more specific look at the hero as a kind of sacrificial officiant, someone who sheds blood—and for a purpose. It is time to examine these two finales, the victimal sacrifice and the death dealing of the hero; to take up two modalities of death, and either rejoin them or separate them even farther.

Locating the function of sacrifice in societies where blood sacrifice is a central and vital religious rite has been much in vogue in recent years, as witness the wide scholarly and lay audience claimed by studies such as René Girard's *Violence and the Sacred* and Walter Burkert's *Homo Necans*.[120] The anthropological literature is especially rich in analyses of societies in which sacrifice to spirits or to some divine power occurs or once occurred; and this has been supplemented by scholarship both in the history of religion and, even more particularly, in the work of the French scholars following Louis Gernet, who amiably claim to be "anthropologists of the Classical world."[121] The analytical pursuit of the utility of social sacrifice goes back at least to Jane Harrison's *Themis* (1912), where that scholar identified two basic sacrificial modes: the *do ut des* or "contractual" sacrifice, in which men and gods ritually joined to share the sacrificed animal commensally, and the *apotropaic* sacrifice, the holocaust in which the victim is dedicated entirely to the terrible punitive god or gods, to persuade these powers to leave the scene and remit their punishment, whatever it might have been.[122] This second sort of sacrifice highlights certain possibilities for the present study, to which I will return.

I speak very broadly here, and of course my focus is on the classical Mediterranean Old World and the Indo-European context generally, and does not include New World societies such as the Mesoamerican Aztec, in which the ever-flowing blood of human sacrifice was the precious fuel that kept the whole cosmic order going.[123] Indeed this was a society in which the very meaning of the word "sacrifice" needs to be very carefully surrounded and dissected;[124] but for my more limited purposes, that part of religious activity involving contractual animal sacrifice (in which the Greco-Roman world plays a central role because of all the research done in that field) presents a social drama of ordering process and control: the regularized sequences in which a specific, "proper" victim is killed, the identification of sacred topoi, the specialized officiating personnel, the pronunciation of normative and precise formulas, the exact division and disposition of the sacrificial products, all are combined in rigid sequence to set up an axial orientation and connection between men and the divine. The individuals who must perform key aspects of the sacrifice—king, priest, or priest-king—are undoubtedly standing and acting, at least in the Indo-European tradition, as representatives of sacred sovereignty, of the Dumézilian First Function.[125] In the simplest calculus bearing on this socioreligious moment, these sacred specialists are empowered not only to connect the animal world to the divine realm but also to create that commensal event in which gods and men are for a time symbolically reunited at the sacralized meal. The creation of a sacrificial topos is also very important, and if a permanent altar does not exist, another temporary one will be very efficiently marked off.[126]

The connection to the supernatural realm is now established according to traditional rites; this is true even (or especially) for that very special ritual in which a human being is sacrificed, whether as a scapegoat, a "most sacral" being, or however else the victim is set apart and doomed. In this last case an extraordinary bargain seems to be struck with the gods, and human sacrifice either represents the most extreme response to an apotropaic (or taboo-raising) situation, such as a natural or human disaster of singular magnitude, or an almost casual indulgence, in which the victims are identified by their depotentialized, servile or defeated, prisoner-of-the-spear status.[127] The Homeric poems, with the expanded *historia* and commentaries that densely surround them, provide examples of both subtypes: in the sacrifice of Iphigeneia,[128] and the contrasted sacrifice of twelve Trojan youths—*dôdeka de Trôôn . . . hueas*—by Akhilleus at Patroklos's funeral pyre (*Il.* XXIII.175–76).

SACRIFICE AND THE HERO

Akhilleus's grim act of revenge-in-sacrifice at Patroklos's pyre returns us again to our focal point, the hero as sacrificer. The *Iliad* shows us a qualitative as well as a quantitative difference between the purposive sacrifice of the twelve Trojan lads and the frequent refusal of mercy by a victorious hero to a surrendered foe. The sacrifice is made in cold blood, for example, although the supremely vengeful *mênos* (or *akhos?*) of Akhilleus is also fed in what we would call a particularly savage action, and Akhilleus's act of throat cutting cannot be considered an execution. That is a juridically sanctioned practice that the hero would consider demeaning. It would probably be fair to say that these sacrificed foes have been reduced, by their captive status, to the symbolic posture of slaves, or even animals. The true warrior-hero would rather sacrifice an armed foe—or, in the end, himself.

The hero's death offering is rarely made in a specific, sacralized place or space that calmly replicates a divine-human axis, but on the broken, bloody, and disordered field of combat. Moreover, his sacrificial act (which in most cases cannot be called a true sort of ritual) has no set form, and all the fighters are potential victims, but there is a recognizable sequence: the unavoidable blow with edge or stab with point, the stricken warrior's fall, and the "baptism of blood," to recall another sort of ritual. Now the victim is surely revealed. This sacrificer-sacrificed motif of the chosen victim does not appear in every heroic-epic source, and may not be easy to find when it does; like many another analytic insight and construct, it is often recoverable only by inference. In the *Chanson de Roland,* for example, the Frankish heroes ask that their *own* deaths shall honor their king: *Por nostre rei devom nos bien morir* (LXXXIX.1128), and their fierce warrior-priest, Bishop Turpin, follows with the old and often-repeated clerical promise that the fallen Franks shall surely gain Paradise through their martyr-doom.[129] (The Saracens, on their side, have no promise of Paradise, though the epic says that they had "offered" to their idols [again they are conventionally depicted as idolatrous pagans], and when the "idols" did not deliver victory, they were angrily smashed.)[130] A kind of self-sacrifice is seen in this bloody epic, but not the imputed sacrifice of the other warrior. The *Iliad,* which is rich both in animal and in human sacrifice, sends its dead warriors' souls to Hades, at once the place and sign and god of death. Obviously there can be no sacrifice to the war-god, at least not by the Achaeans, when Ares himself is supposed to be enrolled and active on the Trojan side; and in fact the most famous dedication of this poem is not to a god at all but to a dead mortal hero: Akhilleus will not permit Patroklos's funeral ceremonies to go forward until he can bring back and dedicate the armor and the head (*teukhea kai kephalên*) of Hektor—along with the twelve Trojans he sacrificed at his friend's funeral pyre (XVIII.335ff.).

I will return to the *Iliad* and to this "making sacred" presently, but at the moment I want to note that our emphasis on the religious or sacral or pseudosacral element in the war sacrifice should not be carried too far; much more potent is the personal element, which dictates that the enemy must die because the enemy has killed someone to whom the warrior-hero was affectively attached. This is a complicated way of returning to that prime paradox of heroism, that despite the fact that he proclaims himself an isolate, and demands that he be seen to act or stand alone, the hero, even when he is supposedly severed from society as an outlaw or an eternal exile, is in some way tied to others, few or many, whose deaths he is bound to avenge.

Vengeance, as a blood sport, can take many different forms. One embodies the classic reciprocity of the blood feud: a capable and responsible adult male is required to shed blood for blood when one of his kin group is attacked; and when the clan, kinship, or classificatory "blood" membership is figured expansively or inclusively, this means that blood vengeance is allowed, almost impersonally, against any capable male of the offending kin group. Specific act or guilt is irrelevant, and the avenging act need not be particularly heroic; other than (usually) safeguarding from attack those not regarded as culpable, like women or young children, the avenger of blood is authorized to strike from ambush, to use surprise or subterfuge, or to act in any other way not prohibited by the "unwritten law" governing the conduct of the blood feud.[131] The gravamen standing or lurking behind the practice of blood feud is simply that: kin blood has been shed, and the honor, name, and integrity of the offended group is only reestablished by an equally bloody counterstroke. The personal element or value can be very weak indeed in such an affair. So can the heroic.

Another variation on the theme of blood vengeance is the custom that supposedly ruled the ancient Germanic *comitatus* and similar warrior associations. The *comitatus* was held together, according to Tacitus, by mutual oaths sworn to and by the war band leader, and one of these obligated the warriors not to survive their fallen chieftain: *iam vero infame in omnem vitam ac probrosum superstitem principi suo ex acie recessise.*[132] Here what we can probably call a quasi-religious sanction calls for the deaths—in truth, the sacrifice—of the whole war band when its leader fell; the chieftain's death demands a full payment or toll of lives, including—but not only—the lives of his foes. The Anglo-Saxon *Battle of Maldon* provides evidence of something like this death pact, although Brihtnoth's Saxons may not have been strictly oath-bound to him. In fact the vital sense of the warrior *communitas* suffusing the fighters of one side or the other in any battle or armed confrontation seems to demand a generalized avenging response, often expressed as "paying back" the enemy for the losses of one's own side.[133]

As we might expect, however, more personal flavor is widely present in epic-heroic narratives. With his *amis* Olivier's death, Roland *ad doel, si fut maltalentifs* (translated by Terry as "grieving, and filled with bitter rage") rides headlong into the "Spanish" enemy's ranks and "sends twenty to their deaths" (*en ad getet mort .XX*).[134] In the *Nibelungenlied* a singularly noisy and gore-spattered sequence (in *aventure* 38) begins when Sigestap, the nephew of Dietrich of Verona, is cut down by the saturnine and bloody-minded Nibelung Volker the Fiddler; the dead youth is avenged by Old Hildebrand—*daz rach der alte Hildebrant*—who slays Volker, which spurs "hard" Hagen of Troneck to a terrible vengeance in his turn: *owê wie harte Hagene den helt dô réchén began!*[135] This brutal *aventure* ends with only Hagen and Gunther left standing among the Nibelungs, and all of Dietrich's men slaughtered, but in fact most of the *Nibelungenlied* is a tale of condign, terrible vengeances. The *Iliad,* always our first and in many ways our most complicated epic-narrative exemplar, has any number of personal encounters in which the fall of one fighter is balanced by the death of his slayer, although the bias of the poet tends to let the Trojan warriors fall unavenged, as especially in books V and VI. The powerful, penultimate sequence in book XVI that ends with the death of Patroklos begins when Patroklos spears the Lycian chieftain Sarpedon, son of Zeus (481–84); Patroklos will then fall to Hektor—and to Apollo's intervention. Of course, the skein of fate now winds on to Hektor's death at Akhilleus's hand, with yet another divine, enabling interference.[136]

The final vengeance of Akhilleus brings us back again to the theme of sacrifice, but Akhilleus offers the body of Hektor and the twelve pitiable Trojan boys not to a god but to dead Patroklos himself. This act has a special—one might even say an atheistic—flavor to it, which in various ways permeates the Homeric poem; and although the grand and sanguinary *Iliad* provides us with a series of correlated imaginal signs surrounding the warrior's sacrifice of his opponent, none of them involves what we would call the real thing, battle-sacrifice to a god. For that we have to turn to the death imagery of the Norse sagas and the Eddic poems. Here we find that the dark nature of the god Óðinn, his grim regnancy and his great powers, puts us on the right track—although, in true Óðinnic fashion, the god does not make the task easy. In pagan Scandinavia, Óðinn was closely associated with the battle dead. As Valfoðr he is lord of Valhöl, where he "each day chooses weapon-slain warriors" (*Grimnismál* 1, 8); those blessed chosen are the consecrated *einherjar*, the formidable "single champions" (as in *Vafþruðnismál*, 40, 41). When we move from the deep-mythic atmosphere of the Eddas to the sagas, we are still connected to Óðinn (at least in the sagas set in pagan times) because we are likely to find our ritual-sacrificial language not in the saga narratives themselves but in the interpolated verses of the warrior-skalds, who can boast of possessing Óðinn's own poetic gift—and who also kill.

The skald whose poetry celebrates his own or another's battle prowess often makes the connection between the death-god or -goddess and his or her human votary, and our first problem is to decode the often complicated symbolic language and allusive kenning constructions of which these verses are so frequently built. Recall that the warrior-trickster-skald Egill, after "saving his head" through hypocritical praise of King Eiríkr, had the king "leave the dead that Óðinn saw" (*en Viðrir sá / hvar valr af lá*—Viðris was one of Óðinn's many code names, the *Óðinn-heiti*).[137] What the god "saw" was, evidently, the acceptable blood sacrifice (*blót*) laid out for him. Elsewhere Egill employs a standard skaldic encryption for killing a foe: "wolf and eagle walk / through the king's kin" (*gengr úlfr og orn / of ynglings born*).[138] (Animals, especially the eagle, the wolf, and the raven, are attached to and reverberant of Óðinn as battle-god.) Similar imagery threads throughout these stories, as in *Eyrbyggja saga*, where Þórarinn the Black four times uses the image of scavenging ravens tearing the flesh of the dead,[139] or *Kormáks saga*, in which Kormák's verse claims that he "sated wolves on weapon-slain warriors' bodies." Bersi's *vísur*, in the same saga, have this warrior feeding both wolves and ravens to satiety.[140] In fact, Bersi makes the connection between those he has slain—offered to the wolves—and the good welcome the god Óðinn will grant him at last: "I oft fed wolves And I shall be welcome with Óðinn in the world to come."[141] But Egill also crafts another sort of image, after he slew Berg-Onund: he "bestowed a blood-coif / On Earth, Óðinn's bed-mate."[142] We know from the Eddic *Grimnismál* that Freya claims half of the battle dead (stanza 14), and this notion appears as late as *Grettis saga*, when Grettir the Strong, a nominal Christian, refers to the "stealthy goddess of death" who had thought to claim his life in Norway, and this surely must be Freya.[143] Freya's interference, it may be said, complicates a picture of "offering" already sufficiently murky, as befits any scenario in which Óðinn is even tangentially involved. In my computation, the sacrificial relationship of the warrior to Óðinn is approximately as follows: (a) before the two sides come together in pitched battle, Óðinn consecrates all the forthcoming battle dead to himself, by spearcast over the hosts (*Völuspa,* stanza 24); (b) Óðinn may himself kill warriors, and so feed his wolves, the "greedy ones" (*Grimnismál,* stanza 19); (c) the warrior, as Óðinn's votary, sheds his enemies' blood specifically for Óðinn (and for Freya too); or, (d) more commonly, the warrior sacrifices by feeding the feral corpse feeders, Óðinn's beasts, the gray wolf, raven, or eagle.

Whatever battle sacrifice is good in the Val-Father's eyes, or eye, he is *never* a trustworthy god, and to bargain with him is always to bargain in vain. He may be self-named Gagnroth, "giver-of-good-counsel" (*Vafþruð-nismál,* stanza 8ff.) but his worshipers know, or ought to know, that he operates outside or beyond merely human judgment, and his counsel is dark: Óðinn may uphold a warrior or cast him down, according to his divine whim. In *Völsungasaga* King Sigmund is unknowingly fighting his last battle, for Óðinn appears before him and holds up his spear so that Sigmund's sword, the gift of Óðinn himself, *sverði . . . ór stokkinum*[144] (breaks on the god's spear); Sigmund's doom is sealed (chap. 11). Egill Skalla-grímsson is without doubt the complete Óðinn-warrior, but in his *Sonatorrek* (Lament for my Sons), a long sad poem of his old age, he accuses Óðinn of breaking faith with him, of taking his sons as a sacrifice, leaving behind his skaldic gift but also "hatred" (*fjendr*)—his not yet impotent hatred of the untrustworthy god himself. Óðinn breaks his word, the hero's sword, or anything else that pleases him as he sets in train the destiny that forces the warrior's fall. In the *Sonatorrek,* Egill calls the old god "wolf-killer" (*úlfs of bági*); and although this may refer to the mythical Fenris-wolf, it also suggests that the warrior who feeds the wolves is a man-wolf himself, and that Óðinn will cause him to be slain in his own turn by some other man-wolf.[145]

Such a conceit leads us back to the animal symbolism that clusters around blood sacrifice. If the ordinary socioreligious sacrifice uses a chosen animal to connect man to the divine, with the ritual specialists joining these two disparate realms, then the battle sacrifice, on one interpretive level, hands the fallen *man* over to the animal world. In the place of the careful ritual in which the sacralized beast is killed, its blood divided and disposed of, its body dismembered and the parts distributed according to right order and tradition, men in battle are furiously slain by men, their shed blood is drunk up by the thirsty earth (that dust of which Homer so often speaks), and their dead and abandoned bodies are torn and devoured by the waiting carrion eaters. So runs a master motif in any number of heroic epics, from the

Iliad, with its unforgettable first image of those loathsome scavengers who feed on the dead, *kunessin oiônoisi te pasi,* onward. The Irish Celtic *Táin* allows the fallen to be a fit prey for ravens;[146] the *Chanson de Roland* wants the heroic Frankish dead to be given proper Christian burial, lest they be "eaten by wolf, pig, or dog" or by "lions and wild beasts."[147] The Old Russian *Slovo* says that "the eagles' shriek calls the beasts to feed on bones," "the beasts have licked up the blood," and "often the ravens croaked, sating themselves on the dead."[148] The animal as the dark guest at the feast of the "sacrificed" human dead is a nearly universal motif in the heroic-epic sources.

At this point our perpetually interstitial hero is placed (to use again the old but always valuable Norse images) between the war-god Óðinn and Óðinn's wolf; and certainly he displays aspects and attributes of both god and animal. But when he, the warrior, sends other warriors' souls or spirits to Hades or Hel, and throws their emptied bodies down to become a dinner *al fresco* for the scavengers, he must accept that he too can suffer this fate, and thus pass from sacrificer to sacrificed. He holds and wields the sharp instruments of bloodletting: he is himself an animate weapon, "smithed" into the form of the perfect killing tool: so he knows that swords can be broken in the end, that every human hero dies, and that he ought to be prepared for, indeed to search out, that "good" battle death. *How* he dies is of great importance, for although he hopes to trade his self-sacrifice for eternal fame, for his name to be celebrated no matter what might happen to his body, he also must hope to avoid the carrion feeders and receive a proper sepulture. But there can be no guarantees, and violent death is and should always be the hero's fitting end. Undoubtedly this heroic posture, of the sacrificer willing to be sacrificed, is a tremendous part of the sway the hero holds over those who celebrate, even worship his ancient and powerful image. Another part of the fascination must have to do with the killing of a human being as an ultimate taboo; and the killer killed is doubly involved in a form of human sacrifice. A final aspect involves yet another, even more intensely viewed and forbidden phenomenon: how this sacrificial victim, even when it is human, may be not only slain but eaten.

The suggestion of heroic cannibalism, given the sequence of important taboo violations we have been following and the conjoined series of raptor and carnivore images attached to this figure, is not at all far-fetched. The hint of cannibalism in the *Iliad* has attracted a good deal of appalled attention, but what are we to make of the "toast to the dead" or "drinking to the dead" (that is, the dead Siegfried) in the *Nibelungenlied: nu trinken wir die minne und gelten des küneges win?*—that is, the warriors are "paying" for the

Hunnic king's wine by pouring out another red fluid, and grim Hagen, more barbarous than any Hun, begins the repayment at once by beheading Etzel's and Kriemhild's little son Ortlieb: "The blood flowed down the sword to his hand" (*Daz im gegen der hende ame swérte vlôz daz bluot*). [149] We are not discussing vampirism here, but rather a horrendous metaphor that identifies shed blood as "wine red and warm."[150] The more fantastic hero tales (the aforementioned *Hrólfs saga Kraka,* along with an entry in the *Landnámabók*) demonstrate how bizarre transformations, whether for good or for ill, can occur when the blood of a monstrous ("unfit") being or carnivore is drunk or its flesh eaten: when a human being reverses and perverts his acceptable diet and feeds on the thing that usually feeds on man. Given the animalized and even the teratic or ogrish character that can appallingly appear in an enraged, *wuote,* or *berserksgangr* hero, where will the line be drawn? Our exercise in the investigation of tertiality has come at last to this: to our hero imagined to be simultaneously perfect man and perfect monster.

7 THE FINAL HERO:
BEYOND IMMORTALITY

Dimé cómo mueres, y te diré quién eres
Tell me how you die, and I will tell you who you are
—Octavio Paz, *El laberinto de la soledad*

The more or less constant premise of this study has been that the particular phenomenon of heroism under discussion is in the main controlled, or at least influenced, by what Georges Dumézil called the Indo-European *idéologie*. With the exception of the Georgian *Lord of the Panther's Skin* and an occasional exotic example from beyond the Indo-European camp, the epic materials on which I have drawn for this study were formed and created in one or another (or several combined) Indo-European languages.[1] Unless we are very careful, this could lead to circularity: taking a hero tale expressed in an Indo-European language and then declaring that this guarantees an embodiment of some underlying Indo-European *idéologie*. Instead it is my contention that a specific Indo-European patterning impulse can be discerned in the major biographical, topical, and developmental themes of heroism as we know it, and that these themes, if not invariably and uniquely visible in an Indo-European context, are likelier to occur there than anywhere else. Certain others are not only central but dominant in the Indo-European "family" of epics, the most salient and in many ways the most troubling of which is the death of the son.

The Sohnes Todt Theme

This is one of the most notorious and specifically Indo-European "markers" in the collected Indo-European heroic epos, which seems to emerge most clearly not only as a common Indo-European narrative element but as a *characterological* one. It involves that deadly duel between heroic son and heroic father in which the son will die at the father's hand—an extreme but not a rare case of the agonistic relationship between generations contained in the typical (even the quintessential) hero tale. For Jan de Vries, who was concerned early on with the motif of the "heroic" generational conflict, there was no question but that a genuine Indo-European leitmotiv was apparent in what he termed the *Vater-Sohnes-Kampf*.[2] A. T. Hatto then examined what he also saw as the four canonical exemplars of this conflict in the collectivity of Indo-European epic: Rustam and Sohráb (Persian), Hildebrand and Hadubrand (Germanic), Cú Chulainn and Connla (Irish Celtic), Il'ya of Murom and Sokol'nichek (Russo-Slavic). Hatto considered the brief and fragmentary Germanic exemplar the most complete and unalloyed version, deserving of the "highest grade" for thematic power and schematic purity,[3] but in fact the evidence of this central, paradigmatic confrontation is wider, and the variations within it more evocative and deeply convoluted, than any analysis of the canonical four epic incidents would suggest.[4]

The Ossetian Nart tales, as we often have seen, are full of wonderfully enigmatic and anomalous generational acts and sequences, but they also contain more ordinary births. One such occurs when the Nart Uryzmæg has a son, the "fils sans nom" in Dumézil's translation, with Satána, the "mother of Narts." Satána sends the boy to the Submarine Kingdom; Uryzmæg later meets him there and kills him "by accident" in a fight. In the old, received manner,[5] neither was known to the other. This redaction also involves heterogamy (marriage or mating to a woman defined as completely "other" beyond the definition of simple exogamy) because Satána is a figure of supernatural origin and powers. Moreover, the son's lack of a proper name appears to be a fitting parallel to that missing or obscured token of recognition between father and son in the canonical version of the theme.

The Norse-Icelandic *lygisögur* give us the case of Arrow-Odd (Örvar-Oddr) and his son Vignirr, begotten on the giantess Hildigunn in Giant-Land and raised there in the canonical fashion. At the age of ten, and already displaying his monstrous maternity in his extraordinary size and strength, Vignirr joins his father, but he is soon gruesomely killed after a hard-fought duel by the trollish and inhuman Ogmunðr Eyþjof's-Killer. But Ogmunðr lays the blame for the precocious Vignirr's death at Arrow-Odd's door, saying that it would not have happened if Ogmunðr and Odd had been reconciled as the troll creature had asked. In *this* rendition of the theme, heterogamy and "exile" are clearly laid out, while an inhuman potency slays the son, apparently because of his father's stubbornness. This death, however, is not by the father's own hand.[6]

The Old French *chansons de geste* include the story of *Gormont et Isambard*. In this tale, evidently drawn from an historical core, a Viking raid into the Frankish realm is converted into a Saracen incursion; various changes are rung on the themes of kingship, ethnic identity, and other political and social problems,[7] and the father-son conflict is deflected toward a tense subject-monarch relationship. Thus Isambard goes into exile with the heathen "Sarrazins" because King Louis had wronged him; Louis is transformed into the "distancing" father figure.[8] While he is fighting on the Saracen side, Isambard and his real father, Bernard, meet in battle and exchange blows without recognizing each other, but in the end it is four French knights, again substituting for the father, who mortally wound Isambard—"but they did not know who he was" (*mais ne l'unt pas reconeu*).[9] This Old French reflex of the theme has no strange or exotic marriage, splits off the "displacement" theme, shrinks from placing the death of the son into the father's hands, and yet maintains a faint but intact outline of the original plot.

In another Old French source, the *Perlesvaus*, we find that Arthur had a son by Guinevere, Lohort or Lohout, and that this promising young man was treacherously killed by Sir Kay after Lohout had killed a giant and was, as was his custom, sleeping on his fallen foe's body. Kay beheaded both Lohout and the giant and took the latter's head back to Arthur to falsely claim the victory. Rather later in the tale Kay's base deed is revealed, but he is not punished; he simply leaves the court.[10] Here Kay appears to revert back to his older, more powerful and malignant persona; is he also reclaiming that "twinned" status he once shared with King Arthur? The king's inaction in the face of Kay's killing of Lohout is otherwise difficult to explain.

All of the above examples might be called miniatures, reduced reflexes of the original *Sohnes Todt* theme. The Armenian epic *David of Sassoon*, however, presents an almost classic confrontation between father and son—yet it, too, reveals an important variation. The eponymous hero of this epic, David, begets a son, Mher (or Pokr Mher), on a foreign woman in another, "Arab" land. In paradigmatic fashion this son is raised apart from his father but with the usual token of recognition, in this case a golden ring; the two eventually meet and, unknown to each other, fight. The fatal conclusion, however, does not come with David's killing his son, but in this: that before he recognizes Mher, he curses him. David then goes on to his own fated end (to be slain by his own illegitimate, Amazonian daughter), and the epic ends as Mher departs this world, to become the childless cave sleeper, the undying one of Armenian heroic legend. In this case generational sequence has been convoluted, but the essential character of the fated confrontation between heroic generations remains: father dooms son through the condemnatory power of his paternal curse.[11]

The filicidal potency of a father's curse, its truly mythic power, brings us around again to that Oedipal drama to which the *Sohnes Todt* motif is archetypically reversed and counterposed. We remember that Oedipus unknowingly slew his own father, but he also—knowingly, for cause, filled with the red choler, the *orgē* that indelibly marks his character and all of his condemned Kadmean line—cursed his sons, and this curse surely prepares and activates the "bad death" the two young men would suffer later at each other's hands.[12] And we recall that the ramifications of the prepotent father's curse also figure prominently in the later part of the career of the hero-king Theseus, Oedipus's erstwhile protector in the last episode of his high drama at Colonos, for he too cursed and so must have caused the death of his son Hippolytos.[13] Theseus's curse is called forth by twisted or lying evidence; even farther from the filicidal scenario would be the act of the hero Herakles (often "doubled" with Theseus) who, sorely afflicted by *lyssa* or *mania*, slays his own children.[14] The Theseus-Hippolytos drama makes explicit the subtheme of sexual jealousy between two male generations, to which I will presently return. Before that, however, I want to examine a series of aspects exploring confusion, recognition, and comedy.

Confused, Comic, and Sexual Variations

The late Henri Grégoire, in the course of a long and detailed scholarly exegesis of the great Byzantine Greek popular or border epic, the *Digenes Akrites,* investigated a variety of father-son encounters. Grégoire assiduously, even obsessively searched out what he believed to be the actual historical surround of the *Digenid* tale, employing, among other sources, a very long old demotic Greek ballad entitled *To tragoudi tou giou tou Andronikou,* the *Song of the Son of Andronikos.* Here, as in the *Digenid* itself, we have the hero's father wed or mated in a foreign land, and the later encounter of the son who results from this mating with his father, but in this particular narrative, after a hostile or threatening introduction, the father *does* recognize the son and welcomes the reunion. For Grégoire this balladic episode parallels the begetting of the Two-Raced (*Digenid*) Basil the Akritic, the Borderer, his father the Emir's return to Romania, and the reuniting of the two.[15] Rather than fatality, a kind of "testing" seems to be at the base of this rendition of the father-son conflict, a conflict Grégoire calls *to pagkosmio thema*, a "universal theme," and which he easily connects with the harsher or deadlier Persian and Germanic examples of the conflict.[16]

The comedic version of the father-son encounter, which in many ways resembles the meeting in *The Son of Andronikos*, takes us back to medieval Europe and involves Rainouart, the "slow" and "blackened" comic hero of the Guillaume Cycle of *chansons de geste*, and his "Saracen" son Loquifer (or Maillefer).[17] Rainouart, of course, follows the heroic trajectory at one exaggerated remove, so in this comic instance he meets and fights with the son he had never known, but again there is no fatality. Instead we have recognition and "incorporation"—through the baptism of the heathen son. (In the *Digenid* the Moslem emir, the hero's father, is the one baptized.) The theme turns serious again, however, when sex rears its head.

The theme of the older man confronting and compassing the death of the younger emerges in various encounters pitting uncle against nephew (mother's brother, sister's son). The two, instead of acting within a fully normative framework of affection, mutual obligation, and reciprocity expressed in the relationship of the avunculate, break this frame entirely by introducing sexual rivalry and subsequent betrayal. The Old Irish stories describing the fatal rivalry of Conchobar and Noisiu over Dierdre, or of Finn and Diarmaid over Ghráinne, clearly set out the pattern, and at least some versions of the most famous example of all, the story of Tristan and Isolde, put Tristan's death squarely in King Mark's hands. The point, in this variation, is that the classificatory "son" is killed, and the classificatory "father" is responsible for his death.[18] The new element is the introduction of the younger woman as an object of sexual rivalry: the confrontation is not a contest of warrior excellence but of sexual primacy, and the term "the better man" takes on a thoroughly new meaning.

Yet another instance, which brings these uncle-nephew confrontations sharply back to the main thrust of my argument, occurs in the *Iliad* (IX.444–84), where old Phoinix describes how and why he fled "from strife with my father Amyntor." Because Amyntor had favored his young concubine over Phoinix's mother, the betrayed woman besought her son to have relations beforehand (*promigénai*) with this concubine, to make the old man, by invidious comparision, hateful to the younger woman. But Amyntor found out and "cursed me thoroughly," Phoinix says, enjoining in particular that Phoinix should never himself beget any child.[19] Phoinix considered killing his father but forbore, "that I might not be called a parricide [*patrophonos*] among the Achaeans" (461). Phoinix's relatives and friends tried to keep him at Amyntor's court but he fled to Peleus, Akhilleus's father.[20]

This last episode constructs a complicated variant on our theme: (a) the father again reverses the generative-sexual norm, in parallel to the two uncles in the Celtic citations; (b) the son's interference in this malformed relationship brings down the paternal curse, so that (c) like the Armenian hero Pokr Mher, Phoinix will have no child, that is, will be "dead"; (d) Phoinix considers killing his father "with the sharp bronze" (*oxei khalkô*), but instead he (e) flees to where he finds a second, fostering relationship with Peleus. This is a cross-fertilizing rendition of our base theme, touching and connecting numerous other cores of the story: sexual jealousy and generational reversal, the sterilizing curse, a threat of parricide avoided, and removal to a parallel but artificial generational scheme.

The Death of the Son Explained

Why is the *Sohnes Todt* theme, and particularly its primary format, so important? What motivates the act and drama? And how can such a theme be identifiable as peculiarly Indo-European?

Various heroic-epic contexts in which the theme is visible make a point of the tremendous heroism the hero's son would inevitably have displayed—had he lived. Cú Chulainn's son and victim, Connla, says this of himself; Arrow-Odd's son Vignirr, according to his killer, would have been "the bravest and toughest in all Scandinavia"; and, in a slightly variant instance, the mortally stricken Sohrâb was not cured by King Kâvus because of what the king knew a son of the tremendous Rostam would surely become. The son's death, in my view, defines and restricts the usually irresistible heroic nature: enough is enough, and even heroism has its limits. It cannot be allowed to grow, and its ferocious powers take form and be actualized, beyond a certain set point. We should probably call this a narrative-imaginative limitation expressed by means of the theme, and one thus detached from the hero's own judgment and motivation.

The most salient characteristic of our central drama, the slaying of hero's son by heroic father, is absolutely opposed to the more familiar Oedipal myth-drama. If this other and more familiar theme is read positively, it conforms or constrains that old confrontation to a pattern that truly expresses and supports progression-in-succession: it points to the creation of a new order that defeats and replaces a resistant, a "stand-fast" old order as the son by necessity replaces the father. The *Sohnes Todt* drama explicitly halts and reverses this claim and this arguably progressive temporal movement. Instead of the achievement of a new, a "next" or succeeding order, the clearing away of a past (even or especially through the extraordinary—*but necessary*—violation of the parricide taboo), we have an aborting of forward temporal movement, the destruction of the future, even a decisive turn toward death as a solution and a last act: the paradigmatic hero-as-father, after killing the next heroic generation, sooner or later seeks and finds his own death. A psychoanalytic bias or sensibility would probably find, in this drama, two forms of suicide: killing the self after killing the extension of self. A distrust, even a hatred of future time must be the key element here: the hero again is singularly isolated, and has acted to isolate himself, in a perpetual, epical present time.

The hero's sexual and maturational identity is also put at risk by his engendering of a son; the sometimes celibate, sometimes predatory pattern of a typical hero's sexuality is somehow perverted or betrayed by the dubious, atypical achievement of heroic fatherhood. The essentially *adolescent* image of the hero may also be recalled here: the hero who becomes a father has moved too far into the adult world, even if his marriage or mating occurs far away, out of sight, in an ectopic or heterotopic "otherwhere." The normative sexual role is thus reset or reestablished when he kills his own progeny. We might also ask how far and in what way the hero's son may be marked and contaminated by the "foreignness" of his birth and maternity. This in itself raises an obvious question, because the hero's own generation is also frequently extraordinary. The son merely repeats (or intensifies) the pattern, so why must he be doomed? The only answer is, Why not? No one should ask for fairness in the doings of heroes.

Finally, the theme maintains once again the character of the hero as an ultimate solidity, resting in a kind of impermeable (and solidly Second Functional) state. His particular excellences remain intact; they are only temporarily transmitted to any son or heroic heir and are won back from that slain heir. The hero-father claims and defends a posture and a character that is unyielding and absolute, a perfection in ultimate solipsism. This might be called the final, architectonic motif in the *Sohnes Todt* scenario.

A PECULIARLY INDO-EUROPEAN THEME?

The Indo-European identification of the theme remains. I think the answer lies in the heart of Dumézil's Second or Warrior Function, as the hero is a distillation or crystallization of all of the powerful valences of that function, and especially in its relationship to the "framing" First and Third Function. Elsewhere I have tried to set King Oedipus into an acceptable Indo-European formula as a "sinning" king *and* hero, but I do not think that "Oedipal" parricide is, in its essence, an Indo-European theme—although parricide and regicide do occasionally occur in the Indo-European heroic epos.[21] In the Indo-European perception of royalty/sovereignty the death, more or less sacralized, of the old king does not seem to be required to fertilize, renew, or revitalize society and land or realm: whether or not this is a relict of an archaic nomadic or preagricultural stage is not a matter for me to decide or even to trifle with at this point.

Collectively the Indo-European heroic epics show the hero detached from and opposed to the royal (and the paternal) in any number of complex ways, but with very rare exceptions the young hero does not actually attack, throw down, kill, and replace the old figure of paternal authority, be he familial or regnal. The Sovereign Function, it seems, may be depotentialized, marginalized, derogated by the warrior-heroes who act in the Second Function, but it is not to be destroyed as a Function; it remains an ally of sorts against the hidden powers and threats of the Indo-European Third Function.[22] As this alliance or ligature is significant for the *Sohnes Todt* theme, it means that the father—the first generation—may act or be seen as an enemy to his hero-son, the second generation, but it is the *third* generation, the hero's own son, aspirant to his father's power and position, who is often at deadly risk. (Or, in another symbolic expression analyzed by Grisward, the red tree, which symbolizes the hero, is infertile: it bears no fruit.)[23] There are even grimmer reflexes of the *Sohnes Todt* theme, in which the doomed son is not merely a victim of the father's superior valor but is actually sacrificed by the father's hand or at his order. This enormity, in the Indo-European context, moves into the area of magical manipulation, and such a sacrifice is usually undertaken so that some particular gain or prize might be won by the father. In the Norse *Jómsvíkingasaga*, for example, Jarl Hákon enlists the powerful aid of two witch figures or goddess-sorceresses, Þórgerðr Holgi's-bride and her sister Irpa, through the blood sacrifice of his youngest son, Erling;[24] and in a brief sentence or two in "The Prince of Tver," one of the Russian *byliny*, an even more comprehensive enormity is set out: the lieutenant of a Khan is given a city to rule because, at the Khan's order, he had stabbed his own son and drunk his blood.[25] Filicide of this sort, and particularly the latter example, is caught in a web of significances like an ugly but fascinating bug, and any act of filicide, as I have suggested elsewhere, can be construed as a serious delict against the Third Function.[26] These two cases, however, add certain other features and violations, and indeed the *bylina* can be said to simultaneously activate the subsistent powers of the following: the "Abrahamic" sacrifice, an act of total obedience demanded by an authority; the theme of the "bad king," with the extra horror, in the unnamed Khan's gruesome order, of how a foreign and pagan ruler might be expected to act; the magical power of precious human blood, shed to achieve some goal otherwise unattainable; the *Sohnes Todt* theme, though in neither case is a duel apparent; and the "forbidden blood" theme. As we have seen cowards (in *Hrólfs saga Kraka* and *Perlesvaus*) converted to heroism by blood in one form or another, so we have here not the shedding of a monster's blood (an alien and inhuman being) but the shedding and/or drinking, nearly literally, of one's *own* blood.

A distrust, even a hatred of the future may be the key element in this confrontation. The heroic drama as a total narrative image and creation, with its self-destructive violence, its *sensations forts*, its celebration of the agonic, and its shaping of the evanescent moment, fits best into a time when ordinary order has been degraded and any attraction the future might hold has been thrust aside. Indeed it is gratefully traded for that "epic past," that disjunct and distant temporality so often noted as encasing and operative in the epic narrative frame. This is a true psychic reversion and retreat, and it is accompanied by the celebration, in the hero-tale, of other retrogressive events and characteristics: the ignoring or truncation of sexuality and familial continuation, the derogation of long life and old age, and, symmetrically, the obsessive concern with a "good" and fitting early death for the epic hero himself. Even the eternal fame that is supposed to be won by heroic deed and heroic death is left as a vague and unorganized assurance: "So long as men remember"—or so long as that old invention, the hero's tale, is passed on, verbally or otherwise, by a human society with its gaze fixed on and into the heroic past: by a human society uneasily backing, as it were, into an uncertain, unpromising, and most definitely unheroic future.

Such an attitude slips into all of these general schemes explaining epical creation in past ages; it also, in a period closer to our own time, fits that psychosocial atmosphere redolent of uncertainties and historical disasters, the aftermath of shattered social and political order that ushered in the romantic era, when the archaic hero type and his specifically shaped violence were rediscovered and honored once more. The newly converted acolytes of the hero were not only looking to the past, but, it seems, had consciously closed off part of the future. Science and invention and humanism and progress have not, it seems, much relieved us of the strong temptation of the bloody, the retrograde, and the irrational.

Yet there must be other connections that humankind reaches for in its hunger for the hero and the hero's epic story. Fear of the future, dream of the past, death figured as ennobled and ennobling (not casual or banal or meaningless), or the hero created as a human cynosure, a living, moving sculpture made to strive fiercely against whatever enemies for an impressive little space of time: is this all of his attraction? It may explain a lot of it, and the core of the heroic drama has enormous power. Epic poets, however, can also reach their audience in more subtle ways, and their genial talent (no matter how it may differ from song to song or tradition to tradition) reveals depth, dimensionality, variation even as it always concentrates on its fatal subject. The hero is forever cast in human terms, even when the *morphos* is superhuman, and this essential humanity of the hero-subject is immediately sensed and appreciated by the song's audience (as is the marvelously mixed supporting cast that appears over and over in these epics). Thus the untried and callow Meho, son of Smail, in the Moslem Serb epos, threatens to cross the border and take service with the ancient Christian enemy if he can find no sufficiently glorious enterprise on his own side; the heroic El Cid suppresses his true feelings and common sense in marrying off his daughters to the unspeakable but aristocratic Infantes de Carrión; the knight Grevier, in *Raoul de Cambrai*, so hot to avenge his uncle Raoul, becomes a caricature of the angry young hero and, in essence, makes a bumptious fool of himself. Epic stylization, exaggeration, and the use of the formulaic devices so common in the genre may mask somewhat these descriptions and fuller explorations of character, and indeed the epic's human touch, despite the frequently grim nature of the central theme, can place this particular genre in a more subjectively interesting category of contrivance or art, between the overtransparent and crystalline cliché on the one hand, and the decadent playfulness of the later romances, or even the psychological convolutions of the modern novel, on the other. I return to this obviously powerful aesthetic, deictic, and emotional theme in the coda ending both this chapter and the book.

THE CONSTELLATIONS OF HEROISM

Investigations of the hero seem continually to produce the most solid and marmoreal result, only to have it dissipate before our very eyes. Eccentric, puzzling, even maddening variations turn our firm structures into chaos, and the very notion of laying out a linear continuum of heroism or heroic types, which seemed an attractive idea at first, begins to lose its presumptive validity and value. Any two poles (as of nature/culture) that may at first seem to organize the data now become too flat, unfeatured, or unidimensional. A more flexible and comprehensive armature is surely needed—if it can be assembled.

A Grid of Heroism

To begin to set up a paradigmatic expression or schema, let me take three familiar warrior-heroes from the *Iliad*—Akhilleus, Odysseus, and Diomedes—and set each of them in a *morphos* or hard characteristic category. Figure 1a presents a "base" grid: on it, or to it, can be hooked or fitted a number of other "heroic" grid segments, as we will presently see—I hope. The three apices of the triangle are identified by characteristic subtypes of heroism, or of salient features or factors: *surface brilliance* is Akhilleus's marking factor; *depth, complexity, occlusion* belong to Odysseus; *solidity* and *strength* are invariably projected for Diomedes.

Figure 1a uses only three players in the large-scale heroic drama of the *Iliad*; it omits the matter of that fatal *mênis* that drives the epic, springing from the great rivalry between Agammemnon and Akhilleus (see diagram in figure 1b, the grid on royal heroism). It also omits other oppositive tensions, such as the subsidiary rupture between Odysseus and Telemonian Aias, although this can be figured as a slightly reduced but similar version of the antagonistic relationship between Odysseus and Akhilleus; but this rendering does allow for the *simultaneity* of grid formations, so that a three-dimensional situation, with grid behind grid, is certainly possible (see below, figure 4a). The grid also leaves out an intermediating figure like Nestor, with his old man's salving and gnomic "wisdom"—which must be somehow related to Odysseus's wiliness, though it is surely more positive in its valence. (Nestor, of course, also belongs on the royal grid.) And obviously the diagram omits the players on the Trojan side, especially their great champion, Akhilleus's foe and prey, Hektor. Finally, of course, the great difficulty in using figures from the *Iliad* to give body to a theory of relational tensions is that these abstracted characters always come roaring back from any abstractive attempt; they are so filled with imaginal and affective life that they are liable to push any mere theory out of shape.

Nevertheless this triangular schema does, I think, clarify the lines of relationship (or relational vectors) of *cooperation, noncooperation,* and *rivalry* among the three players and their three clusters of salient characteristics. These relational vectors are realized and identified in the communicative (or confrontational) codes and modes of *arms/combat* and of *speech.*

1. The combinatory possibilities of *depth, occlusion* and *strength, solidity* are personalized in the relational nexus of Odysseus and Diomedes, aligning a strong-arm and "chivalric" figure, here Diomedes, with an epical trickster, whose talents are made most apparent in the related realms of craft, guileful speech, and guileful practice. The one figure's attributes balance the

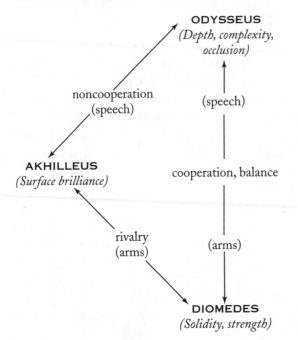

ODYSSEUS
*(Depth, complexity,
occlusion)*

noncooperation
(speech)

(speech)

AKHILLEUS
(Surface brilliance)

cooperation, balance

rivalry
(arms)

(arms)

DIOMEDES
(Solidity, strength)

FIGURE 1A. THREE WARRIOR TYPES

other's, so that they make up a cooperative, almost a symbiotic unity, a true example of a heroic team.

2. *Surface brilliance,* the mark of Akhilleus, is not a simple or unmodifed quality, nor is Akhilleus simply the odd man out in figure 1a. Instead he introduces a specific and complex tension. His furious and savage herohood, his "lionlike" animal image (which in fact is a morphism or mask he seems to adopt almost physically in the poem), fairly obscures his considerable powers of human intelligence, again marked through speech.[27] In speech he can be almost painfully clear and honest, in self-proclaimed contrast to Odysseus, whose hidden agenda and tricking talk Akhilleus so unreservedly abhors. He is not, then, presented as a *rival* to Odysseus but regards himself as essentially different and separated from—that is, noncooperative with—the man of many wiles. Moreover, in Akhilleus sight and speech are transparent but not complete; as James Redfield put it, he "sees the situation so clearly because he sees only one part of it" (as we usually see only part of him, his scintillant surface), and he speaks exactly to what he sees. Again compared with Odysseus, the true warrior-champion sees one aspect clearly, whereas the wily one sees every aspect but may not truly report what he sees or knows.[28] I am inclined to think that behind or around Akhilleus, whose force field is so strong, would cluster those magnetically

drawn to him by some imitative inclination or by their code-enforced rivalry: Patroklos, for example, or Telemonian Aias (also negative and non-cooperative to Odysseus), who killed himself later, as we have seen, over a question of the invariant calculus of personal honor. Foredoomed Hektor, the ultimate enemy, is pulled into this force-field as well.

3. In his saturnine strength and impervious solidity, Diomedes remains the least complicated figure in this grid; because of that he may command less of our interest. We know that he is laconic: even in that ritualized, "chivalric" exchange (in book VI) with the Trojan Glaukos, his speech is a quarter the length of his enemy's; and despite the occasional excesses of his war fury, he does not display the convulsive rages of Akhilleus—to whom he is simply a warrior-rival for the Homeric hero's grand prize and appellation *aristos Akhaiôn,* "best of the Achaeans."[29] His position is thus bifaceted but unambiguous: cooperative to the wily Odysseus, rival to Achilleus, and remaining quite untroubled by any interior questionings or agitated by any frenzied, schizoid anger. He is nearly, in fact, a "pure" warrior, a figure sprung from the irreducible physical core of heroism, although in this epos, as we have seen, he is drawn slightly off-center because he does not have to accept the hero's early death—nor, in fact, does he appear to win the "lasting glory" of those who rush to accept it.

In demonstrating something close to "pure" warriorhood (though not, in essence, pure herohood), he makes a significant contrast to Akhilleus, whose double-edged character seems to place him directly in that category of warrior-heroes who "split" their Second Function place and actions (the cleavage between a rational-human and an irrational-animal valence). Such a scission can never be comfortable or easy for the "doubled" warrior-hero, even when (as in the case of the Welsh hero-warlock Cei) the two aspects are clearly and cleanly separated, as they were at an early point in the long evolution of his particular legend. Cei's archaic, towering champion's stance, as set forth in the old Welsh *Triads,* is hardly apparent in *Culhwch ac Olwen,* for now it jostles with those tricksterish skills of plan and craft that emerge when he is teamed with another "pure" champion and strong arm, the square and stable Bedwyr.[30] Cei's later career charts a steady narrative decline: he loses his warrior's prowess and even his trickster's skills, and all he has left is the long life that the crafty tend to live.

Akhilleus and Diomedes illustrate another kind of asymmetrical balance, oddly enough, in the area of filiation and paternity, of time figured generationally. Diomedes' father was the savage, even bestial Tydeus, who so venomously rampages in Aeschylus's *Seven against Thebes,* and it is fair to say that Diomedes inherited the energetic part of his heroic *aretê* from this father, while adding his own more measured, nearly chivalric individuality. Akhilleus seems to have passed only his unhinged ferocity to his own son, Neoptolemos, who will eventually slaughter both old Priam, Hektor's father, and Hektor's small son Astyanax. It is the signal, bald brutality of these merciless acts, slaying both the eldest and the newest generation of the Trojan royal house, that finally ends the great, paradigmatic war.[31]

A Grid of Royalty

All of the great heroes of the *Iliad* are also kings in their own right, even if "kingship" in this context means, mainly, to be a war leader, a polemarch. Let me attempt in figure 1b to build another grid in order to rearrange some of the possibilities within this category. One can parse this particular grid of "heroic royalty" in various ways, one of which is the *communicative* mode: speech or, in this situation, what each figure or persona "speaks for." Agamemnon, occupying the office of "legitimate king," speaks (however ineptly at times) for the special rights of that particular sort of monarchy (derivative, not absolute) he occupies as *primus inter pares* among the other Achaean kings. Akhilleus, a war leader who always leads by effortful personal example, speaks, as he acts, for himself, and thus for a kingship strongly mixed with and mediated by the warriorlike heroic. Nestor, representing the "old king," speaks for a kingly mode rich in accumulated experience; his conceptual base seems to be set much more in the experiential and practical realm than in any sacralized sense of a supreme royalty.

Another analytic positioning might place a temporal marker in the grid. We now see that Akhilleus operates in the instant, as he is known to be "strikingly lacking in both forethought and afterthought";[32] Agamemnon, who as a "legitimate" king must accept that his tenure rests in Zeus's hands (Zeus who gave him that sign of sovereignty, the palladial scepter), operates within a limited or circumscribed temporal frame; Nestor obviously operates in durative or experiential time, which represents a dense "historical" assemblage or accumulation of considered acts and reactions.

Between Akhilleus and Nestor the differentiating element is *dimensionality* or depth (the single, utterly clear, unidirectional view of the fighting king-hero versus the deep, multidimensional outlook of the "old king" who has survived so long and will continue to survive). The relational tension between Agamemnon and Nestor is a little harder to detect, but royal *experience* is the key, as in book IX.104–6, in which Nestor unequivocally puts his accumulated years and consequent wisdom into the balance—"I am

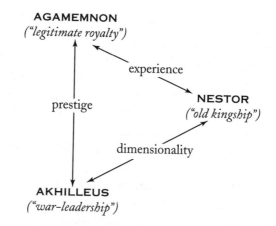

FIGURE 1B. THE GRID OF ROYALTY

older," (*hôs seio geraiteros . . . einai*)—and counsels Agamemnon to make peace with Akhilleus. None of the Achaeans, including Agamemnon himself, can gainsay this product of his ripened mind, or its persuasive force. The truth is that Nestor's complex and matured thought, and the uses to which he puts it, sets him into a category close to that of Odysseus; and this return to the trickster, with his slanted relation to the hero, helps bring us to another ambiguous and slanted realm, that of the magical or supernatural.

Aspects of the Supernatural

Supernature has a predictably ambiguous place in this series of constructed grids illustrating heroic relationships and identifiable subtypes, and the problem can be laid out from a number of perspectives. A vertical-topical scheme or arrangement would show supernature maintained as a separate entity and creation, positioned "over" the human terrain and topos, with the heroic active zone plotted or poised somewhere between the superior and supernatural and the ordinary or profane human zones. (How this topical placement works itself out within the heroic drama will differ from epic tradition to epic tradition.) Supernatural powers—personalized as individual and identifiable gods—are often involved in act one, the generation of the heroic individual, but that divinely begotten hero rarely inherits any specific, indelibly divine, or supernatural powers. Super*nature* is routinely transmuted into the heroic-super*human* in the form of the hero's "unnatural" rate of maturation, exceptional physical morphisms, and such precocious enhancements as phenomenal strength, endurance, and speed, but it remains a separate realm usually distrusted by the poets themselves as they shift the narrative of the story from a mythic to an epic format.

Another view rules in the heroism of the North, at least in that fine and commodious if mixed source, the collection of Norse-Icelandic family sagas. There the manipulators of the supernatural are usually sorcerers and other uncanny but human operatives; only very rarely does an identifiable pagan god or goddess appear. Nor does the Christian God have much direct concern or miraculous play in this genre. The occasional supernatural intrusions add variety and complication to the given story line, with results that extend from the irritating and casual to the fatal. Reflecting the off-handed, cool, and even ironical tone that typifies the emotional field of the average family saga, the Otherness of the supernatural is almost never dramatized or overdrawn, and consequently it is up to us as audience to inject emotional colorations. (This allows us to see something like psychological stress or damage coming to a protagonist through some magical intervention.) In other plot situations a supernatural element reinforces fate, or reflects a bad turn of "luck," *ógæfa*—a key to and perpetual dominant in the Norse saga's thoughtworld. An example of the confusion of these possibilities is apparent in *Kormáks saga*, in which the hero is apparently unable to consummate his long time attraction to the lady Steingerðr; he wins her from other men but cannot hold her for himself, as a result either of a "magical paralysis" (a sorceress's vitiating curse was once aimed at him) or because of his own innate "fateful indecision."[33] Kormák is also confronted with another, more common magical interposition, one frustrating his warrior's physical prowess. Because of a sorcerer's magic his sword will not bite on a rival, Þórvaldr, in either of two duels, so Kormák falls back on brute strength and first breaks his opponent's ribs, and then his shoulder blade, with his sword edge.[34] Here he uses the heroic sword as a club, the most primitive of weapons—yet also at times the weapon of magical anomaly. We might recall that the saga hero Egill Skalla-grímsson, in his own story, is frustrated in the same way by the sorcerer-opponent Atli the Short, whereupon he fells the sorcerer at last and tears out his throat with his teeth (chap. 65). Once more, "brute" or animal energy is used to counteract or overleap the perverse, blocking, or frustrating subtleties of the magical act with its patent connection to an inhuman Otherness. Even a Norse adventure romance like "Bósa ok Herrauðr," rife with magic and magicians and their supernatural impedimenta and fantasy fireworks, sets a firm limit to supernature: Bósi, though he is the crafty one among the tale's heroes, had supposedly limited his own tutoring in sorcery because he wanted to be known "in his own saga" more for his exceptional but human gifts, and at the end of this rowdy and unbuttoned saga all the ancillary sorcerers and magicians, black *and* white, violently and conveniently cancel one another out and vanish from the scene.

Somewhere between but also beyond the attitudes of these two traditions would lie the Ossetian Nart tales, in which the inhuman and transhuman conceptions of the main players (specifically of the heroes Soslan and Batradz, but also of Satána, the "mother" of the Narts) prefigure an ambience in which the human and the inhuman are marvelously mixed or confused. In these Nart tales the "gods" interpenetrate the mortal heroic world, as we find when Uastyrdji, a sort of roughly defined sky-god or horse-god (his name is an Ossetian transcription of Saint George), descends and perversely fathers Satána on a dead and entombed old woman after whom he long had lusted; but the Nart heroes themselves are not confined merely to their own earthly sphere—and there is a whole host of intermediate spirits to be dealt with as well.[35] Thus the Nart hero Uryzmæg journeys down to the submarine realm of the Spirit of the Sea, while the sprightly daughter of that spirit, "la Belle Djerasse," finds her way to dry land to be eventually married to a Nart.[36] The bumptious and choleric Hero's Hero of the Narts, steel-skinned Batradz, "having become a man, remained concealed in the sky"—rather a strange posture and placement—and he must be called down by the other Narts from this *locus incognitus* when they need him.[37] The Narts also live amid a variety of other spirits; with a familiar touch of *illo tempore*, one tale tells us that "At that time"—the time-past of epic narrative—"the Narts and the spirits ate and drank together," and yet these spirits are often the antagonists of the Narts and especially of the uncontrollable Batradz, who in one of his turbulent adventures kills one spirit and brutally manhandles another. In their turn, these much-abused spirits finally compass Batradz's death with their successful appeal to an overgod, who is called the—Christian?—God of Heaven.[38] All in all, in this little corner of the Caucasus in which the heirs of the Scyths and Alans still live, we have a lively, archaic, naively formed conflation of human and superhuman, natural and supernatural, with narrative scenarios played out by a sprawling cast that includes gods, spirits and *jinn,* Nart heroes, and ordinary nonheroic or common human beings—the latter, as is normal for the epic tale, playing little real part in these legends. Dumézil was long aware of the striking resemblance of these Caucasian Ossete tales to certain of the Irish Celtic mythic and epic cycles, and indeed it is easy to spot similarities between the two heroes Batradz and Cú Chulainn, the interferences of divinities in both families of sources, even the familial likeness of the spirits in the Nart narratives to the Irish *síd* (as the latter, for example, are seen in their separate world in a tale like the *Serglige Con Chulaind*, or in the stories of Finn and his *fénnidi*).

We can demonstrate that the supernatural realm always abuts, is always potential, behind or beyond any tale set in the heroic zone. Despite that, however, the uttermost nonhuman other still may not be acknowledged in our epic sources, and thus may be kept almost entirely outside the frame of heroic adventure, as in the *Chanson de Roland* and other Old French chanson cycles. Another treatment may imagine the supernatural as merely vestigial (like the intrusive, unconvincing, Hydra-like serpent monster-rapist who appears in the Byzantine Greek *Digenid*) or as a casual operation of little significance (as with the divs in the Georgian *Lord of the Panther's Skin*). Even the dragon-fight of the Germanic Sigurd-Siegfried, intrinsic to the archaic action of the *Völsungasaga*, becomes no more than an anecdote in the *Nibelungenlied,* tied only to the hero Siegfried's near invulnerability, which the remorseless Hagen bitterly breached. Near invulnerability, a partial or faulted supernatural protection, is a peculiarly heroic gift or characteristic, because, in the most elementary way, it reveals the *limits* set to the uncontrolled heroic persona and career. But the teratic-supernatural realm, despite an occasional casual appearance, can still be a serious matter in the northern realms, and it seriously confronts the hero in an epic like that of Beowulf, who in his youth won fame by battling and defeating those two ogrish monsters in the Dane-land, and who was mortally wounded by the dragon he slew in his old age, in his own Geatish kingdom. These two supernatural encounters neatly frame the great Anglo-Saxon epic, which is otherwise a northern confabulation of human-heroic warriors' violence, invasion, rapine, and plunder.

Separated from the supernatural trial or the proofing-and-proving of a hero-warrior is our old and complicated friend the trickster, the figure, among all the constellations of heroism, most likely to stand between the heroic and the supernatural. His powers of mind can negate, befool, or bypass the threats of the destructively monstrous, and sometimes foil even the terrible embodiments of supernature themselves, at least when the gods descend into a vulnerable pseudohumanity.

A Grid of the Trickster

The heroic trickster is able to solve many, if not all, of the problems presented him in the heroic epic, but his essential humanity is made clear in his errors and gaffes, which are often at his own expense. True to his type, the trickster "plays" with reversal, which separates him from the sorcerer, whose entire being is very seriously enclosed in the reversed or contrary universe of the magical. The trickster and his tricks may (or may not) be temporarily foiled, but the sorcerer's dark powers *must* be defeated, if not by the trickster then by the most primitive brute force. Peredur-Percival uses his naive, unfettered strength to beat down the malignancy of witches, and in the North sorcerers are seized, "bagged" about the head to block the power of their evil eye, and then beaten to death on the liminal foreshore of the sea.[39] The lesson from the Norse sagas, at least, is clear: this danger-ous if temporary eruption from another, magical sort of reality cannot be allowed to maintain its force in the human world.

The trickster, in one approach to the grid in figure 2, adapts or reacts to the supernatural in a "hot" way (recalling the passion or heat of Cei in his trickster, shape-changer mode from *Culhwch ac Olwen*), filling the dramatic foreground with action and confusion, mixing images, alternating between the combative and the manipulative. The sorcerer is cool or "cold," and obvi-ously manipulative, projecting his or her magical malice in one direction and using a predictable tool kit of malignant acts and gestures. (This, at any rate, is how the witch-sorcerer usually behaves in the epic context.)[40] Gen-der enters the grid because the formula so often casts the sorcerer as a witch or old hag, though occasionally as a young woman (or a seductive *foreign* young woman, like the sexually dangerous Queen Gunnhildr of Norway, who shows up in the *Eigla* and elsewhere); the reprehended *seiðr*, seen as a heavy-caliber, perverted woman's magic, displays an aspect of the gender problem in magic as well. Trickster, especially in his frequently shamanis-tic modality, "plays" with the feminine-chaotic zone by adopting transves-

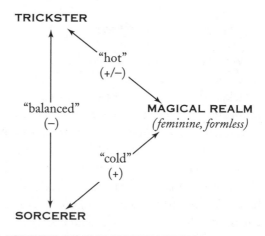

FIGURE 2. THREE ASPECTS OF THE SUPERNATURAL

tite disguises, by his formless or disheveled appearance, and even by his unheroic taste and propensity for erotic adventures or misadventures.

Thus Odysseus, the survivor, who is a highly ambiguous fighter in the
Iliad, evades, in his own travel tale, the monstrous if stupid malice of Polyphemos and the sex-sorcery of Kirke and Kalypso; sometimes he can save
most of the warriors with him, though his protective kingship or chieftainship cannot survive at last against the harsh opposition and malignant
manipulations of the great god Poseidon. An even better case might be
made for those tricksters whose powers are even closer to the shamanistic
(the shaman, we remember, is Eliade's "hero of the supernatural"),[41] like
Tale of Orasacs in the Serbo-Croat heroic songs, Bósi the Joker in his own
Norse adventure romance, and especially the Welsh Cei. Part of the strangeness of the Welsh tale *Culhwch ac Olwen* emerges when Cei, who played
such a key role in the early, preparatory adventures involving Wrnach the
Giant, the rescue of Mabon, and the tricking of Dillus Greatbeard, is forced
out of the quest by Arthur's inexplicable insult—though in fact Arthur was
not left without that often vital tricksterish and magical aid Cei had earlier provided, as one of the men still questing with him would be Menw
Teirgwaedd, whom the text calls a magician and shape changer.[42] And
even though the latter part of this narrative is more of a furious running
battle, in which a warrior's bloody and immediate sword skills are more useful than a trickster's cunning, this tale is nevertheless shot through with the
usual Celtic intermixture of the zones of humanity, nature, and supernature. However else the tale may resemble and repeat certain aspects of the
true epic, the protomythic atmosphere is very strong, whatever the authorial intent.

The Grid of Heroic Aspects

In some respects we have seen the hero increasingly cut down to a certain
hard and resistant purity or essentiality—but then we encounter the richly
"blackened" hero. This sort of hero shares the trickster's disheveled state
in one way, touches the "naive" or slow hero at another point, and reaches
toward the comic zone of wildly antic and uncontrolled reversals. In fact
his combinatory aspect divides him, for we can take the "slow" hero as occupying a preheroic mode (in the sense of a developmental line), while the
"blackened" hero is, if rightly placed, probably what ought to be called post-
heroic.[43] Perhaps another triangular grid is called for, this time using the
trickster—already firmly attached elsewhere to our heroic core—as its first
apex.

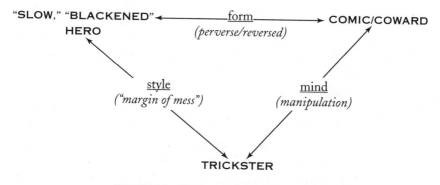

FIGURE 3. TRICKSTER AND OTHERS

The trickster holds the grid in figure 3 together and connects it to the triangular nexus, or nexi, of the normative hero, though he is not alone in this, for the "slow" hero is always intended eventually to achieve fully heroic status, when he will leave behind his ignorantly or naively unwarriorlike or unknightly character. In truth, because the variable figures in this grid consist of such fluid, shifting, and even contradictory components, they will often sidle into one another's territories or borrow one another's morphisms or personae; and they are never as severely constrained as the heroic subtypes we have identified, who are positioned closer to the harder-edged, obdurate heroic core. A cowardly character like the coward knight in *Perlesvaus,* or Hottr in *Hrólfs saga Kraka,* or Prince Virâṭa, a reluctant charioteer in the *Mahâbhârata,* is finally pulled or pushed by a heroic tutor into something resembling true herohood.[44] These more or less comic actors, in *their* characteristic careers, overleap the typical "slow" hero, especially one of the type who (like Peredur/Perlesvaus/Percival) is gradually trained and guided toward a truly heroic final apparition.[45]

Despite the informality of the categories, the axis connecting "slow/ blackened" and "comic/coward" emphasizes form or the formal: the comic/ coward *reverses* the forms of the heroic, the "slow" hero perverts it by his singular lack of heroic precocity. Trickster and the "slow" or "blackened" hero, on the other hand, share a certain *stylistic* tendency in their play with and even residence in what Barbara Babcock calls the "tolerated margin of mess," the ambiguous place of blurred and ragged outlines.[46] Some element of sexual adventuring or shamelessness, or simply of a recognizable and ordinary (and therefore unheroic) erotic drive, is also possible in both of these subtypes. Finally, the trickster and the comic/coward are synchronized in their display of sharply unheroic mental powers and a realistic (again, unheroic) incisiveness and clarity of thought, though the trickster dominates and makes continual use of this mental quality, whereas the comic/coward actor only displays it (or plays around with it) temporarily.

The temporal dimension also reappears in this triangular grid. The comic/coward presents himself in a particular location and situation, a specific point in time, and makes a singular or unique statement of norm reversal; the "slow" hero stretches out and even "wastes" durative time (compared with the aggressive, early-maturing, and always impatient hero); and one characterization of the "blackened" hero, recalling the ancient Iliach mac Cass in the Irish *Táin* or even the grizzled and scarred Starkaðr, marks him as a victim of age too-long endured. The trickster, as the survivor but also as the penetrator and manipulator of unique situations, is comfortable in all these modes of secular temporality: he is defined as the one who can plan (penetrating the future, manipulating its possibilities), execute a plan (taking immediate and reactive action), and lie—that is, rearrange past and present time (and the events thereof)—to suit himself.

The Grid of Life

Although the epic hero is involved with the inevitabilities of human intercourse in ways that are often roughly contoured and obscure, the processes of life nevertheless affect him: he must react to them, however crudely, blindly, or even perversely at times. Even if his genesis is extraordinary (which it usually is), he becomes a necessary part—though frequently a dangerous and recalcitrant part—of human society. Though it is possible to construct a grid for him plotted along the vital lines of sexuality, blood and kin ties, and other normative aspects of human social existence, it is not an easy process. The chief difficulty lies in the way the heroic individual tries to escape the net both of familial-parental (especially paternal) authority and what we might call the shapes and obligations of ordinary human affection—here meaning the inclusive, adhesive forces of emotional commitment, either to family or to a woman who might become his wife (and thus allow him to continue the family line).

The grid presented in figure 4a puts the individual hero at the apex of four intersecting triangles. His solitary position may be modified by any of the four "boundary" figures—wife, father, brother, son—but the left-hand triangle (A/B/D) is marked or dominated by negative and aggressive acts or potential acts on his part, whereas the right-hand triangle (A/C/E) displays a contrasting positive or at least balanced value in potential or act. The two upper, familial foci represent the family in a sexual, reproductive, and emotional focus (B) and as the focus of generational authority (D). Note

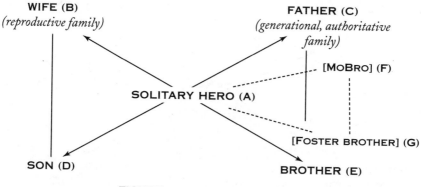

FIGURE 4A. FIRST "LIFE GRID"

that in the right-hand triangle the central hero, though he resists or is at best neutral to paternal authority and to fraternal companionship or aid, is more positively inclined to the classificatory kin figures of uncle (mother's brother) and foster brother (who make up another triangular insert, A/F/G, arranged "behind" the first, in another dimensional extension). On the left hand the line of force is essentially contrary, negative: the solitary hero resists ordinary marriage and the blandishments of the reproductive family, and he is often deadly to the son who might be born from some adventurous failure or rupture in his solitary resolve. (Remember the *Sohnes Todt* conflict: the hero resists the future.)

A second "life grid" diagram can be drawn as shown in figure 4b, but in this case each of the four terminal points has been subjected to a morphological "softening," a sublimated or abstractive process. Figure 4b replaces the four figures in the previous grid's design with four *ideas* or abstract concepts, and constructs what might be called a "soft" or cooperative grid describing the same, or approximately the same, foci or modes in the hero's life. For the paternal authority figure we substitute a "good" maternal focus (C), with her protective and nurturing imaginal aspect (Thetis to Akhilleus, Aphrodite to Aeneas, Aalais to Raoul of Cambrai). For the hero's antagonistic or intrusive brother we substitute the heroic companion (E), who is the voluntary or chosen aide to the central hero (note that this figure can also be attached to the hero in the "death diagram" in figure 5). These emendations are easy; the left-hand substitute presents a bigger challenge.

Two possibilities present themselves: either the stringencies of the family calculated as a purely reproductive nexus are here replaced by a "romantic" connection (B) to the cult of the ladylove, or the affective (but theoretically asexual) ties of *cortoisie* bind the knight (that is, a sexual or at least a procreative sign is replaced by a sublimated image). The fourth figure (D)

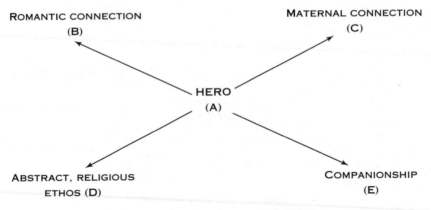

FIGURE 4B. SECOND "LIFE GRID"

is problematic or arguable but still tempting: for the hostile, darkly personal tension created by the anomalous hero's son I have substituted an abstract or religious ethos, as objectified, for example, in the persuasions of Christian knighthood (that is, the Graal quest), or the force emanating from the "crusading" idea or some similar aggrandizement of a religious faith, or perhaps even military monasticism. The future is softened to fit an asexual ethicoreligious statement or plan in lieu of the assault on future-time implicit in the hero's slaying of his own son. The future, the *telos*, is sacralized, the body made ephemeral. Possibly these last two figures could be reversed.

The Grid of Death

The grid in figure 5 brings an end to the hero's time and to any future in this world, and uses death, always a principal player in the eternally refigured heroic drama, as a reagent. We see the heroic trickster here again serving as an anchor, in fact the anchor of a doubled grid, devised because of significant variables that may be inserted into the old theme of heroic death. Perceived in one way, death is a culminating and scissive event, set against the adhesive process by which hero is bonded in some way to hero. The first (lower) section is essentially the Odysseus-Akhilleus-Diomedes triangle redrawn (figure 1), but the new vectors put Akhilleus into the role of the young hero who *achieves* (and is self-realized in) death; Odysseus as the trickster who *outwits* death; and Diomedes as the old hero. I have called Odysseus a survivor, but in fact the true heroic trickster once again "plays" death like an angler or, better yet, like a bullfighter: he interferes in death's realm, agitates death's *regula,* and as often as not escapes death's trap,[47] because death, to the trickster and *his* drama, seems to be a particular kind of powerful but not very bright antagonist, to be tempted, outmaneuvered, and outwitted. As for Diomedes, he doggedly perseveres. As with Bedwyr and Herrauðr and other strong-arm partners to trickster-figures, his death is consistently put off, perhaps until he survives beyond the narrative frame or range of his particular epic.[48] The three actors repeat their relationships configured by force and by rationality.

The new grid (which actually forms a double triangle extending, dimensionally, beyond the first) adds a fourth figure, another kind of heroic partner, one who is actually drawn into death through his association with the young hero, the veritable death-bound one. Patroklos finds his place here, who is doomed because he imitates (but does not, interestingly enough, think to rival) the peerless Akhilleus. Like Diomedes, he is an ancillary or "twinned" figure, but his considerable (though not quite overwhelming) personal powers, along with the fatal urge to imitate his younger partner, take him into a deadly confrontation from which his bravery cannot help him to escape. On the other hand, when we insert a hero-partner like the *Chanson de Roland*'s Olivier into these grids, we create a slightly but significantly different connection. Olivier is tied to Roland, who is positioned as the young hero, but his distinguishing quality is good sense or prudence; when Roland ignores it, the Frankish host is doomed. Olivier's wisdom (which, in strictly heroic terms, makes him rather trickster-like) is not enough to save him, as Patroklos's furious and eventually vain imitation of Akhilleus

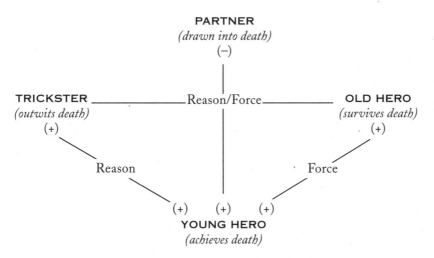

FIGURE 5. THE GRID OF DEATH

also fails in the end. Both partners are killed, though for very different reasons, because of their link to the deadly higher voltage of the self-doomed young hero.[49]

A final relation: the young hero lives and acts in a distinctive force field, one that we can describe at this point as converting death, the great negative, into a positive, because this hero, in his search for fame, concentrates his energies so powerfully into his *agôn* with death. This fatal force is met and countered by the trickster at one angle, whose different persona and ethos give him a particular, shielded advantage, and matched by the consummate warrior's *aretê*, the excellence of the old hero, at another. This force, however, reaches to and overwhelms the subordinate partner, who can neither match nor ignore it, and so becomes its victim.

CREATING THE HERO

The dark fascination of the heroic death search leads to a question that we have not examined until now: why the hero? Why is he created? There are numerous answers, the first of which is—unheroically?—socioeconomic.

A Class Act?

The simplest response to the question, Why the hero? makes him the specific imaginative creation of a specific sociopolitical group, whose ethos he constructs and supports in and by his *muthos*. The "sword" nobilities, with their combat-linked ideals, their scornful view of society and its rational organizations, their immoderate and self-authenticated élite posture, seem simultaneously to create the heroic image and to follow the image they create, especially with the help of their celebratory bards. The fact that the epic as a genre can be rooted in older songs celebrating this or that warlike exploit (even more so, this or that admired behavior or isolate style), and the deep and abiding attraction of violent, even fatal confrontation, appears to connect the hero-warrior firmly to a class or caste or nobiliary elite, to the dominant social dimension so well expressed in Dumézil's concept of a *fonction guerrière*.

In the same way, the felt sense of "epic past" fits into the peculiarly myopic and limited historical vision of a sword nobility: this group looks to an authentic-heroic past always identified as a departed "great age," sadly different from the stunted and undistinguished present, but still able to serve up models and mores worthy of whatever emulation can be possible in a decayed latter day. The parallel or reinforcing idea is that aristocratic *aretê* has its own origins in a past made distinct not by time but by type, a qualitatively distinct aeon semimythic in its essence. The same congruence takes place. This means that the authentic difference marking off the fighting nobles' selves and their lineages from the easily despised generality of their society can be assigned to the same vague origin, to that potently creative time once occupied by the hero. Their "time" is his "time"; their forebears were in some vague sense the hero's admiring peers. In this imagining, they composed his social context.

In the ordinary way of things a noble family would not try to claim direct descent from a hero, because the hero's isolate and afamilial character is notorious. Collateral descent might be permissible, however, and we also know the special cases of some family-founding saga heroes, or of a certifiably historical figure like El Cid Campeador, who had daughters if not sons. An aristocratic elite can better claim a kind of spiritual filiation from some hero, as this elite admires, recollects, and passes on the tales of heroic deeds and deaths, or even as it continues to use heroic names: noble *nomina* recapitulate heroic *numina*. The other characteristic image of blood, literally and liberally flowing from the fount of heroic violence and all its separate deadly acts, truly ties the hero and the war-making, fighting aristocratic elite more closely together than any tie of blood figured as "genetic" proof of familial descent. The hero pays for the right and privilege of death dealing with his own blood, as his glory is figuratively transfused with the blood shed by others, and the warrior aristocracy faithfully imitates what it considers a desirable bargain and exchange. If the heroic epicdrama often ratchets up the tale of bloodshed past any reasonable or even possible reality, to explode in a frantic fantasy of violence, the aristocratic imitators will still insist on their right to follow along in the imaginal pattern to the limit of their personal skill and resources. They maintain the inevitable component of individual confrontation and combat, the necessity of the recognizable and worthy opponent, and the brutally agonic focus of life. At the core of the aristocratic imitative idea is the same "heroic" vision of an integral personal essence, called by whatever name; and it must at all times be forcefully defended, violently proved "on the body" of any challenger.[50]

The Popular Hero

At the same time, the power of the heroic icon cannot be limited only to an aristocratic, or warrior-aristocratic, following, however persistent that following's claim. This icon is too complex; it goes far beyond the limits of the nobiliary mental horizon and penetrates deeply into the generic human psyche from which it sprang. An aristocracy may try to monopolize, even try to embezzle the heroic ideal, but that ideal exerts a far broader sway than any elite group can contain.

The European nineteenth century saw the simultaneous rise and florescence, if by no means the original invention, of a cult of heroism and of the wider notion of a reborn "people" or nation; when these two combine, we suddenly have the image of the national hero, in which various and even conflicting currents may run. Heroic epic is almost by definition connected to the common (if not the vulgar) tongue in which it appears, or at least, as in the Homeric poems, to a special epical linguistic mode considered "authentic" in its recognizably archaic tones and shapes. In fact, its archaism is factitious, contained in that *langue* of "time past" standard for the epic. (This is a separate problem from the distancing factor appropriate to identifying and viewing the past action of the epic.) Yet the language of the epic seems not so much a popular language, in the sense that it springs from a specific, demotic folk, as a coded communication that is usually anticenter, even antiestablishment, but by no means propopular. In Dumézilian terms, it is the expressive mode of a warrior's Second Function with a possible admixture of the language either of the First Function or, in rare cases, of the Third, but it is specifically made quite distinct from the "sacral" or First Function language of the Center, be it "courtly," legal, bureaucratic, or priestly. Epic language does not have or need a particularly large or complex descriptive vocabulary, and its specialized subvocabularies and formulas mainly have to do with descriptions of the coruscating surface of the warrior, details of quest or deadly battle, ponderous exchanges of honor between heroes, and so on.[51]

The heroic-epic narrative sustains a "national" identity or consciousness only by implication. The central hero is detached from any sense of national or ethnic affiliation by his solipsistic individualism, his studied self-exclusion from *any* group identification, his disdain for or distrust of all of the "legitimate" abstractions that accompany any process of social and political organization. The hero type whom we have seen operating on some far border, or the ectopical or atopical knight errant abroad in his wanderings, demonstrates how far the special sense of a heroic topos can take him from an ethnic or national description and limitation, and other aspects of his liminoid status do the same. (The case of the "Irish" hero, the magnificent Cú Chulainn, is symptomatic, for he is not of Eirenn—he is not even fully of Ulster, of the Ulad for whom he rejoices to fight.) At the same time the hero does have an identity beyond the purely atomistic and personal; part of this identity *is* formed by language, part by some eminent sense of who "we" are—we who are undoubtedly separate from what "they are."[52] The Homeric *Ur*-epos very clearly distinguishes the favored Achaeans from the Trojans, and not just by much-worn formulaic adjectival formations such as "well-greaved" or "long-haired" for the former, "horse-taming" for the latter.[53] The two sides, however similar their equipage and tactics (and despite the fact that, as is usual in the epic, they have no difficulty whatsoever in conversing), are never to be confused with one another: Achaeans are Achaeans, Trojans are the enemy, and they are located "over there," in the beleaguered city on the other side. The hero may act as if he were merely playing a game when choosing sides, but he will rarely deviate from that singular allegiance. On the other hand, we cannot simply ignore that part of the heroic game in which sides really *are* chosen, for of course when the hero joins one side or the other his archetypical, heroic individualism is somehow compromised.

The hero's isolation and uniqueness notwithstanding, the history or narrative development of the heroic tale makes clear the ligatures that tie the hero to his people or his place. The Serbian Christian folk epos describing Prince Marko Kraljević's heroic deeds naturally pits him against the Moslem Turks, as well as the occasional liminoid, brigandish foe, like Mujo the Highwayman. The Serbian Moslem heroic songs are sure that their eternal enemies are the various Christian monarchs and their infidel hosts on the other side of the border, but they also, as in the *Wedding of Smailagić Meho*, scornfully identify turncoat or traitorous Ottoman officials, like the corrupt and evil Vizier of Buda. So-called popular or folk-epic heroes may somehow be connected to an ethnic base or sense of membership, as in the Russian subtype of *byliny* called "Kievan." Here the peasant folk-hero Il'ya of Murom fights "for the Russian land" and for the Christian, meaning the Orthodox, faith, while the collective opposition is likely to be called "Tatar" (the Tatars are identified as the archetypal heathen enemy of the Russian land) even when Polish or Lithuanian foes are in fact meant.[54] These *byliny* do not merely divert themselves with ordinary secular history, however redrawn: at times they also monstrify their hero's foe, turning that adversary back into a mythical potency, a devouring dragon, or an ogrish giant. By no means are they the only popular hero tales to reawaken and reuse mythic characters and formulas.[55]

The Limits of Fantasy

Investigations into what would seem to be a parallel imaginative creation of a potent-impressive type, the *charismatic* leader or figure of power, have suggested that the deep origin of this type lies in the earnest human desire to rebuild or resuscitate a kind of super nurturant, ever-providing caregiver-parent, perfect and powerful and protective of the individual self in every respect. Fantastication or fabulism, in this view, will construct such a figure on the template of paternity (or a combined ideal of beneficent paternity and maternity, like the Jungian Good Parents), but how can we do this with the heroic persona? Can we find a fantasized big brother—not Orwell's grim invention, but the imagined older brother to ego—who displays a stronger, swifter, more powerful persona? The notion is tempting. Here is the condensation of *like/not like,* close to the heart of the image-maker yet essentially detached from him, invested with all the lively powers of a younger generation (ego's generation) yet soon maturing toward his own destiny, strong in all his imagined perfections. And yet this fraternal-familial image doesn't quite fit. The problem is that in the construction or projection of the heroic icon, ego forever invents and reinforces only ego: the invented hero must in some sense truly be self, or at least some significant part of self, and not self's brother.

One of the puzzles attendant on shifting the concept and the various explanations of charisma toward our understanding of the hero is the fact that charisma is usually associated with the assumption by the charismatic figure of a *leadership* role in a society. Admittedly, the Weberian notion of charismatic leadership can stress its irrational base and ephemeral character, but if we take "leadership" to mean some form of recognized precedence (at least) or dominance (in major), we will have to be careful to fit our hero to the received definition, because although a hero will always resonate to some of the motive aspects of charismatic leadership and power, he is both defined and *self*-defined as a "leader" only in a very special, limited, and task-specific sense. Heroic leadership as such is ever a debated matter. It is mainly or even essentially exemplary; the hero's directive power or force lies in what he does, and his lesson is almost a casual "do as I do—if you can." Only rarely (if ever) will it be "do as I say," not only because of the limits on communication or speech placed on the heroic figure but also because of the important assumption, on the part of the hero *and* his audience, that the ordinary human being, even the proudest, most arrogantly imitative warrior-noble, can never "do" exactly what the hero does—except, possibly, die.

When the hero's acts are organized or crystallized into a sort of code that a nobiliary sword elite is obliged to observe and try to follow, we have the direct transference of the heroic act into the hands of his imitators.[56] But this is merely mimesis; the heroic *paideia* or his display of exemplary acts is not leadership in any strict definition. The fact is that trying to penetrate the mystery of why the hero is identified as such requires us to recognize that hero worship may spring from a great depth and unpenetrated darkness in the hearts of the hero worshipers, an area closed off to the ideal-causal formation and even to the rational mind. Which brings us back again to the Weberian concept of charisma.

There is some confusion in Weber's own original statements, in which he describes "pure" charisma as it might be embodied in hero-warriors like Akhilleus and Cú Chulainn: truly heroic figures inflated by the pure irrational rage of battle. (This could also include berserkers or those old Welsh "champions before the host.") It is true that such a heroic battle leader, inflamed against the foe to the point of a ferocious incandescence, can force or induce imitation on the part of others who are affected, even bespelled by him and his warlike deeds. But heroes, though paradigmatic, are not, as I have already insisted, usually *in authority*. Roland's ill-fated command simply attaches the other paladins in the Frankish rear guard to his own willful dead end; Akhilleus is war king of a people or tribe, the Myrimidons, but he never seems to be concerned to lead or *direct* them as a polemarch might, except by his example.[57] And yet again, the hero does and must shape his image to, and respond to some need in, his secular audience, defined not as his imitators but as an audience made up of his wider society, whichever one eventually claims him.

In our recreation of the heroic drama, the central focus is at base extrafamilial; the hero, in terms of the revelation of psychological deeps and efficient structures, in no way represents any projective imagining of a parental "caregiver" kept in the human infant's archaic recollection or formulation. Quite the contrary: in the hero's tale we do not have the signs of nurturant life but the straightly marked-off pathway toward finality, termination, and personal death. Can we argue, then, that the hero gains his imaginative place and power because "he died for us" or "for me"? Certainly such a notion is possible, though here projected far from any truly salvific intent or event, as of a martyred saint, prophet, or god-man. No hero is likely to be merely a passive or helpless victim; he expects to be brought down, with great difficulty and violence, by the savage force he understands so well, and the foes he has defied. His martyrdom, therefore, is a very special manifestation of *marturia* read as close to the original: he "witnesses" his inescapable portion of death, however he may seek it out and accept it.

Another aspect, perhaps even another function, of the heroic death drama or final *agôn* appears in a number of epic contexts as a kind of simple if sinister dialectic. The heroic drama's finale always seems to generate, even to glory in, a display of dramatic opposites: the heroic one, isolated, is contrasted to the pullulating enemy multitude; a cold, hard-plated, sculptural heroic attitude and careless pose explodes into the whirling blood-red heat of action; the solitary, erect hero-warrior figure, stricken, falls like a tree and never rises again; the vital representative of furious life actually seeks out and "lives" in death. How did the original epic audience react to this? There is no real way of telling, although we do know that that audience's experience and reaction was much less vicarious than ours. Perhaps we can presume a combination of exhilaration and resignation, excitement and a kind of ritualized regret, as in the *Chanson de Roland,* in which most of the song's laisses end with the trisyllable 'AOI,' which appears to be a bleak cry of regret and mourning, repeated time after time throughout the poem. An element of shock, of course, is intended from these jarring contrasts; we have dislocation and disequilibrium—but also the grimmest certainty. The old tale cannot end but one way.

The process of shock and of dislocation is subject to certain limits. It is again important to note that no specifically *magical* sleight of hand will interfere in the hero's final transformations: he doesn't manipulate the supernatural to rupture and disintegrate further profane reality, although magic is often used against him. Thus the great personal force of the hero, always keeping its operative core in his superhuman character and dimension, is the more pathetically borne down and slain, though it is never finally defeated. We also know that the idea of a "fair fight" is largely irrelevant (if not impertinent) in the last heroic confrontation: the hero never makes optimistic assumptions about the fairness of life, nor does he naively question the unfairness of an early death or the malignancy or randomness of those accidents ruling human fate. He insists on quite the opposite: on the perpetual dramatic value of standing at last outnumbered, doomed, and fated to die. If he is able to strike that reciprocal bargain in exchanging his young life for a fitting death and a place hardened in memory and imagination forever, his very exceptionality earns him such a chance to take part in so very rare a game.

One mark of our times is that we continually try to fit this death-bound hero into some sort of understandably human psychological frame. How else is the hero's recognized and self-conscious (in the root sense) exceptionality, his essential difference from all other "powerful ones," as well as from the ruck of ordinary humanity—how is this invented, separate state reflective of or connected to the structures and needs of the deep psyche? Some responses from those concerned with plumbing and explaining this deep psyche and its conformations have been scattered throughout this study, but we have seen that the "triumph of the young male" implicit in the Oedipus drama as Freud and his followers redrew it is contravened by the more dominant theme of the filicidal, not parricidal, Indo-European hero. The Jungian approach is perhaps more helpful, but the developed Jungian delineation of the heroic exfoliation into full, mature ego consciousness (as presented, for example, by Erich Neumann) has to be severely modified for our epic hero as he takes his willful plunge toward death. The main lines of psychoanalytic and depth-psychological inquiry have not gotten us much forrader in our specific quest, fascinating as the elaboration of these canons in one or another chosen heroic matrix may be; yet I think it necessary to try them again, and I will do so presently.

The investigation of charisma as it might be explained in psychological terms leaves us some hints, but if there is nothing parental and nurturing about the hero, if the "deep imagos of archaic care" are not called up, what archaic imagos *are* found in this figure?[58] One suggested line of investigation branches off from a reconstruction or "attribution" of segments of the human psychic apparatus, in which four segments of that apparatus respond to or specifically enhance the "charismatic" particularities: uncanniness, excellence, sacredness, and omnipotence.[59] Our epical hero fits securely into only one of these attributes: excellence, which is an easy translation of the Greek heroic *aretê*. Following the attributive structure underlying this notion, the hero would be immediately responsive to the needs of the (societal) superego, though we might see a partial heroic activation of others. (According to this theory, for example, the imputation of uncanniness would respond to the instinctual id.)[60] But in fact the most intensive psychological voltage, considered both subjectively (produced within the hero) and objectively (produced within his audience), seems to flow most strongly from the peculiarly *adolescent* placement of our heroes; such a conclusion has been suggested more than once in earlier pages of this study. The powerful contradictions and hypertrophied special dynamics that characterize and afflict this liminoid human male state are, in a heroic persona, inflated and made even more tenacious and impressive: extraordinary physical strength and maturity often conjoined with a moral and intellectual deficiency or even vacuum; a significantly ambiguous attitude toward familial and social norms combined with the most florescent and indomitable if simplistic sense of self; the overwhelming "presentness" that forcefully repudiates the importance of both past and future; an uneven and frequently neutral sexual identity (and a sexuality easily turned toward confrontation and *agôn,* and frequently marked by a flagrant if paradoxical gynophobia— the attraction/repulsion syndrome). Even the persistent and pervasive appeal of death itself, with an allied and consequent notion of the supreme benefit, of winning deathless fame and "name," marks both the adolescent and the hero. We might have to reconsider and separate the subjective and the objective appeal of this state as it may reinforce the psychic appeal of the hero, but the heroic mode is undoubtedly contaminated by adolescent psychological affects, however highly polished and intricately decorated.

If these further attempts to invoke a specific psychological theory fail to satisfy us and the needs of our argument, we may be forced back to some extent upon the already noted theories of Chadwick, Bowra, and Levy explaining those historical shocks and spasms that lead to the appearance of heroic-epic narratives. "Variability of the environment outside its accustomed range typically elicits a need for stabilizing leadership" is one sociologist's view,[61] yet the heroic mode displays not just, or not even, a re-stabilizing of "omnipotence," but also the newly created and reinforced importance of confrontation—and perhaps a move toward something like heroic *blood sacrifice* (with the hero as both officiant and victim) in order to recover some sort of eventual stability. Heroism, says William James, is consecrated by death.[62] Yet the "order" recovered from the sacrifice has an unusual conformation, and the "stability" achieved needs more examination, definition, and explanation.

God, Man and Society

As I began with the Greek hero, so must I return, for whatever enlightenment the solving of his "problem" might bring. In his brilliant, if unfortunately posthumous, essay, "The Heroic Paradox,"[63] Cedric Whitman meditates on the hardest center of Greek heroism, Akhilleus, who in his view alternates between a search for a "divine" autonomy and the desire to be reconnected to humanity: "A man may assert his divine absolutism and thus in some sense 'become a god,' but then also after some fashion he ceases to be a human being, and he has no communication with anyone."[64] For Whitman, the reconnection to humanity *and* the aspiration toward divinity are accomplished in the heroic death drama, "the only assertion by which mortality and divinity can coincide."[65] The paradox is clear, but the "absolute" that Akhilleus (and any Greek hero) attains is the self-chosen death. He is less concerned with that *kleios* that so many others say is necessary to the hero, that fame everlasting, the song sung by his people to celebrate him, his deeds, his death. What we have, in a phrase, is a song about a dance: the steps, simple or complexly plotted, danced by the hero as he moves through his parabolic life, finally footing a *Totentanz* for one, always only one, lonely figure.[66]

Very few epics display the complex relationship of human hero to god or divinity *and* to human society as the ancient Greek. In the North, the pagan heroes usually take Óðinn for their war-god, and in doing so they seem to accept the casual, savage intervention of this grimly playful and utterly untrustworthy old god in their deadly affairs; it is as if he personifies the invariant and ever present chance and changeability of the wager of battle. The warrior-hero, caught between the supernatural image of his own god on the one hand, and of Óðinn's corpse-tearing wolf or carrion-crow on the other, not only accepts but even glories in this perilous interposed place. Such a scheme is somewhat, though not exactly, like the depiction of the Greek hero as a man, even if a superman, caught between god and animal. Other epic traditions merely put their statement of man and the divine into the framework of faith and belief; religion discovers to us what we are, only as we are compared with the unbelieving other. But every epic tradition in some way demands a description or definition of that social framework against which the hero reacts, to which he may be most dangerous, which he may defend, and which he knows will sing of his sword dances—especially the last, most dramatic, and most fatal dance of all.

THE FINAL DISCONNECTION

Who will count all the words, through all the ages, dedicated to death and how we deal with it? We ought to keep this thought in mind not least because the red thread that runs throughout this study is the persistent presence of the violent and of those dead by violence; our subject, the hero-warrior, is a primary violator of the ancient, supposedly strict taboo against shedding the "blood of one's brother." He follows Cain, and ever kills his own kin. At the very least this means that the hero, that prince among dealers of death, may be one of the targets of an extraordinary range of views debating what death is, and how humankind deals with this ultimate departure and terrible reality. The range reaches from the philosophical and the ethicoreligious (and, of course, the theological) to what has often been substituted for religion and philosophy in our day, the theoretical postulates and perceptions of the psychologist and (especially) the psychoanalyst.

In this last category alone, the literature is vast, and I am purposely nar-

rowing my field to a relatively few figures, with the best excuse that two of
these, Robert Jay Lifton and Ernest Becker, particularly Becker, put "heroism" in some sort of specific focus.[67] In both of these cases, and probably in
the great majority of instances in the psychological field regardless of theoretical or ideological orientation, the deep concern with analyzing the human attitude toward death has been powerfully motivated by the history of
this century, which after two decades had suffered the endless and point-
less slaughter of the Great War, then saw another world conflict involving
even more widespread destruction and catastrophic loss of life, and has
throughout endured revolutions, state-engineered famines, genocidal "incidents," and mass exterminations of peoples, both mechanized and ran-
domized, purposeful and horribly casual—a pullulating list of insane and
banal deaths. Finally came the appearance (and use) of an ultimate weapon
of mass annihilation so dreadful that the actual extinction of much of human civilization seemed possible if not assured: in our time we have before
our eyes an apocalyptic vision of *total* death.

Certainly we of the twentieth century can claim no monopoly on the
spectacle of mass death and its attendant horrors: the slaughters accompanying the growth of Middle-Eastern empires and Rome's triumphs, the
disastrous Eurasian campaigns of the Mongols and of Tamerlane, the drastic depopulations of France during the Hundred Years' War and Germany
at the end of the Thirty Years' War, the genocidal impact of the European
Conquista on native populations in the Americas, the terrible toll of the
African and other slave trades, the effects of "natural" plagues and pan-
demics from ancient Athens through seventeenth-century London—these
would be only a tiny fraction of the list. Great killings and dyings we have
had aplenty throughout human history, but the analysts of past death and
disaster have, in the West, mainly been churchmen, together with the occasional historian and moral philosopher. Our experts on death nowadays
most often root themselves in the psychological revolution.

The insights these mind experts bring to the study of our central hero
vary from the diverting to the bizarre (or perhaps both together?), and they
often strike a curious balance between the useless and the fruitful. Thus
Lifton, for example, sees threatened masculinity, translated into the dubious or at least arguable old context of the Freudian "castration complex," as
the heart of the warrior ethos,[68] and "pseudo-heroism" as the primary heroic obsession with death. Killing for the sake of killing, in his view, can
only be destructive; to him it is the dark foundation of a death culture, or
even the terrible and ultimate psychic seed (along with a feckless and literally demoralized Science), that would generate the supreme death-machine,

the atomic or hydrogen bomb. Yet Lifton also believes that death can be defeated through what he calls "symbolic immortality," a phenomenon he defines as "to know death and still transcend it."[69] Several of the scenarios he outlines for this immortality closely approach our heroic frame of possibility.

Lifton also believes that "an increased capacity to imagine . . . the end of the self can release powerful, revitalizing energies,"[70] and that maturation, the process of ego-individuation, is built on the sensible acceptance of one's death. We know, however, that the hero sensibly (perhaps too sensibly, or even avidly?) accepts the idea of his death, yet throughout our epic-heroic sources we have uncovered a fundamentally adolescent persona. He is *not* psychically mature, though he is certainly individuated, and his most typical stance combines extraordinary physical maturity with a grossly underdeveloped moral and psychic apparatus.[71] Sexuality is also immature and lacking in force, though of course one could argue that it is merely sublimated or repressed.

Ernest Becker would insist, however, that humankind's primary repression is not of sexuality but of death.[72] A corollary is that "One way of looking at the whole development of social science since Marx and of psychology since Freud is that it represents a massive detailing and clarification of the problem of human heroism."[73] Yet a book apparently devoted to our very subject, and ending with a chapter entitled "What Is the Heroic Individual?" still seems to skirt our main problem. The analysts we cite here continue to have trouble with the very heart of the heroic "idea"; the hero seems constantly to slip away from them. If Lifton is too narrow and repressive, Becker is too tolerant: his "heroic individual" is too sane, too balanced, too realistic, to resemble our iconic epical hero. Becker's hero remains merely an elegant model, useful for defeating, through his realism and sangfroid, the human neurosis that is "the denial of death." But he has little to do with our archetype.

The closest approach may well be Freud's notion of a "death instinct," destructive *Thanatos* in mortal combat against productive *Eros*, although the theory has come under considerable assault in recent decades even within the psychoanalytic community. Lifton, for one, finds it lacking to say the least, and yet our hero seems to be so temptingly planted in this instinctual zone that we might pursue the connection a little further.

Norman O. Brown locates instinct itself as "a borderland concept between the human and the animal," and this *Zwischenland* undoubtedly is where the hero often is born, lives, tours, discovers, acts—and dies.[74] Yet although the hero may draw his powers from some "reservoir" of instinct—

the animal, *sensible* body, or more abstractly the id—he is not marked by what Brown sees as the prime mental characteristic of the ordinary human "man-animal": he is not possessed, certainly not dominated, by the *neurotic* conflict between these two primary psychic elements. The hero is not conflicted within himself, however devoted he may be to conflict and to the agonistic; his interiority is not in the least riven by neurotic doubts, pressures, and tensions. If he bodies forth the deep and feral power of instinct, and (in this view) preeminently represents the threat of *Thanatos* or death instinct, he does so without generating any crisis between life instinct and death instinct in his psychic core. Is this violent lucidity, this internal integrity, one part of his true herohood, his perceived difference from ordinary humanity? (Most of the rest of us, feeble and nonheroic as we are, *are* conflicted and riven, after all.) Brown eventually separates the Freudian thanatic-instinctual drive into three elements, one of which he finds particularly suited to our heroic character's drive toward death, his imagined thanatogenesis and fitting thanatography: the third or sadomasochistic element.[75] Here the hero is finally and absolutely detached from Eros, and finally and absolutely devoted to that special—divine?—power, the power to take life; but yet again, Freud's original must be modified in our case, because the hero does not fear death. Instead he is involved in his own particular way in what Brown, following a Hegelian line, describes as the dialectical process constructing or resulting in "the consciousness of death," "the desire to die being transformed into the desire to kill, destroy or dominate" and in "a struggle to appropriate the life of another human being at the risk of one's own life."[76] The hero is always aware that he is on the way to death (which may or may not be read as a *desire* for death), and he continually and knowingly risks his own life in order to take life.

We seem to have part of the puzzle, and perhaps now we are very close to the heart of the drama. The hero is embedded in the reality of death as a death dealer, but in no case does the death of the opponent or victim release the hero from the peril of death: very much the opposite is true. The ordinary psychoanalytic viewpoint would disagree ("the death fear of the ego is lessened by the killing, the sacrifice, of the other; through the death of the other, one buys oneself free from the penalty of dying, of being killed"),[77] but of course we know that from the *Iliad* onward, the hero has no doubt that he must and will die, not only because he puts himself in the way of death but also because the eternal balance of life with death must be maintained. The hero accepts this inescapable fact. Indeed the complete reversal of Rank's observation is laid out with the usual Homeric clarity in Sarpedon's well-known speech to his comrade Glaukos in *Iliad* XII.310–

28. After remarking that the two of them have earned their appropriate rewards as hero-kings by standing foremost with the Lycians in the battle, *epei Lukioisi meta prôtoisi makhontai,* Sarpedon (a mortal son of Zeus himself) moves to a vital second point. If he were "ever ageless and immortal"— *aiei . . . agêrô t' athanatô*—he would be long gone from the combat, which would have no meaning for him: "But now, seeing that the spirits of death stand close about us in their thousands, no man can turn aside and escape them, let us go on and win glory for ourselves, or yield it to others."[78] One cannot kill oneself free of death: it will be there, it is all around us, so we must make the best and most glorious death we can, if death is our portion—as eventually it must be.[79]

In the confrontation between Eros and Thanatos, the hero images and directs the irruption of thanatic instinct, and yet he does not totally lose self. He is not reabsorbed into primal chaos, as a Jungian like Neumann would say; he goes violently, passionately into death, both because he has been honored in life *and* because he will leave something behind, the memory of glory, of honor won, paid for, and fulfilled. Thus he has no fear of death; but does this, by itself, secure his heroic eminence? Surely it is important, even vital to the final image left behind for others to sing and celebrate. Is this merely narcissism, some inflated sense of an image of self too important ever to be allowed to perish? Probably not: for one thing, the hero requires no reflecting surface to tell him about his own surface or his essence. Both (they are the same) are perfectly and consciously known.

Perhaps, for our lesson, we must return to the *sacral* importance of the limen, the threshold, the interstice, and those who occupy such a place. Reckoning from his first, physical placement, the hero stands in the adolescent state physically—and psychically. He is part of but yet escapes id and instinct, the animal image and potency, yet still is not fully part of ego, matured psyche and self. The *solidity* of his constructed image confuses us; his outlines are so marmoreally clear that we try to force him into the most inclusive and clearest categories, where he simply will not fit. His self-accepted position in the most final scheme of death confuses us even more— but it also, obviously, exhilarates us. Perhaps we see him as he stands *beyond immortality;* casual and even oblivious to what might be precisely remembered of him; self-secure in this, that he lived to act, which usually meant to kill, and that he played a prime part in a drama shaped by inevitable but not tragic forces; that he was able to stretch the human far into the superhuman, and yet by accepting death and thus dying, kept the old bargain with his ultimate humanity.

Death therefore *is* the limit—the *only* limit—the hero accepts without demur. His "megalomania" (in Becker's word) has this impermeable and perfect boundary, the hardest of all limiting outlines.[80] He not only says "I am what I am" but then tells us that "I will stop being what I am"—and yet he will remain, in some important sense, *intact*, whether or not his name and fame perdure in time. He has won free into another air, free even from the consideration and constraint of reward.

THE HEROIC PLANE: AN EAGLE'S VIEW

At the end we must confess that, if only for our sins, the heroic story continues to have the most shocking, enduring, and powerful aesthetic impact on us; and although it is true that almost any heroic tale will be largely framed in an antique accord with certain preset and closely considered rules, it is equally true that the vast, sometimes ill-focused *energy* that permeates each narrative will always remain no matter how formally it may be circumscribed. However naive or sophisticated its forms, the hero tale leaves an indelible impression of this energy—an energy that erupts through even the most ham-handed or maladroit original creative urge, the crudest or most banal conception, the most anachronistic or hypersophisticated translation. Sculpted into the simplest themes and portions, the most potent images of life and death are hacked away from the mundane and profane world, isolated into liturgies somehow made visible—even, one may be permitted to say, in some way sacralized.

> Variedes tantas lancas premer e alcar
> tanta adagara foradar e passar
> tanta loriga falssar e desmanchar
> tantos pendones blancos salir vermejos en sangre
> tantos buenos cavallos sin so duenos andar.
>
> So many lances seen rising, dipping
> So many shields pierced and split
> So many mail-coats broken and darkened
> So many lance-pennons pulling free, red with blood
> So many good horses running free, riderless.[81]

This is a passage taken almost at random, from the *Cantar* or *Poema del Mio Cid*, selected for its iconic yet plastic rendering (to borrow from the art historian's vocabulary) of impressions of color and motion. Human actors as such are not present here; this is a kind of epical panning shot, an abstraction of the movements of light-cavalry warfare that still leaves the most powerful visual (and visceral) imaging; of brutal yet exhilarating noise and pounding confusion, of riders' chain mail broken and "darkened" by dirt and sweat and blood, while in a terrible contrast, white lance-pennons are suddenly dyed bright red as the thrust lance points *salir*, pull free. The "lightness" of this epic's language cannot disguise, in fact enables, our cinematic impression of one small part of a whirling battlescape of mailed horsemen; and if we simply allow the epic images to flash by for a moment, as on a tape or segment of film, we might almost be able to *join* the epic battle ourselves, to free our minds of the constrictions of theory and even of the adamantine rules of scholarship, and arrive at a final (or primary?) and more immediate apperception of this literary form. Each of us could make his own selections at this point; these are a few of my own, chosen not from any literary-theoretical bias, but only because of the sharp, prismatic impact they have on the reader:

➤ Hard-edged, black-humored, percussive, and relentlessly brutal, yet its stolid rhythms can be suddenly pierced by acute bursts of a subdued and eerie beauty: such is the *Nibelungenlied*. Jan de Vries described it as "like a good hunk of boar's meat smothered in a delicious sauce from the French kitchen," but to my mind that Frenchified sauce is a faint hint, a mere *soupçon*, and the dominant flavor is much more rank, the smell more that of the butcher's shop—or a barbecue.[82]

➤ Almost perversely romantic in its celebration of a paradisal isolation, with rhapsodies on the casual heroic adventure, a naive-mythic voice combined with folk themes that put ordinary salt into the narrative but can sometimes soar as well (*hê perdika exepetasen, ho hierax tên edekhthe*, "the partridge flew out and the falcon caught her"): that is the Byzantine Greek *Digenid*.

➤ Balladic brio and stark fatalism, an engagingly adolescent quality in the poetry and especially in the rhymes, yet we know it to be a great, perhaps the greatest requiem for valor foundered, overwhelmed, and finally lost; surface is openly depicted and praised and subtlety is rare, and in its own rite of violence it has no identifiable father and some very odd sons: the unique *Chanson de Roland*.

➤ Another and even starker account of lost heroism: the old Russian poem of epic disaster, the *Slovo o polku Igoreve*. Its hard exoskeleton is formed of formula and trope, yet the affective atmosphere is of an almost hypnotic elegiac regret, and a kind of fine if futile defiance. Its periods roll like Slavic drums celebrating both marriage and death;[83] its condensed and even cryptic images blend the natural world with the human in striking and singing ways:

Prysnu more polunoschi,
idut' smortsi m'glyami,
Igorevi knyazyu Bog' put' kazhet'
iz' zemli Polovetskoi na zemlyu Ruskuyu,
k' otnyu zlatu stolu.

The wave rolls high on the midnight sea/pillars of mist arise
God shows the way to Prince Igor
From the Polovetsian land to the Russian
to his father's golden throne.[84]

➤ The magical realism of so many of the sagas, the magic woven and warped throughout the undecorated and sparsely conformed yet complicated stories, but especially contrasted in the showoffish mind and convoluted word-art of the warrior-skalds, fitting a phrase to a boasted and bloody deed. Who can forget the words old Njál did not speak when he wrapped himself, his wife, and their little grandson in a steer hide, and waited for the fire?

➤ Wit and wordplay and mind-play, ornate decoration and marvelous contriving mark the Old Irish *epos,* in which the *fili*'s great poetic art interferes in, interpenetrates, and dominates the tale. Here a ready phrase is *Ni anse,* "easy to say"—but of course it isn't easy to say, and only the poet's never forgotten skills make the old brag work. Battle and war are ever celebrated, and yet the *filid* knew what it all comes to in the end; utter hyperbole is followed by the coldest and starkest evidence. At a battle's close, "Pride and shame lay there side by side" *(Roboi úall 7 imnáire and leth for leth).*[85] And no cast of characters could ever be louder, brighter-hued cartoons of an old, pagan, violent Celtic glory.

➤ A real and pervasive sense of a deep-archaic mind transmitted, lively wonder tales from the old mountains but with a reverberant folk memory of the even older Scythian horseman's wide plain and wandering life in war; florient and unabashed anomaly, combined with a solid tragic-heroic vision. These are the Ossete tales, composed of the living green memory of their long-lost race of strange heroes, the irrepressible Narts.

➤ Finally, and first, the *Iliad.* Nearly everyone who truly experiences this epic will build his or her own theory of why, and how, the thing spreads its ever young and glorious appeal. Barbaric and splendid as Mykenean-worked gold, mastering us with the poignant master phrase, it breaks out of the familiar (even, by now, the cliché) to astound us with a flash of agonizingly sharp image and unbearable impress. The *Iliad* could never have a peer. We know that it was subtly and brilliantly cut from a larger body of epic, ballad, memory, yet still it retains an expansive verbal loquacity, especially in its long discurses, which are *not* representative of the "epic." And yet what a fabulous world it invents, and what power it weaves by splicing explosive brevity into its more meditated *mise-en-scène*. "Die, then!" ends a typical armed debate, with the bleak and bitter words pronounced by Akhilleus the ever victorious and self-doomed. Who cannot be caught and held in its net?

Each of these epical contexts contains and projects a significantly varied version of the heroic icon or type. Each has its own way of informing us about its hero or heroes, and of coloring, promoting, and, to some degree, even of explaining them. Each attracts us in its own way, with its own affect, and that affect reaches though the different masking mists of a different thoughtworld, through the perils of collection and translation and through the long tale of years. Each holds its hero in its own way. Each graphically proves that behind the *aitios* of the hero tale, the causes of the creation of the great icon lies the deadly attraction of the hero himself. *Caedo, ergo sum.* Perhaps we should be ashamed to find his image so appealing, to find death and death dealing so powerful a stimulus. Perhaps—but if we are honest, we will make that admission: there it is, and there we are. No artificial fantasy can dig deeper into, and more agonizingly use, our need to see some lesson drawn from the violence that is ever human, that surges so terribly in our humanity.

NOTES

ABBREVIATIONS

AIT *Ancient Irish Tales.* Edited by Tom Peete Cross and Clark H. Slover. 1936. Reprint, Totowa, N.J.: Barnes & Noble, 1969.

"BoH" "Bósa ok Herrauðr." Edited by G. Jónsson and B. Vilhjálmsson. Fornaldarsögur Norðulanda, vol. 2. Reykjavik: Bokantgafen Forni, 1944. Translated by H. Pálsson and P. Edwards in *Seven Viking Romances*, 195–277. Harmondsworth: Penguin, 1985

CMT *Cath Maige Tuired. The Second Nattle of Mag Tuired.* Edited and translated by Elizabeth A. Grey. Irish Text Society 52. Naas, 1982.

CO *Culhwch ac Olwen.* Edited by Rachel Bromwich and D. Simon Evans. Caerdydd: Gwasg Prifysgol Cymru; Cardiff: University of Wales Press, 1988. Edited and translated by P. K. Ford in *The Mabinogi and Other Medieval Welsh Tales*, 119–57. Berkeley: University of California Press, 1977.

DS *Sassowntsi David. David of Sassoon.* Translated by A. Shalian. Athens: Ohio University Press, 1964.

EG *Egil's Saga.* Translated by H. Pálsson and P. Edwards. Harmondsworth: Penguin, 1976.

EgS *Egils saga Skalla-Grímssonar.* Edited by Óskar Halldorsson. Íslensk Úrvalsrit í Skólaútgáfum. Reykjavik: IÐUNN, 1983.

EIMS *Early Irish Myths and Sagas.* Edited and translated by J. Gantz. Harmondsworth: Penguin, 1985.

"EoÁ" "Egill ok Ásmunðr." In *Egils saga einhenda ok Ásmunðr berserks-jabana*, 323–65. Edited by G. Jónsson. Fornaldarsögur Norðulanda 3. Reykjavik: Islendingasagnaútgafen, 1954. Translated by H. Pálsson and P. Edwards in *Gautrek's Saga and Other Medieval Tales*, 91–120. New York: New York University Press; London: University of London Press, 1968.

EyS *Eyrbyggja saga*. Edited by E. O. Sveinsson. Íslensk Fornrit 5. Reykjavik: Hið íslensk fornritafélag, 1934. Translated by H. Pálsson and P. Edwards. Toronto: University of Toronto Press, 1973.

GiS *Gísla saga Súrssonar*. Edited by. B. Þórólfsson. Íslensk Fornrit 6. Reykjavik: Hið íslensk fornritafélag, 1943. *Gisli's Saga*. Translated by G. Johnston. Toronto: University of Toronto Press, 1963.

GRO Grottaferrata manuscripts I–VIII.

GrS *Grettis saga Ásmunðarsonar*. Edited by G. Jónsson. Íslensk Fornrit 7. Reykjavik: Hið íslensk fornritafélag, 1936. *Grettir's Saga*. Translated by D. Fox and H. Pálsson. Toronto: University of Toronto Press, 1974.

GtS *Gautrekssaga*. Edited by G. Jónsson. Fornaldarsögur Norðulanda 3. Reykjavik: Bokantgafen Forni, 1950. Translated by H. Pálsson and P. Edwards in *Gautrek's Saga and Other Medieval Tales*, 23–55.

HsK *Hrólfs saga Kraka*. Edited by D. Slay. Editiones Arnamagnæanæ. Copenhagen: Einar Munksgaard, 1960.

JS *Jómsvíkingasaga*. Translated by N. F. Blake. Icelandic Texts. London: Thomas Nelson & Sons, 1962.

KS *Kormáks saga*. In *Vatnsdæla saga*. Edited by E. O. Sveinsson. Íslensk Fornrit 8. Reykjavik: Hið íslensk fornitafélag, 1939. Translated by L. M. Hollander in *The Saga of Kormák and the Sworn Brothers*. New York: Princeton University Press for the American Scandinavian Foundation, 1949.

Ldn *Landnámabók*. Edited by J. Benediktsson. Íslensk Fornrit 1. Reykjavik: Hið íslensk fornritafélag, 1969. Translated by H. Pálsson and P. Edwards. Winnepeg: University of Manitoba Press, 1972.

LjS *Ljósvitninga saga*. In Theodore M. Andersson and William I. Miller, *Law and Literature in Medieval Iceland: Ljósvitninga saga and Valla-Ljóts saga*. Stanford: Stanford University Press, 1969.

LPS *Vep'khistqaosani. The Lord of the Panther-Skin (by Shota Rustaveli). A Georgian Romance of Chivalry*. Translated by R. H. Stevenson. Albany, N.Y.: SUNY Press, 1977.

LxS   *Laxdæla saga.* Edited by. E. O. Sveinsson. Íslensk Fornrit 5. Reykjavik: Hið íslensk fornritafélag, 1934. Translated by M. Magnusson
and H. Pálsson. Harmondsworth: Penguin, 1978.

NjS   *Brennu-Njáls saga.* Edited by E. O. Sveinsson. Íslensk Fornrit 12.
Reykjavik: Hið íslensk fornritafélag, 1954. *Njal's Saga.* Translated by
M. Magnusson and H. Pálsson. Harmondsworth: Penguin, 1960.

SCHSI   *Serbo-Croat Heroic Songs.* I. *Novi Pazar: English Translations.* Collected by M. Parry, edited and translated by A. B. Lord. Cambridge,
Mass.: Harvard University Press; Belgrade: Serbian Academy of Sciences, 1954.

SCHS II   *Serbo-Croat Heroic Songs.* II. *Novi Pazar: Serbo-Croatian Texts.* Collected by M. Parry, edited and translated by A. B. Lord. Cambridge,
Mass.: Harvard University Press; Belgrade: Serbian Academy of Sciences, 1953.

SCHS III   *Serbo-Croatian Heroic Songs.* III. *The Wedding of Smailagić Meho.*
Translated by A. B. Lord. Publications of the Milman Parry Collection. Text and Translation Series 1. Cambridge, Mass: Harvard University Press, 1974.

TBDD   *Togail Bruidne Da Derga. The Destruction of Da Derga's Hostel.* Edited
by E. Knott. Medieval and Modern Irish Studies 7. Dublin, 1936.
Translated in *EIMS*, 60–106; in *AIT*, 93–126.

TDAG   *Tórnigheacht Dhiarmada agus Ghráine. The Pursuit of Diarmuid and
Grainne.* Edited and translated by Nessa Ní Shéaghda. Irish Text
Society 47. Dublin: Dublin University Press, 1967. Translated in
AIT, 370–421.

TI   Gottfried von Strassburg. *Tristan.* Edited by F. Ranke. In *Gottfried
von Strassburg: Tristan und Isolde.* Zurich: Weidman, 1967. Translated by A. T. Hatto in *Tristan of Gottfried von Strassburg.* Harmondsworth: Penguin, 1960.

TYP   *Trioedd Ynys Pryddein. The Welsh Triads.* Translation and commentary by Rachel Bromwich. Cardiff: University of Wales Press, 1961.

VölS   *Völsungasaga. The Saga of the Völsungs.* Translated and edited by
R. G. Finch. Icelandic Texts. London: Thomas Nelson, 1965.

INTRODUCTION: THE BOOK OF THE HERO

1. An article by Spyros Vryonis gave me important information on the
reputed origins of Byzantine aristocratic families of the tenth century. East Rome,
as is not often the case, could actually show a military aristocracy coming into historical being and then remythizing its past: see S. Vryonis, "Byzantium: The Social

Basis of Decline in the Eleventh Century," *Greek, Roman and Byzantine Studies* 2, no. 2 (1959): 161–68.

2. That is, beyond the "core" to heroic (or "heroic") tribal societies of the Caucasus, the Finno-Lappish zone to the northeast of Europe, and in a certain number of cases to nomadic Central Asia, though I have arbitrarily taken particularly useful instances from heroic sources originating outside this focal zone and its extensions.

3. The most useful introduction to Dumézil's work in English remains C. Scott Littleton's *The New Comparative Mythology: Anthropological Assessment of the Theories of Georges Dumézil*, 3d ed. (Berkeley: University of California Press, 1982), though we now have Wouter Belier's *Decayed Gods: Origin and Development of Georges Dumézil's "Idéologie Tripartie"* (Leiden: E. J. Brill, 1991), a cool, rather dry, well-organized, but at base tone-deaf study of Dumézil's theories. Bernard Sergent's *Les Indo-Européens. Histoire, langues, mythes* (Paris: Payot, 1995) puts forward a view more respectful of Dumézil's work. Didier Eribon's recent *Faut-il brûler Dumézil? Mythologie, science et politique* (Paris: Flammarion, 1992) is especially important because it thoroughly, precisely, and devastatingly counters most of the grotesque and, I must say, dishonest attempts made in recent years to condemn Dumézil's scholarship *tout à fait*, as diminished by his supposed fascistophilic and even pro-Nazi inclinations.

4. Eribon, *Faut-il brûler Dumézil?*, 224.

5. Some also appeared, in truncated form, in German in Adolf Dirr, *Kaukasische Märchen* (Jena: E. Diderichs, 1920), trans. L. Menzies as *Caucasian Folktales: Selected and Translated from the Original by Adolf Dirr* (New York: Dutton, 1925).

6. Brendan Gill, *Here at the New Yorker* (New York: Da Capo, 1997), 384.

7. The curious and the suspicious may find a translation of Skalla-Grímr's words in chap. 25 of *Egils saga*, in *ES*, p. 67.

CHAPTER 1: THE HERO FROM ON HIGH

1. Cited in Daniel Madelénat, *L'épopée* (Paris: Presses Universitaires de France, 1986), 53, n. 6. Madelénat believes that the "sens épique" of the word was already much reduced: "le héros d'un roman n'est souvent que le mediocre protagoniste d'une histoire sans grandeurs."

2. James Thurber, "The Greatest Man in the World," in *The Middle-Aged Man in the Flying Machine* (New York: Harper & Bros., 1935). The president of the United States, among other horrified notables, conspires to have this unfortunate tipped out a skyscraper window, so as to maintain his "heroic" image. For Lindbergh's peculiar and permanent appeal, see Modris Eksteins, *Rites of Spring: The Great War and the Birth of the Modern Age* (Boston: Houghton Mifflin, 1989), 242ff.

3. Michael Foucault, *Folie et déraison. Histoire de la folie á l'âge classique* (Paris: Plon, 1961); trans. R. Howard as *Madness and Civilization: A History of Insanity in the Age of Reason* (New York: Pantheon, 1965).

4. J. E. Fontenrose, *The Ritual Theory of Myth* (Berkeley: University of Cali-

fornia Press, 1966), 40. He further notes that the individual supernatural being is contrasted with the ancestral dead of a family, or with the *Manes,* beings worshiped in public as "the dead in general" (46).

5. K. R. Bradley, *Slavery and Rebellion in the Roman World: 140B.C.–70B.C.* (Bloomington: Indiana University Press; London: B. T. Botsford, 1989), 40, and n. 34, citing Athenaeus.

6. Pausanias, IX.xxxviii.5. The edition used is Pausanias, *Periêgêsis,* trans. W. H. S. Jones, Loeb Classical Library (Cambridge, Mass.: Harvard University Press; London: Heinemann, 1979).

7. Gregory Nagy, *The Best of the Achaeans: Concepts of the Hero in Archaic Greek Poetry* (Baltimore: Johns Hopkins University Press, 1981).

8. See A. M. Snodgrass, *The Dark Age of Greece: An Archaeological Survey from the Eleventh to the Eighth Centuries* (Edinburgh: University of Edinburgh Press, 1971).

9. A. M. Snodgrass, "Les origines du culte des héros dans la Grèce antique," in *La mort, les morts dans les sociétés anciennes,* ed. G. Gnoli and J.-P. Vernant (Cambridge: Cambridge University Press; Paris: Editions de la Maison des Sciences de l'Homme, 1982): 107–19.

10. J.-P. Vernant, "La belle mort et le cadavre outragé," in Gnoli and Vernant, *La mort, les morts,* especially 53ff.; see also D. A. Miller, "Indo-European 'Bad Death' and Trifunctional Revenants," *Incognita* 1, no. 2 (1990): 143–82.

11. C. Berard, "Récuperer la mort du prince: Héroisation et formation de la cité," 89–105, and Nicole Loraux, "Mourir devant Troie, tomber pour Athènes: De la gloire du héros à l'idée de la cité," 27–43, both in Gnoli and Vernant, *La mort, les morts.*

12. K. Kerényi, *The Heroes of the Greeks,* trans. H. J. Rose (New York: Thames & Hudson, 1978), 128–206.

13. J.-P. Vernant, "The Historical Moment of Tragedy in Greece. Some of the Social and Psychological Conditions," in J.-P. Vernant and P. Vidal-Naquet, *Myth and Tragedy in Ancient Greece,* trans. J. Lloyd (New York: Zone, 1988), 25.

14. Aristotle, *Poetics,* 1449b.28.

15. J.-P. Vernant, "Tensions and Ambiguities in Greek Tragedy," in Vernant and Vidal-Naquet, *Myth and Tragedy,* 33. Vernant quotes Wilhelm Nestle's statement that tragedy is born "when myth starts to be considered from the point of view of a citizen." In Nestle, *Vom mythos zum Logos,* 2d ed. (Stuttgart: Kromer, 1942). For the Greek sense of the separation of the heroic from the quotidian time frame see C. W. Fornara, *The Nature of History in Ancient Greece and Rome* (Berkeley: University of California Press, 1988), 4–10.

16. Vernant, "Tensions and Ambiguities," 33.

17. Ibid., 38.

18. Madelénat, *L'épopée,* 124–25.

19. The masking or self-disguising of the trickster-hero belongs to another category of our type; see chapter 5.

20. Charles Segal, *Dionysiac Poetics and Euripides' Bacchae* (Princeton: Prince-

ton University Press, 1982), also J.-P. Vernant, "The Masked Dionysus of Euripides' *Bacchae*," in Vernant and Vidal-Naquet, *Myth and Tragedy*, 381–412.

21. Vernant, "Historical Moment," 25, and "The God of Tragic Fiction," 186, both in Vernant and Vidal-Naquet, *Myth and Tragedy*.

22. As in *Aen.* X.312–13, when Aeneas killed the Rutilian Theron, *virum qui maximus ultro Aenean petit;* Fitzgerald, catching the nuance precisely, translates this as "the giant Theron who left ranks to encounter him" (304). The individual encounter, which is the norm and rule in the *Iliad*, is not at all to Virgil's Roman taste, since it obviously violates proper military discipline. For the text and translation, see *Aeneid*, in *Vergili Opera*, ed. R. A. B. Mynors, Scriptorum Classicorum Biblioteca Oxoniensis (Oxford: Clarendon, 1976), and *The Aeneid/Virgil*, trans. Robert Fitzgerald (New York: Random House, 1983).

23. R. Janin, *Constantinople byzantine: Développement urbaine et répertoire topographique*, 2d ed. (Paris: Institut Français d'Etudes Byzantines, 1964), 73. A crude fifteenth-century sketch of this statue is put as frontispiece in the Loeb Classical Library edition of Procopius of Caesarea's *Peri ktismatôn = On Buildings*, trans. by H. B. Dewing (Cambridge, Mass.: Harvard University Press; London: Wm. Heinemann, 1954). For some of the extraordinary transformations and reeditions of the story of this greatest of Homeric heroes, see Katherine Cullen King, *Achilles: Paradigms of the War Hero from Homer to the Middle Ages* (Berkeley: University of California Press, 1987).

24. Justinian himself tried to regain parts of the Latin-speaking ex-imperial possessions, and reigned "on the cusp" between the period when Latin and Greek traditions coexisted in East Rome and the period when Greek language and culture regained a complete hegemony there.

25. K. Krumbacher, *Geschichte des byzantinischen Literatur (527–1453)*, 2d ed., in *Handbuch d. klass. Altertums-Wissenschaft*, ed. I. von Muller, vol. ix, i (Munich, 1897); also, more recently, N. G. Wilson, *Scholars of Byzantium* (Baltimore: Johns Hopkins University Press, 1983).

26. Dante, *Inferno*, Italian text with English translation by J. D. Sinclair (New York: Oxford University Press, 1964). For Rome and Troy, see N. O. Brown, "Rome: A Psychoanalytic Study," *Arethusa* 3, no. 1 (Spring 1974): 95–101.

27. The confrontational nexus of the Persian *Shâh-nâma* pits two races against one another, the Persian against the Turk, that is, Iran against Turan.

28. See, e.g., G. Goetinck, *Peredur: A Study of Welsh Tradition in the Grail Legends* (Cardiff: University of Wales Press, 1975), and P. Matarasso, *The Redemption of Chivalry: A Study of the Queste del Sant Graal*, Histoire des Idées et Critique Litteraire, vol. 180 (Geneva: Droz, 1979).

29. Specifically the greatest, Cú Chulainn, but also King Conchobar mac Nessa: see *The Phantom Chariot of Cú Chulainn*, in *AIT*, 347–54; from J. O'Beirne Crowe, "Siabur-charpat Con Culiand," *Journal of the Royal Historical and Archaeological Association of Ireland*, 4th ser., 1 (Dublin, 1871): 371–448.

30. J. Grisward, *L'archéologie de l'épopée médiévale: structures trifonctionelles et mythes indo-européennes dans le Cycle des Narbonnais* (Paris: Payot, 1981), 137ff.

31. Julia Kristeva, *Desire in Langauge: A Semiotic Approach to Literature and*

Art, ed. L. S. Roudiez, trans. T. Gora, A. Jardine, and L. S. Roudiez (New York: Columbia University Press, 1980).

32. This theme will be touched on below, when the sexual aspect of the hero is investigated.

33. Though members of the opposition were called Cavaliers, we are told that the chivalric idea influenced even John Bunyan (!) and others of the Parliamentary Puritan persuasion, being identified as a reflex of "godly warfare": see William Hunt, "Civic Chivalry and the English Civil War," in *The Transmission of Culture in Early Modern Europe*, ed. A. Grafton and A. Blair, S. C. Davis Center Publications, Princeton University (Philadelphia: University of Pennsylvania Press, 1990), 206–13.

34. My focus is restricted to Europe, though parallels are certainly apparent in the law or "code" of the baronage (the *kšatriya*, or warrior caste) in the *Mahâbhârata*, or the norms demanded for "knightly" behavior as seen in the Persian or Caucasian hero-narratives.

35. See G. Kipling, *The Triumph of Honour: Burgundian Origins of the Elizabethan Renaissance* (Leiden: Leiden University Press, 1977); M. G. A. Vale, *War and Chivalry: Warfare and Aristocratic Culture in England, France and Burgundy at the End of the Middle Ages* (London: Duckworth, 1981).

36. The text used in this study will be *The Epic of the Kings: Shâh-nâma, the National Epic of Persia, by Ferdowsi*, trans. R. Levy, rev. A. Banani (London: Routledge & Kegan Paul, 1985). Rustaveli's Georgian *Vep'khistqaosani*, which is heavily Persified, is not so much a national epic (it contains no theme of heroism in defense of this ethnos) as an Orientalized, knightly *jeu d'esprit*; see *LPS*.

37. Kristeva, *Desire in Language*, 49.

38. Bernal Diaz del Castillo, *Istoria verdadera de la conquista de la Nueva España*, dir. M. Artigas (Mexico City: Perrua, 1955), I.xx, e.g. For the hero and booty, see the career of Egill Skalla-Grímsson, below.

39. Ibid., II.xxxix; VI.lxxxiv; VII.lxxxvii.

40. Ibid., VI.lxxxii. Velasquez was killed on the *noche triste*, 30 June 1520, when Cortés's army had to retreat from the Aztec capital, Tenochtitlán.

41. Cited in Martín Menéndez y Pelayo, *Orígenes de la Novela*, in *Edición Nacional de las Obras Completas de Menéndez y Pelayo* (Madrid: G.S.I.C., 1943), 1:370, n. 71.

42. D. Quint, "Epic and Empire," *Comparative Literature* 41, no. 1 (Winter 1989): 5–13.

43. Luis de Camoes, *Os Lusiadas = The Lusiad*, ed. F. Pierce (Oxford: Clarendon Press, 1973), 2.49–55, especially 53–54; Quint, "Epic and Empire," 13.

44. Quint, "Epic and Empire," 11–12, 16ff.

45. D. Quint, "The Boat of Romance and Renaissance Epic," in *Romance: Generic Transformation from Chrétien de Troyes to Cervantes*, ed. K. Brownlee and M. S. Brownlee (Hanover, N.H.: University Press of New England, 1985), 182–83; Quint, "Epic and Empire," 25.

46. For Milton to take Europe's conquests as a sign of an allegiance to Mammon is perhaps understandable, as he would also have no truck with any victory of

the true faith won by papists. The matter of the winning of material wealth must be handled in a gingerly fashion even by proponents of "imperial epic" behavior; Quint ("Boat of Romance," 186–91) recalls that the hero-imitating *caballeros* (or *cavalheiros*) denigrated trade as such; booty was one thing, profit another. A proper hero would never be a "fortune hunter" (!) and Camoes, for instance, must therefore play down the mercantile aspect of "discovery" (ibid., 187).

47. In Wagner we are looking at stylized but powerfully expressed emotions, *sensations fortes*, themes of death and glory—all apart from the actual borrowing of a framework of heroic epos.

48. Georg Lukács, *The Historical Novel*, trans. H. Mitchell and S. Mitchell (London: Merlin, 1982), 19–30.

49. Thomas Carlyle, *On Heroes, Hero-Worship and the Heroic in History* (London: Oxford University Press, 1968), 7.

50. S. Hook, *The Hero in History: A Study in Limitation and Possibility* (Boston: Beacon, 1955).

51. As Udo Strutynski is demonstrating in a book still in process, the Wagnerian superdramatization of a Twilight of the Gods repeats an old but persistent distortion of Germanic myth. Following an Indo-European pattern, the disintegration of one divine-cosmic structure would be followed by a new creative reconstruction: a *cyclic* movement is most likely.

52. R. LeBrun, *Joseph de Maistre: An Intellectual Militant* (Montreal: McGill-Queen's University Press, 1988); also C. M. Lombard, *Joseph de Maistre* (Boston: Twayne, 1976), and see now Isaiah Berlin, "Joseph de Maistre and the Origins of Fascism," in *The Crooked Timber of Humanity: Chapters in the History of Ideas* (New York: Alfred Knopf, 1991), 91–174, where Berlin sets de Maistre down not as a leftover feudalophile or neomedieval obscurantist, but as born before and not after his time, a genuine protofascist.

53. Temporal distance is also built into the Byronic romance inventions; his Advertisement to *The Giaour* sets the story in an "earlier time," and temporal detachment is implicit in *The Corsair* as well.

54. See D. Skiotis, "The Nature of the Modern Greek Nation: The Romaic Strand," in *"The Past" in Medieval and Modern Greek Culture*, ed. S. Vryonis, *Byzantina kai Metabyzantina*, vol. 1 (Malibu, Calif.: Undena, 1978): 155–62; John Th. Kakridis, "The Ancient Greeks and the Greeks of the War of Independence," *Balkan Studies* 4 (1963): 258–59.

55. See Skiotis's specific reference to the guerrilla chief Makriyannis; "The Nature of the Modern Greek Nation," 161.

56. A. Politis, *To demotiko tragoudi—Klephtika* (Athens: Themelio, 1981).

57. Two of the best-known, though quite different examples of Mexican popular-revolutionary leadership, Emiliano Zapata and Francisco (Pancho) Villa, were eventually and probably inevitably eaten by the new order they helped to create, Zapata in 1919, Villa in 1923. Villa (*né* Doroteo Arango) had an acknowledged bandit past. For Zapata, see J. Womack, *Zapata and the Mexican Revolution* (New York: Vintage, 1970). For the *serrano* and related phenomena in the Mexican Revolution, I can but digest a small segment of Alan Knight's massive (twelve hun-

dred pages in two volumes) but exceptionally delicate and precise dissection of this series of events, the parties and the players: Knight, *The Mexican Revolution*, 2 vols. (Lincoln: University of Nebraska Press, 1986). Both Zapata and Villa attained heroic and even mythic status through assassination, especially Zapata, the *agrarista* hero of Morelos.

58. For the *corrido*—a relatively modern verse form—see Vicente T. Mendoza, *El corrido mexicano* (Mexico: Gráfica Pan-Americana, 1954), and Merle E. Simmons, *The Mexican CORRIDO as a Source for Interpretative Study of Modern Mexico (1870–1950)* (Bloomington: Indiana University Press, 1957); for an analysis of a "border" *corrido* with a fascinating mix of verifiable history, mythicized character, and imaginative folklore, see Américo Paredes, *"With His Pistol in His Hand": A Border Ballad and Its Hero* (Austin: University of Texas Press, 1973).

59. E. Hobsbawm, *Bandits,* rev. ed. (New York: Pantheon, 1981), 17–29. The case of Jesse James is instructive. Novelistic and especially cinematic images of the Western outlaw, reflecting a majority (if not a "high") cultural attitude, until fairly recently demanded a *moral* resolution in its working up of heroic legend (as a cliché, the black hat/white hat differentiation and opposition). This is certainly foreign and anachronistic in respect to the older or original epic hero context.

60. The North American balladic support for these social bandits is probably best summed up in the social-satirical line "I've never known an outlaw / Drive a farmer from his home," contrasting the essential *gemeinschaftlich* morality of the so-called criminal with the unfeeling carelessness of the "system" personified in the rapacious banker: Woody Guthrie, "The Ballad of Pretty-Boy Floyd." Emotional if not social symmetry is reestablished when the banker is himself made a victim of the "social bandit."

For another analytic aspect of the phenomenon of the outlaw, one deriving from Orlando Patterson's concept of "social death," see Hans-Peter Hasenfratz, *Die Toten Lebenden: Eine religionsphanomenologische Studie zum sozialen Tod in archaischen Gesellschaft: Zugleich ein kritischer Beitrag zur sogenannten Strafopfertheorie.* Zeitschrift für Religions- und Geistesgeschichte (Leiden: E. J. Brill, 1982).

61. Karl Marx, *The German Ideology,* "On Feuerbach," essay 3, ed. R. Pascal (New York: International Publishers, 1947), 71–72, 76.

62. Mikhail Lermontov, *A Hero of Our Time,* trans. by V. Nabokov and D. Nabokov (Garden City, N.Y.: Doubleday, 1958); I cite the Russian text *Geroe nashego vremeni,* ed. D. Shamova (Moskva: Detlit, 1957).

63. Grushnitski could not "know" other people "because all his life he had been occupied with himself alone" (*potamu chto zanimalsya tselnyu zhizn' odnim sobayu*: Lermontov, *Geroe,* 90; Lermontov, *Hero,* 85). He also wanted to be "the hero of a novel" but was probably a coward.

64. Lermontov, *Geroe,* 169–70; Lermontov, *Hero,* 185–86.

65. "Deepest melancholy" (*globokoy grusti*): Lermontov, *Geroe,* 65; Lermontov, *Hero,* 57; living "out of curiosity" (*iz lyubopystva*): Lermontov, *Geroe,* 148; Lermontov, *Hero,* 158. Pechorin's soliloquy following these pages outlines the fatalism that will be the theme of the last part of his journal.

66. For nature, see the first pages of "Bela," (Lermontov, *Geroe,* 23–24; Ler-

montov, *Hero,* 3); for the Chechen *dzigit,* see, e.g., Baron von Haxthausen, *The Tribes of the Caucasus* (London: 1835), and now L. Branch, *The Sabres of Paradise* (New York: Carroll & Graf, 1984), 48–50.

67. A. Lord, *The Singer of Tales* (New York: Athenaeum, 1968).

68. P. Sébillot, *Le folk-lore de France,* 5 vols., Librairie Orientale et Américaine (Paris: E. Guilmote, 1904–7). Folklore is a broader category than folktale, but certainly may (in the form of local traditions, songs, sayings, or other folk productions) contain evidence on the hero.

69. Antti Aarne, *Verzeichnis der Märchentypen,* FFCommunications, no. 3 (Helsinki, 1910), revised by Stith Thompson and published as *The Types of the Folk-Tale,* FFCommunications, no. 74 (Helsinki, 1928) and usually referred to as Aarne-Thompson. In Thompson's own *Motif-Index of Folk Literature: A Classification of Narrative Elements in Folktales, Ballads, Myths, Fables, Medieval Romances, Exempla, Fabliaux, Jest-Books and Local Legends,* 6 vols. (Bloomington: Indiana University Press, 1955–57), see introduction (9–27) and biography and abbreviations (37–58) for a summary of work in the folktale to that date.

70. See Franz H. Baüml and Edda Spielmann, "From Illiteracy to Literacy: Prolegomena to a Study of the *Nibelungenlied,*" in *Oral Literature: Seven Essays,* ed. J. J. Duggan (New York: Barnes & Noble, 1975), 62–73.

71. These manuscripts were still being brought to light as late as the early part of the nineteenth century: a manuscript of the "barbarous" *Nibelungenlied* was discovered in 1784; *Kudrun,* in the same cycle, in 1830: see Jan de Vries, *Heroic Song and Heroic Legend,* trans. B. J. Timmer, Mythology Series (Salem, N.H.: Ayer, 1988), 61.

72. To take an example from another literary genre, Anglophone readers of Dostoievsky often depend on the Constance Garnett translations, and our view of this artist has long been conditioned by her harsh, jagged, "neurotic" prose (she also was not completely competent in the Russian language, though she had a great enthusiasm for it); the style she created was not in fact Dostoievsky's true style, as one may see in Sidney Monas's translation of *Crime and Punishment* (New York: New American Library, 1968), where the text is smoother, even sophisticated in its flow, and certainly very much closer to the Russian original.

73. Of the epical and other evidence dealt with below, we can safely assume that when a single author-creator is identified, he (like Shota Rustaveli in the case of the Georgian *Vep'khistqaosani*) based his creation on an inheritance of traditional materials. Such a dependence is acknowledged in Ferdausi's *Shâh-nâma:* see Wm. L. Hanaway, "The Iranian Epics," in *Heroic Epic and Saga: An Introduction to the World's Great Folk Epics,* ed. Felix Oinas (Bloomington: Indiana University Press, 1978), 76–77. Virgil and his *Aeneid* make a slightly different case.

74. See Ward Parks, "Orality and Poetics: Synchrony, Diachrony and the Axes of Narrative Transmission," in *Comparative Research on Oral Traditions: A Memorial for Milman Parry,* ed. John Miles Foley (Columbus, Ohio: Slavica Publishers, 1987), 511ff.

75. Another earlier audience may be made up of learned, urban and in some sense bourgeois scholars, such as those who as self-identified Ancients supported

the rediscovered canons of Aristotle's *Poetics* in the early sixteenthth century, as these canons pertained to unity in narrative (present in the epic, absent in the "romance"); see R. Cohen, "Afterword: The Problem of Generic Transformation," in Brownlee and Brownlee, *Romance*, 265–80.

76. "The true epic poet," writes Jan de Vries, "believes in his heroes, especially in the ideal which they represent." See de Vries, *Heroic Song and Heroic Legend*, 52–55.

77. In particular the late Henri Grégoire; see *Autour de l'épopée byzantine* (London: Variorum, 1975).

78. Madelénat, *L'épopée*, 135, 137–48.

79. Ibid., 143.

80. Dumézil's theory of the persistence of Indo-European mythographic patterns, such as the motif of interfunctional war, is given resonance, I am convinced, in the *Ur*-epos that underlies the confrontation used by Aeschylus in the *Seven against Thebes:* see D. A. Miller, "In Search of Indo-European Interfunctional War," in *Studies in Honor of Jaan Puhvel*, vol. 2, *Mythology and Religion*, ed. J. Greppin and E. Polomé, *JI-ES* Monograph Series, 21 (1997): 202–24. Much is changed in Aeschylus's tragedy, and the "interfunctional war" is more clearly established in the account of the *Seven* contained in Apollodorus, where much more archaic arrangements are visible; see the *Bibliothêkê*, trans. J. G. Frazer, Loeb Classical Library (Cambridge, Mass.: Harvard University Press; London: Heinemann, 1976), III.iv.1–vii.6.

81. F. Oinas, "Folk-Epic," in *Folklore and Folklife: An Introduction*, ed. R. Dorson (Chicago: University of Chicago Press, 1972).

82. See Baüml and Spielmann, "From Illiteracy to Literacy"; and for a modern (however archaic) reflex, note the confusion in historical reality contained in the Serbo-Croat heroic songs collected by Parry and Lord: see *SCHS* III, 13ff.

83. Madelénat, *L'épopée*, 139–48. Paul Zumthor also identifies the recently discovered and translated Philippine *Ulahingan* (an epic of the Manobo, non-Moslem indigenes of Mindanao) as a myth-epic. Zumthor, *Introduction à la poésie orale* (Paris: Editions du Seuil, 1983), 112–13; and *Ulahingan: An Epic of the Southern Philippines*, ed. and trans. E. Maquiso (Dumanguete City: Silliman University Press, 1977).

84. Zumthor, *Introduction*, 111; for C. M. Bowra, see *Heroic Poetry*, 2d ed. (New York: Macmillan, 1972), 29–30, 70–78. Zumthor (107) describes and criticizes Bowra's theory of the development of the epic as over-"genealogical," deriving from Bowra's use of the scheme of the Chadwicks' *The Growth of Literature;* the "shamanist" type in this reading is *anterior* to the "historic" epic out of which, in theory, the latter grows. Cf. N. K. Chadwick and H. M. Chadwick, *The Growth of Literature*, 3 vols. (Cambridge: Cambridge University Press, 1932–40).

85. Oinas, "Folk-Epic," 100.

86. The text translation used hereafter will be *Kalevala = The Old Kalevala and Certain Antecedents*, comp. E. Lönnrot, trans. F. P. Magoune Jr. (Cambridge, Mass.: Harvard University Press, 1969).

87. See now Juha Y. Pentikainen, *Kalevala Mythology*, trans. and ed. R. Poom

(Bloomington: Indiana University Press, 1989). The territory that gave birth to the *Kalevala* itself occupies a position between the Scandinavian-Icelandic zone and the Slavo-Russian, and how these three epical zones influenced one another is not at all clear.

88. Madelénat, *L'épopée,* 159: the Homeric hero "surpasses the gods in moral dignity."

89. Or in the case of the *Táin,* great and perilous queens, laden with pride and sexual energy, like Medb.

90. See J. Nagy, *The Wisdom of the Outlaw: The Boyhood Deeds of Finn in Gaelic Narrative Tradition* (Berkeley: University of California Press, 1985), 37, and s.v. *síd, síde.*

91. Jan de Vries, *La religion des Celtes,* trans. L. Jospin (Paris: Payot, 1984), from *Keltische Religion* (Stuttgart: Kohlhammer, 1970).

In one of the Norse saga subtypes, the *fornaldar sögur* or sagas of far-off times, we will also find that the gods (usually Óðínn) can make an occasional appearance: Óðínn and Þórr in *Gautreksaga* (VII); Óðínn, more or less disguised, in *Völsungasaga* (X) and in Saxo Grammaticus's version of the tale of Hadingus: *Gesta Danorum = History of the Danes,* trans. P. Fisher, ed. H. R. Ellis Davidson (Totowa, N.J.: D. S. Brewer; Cambridge: Rowman & Littlefield, 1979), I.20ff. The latter two cases show Óðínn specifically as god of the dead: see H. R. Ellis Davidson, *The Road to Hel: A Study of the Conception of the Dead in Old Norse Literature* (Westport, Conn.: Greenwood, 1977), 174ff. The strong impression in this kind of saga is of a fragmentary reminiscence of that time when the gods were more familiar to mankind; a widely distributed notion in terms of a reading of the "past."

92. Madelénat, *L'épopée,* 171; the chronicle is that of Einhard, *Vita Caroli Magni = Einhard's Life of Charlemagne,* ed. H. W. S. Garrod and R. B. Mowat (Oxford: Oxford University Press, 1915), II.9.

93. Oinas, "Folk-Epic," 103. An older epic such as the (Old Russian) *Slovo o polke Igoreve,* plotting a disaster similar to what occurred in the *Chanson de Roland,* evidently does not fall within Oinas's folk-epic rubric.

94. Madelénat, *L'épopée,* 161.

95. For an examination of the composite hero tale and wonder tale, see Gwyn Jones, *Kings, Beasts and Heroes* (London: Oxford University Press, 1977), 123ff.

96. Jessie Crosland, *The Old French Epic* (Oxford: Oxford University Press, 1951), 17. William Calin, *A Muse for Heroes: Nine Centuries of the Epic in France* (Toronto: University of Toronto Press, 1983), 57–82, separates out *Huon de Bordeaux* and its lineal descendants as not fitting easily into any one of the three traditional *chanson* cycles.

97. Crosland, *Old French Epic,* 215.

98. See William C. Calin, *The Old French Epic of Revolt: Raoul of Cambrai, Renaud de Montauban, Gormond et Isembard* (Geneva: Droz; Paris: Minard, 1962).

99. Note that Crosland assigns *Gormond et Isembard* to no category, because Isembard is sympathetic though a *margariz* (*Old French Epic,* 190–91), whereas Calin has no difficulty in putting this poem in the "rebel" category (*Epic of Revolt,* 101).

100. Calin, *Epic of Revolt*, 111.

101. Peggy Schine Gold, *The Lady and the Virgin: Image, Attitude and Experience in Twelfth-Century France* (Chicago: University of Chicago Press), 18ff., 24, 37–42.

102. Madelénat, *L'épopée*, 162. In *Isenbard et Gornmond* a Viking invasion and the battle (Cayeux) that stopped it are Saracenized (as was the actual Basque enemy at the historical Roncevaux): see Calin, *Epic of Revolt*, 48ff.

103. One example: according to Gregory of Tours, the Geatish king Hygelac was killed by the Franks; see *Historia libri decem*, iii, 3, in A.D. 521.

104. Zumthor, *Introduction*, 111; yet "no epic is totally without an historical ingredient" (112).

105. De Vries, *Heroic Song and Heroic Legend*, 64. We might add Hagen, as a reflection of an archaic-mythic type: see chapter 5, for the "Red Knight."

106. See D. A. Miller, "The Twinning of Arthur and Cei: An Arthurian Tessera," *JI-ES* 17, nos.1–2 (Spring–Summer 1989): 47–76.

107. For the text see *JS*.

108. A distant parallel to this theme is visible in the Old Russian *Slovo o polku Igoreve* where Prince Igor survives the slaughter of his host by the Polovtsi and—like Vagn—weds a daughter of the enemy.

109. See D. A. Miller, "Functional Operations and Oppositions in the Thought-World of the Sagas," *History of Religions* 29, no. 2 (November 1989): 115–58.

110. As in de Vries, *Heroic Song and Heroic Legend*, chap. 10, "The Historical Background of Heroic Legend," 194–209.

111. Most recently, see J. P. Mallory, *In Search of the Indo-Europeans: Language, Archaeology and Myth* (London: Thames & Hudson, 1991), and most idiosyncratically, Colin Renfrew, *Archaeology and Language: The Puzzle of Indo-European Origins* (New York: Columbia University Press, 1988). For Mallory's comments on Renfrew, see *Search*, 166–68.

112. H. M. Chadwick, *The Heroic Age* (Cambridge: Cambridge University Press, 1912), 439, 448. To illustrate the latter circumstance, he cites Teutonic, Ser(b)ian, and Welsh Cumbrian heroic literatures. He could not yet, in 1912, make the same case for the Homeric Achaeans.

113. Ibid., 442–43, 461.

114. Ibid., 440.

115. C. M. Bowra, "The Meaning of a Heroic Age," Earl Grey Memorial Lecture, 1957, in his *In General and Particular* (London: Weldenfeld & Nicolson, 1964), 63–84.

116. Ibid., 64. Bowra wrote after two World Wars and every sort of violence had perturbed the century; one might say that he had been sensitized to violence, if not to heroic violence.

117. Ibid., 67.

118. Ibid.

119. Ibid., 70. This is the most opaque of Bowra's observations.

120. Ibid., 71.

121. Ibid., 75; for Marko see below, p.73ff. The emotional ambience of the old

Russian *Slovo o polku Igoreve,* while marked by expressions of doom and disaster, does not quite fit this mode. The motif of doom and defiance in the last part of the *Nibelungenlied* or in *The Battle of Maldon* is also discrete from what I perceive to be Bowra's category.

122. William Sayers is of the opinion that in a saga like Grettir's, part of the tension and pathos results from a consciousness of "old heroism," of a mode of heroic behavior now outmoded (personal communication). Note also Peter Hallberg's remarks on the "heroized" stylization of violence in pagan Iceland undertaken in the later Sturlung period: *The Icelandic Saga,* trans. P Schach (Lincoln: University of Nebraska Press, 1962), 28–29.

123. Tacitus, *Germania,* xiv.

124. See below, p. 345ff.

125. Bowra, "Heroic Age," 75.

126. Ibid., 77.

127. In fact Frye uses the naive/sentimental categories, but to distinguish the folktale or *Märchen*-type of romance (naive) from the sentimental read as the "extended and literary development of the formulas of naive romance"; in Northrop Frye, "The Word and World of Man," in *The Secular Scripture: A Study of the Structure of Romance* (Cambridge, Mass.: Harvard University Press, 1976), 3.

128. See Marshall McLuhan, *Understanding Media: The Extensions of Man* (New York: McGraw-Hill, 1964), especially chap. 2: "Media Hot and Cold." "A Hot medium is one that extends one single sense in 'high definition.' High definition is the state of being well filled with data" (22); "speech is a Cool medium of low definition, because so little is given and so much has to be filled in by the listener" (23).

129. M. M. Bakhtin, "Epic and Novel," in *The Dialogic Imagination: Four Essays,* trans. C. Emerson and M. Holquist, ed. M. Holquist (Austin: University of Texas Press, 1981), 14, 15, 16, 30. Translated from Bakhtin's *Voprosy literatury i estetiki* (Moskva: Khudozh. Lit., 1975).

130. Madelénat, *L'épopée,* 128. The relationship is stated as this type "rappellant la fantasie du conte ou annoncent la nonchalance anomique du roman."

131. For Aristotle's *Poetics,* Ariosto, and the Italian combat between the schools, see Quint, "Epic and Empire," 7. For the old *Querelle,* see Hans Baron, "The *Querelle* of Ancients and Moderns as a Problem for Renaissance Scholarship," *Journal of the History of Ideas* 20, no. 1 (January 1959): 3–22; also, exhaustively, H. Gillot, *La querelle des anciens et des modernes en France* (Paris, 1914). For the deep background to this controversy, see Adolf Buch, "Aus der Vorgeschichte der *Querelle* des anciens et des moderns in Mittelalter und Renaissance," *Bibliothèque d'Humanisme et Renaissance* 17 (September 1958): 17–38.

132. See Baron, "The *Querelle*," 5–6.

133. Frye, *Secular Scripture,* 4. So Sir Walter Scott, in the nineteenth century, exposes and uses plots that would have been familar to the Greek "romancers" of the Hellenistic or late antique period. Not everyone agrees with this view: see the introduction (by the editors) in Brownlee and Brownlee, *Romance,* 3ff.

134. See Erwin Rohde, *Die griechische Roman und seine Vorlaüfer* (1876; reprint,

Hildesheim: G. Olms, 1960); Ben Perry, *The Ancient Romances: A Literary-Historical Account of Their Origins* (Berkeley: University of California Press, 1967); Arthur R. Heiserman, *The Novel before the Novel: Essays and Discussions about the Beginnings of Prose Fiction in the West* (Chicago: University of Chicago Press, 1977).

135. At least laughter kills "epic distance"; Bakhtin, "Epic and Novel," 35. The problem of laughter in the epic needs more work, and this may be one of this critic's overstretched *dicta*. Laughter is not absent, as we know, from the *Iliad*, though the "unquenchable laughter" (*asbestos . . . gelos;* I. 599) raised by the gods at Hephaistos, or the Argives' laughter aimed at Thersites (II.215, 270) is cruel laughter, laughter used as a weapon. The figure of the trickster, and his place in the epic, also enters at some point in this discussion.

136. See Robert M. Torrance, *The Comic Hero* (Cambridge Mass.: Harvard University Press, 1978).

137. Frye, *Secular Scripture*, 39.

138. As Cedric Whitman, in *Homer and the Heroic Tradition* (Cambridge, Mass.: Harvard University Press, 1958), remarks on epic: "Everywhere can be found, reshaped according to shifting cultural traditions, the ideal hero, *chevalier sans peur et sans reproche,* the crafty hero, the boaster, the grim and aging warrior, the slightly buffoonish hero, the aged king, the warrior virgin, the wise counsellor, or the young reckless fighter" (155). Of course, these images are kept in their separate formulations; one finds no development or shift from one to the other.

139. Oinas, "Folk-Epic," 103; Frye, *Secular Scripture*, 83.

140. Frye, "Our Lady of Pain: Heroes and Heroines of Romance," in *Secular Scripture*, 74ff.

141. G. Dumézil, *The Destiny of a King*, trans. A. Hiltebeitel (Chicago: University of Chicago Press, 1973), 123; Dumézil sets up a series of contrastive statements on virginity/chastity, with the former marked by instability and liminality, the combination of threat and promise, magical powers and a "hot" potentiality.

142. See, e.g., the tale of "Bósa ok Herrauðr," in "BoH" and translated in H. Pálsson and P. Edwards, *Gautrek's Saga and Other Medieval Tales* (New York: New York University Press; London: University of London Press, 1970), 57–88, reprinted with minor changes in *Seven Viking Romances*, ed. H. Pálsson and P. Edwards (Harmondsworth: Penguin, 1985), 199–277.

143. "Bósa ok Herrauðr" is a good example of such an intertwined scenario. Oinas cites the Don Juanesque figure of Lemminkäinen called Kaukamieli in the Finnish *Kalevala*, whom he regards rather uneasily as "flighty," which is a certifiable trickster's characteristic in several senses: Oinas, "Folk-Epic," 104; *Kalevala*, *Runo* 17 (91ff.).

144. Especially in that narrative sequence that eventuates in the Christianized *Graal* story: see Goetinck, *Peredur*; Pauline Matarasso, *The Redemption of Chivalry: A Study of the* Quest del Sant Graal. Histoire des Idées et Critique Litteraire, vol. 180 (Génève: Librairie Droz, 1979). For aspects of the virgin and others, see Frye, *The Secular Scripture*, chap. 3, "Our Lady of Pain: Heroes and Heroines of Romance."

145. For the quest component in the normative heroic series of adventures, see chapter 3, pp. 162–64.

146. Pálsson and Edwards, *Seven Viking Romances*, 8, introduction.

147. Quint, "The Boat of Romance," 174, 179.

148. Ibid., 182.

149. Quint, "Epic and Empire," 15: the "romance episode . . . resists fitting into the teleological scheme of epic." Erich Auerbach sees that already in a "song" like the *Chanson de Roland* the narrative moves "by progresion and retrogression" and "never flowing, as in that of the antique epic" (*Mimesis: The Representation of Reality in Western Literature [New York: Doubleday, 1953]*, 91–92); "periodicity and flow of discourse are not among the characteristics of this style" (93).

150. C. Segre, "What Bakhtin Left Unsaid: The Case of the Medieval Romance," in Brownlee and Brownlee, *Romance*, 34. Segre also sees in the type called the *roman d'antiquité* a "real intermingling of the two genres" of epic and romance (35).

151. Though a semioticist like Todorov asks where genres come from, and answers himself: "simply from other genres." Tzvetan Todorov, *Genres in Discourse*, trans. C. Porter (Cambridge: Cambridge University Press, 1990), 15.

152. Tzvetan Todorov, "Le retour de l'épique," in *Literary Theory and Criticism: Festschrift Presented to Réne Wellek in Honor of His Eightieth Birthday*, vol. 1, *Theory*, ed. J. Strelker (Bern: Peter Lang, 1984), 607.

153. On the part of some Icelanders, at least; Iceland's literary establishment, closely connected to the Danish establishment, pursued the orthodox themes and studies of the European literati up to and through the Enlightenment.

154. And, of course, "king tales" such as the *Heimskringla;* these are "heroized" kings, and see below (pp. 178–82) for the usual saga-heroic attitude to the monarch.

155. See N. Chadwick, *Russian Heroic Poetry* (Cambridge: Cambridge University Press, 1932), with reference to the Novgorodian merchants Sadko (136–40) and Vasily Buslaev (143–55). Pertinent *byliny* are printed in P. V. Kir'evskii, *Pesni sobraniya P. V. Kir'evskim' izdany obshchestvom' lyubitelei rossiyskoi slovesnosti* (Moscow: Tipografii P. Bakhmetev, 1870), chap. 5, 41ff. (for Sadko), and P. N. Rybnikov, *Pesni P. N. Rybnikovym'*, 2d. ed., A. Ye. Gruzinski (Moscow: Sotrudnik' Shkol', 1909), 1:368–74 (for Vasily Buslaev). The latter's primitive and comic heroic strength is displayed in line 12: "whose arm he grabbed, the arm came off; whose leg he grabbed, that leg came off" (*kogo dernet' za ruku, ruka proch'; kogo devnet' za nogu, noga-to proch'*). Cinematophiles may recall that the merchant-warrior Vasily Buslaev is featured as a comic character in Eisenstein's great film, *Alexandr Nevskii.*

156. See the editors' introduction in Brownlee and Brownlee, *Romance;* and also Calin, *A Muse for Heroes: Nine Centuries of the Epic in France.*

157. Lukács, *The Historical Novel*, 30–38.

158. See the extraordinary focusing essay by Hans Blumenberg, *Arbeit am Mythos/Work on Myth*, trans. R. M. Wallace (Cambridge, Mass.: MIT Press, 1985), 3–33.

159. The Waffen SS, the elite "black corps" of Hitler's Germany, openly tapped into the perceptual fund of archaic heroism in its unit nomenclature; see the 5th

Panzerdivision "Wiking," the Waffen-Grenadier-division "Charlemagne" (made up of French volunteers), Albanian and Hungarian units named after Skanderbeg and Hunyadi respectively, and—prophetically and pathetically—a "forlorn hope" unit recruited in the storm of the last days, the 38th Panzergrenadierdivision "Nibelungen." From a very large bibliography, see George H. Stein, *The Waffen SS: Hitler's Elite Guard at War, 1939–1945* (Ithaca: Cornell University Press, 1984).

160. A. van Gennep, *The Rites of Passage*, trans. M. A. Vizedom and G. E. Caffee (Chicago: University of Chicago Press, 1960), 65–115.

161. Out of the large bibliographies available on each of these topics, I can make a small selection. Most of these topics will be dealt with in more detail in the following chapters: for one area, on blood vengeance, see now Christopher Boehm, *Blood Revenge: The Enactment and Management of Conflict in Montenegro and Other Tribal Societies* (Philadelphia: University of Pennsylvania Press, 1987), bibliography, 253–58.

162. See, e.g., J. Nagy, *Wisdom,* for an extensive bibliography.

163. M. E. Meeker, "The Twilight of a South Asian Heroic Age: A Rereading of Barth's Study of Swat," *Man,* n.s., 14, no. 4 (1980): 683.

164. The volume in the American Museum Sourcebooks in Anthropology series edited by Paul Bohannon entitled *Law and Warfare: Studies in the Anthropology of Conflict* (Garden City, N.Y.: Natural History Press, 1967) shows this in a crude page count: three hundred pages refer to "The Judicial Process," about a hundred to "Feuds, Wars and Raids."

165. C. H. Wedgewood, "Some Aspects of War in Melanesia," *Oceania* 1 (1939–31): 5–33, especially 25–28; see, for Highland peoples, M. J. Meggitt, "Enga Political Organization," *Mankind* 5 (1957): 133–35, and more extensively *Blood Is Their Argument: Warfare among the Mae Enga Tribesmen of the New Guinea Highlands,* Explorations in World Ethnology (Palo Alto, Calif.: Stanford University Press, 1977) for the Mae Enga; for Siane examples, R. F. Salisbury, *From Stone to Steel* (Cambridge: Cambridge University Press, 1962), 26–27.

166. M. E. Meeker, *Literature and Violence in North Arabia* (Cambridge: Cambridge University Press, 1979), especially chap. 7, "Heroic Skills and Beastly Energies," 11–150.

167. E. E. Evans-Pritchard, *The Nuer: A Description of the Modes of Livelihood and Political Institutions of a Nilotic People* (1940; reprint, Oxford: Clarendon, 1963), and *Nuer Religion* (Oxford: Clarendon, 1956). In the later volume, see pp. 45–47 for war songs and a look at the *buk* or air-spirits who dominated war making.

168. For the former, see Meeker, "Twilight"; for the latter, Lincoln Keiser, *Friend by Day, Enemy by Night: Organized Vengeance in a Kohustani Community* (Fort Worth, Tex.: Holt, Rinehart and Winston, 1991).

169. Louis Gernet, *Droit et société dans la Grèce ancienne,* Publications de l'Institut de Droit Romain de l'Université de Paris, vol. 13 (Paris: Receuil Siey, 1955); *The Anthropology of Ancient Greece,* trans. J. Hamilton and B. Nagy (Baltimore: Johns Hopkins University Press, 1981).

170. "Like an ethnologist who, beginning with the dawn of civilization, sets out

to a distant land, he would never abandon his quest, and would understand the people from within and without, with the twofold perspective of native and foreigner": J.-P. Vernant, in the preface to Gernet, *The Anthropology of Ancient Greece*, viii.

171. The quotation is from Bernard Knox, in his foreword to P. Vidal-Naquet's *The Black Hunter: Forms of Thought and Forms of Society in the Greek World*, trans. A. Szegedy-Maszak (Baltimore: Johns Hopkins University Press, 1986), xii.

172. Vidal-Naquet, "The Black Hunter," in *The Black Hunter*, 106–28.

173. In the collection of essays by both Vernant and Vidal-Naquet, published first as *Tragedy and Myth in Ancient Greece*, trans. J. Lloyd (Brighton: Harvester Press; Atlantic Highlands, N.J.: Humanities Press, 1981) and then expanded to two volumes in one, with the same title and translator (New York: Zone, 1988) see, e.g., Vernant's "Oedipus without the Complex," 63–86 in the first collection; 85–111 in the second.

174. M. Detienne, *L'invention de la mythologie* (Paris: Gallimard, 1981) = *The Creation of Mythology* trans. M. Cook (Chicago: University of Chicago Press, 1986); *Dionysos mis à mort* (Paris: Gallimard, 1977) = *Dionysos Slain*, trans. M. Muellner and L. Muellner (Baltimore: Johns Hopkins University Press, 1979); *Dionysos à ciel ouvert* (Paris: Hachette, 1986) = *Dionysos at Large*, trans. A. Goldhammer (Cambridge, Mass.: Harvard University Press, 1989). On the last publication, see my brief review in *Incognita* 1, no. 1 (1990): 97, where I suggest that Detienne perhaps has gone too far in his Dionysian playfulness.

175. Nicole Loraux, *L'invention d'Athènes. Histoire de l'oraison funèbre dans la "cité classique"* (The Hague: Mouton, 1981).

176. See B. Knox's foreword to Vidal-Naquet, *The Black Hunter*, xi–xv. Some idea of the problem is reflected in Vidal-Naquet's claim, in "The Black Hunter," that his intention is "to detect polarities expressed not in book-thinking but in social institutions" when the "social institutions" he seeks are only accessible, so far as the ancient Greeks are concerned, in book-borne, never direct, testimony (114).

177. C. Lévi-Strauss, *Mythologiques I: Le cru et le cuit.* (Paris: Plon, 1964), 12.

178. James A. Boon, *From Symbolism to Structuralism: Lévi-Strauss in a Literary Tradition*, Explorations in Interpretative Sociology (Oxford: Basil Blackwell, 1972), 127.

179. James A. Boon, *Other Tribes, Other Scribes: Symbolic Anthropology in the Comparative Study of Cultures, Histories, Religions and Texts* (Cambridge: Cambridge University Press, 1982) 14, for the realist-naturalist affinity; Boon associates Geertz to William James through an ingenious linking of their view of *negation;* see *Tribes/Scribes*, 138ff.

180. Boon, *Tribes/Scribes*, chap. 7, "Structuralism/Romanticism, reciprocally," and especially p. 228, where the author suggests that romanticism can replace the "alliance" with structuralism he proposed for French symbolism in *From Structuralism to Symbolism.*

181. C. Lévi-Strauss, *Structural Anthropology*, trans. C. Jacobson and B. G. Shoepf (New York: Basic Books, 1963), 213ff.

182. For a critique of the discipline and its ability to deal with ideology, see

Talal Asad, "Anthropology and the Analysis of Power," *Man,* n.s., 14 (1979): 607–27.

183. Meeker, "Twilight," 683–85.

184. T. Parsons, "The Life and Work of Émile Durkheim," in É. Durkheim, *Sociology and Philosophy* (New York: Free Press, 1974), lx, lxii.

185. C. Lévi-Strauss, *The Scope of Anthropology,* Inaugural Lecture, Chair of Social Anthropology, Collège de France, 5 January 1960, trans. S. O. Paul and R. A. Paul (London: Jonathan Cape, 1967), 8ff. Mauss is inserted into this sequence as Durkheim's "pupil and successor."

186. Boon, *Tribes/Scribes,* 68.

187. Reinhold Bendix, *Max Weber: An Intellectual Portrait* (Berekeley: University of California Press, 1977), 85.

188. M. Weber, *Wirtschaft und Gesellschaft,* 2d ed. (Tubingen: J. C. B. Mohr, 1925): 2:356 and 373–85 for feudalism generally; also *Theory of Social and Economic Organization* (New York: Oxford University Press, 1947), 175.

189. Boon, *Tribes/Scribes,* 72–73.

190. See Bendix, *Max Weber: An Intellectual Portrait,* 479–81.

191. The shaman, "hero of the spiritual zone," is another matter. For the essential antireligiosity of the warrior, see Weber, *Wirtschaft und Gesellschaft,* 1:270.

192. M. Weber, *On Charisma and Institution Building: Selected Papers,* ed. and introd. S. N. Eisenstadt (Chicago: University of Chicago Press, 1968), 48; all excerpts taken from his *Theory of Social and Economic Organization,* trans. A. R. Henderson and T. Parsons (New York: Macmillan, 1947).

193. Weber, *On Charisma,* 48–49.

194. Ibid., 48.

195. Ibid., 51–52.

196. Littleton, *The New Comparative Mythology,* 11–19.

197. See ibid., pt. 3, 153–203, and now Didier Eribon, *Faut-il bruler Dumézil?* (see introduction, n. 3), for Eribon's brilliant dissection of a late and particularly perverse personal assault on Dumézil.

198. G. Dumézil, *Mitra-Varuna: essai sur deux réprésentations indo-européennes de la souveraineté,* 2d ed., Collection "La Montagne Sainte-Geneviève," vol. 7 (Paris: Gallimard, 1948); trans. D. Coltman as *Mitra-Varuna: An Essay on Two Indo-European Representations of Sovereignty* (New York: Zone, 1988).

199. See below, p. 245.

200. Hertz was killed in action in 1915; he was predicted (had he lived) to have been a *sociologue* equal to Mauss: see R. Needham, ed., *Right and Left: Essays on Dual Symbolic Classicification* (Chicago: University of Chicago Press, 1973).

201. Marie Delcourt, *Légendes et cultes des héros en Grèce,* Collection "Mythes et Religions," ed. P.-L. Couchoud (Paris: PUF, 1942), p. 54. Other monographs include the path-marking *Stérilités mystérieuses et naissances maléfiques,* Bibliothèque de la Faculté de Philiosophie et Lettres de l'Université de Liège, fasc. 83 (Liège, 1938); 2d ed. (Paris: Societé d'Edition Les Belles Lettres, 1986); *Oedipe ou la légende du conquerant,* Bibliothèque de la Faculté de Philosophie et Lettres de l'Université de Liège, fasc. 104 (Liège, 1944); and *Oreste et Alcméon: Étude sur la*

projection légendaire du matricide en Grèce, Bibliothèque de la Faculté de Philosophie et Lettres de l'Université de Liège, fasc. 151 (Liège, 1959).

202. Several of her monographs, specifically *Héphaistos* and *Oedipe*, have recently been reprinted in France in the collection "Confluents Psychanalytiques," together with brief explorations by other scholars directed from a more strictly psychoanalytic viewpoint: in Andre Green, "Héphaistos, la magie d'Héphaistos," in *Oedipe, ou la légende du conquérant*, 2d ed. (Paris: Société d'Edition Les Belles Lettres, 1981), the addition is "'Oedipe Roi,' selon Freud," by Conrad Stein.

203. Marie Delcourt, *Hermaphrodite: Myths and Rites of the Bisexual Figure in Classical Antiquity*, trans. J. Nicholson (London: Studio Books, 1961).

204. Hayden White, the author of *Metahistory: The Historical Imagination in Nineteenth-Century Europe* (Baltimore: Johns Hopkins University Press, 1973) and more recently *Tropics of Discourse: Essays in Cultural Criticism* (Baltimore: Johns Hopkins University Press, 1978).

205. S. Freud, *Totem and Taboo: Some Points of Agreement between the Mental Lives of Savages and Neurotics* (1912–13), trans. J. Strachey (New York: Norton, 1950), 125–26ff.; see R. Eisner, *The Road to Daulis: Psychoanalysis, Psychology and Classical Mythology* (Syracuse, N.Y.: Syracuse University Press, 1987), 1–33, "Oedipus and His Kind" for the development of Freud's thought on Oedipus, from *The Interpretation of Dreams* (1900), trans. J. Strachey (New York: Avon, 1965), 294–97, to the canonical account in *Introductory Lectures on Psychoanalysis* (1916–17), trans. J. Strachey, in *The Standard Edition*, ed. J. Strachey, vol. 16 (London: Hogarth, 1967), 327–38.

206. See Eisner, *Daulis*, 6 and n. 19; and, for an older but still acceptable run through the tangles of the Matter of Oedipus in psychoanalysis, see P. Mullahy, *Oedipus, Myth and Complex: A Review of Psychoanalytic Theory* (New York: Grove, 1955).

207. Especially as an "intruder" according to W. T. H. Jackson's formula, in *The Hero and the King: An Epic Theme* (New York: Columbia University Press, 1982); see below, pp. 179–80.

208. O. Rank, *The Myth of the Birth of the Hero*, trans. F. Robbins and S. Jelliffe, Nervous and Mental Disease Monographs (New York, 1914); in *The Myth of the Birth of the Hero and Other Writings*, ed. P. Fruend (New York: Vintage, 1964). Freud, in *Moses and Monotheism*, trans. K. Jones (New York: Random House, 1937), 7, referred to Rank in 1909 as "still under my influence" while in Freud's *Group Psychology and the Analysis of the Ego* (1921; reprint, New York: Norton, 1959) a postcript was added "written under the influence of Rank" according to Eisner, *Daulis*, 194. A reciprocal influence is, of course, quite possible.

209. See Eisner, *Daulis*, 17; Freud on "lying fancies" is in *Group Psychology*, 68. In the context, it is true, he seems to be referring to one *kind* of myth.

210. Erich Neumann, *The Origins and History of Consciousness*, trans. R. F. C. Hull, Bollingen Series 42 (Princeton: Princeton University Press, 1973).

211. See Eisner, *Daulis*, 177–80, 195, with specific reference to J. Friedman and S. Gassel, "Odysseos: The Return of the Primal Father," *Psychoanalytic Quarterly* 21 (1952): 215–23, and "Orestes: A Psychoanalytic Approach to Dramatic Criti-

cism," *Psychoanalytic Quarterly* 20 (1951): 423–33, also R. Caldwell, "Psycho-analysis, Structuralism and Greek Mythology," *Phenomenology, Structuralism, Semiology, Bucknell Review* (April 1976): 209–30.

212. And so, by the way, combining ritual and mythic evidence. See E. R. Leach, *Claude Lévi-Strauss*, rev. ed., Penguin Modern Masters (Harmondsworth: Penguin, 1976), 65: "When, like Frazer, [Lévi-Strauss] roams about the ethnographies of the whole world, picking up odd details of custom and story to reveal what he presumes to be a single message inherent in the architecture of the human mind." This criticism Boon (*Tribes/Scribes*, 18) apostrophizes as "such is the fashion."

213. Boon, *Tribes/Scribes*, 10.

214. Ibid., 21; A. M. Hocart, *Kingship* (London: Oxford University Press, 1927), and *Kings and Councillors: An Essay in the Comparative Anatomy of Human Society* (Chicago: Chicago University Press, 1970).

215. I. C. Jarvie, *The Revolution in Anthropology* (London: Routledge & Kegan Paul, 1967), 175. Though Jarvie (in a style Boon, *Tribes/Scribes*, 11, calls "tabloid-like" and I would call "handless") wants to move, as he insists, *either* "back to Frazer" or "over to Lévi-Strauss."

216. Jarvie, *Revolution in Anthropology* , 43.

217. R. Ackermann, *J. G. Frazer: His Life and Work* (Cambridge: Cambridge University Press, 1987). The biography is most pleasantly free of psychobabble, for Frazer was what he wrote; words truly *were* his life.

218. F. R. Somerset, Lord Raglan, *The Hero* (London: Pitman & Sons, 1936; 2d ed., New York: Vintage, 1956; reprint, Westport, Conn.: Greenwood Press, 1975). This is the only work for which this scholar is remembered now, though his later *The Origins of Religion* is also emblematic of what Joseph Fontenrose has called his "strange compound[ing] of lucidity and absurdity." Raglan, *The Origins of Religion* (London: Watts, 1949); Joseph Fontenrose, *The Ritual Theory*, University of California Publications, Folklore Series 18 (Berkeley: University of California Press, 1971), 2, n. 1.

219. See Fontenrose, *Ritual Theory*, 1.

220. Raglan, *The Hero*, 97.

221. Ibid., 278–80.

222. In Theodore Gaster, *Thespis: Ritual, Myth and Drama in the Ancient Near East* (New York: Doubleday, 1961); see Fontenrose, *Ritual Theory*, 50.

223. Raglan, *The Hero*, 123. Does he mean "unfamiliar" things? In any case, Raglan was, of course, quite mistaken.

224. Ibid., 161; see Fontenrose, *Ritual Theory*, 8, n. 17.

225. Raglan, *The Hero*, 174–75.

226. Fontenrose, *Ritual Theory*, 24–25; see also Wm. Bascom, "The Myth-Ritual Theory," *Journal of American Folklore* 70 (1957): 103–14.

227. See Kenneth Roberts, "Education," in *The Kenneth Roberts Reader* (Garden City, N.Y.: Doubleday, Doran, 1945), 130–34. Robert's prewar observations fit with Lord Raglan's authorial time span.

228. R. B. Onians, *The Origins of European Thought, about the Body, the Mind, the Soul, the World, Time and Fate. New Interpretations of Greek, Roman and Kindred*

Evidence, also of Some Basic Jewish and Christian Beliefs (1951; reprint, Cambridge: Cambridge University Press, 1988).

229. Ibid., 13.

230. Ibid., 200 (emphasis added).

231. See ibid., 215ff., especially with the human image assimilated to plant life, as Latin *sucus* or the "sap of life."

232. Joseph Campbell, *The Hero with a Thousand Faces*, 2d ed., Bollingen Series 17 (Princeton: Princeton University Press, 1968).

233. Ibid., 20.

234. Recent reports and reestimations of Campbell's personal idiosyncracies, in which the shaman of "bliss" is excoriated for elitism, racism, sexism, and neofascist tendencies, appear to say something about the man, and little about his scholarly bent. I confess to a belief that these two realms may have little to do with each other—and that the final value of a scholarly work proceeds *ex opere operata*. Other and similar attacks have been launched at Mircea Eliade and Georges Dumézil, on the grounds that these scholars, at some point in their respective careers, made obeisance to extreme rightist (nationalist, authoritarian) politics and beyond this, even to fascist and to Nazi racial ideologies. These attacks, in my view, have their origins in a mélange of confused motivations, from the vulgar Marxist, to the revision-at-any-cost absurdity, to a simple or purposeful misapprehension or misreading of the *Geist* of the 1930s, when Eliade and Dumézil are supposed to have committed their sins. In any event, the total body of work of Eliade and Dumézil will almost certainly survive such attacks, and Campbell's work should be subjected to the same test of time and utility.

CHAPTER 2: THE HEROIC BIOGRAPHY

1. G. Nagy, *Best of the Achaeans* (see chap. 1, n. 7).

2. Kerényi, *The Heroes of the Greeks*, 308 (see chap. 1, n. 12).

3. Ibid.

4. See G. Nagy, *Best of the Achaeans*, 253ff., for Thersites as a vestigial "blame-poet"; for Egill see below, chapter 4.

5. Pausanias, X.vi.1 (see chap. 1, n. 6).

6. See G. S. Kirk, *The Nature of Greek Myth* (Harmondsworth: Penguin, 1974), 109.

7. Kerényi, *Heroes of the Greeks*, 134.

8. Ibid., 45ff., especially 47; for Theseus, see D. A. Miller, "The Three Kings at Colonos: A Provocation," *Arethusa* 19, no. 1 (Spring 1986): 75, n. 46.

9. *Mahâbhârata*, trans. and ed. J. A. B. van Buitenen (Chicago: University of Chicago Press, 1973), 1 (7) 104 (p. 241).

10. In *Pwyll Prince of Dyfed*, in *The Mabinogion and Other Medieval Welsh Tales*, trans. and ed. P. K. Ford (Berkeley: University of California Press, 1977), 50–55; see also D. A. Miller, "Indo-European Protoforms in Three Heroic Conception-Narratives," *Incognita* 1, no. 1 (1990): 39–44.

11. *The Superhuman Life of King Gezar of Ling*, trans. and ed. A. David-Neal and Lama Yongdon (New York: Arno Press, 1978), 68, 91, 98–99.

12. Pausanius, IV.xiv.7: *daimona ê theon drakonti eisasmenon*.

13. Plutarch, "Alexander," in *Lives*, trans. B. Perrin, Loeb Classical Library (Cambridge, Mass.: Harvard University Press; London: Heinemann, 1971), II.4, 6.

14. Plutarch, "Alexander"; and *Romance of Alexander the Great by Pseudo-Callisthenes*, in *Lives*, trans. A. M. Wolohogian (New York: Columbia University Press, 1969), 33.

15. See V. Belmont, "La coiffe et le serpent," *Échanges et Communications* (Paris) 2 (1970): 1223–28.

16. D. H. Low, *The Ballads of Marko Kraljević* (New York: Greenwood Press, 1968), 131. In the Serb context the snake-dragon image for the hero is not uncommon: see *SCHS* III, for the hero (Meho) as "golden dragon" (93); as "dragon's son" (100); dragon images for both hero and standard-bearer (109).

17. Pausanias, X.xxxiii.9ff.

18. Though we note that an Albanian hero, Mujo (the Albanian epic tales closely parallel those of the Serbs) was cared for when wounded by a snake *and* a wolf, with some other assistance from a *zonia* (the Albanian version of the Serbian *vila* or water-sprite) and a hound: St. Skendi, *Albanian and South Slavic Oral Poetry*, Memoirs of the American Folklore Society 44 (1954): 113.

19. Two Balkan sources refer to the healing of the hero Mujo's wounds: in *SCHS* I, 161, the wounds are healed by a snake spitting into them and hounds licking them; in an Albanian version (Skendi, *Albanian and South Slavic Oral Poetry*, 113) the same hero—here identified as Albanian—is cared for by the snake and the wolf, with some assistance from a hound and the Albanian supernatural female.

20. N. Chadwick and V. Zhirminsky, *Oral Epics of Central Asia* (Cambridge: Cambridge University Press, 1969), 157.

21. Low, *Marko*, 472; Skendi, *Albanian and South Slavic Oral Poetry*, 67.

22. *SCHS* III, 183.

23. Kerényi, *Heroes of the Greeks*, 236. Perithoös's divine-monstrous parental associations make him especially open and apt to the Thesean connection: Theseus's "divine" father was Poseidon, but in *human* form (see the next paragraph).

24. *Pwyll Pendeuic Dyfed* in, e.g., *Y llvyr Gwyn Rhydderch = The White Book of Rhydderch*, ed. J. Gwenogvryn Evans, Series of Old Welsh Texts, vol. 7 (Pwllheli, 1907); *Compert Con Culainn* (in two versions) in *Compert Con Culainn and Other Stories*, ed. A. G. van Hamel, Medieval and Modern Irish Series, vol. 3 (Dublin, 1933), 1–8.

25. Miller, "Indo-European Protoforms in Three Hero Conception-Narratives," 46.

26. R. S. Loomis, "The Strange History of Caradoc of Vannes," in *Franciplegia: Medieval and Linguistic Studies in Honor of Francis Peabody Magoune, Jr.*, ed. Jess Bessinger and Robert P. Creed (New York: New York University Press, 1965),

232–39. *CO*, 38.1075–76, and Ford, *Mabinogion*, 153, for Arthur's remark on the boar: *Brenhin uu, ac am y bechawt y rithwys Duw ef yn hwch;* see also Ford, *Mabinogion*, introduction, 15–16, for the Welsh conflation of "boar" and "chieftain" and other information on their swine-born heroes, including Culhwch himself.

27. Low, *Marko*, 30–33; for human speech, 82; for drinking, 52, 128.

28. Ibid., 182.

29. *Il.* XIX.405ff.

30. *Gezar of Ling*, 68, 148.

31. Kerényi, *Heroes of the Greeks*, 51.

32. Low, *Marko*, 9.

33. *DS*, 181.

34. Alwyn Rees and Brinley Rees, *Celtic Heritage: Ancient Tradition in Ireland and Wales* (London: Thames & Hudson, 1961), 232.

35. *DS*, I (4): 12–14.

36. Kerényi, *Heroes of the Greeks*, 78.

37. Ibid., 154–55. The horse of Alexander, Bucephalos, is called a "man eater" in Plutarch, *Alexander Romance*, 34.

38. M. Detienne, "Athena and the Mastery of the Horse," *History of Religions* 11 (1971): 167–68, 173–74. However, note that in Pausanias, V.xv.5–6 Poseidon *hippios* and Hera *hippia* are paired, and also Ares Horse-God and Athena Horse-Goddess; he is describing the altars at Olympia in Elis, placed near the chariot racecourse. We might note that in terms of hero images, the *falcon* is often present (looking for a few examples to the simile language of the Byzantine Greek *Digenid*, or, in the Russo-Slavic *byliny*, to Il'ya of Murom's doomed son Sokol'nichek, "Little Falcon"): the falcon is essentially a wild animal barely brought under control or "tamed."

39. Gilbert Durand, *Les structures anthropologiques de l'imaginaire. Introduction à l'archétypologie générale* (Paris: Bordas, 1969), 78; Durand cites (for the death horse) the early monograph by L. Malten, *Das Pferd in Totenglauben. Jahrbücher des Deutsches Archeologisches Institut* 29 (1919).

40. Thompson, *Motif-Index*, vol. 6 (see chap. 1, n. 69).

41. D. Biebyck, *Hero and Chief: Epic Literature from the Bunyanga (Zaire Republic)* (Berkeley: University of California Press, 1978), 145, n. 32.

42. David McKnight, "Man, Women and Other Animals: Taboo and Purification among the Wik-Mungkan," in *The Interpretation of Symbolism*, ed. R. Willis (New York: ASA Studies, 1975), 83.

43. H. Schärer, *Ngaju Religion: The Conception of God among a South Borneo People*, trans. R. Needham, Koninklijk Instituut voor Taal-, Land- en Volkenkunde, ser. 6 (The Hague, 1963), 29.

44. S. Tambiah, "Animals Are Good to Think and Good to Prohibit," *Ethnology* 8, no. 4 (October 1969): 435, 441.

45. J.-P. Dumont, *Under the Rainbow: Nature and Supernature among the Parare Indians* (Austin: University of Texas Press, 1976), 131–33.

46. *Il.* I.4.

47. *Il.* VI.345, 354: *emeio kunos kakomêkhanou okryoessês*, and also I.356;

P. Friedrich, "Defilement and Honor in the *Iliad*," *JI-ES* 1, no. 2 (Summer 1973): 121.

48. Tambiah, "Animals Are Good to Think," 435. The derogation of the ambiguous, "boundary-breaking" dog is seen as well among the Keram of Papua–New Guinea: though an animal, the dog is set into the same imaginal category as the cassowary and man himself, and the killer of any of the three is considered unclean: R. Bulmer, "Why Is the Cassowary Not a Bird? A Problem of Zoological Taxonomy among the Keram of the New Guinea Highlands," *Man*, n.s., 2 (1967): 14–15. Dogs are "adopted" by their owners and are regarded, like men, as having spirits (19).

49. *Marko the Prince: Serbo-Croat Heroic Songs*, trans. A. Pennington and P. Levi (New York: St. Martins, 1984), 121.

50. Miller, "Indo-European Protoforms in Three Heroic Conception-Narratives," 40.

51. Patricia Kelly, "The *Táin* as Literature," in *Aspects of the* Táin, ed. J. P. Mallory (Belfast: University Presses, 1992), 74–75, citing especially the work of Kim McCone: "*Aided Celtchair maic Uthechair:* Hounds, Heroes and Hospitallers in Early Irish Myth and Story," *Ériu* 35 (1984): 1–30; "Hund, Wolf und Krieger bei den Indogermanen," in *Studien zum Indogermanischen Wortschatz*, ed. W. Meid (Innsbruck: Institut für Sprachwissenschaft der Universitäts Innsbruck, 1987), 101–54.

52. See J. Nagy, *Wisdom*, 44 and nn. 19 and 20 (see chap. 1, n. 90).

53. T. Ó Cathasaigh, "The Sister's Son in Early Irish Literature," *Peritia* 5 (1986): 137, 148–49, 150.

54. In addition to the hero Mujo mentioned above, Saxo tells us that the Danish hero Ole's dog cured his master by licking his wounds: Saxo, *Gesta Danorum*, I.230.

55. *CO*, 25, 36, 41; in Ford, *Mabinogion*, 141, 152, 156. Gwyn Jones says that Arthur's dog Cafall was probably not a dog but a horse!: see *Kings, Beasts and Heroes*, 87, n. 1 (see chap. 1, n. 95).

56. *DS*, 122; *Digenes Akrites*, trans. by J. Mavrogordato (Oxford: Clarendon, 1956), GRO IV, lines 739–40 (pp. 18–19); *Shâh-nâma*, 49 (for Rostam "roaring like a lion"), 75 (described by his son as "that lion of a man") (see chap. 1, n. 36).

57. Durand, *Les structures anthropologiques*, 91.

58. Rees and Rees, *Celtic Heritage*, 232.

59. P. Brown, "Rise and Function of The Holy Man in Late Antiquity," *Journal of Roman Studies* 61 (1971): 83, 92; reprinted in Brown, *Society and the Holy in Late Antiquity* (Berkeley: University of California Press, 1982), 105, 119.

60. T. Ó Cathasaigh, *The Heroic Biography of Cormac mac Airt* (Dublin: Dublin Institute of Advanced Studies, 1977).

61. Pausanius, X.xiv.7. One of the characteristics of a sacred precinct, of course, may be to reverse profane realities. Note too that this Pausanian tale reverses the image of the "bad wolf"—the natural wolf?—seen in X.xxxiii.9ff., cited above.

62. For the *Wilde Jagd*, see H. Bachtold-Staubli, *Handwörterbuch des deutschen Aberglaubens* (Berlin: Walter de Gruyter, 1935), s.v. "Wilde Jagd" = "Nachtjagd,"

cols. 796–802, and Hans von Beit, *Symbolik des Märchens. Versuch einer Deutung* (Bern: A. Franke, 1952), s.v. "Wilde Jagd"; for the Balt folklore, see R. Ridley, "Wolf and Werewolf in Balt and Slav Tradition," *JI-ES* 4, no. 4 (Winter 1976): 325.

63. M. Eliade, *Zalmoxis, the Vanishing God: Comparative Studies in the Religion and Folklore of Dacia and Eastern Europe*, trans. W. R. Trask (Chicago: University of Chicago Press, 1972), 16–18.

64. Jones, *Kings, Beasts and Heroes*, 129. Old Norse text in *HsK*.

65. *Le haut livre du Graal: Perlesvaus*, ed. W. Nitze and R. Jenkins, vol. 1, *Text, Variants and Glossary*, Modern Philology Monographs of the University of Chicago (Chicago: University of Chicago Press, 1932), lines 1360ff.

66. Baudouin suggests this from the evidence of the *Râmayana*, terming Râma and the Monkey King "doublets": the repellent traits are *projetés sur son double*. Charles Baudouin, "Présences," in *Le triomphe du héros: Étude psychalytique sur le mythe du héros et les grandes épopées* (Paris: Plon, 1952), 12.

67. Again, if the dog did not somehow approach the human image, this derogation would not, I think, appear. See Tambiah, "Animals Are Good to Think," 428.

68. See L. de Heusch, *Essais sur le symbolisme de l'inceste royale en Afrique* (Brussels, 1958).

69. Ibid., 132.

70. See Franz-Rolf Schröder, *Germanische Heldendictung: Ein Vortrag nebst einer Studie zur Heroisierung des Mythes*, in *Philosophie und Geschichte* 55 (1935).

71. G. Dumézil, *From Myth to Fiction: The Saga of Hadingus*, trans. D. Coltman (Chicago: University of Chicago Press, 1973), 53, n. 5.

72. Kerényi, *Heroes of the Greeks*, 305–6, citing the Scholion on Euripides' *Orestes*, 15, and Hyginus, *Fabulae*, 254; see also D. A. Miller, "A Note on Aegisthus as 'Hero,'" *Arethusa* 10, no. 2 (Fall 1977): 261–62.

73. Miller, "Indo-European Protoforms in Three Heroic Conception-Narratives," 40.

74. In M. A. O'Brien, *Corpus genealogiarum Hiberniae* (Dublin: Dublin Institute of Advanced Studies, 1962); 154; cited in Donnchadh Ó Corráin, "Irish Origin Legends and Genealogy: Recent Aetiologies" in *History and Heroic Tale: A Symposium*, ed. T. Nyberg, I. Pio, P. M. Sorensen, A. Trommer, Proceedings of the Eighth International Symposium organized by the Center for the Study of Vernacular Literature in the Middle Ages held at Odense University, 21–22 November 1983 (Odense: Odense Universitetsforlag, 1985), 51–87.

75. Rees and Rees, *Celtic Heritage*, 229, citing the cases of Daolgas and Tuan.

76. *HsK*, chap. 9; Jones, *Kings, Beasts and Heroes*, 139.

77. Another father-daughter incest is noted by Dumézil, *Hadingus*, 53, n. 5.

78. *Shâh-nâma*, XVI-XVII.219, 223–24 (see chap. 1, n. 36). Darâb, like Cú Chulainn and Finn mac Cumaill, is too strong as a youth for the youngsters who have banded against him. Another Boy Troop instance is given in the *Shâh-nâma*, in describing the youth of Shâpur: XXIV.iii.274.

79. Like the Algonquian Manabozo "sinning" with his grandmother and sister, or the Polynesian Maui with his mother and sister; L. Makarius, "Le Mythe

du 'Trickster,'" *Revue de l'Histoire des Religions* 175 (1969): 27, 28, 32. Maui also murders his maternal uncle, another enormity.

80. Dumézil, *Hadingus,* 10, 53, 70; Saxo, *Gesta Danorum,* I.23 (see chap. 1, n. 91).

81. *VölS,* chap. 7 (p. 9); *Beowulf,* in *Beowulf and the Fight at Finnsburg,* ed. F. Klaeber, 3d ed. (Boston: Heath, 1950), lines 879, 889.

82. *VölS,* chap. 8 (p. 10).

83. Plutarch, *Alexander Romance,* 41.

84. *Coir Anmann,* trans. W. Stokes, in *Irische Texte* III (Leipzig, 1902), 333. Lugaid is aid to have begotten a second heroic generation, his son Crimthanu, upon his own mother.

85. Rees and Rees, *Celtic Heritage,* 233ff.

86. *Tochaid Étain,* in *Lebor na hUidre = The Book of the Dun Cow,* ed. R. J. Best and O. Bergin (Dublin: 1929), 325.

87. de Heusch, *Essais sur le symbolisme de l'inceste royale en Afrique;* Rees and Rees *Celtic Heritage,* 229, with other instances of the "swallowed seed" that eventuates in a remarkable birth.

88. Miller, "Indo-European Protoforms in Three Heroic Conception-Narratives," 38–39; see Dumézil, *Le livre des héros: Légendes sur les Nartes,* Collection Caucase (Paris: Gallimard, 1965), 69 (for the conception of Soslan), 178 (for the conception of Batradz); and cf. Dumézil's older work on the Ossete tales, *Légendes sur les Nartes, suivies de cinq notes mythologiques.* Bibliothèque de l'Institut Français de Leningrad, vol. 2 (Paris: Institut d'Etudes Slaves, 1930).

89. R. Bezzola, "Les Niveaux," in *Mélanges de langue et de literature du Moyen Age et de la Renaissance, offerts à Jean Frappier,* Publications Romaines et Françaises (Geneva: Librairie Droz, 1970), 1:89–114. For some concluding remarks on the incest prohibition from an anthropological viewpoint, see Roy Wagner, "Incest and Identity: A Critique and Theory on the Subject of Exogamy and Incest Prohibition," *Man,* n.s., 7, no. 4 (1972): 601–13.

90. *VölS,* chap. 2 (p. 2): *ok sásveinn var mikill vexti þá er hann kom til, sem ván var at.*

91. *SCHS* III, 89.

92. Rabelais, *Gargantua,* author's preface, and further remarks by the hero Gargantua: "l'appetit vient en mangeant," in the *Oeuvres complètes de Rabelais,* ed. A. Lefranc et al. (Paris: Champion, 1913), vol. 1.

93. *The Mabinogion,* trans. G. Jones and T. Jones, Everyman's Library (London: Dent, 1957), 138.33–36, " . . . *a meint milwr ae praffter yndaw ac oetran mab arnaw.*" G. Goetinck says that this is a common poetic conceit (which is true), but that in this instance there is also a reference to Otherworld beings "taller than mortals": Goetinck, *Peredur,* 13 (see chap. 1, n. 28).

94. Rees and Rees, *Celtic Heritage,* 244.

95. *Táin Bó Cúalnge: From the Book of Leinster,* ed. C. O'Rahilly, Irish Text Society 49 (Dublin: Dublin Institute for Advanced Studies, 1967), 158–71; *The Táin,* trans. T. Kinsella (Oxford: Oxford University Press; Dublin: Dolmen Press, 1969), 76–92. The quotation by Cú himself comes from the late (later than the

Táin) Siaburcharpat Con Culaind = The Phantom Chariot of Cú Chulainn, ed. and trans. J. O'Beirne Crowe, in *Journal of the Royal Historical and Archaeological Association of Ireland,* 4th series, 1 (Dublin, 1871): 371–448; in *AIT,* 350.

96. *Macgnimartha Finn* = "The Boyhood Exploits of Finn," trans. K. Mayer, in *Ériu* 1 (1904): 180–90.

97. *Digenes Akrites,* GRO IV, line 1069 (pp. 70–71); lines 1101–69 (pp. 74–77).

98. Ibid., line 1007.

99. *LPS,* 50–51. In this Georgian epical context the lion has other symbolic meanings, i.e., as (a) a sign of virility, excellence, royalty (the "lion's whelps" [the king's children] are equal, be they male or female," 8); (b) an identification, specifically with the "wild" or wandering knight in his mad or *destrait* phase: "alone he roams mad with the brutes" (108, 122). Note also Tariel's assimilation to the animal world, and his strange behavior, when he encounters a lion and a panther mating; he kills the lion and tries to *kiss* the panther, which of course savages him, and so he kills it (her) as well (109).

100. *Kitune Shirka,* trans. by A. Waley, in *Botteghe Oscure* 7 (1951): 217.

101. *DS,* I (2) 15 (45–46); and see also the eponymous hero David's magical growth in III (5) 12 (261); the more typical hero is the last of the House, Pokr Mher: III (2) 2 (327).

102. *ES,* chap. 31; Old Norse text in *EgS;* for the *mikill og sterker* child.

103. Ifor Williams, *Chioedd Taliesin = The Song of Taliesin* (Caerdydd: Gwasg Prifysgol Cymru; Cardiff: University of Wales Press, 1957), 7.

104. From Dumézil by way of Brinley Rees, "Georges Dumézil et les traditions celtiques," in *Pour un Temps/Georges Dumézil* (Paris: PUF, 1982): 271–82. For a more detailed view of the Óðinn-warrior, see below, chapter 4.

105. *Digenes Akrites,* GRO IV, lines 94–96 (pp. 70–71).

106. William Sayers, "Warrior Initiation and Some Celtic Spears in the Irish and Learned Latin Traditions," *Studies in Medieval and Renaissance History* 11 (1989): 90. Sayers sees the mysterious weapon wielded by this hero, the *deil chlis,* as a juvenile weapon, almost a toy: "a weapon that is not a weapon" (106).

107. Thompson, *Motif-Index,* L100–199; see especially L101; for the large number of the type seen in the North, see Inger Boberg, *Motif-Index of Early Icelandic Literature,* Bibliotheca Arnamægnæana, vol. 27 (Copenhagen: Einar Munksgaard, 1966), L100–L199.

108. Miller, "Other Kinds of Hero: The Coward Knight and Intelligence Embattled," *Journal of Indo-European Studies* 27 (Spring–Summer, 1999): 1–15.

109. *Perlesvaus,* 1401, *il ne vient de guerre se non max.*

110. *Beowulf,* 2183ff.; Saxo, *Gesta Danorum,* IV.101.

111. Saxo, *Gesta Danorum,* VII.221; see *Peredur mab Efrawg,* in Jones and Jones, *Mabinogion,* 183–87. Peredur is transmuted into the later Perlesvaus/Perceval/Parzifal.

112. *GtS,* 6.9–11, from the Old Norse edition by G. Jónsson. Fornaldarsögur Norðulanda 3 (Reykjavik: Bokantgafen Forni, 1950); *Orms Þattr Storolfsson,* trans. J. Simpson, in her *The Norsemen Talk: A Choice of Tales From Iceland* (London: Phoenix House; Madison: University of Wisconsin Press, 1965), 198.

113. *GrS*, chap. 14. A *berserkr* is one who eats unfit things; see also H. E. Ellis Davidson, "Loki and Saxo's Hamlet," in *The Fool and the Trickster: Studies in Honor of Enid Welsford*, ed. Paul V. A. Williams (Cambridge: D. S. Brewer; Totowa, N.J.: Rowman & Littlefield, 1979): 3–17.

114. Low, *Marko*, xxxv.

115. *Hreiðars Þattr heimska*, in Simpson, *The Norsemen Talk*, 119–32.

116. G. Dumézil, *Contes et legendes des Oubykhs*, Travaux et mémoires de l'Institut d'Ethnologie 60, Université de Paris (Paris: Institut d'Ethnologie, 1957), 40–49, for three versions of the story "La fin de la liquidation des vieillards."

117. Or, as a different scholar expansively termed it in another, Byzantine epic context, *to pankosmio thêma*. See Henri Grégoire, *Ho Digenês Akritas: Hê Byzantinê epopoi'i'a stên istoria kai sten poiêsê* (New York: National Herald, 1942), 26ff. According to Edith Kern, *The Absolute Comic* (New York: Columbia University Press, 1980), the essence of tragedy, as compared to comedy, is the *real* death of the son, not the "comic death" of the father (25).

118. The death of Sohrâb, in *Shâh-nâma*, V.xiv–xx (pp. 67–79); of Connla, in Kinsella, *Táin*, 44, from the Old Irish text in van Hamel, *Compert Con Culainn*, 9–15; the text of the fragmentary *Hildebrandslied* is in *Das Hildebrandslied. Eine geschichtliche Einleitung für Laien, mit Lichtbildern der Handschrift, Alt- und Neuhochduetsche Texten*, ed. Georg Baesecke (Halle: Max Niemayer, 1945); the tale of Il'ya and his son in Rybnikov, *Pesni*, I.425–31; II.637–38 (see chap. 1, n. 155).

119. Jan de Vries, "Das Motiv des Vater-Sohn-Kampfes im Hildebrandslied," *Germanisch-Romanisch Monatschrif* 34 (1953): 257–74; see also A. T. Hatto, "On the Excellence of the 'Hildebrandslied': A Comparative Study in Dynamics," *Modern Language Review* 68 (1973): 820–38. In the present study see chapters 6 and 7, pp. 316–17, 345–54, for further discussion of this theme.

120. C. Lévi-Strauss, "The Structural Study of Myth," in *Structural Anthropology*, trans. by C. Jacobson and B. G. Shoepf (New York: Basic Books, 1963), 430ff.

121. Kerényi, *Heroes of the Greeks*, 224.

122. Ibid., 186–87.

123. *DS*, 364. Pokr Mher's fate of childlessness and yet "continuation" appears to be a result of his father's curse.

124. Practically speaking, of course, the hero must be allowed time to engender a son, though normative, sequential, or developmental time lines are seldom followed in the heroic career or *bios*.

125. GRO I, line 277 (pp. 18–19).

126. Rees and Rees, *Celtic Heritage*, 238.

127. Kerényi, *Heroes of the Greeks*, 46.

128. See Miller, "Indo-European Protoforms in Three Heroic Conception-Narratives," 39, 43–44.

129. *Shâh-nâma*, XVI.i.221–22. Dârâb was raised by a lowly cloth-fuller, eventually tested, and finally revealed and crowned king by this same mother, Queen Homây: XVI.v.228.

130. J. Nagy, *Wisdom* 70 (see chap. 1, n. 90): Nagy's translation of "óclach for topur thuli/ní bí errach senduni" from the *Fíanaigecht*, trans. and ed. K. Meyer,

RIA Todd Lectures Series 16 (Dublin, 1910), 20. The *óclach*, as defined as a reasonably experienced though young warrior, may be contrasted with the *gilla*, or "boy warrior," who is even less under control: Nagy, 67. Another debate between young and old is given in Saxo's account of the hero Hadingus (Saxo, *Gesta Danorum*, VIII.25).

131. *ES*, chap. 40, 94; *EgS*, p. 128.

132. *ES*, chap. 40, 95; the *ambatt* and *fjolkunnug* Þórgerdr Brak. Skalla-Grímr's supernatural powers are seemingly diverted by or drawn to the sorceress; Egill inherited *some* magical powers but not, in this case, enough.

133. *GrS*, chap. 16.

134. *VölS*, chap. 8 (p. 10).

135. *VölS*, chap. 8 (pp. 10–11).

136. *VölS*, chap. 10, (pp. 18–19); chap. 13 (pp. 21–22).

137. *Shâh-nâma*, VI.xix (77); for Cú Chulainn and Connla, see Kinsella, *Táin*, 44; from *Aided Oenfir Aífe*, in van Hamel, *Compert Con Culaind*, in *Compert Con Culaind and Other Stories. Medieval and Modern Irish Series* 3 (Dublin: DIAS, 1933), 11–15.

138. Low, *Marko*, 8–9.

139. *SCHS* III, 96.

140. *Gezar of Ling*, 68.

141. *Cantar del Mio Cid. Texto, gramatica y vocabulario*, vol. 3, *Texto del cantar y adiciones, ed.* R. Menendez Pidal, 4th ed. (Madrid: Espasa-Caepe, 1969); see W. S. Merwin's fine translation, *Poem of the Cid* (New York: New American Library, 1975).

142. See the family tree of Guillaume in *Guillaume d'Orange: Four Twelfth-Century Epics*, trans. and ed. J. M. Ferrante (New York: Columbia University Press, 1974), 11.

143. W. O. Farnsworth, *Uncle and Nephew in the* Chansons de Geste (New York: Columbia University Press, 1913), 201ff. (213–14 for Roland as the *son* of Charlemagne).

144. *Peredur mab Efrawg*, 190–91; in Chrétien de Troyes's *Percival* the hero's mother's brother is not the Fisher King but his father, the Hermit King: see Goetinck, *Peredur*, 31, 32.

145. Chadwick, *Russian Heroic Poetry*, 196, lines 63ff. (see chap. 1, n. 155); Russian source in Kir'evskii, *Pesni*, VI.55ff. (chap. 1, n. 155).

146. Miller, "Indo-European Protoforms in Three Heroic Conception-Narratives," 40–41.

147. Tacitus, *Germania*, ed. J. G. C. Anderson (Oxford: Clarendon, 1938); in *The Agricola and the Germania*, trans. H. Mattingly, rev. S. A. Handford (Harmondsworth: Penguin, 1970), 20.4; on the avunculate, see Ó Cathasaigh, "Sister's Son," 127.

148. Ó Cathasaigh, "Sister's Son," 130.

149. Ibid., 145ff.

150. Kinsella, *Táin*, 164ff.; O'Rahilly, *Táin*, 207; Ó Cathasaigh, "Sister's Son," 148–49.

151. *Longes Mac n-Uislenn*, ed. and trans. V. Hull, MLA Monographs 16 (New York, 1949); in *EIMS*, 256–67, and in *AIT*, 239–47; *Tórnigheacht Dhiarmida agus Ghráinne*, ed. and trans. Nessa ní Shéaghdha, Irish Texts Society 48 (Dublin: Dublin Institute for Advanced Studies, 1967); in *AIT*, 370–421.

152. Rees and Rees, *Celtic Heritage*, 283.

153. *TYP*, T 71.

154. Rees and Rees, *Celtic Heritage.*, 283ff.; in *TI*, 341. Compare, however, the version of the tale in the Italian *La Tavola Ritonda*, where King Marco *is* made responsible for Tristano's death: *La Tavola Ritonda = Tristan and the Round Table*, trans. A. Shaver, Medieval and Renaissance Studies and Texts 28 (Binghampton, N.Y.: Center for Medieval and Early Renaissance Studies, 1983).

155. Rees and Rees, *Celtic Heritage*, 293: "women's men."

156. Neumann, *Origins and History of Consciousness*, 182–83 (see chap. 1, n. 210).

157. See Lévi-Strauss, *Structural Anthropology*, 42–45 (see chap. 1, n. 181).

158. Émile Benveniste, *Indo-European Language and Society*, trans. E. Palmer, Miami Linguistic Series, no. 12 (Coral Gables, Fla.: University of Miami Press, 1973), 368–70.

159. For the Old Norse version, see "BoH."

160. Saxo, *Gesta Danorum*, I.22–24; Dumézil, *Hadingus*, 58ff.

161. J. Nagy, *Wisdom*, 99ff.

162. Ibid., 103.

163. Kinsella, *Táin*, 29–31; from the *Tochmarc Émire*, in van Hamel, *Compert Con Culainn*, 17ff.

164. *Beowulf*, 2428ff.

165. *ES*, chap. 26.

166. *Víga-Glúms saga*, in *Eyfirðinga sögur*, ed. J. Kristjansson, Íslensk fornrit 9 (Reykjavik: Hið íslensk fornritafélag, 1956), chap. 6. Bremmer's remark that Glúmr is treated "exceptionally well" by his grandfather (70) is true, but only after Glúmr had proved his lineage by beating up a particularly obnoxious berserk named Bjórn.

167. See Jesse Byock, *Feud in the Icelandic Saga* (Berkeley: University of California Press, 1982), 140, for *Droplaugarssaga*, chap. 5, and also in *Laxdæla saga* (chap. 16), for the fostering of Hoskuldr's illegitimate son Oláfr the Peacock, so as to gain Hoskuldr's friendly support (247).

168. *Sturlinga saga*, trans. J. McGrew, Library of Scandinavian Literature (New York: Twayne, 1970), 1.25; Old Norse edition by J. Jóhanneson, M. Finnbogason, and K. Eldjárn (Reykjavik: Sturlunguutgafan, 1946), vol. 1.

169 The hero himself notes that "Chariklo and Philyra, his wife and mother [and] the Centaur's virgin daughters reared me"; see Kerényi, *Heroes of the Greeks*, 249.

170. Ibid., 309, 318.

171. According to Jan Bremmer, Theseus, his son Hippolytos, Aigyptos, and Pyrrhos were all raised by the mother's father: "Avunculate and Fosterage," *Journal of Indo-European Studies* 4, no.1 (Spring 1976): 68. Bremmer also lists Kisses, a

typographical error for Kisseus, who in fact (*Il.* XI.221) was the mother's father (*mêtropatôr*) who raised the hero Iphidamas.

172. Gernet, "Fosterage et légende," in his *Droit et société dans la Grèce ancienne,* 27 (see chap. 1, n. 169).

173. Bremmer, "Avunculate and Fosterage," 71.

174. Ó Cathasaigh, "Sister's Son," 130.

175. *TYP,* 306.

176. J. Nagy, *Wisdom,* especially 100–102, and s.v. "Fosterers," "Fosterage."

177. See Bremmer, "Fosterage and Avunculate," 71–75, for his view of Bachofen and *Mütterrecht.*

178. Rees and Rees, *Celtic Heritage,* 292; adding "to a female son," but the femininity they identify in the son only makes its appearance in the sister's son identified as young lover, the wife stealer.

179. Evans-Pritchard, *Nuer Religion,* 166 (see chap. 1, n. 167).

180. Ibid.; his curse can affect the fecundity of his nephew's cattle, while a *mother's* curse can affect a man's own potency. See also Lévi-Strauss, *Structural Anthropology,* 43.

181. Delcourt, *Oreste et Alcmaeon: Étude sur la projection légendaire du matricide en Grece,* 15.

182. Saxo gives us an instance of brother killing (half) brother, in VIII.223ff. Hildigerus is mortally wounded by Hal(f)dan; when Hal(f)dan later marries, his wife cannot conceive. He goes to Uppsala (where both Freya and Óðinn are potent) "to try to secure her fruitfulness," and "the oracle" there has him propitiate his brother's ghost. His wife then conceives. See Ellis Davidson, *History of the Danes,* 2:119, n. 99 (see chap. 1, n. 91). The "oracle" and "propitiation" seem to emerge from Saxo's classical reading.

183. Saxo, *Gesta Danorum,* III.82–90.

184. Ibid., VII.201–3.

185. Yet Saxo also gives us the tale of Harald War-Tooth (Hildetan), who supported and protected a sister's son, Ring; but Ring and another sister's son, the uncanny Oli, turned against Harald. He was killed in battle against them by none other than Óðinn—who had always been his friend. But this anecdote of destiny probably has to do more with the ambiguous and often dangerous character of the god Óðinn than with the avunculate proper. See Saxo, *Gesta Danorum,* VII.225–28; VIII.243. Oli would be killed for money by the old hero Starkaðr, as the third of Starkaðr´s "warrior's sins": Dumézil, *The Destiny of the Warrior,* trans. by A. Hiltebeitel (Chicago: University of Chicago Press, 1970), 87ff.

186. Gottfried von Strassburg, *Tristan,* 50, 63; *Raoul of Cambrai: An Old French Epic,* trans. Jennie Crosland (New York: Cooper Square, 1966), IV.

187. *MacBeth,* V.vi.

188. *Shâh-nâma,* VI.47–48.

189. See Miller,"Bad Death," 143–82 (see chap. 1, n. 10), where my focus is on a putative Indo-European theme: the appearance of the undead-dead according to a Functional (in the Dumézilian sense) construction. The cluster of revenants I identify as Third Function are so labeled because of sexual activity between the liv-

ing and the "dead," with the possibility of the actual generation of life from a dead partner. The Nart narrative is paralleled by a tale repeated in the *Prodigia* of the eccentric thirteenth-century scholar Walter Map, while in the "Helgi Poems" found in the *Poetic Edda* we have a series of "rebirths" of the hero Helgi, the last after his love, the Valkyrie Sigrun, goes into the grave-howe of the second Helgi. The theme of reincarnation found here creates a separate problem.

190. Saxo, *Gesta Danorum,* II.50–51.

191. See H. Sieber, "The Romance of Chivalry in Spain. From Rodríguez de Montalvo to Cervantes," in Brownlee and Brownlee, *Romance,* 208 (see chap. 1, n. 45), citing J. Fogelqvist, *El Amadís y el género de la historia fingida* (Madrid: Porrua, 1982), 127–28.

192. Kerényi, *Heroes of the Greeks,* 111, citing Pindar's *Nemean Odes,* 10.79. For the Indo-European import of the Twins, especially as a Third Function marker, see Donald Ward, *The Divine Twins: An Indo-European Myth in Germanic Tradition,* Folklore Studies 19 (Berekely: University of California Press, 1968).

193. Kerényi, *Heroes of the Greeks,* 36ff.

194. Ibid., 184.

195. Ibid., 41.

196. Ibid., 34.

197. Ibid., 69, 72, 184.

198. For Thompson, *Motif-Index,* H1242 "youngest brother succeeds;" L0–L72, for "victorious younger child." The various Caucasian *contes* studied and translated by Dumézil, which often show a strong folktale or wonder-tale component, have a triumphant younger son in the Lazian tale "Le prince dans le monde souterrain", where two older brothers fail and the younger succeeds in a subterranean adventure: G. Dumézil, *Contes Lazes,* Travaux et Mémoires de l'Institut d'Ethnologie 27 (Paris, 1937), 78–106.

199. I *Sam.,* xvi; see Geo Widengren, *Sakrales Königtum in Alten Testament und im Judentum* (Stuttgart: W. Kohlhammer, 1955), 54ff., and D. A. Miller, "Royauté et ambiguité sexuelle," *Annales E.S.C.* 3, no. 4 (May–August 1971): 642–43.

200. Miller, "Royauté et ambiguité sexuelle."

201. Kerényi, *Hero of the Greeks,* 132.

202. Daniel F. Melia, "Parallel Versions of the Boyhood Deeds of Cuchulain," in *Oral Literature: Seven Essays,* ed. K. Duggan (New York: Barnes & Noble, 1975), 33, with a citation to G. Dumézil's *Horace et les Curiaces* (Paris: Gallimard, 1942), 105.

203. G. Nagy, *Best of the Achaeans,* 103; Nagy thinks that Patroklos's name itself dissects into *patro-klees* 'glory of the men of old'; Akhilleus achieves "glory" through Patroklos, as the latter receives *akhi* 'grief', through Akhilleus's fault (111).

204. *Chanson de Roland,* LXXXVII.1093.

205. CXLIX.795ff.

206. See below, pp. 276–81.

207. *Shâh-nâma,* X.153ff. The tone of the *Shâh-nâma* emphasizes outrageous and untrammeled ego, and any kind of cooperation, even between close kin, seems to be at risk; we have seen how father kills son in the story of the ill-starred Sohrâb,

and the final bane of the hypermachic Rostam will be his half brother Shaghâd, who devises Rostam's end but is killed by the hero before Rostam himself dies: XIV.211–12, 216.

208. See Miller, "The Twinning of Arthur and Cei" (see chap. 1, n. 106).

209. *CO*, 34–35; Ford, *Mabinogion*, 150–51.

210. Miller, "Functional Operations and Opposition," 128–30 (see chap. 1, n. 109). These two types or identifications were discovered by Dumézil in the course of his investigation of the archaic narrative (in Saxo and elsewhere) describing the strange long-lived warrior called Starkaðr, Strakaðr the Old, but it is in Egill's saga that the two warrior types are perhaps most clearly delineated.

211. *CO*, 10 ("no server," etc.: *ny byd gwasanaythur na swydvr mal ef*), 14; Ford, *Mabinogion*, 128–29, 132.

212. J. Nagy, *Wisdom*, 17ff.

213. *Mahâbhârata*, 4 (p. 46) 13 (p. 47), 14 (p. 49) for the derogation of Kicaka, "son of a *suta*."

214. *The Laws of Manu*, trans. G. Buhler (New York: Dover, 1969), X.11: "From a Kshatriya by the daughter of a Brahmana is born (a son called) according to his caste a Suta . . . "

215. *Mahâbhârata*, 4 (p. 47) 38.

216. O'Rahilly, *Táin*, 34, 172 (line 1240), *ní gonaim aradu nó echlachu nó áes gan armu*. Cú Chulainn (and the text) often use the informal *gilla* 'boy' for charioteer or driver, as in this same passage (line 1230), as well as *ara(i)d.* In the translation of the *Táin* by Kinsella, which collates other versions of the narrative in addition to the Book of Leinster redaction used by O'Rahilly, Cú Chulainn's encounter with Orlam's charioteer ends with the death, by the hero's slingshot, of the charioteer, whose name (Fertadil) is given, and the statement: "It is not true, therefore, that Cúchulainn didn't kill charioteers; he killed them if they did wrong" (96). This text does not give Cú Chulainn's exculpatory remark.

217. For some other, marvelous powers and characteristics of the charioteer Laeg, see William Sayers, "Three Charioteering Gifts in *Mesca Ulad* and *Táin Bó Cúalnge: immorchor ndeland, foscul ndírich, léim dar boilg*," *Ériu* 32 (1981): 163–67.

218. *EIMS*, 79ff.

219. *Il.* V.608–9, *ein heni diphrô eontes*, and see V.13.

220. Or, for that matter, *Hera* driving and Athena beside her arrayed for war, V.737ff., or Athena herself taking the reins with Diomedes beside her: "a dread goddess and the best warrior" (839) rolling on against Ares.

221. Caesar, *De Bello Gallico*, IV.33: *et per temonem percurrere et in jugo insistere;* some of the "feats" performed by Cú Chulainn and others in the *Táin* must be exaggerations of these tricks.

222. A fourth figure, Herrauðr's illegitimate half-brother Purse, is killed by Bósi (chap. 4); the strongest personal adhesive in this tale is the *fostrbræðrum* of the two in the title.

223. *SCHS* I, 190, 201, 433.; Omer the Standard-Bearer is also mentioned in *SCHS* III, 162.

224. Low, *Marko*, 22–24; in the Pennington-Levi translation of the Marko

songs we find Alil-aga, named as Marko's "brother-in-god," who is obviously a Moslem: Pennington and Levi, *Marko the Prince*, 49.

225. Low, *Marko*, 130; for another kind of adventure with a *vila*, see Pennington and Levi, *Marko the Prince*, 33ff.; this *vila* has injured one of Marko's friends and has to be disciplined.

226. Skendi, *Albanian and South Slavic Oral Epic Poetry*, 121, for the "tavern maid" Ruza.

227. E. Stenboch-Fermor, "The Story of Van'ka Kain," in *Slavic Folklore: A Symposium*, ed. A. Lord, Bibliographical and Special Series, vol. 6 (Philadephia: American Folklore Society, 1956), 61–62.

228. In vv. 1533–47 (pp. 86–91) Hagen steals the clothing of the "nixies" and forces them to prophesy for him.

229. C. Scott Littleton, "Some Possible Indo-European Themes in the *Iliad*," in *Myth and Law Among the Indo-Europeans: Studies in Indo-European Comparative Mythology*, ed. J. Puhvel (Berkeley: University of California Press, 1970), 237; Ward, *The Divine Twins: An Indo-European Myth in Germanic Tradition*.

230. *SCHS* III, 102, 136.

231. C. Muscatine, "Courtly Literature and Vulgar Langauge," in *Court and Poet: Selected Proceedings of the Third Congress of the International Courtly Literature Society*, ed. G. S. Burgess (1980; reprint, Liverpool: Francis Cairns, 1981), 2.

232. Saxo, *Gesta Danorum*, VI.177–78, 181.

233. *CO*, 10, 13; Ford, *Mabinogion*, 129, 131; Bedwyr also has a daughter in this list.

234. According to Tauno Mustanoja, most critics "refuse to believe that Beowulf was maried to Hygd [Hygelac's widow] or to any woman whatsoever." In "'Beowulf' and the Tradition of Ritual Lamentation," *Neuphilologische Mitteilungen* 68 (1967): 12, referring to *Beowulf*, 3150–55.

235. Katherine Callen King, who follows Akhilleus's story and iconography from the original Homeric epic through two millennia (to the thirteenth-century Italian Guido delle Colonne's *Historia Destructionis Troiae*), shows how his extraordinary sexual passions are differently viewed and treated at different times. She lists his liaisons with the war prize Briseis, the Amazon Penthesileia, and in his wider legend the unfortunate Polyxaena, as well as with Deidameia, mother of his uncontrollable son Neoptolemos, together with Helen and Medea. See King, *Achilles: Paradigms of the War Hero from Homer to the Middle Ages* (Berkeley: University of California Press, 1987), 171–217. For another estimation and judgment of the sexual antics of Akhilleus and their psychological significance, see W. Thomas MacCary, *Childlike Achilles: Ontogeny and Philogeny in the* Iliad (New York: Columbia University Press, 1982). This view from the Freudian vantage point is ingenious, if not entirely convincing.

236. See G. Nagy, *Best of the Achaeans*, 279, citing Proclus; and see Kerényi, *Heroes of the Greeks*, 355 for the addenda to the Akhilleus legend that have him married, in the afterworld, either to Helen or to the great witch Medea. The postmortem marriage to Medea would connect Akhilleus's warrior legend to the "supernatural wife" motif.

237. GRO VI, line 838 (pp. 214–15).

238. Low, *Marko,* 104ff.

239. *Kitune Shirka,* 225.

240. Skendi, "Oral Epic," 121.

241. A subtype, the Amazon instructress, appears especially in the Celtic materials; Scathach, who taught the usages of war and arms to Cú Chulainn and others, is one of these (see above, n. 147). Also note the "nine witches" in the Welsh tale *Peredur mab Efrawg* who teach the naif Peredur the use of arms: Jones and Jones, *Mabinogion,* 198–99, 226–27.

242. Plutarch, *Alexander Romance,*145.

243. See P. Arant, "Concurrence of Patterns in the Russian *bylina,*" *Journal of the Folklore Institute* 7 (1970): 81. The hero Dunaj secures both a bride for his Prince Vladimir and the bride's Amazonian sister, Nastas'ya, for himself; when Dunaj brags of the conquest Nastas'ya challenges him, and the rest follows. For other Old Russian Amazons, see "The Healing of Il'ya" for the *polenitsy:* Chadwick, *Russian Heroic Poetry,* 60, line 32 (in Kir'evskii, *Pesni,* I.1ff); also "The Youth of Churilo" in Chadwick, *Russian Heroic Poetry,* 92, line 6. (in Rybnikov, *Pesni,* II.524: *vse palenitsy udaliye,* "all the bold fighting-women").

244. Kerényi, *Heroes of the Greeks,* 41, 159–163.

245. Ibid., 240–41.

246. *Aen.* XI.571–2.

247. *SCHS* II, 183–90. On the Moslem side the hero Đerdelez Alija marries the Amazon Fatima, who evidently is a horsewoman of note: *SCHS* II, 88.

248. *DS,*106.

249. *The Nibelungenlied,* trans. by A. T. Hatto (Harmondsworth: Penguin, 1981), v. 10, p. 93; Middle High German version in *Das Nibelungenlied. Mittelhochdeutscher Text und Ubertragung* ed. H. Brackert (Frankfurt am Main: Fischer, 1979), v. 680, pp. 150–51 (the Middle High German version will be cited here).

250. *Kitab-i Dede Korkut, The Book of Dede Korkut,* ed. and trans. F. Siemer, A. Uysal, and W. Walker (Austin: University of Texas Press, 1972), 46ff.

251. R. Eisler, *Man into Wolf: An Anthropological Interpretation of Sadism, Masochism and Lycanthropy. A lecture delivered at a meeting of the Royal Society of Medicine* (London: Spring Books, 1951), 156ff, n. 116; Kerényi, *Heroes of the Greeks,* 116–17.

252. J.-P. Vernant and Françoise Frontisi-Ducroux, "Features of the Mask in Ancient Greece," in Vernant and Vidal-Naquet, *Myth and Tragedy,* 197 (see chap. 1, n. 13).

253. Saxo, *Gesta Danorum,* I.23.

254. *Beowulf,* 1931ff; see F. Klaeber, *Beowulf and the Fight at Finnsburg,* 3d ed. (Boston: Heath, 1950), 195 for note.

255. Miller, "The Three Kings at Colonos," 57–58.

256. "BoH," chap. 2, 200.

257. *Saga Heiðriks Konungs in Vitra = The Saga of King Heidrek the Wise,* trans. C. Tolkein (London: T. Nelson & Sons, 1960), chaps. 10–20.

258. See, e.g., the *Helgi Lays (Helgakviða),* in *The Poetic Edda,* trans. L. M. Hol-

lander, 2d ed., rev. (Austin: University of Texas Press, 1986), 169ff., and see N. K. Chadwick, "Thorgerðr Holgabruðr and the *trollaping:* A Note on Sources," in *The Early Cultures of North-West Europe,* ed. C. Fox and B. Dickins, H. M. Chadwick Memorial Studies (Cambridge: Cambridge University Press, 1950), 413ff.

259. Low, *Marko,* 42ff.

260. For Indo-European "forced" (called in the Indic-Sanskritic context "demoniacal") marriage, see Calvert Watkins, "Studies in Indo-European Legal Language, Institutions, and Mythology," in *Indo-European and Indo-Europeans: Papers Presented at the Third Indo-European Conference at the University of Pennsylvania,* ed. G. Cardona, H. M. Hoenigswald, and A. Senn (Philadelphia: University of Pennsylvania Press, 1970), 323–24, s.v. *usurpare.*

261. *TYP,* 410; see Miller, "The Twinning of Arthur and Cei," 50–52 (see chap. 1, n. 106).

262. Miller, "Twinning of Arthur and Cei," 67–69.

263. Kerényi, *Heroes of the Greeks,* 316; Apollodoros, *Bibliothêkê,* III.xii.5 (chap. 1, n. 80).

264. As Hektor to Paris: *Il.* III.38ff, and III.454, "hated by all."

265. Whether or not the city of Ilium can be deposited right in the Third Function, as Littleton suggests, is still debated: Littleton, "Some Possible Indo-European Themes," 232–37. See now Bernard Sergent, *Les trois fonctions indo-europénnes en Grèce ancienne,* vol. 1, *De Mycènes aux Tragiques* (Paris: Economica, 1998): 37–84, and especially 32–37.

266. Grisward, *Archéologie.*

267. Ibid., 260, nn. 41–46. Grisward cites other Indo-European evidence, including the Roman and the Germanic (but not, one would think, the Achaean Greek), in which long "feminine" hair marks the Third Function. He notes that the "mythologie de la chevalure" displays two poles, "force" and "beauty," of which the former signifies the uncircumscribed *masculine* power. See now D. A. Miller, "On the Mythology of Indo-European Heroic Hair," *JI-ES* 26, nos. 1 and 2 (Spring–Summer, 1998): 41–60.

268. Grisward, *L'archéologie,* 229ff., and Miller, "The Coward Knight."

269. *Yvain,* 2513; and see Gold, *The Lady and the Virgin,* 24–25 (see chap. 1, n. 101), for *Yvain.*

270. J. Bremmer, "An Enigmatic Indo-European Rite: Paederasty," *Arethusa* 13, no. 2 (Fall 1980): 282ff.

271. Ibid., 288, nn. 84–87. Redactions of the archaic Irish and Welsh materials undertaken when Christianity had gained a dominant influence in these Celtic lands might well have wiped out any mention of practices abhorrent to Christian morality. Otherwise we might expect to find evidence in, for example, descriptions of the *fénnidi,* a typically excluded initiatory (and fostering) group of young males.

272. Kerényi, *Heroes of the Greeks,* 89–90.

273. For the view of the psychoanalytically inclined classicist Georges Devereux, see his "Retaliatory Homosexual Triumph over the Father: A Clinical Note on the Counteroedipal Sources of the Oedipus Complex," in *Basic Problems of*

Ethnopsychiatry, trans. B. M. Gulati and G. Devereux (Chicago: University of Chicago Press, 1980), 138–47.

274. Bremmer, "Paederesty," 291–92.

275. See Theodore M. Andersson and William Ian Miller, *Law and Literature in Medieval Iceland: Ljósvitninga saga and Valla-Ljóts saga* (Stanford: Stanford University Press, 1989), 165 ff. and n. 76. The specific instance here is a charge of effeminate perversion leveled against Gudmundr the Powerful by one Þórkell Hake—an accusation apparently without any foundation in fact, and which eventually led to Þórkell's violent death.

276. *ES*, chap. 57, 148; *EgS*, chap. 58, 209.

277. I am unaware, though I am willing to be informed or instructed, of any hint of lesbianism in the northern sources (that is, true lesbianism as distinct from mannish and therefore unseemly behavior on the part of women).

278. Among the Bumin-Kuskusmin of the New Guinea Highlands, male seed "lost" in a man's wife, in the ordinary course of copulation, is as soon as possible replenished by the husband when he fellates the wife's brother (personal communication by F. J. Porter-Poole). Other Papuan-Melanesian societies may not go this far, but do regularize a state of extraordinary antagonism, almost a gender warfare, between men and women, with a strong emphasis on the contaminative power of the feminine.

279. *Tochmarc Émire*, 16–68; translated in *AIM*, 155.

280. J. Nagy, *Wisdom*, 95, citing *The Book of Leinster*.

281. *CO*, 42; Ford, *Mabinogion*, 57.

282. See W. Sayers, "Concepts of Eloquence in *Tochmarc Émire*," *Studia Celtica* 24–25 (1989–90), 120–59.

283. *LS*, chap. 23, 99–100; Old Norse text edited by E. O. Sveinson, Íslensk Fornrit 5 (Reykjavik: Hið íslensk fornritafélag, 1934). Note the remark of Theodore Andersson, in his *The Icelandic Family Saga: An Analytic Reading* (Cambridge, Mass.: Harvard University Press, 1967), 233: "There is no love dialogue, no love psychology, no love analysis, no verbal play, and no homage to the mystery."

284. *LS*, especially chaps. 32–57, 117–91; in the end she became "a deeply religious woman": 76.235.

285. *GiS*, 6.17, 7.25. For brothers-in-law as *antagonists*, not close friends, see *Landnámabók*, 149.

286. *NjS*, 77.171. Yet note that Lars Lönnroth, in *Njáls Saga: A Critical Introduction* (Berkeley: University of California Press, 1976), 65, refers to Hallgerðr as a "primadonna of the Brynhildr type."

287. See J. Redfield, *Nature and Culture in the* Iliad: *The Tragedy of Hector* (Chicago: University of Chicago Press, 1975), and H. Montsacré, *Les larmes d'Achille: Le héros, la femme et la souffrance dans le poésie d'Homère* (Paris: Albin Michel, 1984).

288. R. Bespaloff, *On the Iliad*, trans. M. McCarthy, Bollingen Library (New York: Harper & Row, 1962), 39. This is a short but singularly acute study.

289. *DS*, 310, 321–23. The fate of David can of course be tied to the theme of a woman's revenge. Earlier in the epic the enchantress Deghtzoun Dzam merely hears of the exploits of Sanasar and falls in love with him (II.2.65), and this theme

is replicated with David and Khantout (II. [II] 1. 293). There may be an echo of the "marriage to sovereignty" motif here: the Caucasian-Celtic "ideological" nexus is clear enough in a number of cited instances.

290. The Old French *chansons de geste* may display a particular subtype, in which heroism is nearly subordinated to other constricting patterns and especially to "lignage," meaning "family ties," an area in which women may be and are more important: see P. Matarasso, *Recherches historiques et littéraires sur "Raoul de Cambrai"* (Paris: Nizet, 1962), 411–12, for the "chanson de lignage."

291. Delcourt, *Légendes et cultes,* 54 (see chap. 1, n. 201).

292. Skendi, "Oral Epic," 40–41.

293. *Historiae Alexandri Magni Macedonis = The History of Alexander* by Q. Curtius Rufus, trans. J. C. Rolfe, Loeb Classical Library (Cambridge, Mass.: Harvard University Press; London: Wm. Heinemann, 1956), 3.5.5, 3.5.10. Alexander's fear of "death in his bath" may echo an Indo-European pattern: the water death is assigned to the Third Function. See Donald J. Ward, "The Threefold Death: An Indo-European Trifunctional Sacrifice?" in Puhvel, *Myth and Law among the Indo-Europeans:* 123–42.

294. Saxo, *Gesta Danorum,* VIII.247: "adeo quondam rei bellicae deditis morbo oppetere proboscum existimatum est."

295. *KS,* chap. XI.

296. On the "good death," see Wilhelm Schultze, "Der Tod des Kambyses," *Sitzungsberichte der Königlich Preusischen Akademie des Wissenschaft* (1912), Bild II: 685–703ff.

297. M. Douglas, *Purity and Danger: An Analysis of Concepts of Pollution and Taboo* (London and Henley: Routledge & Kegan Paul, 1966), 169, 177–78.

298. Saxo, *Gesta Danorum,* I.35; Dumézil, *Hadingus,* 13–14.

299. Saxo, *Gesta Danorum,* VIII.252.

300. *ES,* chap. 85, 236–37; he dies after hiding his treasure, just as his father Skalla-Grímr had done (58, 150).

301. Grisward, *L'Archéologie,* 124 (see chap. 1, n. 30).

302. Dumézil, *Destiny of a King,* 58–59 (see chap. 1, n. 141).

303. *Aen.* X.745–46 for *ferreos . . . somnus;* XI.110 for *Martis sorte;* X.583 for *belli finis et ævi.*

304. Pennington and Levi, *Marko the Prince,* 65.

305. *Chanson de Roland,* ed. et trans. J. Bédier (Paris: L'édition d'Art, 1931); *The Song of Roland,* trans. P. Terry, Library of Liberal Arts (New York: Bobbs-Merrill, 1965), CXXVII.1685, CXLIII.1928–30.

306. *EIMS,* 91; Rees and Rees, *Celtic Heritage,* 330.

307. *GrS,* chap. 82.

308. For the "logic of death" in the *Iliad,* see Redfield, *Nature and Culture in the Iliad,* 19ff.

309. G. Nagy, *Best of the Achaeans,* 32.

310. Pennington and Levi, *Marko the Prince,* 59; also in Low, *Marko,* 130.

311. Pennington and Levi, *Marko the Prince,* 60; Low, 131.

312. *Chanson de Roland,* CLI.2050.

313. *Chanson de Roland*, XXXI.1726.

314. *Digenid*, GRO VIII, lines 35–36 (pp. 234–35).

315. *Digenid*, GRO VIII, lines 195–96 (pp. 242–43).

316. *Nibelungenlied*, vv. 899, 905, 980–82; Middle High German text, 200–201, 216–19.

317. Kerényi, *Heroes of the Greeks*, 353.

318. Ibid., 200–201.

319. *NjS*, chap. 77.

320. J. Nagy, *Wisdom*, 88 and n. 34. Note also that Cumall will die "once he marries" (90).

321. I have just made mention of the shadow, and to a degree this aspect of the heroic psyche emerges in fatality through self-limitation, or the rupture of self-limiting taboos.

322. Rees and Rees, *Celtic Heritage*, 327.

323. *Agallamh na Seanórach*, ed. by Nessa Ní Shéaghdha, 3 vols. (Dublin: 1942–45); translated in *AIT*, 150.

324. *AIT*, 337–38; Rees and Rees, *Celtic Heritage*, 331–33.

325. *EIMS*, 103–5; Rees and Rees, *Celtic Heritage*, 327ff.

326. *Chanson de Roland*, LXXXV; *JS*, chap. 21.

327. *ES*, chap. 22.

328. Rees and Rees, *Celtic Heritage*, 376.

329. Ellis Davidson, *The Road to Hel*, 70 (see chap. 1, n. 91).

330. Ibid., 72. See now Britt-Mari Näsström, *Freya—The Great Goddess of the North*, Lund Studies in History of Religions, 5 (Lund: University of Lund, 1995) for Freya as an omnifunctional goddess.

331. *GiS*, chap. 29. This marked friendship of the Third Function deity and spokesperson toward Gísli must be connected to the dramatic core of his saga, that is, his abandonment of his own kin and his perverse affection for his wife's family; i.e., he had left the normative social organization and gone over to his wife's kin, a clear violation of agnatic familial solidarity as traditional Norse-Icelandic culture viewed it.

332. Rees and Rees, *Celtic Heritage*, 336; see in *The Death-Tales of the Ulster Heroes*, ed. and trans. K. Meyer, Royal Irish Academy Todd Lecture Series 15 (Dublin, 1906), 32ff.

333. Rees and Rees, *Celtic Heritage*, 337.

334. *DS*, 334.

335. Rees and Rees, *Celtic Heritage*, 337–338.

336. The sleeping king is a folk figure whose roots go deep into myth. The best known are Charlemagne, Frederick Barbarossa, Frederick II, the Byzantine emperor Constantine V (who won his never-dying status even though he was an Iconoclast [a heretic]), and Baldwin of Flanders: see N. Cohn, *The Pursuit of the Millennium* (Fairlawn, N.J.: Prentice-Hall, 1957), 57–58, 81; and H. R. Ellis Davidson, "Folklore and History," in her *Patterns of Folklore* (Ipswich: D. S. Brewer; Totowa, N.J.: Rowman & Littlefield, 1978), 17–18. All of these are historical figures; to them we should add the legendary Arthur, *rex quondam et futurus*. The cluster of ideas

behind this image surely has as a foundation the notion of the king who, in his *saeculum*, is sleepless; according to a reliable source, the late Ernst Kantorowicz was working on the theme of "the king as insomniac," but this study remains, unfortunately, unfinished. According to Orphic beliefs the king cannot be bound by Sleep, though Sleep (*hupnos*) or Night affects and binds both gods and men: see M. Delcourt, *Héphaistos, ou la légende du magicien*, Bibliothèque de la Faculté de Philosophie et Lettres de l'Université de Liége, fasc. CXLVI (Paris: 1957), 22, 25. The king, when his earthly reign is past, is then permitted sleep, a closely related theme to the king in the mountain: see W. A. Chaney, *The Cult of Kingship in Anglo-Saxon England: The Transition from Paganism to Christianity* (Berkeley: University California Press, 1970), 97, n. 48. According to the Sibylline tradition the king or emperor who rises from deathless sleep to save his people occupies the first stage in the apocalyptic tradition; the second stage belongs to the Antichrist, the third to Christ returning: Cohn, *Millennium*, 17.

Ellis Davidson suggests that parallel to or developing from the sleeping king is the legend of the historical king who, following his supposed death, is said to take up a completely different persona. Her examples are Olaf Trygvasson of Norway in the eleventh century and Tsar Alexander I of Russia in the nineteenth: the common factors are (a) the transmutation of a powerful secular figure into an unknown, mysterious holy man, and (b) a search for salvation or even sanctification through, it is hinted, a long term of penance: in *Patterns of Folklore*, 15–16.

337. Miller, "Bad Death," 147–48, 156–58.

338. Ibid., 157–58.

339. *DS*, 366ff.

340. Low, *Marko*, 183; Skendi, "Oral Epic," 41. The second version is a legend of Nogatin. The Moslem singers of tales allow the sleeping cave to Prince Marko but make it more of a punishment: according to their version his cave is uncomfortably icy: *SCHS* I, 115, 363.

341. Kerényi, *Heroes of the Greeks*, 245–46, citing Plutarch, *Theseus*, in *Plutarch's Parallel Lives = Ploutarkhoi bioi paralleloi*, vol. 1, trans. by B. Perrin, Loeb Classical Library (Cambridge, Mass.: Harvard University Press; London: Wm. Heinemann, 1982), 36.2: *thêke te megalou sômatos aikhmê*.

342. Pausanius, IV.xxxii.4.

343. *Poema de Cid/The Poem of the Cid*, trans. W. S. Merwin (New York: New American Library, 1959), chap. 152; *Nibelungenlied*, v. 6 (pp. 6–7); *Chanson de Roland*, LXXXIII, CXV.

344. *Digenid*, GRO IV, line 96 (pp. 70–71): *arti pothô dexasasthai kai to genos lamprunai*. Digenes *may* be merely saying "to cast my family in a good light."

345. O'Rahilly, *Táin*, 1433 (pp. 39, 177) for Cú Chulainn "renowned in song"; 910–11 (pp. 25, 163) for his naming: *dáig concechlabat fir Hérend 7 Alban in n-ainm sín . . . bat lána beóil*. For Fergus's fame, 429 (pp. 12, 149).

CHAPTER 3: THE FRAMEWORK OF ADVENTURE

1. *CO*, 3 (lines 11–12); Ford, *Mabinogion*, 123 (see chap. 2, n. 10).

2. *Shâh-nâma*, V.ii.38 (see chap. 1, n. 36).

3. Though see B. Lincoln, "The Indo-European Cattle-Raiding Myth," *History of Religions* 16, no. 1 (August 1976): 42–65, and also *Priests, Warriors and Cattle: A Study in the Ecology of Religions*, Hermeneutics: Studies in the History of Religions 10 (Berkeley: University of California Press, 1981).

4. Information derived from a narrative recorded by the Austrian ethnographer Alois Musil in the first years of this century, as repeated and analyzed in Michael E. Meeker, *Literature and Violence in North Arabia*, 54 (see chap. 1, n. 166).

5. Ibid., 118.

6. Lincoln, "Cattle-Raiding Myth."

7. *HsK*, cited in Jones, *Kings, Beasts and Heroes*, 136 (see chap. 1, n. 95).

8. GRO VII, lines 14, 42 (pp. 216–17, 218–19); the hideout, *en tê kryptê tou lophou*, is in GRO VI, line 526 (pp. 194–95).

9. G. Dumézil, *Ancient Roman Religion: With an Appendix on the Religion of the Etruscans*, trans. P. Krapp (Chicago: University of Chicago Press, 1970), 1:235, as against H. J. Rose, *Some Problems of Classical Religion: Mars Eitrem Conference, Oslo, 1955* (Oslo: Universitets Forlaget, 1958), 1–17, who sees Mars and Silvanus as separate, not "confounded." The Irish Celtic case may give a better reading, for here war-god and forest-god are both separate *and* confounded.

10. *Aen.* VI.765.

11. Dumézil, *Ancient Roman Religion*, 344, 411ff., and 418ff. for *Rudra*.

12. Tacitus, *Germania*, 5, 9.

13. *VölS*, chap. 6; *Germania*, 20; though these *subterraneos* mainly seem to be hiding places for crops, *frugibus*.

14. Caesar, *De Bello Gallico*, VI.30. Of that Hyrcanian forest also mentioned in Tacitus, Caesar writes that "no man of the Germans can say he has reached the edge of that forest [*ad initium eius silvae*] or knows where it begins [*ex loco oriatur*]" (VI.25).

15. Caesar, *De Bello Gallico*, VI.34.

16. J. Nagy, *Wisdom*, 55, 58 (see chap. 1, n. 90).

17. The "grant" is contained in the *Colloquy of the Ancients* (*Accalamh na Senórach*), translated by J. Nagy in *Wisdom*, 30; see also p. 226, n. 7 for this source.

18. J. Nagy, *Wisdom*, 137, for the *fili* and the tree.

19. Ibid., 62–64.

20. See below, p. 268.

21. J. Nagy, *Wisdom*, examines the opposed occupations in dealing with the *gilla* (124ff.), and with Finn as *rígfénnid*, "chief of the *fianna*" (42ff.; see also 120).

22. Ibid., 136, 160, 175, 192, 194–95; for avoiding death, 62.

23. See, for example, the water-born Kourkis Jelaly in the *Sassowntsi David*—though the heroes of the Armenian epic are themselves often associated with lakes. Indeed, their heroic line supposedly originated in the mysterious and sacred

Lake Van. *DS*, I. 15 (44–45) (see chap. 2, n. 33). This supernaturally long-lived horse must be retamed by its heroic owner generation after generation, and it finally goes "into the mountain" with Pokr Mher, last of the heroic Sassoon line: IV. 4 (369).

24. *JS*, chap. 33 (see chap. 1, n. 107).

25. *Beowulf*, 210–28 (see chap. 2, n. 81).

26. *ES*, chap. 40.

27. As when Egill's ship was mysteriously drawn to York, presumably through Gunnhildr's magic: *ES*, chap. 49.

28. *Od.*, I.78; V.377.

29. Rees and Rees, *Celtic Heritage*, 40 (see chap. 2, n. 34); in their *Ur*-mythic attack on Ireland, in the time of Partholon, the Fomoirean ships, led by the ogress Lot, carried three times as many women as men (31).

30. *VölS*, chap. X (see chap. 2, n. 81); Low, *Marko*, 76 (see chap. 2, n. 16). For Hadingus see Dumézil, *From Myth to Fiction*, 45–46 (see chap. 2, n. 71); Hadingus at one point is cursed with a fate very similar to that of Odysseus: "at sea thou shalt be tossed, an eternal tempest shall attend the steps of thy wandering," because he, like Odysseus, had killed or injured the wrong monster: Saxo, *Gesta Danorum*, I.29 (see chap. 1, n. 91).

31. Ellis Davidson, *The Road to Hel*, 39–41 (see chap. 1, n. 91).

32. Ibid., 42–43.

33. Dumézil, *Le livre des héros*, 60ff. (see chap. 2, n. 88) (a tale called "Le dernier butin d'Uryzmæg"). In his notes to this narrative Dumézil reminds us that the Scythian ancestors of this Caucasian people used the "floating coffin" as a method of suicide: citing Pliny, *Natural History*, iv.26.

34. GRO IV, line 474 (pp. 102–3).

35. GRO IV, lines 971–73 (pp. 132–33). Between the heroic attitude of a Digenes and the traditional peasant distrust of the city (as in Robert Redfield, *The Primitive World and Its Transformations* [Ithaca, NY: Cornell University Press, 1957], 54ff.) would be the opinion of the Ukrainian guerrilla leader of "peasant-anarchists" Makhno: "the cities always give out a smell of dying and betrayal"; Nestor Ivanovitch Makhno, *La revolution russe au Ukraine (mars 1917–avril 1918)* (Paris: Brochure mensuelle, 1927), 297.

36. Jackson, *The Hero and the King*, 12ff., 15, and often (see chap. 1, n. 207): this is Jackson's primary image.

37. As late as the sixth century A.D. the Byzantine historian Procopius, in his *Peri ktismatôn*, pointed to the "rulerless" (*anarkhoi*) Caucasian Tzani, who follow a "beast-like existence" and who are to be tamed, and *eukosmia* thereby promulgated, by the introduction of cities according to imperial command: *Peri ktismatôn*, III.vi.2ff. (see chap. 1, n. 23).

38. Jones, *Kings, Beasts and Heroes*, 11 (see chap. 1, n. 95) ; Beo-wulf here is read as "Foe (wolf) of bees," that is, a bear.

39. *Nibelungenlied*, vv. 1935, 2078, 2099; Middle High German text: 170–71, 200–201, 204–5 (see chap. 2, n. 249).

40. "BoH," chaps. 12, 13.

41. We have to assume that Herrauðr is the "tall, handsome man" in a scarlet tunic who assaults the king; for some reason he is not named. Bósi is disguised by wearing another man's skin.

42. Saxo, *Gesta Danorum*, VI.169 (and 186ff.).

43. Ford, *Mabinogion*, 63, 64 (see chap. 2, n. 10).

44. It seems likely that the iron house in the *Branwen* story, with iron known to be a prophylactic against the "old magic," and the craft and power of the assembled smiths, is detailed to make the effort against the giants seem more potent.

45. Text in *TBDD*, translation in *EIMS*, 103. All water in the hostel is used up fighting the fires, and Conaire's magically induced thirst causes him to send a needed champion in search of more water: the elements are used against him (Rees and Rees, *Celtic Heritage*, 330). Compare the Nart tale, "La mort de Batradz" in Dumézil, *Le livre des héros*, 233ff., where this uncontrollable hero is finally done to death, broiled in his steel skin by the heat of the sun-divinity.

46. Rees and Rees, *Celtic Heritage*, 334–35, 338–40.

47. J. Nagy, "Shamanic Aspects of the *Bruidhean* Tale," *History of Religions* 20, no. 4 (November 1980): 310–14; Nagy collected and examined the Fenian stories of hostile supernatural hosts in the *bruidhne*, and believes that these adventures conceal a shaman's Otherworld journey, a journey during which the adventurer risks injury or death to gain supernatural knowledge.

48. Dumézil, *Le livre des héros*, 200–201: the tale is "Batradz sauve les plus illustres des Nartes." The hero Batradz is called down, presumably "from above" (he has a semidivine or perhaps a demonic persona added to the heroic), to save the threatened Narts.

49. *Ldn*, chaps. 229, 356, 217.

50. *Ldn*, chaps. 42, 348.

51. *Ldn*, chap. 24; *Hænsa-Þoris saga*, ed. S. Nordal and G. Jónsson, Íslensk Fornrit 3 (Reykjavik: Hið íslensk fornritafélag, 1938), c. 11; in fact a second burning was threatened by the arsonous Tongue-Oddr and was only just prevented by Tongue-Oddr's brother Þóroddr, who was in love with the prospective victim's daughter (chap. 17). Andersson, *Family Saga*, 115 (see chap. 2, n. 283), believes that this saga should properly be *Blund-Ketils saga*, inasmuch as the burning (as in the *Njála*) "stands at the center of the action."

52. *Vatnsdæla saga*, ed. E. O. Sveinsson, Íslensk Fornrit 8 (Reykjavik: Hið íslensk fornritafélag, 1939), chap. xxviii; also in *The Vatnsdaler's Saga*, trans. Gwyn Jones (Princeton: American Scandinavian Foundation, 1944).

53. *Hallfreðar saga*, in *Vatnsdæla saga* , chap. 1.

54. *EyS*, chap. 31.

55. *Guðmundar saga dyri*, in *Sturlunga saga*, ed. J. Jóhannesson, M. Finnbogason, and K. Eldjárn (Reykjavik: Sturlunguútgáfan, 1946), 1.14, 17; trans. J. McGrew, Library of Scandinavian Literature (New York: Twayne, 1970).

56. *Hrafns saga Sveinbjarnarssonar*, in *Sturlunga Saga*, chap. 19.

57. See Lönnroth, *Njáls Saga: A Critical Introduction*, with bibliography, 249–60 (see chap. 2, n. 286).

58. Andersson, *Family Saga,* 304; Byock, *Feud in the Icelandic Saga,* 161ff., 190 (see chap. 2, n. 167).

59. *LxS,* chap. 64.

60. *CO,* 31 (lines 849–50); Ford, *Mabinogion,* 147.

61. *CO,* 32 (lines 886ff.); Ford, *Mabinogion,* 148.

62. *CO,* 35 (lines 998–99); Ford, *Mabinogion,* 151.

63. Ford, *Mabinogion,* 50–52.

64. Ibid., 80ff.

65. One possibility for the cause behind the occultation of the newborn is the desire by the Otherworld to sequester a "dangerous" heroic individual, because he will be sure to act powerfully in both realms, sacred and profane.

66. *Ragnar saga loðbrókar,* in *Fornaldarsögur Norðulanda,* ed. G. Jónsson (Reykjavik: Islendingasagnaútgáfen, 1954), vol. 1, chap. 15; in parallel with a hero like Beowulf, Ragnar defeated a monster-dragon at the start of his saga career (in "BoH," chap. 16), and was the victim of a similar monster or monsters at the end of it.

67. See W. Sayers, *"Guin agus Crochad agus Gólad:* The Earliest Irish Threefold Death," in *Proceedings of the Second North American Congress of Celtic Studies, Halifax, 1989,* ed. Cyril Byrne (Halifax: Chair of Irish Studies, St. Mary's University, 1990), 65–82; Sayers also cites the *Corpus Juris Hiberniae,* ed. D. A. Binchy (Dublin, 1975): p. 1927, lines 20–21.

68. GRO IV, lines 1050–52 (pp. 138–39).

69. GRO V, line 22 (pp. 142–43); VI, line 288.

70. GRO VIII, lines 206–7 (pp. 244–45); see also Grégoire, *Ho Digenês Akritas,* 37 (see chap. 2, n. 117).

71. GRO VI, lines 121ff. (pp. 168–69), e.g.

72. The historical El Mio Cid died in A.D. 1099; see *Poema/Poem,* vii (see chap. 2, n. 343); now see also Richard Fletcher, *The Quest for El Cid* (New York: Knopf, 1990). The "historic" Digenes *may* be assigned to the eighth-ninth century: see Grégoire, "The Historical Element in Western and Eastern Epics," in his *Autour de l'épopée byzantine* 527 (see chap. 1, n. 77), and also in his *Ho Digenês Akritas,* 36.

73. *Poema/Poem,* 104 (pp. 186–87): *la barba que tan aínal creçió.*

74. See, e.g., Grégoire, *Ho Digenês Akritas,* 3ff.

75. *Poema/Poem,* 46 (pp. 98–99), the Moors send their prayers with El Cid: *nuestras oraciones váyante delante!;* 83 (pp. 144–45), Abengalbon: *mio amigo es de paz* (see also 126, pp. 228–229); 118 (pp. 212–13), the Cid to Bucar: *saludar nos hemos amos, e tajaremos amiztat.*

76. *Poema/Poem,* 110 (pp. 196–97).

77. Two motifs in the *Poema* may show a weak survival of motifs more common in other heroic tales: (a) the lion kept captive by the hero (which affrights the brothers of Carrión) demonstrates the hero's power over this iconic carnivore: *Poema/Poem,* 112 (pp. 202–3); (b) the Forest of Corpes, where the Cid's daughters are maltreated and abandoned, is depicted as a typical wilderness, with "trees so

tall they brush the clouds, and its wild beasts that roam about": *Poema/Poem*, 128, 129 (pp. 232–33, 236–37).

78. Lord, *The Singer of Tales* (see chap. 1, n. 67); see also J. M. Foley, "The Oral Theory in Context," in *Oral Traditional Literature: A Festschrift for Alfred Bates Lord*, ed. J. M. Foley (Columbus, Ohio: Slavica Publishers, 1980), 27–122.

79. *SCHS* III, 112, 122f.

80. The Serbian bard Avdo, for example, who sang "Smailagić Meho," substitutes a ficticious "river Klima" for Buda's river, though he also knows of the Danube: *SCHS* III, 118 and n. 61 (256–57), 127.

81. *Slovo o Polku Igoreve*, trans. into modern Russian by D. Likhachov, trans. into English by I. Petrova (Moscow: Progress Publishers, 1981), 34–35, 36–37.

82. Ibid., 50–51.

83. Ibid., 57.

84. *ES*, chap. 70 (*EgS*, chap. 71): because "the king has ill will towards him," *Er konungi . . . allilla til hans.*

85. Kerényi, *Heroes of the Greeks*, 185–86 (see chap. 1, n. 12).

86. Ibid., 102; see also Antiope, sent mad by the god Dionysos, who "punished her with wanderings" (38), and also the grave disorientation of Agave, another victim of Dionysos (32). Among other cases, Atalante's "amorous madness" can be read as more or less hysterical (118), while the madness of Aias that led to his suicide seems to have come from massive frustration: not winning the champion's prize at Akhilleus's funeral games, and, much worse, losing the prize to hated Odysseus: 324.

87. Chrétien de Troyes, *Yvain = Le Chevalier au Lion*, in *Les romans de Chrétien de Troyes*, ed. Mario Roques (Paris: Les Classiques Français du Moyen Age, 1952); *The Complete Romances of Chrétien de Troyes*, trans. D. Staines (Bloomington: Indiana University Press, 1990), 2774ff.

88. *Slovo*, 40–41.

89. See Marcel Detienne and J.-P. Vernant, *Cunning Intelligence in Greek Culture and Society*, trans. J. Lloyd (Chicago: University of Chicago Press, 1991), s.v. "Athena."

90. E. Auerbach, *Mimesis: The Representation of Reality in Western Literature* (New York: Doubleday, 1953), chap. 1, "Odysseus' Scar."

91. For Uastyrdji's extraordinary rape, see the Russian translation of the Ossetian *Narty Kajsytæ* in *Narty, epos ossetinskaya naroda*, trans. and ed. V. Abaev et. al. (Moskva: Akademiya Nauk SSR, 1957), 87–90; A. Dirr's version is in his *Kaukasische Märchen* (Jena: E. Diederichs, 1920), with an English translation in *Caucasian Folk-tales: Selected and Translated from the Original by Adolf Dirru*, trans. L. Menzies (New York: Dutton, 1925). For other various Ossetian concepts of the supernatural in their Nart tales, see Dumézil, *Le livre des héros*, 44–54 ("Le fils sans nom d'Uryzmæg"), 69–70 ("Naissance de Soslan"), 233–38 ("Mort de Batradz").

92. Starkaðr's tale is connected at its beginning to the mythic world in which Þórr is the divine giant fighter of the Aesir, and it is Starkaðr's giant ancestry that evidently offends this god.

93. In *Ldn*, chap. 68: Þórir Grímsson (Sel-Þórir), when old "and blind," saw

(?) a "huge, evil-looking" man row up Kald River in an enormous iron boat, debark, walk to a farm called Hrip, and begin digging "at the gate of the sheep fold." During the night a volcanic eruption occurred at that place. Here we seem to have a Vulcanic figure, a smith-and-fire-spirit or -god (the text adds, unnecessarily, that Þórir and his kin were all pagans). Oláfr's dream of Freya is in *LxS*, chap. 32.

94. *EyS*, chap. 4; for the instance of Hrafnkel Frey's-Priest (Freysgoða) in his short saga, and specifically for Hermann Pálsson's exposition and treatment of this saga not as a record of pagan cultic activity and belief but as a "morality play," see Pálsson, *Art and Ethics in Hrafnkel's Saga* (Copenhagen: Einar Munksgaard, 1971); for the saga itself, *Hrafnkels saga Freysgoða*, in *Nordisk Filologi*, ed. J. Helgason (Copenhagen: Einar Munksgaard, 1950); translated in *Hrafnkel's Saga and Other Stories*, trans. H. Pálsson (Harmondsworth: Penguin, 1980): 35–71. The hero, Killer-Glumr, of *Víga-Glúms saga* is also made out to be an adherent of Frey, though eventually he became a Christian: see chaps. 5, 9, 19.

95. Ellis Davidson, *Hel*, 69ff. (see chap. 1, n. 91); Snorri, *Grimnismál*, in *The Poetic Edda*, trans. L. Hollander, 2d ed. (Austin: University of Texas Press, 1986), strophe 37.

96. Ellis Davidson, *Hel*, 68, 71ff.

97. J. Nagy, *Wisdom*, 39: "in Irish mythology generally, we can see that the difference between this world and the other world is more of degree than of kind. . . . The otherworld is different . . . because the fundamentals of civilization, both the good and the bad, are perfectly idealized there."

98. See Ford's introduction to his *Mabinogion*, 4–10.

99. See chapter 2, p. 127 above.

100. J. Nagy, *Wisdom*, 178.

101. Ibid., 130, 173.

102. Nagy sees Finn's untimely graying as providing a further processual mark on this hero as he transcends temporal divisions and remains caught "between youth and senility": ibid., 160. In the Norse-Icelandic context early graying was regarded as a suspicious and troubling mark on a man: see below, chapter 7.

103. J. Nagy, *Wisdom*, 154–55.

104. G. Nagy, *Best of the Achaeans*, chap. 14, 253ff. (see chap. 1, n. 7), for Thersites as the "worst of the Achaeans."

105. Dumézil, *Contes Lazes*, 78–106 (see chap. 2, n. 198); see Thompson, *Motif-Index*, D859.2, F80ff, H1250ff, H1270ff. (see chap. 2, n. 40).

106. Kerényi, *Heroes of the Greeks*, 51.

107. Ibid., 178–79.

108. Ibid., 239.

109. Kirk, *The Nature of Greek Myth*, 109 (see chap. 2, n. 6).

110. Miller, "The Three Kings at Colonos," 57 (see chap. 2, n. 8). There are other Otherworld journeys in our sources: Saxo has the hero-king Hadingus visit the Netherworld (led there by a supernatural woman). Some of the inspiration for this journey may have been Saxo's classical learning, but other influences are pos-

sible as well: Saxo, *Gesta Danorum*, I.30–31, and see Ellis Davidson's note, 2:35, n. 58 (see chap. 1, n. 91).

111. Kerényi, *Hero of the Greeks*, 286.

112. *Aen.* VI.720ff.

113. Rees and Rees, *Celtic Heritage*, 183–88 on the *síd* and their "mounds." Icelandic folklore constructs a very similar world for the "elves," called *huldufolk* or "hidden people," who are "barely distinguishable from human beings, . . . having homes, social relationships, and often a religion closely mirroring the human pattern"; Jacqueline Simpson, *Icelandic Folktales and Legends* (Berkeley: University of California Press, 1979), 14–15. They may live underground (18), or on the "Lower Road" (50; cf. a well-known Scottish ballad), or even in a lake (54). Some Irish-Celtic influence on the Icelandic folktale is not impossible.

114. Another malignant power besides the dead may inhabit the grave barrow, at least in the later Icelandic imagination: trolls reside there in *Sigrgarðs saga frækna*, available in Agnete Loth, *Late Medieval Icelandic Romances*, Editiones Arnamagnæanæ, ser. B, vol. 5 (Copenhagen, 1962–65): chaps. 14–15, 90–93.

115. Rees and Rees, *Celtic Heritage*, 136–37, citing the *Finnaigecht*, ed. and trans K., Meyer Royal Irish Academy Todd Lectures 16 (Dublin, 1910), 58ff.

116. *Cath Maige Mucrama: The Battle of Mag Mucrama*, ed. and trans. Máirín Ó Daly, Irish Texts Society 50 (Dublin: Dublin University Press, 1975), 156–57; J. Nagy, *Wisdom*, 81–82; see also Tomás Ó Cathasaigh, "The Theme of Lommrad in *Cath Maige Mucrama*," *Éigse* 18 (1981): 216, n. 11.

117. K. Meyer, "Finn and the Man in the Tree," *Revue Celtique* 25 (1904): 344–49; J. Nagy, *Wisdom*, 129–30.

118. *Macgnimartha Find = The Boyhood of Finn*, ed. K. Meyer, in *Revue Celtique* 5 (1882): 195–204, trans. K. Meyer, in *Ériu* 1 (1904): 180–90, and also in J. Nagy, *Wisdom*, appendix I, 209–21.

119. J. Nagy, *Wisdom*, 178.

120. Rees and Rees, *Celtic Heritage*, 336.

121. The fantasy romance "Egill ok Ásmunðr" ("EoÁ," 3:323–65) has Queen Eagle-Beak, ruler of Jotunheim (Giant-Land) relating a tale-within-a-tale in which she visits *undirheimar* or *undirdjup; underheimar* is ruled by King Sujar ("Snow"), whereas in *undirdjup* Óðinn is the Chief of Darkness, *hofþingi myrkranna*—an interesting conceit, reconnecting Óðinn to Hel: chap. 13. "Egill ok Ásmunðr" is a wild and woolly story influenced by a number of non-Norse sources, evidently including the Polyphemos encounter in the *Odyssey* (chap. 10). Some Icelandic sources suggest that trolls, who are nonhuman monsters, also can inhabit grave howes but the passage in "Egill ok Ásmunðr" cited by Boberg, *Motif-Index*, F455.1.1 (see chap. 2, n. 107, *tyrfd ok trollum gefin*, simply means "put under ground (under sod, "turfed") "and given to the trolls" (chap. 12). Generally trolls are assigned by the saga men to the nonhuman wild, to natural places such as cliffs, caves, and fell lands: Boberg, *Motif-Index*, F455.1.2; but see note 114 in this chapter.

122. *GrS*, chap. 18.

123. *Ldn*, chap. 174. For the continued history of the sword Skofnung, the

"Gleaner," see *KS*, chap. 9 and *LxS*, chaps. 57, 58, 78. See also Jones, *Kings, Beasts and Heroes*, 161–62.

124. *Flateyjarbók, Oláfs saga Helga*, II.7.5–7.

125. See Ellis Davidson, *Hel*, 111–16. It is tempting to identify the elves as spirits of health and plenty, which would probably set them into Dumézil's Third Function, but this cannot be confirmed because they are different from both the Aesir and the Vanir. *Alfar* may be associated with mounds, however, and therefore demonstrate a Norse parallel to the Irish Celtic supernatural *síd*-dwellers.

126. See Miller, "Bad Death," 155–56 (see chap. 1, n. 10).

127. *Flateyjarbók, Oláfs saga Helga*. II.106, p. 135.

128. *EyS*, chap. 4; also *Ldn*, chap. 85.

129. *EyS*, chaps. 4, 11, 13.

130. *NjS*, chap. 14.

131. Fontenrose, *The Ritual Theory of Myth*, 47 (see chap. 1, n. 4): citing J. G. Frazer, *The Golden Bough: A Study in Magic and Religion*, 3d ed. (London: Macmillan, 1912), 2:29–33, for trees, and Ovid, *Metamorphoses*, for springs (Byblis, Arethusa).

132. W. Burkert, *Structure and History in Greek Mythology and Ritual* (Berkeley: University of California Press, 1979), 116.

133. V. Propp, *Morphology of the Folktale*, trans. L. Scott, *International Journal of American Linguistics* 24, no. 4 (October 1958) = Publication 10 of the Indiana University Research Center in Anthropology, Folklore and Linguistics, vol. 20.

134. Campbell, *The Hero with a Thousand Faces*, 30 (see chap. 1, n. 230).

135. Ó Cathasaigh, *The Heroic Biography of Cormac mac Airt* (see chap. 2, n. 60); de Vries, *Heroic Song and Heroic Legend*, 211ff. (see chap. 1, n. 71).

136. *ES*, chap. 75.

137. Kerényi, *Heroes of the Greeks*, 219–24.

138. Ibid., 251. "Lasting happiness," of course, is inapposite in respect to the most final aspects of the heroic *muthos*.

139. All motifs may be mixed in some forest of ever-night, which the light of day never reaches; note also that in the ancient (and modern) Greek view "silent midday," the opposite of midnight, was an ambiguous between-time, literally a "panic" time when that wild godling or some other mischievous spirit might appear to frighten humans.

140. The reverse is also known, of course, when the hero spends what is calculated as near to a lifetime in the separated Otherworld realm and time—wooing, marrying, having children, growing old—and on his return to human time has been "gone" only a matter of a day or a night.

141. Kerényi, *Heroes of the Greeks*, 266: "The dark son of Helios and his dwelling were like Hades and his house." See also Neumann, *Origins*, 171ff. (see chap. 1, n. 210), for the "destructive, negative" father.

142. In respect to the adventure of the dragon's teeth and of the sown men, the Spartoi: see Kerényi, *Heroes of the Greeks*, 264–66.

143. The widespread Indo-European motif pattern of the cauldron of life is especially and frequently visible in the Celtic context, but Greece affords us this

example as well as that contained in the myth of Pelops: see W. Burkert, *Homo Necans: The Anthropology of Ancient Greek Sacrificial Ritual and Myth*, trans. P. Bing (Berkeley: University of California Press, 1983), 99; and see Miller, "Bad Death," 153–54.

144. For a sharp critique of some of the more recent and *outré* interpretations of the Graal legend as Chrétien de Troyes had decorated and reedited it, see Pierre Gallais's first chapter, "Déraissoner sur le Graal?" in his *Percival et l'initiation: Essais sur le dernier roman de Chrétien, ses correspondences "orientales" et la signification anthropologique* (Paris: Editions du Sirac, 1972).

145. Goetinck, *Peredur,* 122 (see chap. 1, n. 28).

146. Ibid., 231.

147. Ibid., 257.

148. Ibid., 281–83. Jean Markale, the indefatigable Breton Celticist, places the anonymous *Perlesvaus* under the same "primitive" rubric as *Peredur* but differentiates its hero as one who "sait ce qu'il veut," replacing "un héros imbécil qui accede par hazard aux mystères de l'exstase divin": *Le Graal,* Collection "Question de," ed. M. de Swedt (Paris: Editions Retz, 1982), 88. In *Perlesvaus* the vengeance quest is open and central and violent: "Rarement oeuvre 'courtoise' a été plus sanglante, plus violente" (ibid.), and Markale sees this violence as redolent of "l'idée de croisade" so dear to the dour Clunaic spirit (89). One might question the "imbecility" of Peredur's progress, recalling the hero-as-fool theme, but *Perlesvaus* does bridge effectively over to the Continental redactions of the sacred quest.

149. Though Markale notes (*Graal,* 116ff.) that an anonymous *Elucidation* of the *Perceval* and its themes not only reintroduced the theme of an Otherworld figure attacked and then revenging itself on the attacker, but depicted the Graal itself as "un objet magique paiën" (118) and painted a renewed Celticism, and even paganism, onto the backdrop of the quest.

150. Goetinck, *Peredur,* 206.

151. Matarasso, *The Redemption of Chivalry,* 114 (see chap. 1, n. 28).

152. Ibid., 120. In terms of color symbolism, Galaad, as red knight (symbolizing the salvific sign of Christ's shed blood), has exactly reversed the usual Second Function significance of this color, which ordinarily represents blood shed in battle and the choleric battle-heat of the warrior.

153. See Markale, *Graal,* 186–99.

154. *CO,* 21ff. (lines 570ff.); Ford, *Mabinogion,* 137ff.

155. See *CO,* 33 (lines 930–31); Ford, *Mabinogion,* 149, for the "two pups" of Rymhi, evidently a supernumerary segment of the quest.

156. *CO,* 25 (lines 668–69); Ford, *Mabinogion,* 141.

157. *CO,* 28 (lines 753–54); "A'm harglwyd gar Arthur . . ."; Ford, *Mabinogion,* 144.

158. *CO,* 35 (lines 977–982); Ford, *Mabinogion,* 151. See Miller, "The Twinning of Arthur and Cei," (see chap. 1, n. 106).

159. *CO,* 42 (lines 1238–41); Ford, *Mabinogion,* 157.

160. Jones, *Kings, Beasts and Heroes,* 68; Thompson, *Motif-Index,* 513, 513A.

161. Jones, *Kings, Beasts and Heroes,* 77.

162. Joan N. Radner, "Interpreting Irony in Medieval Celtic Narrative: The Case of *Culhwch ac Olwen,*" *Cambridge Medieval Celtic Studies* 16 (Winter, 1988): 41–59; especially 51. Radner tries to fit the currently fashionable rhetorical trope of irony to *CO;* my own reaction to such a tactic is that Radner fails to, in fact cannot, reconstruct the medieval mind-set to which such "irony" might appeal; in other words, her semiosis is essentially anachronistic. But she takes the tale seriously (45).

163. John Layard, *A Celtic Quest: Sexuality and Soul in Individuation. A Depth-Psychology Study of the Mabinogion Legend of Culhwch and Olwen* (Dallas: Spring Publications, 1985), 31. Two prisoners, two boars, two giants, and so on, are seen by Layard as symbolic male/female pairs: 88–89.

164. *LPS,* introduction, xvii.

165. Rustaveli's work is regarded as a primary Georgian cultural artifact, and copies are still given to newlywed brides as a foundation stone (along with language and religion) of a properly constituted household and of the Georgian nation at large.

166. *LPS,* 61.

167. In fact, Avtandil's loyalties appear divided along—in Dumézilian terms—trifunctional lines: to his king (First Function), to his warrior-comrade (Second Function), and to his ladylove (Third Function). Any identifiable Indo-European elements in this Georgian tale could come either from the strong Persian influence (on medieval Georgia and on Rustaveli specifically) or from other, contiguous Indo-European-speaking peoples of the Caucasus.

168. *LPS,* 114–23.

169. *LPS,* 150.

170. *LPS,* 200.

171. *LPS,* 203, 88. Weeping used as an instrument of persuasion is seen in an exchange between Avtandil and Tariel's sister Asmat, who shares her brother's wilderness cave: 29.

172. *LPS,* 113.

173. *LPS,* 66, 93–97.

174. Stevenson's introduction, ibid., xvii; *LPS* transmutes the "romance" between lovers seen in such possible models as *Visramiani* and *Leyla and Majnun* (the first Georgian, the second Persian) into a more complex knot of affective ties. What this Georgian epic is emphatically not is any sort of paean to what a Soviet commentator (A. G. Baramidze in his "Georgian Perspective" appended to this translation: 226) has called "unshakeable faith in the ultimate triumph of justice." The narrative is a fine baroque invention with no more political or social conscience than any other aristocratic-poetic celebration of the knightly or warrior-hero ethic.

175. Neumann, *Origins,* 213–19.

176. The feminine as it is reflected in the Thesean legend always projects the feeling of eventual ill fate; he cannot cooperate with its dense and multiform powers for long, for his masculinity appears to be too primitive: see Miller, "The Three Kings at Colonos," 55–58, for Theseus as the extreme or hypermachic type.

177. *Od.* XI (90ff. for the prophecies of Teiresias). Almost certainly that trickster's role is what protects Odysseus in this scene.

178. *CMT,* chap.146 (pp. 66–67).

179. *Raoul de Cambrai,* CLXXIII, CLXXXIX (see chap. 2, n.186). Auerbach comments that in the *Roland* "strata other than that at the top of the feudal system simply do not appear" (*Mimesis,* 106 [see chap. 1, n. 149]).

180. "Meier" is a caricature of the robber-knight, who feels himself *hochvertigen* because he was sponsored at his baptism by a noble knight (485–86) and, even more so, because his mother had had relations with a noble knight while he (Meier) was in the womb (*do kom zuo ir gekrochen ein vil gefueger hoveman:* 1377–78). "Meier" of course translates as "steward," the despised representative of another power. See *Die Mare vom Helmbrecht (von Wernher dem Gartenaere),* ed. F. Panzer, Altdeutsche Textbibliothek, no. 11 (Tubingen: Max Niemayer, 1960); in *Peasant Life in Old German Epics:* Meier Helmbrecht *and* Die arme Heinrich, ed. and trans. C. H. Bell, Records of Civilization Series (1931; reprint, New York: Columbia University Press, 1959).

181. The "enemy as mass"—often in magically figured numbers—works its effect in another way as mere numbers are derogated and singularity is advanced, as we have seen in more than one heroic death drama.

182. H. W. Bailey, "Ossetes," in A. T. Hatto, *Traditions of Heroic and Epic Poetry,* vol. 1, *Traditions,* Publications of the Modern Humanities Research Association, vol. 13 (London: 1989), 246. The father of Syrdon, the Nart trickster whose role in the tales greatly resembles that of the Norse Loki, was supposed to be a *san lag:* Bailey, 250.

183. Such a presumed promotion may not have a good end: Beowulf, the conqueror of monsters, will be the *god cyning* of the Geats, but also will eventually be helpless before a malignant destiny. The king's champion, standing for the king, is extremely vulnerable as well.

184. *LPS,* xix.

185. *Shâh-nâma,* VI.xx.79–80 (see chap. 1, n. 36): The arch-hero Rostam, having mortally wounded his son, sends to King Kâvus for a panacea to heal Sohrâb, but the king refuses, because if Sohrâb lived Rostam would wax even greater, and he is already (in Kâvus's eyes) the king's "enemy."

186. *Nibelungenlied,* v. 110 (pp. 28–29) (see chap. 2, n. 249), for the boast; the quotation is from Stephen L. Wailes, "The *Nibelungenlied* as Heroic Epic," in Oinas, *Heroic Epic and Saga,* 126 (see chap. 1, n. 73).

187. Jackson, *Hero and King,* 54, 63; the emperor's "moral weakness" is culpable.

188. Auerbach, *Mimesis,* 88.

189. Jackson, *Hero and King,* 64.

190. Grisward, *L'archéologie,* 220 (see chap. 1, n. 30). Other *chansons* (such as *Renaud de Montauban*) make Charlemagne himself the king-villain, while such a strange work as *Le pélérinage de Charlemagne* turns the whole king-hero relationship into a huge joke: *Le pélérinage de Charlemagne,* ed. A. J. Cooper (Paris: A. Lahure, 1925).

191. Jackson, *Hero and King,* 73; Grisward, *L'archéologie,* 221; also note that

sovereignty, the First Function office, is assigned to certain of the sons of Aymeri, following a pattern first discerned by Dumézil: Grisward, 171–82.

192. Jackson, *Hero and King,* 74.

193. For example, *Ldn,* chaps. 85, 134, 135, 139, 155, 156, 267, 341.

194. *Ldn,* chap. 85, *EyS,* chap. 3; see Miller, "Functional Oppositions," 127ff. (see chap. 1, n. 109).

195. Miller, "Functional Oppositions," 127.

196. Ibid., 117–23, with references to *Jómsvíkingasaga.*

197. Ibid.,136–43, referring to"BoH"; see, in the Pálsson and Edwards's volume *Seven Viking Romances* (see chap.1, n. 142), the appearance of King Godmunðr in the tale *Helgi Thorisson:* c. 2–3.

198. Miller, "Functional Operations."

199. Dumézil, *Mitra-Varuna,* 80ff., 125ff. (see chap. 1, n. 198).

200. See Ellis Davidson's introduction (2:8ff.) to Saxo, *Gesta Danorum.*

201. See D. A. Miller, *Imperial Constantinople* (New York: John Wiley, 1969), 82ff., for theoretical and iconic hints at the guidelines to delegated power in the Byzantine imperium; see also Miller, "The Emperor and the Stylite: A Note on the Imperial Office," *Greek Orthodox Theological Review* 15, no. 2 (Fall 1970): 207–12; and Needham, *Right and Left: Essays on Dual Symbolic Classification* (see chap. 1, n. 200).

202. On Starkaðr: Dumézil, *The Destiny of the Warrior,* 82–95 (see chap. 2, n. 185); *The Stakes of the Warrior,* ed. J. Puhvel, trans. D. Weeks (Berkeley: University of California Press, 1983), 9–50.

203. *GtS,* chap. 7; Saxo, *Gesta Danorum,* VI.170ff.

204. Miller, "Functional Operations," 127–29.

205. Calin, *Epic of Revolt,* 132 (see chap. 1, n. 98): for the *démesuré* in his "negligence of thought" and "wild displays of violence" against authority or "society as a whole."

206. O'Rahilly, *Táin,* 14, 151 (line 496) (see chap. 2, n. 95): Fergus says "this is a champion's bond, not the bond of a madman," *iss naidm níad, ní nasc fir mir.*

207. For a small sampling, see the Kinsella, *Táin,* 54ff.; O'Rahilly, *Táin,* 25–26, 163–64 (lines 921ff.) (see chap. 2, n. 95). It should be recalled that Cú Chulainn was not an Ulsterman on both sides of his parentage, no matter how this parentage is figured.

208. J. Nagy, *Wisdom,* 41–79.

209. *TYP,* T. 20, T. 37R, T. 54; and see Miller, "The Twinning of Arthur and Cei," 47–76.

210. Miller, "Twinning of Arthur and Cei"; see also J. Grisward, "Uter, Artur, Pendragon et l'idéologie royale des indo-européens: Structure trifonctionelle et roman arthurienne," *Europe. Le Moyen Age Maintenant* (October 1983), 111–20.

211. The *Pa Gur* is contained in the *Llyvyr Du Kaer Vryddin = The Black Book of Camarthen,* ed. J. Gwenogvryn Evans, Series of Old Welsh Texts, vol. 5 (Pwlheli, 1906), 94; a partial translation is in Jones and Jones, *Mabinogion,* xxiv (see chap. 2, n. 93), and Miller, "Twinning of Arthur and Cei," 58–59.

212. See above, p. 104.

213. *TYP,* T. 12, for Arthur described as a "frivolous" or "scurrilous" bard.

214. *Peredur mab Efrawg,* in Jones and Jones, *Mabinogion,* 187–89.

215. See Grisward, *L'archéologie,* 66, 262ff., for the derogated position of the seneschal. Yet in Wolfram's *Parzifal* Cei, called Keie, is given a more sympathetic character, as a "brave and loyal man" who "separated Tricksters and hypocrites from the noble folk" (Goetinck, *Peredur,* 96, n. 131 [see chap. 1, n. 28]). Goetinck sees this attitude as closer to the Welsh material, which points to a fund of different material on Cei/Kay available to (or invented by) the Continental authors (102, 128 and n. 222).

216. *TYP,* T. 21; Cei as one of three *Taleithyavc Cat.* The third great hero is Huail Mac Caw.

217. See Miller, "Twinning of Arthur and Cei," afterword, 66–69.

218. Like Arthur of the *TYP,* Huail does not or cannot claim the fully sovereign office.

219. In the perverse case described in the *Nibelungenlied,* Siegfried actually subdues Brunhilde sexually while in the king's physical guise, and no good comes of this, either.

220. This theme has apparently degenerated, since the narratives describing the "triangle" rarely allow the younger man to actually succeed to the kingship.

221. J. Nagy, *Wisdom,* 52, 61ff.

222. Jackson, *Hero and King,* 15.

CHAPTER 4: THE HERO "SPEAKS"

1. *SCHS* III, 101. This description of the hero ends with the explanation that he needed no watch, for he wore a set of plumes that, rather than "nodding terribly" *à l'Iliade,* revolved "three or four times an hour."

2. *Digenes Akrites,* GRO IV, lines 249, 251 (pp. 80–85).

3. *CO,* 3, lines 60ff.; Ford, *Mabinogion,* 123 (see chap. 2, n. 10).

4. *Mahâbhârata,* 4 (47) 30; p. 75 (see chap. 2, n. 9).

5. *Poema/Poem,* 137 (pp. 258–59) (see chap. 3, n. 72): *rançal tan blanca commo el sol,* etc.

6. *LxS,* chaps. 20, 21.

7. Lord, *The Singer of Tales,* 30–67 (see chap. 1, n. 67).

8. D. A. Miller, "Une théorie unifiée de la royauté et de l'aristocratie," *Annales E. S. C.* 33, no. 1 (January–February 1978): 10.

9. In some epical sources, including the *Chanson de Roland,* we may again hear an echo of the archaic Indo-European theme of interfunctional war. This theme, as Dumézil reconstructed it, reflects the *guerre du fondation,* when the first two *fonctions* of the Indo-European triad fought the third, resulting in the coalescence or melding of the two: see G. Dumézil, *Les dieux des Germains: Essai sur la formation de la religion scandinave,* 2d ed., rev., Collection "Mythes et Religions," ed. P.-L. Couchard (Paris: PUF, 1959), 3–37; *From Myth to Fiction: The Saga of Hadingus,* 95–105 (see chap. 2, n. 71). As this theme is fragmented and redone, the "enemy" is given particularly rich and costly equipment and dress—wealth clearly

is a Third Function characteristic—whereas the favored side is sterner, plainer, and more openly warlike: see Joel Grisward, "L'or corrupteur et le soleil arreté ou la substructure mythique de la *Chanson de Roland*," in *Georges Dumézil. Cahier pour un Temps* (Paris: Pandora, 1981): 257–70, for the Roland epic.

10. *Heike Monogatari. The Tale of the Heike*, trans. H. Kitagawa and B. Tsushida (Tokyo: University of Tokyo Press, 1978), vol. II, chap. XVII, p. 491.

11. A little onward from the description given immediately above, another character is roundly criticized, because "he has no elegance," ibid., p. 494.

12. "Dressing" the hero may also subsist as a particular scene in certain types of heroic adventures as a kind of formal preparation, especially for battle.

13. The subject of symbolic color (especially concerned with the Warrior Function) will be taken up again in chapter 5. See E. Lyle, "Dumézil's Three Functions and Indo-European Cosmic Structure," *History of Religions* 22, no. 1 (August 1982): 25ff.

14. *EyS*, chap. 44.

15. "EoÁ," chap. 6; p. 235 in Pálsson and Edwards, *Seven Viking Romances* (see chap. 1, n. 142).

16. "Arrow-Odd" ("Ölvir-Oddr"), chaps. 1, 27; pp. 27, 108 in Pálsson and Edwards, *Seven Viking Romances*.

17. *LxS*, chap. 21.

18. *NjS*, chap. 33, 93.

19. See *Fostbræðra saga*, ed. B. K. Þórólfsson and G. Jónsson, Íslensk Fornrit 6 (Reykjavik: Hið íslensk fornritafélag, 194), 129.

20. Cf. Gerschel, "Une épisode trifonctionel," 129. But note that in *EyS*, chap. 18, 64, the magic tunic made by the witch Katla for her son Oddr is "reddish brown," with two possible interpretations (1) that as in Arrow-Oddr's case a color in the red range can be "powerful" or magical, or (2) that the red-brown color is meant to recall a "contaminated," in-between color, as suitable for magic as gray or dappled gray (see below, pp. 293–95).

21. *GiS*, chap. 16.

22. *Hrafnkels saga Freysgoða*, chaps. 6, 18, and see Pálsson's introduction, p. 25 with n. 8 in *Hrafnkel's Saga and Other Stories* (see chap. 3, n. 94).

23. *Ldn*, chap. 168.

24. Kinsella, *Táin*, 61–2; O'Rahilly, *Táin*, 6, 143, lines 220 (see chap. 2, n. 95).

25. *Táin*, Kinsella, 146; O'Rahilly, *Táin*, 59, 199, line 2179. In the *Fled Bricrend* or "Bricriu's Feast," Cú Chulainn maintains his canonical color with red spear, red shield, and crimson tunic: see *AIT,* 265; *EIMS*, 235; Old Irish version, ed. and trans. George Henderson, Irish Text Society 2 (Dublin, 1899).

26. That is, Fergna mac Finnchaime or Findchonna: Kinsella, *Táin*, 233; O'Rahilly, *Táin*, 125, 261, lines 4517–25.

27. As in Kinsella's translation of the *Táin* (159) translating line 2380, *in riastarde;* O'Rahilly, *Táin*, 65, 205.

28. *Il.* III.229, XI.820, XXI.527.

29. *Il.* III.227, VII.155. Athena, chivvying the wounded hero Diomedes in V.801, refers with approval to Diomedes' father Tydeus: "Tydeus was small in stature,

but a fighter." Note that in the iconic presentation of such a hero as Akhilleus his huge size must be emphasized, as in the frequently reproduced black-figure vase painting in which a smaller Aias carries off the massive dead body of Akhilleus: see T. H. Carpenter, *Art and Myth in Ancient Greece: A Handbook* (London: Thames & Hudson, 1991), pl. 329.

30. *Aen.* VII.784, VIII.367, X.768.

31. *Shâh-nâma*, VI.i.48 (see chap. 1, n. 36).

32. *Shâh-nâma*, Vi.xvii.72.

33. *VölS*, chap. 23: a "sign of his height" (*mark um hans hæd*) was that when he wore the sword Gram, which was over five feet long, the scabbard tip would just brush the tops of a field of unharvested rye.

34. Saxo, *Gesta Danorum*, VIII.252 (see chap. 1, n. 91).

35. *CO*, 14, lines 387–8; Ford, *Mabinogion*, 132 (see chap. 2, n. 10). Cú Chulainn's physical appearance is at all times ambiguously or confusingly drawn: he is the "beardless boy," the "little champion" of the Ullaid, and so he seems to have a boy's size, yet his massive battle harness—"twenty-seven tunics of waxed skin," and so on—would fit a giant. (See Kinsella, *Táin*, 146; O'Rahilly, *Táin*, 61, 201, lines 2224–5; and contrast this with the armor of Finn mac Cumaill, in *AIT*, 432.) And when he dueled with his foster brother Ferdiad, and was frustrated so that his battle rage seized him, "he blew up and swelled . . . mottled and terrifying, and the huge high hero loomed straight up over Ferdia." See Kinsella, *Táin*, 195; O'Rahilly, *Táin*, 92, 228, lines 3317–20.

36. *Erec et Enide*, in Roques, *Les romans*, 5847; Jean Frappier, *Chrétien de Troyes: The Man and His Work*, trans. by R. J. Cormier (Athens: Ohio University Press, 1982), says that Chrétien would not "have us admire strength or prowess for their own sakes," but demands equilibrium and moderation.

37. *Raoul de Cambrai*, CLX (see chap. 3, n. 179).

38. Kinsella, *Táin*, 205; O'Rahilly, *Táin*, 99, 234, line 3591: "rough play of weapons," *ro marbus dom garbchluchi*.

39. R. Caillois, *Man, Play and Games*, trans. by R. Barash (New York: Free Press, 1961), 23–26.

40. *Fíanaigecht*, ed. and trans. by K. Meyer, Royal Irish Academy Todd Lectures 16 (Dublin, 1910); see *AIT*, 430.

41. Bailey, "Ossete tradition," in Hatto, *Traditions*, 238 (see chap. 3, n. 182).

42. GRO IV, line 132 (pp. 74–75), *petasas hôs aetos;* line 142, *hôsper pardos exebê;* GRO VI, line 149 (pp. 170–71), *ou gar enikêsen eme hippos pote eis dromon.*

43. *Peredur mab Efrawg*, in Jones and Jones, *Mabinogion*, 183–84 (see chap. 2, n. 93).

44. See *Il.* XX.410–14 for Polydoros, another son of Priam, who "in swiftness surpassed all" and was speared by Akhilleus because this swiftness took him too close to the champion.

45. Recall Durand, *Structures anthropologiques de l'imaginaire*, 78–79 (see. chap. 2, 39). Mobility with its accompaniment, celerity, is of course a prime sign of the border, but My Cid is probably talking about increased opportunities for plunder

when he says, in laisse 54 of his poem (106–7), "that one who stays in one place he will grow poor" *(qui en un logar mora siempre, lo so puede menguar)*.

46. In *Sancti Bernardi opere,* ed. J. Leclercq and H. M. Rochais (Rome, 1960), vol. 3. See Georges Duby, *The Legend of Bouvines: War, Religion and Culture in the Middle Ages,* trans. C. Tihanyi (Berkeley: University of California Press, 1990), 99–100; Alan Forey, *The Military Orders from the Twelfth to the Early Fourteenth Centuries* (Toronto: University of Toronto Press, 1992), 11ff.

47. Saxo, *Gesta Danorum,* VI.195. See now Miller, "On the Mythology of Indo-European Heroic Hair," *JI- ES* 26, nos. 1–2 (Spring–Summer 1998): 41–60.

48. Grisward, *L'archéologie,* 260 (see chap. 1, n. 30).

49. Gregory of Tours, *Libor histoire francorum,* II, 9; see J. M. Wallace-Hadrill, *The Long-Haired Kings* (Toronto: University of Toronto Press; London: Medieval Academy of America, 1982), 154ff.

50. Alan Harrison, *The Irish Trickster,* Folklore Society, Mistletoe Series 20 (Sheffield: Sheffield Academic Press, 1989), 44–47, citing J. O'Donovan, *The Ancient Laws of Ireland* 3 (Dublin, 1873), 354.

51. Diodorus Siculus, *Bibliothêkês Historikês,* trans. C. H. Oldfather, Loeb Classical Library (London: Wm. Heinemann; Cambridge, Mass.: Harvard University Press, 1970), V.28.

52. That is, it follows the Indo-European tripartite color scheme. For the Celts, see W. Sayers, "Early Irish Attitudes toward Hair and Beards, Baldness and Tonsure," *ZCP* 44 (1991): 160.

53. Ibid., 161; citing Kim McCone, "Werewolves, Cyclopes, *Díberga* and *Fíanna.*"

54. Sayers, "Irish Attitudes," 187.

55. J. Nagy, *Wisdom,* 152 (chap. 1, n. 90); but *mael* can also, on the obverse, mark the druidical or another ambivalent status. See Sayers, "Irish Attitudes," 164, 174ff.

56. *Meier von Helmbrecht. Die Mare vom Helmbrecht von Werner dem Gartenaere,* ed. F. Panzer, Altdeutsche Textbibliothek, no. 11 (Tübingen: Max Niemayer, 1960); *Peasant Life in Old German Epics: Meier Helmbrecht and Der Arme Heinrich,* ed. and trans. C. H. Bell, Records of Civilization, Sources and Studies (1931; reprint, New York: Columbia University Press, 1959), 12.432, and 1896–99.

57. GRO IV, line 373 (pp. 92–93).

58. GRO V, line 186 (pp. 152–53) and GRO IV, line 1024 (pp. 136–37).

59. *Nibelungenlied,* v. 87 (pp. 24–25) (see chap. 2, n. 249).

60. *Chanson de Roland,* CXXIV.1639–41 (see chap. 2, n. 312). Grandoine knows Roland by his physical appearance, his *fier visage,* and so on.

61. *Peredur mab Efrawg,* in Jones and Jones, *Mabinogion,* 187.

62. "BoH," chap. 12.

63. *Beowulf,* 260–63, 343 (see chap. 2, n. 81). Jackson, *Hero and King,* 30 (see chap. 1, n. 207), sees as the "insulator" in *Beowulf* and other Germanic epics one he calls the "recognition nobleman."

64. Translated in Jones and Jones, *Mabinogion,* xxiii ff.

65. *CO,* 4–5, lines 104–5ff.; Ford, *Mabinogion,* 124.

66. *CO*, 7, lines 168–69; Ford, *Mabinogion*, 126.

67. See Miller, "Twinning of Arthur and Cei," 58–61 (see. chap. 1, n. 106).

68. *CMT*, chaps. 53–74 (pp. 38–43).

69. In the Kinsella, *Táin*, 77–78; O'Rahilly, *Táin*, 21–22, 159, lines 768ff.

70. *DS*, III (v. II) 5 (304–5).

71. GRO I, line 159 (pp. 12–13), *peiran te kai andreian*.

72. Norman Daniel, *Heroes and Saracens: An Interpretation of the* Chansons de Geste (Edinburgh: Edinbugh University Press, 1984), 36–37. In contrast, the *Digenid*, though certainly written from a Christian point of view, has a relatively knowledgable and even friendly view of Islam; see GRO I, lines 100ff., where the emir is entreated, and the hope raised that he will "see the Prophet's Tomb, and hear the consecrated prayer" if he be merciful.

73. Daniel, *Heroes*, 35, 107.

74. *CO*, 3, 7, lines 58, 170; Ford, *Mabinogion*, 123, 126.

75. See *NjS*, chap. 25, for example.

76. *LxS*, chap. 13.

77. Daniel, *Heroes*, 35.

78. *CO*, 4, lines 104–5; Ford, *Mabinogion*, 124.

79. GRO IV, line 971 (pp. 132–33). The more recent English translation by D. B. Hull is consistently in error in rendering the title as "emperor": *Digenis Akritas: The Twy-born Border Lord* (Athens: Ohio University Press, 1972).

80. GRO IV, line 999 (pp. 134–35); the king is said to regard this statement as "modest."

81. *Beowulf*, 499–606; see also Edward. B. Irving Jr., "What to Do with Old Kings," in Foley, *Comparative Research*, 259–68 (see chap. 1, n. 74).

82. *LPS*, 12–15.

83. *ES*, chap. 25: "að ég mun eigi gæfu til bera að veita þér þá þjónustu, sem ég myndi vilja og vert væri."

84. See Miller, "Functional Operations," 127–33 (see chap. 1, n. 109).

85. *Nibelungenlied*, v. 3 (pp. 28–29).

86. GRO IV, lines 1033ff (pp. 136–37).

87. GRO IV, line 1040 (pp. 136–37).

88. Saxo, *Gesta Danorum*, VI.171–72 (pp. 188–89).

89. Saxo, *Gesta Danorum*, VI.178 (pp. 193–94).

90. *Le Couronnement de Louis*, ed. E. Langlois, 2d ed., rev. (Paris: Honoré Champion, 1966); trans. in Ferrante, *Guillaume*, VII.65–67 (see chap. 2, n. 142).

91. Ferrante, *Guillaume*, XXXV.1493, 1497.

92. Ferrante, *Guillaume*, LXIII.2671.

93. *Aliscans*, ed. G. Rolin (Leipzig: Teubner, 1894); especially LXV and after.

94. *Aliscans*, LXIX.2776ff.

95. Caillois, *Man, Play and Games*, 14–26, 71–79.

96. I note as an aside that the illustration of the typical posture of the medieval knight, when horsed, shows him not as seated, with bent legs, but as standing in his stirrups, that is, with the stirrup irons extended; so he is essentially erect.

97. E.g., *Nibelungenlied*, v. 585 (pp. 130–31): *hei waz starker schefte vor den*

frouwen brast! In *Tristan* see the first section, "Rivalin und Blancheflor": (Hatto, 50 [see chap. 2, n. 154]).

98. For Agamemnon, *Il.* XI.92.

99. *TYP,* T. 21 (p. 37).

100. Caesar, *De Bello Gallico,* IV.33; Polybius refers to the Geisatae who fought naked (*gumnoi*) and who "placed themselves first in the ranks," *prôtoi tes dunameos katestêtan* (*Hist.,* II.28): almost certainly Geisatae are not a tribe, as Polybius implies, but "*gessa*-men," men fighting under a tabu or *geis.* The sight of these self-chosen champions, "in the prime of strength and beauty" (II.29), strongly affected their Roman foes. Didorus Siculus (V.29.2) in his description of the Celtic Cimbri, supports the epiphany of the *gumnoi* or naked champions, who "step out in front of the line" (*proagein tês parataxeôs*) and issue a challenge to single combat (*monomakhian*) to the enemy host.

101. See T. G. E. Powell, *The Celts,* Ancient Peoples and Places, 2d ed. (London: Thames & Hudson, 1985), 140: "The Champion's Challenge is splendidly illustrated by that Indo-European Philistine"; cf. I Sam. xvii.8–10.

102. W. Sayers, "The Jongleur Taillefer at Hastings: Antecedents and Literary Fate," *Viator* 14 (1983): 78, citing Gaimar, *L'estoire des Engleis by Geffrei Gaimar,* ed. A. Bell, Anglo-Norman Texts Society 14–16 (Oxford: Oxford University Press, 1960), 5300.

103. Sayers, "The Jongleur Taillefer," 77; William of Malmsbury, *Gesta regum,* ed. William Stubbs, Rolls Series (London, 1889), vol. 2, bk. 2, par. 242. For Turnus, see *Aen.* IX.56, and note that Turnus is "first in that fight."

104. Sayers, "The Jongleur Taillefer," 81, 78, citing for the beheading *The Carmen de Hastingae proelio of Guy, Bishop of Amiens,* ed. C. Morton and H. Muntz (Oxford: Oxford University Press, 1972), 81.

105. "Battle of Maldon," in *The Anglo-Saxon Poetic Records,* ed. E. van Kirk Dobbie (New York: Columbia University Press, 1942), VI.

106. *Chanson de Roland,* CLXXI.2297–8.

107. *JS,* chap. 35 (see chap. 1, n. 107).

108. *GrS,* chap. 82.

109. *Nibelungenlied,* v. 2352 (pp. 258–59).

110. *JS,* chap. 38.

111. Irving, "Old Kings," 262; with reference to Hrothgar in *Beowulf* and to Charlemagne at the beginning of the *Chanson de Roland.*

112. At this point it is an obvious leap to the best-known royal seating-plan for heroes, the Round Table invented in the later Continental legends of Arthur; in this case the only hierarchical claim was set neither by king nor by warrior, for the empty Siege Perilous could only be occupied by the saintly Galaad, and we have passed beyond the bounds of strictly heroic-epical constraint and theme.

113. Onians, *Origins,* 180–85 (see chap. 1, n. 228).

114. Kinsella, *Táin,* 109; the passage is not included in O'Rahilly's text.

115. *ES,* chap. 64; *EgS,* chap. 65.

116. *Nibelungenlied,* v. 988 (pp. 218–19): *Dô viel in die bluomen der Kriemhilde man.*

117. *Il.* XII.363, XIII.313, and XV.484 for Teukros skilled in sword play.

118. Kinsella, *Táin,* 96–97; O'Rahilly, *Táin,* 34–35, 172, lines 1272ff; *CMT,* paras. 130ff., for Lugh as slinger. The sling also shows up in the *Togail Bruidne Da Derga.* For the considerable variance between the archaeological record in Ireland and the weaponry used and described in the *Táin,* see J. P. Mallory, "The World of Cú Chulainn: The Archaeology of the *Táin Bó Cúalgne,*" in Mallory, *Aspects of the* Táin, especially 131ff. (see chap. 2, n. 51).

119. E. Salin, *La civilisation mérovingienne,* vol. 3 (Paris: 1957): 6, 55–115.

120. See below, chap. 5.

121. See *Haralds saga hárfagr, Heimskringla* III.18. In the Ossete Nart tales we find Uastyrdji giving Soslan his "Frankish sword," which is not however named: Dumézil, *Le livre des héros,* 71ff. (see chap. 2, n. 88).

122. *EIMS,* 213.

123. In "The Death of Fergus mac Leide," and used in a fight with a water-monster, in *AIT,* 486–87. For named swords in Celtic literature, see Donald E. Meek, "The Banners of the Finn in Gaelic Ballad Tradition," *CMCS* 11 (Summer 1986): 36, n. 32.

124. *CO,* 6, lines 159–62; Ford, *Mabinogion,* 125, 129 (for Arthur's weapons); *CO,* 10, line 279 and 41, lines 1193–96; *Mabinogion,* 156, for Bronllafn, the magic knife of Osla Great-Knife.

125. *SCHS* III, 90.

126. *Poem/Poema,* 2434; see *Cantar de Mio Cid. Texto, gramática y vocabulario,* vol. 2, *Texto,* part 4, ed. R. Menendez-Pidal, 4th ed. (Madrid: Espasa-Colpe, 1969), 659–60ff., and s.v. *espada,* for Colada and Tizón.

127. *VölS,* 11.4.

128. *VölS,* 31.117–18.

129. For Balmung, v. 95 (pp. 24–25); taken and used by Hagen (though not named here), v. 1562 (pp. 92–93); Kriemhild beheads Hagen, v. 2373 (pp. 262–63), *daz houpt si im ab sluoc.* Only one other "named" sword is mentioned in this epic, the Dane lord Iring's sword Waske, (v. 2051, pp. 194–95), though mention is im-plicitly made of others: one "of no mean quality" (v. 1696, pp. 120–21), and "a mighty sword" (v. 1895, pp. 162–63: *ein vil starkez wâfen*).

130. Saxo, *Gesta Danorum,* VII.222–23; see also Ellis Davidson's note, 2:116, n. 88 (see chap. 1, n. 91). Among other named blades in Saxo, we have King Ver-mund's sword Skrep (*Gesta Danorum,* IV.108), whose name Ellis Davidson (2:69, n. 33) derives from the Germanic *schrap* 'firm, unyielding'.

131. *GrS,* chap. 17; *ES,* chap. 64; *LxS,* chap. 57; *KS,* chap. 9. Skofnung also appears in *KS,* chap. 9; this saga has more than its share of named blades, for Kor-mák also has Skrymir (chap. XII), while Bersi has two swords, the shorter (Hvit-ing) being the one he used to kill Þórkell (chap. XIV).

132. Hatto, *Nibelungenlied,* p. 401.

133. Low, *Marko,* 71; Pennington and Levi, *Marko the Prince,* 45.

134. *Serglige Con Culainn/*"The Sick-bed of Cú Chulainn," in *AIT,* 176–77; Old Irish text in *Serglige Con Culainn,* ed. Myles Dillon, Medieval and Modern Irish Series 14 (Dublin, 1953), trans. Dillon in *Scottish Gaelic Studies* 7 (1953):

47–88. The text goes on to say that "at that time . . . demons (screamed) from the weapons of men."

135. *Chanson e Roland,*CLXX.2309, CLXXI.2314ff.

136. Pennington and Levi, *Marko the Prince,* "Prince Marko's Death," 66.

137. *ES,* chaps. 23, 61.

138. Saxo, *Gesta Danorum,* II.55, 61.

139. Ellis Davidson, in her notes (2:68) to Saxo, *Gesta Danorum,* says that "Laufi" and "Snytir" are the same sword, but Laufi is described as "unusually long and sharp" (II.55) and definitely is not a *seax,* a "Teuton sword," which Snytir is.

140. *Gunnlaugs saga Ormstungu,* ed. S. Nordal and G. Jónsson, Íslensk Fornrit 3 (Reykjavik: Hið íslensk fornritafélag, 1938); trans. R. Quirk, Icelandic Texts (London: Nelson, 1957), chap. 7.

141. See Ellis Davidson, "The Sword at the Wedding" in her *Patterns of Folklore,* 91–102 (see chap 2, n. 336).

142. *GrS,* chaps. 18, 20.

143. Saxo, *Gesta Danorum,* VII.224–25.

144. *Víga-Glúms saga,* in *Eyfirðinga sögur,* ed. J. Kristjansson, Íslensk Fornrit 9 (Reykjavik: Hið íslensk fornritafélag, 1956); trans. L. M. Hollander in *Viga-Glums saga and the Story of Ogmund Dytt,* Library of Scandinavian Literature, vol. 14 (New York: Twayne Publishers for the American-Scandinavian Foundation, 1972), VI.37. The case of Saint Oláfr is not a straightforward or easy example: the *Flateyjarbók* connects this Oláfr to one King Oláfr *Gierstaðaalfr,* a pagan king of Vestfold, who was neither an eminently successful king nor closely connected kinwise to the later royal saint. Oláfr *Geirstaðaalfr* was, I have suggested, a Third-Function monarch, who did leave a valuable trifunctional gift to his namesake: see Miller, "Bad Death," 155–56 (see chap. 1, n. 10).

145. Ellis Davidson, "Sword," 106.

146. See P. MacCana, "Aspects of the Theme of King and Goddess in Irish Literature," *Études Celtiques* 7 (1955–57): 76–104; 8 (1958): 59–65.

147. Ellis Davidson, "Sword," 107.

148. *Ldn,* chap. 174; *LxS,* chaps. 57, 78.

149. *ES,* chap. 66; *EgS,* chap. 65.

150. Animal ferocity is directly reflected in an incident in the Serbian *Marko* epos: the hero Ban Strahinja kills his Turkish adversary Vlach-Alija with his teeth, like a dog or a wolf: Pennington and Levi, *Marko the Prince,* 128.

151. *LxS,* chap. 29: *ok beið hvergi ryð a.*

152. *LxS,* chap. 30, *er mestr er skaði at.*

153. Oláfr pái has a great ox with four horns, which is slaughtered after it loses one of its horns; Oláfr then has a dream vision of a woman *mikil ok reiðulig,* "huge and red-wrathful," who says that Oláfr had "killed my son and returned him to me mutilated" and that he would see his *own* son "bloodied [*albloðgan*] by my doing": chap. 31. This is surely a vision of "battle Freya." Kjartan, his favorite son, is killed in *LxS,* chap. 49.

154. Cited in Ellis Davidson, *Road to Hel,* 159–60 (see chap. 1, n. 91); *Herver-*

ars saga is included in Guðni Jónsson, ed., *Fornaldarsögur norðulanda*, vol. 2 (Reykjavik: Bokantgafen forni, 1944).

155. *GiS*, chap. 1; the death described is the classic "bad death": see Miller, "'Bad Death,'" 143–44.

156. *GiS*, chaps. 11, 13, 16.

157. See W. Sayers, "The Smith and the Hero: Culann and Cúchulainn," *Mankind Quarterly* 25 (1985): 229–30.

158. *Táin*, Kinsella, 9, 11, 33, 39ff, especially 44–45 for Connla, 136 for Loch, 196–97 for Ferdiad; O'Rahilly, *Táin*, 54, 194, line 2004 for Loch; 92, 229, lines 3348ff. for Ferdiad. The Connla episode is not in O'Rahilly's version of the *Táin*, but in van Hamel, *Compert Con Culaind*, as "the Death of Aife's Only Son" (*Aided Oenfer Aífe*), 9–15 (see chap. 2, n. 24).

159. Sayers, "Smith and Hero," 230: my emphasis.

160. Per Nykrog, *Les fabliaux*, rev. ed., Publications Romaines et Françaises 73 (Geneva: Librarie Droz, 1973), 239. Note that Egill, one of the most notorious Icelandic "head-breakers," wears stone armor in his strange forest adventure toward the end of his saga; this appears to be a magical interpolation: chap. 75. Another Norse source, *Ljósvitninga saga*, tells us that King Haroldr Sigurdarsson, called Hardraða, had a mail shirt with the feminine name "Emma" that could not be penetrated by any weapon: *LjS*, chap. 31. The "proofing" of the hero by means of some sort of magical bath, providing another kind of invulnerability, is a quite different subject.

161. *Il.* XI.440. In Homer a great hero may be undone by the intervention of the gods, who prepare him for death by "loosening" his armor (as Apollo did with Patroklos, XVI.793ff.). This may be interpreted as part of the elaborate calculus involved in bringing down an unconquerable hero-warrior (see above, p. 122ff).

162. *LPS*, 170.

163. *Nibelungenlied*, v. 1981: *sô manegan helm brach*; v. 2003 (pp. 184–85); v. 2219 (pp. 230–31): *Ir swart so scherpfe waren ez enkúnde niht gewegen.*

164. In *Nibelungenlied*, v. 2210.

165. *Chanson de Roland*, CXXIV.1645–46.

166. *Chanson de Roland*, XCV.1246–47.

167. *Coronation*, LX.2609.

168. *Shâh-nâma*, VIII.xxiii.140 (see chap. 1, n. 36).

169. The Irish heroes not infrequently wear "impenetrable" and bespelled body armor; in the Ossetian Nart tales the Nart Soslan possesses the magical cuirass "of Tserek" that puts itself on the hero when the word "battle" is spoken, and renders Soslan (almost) invulnerable: Dumézil, *Le livre des héros*, 96 ("Comment Soslan conquit Beduha") and note on p. 104 (see chap. 2, n. 88).

170. Ford, *Mabinogion*, 184.

171. *Il.* XI.32ff.; see D. L. Page, *History and the Homeric Iliad*, Sather Classical Lectures, vol. 31 (Berkeley: University of California Press, 1976), 270–71, n. 35.

172. F. Zeitlin, *Under the Sign of the Shield: Semiotics and Aeschylus's Seven against Thebes* (Rome: dell'Ateneo, 1982). From an admittedly small sampling of shield devices as they are shown in vase-paintings and other ceramic art, it appears

that the Greek artists made no attempt to assign one device to one hero; there was no accepted "heraldic" convention: see Carpenter, *Art and Myth in Ancient Greece*. Akhilleus too is given a Gorgoneion for his device in a number of examples (pls. 21, 110, 298, 326) but other warriors also carry this device (Aias in pl. 332), and Akhilleus is additionally shown with the Triskeles (pl. 316), a female figure (pl. 313), and what appears to be a wolf (pl. 28).

173. Kinsella, *Táin*, 142; O'Rahilly, *Táin*, 58, 198, line 2142 (not identified as Lugh here); Kinsella, 210–11; O'Rahilly, 101, 235 (line 3633), 103, 238 (lines 3731–2).

174. Kinsella, *Táin*, 187; O'Rahilly, *Táin*, 85, 222, lines 3093–94.

175. Kinsella, *Táin*, 195; O'Rahilly, *Táin*, 92, 228, lines 3311–16.

176. In three of the Four Branches: in "Bronwen" (Ford, 160), a "shield of peace" and also Bendigeidfran's shield (Ford, 69); shields are made, presumably of leather, by the exiles in "Manawydan" (78); and "twelve golden shields," magically manufactured, show up in "Math" (94).

177. De Vries, *Heroic Song and Heroic Legend*, 255 (see chap. 1, n. 71).

178. *Shâh-nâma*, VI.xviii.74; VIII.xxi.135.

179. *Chanson de Roland*, XCVIII.1275–76.

180. *Chanson de Roland*, CXXVIII, and also CXL. See Grisward, *L'archéologie*, 53ff., 253ff.

181. *LPS*, 124–25: "You merchants are cowards and know nothing of fighting."

182. *SCHS* III, 180.

183. Dumézil, *Horace et les Curiaces*, 17 (see chap. 2, n. 202).

184. Kinsella, *Táin*, 150; O'Rahilly, *Táin*, 61, 201, lines 2262ff.

185. Kinsella, *Táin*, 195; O'Rahilly, *Táin*, 92, 228, lines 3317–20.

186. Kinsella, *Táin*, 185; O'Rahilly, *Táin*, 84, 220, lines 3033–36. Note O'Rahilly's slightly differing translation of this stanza.

187. *SCHS* III, 1153. Distortion and swelling may come from other emotional states, as in *Völsungasaga*, when Sigurd's byrnie rings fly apart after his emotional meeting with Brynhild: chap. 29. The exact emotion is not clear here, nor is it in *Egils saga* (chap. 78) when Egill reacted to the news of his son Boðvarr's death: "he grew so swollen that both tunic and hose split apart." Whether Egill's saga borrowed from the Völsung model is moot: see Andersson's discussion in his *Family Saga*, 70 (see chap. 2, n. 283). The idea that strong emotion swells the body of an individual, especially the chest, is already seen in Homer: see Onians, *Origins*, 50ff. Egill's symptomatically swollen body is accompanied by a nearly catatonic state of inaction, but once persuaded out of this state he creates the great, angry poem *Sonatorrek*, the "Lament For My Sons."

188. *ES*, chap. 27, 55, 78.

189. *NjS*, chap. 132.

190. Kinsella, *Táin*, 91; in "Macgnimrada Con Chulaind," in *Stories from the Tain*, ed. J. Strachan (Dublin: Royal Irish Academy, 1944).

191. Michael Nagler, "On Almost Killing Your Friends: Some Thoughts on Violence in Early Cultures," in Foley, *Comparative Research*, 425–63.

192. Ibid., 438.

193. *Mahâbhârata,* I.30–31. (see chap. 2, n. 9)

194. Nagler, "On Almost Killing Your Friends," 451.

195. Kinsella, *Táin,* 44; in van Hamel, *Compert Con Chulaind.* Heroic filicide will be a major topic in chaper 7, below.

196. Nagler sees some differentiation in warrior epical traditions, noting that in the Germanic tradition the discovery of identity is made too late: 436.

197. *Septem contra Thebas,* ed. G. O. Hutchinson (Oxford: Clarendon, 1985), 681–82.

198. *Chanson de Roland,* LXXXIII.1049–51.

199. *Chanson de Roland,* CXXXI.1725, 1731.

200. Andersson, *Family Saga,* 181–82.

201. *GiS,* chap. 33.

202. Andersson, *Family Saga,* 191.

203. *ES,* chap. 64; *EgS,* chap. 65: *fót hjó skáld af Ljóti.*

204. *GrS,* chap. 48.

205. *Nibelungenlied,* v. 2223 (pp. 230–31).

206. Kinsella, *Táin,* 199, 201; O'Rahilly, *Táin,* 94, 230, lines 3440ff. for the long Lament for Ferdiad.

207. *LxS,* chap. 49.

208. *Shâh-nâma,* VIII.xi.117–18.

209. Daniel, *Heroes,* 207–8, 310 (n. 71) and 201–2. Loquifer may be Rainouart's son.

210. See Littleton, "Some Possible Indo-European Themes in the *Iliad,*" 226–46 (see chap. 2, n. 229).

211. But see Andersson, *Family Saga,* 171–73.

212. *Il.* X.454: Dolon pleads "touching his chin with his hand": see Onians, *Origins,* 233ff. In fact Dolon is beheaded, but the head is not taken as a trophy.

213. *Aen.* X.600. See also X.743, Mezentius to Orodes, *nunc morere,* perhaps a parallel to Patroklos.

214. *Aen.* X.523. Just previously to Magus's execution, Aeneas took four captives alive (517–20) to offer at Pallas's pyre, presumably in imitation of pitiless Akhilleus; the blood offering is made in XI.80–82: [the enemy understood] *vinxerat et post terga manus, quos mitteret umbris inferias,* and line 82, "sprinkled the flames with the blood of the slain."

215. Ford, *Mabinogion,* 117.

216. *Peredur mab Efrawg,* in Jones and Jones, *Mabinogion,* 199.

217. Kelly, "The *Táin* as Literature," 81–82 (see chap. 2, n. 51).

218. *Nibelungenlied,* 88–89 (pp. 44–47).

219. Chrétien de Troyes, *Eric et Enid,* in *Arthurian Romances,* trans. W. W. Comfort, Everyman's Library (London: Dent; New York: Dutton, 1975), 40.

220. *Shâh-nâma,* VIII.xxv.145.

221. *Shâh-nâma,* VIII.xxi.135–36.

222. As *Il.* XVII.60, though the verb *enarizo* is more common.

223. *Aen.* XI.7ff. for Mezentius; X.91 for Pallas (Turnus had taken Pallas's swordbelt in X.496: *rapiens immania pondera baltei*).

224. In Jones and Jones, *Mabinogion*, 172. In fact the two are kinsmen.

225. *Nibelungenlied*, v. 2266 (pp. 240–41), "come and get him in the hall . . . where he fell in his blood."

226. Euripides, *Rhesus*, trans. A. S. Way, Loeb Classical Library (Cambridge, Mass.: Harvard University Press; London: Wm. Heinemann, 1978), vol. 1, lines 219–20, 222. The killing of Dolon is offstage, and confirmed in a dialogue between the two Achaeans: lines 591–92. See L. Gernet, "Dolon the Wolf," in his *Anthropology of Ancient Greece*, 125ff., especially 128 (see chap. 1, n. 169), and also see below, p. 239.

227. *Aen.* IX.465–66: the heads of Nisus and Euryalos are displayed, *in hastis praefigunt capita;* XII.511–12, where Turnus kills and beheads two foes and attaches the heads to his chariot rail.

228. *Nibelungenlied*, v. 2025 (pp. 188–89).

229. Chadwick, *Russian Heroic Poetry*, 75 (line 228), 78 (line 120) (see chap. 1, n. 155).

230. *Shâh-nâma*, VIII.xi.118–19, and see, earlier, IV.xvi.34.

231. In Chrétien, *Arthurian Romances*, 13.

232. *GrS*, chap. 82.

233. *GrS*, chap. 18; "EoÁ," chap. 7; for Oláfr *Geirstadsaalfr*, see *Flateyjarbók, Oláfs saga Helga*, II.7, p. 7 (see chap. 3, n. 124); and see Onians, *Origins*, 182ff., for "head" and "thighs" connected in significance.

234. *GiS*, chap. 3.

235. *Serglige Con Culaind* = "The Wasting Sickness of Cu Chulaind," in *EIMS*, 155. Note that the warriors of the Ulaid swear to the accuracy of their count "by the swords on their thighs."

236. *Branwen uerch Llyr*, in Ford, *Mabinogion*, 69.

237. *AIT,* 275; Kinsella, *Táin*, 81; O'Rahilly, *Táin*, 31, 169, line 1129.

238. *EIMS*, 217, 248.

239. Kinsella, *Táin*, 73, 97; O'Rahilly, *Táin*, 16, 153, line 568; 28, 164, line 1005.

240. *AIT,* "Death Tales," 331, 339. Cú Chulainn does *not* take the heads of Ferdiad, or of his son Connla. It is also noted, in the *Táin,* that he left the head of Lethan, one of his early victims, with the body: Kinsella, 97; O'Rahilly, 34, 173, lines 1263–65.

241. *TBDD*, in *EIMS*, 104; *TDAG*, in *AIT,* 389, 395.

242. *Scéla Mucce Meic Dathó*, in *EIMS*, 185–86; *AIT,* 204.

243. *AIT,* 206.

244. Strabo, IV.4, 5; Diodorus Siculus, V.29.4; Ammianus Marcellinus, *Rerum Gestarum*, XXVII.4.

245. Ford, *Mabinogion*, 70; see also *TYP*, T. 37R, for Arthur's brash removal of the head and with it the magical protection extended over the island.

246. "Örvar-Oddr," or "Arrow-Odd," in Pálsson and Edwards, *Seven Viking Romances;* Old Norse in *Fornaldarsögur norðulanda*, ed. G. Jónsson, vol. 2 (Reykjavik: Bokantgafen forni, 1944), chap. 22.

247. *CO*, 35, lines 971–72; Ford, *Mabinogion*, 150.

248. See Thompson, *Motif-Index*, F679.1, F688 and F688.1–4 (see chap. 1, n. 69), for variants on the "heroic shout."

249. See also *Il*. XI.500, XIII.169, XIII.149, XIV.453, 478.

250. In fact the "unquenchable" image is used elsewhere, as in *Il*. XIII.540; *boê d' asbestos orôrei*.

251. *LPS*, 170.

252. *DS*, III (2) 2, 334.

253. J. Nagy, "Fenian Heroes and Their Rites of Passage," in *The Heroic Process: Form, Function and Fantasy in Folk Epic*, ed. B. Almqvist, Séamas Ó Catháin, and Pádraig Ó Héalaí, Proceedings of the International Folk Epic Conference, University College, Dublin, 2–6 September 1985 (Dublin: Glendale Press, 1987), 172–75. The sound is also called *dord* or *andord*.

254. *Nibelungenlied*, v. 1987 (pp. 180–81).

255. *Slovo*, 62–63.

256. *Shâh-nâma*, VIII.xxi.134; xxii.136.

257. Polybius, II.29.

258. Kinsella, *Táin*, 141, see 167 as well; O'Rahilly, *Táin*, 70, 210, lines 2569–71 for the "hero's shout."

259. *CO*, 4–5, lines 108ff; Ford, *Mabinogion*, 124.

260. Rees and Rees, *Celtic Heritage*, 280; *AIT*, 242–43. *EIMS*, 260–61, translates the phrase simply as "singing," not as "melodious war cry." For the heroic shout recorded elsewhere, see Thompson, *Motif-Index*, F679.1, F688, F688.1–4.

261. *CO*, line 745 (p. 28); Ford, *Mabinogion*, 144: *hyt na hanbwyllei neb pei dygwdei y nef ar y dayar*.

262. *Chanson de Roland*, CXXXIV–CXXXV.

263. *Hamðismál*, 18–19; see *The Poetic Edda*, vol. 1, *Heroic Poems*, ed. and trans. U. Dronke (Oxford: Clarendon Press, 1969), 1165.

264. G. Dumézil, *Mythe et épopée*, I. *L'idéologie des trois fonctions dans les épopées des peuples indo-européens*, Bibliothèque des Sciences Humaines (Paris: Gallimard, 1968), 613–16.

265. *Lludd ac Lleuelys*, in Ford, *Mabinogion*, 113–14.

266. Ibid., 115.

267. The connection to Culhwch's narative is provocative: it was Culhwch who threatened to raise abortifacient shouts at Arthur's court, and he himself bore a pig's name: see E. Hamp, "*Culhwch*, the Swine," *ZCP* 41 (1986): 257–59.

268. *Chanson de Roland*, LXXIX.1006–7.

269. *SCHS* III, 80, 94.

270. *SCHS* III, 81, 83: "he looked as if he were dying . . . so downcast and unhappy."

271. *EIMS*, 183–85, especially 185: "Cet thus brought shame on the entire province" of Ulster.

272. Dumézil, *Les dieux des Germains = Gods of the Ancient Norsemen*, ed. Einar Haugen, introd. C. Scott Littleton and Udo Strutynski, Publications of the UCLA Center for the Study of Compartive Folklore and Mythology 3 (Berkeley: University of Califronia Press, 1973), 95.

273. Who or what Unferth, described as Hrothgar's *Þyle*, was or represented is still debated: see Stanley B. Greenfield, "Beowulf" in his *The Interpretation of Old English Poems* (London: Routledge & Kegan Paul, 1972), 77. As a Thersites figure or satirist, Unferth might have been safe from retaliatory violence.

274. *Shâh-nâma*, XIV.viii.203–4.

275. *Shâh-nâma*, VIII.xi.119; see also xxi.135.

276. *Shâh-nâma*, VI.56.

277. That is, *kertomias êd aisima:* XX.202, 433. See G. Nagy, *Best of the Achaeans*, 270, 315.

278. *Aen.* IX.599: *bis capti Phryges;* 617, *o ueve Phrygiae, neque enim Phryges.*

279. Kinsella, *Táin*, 168ff.; O'Rahilly, *Táin*, 81, 219, lines 2947ff.

280. Kinsella, *Táin*, 187. "Squinter" contemptuously refers to Cú Chulainn's deformation or spasm, when he closes one eye.

281. See Miller, "Functional Operations," 123–25.

282. Andersson, *Family Sagas*, 130. The actual insult refers to the fact that the Jarl's father had been killed in a pigsty.

283. *ES*, chaps. 45, 56, 57: Eiríkr is castigated as *Logbrigðir* 'lawbreaker', *bræðra sokkva* 'brother-killer'.

284. Andersson, *Family Saga*, 138–39. Byock omits this saga from his analysis, presumably because its structure is "literary" and dominated by heroic rather than social formulas and schemata: *Feud*, 50ff. (see chap. 2, n. 167)

285. *Bjarnar saga Hítdælakappa*, in *Borgfirðinga sögur*, ed. S. Nordal and G. Jónsson, Íslensk Fornrit 3 (Reykjavik: Hið íslensk fornritafélag, 1938), 168ff.

286. *VölS*, chap. 9.

287. The fond hopes of Rheinhold Aman, and his excellent and entertaining "antiacademic" journal on insults and insulting, *Maledicta*, to the contrary notwithstanding. The insult-series, especially from a tradition in which hyperbolic language is common (as in the *Shâh-nâma*), may also unfortunately remind us of the American frontier braggadocio immortalized (in the exchange between the Corpsemaker and the Child of Calamity) in Twain's *Life on the Mississippi*, chap. 3, but in the traditional heroic narrative context a fatal encounter rather than more bloviating is the consequence and the norm.

288. Kinsella, *Táin*, 168; O'Rahilly, *Táin*, 72, 211, lines 2621ff.

289. Kinsella, *Táin*, 169–71; O'Rahilly, *Táin*, 72, 212, lines 2634–35 does not include Medb's offer of herself. The emphasis on these sensual bribes again reminds us of Dumézil's interfunctional war; do the Four Provinces stand for a Third Function polity?

290. Joseph Harris, "Satire and the Heroic Life: Two Studies (*Helgakviða Hundingsbana* I, 18 and Bjorn Hítdælakappi's *Grámagaflím*)," in *Oral Traditional Literature: A Festschrift for Alfred Bates Lord*, ed. by J. M. Foley (Columbus, Ohio: Slavica, 1980), 323.

291. *CMT*, para. 115: *glám dicenn* carries even more of a magical charge than simple "satire."

292. G. Nagy, *Best of the Achaeans*, 253ff.

293. *CO*, 4, lines 104–5: *teir diaspat*, and so forth; Ford, *Mabinogion*, 124.

294. Harris, "Satire," 322–23: the *male chancun* or "bad songs" feared by Roland (CXV.1517) almost certainly would be sung by a poet-*jongleur*, but as Harris notes, there is no clear indication in the *Battle* that a poetic criticism is specifically feared.

295. Frappier, *Chrétien de Troyes*, 133. See also Auerbach, *Mimesis*, 118 (see chap. 3, n. 90): commenting on the *Yvain* of Chrétien, Auerbach says of Calogrenant that "secretiveness is one of his knightly duties," in contrast to the low *vilain*, who blurts out everything that he knows.

296. For example, Diomedes known for "prudent counsel" despite his youth: *Il.* IX.57–58.

297. See Whitman, *Homer and the Heroic Tradition*, 171–72 (see chap. 1, n. 138); Telemonian Aias credited here for the "brief and grim eloquence that characterizes him."

298. See *Il.* IX.313: Akhilleus reacts to a speech by Odysseus by saying outright how hateful to him is someone "who hides one thing in his mind and says another."

299. Both passages in the *Iliad* featuring this phrase, IV.350 and XIV.83, have Odysseus chiding Agamemnon. Agamemnon is certainly something of a blowhard, but it is noteworthy that his critic is the *polumêtis*, who is notorious for using words too skillfully for an honest man and who was criticized by Akhilleus for his lack of candor in the passage just cited.

300. Montsacré, *Larmes d'Achilles*, 83: "silence is synonymous with virility; confused noise with femininity." The image of the Trojans imaged as ewes bleating for their lambs is also striking, and of course insulting.

301. *EyS*, chap.15.

302. *EyS*; note the anomalous matronymic, usually showing bastardy.

303. *EyS*, chap. 22.

304. *LPS*, 113.

305. The Norse *haugr* never speaks, and the only *draugr*, to my knowledge, to have this power is Glámr, in *Grettirs saga*, perhaps because he had "more power for evil than any other revenant" (*GrS*, chap. 35). For a variation on this notion of how speech is connected to humanity, drawn from the anthropological sources, we are told that among the Maring, of pre-European New Guinea, a man who went "temporarily mad" was referred to as *yu prim*, a "deaf man," one whose hearing has been blocked by a spirit: from C. Lowman-Vayda, "Maring Big Men," *Anthropological Forum* 2 (1968): 216–17. This source is cited by Wm. C. Clarke, who concludes that for the Maring madness = deafness, inasmuch as "rational" signals cannot be received by the afflicted one: "Temporary Madness as Theatre: Wild Man Behavior in New Guinea," *Oceania* 43 (1972–73): 206–20.

306. See, for example, Dumézil's view in his analysis of the Sparlöse Stone from Sweden, where the last of the three royal characteristics is "runic knowledge": "'Tripertita' fonctionels chez divers peuples indo-européens," *RHR* 131 (1946): 53–73.

307. *La Prise d'Orange*, ed. B. Katz (New York: King's Crown Press, 1947); Ferrante, *Guillaume*, I.

308. *DS*, I.(II).10.(98).

309. Here we may detect a strong influence from the sacred *Quran* and a general respect for imperial Ottoman documents. For the Moslem epic, see B. Stolz, "Nihac and Hamza," Multiformity in the Serbo-Croatian Epic," *Journal of the Folklore Institute* 7 (1970): 70ff.; also Low, *Marko*, 44–45, where a letter from the Sultan to Marko is written, even though (or perhaps because) that potentate is being attacked at that very moment. Such an unrealistic conceit surely argues that "writing" is being considered as a sort of "different speech," in this case a cry for help.

310. P. MacCana, "Early Irish Ideology and the Concept of Unity," in *The Irish Mind: Exploring Intellectual Traditions*, ed. R. Kearney (Dublin: Wolfhound; Atlantic Highlands, N.J.: Humanities Press, 1985), 60.

311. *De Bello Gallico*, VI.14; G. Dumézil, "La tradition druidique et l'écriture: Le Vivant et le Mort," *RHR* 122 (1940): 125–26.

312. Dumézil, "Tradition druidique," 130.

CHAPTER 5: FOILS, FOOLS, AND ANTIHEROES

1. See Robert D. Pelton, *The Trickster in West Africa: A Study of Mythic Irony and Sacred Delight* (Berkeley: University California Press, 1980), 1–24, "Interpreting the Trickster," for an excellent overview of the phenomenon.

2. D. Bynum, *The Dæmon in the Wood: A Study of Oral Narrative Patterns*, Center for Study of Oral Literature (Cambridge, Mass.: Harvard University Press, 1978), 162n.

3. B. Babcock, "'A Tolerated Margin of Mess': The Trickster and His Tales Reconsidered," *Journal of the Folklore Institute* 11, no. 3 (March 1975): 150; Hesiod, *Theogony*, 507–12, and see K. Kerényi, *The Gods of the Greeks*, trans. N. Cameron (London: Thames & Hudson, 1974), 212–19.

4. K. Kerényi, "Evil in Mythology," in *Evil*, ed. K. Kerényi, Curatorium of the C. G. Jung Institute (Evanston, Ill.: Northwestern University Press, 1967), 8.

5. Robert Pelton raises a serious question in his important study of the West African trickster: how do we balance an individual trickster figure against the mythic type, or the "shaping of . . . inner and outer worlds, linking the mythical past to the present"? (Pelton, *Trickster*, 12.) The trickster as archetype has not been examined in the context of the Indo-European figure. Dumézil himself, in dealing with the Norse figure Loki, refused to be drawn toward Jung's archetypal ground. See his *Loki*, ed. G. Dumézil, Collection "Les Dieux et les Hommes," vol. 1 (Paris: G.-P. Maisonneuve, 1948): 20.

6. Though we ought to note the hint of an alternative pairing when the *chanson de geste* describes Roland as "brave," Olivier as "wise": LXXXVII.1093.

7. The off-center position of Akhilleus in the epic, his divine-animal ferocity and his emotional complexity, keeps him from any effective partnership with Odysseus, whom he also knows to be a deceiver in speech: see below, p. 000.

8. For a discussion of Odysseus in the *Odyssey* and his putative inclination toward "three categories of peril" (irresponsibility, sex, violence), see Howard C. Clark, *The Art of the Odyssey* (Englewood Cliffs, N.J.: Prentice-Hall, 1967), 48, and

Charles Moorman, *Kings and Captains: Variations on a Heroic Theme* (Lexington: University Press of Kentucky, 1971), 38–39 (for Odysseus's, "errors") and 51–52 for a "doubled" Odysseus.

9. In fact, Bósi and his uterine brother Smidr are actually fostered, by the sorceress Busla, but it is Bosi and Herrauðr who are consistently called *fostbræðra*: "BoK," chaps. 2, 4. See Miller, "Functional Operations," 135–43 (see chap. 1, n. 109).

10. "BoK," chap. 2; "on his own manhood" (*með karlmennsku telja*).

11. To the point where the king-supporting Þórr-warrior is, as Dumézil said, "scarce . . . in Scandinavian literature": *The Destiny of the Warrior,* 90 (see chap. 2, n. 185); though perhaps his type is slightly more common than Dumézil had originally thought. See Miller, "Functional Operations," 115–58 (see chap. 1, n. 109).

12. *JS,* chaps. 9–12.

13. The Hildiridarsons, Hárekr and Hrærekr (both names have associative ties with sorcery and the supernatural) were products of a *lausabrullaup,* a "loose marriage tie" (*ES,* chap. 7), and thus were bastards, as was Fjolnir Tókasson in the Jomsviking narrative. In "Bósa ok Herrauðr" the illegitimate half brother of Herrauðr, Sjodr, also shows features of the "bad councillor": chap. 4. In the *Weltanschauung* of the sagas illegitimacy is sometimes included in the calculus of extraordinary heroic birth (as with Oláfr pái in *Laxdæla saga*), but in the cases under consideration the "bad councillor" is detached from his family and made part of the monarch's bureaucratic *équipe;* in this case bastardy is shown to weaken the family tie and to incline the bastard toward, or facilitate, his self-interested, familial political tie.

14. Kerényi, *Heroes of the Greeks,* 356.

15. Littleton, "Some Possible Indo-European Themes in the *Iliad*," 236 (see chap. 2, n. 229).

16. See Miller, "Aegisthus," 259–68 (see chap. 2, n. 72).

17. L. de Heusch, *Pouvoir et le sacré*, Annales du Centre d'Etudes des Religions, vol. 1 (Bruxelles: Université Libre de Bruxelles, Institut de Sociologie, 1962), 39; C. Préaux, "La légende de Pélops et la royauté sacrée," in the same volume (83–86). In the *Odyssey* (IV.529ff.) Agamemnon is described as having been killed "as one kills an ox in its stall," (535) and after the murder a melee ensues in which all of Agamemnon's men and the twenty whom Aegisthus had picked for the ambush lay dead "in the great hall," *en megaroisan:* 537.

18. Miller, "Aegisthus," 262–63.

19. *SCHS* II, 76, 139.

20. *SCHS* III, 198–99; see D. A. Miller, "The Blackened Hero: Serbian and Celtic Evidence for the Warrior of Reversal," *Mankind Quarterly* 24, no. 2 (Winter 1983): 220.

21. See Oinas, "Folk-Epic," 103 (see chap. 1, n. 81). Janko is not, it appears, a full-fledged reflection of Tale, but borrows something, at least on the surface, from the reversing type.

22. *SCHS* II, 171ff.

23. *SCHS* II, 210, 220; *SCHS* III, 201ff.

24. *SCHS* II, 188.

25. *SCHS* II, 200, 142, 211, 220, 262.

26. *SCHS* II, 203, 204. Here Tale's mace resembles the club or staff of the Irish "good god," the Dagda: with one end the club kills, with the other it restores life (Rees and Rees, *Celtic Heritage*, 35ff. [see chap. 2, n. 34]). The freeing-of-prisoners theme is also seen in the Welsh *Culhwch ac Olwen;* it is one of Cei's responsibilities.

27. *SCHS* III, 203; see H. Wagenvoort, *Roman Dynamism: Studies in Ancient Roman Thought, Language and Custom* (Oxford: Basil Blackwell, 1947), 155ff.

28. Low, *Marko,* 86, 105.

29. Ibid., 25–28, 131. For Cú Chulainn, see the episodes where the *gae bolga* is used, as detailed above, p. 213.

30. Ibid., 110.

31. Ibid., 135–38; *SCHS* II, 112, 193, 211.

32. *SCHS* III, 177.

33. He is already married, to a nagging wife: *SCHS* III, 176. Possibly there is a specific Turkish folk influence made apparent here, taken for example from widely circulated folkloric versions of Sufid exemplary tales concerning that wise fool, the *hodja* Nasruddin: see Idries Shah, *The Sufis* (Garden City, N.Y.: Doubleday Anchor, 1971), 63ff. Some of Tale's baroque *pronunciamentos* have the certified ring of the Wise Fool motif type.

34. Bailey, "Ossetes," in Hatto, *Traditions,* 257 (see chap. 3, n. 182).

35. See Miller, "The Three Kings at Colonos" (see chap. 2, n. 8) and "A Note on Aegisthus as Hero" (see chap. 2, n. 72). For death by suicide (a Heraklean theme), see Dumézil, *Destiny of the Warrior,* 101, and *Stakes,* 41–44 (see chap. 3, n. 202).

36. Dumézil, *Destiny of the Warrior,* 82–95; *Stakes,* 9–49.

37. This we discover in the "debate" between the two Aesir given fully in *GtS,* chap. 7.

38. See John Miles Foley, "Reading the Oral Traditional Text: Aesthetics of Creation and Response," in Foley, *Comparative Research on Oral Traditions,* 185–212 (see chap. 1, n. 74).

39. J. Nagy, *Wisdom,* 19 (see chap. 1, n. 90). The ligature between *fili* and *drui* is formed because of the reliance of both on the great power of the spoken word.

40. J. Nagy, *Wisdom,* 18; *AIT,* 360–69.

41. Rees and Rees, *Celtic Heritage,* 17 (see chap. 2, n. 34).

42. J. Nagy, *Wisdom,* 24.

43. *AIT,* 365.

44. Joseph Nagy believes that nature poetry is in fact "natural" to the *filid/fénnid: Wisdom,* 25. For Beltain and the Celtic calendar, see Emily Lyle, "The Design of the Celtic Year," *Shadow* 1 (1984): 32–41, reprinted in her *Archaic Cosmos: Polarity, Space and Time* (Edinburgh: Polygon, 1990), 75–85.

45. *Fianaigecht,* 68–99 (see chap. 4, n. 40); *AIT,* 427, 428; and note Rees and Rees, *Celtic Heritage,* 354.

46. J. Nagy, *Wisdom,* 33.

47. *Nibelungenlied*, v. 1834 (pp. 150–51); vv. 2002, 2006 (pp. 184–85) (see chap. 2, n. 249).

48. Miller, "Functional Operations," 123–25.

49. Ibid., 125. There is some hint here of the important but difficult-to-authenticate Indo-European motif of interfunctional war: see ibid., 121–23.

50. "BoH," chap. 5, 12.

51. *CMT,* chap. 39 (pp. 34–35); Rees and Rees, *Celtic Heritage* (see chap. 2, n. 34).

52. *CO,* 4, line 104; Ford, *Mabinogion,* 124 (see chap. 2, n. 10).

53. See Rees and Rees, *Celtic Heritage,* 128, for the social position of satirists as a group in Christian Ireland, where they were regarded as either *declassé* or put at the very bottom of the social scale, with prostitutes and "the sons of death and bad men" as the Reeses quote the *Ancient Laws of Ireland* (Dublin, 1901), 3:25.

54. *ES,* chap. 60 [*EgS,* chap. 61]. The poem is a long falsehood but, though it countered a situation in which magic was being used against Egill, it was not itself magical but rather "rational."

55. Unferth in *Beowulf* seems to have some residual satiric powers, though no evident poetic role or talent: see especially lines 1164–65 in the poem.

56. *Il.* XXIV.720; see Foley, "Reading the Oral Traditional Text," 194.

57. G. Nagy, *Best of the Achaeans,* 259–64 (see chap. 1, n. 7).

58. *Gesta Francorum,* mentioned in CXI.1443.

59. GRO III, line 21 (pp. 44–45); *kai tragôdein apêrzato paramuthôn tên korên.*

60. See Babcock, "A Tolerated Margin of Mess."

61. Tucked into the footnotes of *SCHS* III, 177–78 (see pp. 267–68 for nn. 150–53, and 155–58): *govno,* "shit," is one of Tale's favorites, but he reaches full vulgar steam ahead with *psi mu drli majku,* "may a dog screw his mother," a truly Balkan expansion of our pale Anglo-Saxon vulgarity, "son of a bitch."

62. The singer Đemail Zogić so characterized Tale in *SCHS* II, 242.

63. I.e., through the gaping holes in the floor of the chariot: Kinsella, *Táin,* 215–16; O'Rahilly, *Táin,* 108–9, 243–44, lines 3910–11.

64. *CMT,* chap. 93, lines 398–99: he was "unsightly" and "his long penis was uncovered" (*Is ed denucht lebar penntol*). The honorable nakedness of *young* warriors and champions, attested to elsewhere in the Celto-Gaulic world, is another matter entirely.

65. Kinsella, *Táin,* 216, O'Rahilly, *Táin,* 109, 244, lines 3933–34.

66. "BoH," chap. 2.

67. *ES,* chap. 40: Skalla-Grímr's uncanny night-powers increase when he and his son Egill fight until dusk comes on; Egill has to break off the confrontation because of this. Þórgerdr Brak is called *fjolkunnig mjog,* "a great witch" (ibid.).

68. *ES,* chap. 56.

69. *ES,* chap. 45.

70. "BoH," chap. 2; *ES,* chap. 87 (*EgS,* chap. 90: *En fleiri veru Myramenn manna ljóstatir*).

71. Saxo, *Gesta Danorum,* III.84–85, 86 (see chap. 1, n. 91). How Shake-

speare's Hamlet got rid of "the guts" (as in "I'll lug the guts into the neighbour room"; *Hamlet*, III.iv) is still debated.

72. Saxo, *Gesta Danorum*, III.87–90.

73. Saxo, *Gesta Danorum*, introduction to bk. IV, p. 92.

74. Saxo, *Gesta Danorum*, IV.100; later in book IV King Fridlief, Dan's son, uses the same trick (111), which appears again in this century in P. C. Wren's adventure novel, *Beau Geste* (1924) and its various cinematic versions.

75. *TYP,* T. 71, 72, 73.

76. *TYP,* 49 (T. 26).

77. *TI;* English translation by A. T. Hatto (chap. 2, n. 154). See Miller, afterword, in "The Twinning of Arthur and Cei," 66–69 (see chap. 1, n. 106).

78. *TI*, 7340–8225, 8675–11517; Hatto, *Tristan*, 138–49, 155–192; *TI*, 7905–6 (Hatto, *Tristan*, 146) for "saving his own skin"; he is a *paratiere* in *TI*, 8346 (and a *zoubere* or sorcerer in 8336 [Hatto, *Tristan*, 151]); the nearly fatal dragon fight is in *TI*, 10151–55, and Hatto, *Tristan*, 160–61.

79. *TI*, 12436ff. (Hatto, *Tristan*, 205); *TI,* 14764–66 (Hatto, *Tristan*, 236) and *TI*, 15747–48 (Hatto, *Tristan*, 256).

80. The Dahomean trickster-god Legba, a vital example of the type, brought both death *and* culture to mankind: M. Herskovitz and F. Herskovitz, *Dahomean Narrative* (Evanston, Ill.: Northwestern University Press, 1958), 142.

81. M. Delcourt, "The Last Giants," *History of Religions* 4, no. 2 (Winter 1965), 237–38.

82. Kerényi, *Heroes of the Greeks,* 76–78; Kerényi cites Strabo 9.1.17 for Laertes as being Odysseus's foster father or "mortal father."

83. Delcourt, "Last Giants," 241.

84. See Miller, "The Twinning of Arthur and Cei," 53–54.

85. Saxo, *Gesta Danorum*, VIII.247ff.

86. *Oedipus at Colonos*, 1649, 1679–83, 1704–5: "he died as he willed" (*hoion éthelen)* according to Antigone; see Miller, "The Three Kings at Colonos," 70–71.

87. M. Eliade, *The Forge and the Crucible: The Origins and Structures of Alchemy*, trans. S. Corrin, 2d ed. (Chicago: University of Chicago Press, 1978), 34ff.

88. Eliade, *Forge and Crucible,* 105–6 and n. 1.

89. *Beowulf,* 1522ff, 1559–60, 1616; with more on the sword's Otherworldly and "Giant" origins in lines 1687ff.

90. *Hrólf Gautreksson*, ed. G. Jónsson, Fornaldarsögur Norðurlanda (Reykjavik: Bokantgafen Forni, 1954), IV, chap. 15; *Hrolf Gautreksson, A Viking Romance*, trans. H. Pálsson and P. Edwards (Toronto: University of Toronto Press, 1972). For an attenuated but still recognizable rendition of this motif, see *Heiðarviga saga*, where Víga-Styrr (who is himself called an uncontrolled killer, *víga*) is able to kill two berserks with a staff and his bare hands: chap. 11. In *Borgfirðinga sögur*, ed. S. Nordal and G. Jónsson, Íslensk Fornrit 3 (Reykjavik: Hið íslensk fornritafélag, 1938).

91. *Beowulf,* 669–74ff.

92. *SCHS* I, 217.

93. *SCHS* I, 433.

94. Kerényi, *Heroes of the Greeks*, 126, 137; citing Pindar's *Nemean Odes*, 3.22 for Herakles as *hêrôs theos*.

95. Apollodoros, II.4.11.

96. Marie Delcourt details the powers of the "metalworker as magician"; she also separates Hephaistos's more benign force, given that he is a bronzesmith, from the darker powers assigned to the iron-smithing Daktyls, who are his miniatures and also his inferiors. Delcourt, *Héphaistos, ou le légende du magicien*, 12, 50, 80–81, 156, 161, 165, 166–70 (see chap. 2, n. 336).

97. Eliade, *Forge and Crucible*, 95; J. Vansina, *Kingdoms of the Savannah* (Madison: University of Wisconsin Press, 1966), 125, 165. See also L. Makarius, "The Blacksmith's Taboos: From the Man of Iron to the Man of Blood," *Diogenes* 62 (Summer 1968): 25; "Regarded as the possessor of great magical powers, held at the same time in veneration and contempt." The smith, as we shall see, may also be given special social responsibilities beyond his ordinary range of technical skill and capacity.

98. *Shâh-nâma*, II. (8); IV.ii–iii (20–21) (see chap. 1, n. 36); see Eliade, *Forge and Crucible*, 85, n. 3; 86, n. 1. Chingiz Khan was also identified as a "simple smith" before he achieved his Mongol warrior-chieftain epiphany.

99. Makarius, "Blacksmith's Taboos," 34ff.

100. Makarius sees a taboo operative that "still has a compulsive and unchallenged influence, as in certain African societies on the threshold of barbarism and acquainted with work in iron"; ibid., 32.

101. Eliade, *Forge and Crucible*, 79–86, 97–108, 142–52. Jung's researches are laid out in three volumes (12–14) of his *Collected Works* (Bollingen Series 20), *Psychology and Alchemy* (1968), *Alchemical Studies* (1968), and *Mysterium Coniunctionis: An Inquiry into the Separation and Synthesis of Psychic Opposites in Alchemy* (1976), all translated by R. F. C. Hull and published by Princeton University Press.

102. Eliade, *Forge and Crucible*, 102–3.

103. Kerényi, *Gods of the Greeks*, 88, for the Telchines; 84, citing the Scholai on Apollonios Rhodios, 1.1126, and Pausanias, 5.7.6 (see chap. 1, n. 6), for the doubled Daktyloi.

104. Vidal-Naquet, *The Black Hunter*, 9 (see chap. 1, n. 171).

105. Thompson, *Motif-Index*, F450 (see chap. 1, n. 69).

106. See ibid., s.v. "Mines," "Miners."

107. Saxo, *Gesta Danorum*, VI.177.

108. Ibid., 179.

109. *ES*, chap. 25, for Grímr's Gang.

110. A casualty at the Battle of the Althing—in chap. 145—is dragged into "the booth of some sword-grinder"—hardly a respectful term if a smith is in fact meant in this passage.

111. *Ldn*, chap. 179.

112. *Ldn*, chap. 225; in 328 we find two "great fighters and blacksmiths," Vemundr and Molda-Gnup; and in a short poem, Vemundr praises his own two favorite vocations, smithing and killing.

113. N. J. Allen, "The Ideology of the Indo-Europeans: Dumézil's Theory and

the Idea of a Fourth Function," *International Journal of Moral and Social Studies* 2, no. 11 (Spring 1987): 28.

114. Rees and Rees, *Celtic Heritage*, 113.

115. Allen, "Fourth Function," 32.

116. Ibid., 34.

117. G. Dumézil, *Mitra-Varuna: An Essay on Two Indo-European Representations of Sovereignty;* see also Miller, "Functional Operations," 143–52, especially table 1 (151).

118. David-Neel and Longden, *Gezar of Ling*, 272ff. (see chap. 2, n. 11).

119. Kerényi, *Gods of the Greeks*, 84.

120. Bailey, "Ossetes," in Hatto, *Traditions*, 239.

121. Neumann, *Origins*, 213 (see chap. 1, n. 210); Rees and Rees, *Celtic Heritage*, 214.

122. Rees and Rees, *Celtic Heritage*, 250 (and *AIT,* 364). For the modern Scottish Gaelic tradition of Finn as smith, see J. Nagy, *Wisdom*, 33–34.

123. Rees and Rees, *Celtic Heritage*, 238.

124. See above, p. 72, n. 10.

125. Ó Cáthasaigh, *The Heroic Biography of Cormac mac Airt* (see chap. 2, n. 60); Rees and Rees, *Celtic Heritage*, 219.

126. Rees and Rees, *Celtic Heritage*, 257.

127. Van Gennep, *The Rites of Passage*, 65–115 (see chap. 1, n. 160); M. Eliade, *Rites and Symbols of Initiation: The Mysteries of Birth and Rebirth* (New York: Harper & Row, 1975), xiii.

128. The hero Soslan, in Dumézil, *Le livre des héros*, 77 (see chap. 2, n. 88).

129. Kerényi, *Heroes of the Greeks*, 70, 248, 278, 309.

130. Eliade, *Forge and Crucible*, 103ff.

131. Rees and Rees, *Celtic Heritage*, 258.

132. Kerényi, *Heroes of the Greeks*, 222.

133. Allen, "Fourth Function," 29.

134. *Chanson de Roland*, CLXXI.2309; CLXXII.2318: Morianna will be Morgaine or Morgana le Fay, the Fairy Queen. The Serb hero Marko *is* able to break his "razor sword" as he is dying, lest a Turk have it: Levi and Pennington, *Marko the Prince*, 66 (see chap. 2, n. 49).

135. See Miller, "Two Warriors and Two Swords: The Legacy of Starkað," *JIES* 19, nos. 3–4 (Winter 1991): 307–23.

136. *Mahâbhârata*, 1 (6) 57.

137. See Bailey, "Ossetes," in Hatto, *Traditions*, 239ff.

138. Dumézil, *Légendes sur les Nartes*, 60ff. (see chap. 2, n. 88).

139. G. Dumézil, *Romans de Scythie et d'alentour* (Paris: Payot, 1978).

140. Rees and Rees, *Celtic Heritage*, 248; M. Eliade, *Rites and Symbols of Initiation*, 84–85.

141. *EIMS,* 237; *AIT,* 267.

142. *Tochmarc Émire*, in van Hamel, *Compert Con Culaind*, 17ff. (see chap. 2, n. 163); *AIT,* 162–63.

143. See above, p. 195.

144. Sayers, "The Smith and the Hero," 241 (see chap. 4, n. 157).

145. D. A. Miller, "The Blackened Hero," and "Blackened Hero and Heroic Trickster: An Investigation of Congeners," *Mankind Quarterly* 26, nos.1–2 (Fall–Winter 1985): 99–110.

146. The black and ogrish figure will also be featured in the Old Irish Celtic tales; see, for example, the ax-wielding *bachlach* as challenger in the *Fled Bricrend: AIT,* 262–63; *EIMS,* 232.

147. Simpson, *The Northmen Talk,* 119–2 9 (see chap. 2, n. 112). Like Egill, Hreiðar had a long life and many descendents.

148. Ellis Davidson, "Loki and Saxo's Hamlet," 16–17 (see chap. 2, n. 113).

149. Ibid., 11.

150. Ibid., 11–14.

151. *CO,* 35, line 974; Ford, *Mabinogion,* 150. Joan Radner's view of *Culhwch ac Olwen,* that it was conceived as an ironic parody of the adventure tale, and intended to play in this vein from first to last, I do not find convincing: see Radner, "Interpreting Irony in Medieval Celtic Narrative: The Case of *Culhwch ac Olwen,*" 41–59 (see chap. 3, n. 162). The tropes, to my mind, simply do not fit the tale.

152. Dumézil, *Loki,* 174–75.

153. *AIT,* 229; *EIMS,* 201. The two translations differ in certain details.

154. J. J. Ras, "The Panji Romances and W. H. Rasser's Analysis of Its Theme," *Bijdragen voor Taal-, Land- en Volkskunde* 129, no. 4 (1973): 433; J. L. Peacock, "Symbolic Reversal and Social History: Transvestites and Clowns in Java," in *The Reversible World: Symbolic Inversion in Art and Society,* ed. B. Babcock, Symbol, Myth and Ritual Series (Ithaca: Cornell University Press, 1978), 211ff.

155. Ras, "Panji Romances," 414–15.

156. Leszek Kolakowski solemnly and perhaps correctly invests the royal jester with "a philosophy questioning the established absolutes" in his "The Priest and the Jester," *Dissent* (Summer 1962): 233.

157. *Peredur mab Efrawg,* in Jones and Jones, *Mabinogion,* 183–84.

158. In "Aliscans," LXXIV.3159–60.

159. "Aliscans," CXXXII.6157ff; CLXVII.6788.

160. *DS,* II.(1).5–8 (115–19).

161. *AIT,* 362–63, and see above, pp. 85–86.

162. Somewhere in the "reversing" part of the tradition is a place for Unferth the *Þyle,* in the *Beowulf* epic, who seems to have *something* important to do at Hrothgar's Danish court (or, more precisely, in his royal hall), though we have no univocal evidence for any of the roles assigned to him—or rather, we have evidence for a number of very different roles. He is certainly a respected warrior, who finally offers has own "named" sword, Hrunting, to Beowulf, and he could be called a Þórr-warrior because he obviously provides some service to King Hrothgar. (*Beowulf,* 499–523, 1165, 1455–57; the last lines deal with Unferth's gift of Hrunting.) He is also less a jester than a tester, exercising a right to speak disparagingly of intruding heroes, though he is still far from the more dangerous type of, for example, the Celtic satirist. (See Greenfield, *The Interpretation of Old English*

Poems, 101ff. [see chap. 4, n. 273], for a discussion of the various opinions put forth on Unferth. There is a significant lexicographic problem in the fact that "Unferth" can be read either as "spirit-less one" or as "one of great spirit" [103], because the particle *un* in Old English may be either a negative or an intensive.)

Unferth is not quite alone in his uncertain category: A. B. Lord has noted the close similarity between his taunting of Beowulf and Euryalos's taunting of the shipwrecked Odysseus at the Phaiacian court. (Lord, "Beowulf and Odysseus," in Bassinger and Creed, *Franciplegius,* 86–91 (see chap. 2, n. 26); the taunt is in *Od.* VIII.158ff., where Euryalos caustically observes that Odysseus seems to be no athlete but "a captain of sailors, merchants" (*arkhos nautaôn hoi te prektêrês easin*). There Euryalos, too, is surely a warrior, called "equal to Ares Man's-Bane," the war-god himself; Odysseus's response to his gibes is a "flashback" set-piece statement not dissimilar to Beowulf's, and in both cases a sword is given or lent to the maligned hero as an apology for the taunts. I will have to leave these two cases of testing by taunting in this uncomfortable state of confusion, but evidently the taunts are not satirical, and the exchanges have much of the appearance of a formal, even a ritual word duel that does not seem intended to escalate into violence. "Testing," of course, may also be undertaken by a Doorward, as we have seen in the Old Irish and Welsh Celtic contexts.

163. Dumézil, *Destiny of the Warrior,* 78. 87; *Stakes,* 30, 60, for Starkaðr, Indra, Sisupala, and their Second Function delicts.

164. *Cantar del Mio Cid,* 2278ff. (see chap. 2, n. 141); *Poema/Poem,* 128–30 (pp. 234–37) (see chap. 2, n. 343).

165. *Poema/Poem,* 145 (pp. 274–75), a claim made in slightly different form elsewhere in the poem; see L. P. Harvey, "Medieval Spanish" [tradition], in Hatto, *Traditions,* p. 156.

166. Nitze and Jenkins, *Le haut livre du Graal: Perlesvaus,* vol. 1, iv.5.51, lines 1359–60 (see chap. 2, n. 65).

167. For Leriadus, see R. L. Curtis, ed., *Le roman de Tristan (en prose),* vol. 1 (Leiden: Brill, 1963), line 617. From G. D.West's *Index of Proper Names in French Arthurian Prose Romances,* University of Toronto Romance Series 35 (Toronto: University of Toronto Press, 1978), we can extract, in addition to Leriadus, Daguenet "le Coart," who is also "a fool"; Helynan, a handsome and cowardly knight, who is called "le Bel Mauveis"; and Henor, also handsome and a "beau couard." Cowardice is only one marker in this list; clearly these individuals display a tincture of other base or questionable characteristics, from the malignant to the openly clownish.

168. Curtis, *Tristan,* 1400, 1401, 1411.

169. *Ibid.,* 5605–6.

170. Thompson, *Motif-Index,* D1358.1; E714.4.1; *VölS,* chap. 163; *Þiðrekssaga af Bern,* ed. H. Bertelsen, Samfund til udgivelse af gammel nordisk litteratur 34 (Copenhagen, 1905), 2:344.

171. Jones, *Kings, Beasts and Heroes,* 137 (see chap. 1, n. 95); *HsK,* chap. 23.

172. Saxo, *Gesta Danorum,* II.56. The bear-monster of this version would be unlikely because Bjarki was himself a bear, or had a bear "fetch," or double.

173. Lord and Bynum, *SCHS* III, 204.

174. *Carados* (2d version) in *Continuations of the Old French Perceval*, ed. Wm. Roach and R. H. Ivy (1950; reprint, Philadelphia: American Philosophical Society, 1965), vol. 2, line 7195.

175. *Perlesvaus*, 1384-5.

176. Grisward, *L'archéologie*, 38 (see chap. 1, n. 30), citing L. Gautier, *Les épopées françaises*, 2d ed., IV.311.

177. Grisward, *L'archéologie*, 66.

178. *La Mule sans frein*, in *Two Old French Gawain Romances: Le chevalier à l'epée, La mule sans frein*, ed. R. C. Johnston and D. D. R. Owen (Edinburgh: Scottish Academic Press, 1972). Kay will not undertake an adventure unless the damsel involved kisses him first, *Mes il vault qu'ele lou besant* (line 99), and he turns back from the adventure because of fear: *Et Keus en a paor Si grant c'onques mes n'ot gragnor.*

179. For another resemblant figure, consider Queen Isolde's Steward in *Tristan:* he shares the characteristics of the "coward knight" (158, lines 8920ff.); he is accused by the Irish queen of being a "ladies' man" and "robbed of his manhood" (171, lines 9897ff.); and he tries to take credit for the deed of another—in this case, and ironically, Tristan, who in this narrative has the most palpable marks of the trickster. The contrast to Tristan may be as "comic butt" related to "comic hero": see Torrance, *The Comic Hero,* introduction (see chap. 1, n. 136). We have also already noted the special, often contemptible place given to the steward or seneschal in these knightly tales.

180. This argument is more fully worked out in Miller, "Other Kinds of Hero: The Coward Knight and Intelligence Embattled" (see chap. 2, n. 108).

181. H. Muchnic, in "The Coward Knight and the Damsel of the Cart," *PMLA* 43 (1928): 327, located a parallel, of sorts, to the coward knight in Hugh of Rutland's *Ipomedon*, the coward being Ipomedon himself: "Of dedes of armes when they spake / Ipomedon wolde turne his beke / And hye oute of the hall" (44). It is of interest that the Hippomedon of Greek heroic tradition was no coward but one of the "savage"—and arguably Third Function—heroes among the Seven who followed Polyneikes against Thebes, and who was killed there in the assault on the city.

182. Torrance, *The Comic Hero*, 12-36.

183. Ibid., 31. It is possible to be dull while writing on the comic, which is not a sin Torrance commits. His reading of Odysseus's character is idiosyncratic, sometimes provocative, and sometimes merely provoking; his interpretation of the ultimate confrontation between Odysseus and the suitors is simplistic and needs to be balanced, perhaps from M. I. Finley's *The World of Odysseus: Homer and His Age in Archaeology, Literature and History* (New York: Meridian/World, 1963), especially Finley's chapter on "Household, Kin and Community."

184. *Henry IV*, I. v. 1.

185. See B. Berlin and P, Kay, *Basic Color Terms* (Berkeley: University Of California Press, 1969).

186. See M. Granet, *Le pensée chinoise*, La collection "L'Evolution de l'Humanité" (Paris: Albin Michel, 1968), 81.

187. *Popul Vuh*, trans. D. Tedlock (New York: Simon & Schuster, 1985), 71.348, "bowl of earth, bowl of sky."

188. G. Weiss, "Campa Cosmology: The World of a Forest Tribe in South America," *Anthropological Papers of the American Museum of Natural History* 52, no. 5 (1975): 415ff.

189. E. R. Leach, *Culture and Communication: The Logic by Which Symbols Are Connected*, Themes in the Social Sciences (Cambridge: Cambridge University Press, 1976), 57–60.

190. Inga Glendennin, *Aztecs: An Interpretation* (Cambridge: Cambridge University Press, 1991), 243. This Mesoamerican society deployed an almost frighteningly flexible ability to shift and transpose signs and symbols; presumably the "observed" red of human blood, which was freely registered in other sacred iconisms (as in the Flayed God, the "red" Xipe Totec) was redirected in a *hierarchic* intervention of values or valuations, and so made congruent with the supreme and most precious tint of all, the blue-green.

191. See especially E. Lyle, "Dumézil's Three Functions and the Indo-European Cosmic Structure," now in her *Archaic Cosmos: Polarity, Space and Time* (Edinburgh: Polygon, 1990), 7–12.

192. Ibid., 9, citing Dumézil, *Idéologie tripartie*, 26, 98.

193. Another color sign for *richesse*, gold or yellow, can be assigned to the First Function as a reflex of light, radiance, ouranal brilliance.

194. For the woman bewitched by a dwarf in *Göngu-Hrolfs Saga*, see Miller, "'Bad Death,'" 165–66 (see chap. 1, n. 10).

195. P. Vidal-Naquet, "The Black Hunter and the Origin of the Athenian *Ephebeia*," in his *The Black Hunter*, 106–28.

196. Ibid., 110.

197. *Shâh-nâma*, X.1.152.

198. All these individuals' names are taken from West, *An Index of Proper Names in French Arthurian Prose Romances*. Shorter lists could be made up from the tale of Roland's enemies in the *Chanson de Roland*, or of Rainouart's in the Guillaume Cycle, who is himself a bit on the blackened side: see below, p. 349.

199. *Ldn*, chaps. 31, 80, 214, 233; *LxS*, chaps. 6, 54.

200. *Ldn*, chaps. 127, 344; Illugi is mentioned in chaps. 37, 43, 67, 99, 174; Ongul the Black in *Ldn*, chap. 236.

201. For Coal-Beard see *Ldn*, chap. 150; and *LxS*, chap. 24.

202. *Ldn*, chap. 112ff.

203. *Ldn*, chap. 168: *við rauða sciolldu*.

204. *TBDD*, in *EIMS*, 88; in this source we could also note the fatal "Three Reds," supernatural warriors who "were entirely red, teeth and hair, men and horses" and whose coming to Da Derga's hostel preceeds that of Conare the king, who is now doomed to multiply violate his *gessa* (*EIMS*, 69–70).

205. See above, pp. 191–92; Lancelot in Chrétien de Troyes, *Lancelot = Le*

Chevalier de la Charette, in Roques, *Les romans* (see chap. 3, n. 87); in Staines, *The Complete Romances*, 344 (see chap. 3, n. 87).

206. See "The Ossetian Tale" in Lord, *Symposium*, 30, 36 (see chap. 2, n. 227).

207. *Raoul de Cambrai*, XV, XXXII. It is said of the curmudgeonly Red Guerri that "your nephew is ill-disposed of heart, but you are wilder and stranger still" (CLXVIII). See Calin, *Epic of Revolt*, 171–72 (see chap. 1, n. 98).

208. *Yvain*, 780.

209. Grisward, *L'archéologie*, 253, citing J. Frappier, *Étude sur* La Mort le Roi Artu. *Roman du XIIe siècle, Dernière partie du* Lancelot en Prose, 2d ed. (Geneva: Librairie Droz, 1968), 86, n. 6; also Grisward, 253–54. Elsewhere Grisward adds another dimension to the symbolic dimension of the color red, as revealed in the *Quete du Graal: L'arbre rouge*, a tree left over from Adam's Eden, "has no offshoots," and so would seem to demonstrate the essentially infertile aspect of the Second Function (Grisward, "L'arbre blanc, vert, rouge de la Quete du Graal et le symbolisme coloré des Indo-Européens," *Ogam—Tradition Celtique* 35–36 [1983–84]: 114).

210. M. Delcourt, *Pyrrhos et Pyrrha. Recherches sur les valeurs du feu dans les légendes helléniques*, Bibliothèque de la Faculté de philosophie et lettres de l'Université de Liège, fasc. 174 (Paris, 1965), 13–30; L. A. Thompson, *Romans and Blacks*, Oklahoma Series in Classical Culture (Norman: University of Oklahoma Press, 1989), 110–14.

211. *Mesca Ulad*, in *AIT*, 226–27, and *EIMS*, 205; also in the *Siapur-charpat*, in *AIT*, 348, 349.

212. Miller, "Three Kings at Colonos," with reference to Theseus: 55–58, 61.

213. Kerényi, *Heroes of the Greeks*, 329; Delcourt, *Pyrrhos et Pyrrha.*

214. For the Red Knight as Arthur's enemy, see the text of *Percival: Continuations of the Old French Perceval*, vol. 1, *The First Continuation*, ed. Wm. Roach, (Philadelphia: University of Pennsylvania Press, 1949), 945–46; and also Goetinck, *Peredur*, 114ff. (see chap. 1, n. 28).

215. *Wolfram von Eschenbach: Parzifal*, ed. G. Weber (Darmstadt: Insel Verlag, 1963).

216. Goetinck, *Peredur*, 137.

217. *Nibelungenlied*, v. 172 (pp. 42–43) (for "marshall"); v. 1203ff. (pp. 18–19).

218. *Nibelungenlied*, vv. 307 (pp. 70–71), 531 (pp. 118–19).

219. *Nibelungenlied*, v. 873 (pp. 194–95); Mowatt's remark is in the Everyman edition of the *Nibelungenlied*, ed. by O. G. Mowatt (London: Dent; New York: Dutton, 1962), 221.

220. Ford. *Mabinogion*, 27, 61.

221. Ibid., 57.

222. *NjS*, chaps. 120, 123.

223. Lönnroth, in *Njál's Saga: A Critical Introduction*, 131 (see chap. 2, n. 286), concludes rather mildly that Skarpheðinn is a "basically noble but impetuous troublemaker."

224. *AIT*, 120; *EIMS*, 47.

225. *AIT*, 229–30; there is a hint here that he contains interiorly, within him-

self, the good/bad doublet, like Nisien/Efnisien in the Welsh narrative. *EIMS,* 209, gives a different translation: "a gentle blush on one cheek, a furious red blush on the other," and he has some other variations on Dubtach's appearance.

226. *AIT,* 271, 278; *EIMS,* 243–44, 250.

227. *AIT,* 471.

228. Dubtach in fact escapes the fire that destroys Da Derga's hostel.

229. See Jung, *Two Essays on Analytical Psychology,* trans. F. C. Hull, in *Collected Works,* vol. 7, Bollingen Series 20 (New York: Pantheon, 1953), 103, n. 5. The other great troublemaker of the Old Irish epos is Bricriu Memthenga, "Poison-Tongue," but unlike Dubtach Bricriu is not admitted to the heroes' company of the Ulaid: like Thersites, he is given a contemptuous blow (by Fergus, in the *Adventures of Nera,* ed. and trans. K. Meyer, *Revue Celtique* 10 [1889]; *AIT,* 253) and is specifically excluded from the feast he himself gives, that is, the *Fled Bricrend.* His power as a *satirist* is to be feared; he seems to be placed both above and below the ranks of the Ulster warriors.

230. Dáithí ÓhÓgáin, "Magic Attributes of the Hero in Fenian Lore," in Almqvist, Ó Catháin, and Ó Héalaí, *The Heroic Process,* 236 (see chap. 4, n. 253).

231. Thompson, *Motif-Index,* F233.1; F236.1.6; F178.2.

232. Kinsella, *Táin,* 94 (not in O'Rahilly); *EIMS,* 94, for the *TBDD.* For the citation to the *Aided Muirchertaig meic Erca,* see the edition by Lil Nic Dhonnchadha, Medieval and Modern Irish Series 19 (Dublin: DIAS, 1964), lines 7–14, and see a translation by Joan Radner, "Threefold Death," in *Celtic Folklore and Christianity: Studies in Memory of William W. Heist,* ed. Patrick K. Ford, Center for the Study of Comparative Folklore and Mythology, University of California at Los Angeles (Santa Barbara, Calif.: McNally & Loftin, 1983), 196. Two other Otherworldly "green women," Bécuma and Delbchaem, are seen in the *Eachtra Airt* (see Ó Hehir, in Ford, *Celtic Folklore,* 171). But these are all sovereignty goddesses, which adds quite another dimension to the problem.

233. *AIT,* 122; *EIMS,* 100. Joël Grisward (*L'archéologie,* 253ff) examines another difficulty or complication, as unfolded in the *Cycle des Narbonnais,* which maintains a trifunctional scheme of white-red-black—but the Second Function member (Aimer) is a black knight (256). In other ways as well, Aimer proves himself *ce personnage fascinant* (185). In addition, Hernaut, the Third Function seneschal in the *équipe* of the seven sons of Aymeri, is identified as a *roux,* a redhead with a redhead's recalcitrant nature; he has to be trained out of this character's disqualifications in order to do his job. He does not, however, readapt to green; instead, he reverses the Old Irish example (of the "green" warriors from the Otherword punished with a "red" color).

234. Ross G. Arthur, *Medieval Sign Theory and Sir Gawain and the Green Knight* (Toronto: University of Toronto Press, 1987), 50; he adds that the epic hero's marked shield is taken as his "alter ego."

235. Ibid., 51–52.

236. Ronald Dennys, *The Heraldic Imagination* (London: Barrie and Jenkins, 1975), 29. Dennys does not give his own heraldic "court" title, which is uncom-

monly modest for one of these officers; I find from another source that he held the office of Somerset Herald in 1975.

237.   Chrétien de Troyes, *Cliges*, in *Les romans de Chrétien de Troyes*, ed. A. Micha (Paris: Les Classiques Français du Moyen Age, 1957), 65–66; Staines, *Complete Romances*, 142–43.

238.   Arthur, *Medieval Sign Theory*, 106.

239.   Dennys, *Heraldic Imagination*, 47, citing *Le blazon des couleurs en armes, livrées et divisées par Sicille hérault d'Alphonse V roi d'Aragon*, ed. H. Cocheris (Paris, 1960).

240.   Presumably because this tint recalled the first, observed stages of corporeal dissolution in the human body.

241.   For two brief notes investigating some of the possibilities nascent in the Green Knight's devilish or fiendish associations, see D. W. Robertson Jr., "Why the Devil Wears Green," *Modern Language Notes* 69 (1959): 470–72, and Dale B. J. Randall, "Was the Green Knight a Fiend?" *Studies in Philology* 57 (1960): 479–91. In fact Satan, as Prince of the Damned and marshal of the Hellish Host, has to have his own coat of arms; it is found in the thirteenth-century Douce Apocalypse and is blazoned as "Gules, a fess Or between three Frogs Proper," the frogs evidently taken from Rev. 16.13–14. See Dennys, *Heraldic Imagination*, 110–12, and plate, p. 128.

242.   *Sir Gawain and the Green Knight*, ed. J. R. R. Tolkein and E. V. Gordon; 2d ed., ed. N. Davis (Oxford: Clarendon, 1968), lines 150–51.

243.   Ibid., 157ff. The figures who offer to play the beheading game in such later romances as *Carados, Le chevalier à l'epée* and *La Mule sans frein* are not ogres but young and handsome knights.

244.   Ibid., 669ff.

245.   Ibid., 1293.

246.   For the Green Girdle, see Arthur, *Medieval Sign Theory*, 106 ff.; the color itself is neither queried nor analyzed here. For themes of temptation and the beheading game, see Elizabeth Brewer, *From Cuchulainn to Gawain: Sources and Analogues of Sir Gawain and the Green Knight* (Totowa, N.J.: Rowman & Littlefield, 1973).

247.   *Sir Gawain and the Green Knight*, 189.

248.   R. Bernheimer, *Wild Men in the Middle Ages* (Cambridge, Mass.: Harvard University Press, 1952); also F. Tinland, *L'Homme sauvage. Homo ferus et homo sylvestris de l'animal à l'homme* (Paris: Payot, 1968), 3: the latter type is seen in the medieval world view as marked by "sa loyauté et son accord avec les forces de vie."

249.   "Asay" should not, as at least one translation (James Rosenberg's) has it, mean "seduce," but honestly "test": *Sir Gawain and the Green Knight*, 2362.

250.   John Lydus, *Liber de mensibus*, ed. Wuensch (Leipzig: Teubner, 1898), 4.30.

251.   Gawain refuses even to meet the old woman of Bercilac's castle, who is identified as Morgain le Fee, a kind of sinister queen figure whose repulsiveness recalls the archaic Celtic hag of sovereignty. This refusal must keep Gawain secure in his own knightly Second Function.

252.   *NjS*, chap. 116.

253. Jones and Jones, *Mabinogion.*, 194–95.

254. Roman Jakobson and Marc Szeftel, "The Vseslav Epos," *Memoirs, American Folklore Society* 42 (1945): 44.

255. Bruford, "Oral and Literary Fenian Tales," in Almqvist, Ó Catháin, and Ó Héalaí, *The Heroic Process,* 42, 48.

256. P. MacCana, "*Fianaigecht* in the pre-Norman Period," Almqvist, Ó Catháin, and Ó Héalaí, *The Heroic Process,* 76; see also J. Nagy, *Wisdom,* 236.

257. See Dennys, *Heraldic Imagination* 46ff.; the first judgment is that of Sicily Herald, while the disjunct second opinion is that contained in the *Tractatus* of the Welsh scholar-herald who called himself Bado Aureo: John de Bado Aureo, *Tractatus de Armis,* Bodleian Library MS Laud Misc. 733, fol. 9 (68); see also E. J. Jones, *Medieval Heraldry:* Tractatus de Armis, *by Johannes de Bado Aureo (An Enquiry into the Authorship of a Fourteenth Century Latin Treatise* (Cardiff: Lewis, 1943). In the Dumézilian view, Bado Aureo's ranking system and code would put both white *and* black in the First Function!

258. Nibelungenlied, v. 1734.

259. *GrS,* chap. 32. And he came, it is said, from a border area, on the Swedish side of the marches between Norway and Sweden.

260. *GrS,* chap. 13; *Ldn,* chap. 161.

261. *ES,* chap. 60.

262. *AIT,* 334, 336–37.

263. *Raoul de Cambrai,* CLXXXVII.

264. *Le Chevalier à l'épée,* in *Two Old French Gawain Romances: Le Chevalier à l'epée and La Mule sans frein,* ed. by Johnston and Owen, 178 (see n. 178).

265. *Ldn,* chaps. 83, 202.

266. *EyS,* chap. 63; another version of the story has a "dapple-gray" bull, with no known owner, involved in the engendering of the hellish calf.

267. Note Old Norse *grá-leikr* 'malice' and *grá-lika* 'with malice'.

CHAPTER 6: *TERTIUM QUID:* ASPECTS OF LIMINALITY

1. V. Turner, *The Ritual Process: Structure and Anti-Structure* (Chicago: University of Chicago Press, 1969), 95. Turner would modify this definition slightly in *Dramas, Fields and Metaphors: Symbolic Action in Human Society* (Ithaca: Cornell University Press, 1974).

2. See above, p. 266, n. 113.

3. Leach, *Culture and Communication,* 35 (see chap. 5, n. 189), with reference as well to Leach, "Anthropological Aspects of Language: Animal Catgories and Verbal Abuse," in *Mythology,* ed. P. Miranda (Baltimore: Penguin, 1973): 39–67.

4. M. Eliade, *Shamanism and the Techniques of Ecstasy,* Bollingen Series 76 (Princeton: Princeton University Press, 1972), 376. Eliade is, as he should be, careful not to derogate shamanism or its survivals as "primitive": *archaic* is always the operative word.

5. Ibid., 378–79. I hesitate to use the word "students" for those who have

been influenced by Dumézil (many individuals, including myself, never formally studied with the man), and certainly the term "disciples" should be avoided at all costs.

6. See above, pp. 74–76

7. Eliade, *Shamanism*, 412.

8. Ibid., 380ff., 385, but see Britt-Mari Näsström, *Freya—the Great Goddess of the North*, Lund Studies in History of Religions 5 (Lund, Sweden: Novapress, 1995), for an "omni-Functional" Freya.

9. Such as King Harekr in "Bósa ok Herrauðr," chaps. 8, 10, 14.

10. Eliade, *Shamanism*, 409, 390, citing Polyaenus, *Stratêgametôn*, vii.22.

11. A prevision of the stock market? See *Sturlaugs saga Starfsama*, chap. XII, cited in Ellis Davidson, *The Road to Hel*, 126 (see chap. 1, n. 91); *Ldn*, chap. 350.

12. *Ldn*, chaps. 202, 259. Compare Hóttr's "monstrous meal" and its result— the transformation into herohood—in *HsK*.

13. *LxS*, chaps. 35, 36.

14. *GiS*, chap. 19.

15. *EyS*, chaps. 15, 16, 18, 20. Katla practices shape-changing magic; there is a strong current of sexual jealousy running through this episode, and she is finally done in by another witch, her rival Geirrid, and is stoned to death.

16. *Göngu-Hrolfs saga*, ed. G. Jónsson, Fornaldarsögur Norðulanda, vol. 3 (Reykjavik: Bokantgafen Forni, 1959); trans. H. Pálsson and P. Edwards (Toronto: University of Toronto Press, 1980), chaps. 23, 25.

17. Ibid., chap. 2; witch-berserks also appear in chaps. 6 and 8, though the last identified is troll-like in size and strength, but has no supernatural powers.

18. *ES*, chap. 39; also see chap. 37, where Permia is called Bjarmaland.

19. Miller, "Functional Operations," 127–33, 144–47 (see chap. 1, n. 109). It should be recalled that Starkaðr, the archetypal Þórr-warrior as Dumézil saw it but also closely tied to Óðinn's affairs, had the power of superhuman speed when he wished, though on foot: Saxo, *Gesta Danorum*, VI.180 (see chap. 1, n. 91).

20. *Ldn*, chap. 179. The two were to look for "an image of Freyr"—a Third Function deity—"made of silver."

21. *Ldn*, chaps. 15, 20: When Floki's hand is cut off, it returns to him and the wound heals itself; Finn turns himself into a whale, and is finally killed by (and kills) Halfðan's were-dog.

22. *Ldn*, chaps. 5, 19.

23. *Hálfdanar saga Eysteinssonar*, ed. F. R. Shröder (Halle: 1917); trans. H. Pálsson as "Halfdan Eysteinsson" in *Seven Viking Romances*, chaps. 22, 23, 30 (see chap 1, n. 142).

24. Until recently, I was not aware that the Viking explorers of the Greenland area, where shamanism was surely practiced among those the Norse called *skrælings* (native Inuit or possibly Athabascan-speaking Amerindian peoples), located any magical powers among the inhabitants of this western terminus of the Norse-Icelandic world. However, a quick look through the "Vinland Sagas" (*Grænlendinga saga* and *Eiríks saga rauða*) uncovers the following: in *Grænlendinga saga* a strange heavy sleep comes upon the Icelanders just before the Skrælings attack (chap. 5),

and one of the Skrælings appears to send a "double" into the Icelanders' settlement to reconnoitre (chap. 7); in *Eiriks saga* a force of natives proves to be an optical illusion or delusion (chap. 11), and other Skrælings, when pursued, "sank down into the ground" and escaped (chap. 12): *Grænlendinga saga*, in *Flateyjarbók*, ed. M. Þórðarson. *Íslensk Fornrit 4* (Reykjavik: Hið íslensk fornritafélag, 1935); *Eiríks saga rauða*, in *Skálholtsbók*, ed. by S. B. F. Jansson. *Sagorna om Vinland*, v. 1 (Lund: 1944). Both Icelandic sagas are translated by M. Magnusson and H. Pálsson, *The Vinland Sagas* (Harmondsworth: Penguin, 1965), and also by Gwyn Jones, *The Norse Atlantic Saga* (Oxford: Oxford University Press, 1964).

25. Jakobson and Szeftel, "The Vseslav Epos," 29 (see chap. 5, n. 254).

26. Ford, *Mabinogion*, 98 (see chap. 2, n. 10). Their sin was the rape of a virgin, and the two assume both male and female roles in their successive animal morphisms. The transformation is reminiscent of the Norse god Loki's assuming a mare's shape and then throwing Óðinn's mount, the monster horse Sleipnir. Loki's shamanistic attributes are duly noted by Eliade, *Shamanism*, 386, n. 39.

27. Ford, *Mabinogion*, 101ff.

28. J. Nagy, *Wisdom*, 24–25 (see chap. 1, n. 90).

29. Sayers, "The Smith and Hero," 241, 247 (see chap. 4, n. 157).

30. Layard, *Celtic Quest*, s.v. "Cei," and especially 128–31 (see chap. 3, n. 163).

31. *Il.* III.229; XI.820, noting that the adjective "huge" for, for example, Aias makes a specific contrast to the smaller size of the trickster figure, Odysseus.

32. *Shâh-nâma*, VI.i. (48) (see chap. 1, n. 34).

33. The Christian apparition of Fergus is treated anecdotally in *The Triads of Ireland*, ed. and trans. K. Meyer, Todd Lecture Series 13 (Dublin: Royal Irish Academy, 1906), no. 62; in more detail in *De Faillsigud Tána Bó Cuailgne*, "The Story of the Recovery of the *Táin*," edited in K. Meyer, "Die Wiederauffindung der *Táin Bó Cúalgne*," *Arkhiv für celtische Lexikographie* 3 (1907): 2–6; trans. in Kinsella, *Táin*, 1–2 (see chap. 2, n. 95). In the *Agallamh na Senórach*, of which a small portion is translated in *AIM*, 457–68, see p. 459 for the great size of Cailte and Oisín, who were also "called back" by Patrick: "the tall men . . . were not people of one epoch or of one time with the clergy" and "the largest man of them [the latter-day Irish] reached but to the waist . . . or to the shoulder of any given one of the others, and they sitting." I am indebted to William Sayers for these citations.

34. *HsK*, chap. 20; Jones, *Kings, Beasts and Heroes*, 136 (see chap. 1, n. 95); his brother Thorir Houndsfoot has that canine mark; his brother Elgfrothi is elk-shaped from the waist down.

35. *HsK*, chap. 33; Jones, *Kings, Beasts and Heroes*, 149.

36. Kinsella, *Táin*, 77; not included in O'Rahilly.

37. Kinsella, *Táin*, 150–53; O'Rahilly, *Táin*, 61–62, 201–2 (lines 2262–94).

38. See now W. Sayers, "*Airdrech, Sirite* and Other Early Irish Battlefield Spirits," *Éigse* 25 (1991): 45–55.

39. Sayers, "The Smith and the Hero," 239ff.

40. O'Rahilly, *Táin*, 53, 193 (line 1965).

41. Sayers, "Warrior Initiation," 12 (see chap. 2, n. 106). See above, chapter 2,

p. 87, n. 106, for Cú Chulainn's "retention of boyhood arms into young adulthood."

42. King, *Achilles*, 4 (see chap. 1, n. 23).

43. It can safely be said that Judaism, however seminal and prolific in other genres, has generated no specifically epic literature, and that although there may be a trace remnant of Zoroastrian religion in the Persian *Shâh-nâma*, the great opposition in that epic is between Iran and Turan.

44. Daniel, *Hero and Saracens*, 236 (see chap. 4, n. 72). I would say that the heroes of the *chansons de geste* display their faith naively and programmatically.

45. *Chanson de Roland*, XCIII.1212; CXIX.1592.

46. See Daniel, *Hero and Saracens*, 110–17, on "crusades."

47. *Poema/Poem*, 95 (164–65) (see chap. 2, n. 343).

48. *Poema/Poem*, 78 (134–35): *en teirras de Valençia fer quiero obispado, e dárgelo a este buen cristiano.*

49. See Jasper Griffin, *Homer on Life and Death* (Oxford: Clarendon, 1988), 86–91.

50. *Od.* XII.190.

51. *Il.* IV.21, 52–55.

52. For Memnon, see Kerényi, *Heroes of the Greeks*, 352–53 (see chap. 1, n. 12), citing Proclus, *Chrestomathia*, 106.1.

53. The blasphemous Lokrian Aias has somewhat the air, if not the powers, of a Syrdon or a Loki, reduced to human scale; he seems almost to be an unsuccessful trickster figure: see Kerényi, *Heroes of the Greeks*, 325. Unlike Odysseus, this Aias had also incurred the wrath of Athena, and thus had no divine counterweight to set against the hatred of the great sea-god.

54. Hugh Lloyd-Jones, *The Justice of Zeus*, Sather Classical Lectures 41 (Berkeley: University of California Press, 1971), 17.

55. Ibid., 27.

56. Rees and Rees, *Celtic Heritage*, 314–25 (see chap. 2, n. 34); see also H. R. Ellis Davidson, *Myths and Symbols in Pagan Europe: Early Scandinavian and Celtic Religions* (Syracuse, N.Y.: Syracuse University Press, 1988), 182.

57. T. Ó Cathasaigh, "Between God and Man: The Hero of Irish Tradition," *Crane Bag* 2 (1978): 221.

58. Kinsella, *Tain*, 142; O'Rahilly's version has this figure only as "one of my friends from the fairy mounds," *cia dom chardib sídchaire sein:* 58, 198 (line 2148).

59. *AIT,* 335–38; note that Lugh, Cú Chulainn's divine father, has no place in this final drama, as if he could only involve himself when the power of life was in the dominant. On the other hand, there is a point after which divine parents are never able to help their heroic sons; their power, divine or not, has to fail, against fate.

60. *Togail,* in *AIT,* 98; *EIMS,* 66 (for the *gessa*); and *AIT,* 123–25 and *IMS,* 103–4 (for Cú Chulainn's death); see also Rees and Rees, *Celtic Heritage,* 327–31 (see chap. 2, n. 34). Ó Cathasaigh, in *The Heroic Biography of Cormac mac Airt* (see chap. 2, n. 60), deals with another supernatural personification (not, strictly speak-

ing, a goddess), the spirit of sovereignty who "marries" and authenticates the true king.

61. On the other hand, an Ulster Cycle tale like the *Serglige Con Culaind* (Sickbed of Cú Chulainn) shows the Otherworld powers already separated into their own place in the manner of the Fenian tales: William Sayers, personal communication.

62. *AIT,* 215; see *EIMS.* 190.

63. Ó Cathasaigh, *Heroic Biography,* 226.

64. "The Death of Conchobar," in *Death Tales of the Ulster Heroes,* ed. K. Meyer, Todd Lectures Series 14 (Dublin:Royal Irish Academy, 1906): 7. In *AIT,* 346.

65. *Siabur-charpat Con Culaind,* in *AIT,* 354.

66. Freya evidently makes an appearance in Oláfr pái's "fatal" dream in *Laxdæla saga,* chap. 31; two malignant "goddesses" intervene in *Þorleifs Þáttr Jarlsskálds* (pp. 149–50); the two are deities worshiped by Norway's Jarl Hákon of Hlidir, as their work is seen also in *Jómsvíkingasaga* (chap. 32). Occasionally odd sightings and interventions are recorded in the sagas, as when what appears to be some sort of fire-god or spirit of vulcanism shows up in *Landnámabók,* chap. 68. Þórr is rarely seen in a human setting (see Starkaðr's biography). All divine appearances are described ambiguously, often without direct identification (this may, of course, be a later, Christian recension). Óðinn's identity is made known when his aliases are penetrated, usually after he has departed.

67. Ellis Davidson, *Myths and Symbols,* 42.

68. Though we recognize Þórr as a protective god of the Norse familial structure, of what we might call the "contractual" aspects of the family unit.

69. Dumézil, *Destiny of the Warrior,* 82.

70. E. Polomé, "Starkad, Óðin- or Þórr-hero," in *Helden und Heldensage. Otto Gschwantler zum 60. Geburtsdag,* ed. H. Reichert and G. Zimmermann (Vienna: Fassbaender, 1990): 267–85; see also Miller, "Blackened Hero and Heroic Trickster," 104–5 (see chap. 5, n. 145).

71. Miller, "Functional Operations," 127–33.

72. *ES,* chap. 44.

73. *ES,* chap. 56. The name of the god Þórr, as *landás* or "Ase of the Land," is also put into in this curse verse, and Dumézil thus had identified a trifunctional Norse text: see especially "'Tripertita' fonctionnels chez divers peuples indo-Européens," *RHR* 131 (1946): 53–72; also see Belier, *Decayed Gods,* 105–6 (see introduction, n. 3).

74. *ES,* chap. 57 [*EgS,* chap. 58]. Egill advises his men to act "the warrior's part" (*hermannlega)* to kill all they can "and take everything we can get away with (*en taka fé allt, það er vér megum með komast).*

75. *GrS,* introduction, viii–ix. Although, so far as a "Christian and civilized world" is concerned, we might note Lönnroth's comment on thirteenth-century Iceland: by this point the island had been Christianized (and supposedly more intensely civilized as well) for three centuries, yet it suffered from, among other disasters, "feuds longer and more vicious than any described in the sagas": Lönnroth, *Njáls Saga: A Critical Introduction,* 165 (see chap. 2, n. 286).

76. *GrS*, chap. 61. In Norway, Grettir has to undergo an ordeal in church; he would not have been likely to attempt this if he were still a pagan: chap. 39.

77. *GrS*, chaps. 54, 57.

78. Starkaðr actually obeys an order given him by his king, and is *tricked* into killing the king—as he, at the end of his too-long life, would trick a young warrior into killing him.

79. See Miller, "Functional Operations," 131.

80. For the full scope of this theme, see chapter 7, below.

81. The death of Odysseus at the hands of his own unrecognized son (by Kirke) does not attach Odysseus to Oedipus: this must be a fitting trickster's death.

82. Oedipus may exemplfy some aspects of the heroic career—perhaps as a Third Function hero?—but his Oedipal drama hews more closely to another social myth. He returns to the "heroic" mode when he curses, and so dooms, his own sons. See Miller, "Three Kings at Colonos," 58–61, 63, 69–71 (see chap. 2, n. 8).

83. Probably reflected, for example, in the Indic *Mahâbhârata:* the last-born twins, representing the Second Function among the five Pâṇḍavas, Nakula and Sahadeva, are born of their father's second wife, the first three Pâṇḍavas (and the first two Functions) from the first wife: 1 (6) 57: p. 135.

84. Neumann, *Origins,* 216 (see chap. 1, n. 210). Neumann goes on to state that the victory is only possible through the intervention of *positive* aspects of the parental, worked through their agents (Hermes for the Divine Father, Athena for the Great Mother).

85. Eisner, *The Road to Daulis,* 59 (see chap. 1, n. 205); citing Georges Devereux, "Greek Pseudo-Homosexuality and the Greek Mother," *Symbolae Osloenses* 42 (1967): 69–92.

86. Neumann, *Origins,* xv.

87. C. Jung, *The Archetypes and the Collective Unconscious,* trans. R. F. C. Hull, in *Collected Works,* part 9.1, Bollingen Series 20 (Princeton: Princeton University Press, 1980), para. 309.

88. C. Jung, *The Development of Personality,* trans. R. F. C. Hull, in *Collected Works,* part 17 Bollingen Series 20 (New York: Pantheon, 1954), para. 327.

89. Marie-Louise von Franz, *Projection and Re-collection in Jungian Psychology: Reflections of the Soul,* trans. W. H. Kennedy (La Salle, Ill.: Open Court, 1988), 123.

90. Neumann, *Origins,* 351, 352.

91. Ibid., 353.

92. Ibid., 352–53.

93. Redfield, *Nature and Culture,* 36ff. (see chap. 2, n. 287); also Griffin, *Homer on Life and Death.*

94. *Hænsa-Þóris saga,* chap. 22 ; *NjS,* chaps. 128, 129, for the escape of Kari, Njáll's son-in-law.

95. *NjS,* chap 77 .

96. *NjS,* chap. 78, and see Ellis Davidson, *Road to Hel,* 40, n. 1.

97. King, *Achilles,* 7–10.

98. Kinsella, *Táin,* 212; O'Rahilly, *Táin,* 104–5, 240 (lines 3776–86); Kinsella, 212.

99. *TDAG,* Ni Shéaghdha, 575–77; *AIT,* 413–15; J. Nagy, *Wisdom,* 34–35.

100. *Shâh-nâma.,* VI.xx.29–30.

101. Wilhelm Schultze, "Der Tod des Kambyses," *Sitzungsberichte der Königlich Preussischen Akademie des Wissenschaften* (1912), Bild 2: 689–703.

102. See, e.g., Maurice Bloch and Jonathan Parry, "Introduction: Death and the Regeneration of Life," in *Death and the Regeneration of Life,* ed. M. Bloch and J. Parry (Cambridge: Cambridge University Press, 1986), 15–18.

103. With a necessary bow to Robert Hertz's 1909 essay, "La prééminence de la main droite: Étude sur la polarité religeuse," *Revue philosophique* 68 (1909): 553–80, translated by R. Needham as "The Pre-eminence of the Right Hand: A Study in Religious Polarity," in Needham, *Right and Left,* 3–31 (see chap. 1, n. 200). See now Louis-Vincent Thomas, *Anthropologie de la mort* (Paris: Payot, 1975); E. Morin, *L'homme et la mort* (Paris: Ed. du Seuil, 1970); S. C. Humphreys and H. King, *Mortality and Immortality: The Anthropology and Archaeology of Death* (London: Academic Press, 1981); and Miller, "'Bad Death'" (see chap. 1, n. 10).

104. This suicide and its dire cause has to be reconstructed from a compilation of surviving sources: *Od.* XI.544 has Odysseus in Hades, meeting Aias, who is "full of wrath" (*nosphin aphestêkei*) because of his loss (and Odysseus, of course, bobs and weaves and puts the blame on Zeus: XI. 559). Aias's suicide is described in fragments of the Epic Cycle: see *Hesiod: The Homeric Hymns and the Homerica,* trans. H. G. Evelyn-White, Loeb Classical Library (Cambridge, Mass: Harvard University Press; London: Wm. Heinemann, 1964), 508–9; see also T. W. Allen, ed., *Homeri Opera V* (Oxford: Oxford University Press, 1912), 106.20–23, for very brief decriptions from the *Aethiopis* and the *Little Iliad.* Pindar editorializes against Odysseus and the injustice of the games' outcome: *Nemean Odes.* 8.25, "the biggest proportion of honor is given to lying deceit"; see G. Nagy, *Best of the Achaeans,* 225, and n. 5.5 (see chap. 1, n. 7).

105. Saxo, *Gesta Danorum,* VIII.251–52; Saxo suggests that the old hero tried to kill his chosen executioner by tricking him into a position where the decapitated old man's great (i.e., heroic) bodily bulk would fall on and crush him.

106. *Nibelungenlied,* v. 2373 (pp. 262–63); compare the death's of the two Norse Óðinn-warriors, Skalla-Grímr and his son Egill, in *Egils saga* (chaps. 58, 85); both die natural deaths in old age (though Skalla-Grímr's is more "trollish" than that of Egill), but both, like Hagen, had concealed a treasure before dying. For the peculiar "suicide" of the perverse warrior Efnisien, see above, p. 287.

107. See Kerényi, *Heroes of the Greeks,* 323, for the expansion (seen in the Scholion on the *Iliad,* V. 412) on Diomedes' ultimate fate: *Il.* V.407 bluntly says that "whoever fights the Immortals doesn't last long" (*mal' ou dênaios hos athanatoisi makhêtai*) but there is no more said about Diomedes, who wounded both Ares and Aphrodite.

108. Border heroes do die in some of the Serbo-Croat songs that cluster around the figure of Marko Kraljević and have been collected along with his tales

(Marko himself apparently dies a self-willed death: see Pennington and Levi, *Marko the Prince*, 64–68 [see chap. 2, n. 49]).

109. *AIT,* 334–38, from *Brislech mor Maige Murthemni,* in *The Book of Leinster,* vol. 2, ed. R. I. Best and M. A. O'Brien (Dublin, 1956).

110. But Griffin may have cast the "berserker" North too rigidly, especially when the variable evidence of all the sagas is factored in. See *Homer on Life and Death,* 92, 96.

111. Walter Marg, "Zur Eigenart der Odyssee," *Antike und Abendland* 18 (1973): 10; Griffin prefers as a descriptive "the poem of life and death: of the contrast and transition between the two" (95).

112. Ibid., 94.

113. See M. M. Willcock, *A Companion to the* Iliad (Chicago: University of Chicago Press, 1976), 72, referring to *Il.* VI.234–36, the well-known "chivalric" exchange between Glaukos and Diomedes (and also note *Il.* IX. 602–5).

114. The medieval manorial system, insofar as it can be computed in economic terms, settled the warrior on a base in which a dominated and dependent producing group would provide economic autarky. Is this an ideal "heroic" economy?

115. Redfield, *Nature and Culture,* 32–34.

116. The hero is figuratively "swollen" as his reputation grows, but this physical image is subject to death's diminishing power, as the body of the hero usually is.

117. Ibid.

118. Aeschylus, *Septem contra Thebas,* 434.

119. *ES, EgS,* chap. 47, for his poem before the sack and firing by Egill and his men of Lund: *Leiti upp til Lundar/lyða hver sem bráðast* and so on.

120. *Violence et le sacré = Violence and the Sacred,* trans. P. Gregory (Baltimore: Johns Hopkins University Press, 1981); Burkert, *Homo Necans* (see chap. 3, n. 134) and by the same author, *Griechische Religion der archaischen und klassischen Epoche* (Stuttgart: Verlag W. Kohlhammer, 1977) = *Greek Religion,* trans. J. Raffan (Cambridge, Mass.: Harvard University Press, 1985), 55–84.

121. See chapter 1, pp. 55–56. Note, e.g., M. Detienne, *Dionysios Slain* (see chap. 4, n. 174), and M. Detienne and J.-P. Vernant, eds., *La cuisine du sacrifice en pays grec* (Paris: Gallimard, 1979) = *The Cuisine of Sacrifice among the Greeks,* trans. P. Wissing (Chicago: University of Chicago Press, 1989); also P. Vidal-Naquet, "Land and Sacrifice in the Odyssey: A Study of Religious and Mythical Meanings," in *The Black Hunter,* 15–38 (see chap. 1, n. 171), and his "Hunting and Sacrifice in Aeschylus' *Oresteia,*" in Vernant and Vidal-Naquet, *Myth and Tragedy,* 141–19 (see chap. 1, n. 13), particularly for Vidal-Naquet's critical assessment of Burkert.

122. Jane Harrison, *Themis: A Study of the Social Origins of Greek Religion* (Cleveland, Ohio: Meridien/World, 1962).

123. See Burr Cartwright Brundage, *The Fifth Sun: Aztec Gods, Aztec World* (Austin: University of Texas Press, 1979), chap. 9, "The Nuclear Cult: War, Sacrifice and Cannibalism"; for a wider contextual view of Aztec philosophy and theology, Miguel León-Portilla, *Aztec Thought and Culture: A Study of the Ancient Nahu-*

atl Mind, trans. J. E. Davis, Civilization of the American Indian Series, vol. 67 (Norman: University of Oklahoma Press, 1963.

124. See the powerful and original analysis by Inga Glendinnen, *Aztecs: An Interpretation* (Cambridge: Cambridge University Press, 1991), 74: this scholar states that the Spanish *sacrificio* was used as one word to describe several Nahuatl "word clusters," clusters that involved paying a debt but also laying out a feast. In Glendinnen's view the Aztec world view never took *reciprocity* as a given: "no human action, no submission however extravagant, guaranteed response or reward" (76). Reciprocity or "contract" (parallel with the Latin *cura* in terms of sacrifice) conformed more to the Maya religious outlook: see Linda Schele and Mary Ann Miller, *The Blood of Kings: Dynasty and Ritual in Maya Art* (Fort Worth, Tex.: Kimball Art Museum, 1986).

125. Though the *kšatriya* caste—the "barons" in the *Mahâbhârata*—is also authorized to make sacrifices.

126. See *Od.* IX.231; "we lit a fire and offered sacrifice" on the Cyclops' sinister island's forestrand.

127. D. A. See Miller, "Some Psycho-Social Perceptions of Slavery," *Journal of Social History* 18, no. 4 (Summer 1985), 593–94.

128. See Kerényi, *Heroes of the Greeks,* 335, nn. 342–77, for the sources for his complex synoptic account.

129. *Chanson de Roland,* 1134–35, and also CXV.1522.

130. *Chanson de Roland,* CLXXXVII.2600ff., and CCLIII.3492–4.

131. Margaret Hasluck's *The Unwritten Law in Albania* (Cambridge: Cambridge University Press, 1954) is an always fascinating and informative early study; see now Christopher Boehm, *Blood Revenge: The Enactment and Management of Conflict in Montenegro and Other Tribal Societies* (Philadelphia: University of Pennsylvania Press, 1987), bibliography, 253–58; for two differing approaches to feud in the Norse-Icelandic area so important to the present study (and not included in Boehm), see Byock, *Feud in the Icelandic Saga* (see chap. 2, n. 167), and most recently Theodore M. Andersson and William Ian Miller, *Law and Literature in Medieval Iceland* (see chap. 2, n. 275)

132. Tacitus, *Germania,* XIV. And a little later: *principes pro victoria pugnant, comites pro principe.*

133. See the *legal* force in some meanings of Latin *vindico, vindicta.*

134. *Chanson de Roland,* CLIII.2056, 2058. Terry's translation of *maltalentifs* has more force than the modern French *colére,* which Bédier employs in the Oxford edition of this *chanson.*

135. *Nibelungenlied,* vv. 2285, 2289 (pp. 244–45).

136. Patroklos's death is also, more indirectly, avenged by the Achaean Automedon, who "eases his heart" with the killing of the Trojan Aretos, though Aretos is called negligible in rank, and therefore barely fit for a proper taking of revenge: XVII.538–9. For the "logic of death" see Redfield, *Nature and Culture,* 19ff. (chap 2. n. 287).

137. *ES, EgS,* chap. 60.

138. *ES, EgS,* chap. 27.

139. *EyS*, chap. 19.

140. *KS*, chaps. 8, 16, 47.

141. *KS*, chap. 14.

142. This is Pálsson and Edwards' translation of *Bors niðjar felt eg beðju/blóði—Hadd og Froða*, chap. 57.

143. *GrS*, chap. 24. Also in *Grettis saga* the saga hero and skald refers to an enemy he had killed as "embracing the fair earth" (chap. 48). Here we have a recrudescence of the love-death motif, which also shows up in certain images of the Valkyrie (as in the "Helgi Poems" of the *Poetic Edda:* see Hollander, *The Poetic Edda*, 180ff.[see chap. 2, n. 258]), and occasionally emerges in a sequence of *death, sexual experience, rebirth:* see Miller, "Bad Death," 159ff. It is at least possible that this Scandinavian love-death imagery had some influence on the Old Russian *Slovo o polku Igoreve:* see Robert Mann, *Lances Sing: A Study of the Igor Tale* (Columbus, Ohio: Slavica, 1990), 38ff., "Wedding Imagery in the *Slovo.*"

144. *VölS*, chap. 3: "the sword from the tree-trunk."

145. *ES, EgS*, chap. 78.

146. Kinsella, *Táin*, 98, 161, 238; O'Rahilly, *Táin*, 66, 206 (line 2427); 127, 263 (line 4603: *crennait brain braigte fer brunnid fer fuil*).

147. *Chanson de Roland*, CXXXII.1751: *N'en mangeront ne lou ne porc ne chien*; CLXXVIII.2436: *ne beste ne lions*. We have a mixture of wild and of domestic scavengers threateningly named.

148. *Slovo*, 123: *orli klektom' na kosti zveri zovut'*; 494: *a zveri krov'polizasha*; 228–29: *chasto vrani grayakut'/ trupia sebe delyache.*

149. *Nibelungenlied*, vv. 1960–61 (pp. 176–77).

150. The image is used in a traditional Scottish tale repeated by George Macdonald Frazer in his *The Shiek and the Dustbin* (Glasgow: William Collins Sons, 1989), 135–36. The story describes the revenge of a "woman of the Gordons" on those of the despised Gregora who had killed her husband.

CHAPTER 7: THE FINAL HERO: BEYOND IMMORTALITY

1. I take the Georgian epic to be a thoroughly Persified epical artifact, though the point could be made that some of its specificity, its self-conscious Georgian-Caucasian sensibility (especially the lapse or glissade into the heroes' kingly roles and some other decorative motifs and "folkloric" themes) could be taken to provide a strong and even probative contrast to the borrowed Indo-European heroic material. Note that Dumézil, in recording the transmission of the Ossete Nart tales to neighboring, non-Indo-European-speaking peoples, found that the trifunctional schema underlying these tales disappeared: *Mythe et épopée*, 1:479–575 (see chap. 4, n. 264); and Belier, *Decayed Gods*, 73–74 (see introduction, n. 3).

2. Jan de Vries, "Das Motiv des Vater-Sohn-Kampfes in Hildebrandslied: Mit einer Nachschrift des Verfassers," in *Zur germanisch-deutschen Heldensage*, ed. K. Hauck, Wege der Forschung, vol. 4 (Darmstadt: Wissenschaftliche Buchgesellschaft, 1961): 248–84; earlier, Georg Baesecke, "Die indogermanische Ver-

wandtscahft des Hildebrandslied," *Nachrichten von der Gesellschaft der Wissen-schaften zu Gottingen, Phil.-hist. Klasse,* Fachgruppe IV, n.f. 3 (1940): 139–53.

3. Hatto, "On the Excellence of the 'Hildebrandslied'" (see chap. 2, n. 119).

4. For a full exposition of the following theme, see D. A.Miller, "Defining and Expanding the Indo-European *Vater-Sohnes-Kampf* Theme," *JI-ES* 22, nos. 3–4 (Fall–Winter 1994): 307–27.

5. Dumézil, *Mythes et épopées,* 1:564–65; *Légendes,* no. 5, pp. 32–34 (see chap. 2, n. 88); *Livre,* 44–47 (see chap. 2, n. 88).

6. "Ölvir-Oddr" = "Arrow-Odd." Old Norse in Guðni Jónsson, *Fornal-darsögur Noroðulanda,* vol. 2 (Reykjavik: Bokantgafen Forni, 1944), chaps. 18, 22; translated in Pálsson and Edwards, *Seven Viking Romances* (see chap. 1, n. 142).

7. *Gormont et Isambard. Fragment de chanson de geste du XIIIe siècle,* 3d ed., ed. Alphonse Bayet, Les classiques français du Moyen Age, ed. Mario Roques (Paris: Librairie Ancienne Honoré Champion, 1931). Note also P. R. Lonigan, *The* Gormont et Isambard*: Problem and Interpretation of an Old French Epic* (Ann Arbor, Mich.: University Microfilm International, 1976); also Crosland, *The Old French Epic,* 136 (see chap. 1, n. 96), and J. de Vries, "La chanson de *Gormont et Isambard,*" *Romania* 80 (1939): 34–62.

8. *Gormont,* 186.

9. *Gormont,* 626.

10. Nitze and Jenkins, *Le haut livre du Graal: Perlesvaus* VIII.4924–34 (see chap. 2, n. 65), for the killing of Lohout; IX.6344–64 for the discovery of the killing. I am grateful to Professor Linda Malcor for directing my attention to this episode in the *Perlesvaus.*

11. Pokr Mher's—curse-brought?—childlessness, the termination of the line of Sassoon, is of course converted in this epic into the clearest statement of heroic solipsism: "I have had no child, I can have no death." Because life has not been passed on, death cannot enter in.

I should note that V. Ya. Propp recognized the resonance of the old father-son conflict in the Armenian epic: see the excursis on the *boye otsa s synom* in his *Russkoi geroischeskii epos,* 2d ed. (Moskva: Gosudartsvennoe Izdatelstvo Khudozh-estvennoe Literatury, 1958), 261ff.

12. Miller, "Bad Death," 143–44 (see chap. 1, n. 10).

13. Hippolytos, of course, was no rival warrior to his father, and *his* particular fate and tragedy is probably connected to his father's sexual misadventures: see Miller, "Three Kings at Colonus," 64; 75, n. 46 (see chap. 2, n. 8).

14. The children "not known" to the hero, though killed not in battle but in a kind of insane sacrifice: see Kerényi, *Heroes of the Greeks,* 185–87 (see chap. 1, n. 12).

15. *Digenes Akrites,* GRO III, lines 307ff. (pp. 62–63).

16. Grégoire, *Ho Digenês Akritas,* 26 (see chap. 2, n. 117).

17. In *Le moniage Rainouart,* ed. G. A. Bertin, Société des anciens textes français (Paris: Editions A. et J. Picard, 1973), XCI–XCVI.

18. Conchobar and Noisiu in *Longes mac n-Uislenn;* Finn and Diarmaid in *Tórnigheact Dhiarmada agus Ghráinne.* Both the king, Cochobar, and the *rígfénnid*

Finn do have sons of their own body who survive them. The death of Tristan does not come through King Mark's doing in Thomas's *Tristan,* but in the Prose Tristan it does: see, e.g., the fourteenth-century Italian *La Tavola Ritonda,* where the evil King Marco wounds Tristano with a poisoned lance (given the king by Fata Morgana) and so causes his death: *La Tavola Ritonda* = Shaver, *Tristan and the Round Table,* CXXVI–CXXVII (pp. 316–17) (see chap. 2, n. 154).

19. The Greek—*Il.* IX.455–56—says that the father Amyntor will never, by this curse, hold on his knee his son's child.

20. See Willcock, *A Companion to the* Iliad, 105: Willcock notes that there is no clear and good reason for keeping Phoinix at home, especially by means of feasting and sacrifices. I am most grateful to John Peradotto for bringing this example from the *Iliad* to my attention.

21. Miller, "The Three Kings at Colonos."

22. See especially E. Lyle, "Dumézil's Three Functions," in her *Archaic Cosmos,* 6–25 (see chap. 4, n. 13).

23. Grisward, "L'arbre blanc, vert, rouge de la Quete du Graal et le Symbolisme coloré des Indo-Européens," 114 (see chap. 5, n. 209).

24. *JS,* chap. 32.

25. Chadwick, *Russian Heroic Poetry,* 162, lines 75ff. (see chap. 1, n. 155).

26. Miller, "Three Kings at Colonos," 55, 59, 61.

27. See Redfield, *Nature and Culture,* 17 (see chap. 2, n. 287); and now Richard Martin, *The Language of Heroes: Speech and Performance in the* Iliad (Ithaca, N.Y.: Cornell University Press, 1989), s.v. "Achilles."

28. Redfield, *Nature and Culture,* 13, 19; Akhilleus and Odysseus are "mirrored" in their speech.

29. But see Martin, *The Language of Heroes,* 120–30, on Diomedes and word battles.

30. See Miller, "Twinning of Arthur and Cei," 55–56, 61–65 (see chap. 1, n. 106).

31. Neoptolemos seems to inherit his bestial temper not only from his father but from his mother's side as well: from Deidameia's father Lykomedes, "Wolfthought." See Kerényi, *Heroes of the Greeks,* 329, 356; Neoptolemos, like his father, was *Purrhos* 'redhead'. Compare King, *Achilles,* 126 (see chap. 1, n. 23).

32. Redfield, *Nature and Culture,* 22.

33. See Andersson, *Family Saga,* 233–35 (see chap. 2, n. 283); also Hollander's introduction to his translation of the saga (3–8) (see chap. 2, n. 295) and his "The Case of the Skald Kormák," *Monatshefte für Deutschen Unterricht* 35 (1943): 107–15.

34. *KS,* chaps. 22–23.

35. For the bizarre conception of Satána, see Dumézil, "Mort de Æhsar et d'Æhsætæg," in *Livre,* 29–30, and also Miller, "Three Conception Narratives," 38–39 (see chap. 2, n. 10).

36. In the version of the birth of Satána just given (Dumézil, *Livre,* 29–30), the dead mother is this same Djerasse. For Dumézil's last thoughts on Djerasse, Uastyrdji, and some other aspects of the Narts, see "Les jumeaux ossètes" in *Le*

roman des jumeaux et autres essais. Vingt-cinq esquisses de mythologie (76–100) pub-liées par Joël Grisward, Bibliothèque des Sciences Humaines (Paris: Gallimard, 1994), 100–118.

37. In Dumézil, "Batradz et Mukara, fils de la Force," in *Livre*, 192.

38. Dumézil, "Batradz et le Uatsamongæ des Nartes," in *Livre*, 207; "Mort de Batradz," 233–34 (see chap. 3, n. 45).

39. *Peredur*, in Jones and Jones, *Mabinogion*, 199; see *EyS*, chap. 20, for the death of the sorceress Katla.

40. The wizard-kings of the Norse in the *fornaldarsögur* or *lygisögur* are explosive and uncontrolled; their magic is mythic in texture.

41. Eliade, *Shamanism*, 386 (see chap. 6, n. 4).

42. *CO*, 8 (line 199), 15–16 (lines 408–411, 427–28); Ford, *Mabinogion*, 127, 132–33 (see chap. 2, n. 10). In fact Menw shows his shape-changing skills at only one point in the chase: *CO*, 36 (lines 1023–35); Ford, *Mabinogion*, 152.

43. This is a suggestion made by William Sayers (personal communication).

44. This "conversion" of a comic-reversing figure necessitates a drastic, even a tabooed act, best seen when Boðvarr forces Hottr to eat the meat and drink the blood of a monster. In the *Mahâbhârata* the necessary taboo is suggested by the dead body King Virâṭa says is in the tree where Arjuna's great war bow is concealed; in *Perlesvaus* it is the spilling of the coward knight's own blood that "converts" him to true-knightly bravery.

45. Note that a "slow" hero like Rainouart also projects an exaggerated, comic persona. William Sayers suggests that the innocent "slow hero" represents a kind of "pure ore," who is gradually forged into herodom rather then being made almost instantaneously manifest like the normative hero (personal communication).

46. See chapter 5, pp. 272–74, above.

47. We may take it as a rule that only a hero with special connections to the manipulative-magical trickster mode can actually intrude into death's place: Odysseus, of course, Theseus (perhaps successfully, perhaps not)—even Herakles, that complicated figure who combines animal and god in superhuman form.

48. Note that in *Il.* XI.377 Diomedes is struck and wounded by one of Paris-Alexandros's arrows—struck in the foot, like Akhilleus, but only wounded and not mortally.

49. As I noted above, the subordinate partner's death can take its own revenge on the young hero by vitiating his powers: see chapter 2, p. 125.

50. See V. G. Kiernan, *The Duel: Honour and the Reign of Aristocracy* (Oxford: Oxford University Press, 1986), for the multiform aspects of the defense of "honour."

51. This definition puts to one side the exaggerated poetic efflorescence of the Old Irish narratives, where the skills and demonstrations of the *fílid* are still on display; it skirts a mixed, epic chronicle source such as the Persian *Shâh-nâma*, and certainly cannot contain an immense piece of "epic" such as the *Mahâbhârata*.

52. The hero of epic or legend can also be adopted and "nationalized" by the society that succeeds to, even inherits, his own society or segment of society.

53. These descriptive formulaic terms are well known. There is some varia-

tion: *megathumoi,* "great-souled" (with *thumos* as the breath-soul, see Onians, *Origins,* 51ff. [see chap. 1, n. 228]) is first used of the Achaeans but later of the Trojans as well (as in V.102). *Hippodamos,* "horse-taming," is regularly formulaic for the Trojans but is also used at one point for Diomedes (V.899). *Khalkokhitônon,* "brazen-tunicked" (though I have to admit a preference for "copper-jacketed") is used (not frequently) of both sides but in the main for the Achaeans, while "long-haired" and "well-greaved" are applied strictly to the Achaeans. For "well-greaved," see Page, *History,* 245 (see chap. 4, n. 171); for "long-haired," see 243, and for other descriptives in general and an estimation of their historicity, 242ff.

54. Oinas, *Heroic Epic and Saga,* 241–42 (see chap. 1, n. 73).

55. In examining the "tradition" of Old Indian epic, John D. Smith records a contemporary Indian adventure narrative (concerning the life and death of Ompuri, a *dacoit* or brigand in Western India) into which "heroic" or epical elements had already been inserted, and an older tale (the Pabuji "epic" describing a Rajput hero of the fourteenth century) into which both heroic-epic *and* mythic elements had been introduced. East Indian popular mythology of course allows the divinization of its "historic" heroes: Smith, "Old Indian (The Two Sanskrit Epics)" in Hatto, *Traditions,* vol. 1 (see chap. 5, n. 137).

56. Weber did indeed conceive of "charismatic education," the education of a young noble to direct him in the path, or to follow the code, of the hero: T. S. Smith (personal communication).

57. For the Myrimidons as a people or "host" (*laos*) see, e.g., *Il.* II.684: "Myrimidons and Hellenes and Achaeans." Our image of Akhilleus's warriors retains the sense of a faceless mass; in the *Iliad* only the five "leaders" of the Myrimidon host are ever named, and a very few other warriors, in the battle scenes of book XVI.

58. Thomas Spence Smith, "The Release of the Romantic Impulse: Charisma and Its Transformations," *Current Perspectives in Social Theory* 10 (1990): 48.

59. C. Camic, "Charisma: Its Varieties, Preconditions and Consequences," *Sociological Inquiry* 50 (1980): 5–23.

60. Or even a temporary, circumscribed, almost pathetic attribution of omnipotence (responsive to psychic "dependency needs"): ibid.

61. Smith, "The Release of the Romantic Impulse."

62. William James, *The Varieties of Religious Experience* (New York: Longman, Green, 1902), 353.

63. In Cedric H. Whitman, *The Heroic Paradox: Essays on Homer, Sophocles, and Aristophanes* (Ithaca: Cornell University Press, 1982), 19–43.

64. Ibid., 25.

65. Ibid., 28.

66. Setting aside the "companion's death" as a secondary phenomenon.

67. Robert Jay Lifton, *The Broken Connection: On Death and the Continuity of Life* (New York: Basic Books, 1983); Ernest Becker, *The Denial of Death* (New York: Free Press; London: Collier Macmillan, 1973).

68. Becker, *The Denial of Death,* 49.

69. Lifton, *The Broken Connection,* 7.

70. Ibid., 88.

71. This may be the place to reflect once more on the fact that Oedipus had no complex, and that in several versions of his multiplex story he escapes the consequences of his double sin entirely, remarries, fathers more children, and so on.

72. "The terror of death [is] the basic repression," Becker, *The Denial of Death,* 97.

73. Ibid., 1.

74. N. O. Brown, *Life against Death: The Psychoanalytic Meaning of History,* 2d ed. (Middletown, Conn.: Wesleyan University Press, 1986), 79.

75. That is, the *creation* of a death combined with the *description* of such a death; for the sadomasochistic element, see ibid., 97ff.

76. Ibid., 102.

77. Becker, *The Denial of Death,* 99; citing Otto Rank, *Will Therapy and Truth and Reality* (New York: Knopf, 1945), 130.

78. Richmond Lattimore's translation in *The Iliad of Homer* (Chicago: University of Chicago Press, 1961).

79. See Adam M. Parry, "The Language of Achilles," in his *The Language of Achilles and Other Papers* (Oxford: Clarendon, 1989): 1–7.

80. Becker, *The Denial of Death,* 265–66.

81. *Poem/Poema,* cant. 36 (88–89) (see chap. 2, n. 343).

82. De Vries, *Heroic Song and Heroic Legend,* 63. (see chap. 1, n. 71).

83. See Mann, *Lances Sing* (see chap. 6, n. 143) for wedding imagery in the *Slovo.* Mann takes his title from one of the more extraordinary images in the poem: *Kopia poyut' na Dunai,* "the spears are singing on the Duna" (line 547).

84. *Slovo,* 575–79. Prince Igor's life has been spared in the general disaster.

85. *CMT,* chap. 603.

INDEX